For an alphabetical list of correction symbols, see inside back cover. Directions for the use of charts and symbols are in 33

W9-ATE-011

...cal Discussions

SENTENCE STRUCTURE

12 Frag

COMPLETE SENTENCE; FRAGMENT

13 Pred

PREDICATION
13a	Pred a	Subject, verb, complement
13b	Pred b; Eq	Equation with *to be*
13c	Pred c	*Is-when, is-because*
13d	Pred d; Shift	Shifts in structure

14 Paral

PARALLELISM
14a	Paral a	Parallelism in co-ordination
14b	Paral b	Misleading parallelism

15 Sub; Mod

SUBORDINATION; MODIFICATION
15a	Sub	Adequate subordination
15b	Mod	Position of modifiers
15c	DM	Dangling modifiers
15d	Split	Split construction

16 Inc; Comp

INCOMPLETE PATTERNS; COMPARISONS
16a	Inc	Completing patterns
16b	Comp	Comparisons

17 Em

EMPHASIS; SENTENCE PATTERNS
17a	Em a	Postponed subject, expletive
17b	Em b	Substitute subject
17c	Em c; Pass	Passive sentence
17d	Em d	Inverted sentence
17e	Em e	Verb emphasis
17f	Em f	Minor words in emphatic positions
17g	Em g	Rhetorical question

MECHANICS

27 P

PUNCTUATION
27a	P1	End punctuation
27b	P2; RT; CF; CS	Run-together; comma fault
27c	P3	Independent clauses with co-ordinating conjunctions
27d	P4	Series
27e	P5	Non-restrictive modifier
27f	P6	Parenthetical material
27g	P7	Introductory modifier
27h	P8	Geographical, temporal, metrical material
27i	P9	Comma to clarify
27j	P10	Quotations
27k	P11	Colon
27l	P12; Dash	Dash
27m	P13	Parentheses; brackets
27n	P14; No P	Inappropriate punctuation

28 M

MANUSCRIPT FORM
28a	M a; Cap; lc	Capitalization
28b	M b; Ab	Abbreviation
28c	M c; Num	Numbers
28d	M d; Div	Division of words
28e	M e; Tit	Titles
28f	M f; Ital	Italics

29 Sp

SPELLING
29a	Sp a; Apos	Apostrophe; possessive
29b	Sp b; Hy	Hyphenation of compounds
29c	Sp c; Pl; Sing	Plurals
29d	Sp d	Spelling and sound
29e	Sp e	*i-and-e* combinations
29f	Sp f	*y* with endings
29g	Sp g	Doubling and final silent e

34 Gloss

GLOSSARY OF USAGE

If an expression is circled or underlined without reference to this chart, look it up in the index or in the glossary.

...cal Discussions

THEME TOPIC; MAIN IDEA

1-1 Theme idea. 1-2 Limiting. 1-3, 4 Main idea. 1-5 Journal. 1-7 Devices for unity.

PARAGRAPH UNITY; COHERENCE

2-1 Standard paragraph. 2-2, 3 Paragraph structure. 2-4, 5 Topic sentence. 3-1 Revealing plan. 3-2 Transition words. 3-3 Repetition and coherence. 3-4 Word order.

DEFINITION AND DEVELOPMENT

4-2 Methods of definition. 5-1 Fact, judgment. 5-2 General, specific. 5-3 Generalizations. 5-4 Particulars. 5-5 Examples. 5-6 Incident. 5-7 Analogy.

EVIDENCE: INDUCTIVE REASONING

6-1 Induction. 6-2 Types of induction. 6-3 Induction in writing. 6-4 Tests of evidence.

LOGIC: DEDUCTIVE REASONING

7-1, 2 Induction, deduction. 7-3 Middle term. 7-4, 5 Using deduction. 7-6 Assumptions.

ORGANIZATION, OUTLINING

8-1 to 8-5 Analysis, classification. 9-1 to 9-3 Types of organization. 9-4 to 9-8 Outline.

TRANSITIONS, INTRODUCTIONS, CONCLUSIONS

10-1 Revealing outline. 10-2, 3 Transitions. 10-4, 5 Introductions. 10-6, 7 Conclusions.

STYLE AND TONE

11-1 Characteristics. 11-2 Style as mind. 11-3 Reading. 11-4 to 11-6 Tone.

SENTENCE PATTERNS; PREDICATION

12-1 Distribution in grammar. 12-2, 3 Patterns. 12-4 Subject. 12-5 Verbs, complements. 12-6 Developing patterns. 12-7 Clauses. 13-1 Fitting parts. 13-2 Choosing subjects. 13-3 Equation.

CO-ORDINATION, SUBORDINATION

14-1 to 14-4 Co-ordination patterns. 15-1, 2 Subordination patterns. 15-3 Fixed modifiers. 15-4 Clause modifiers. 15-5 Subordination and style. 16-1 Fixed patterns. 16-2 Comparisons.

EMPHASIS: USING PATTERNS

17-1 Postponed subject. 17-2 Substitute subject. 17-3 Passive. 17-4 Position. 17-5, 6 Patterns of emphasis.

VOCABULARY, MEANING, WORD CHOICE

25-1, 2 Dictionaries. 25-3 Vocabulary. 25-4 Meaning. 25-5 Symbolization. 25-6 Abstract, concrete. 25-7 Denotation, connotation. 25-8 Metaphor. 25-9 Contexts. 25-10 Precision.

RESEARCH PAPER; PRÉCIS

30-1 Précis, summary. 30-2, 3 Notes. 30-4 Plagiarism. 31-1 Subject. 31-2 Material. 31-3 to 31-7 Reference books. 31-8 to 31-10 Bibliography. 31-11 Footnote form. 32-1 Style. 32-2 Documentation. 32-3 Research conventions.

ROBERT M. GORRELL *University of Nevada*

CHARLTON LAIRD *University of Nevada*

Moderr

PRENTICE-HALL, INC.
Englewood Cliffs, N. J.

Modern English Handbook

Modern English Handbook

THIRD EDITION

Gorrell and Laird

Second printing.....May, 1963

© *Copyright* 1953, 1956, 1962
by PRENTICE-HALL, INC.,
Englewood Cliffs, New Jersey.

Printed in
the United States of America,
59416—C.
L. C. Cat. No. 62-11982

English Handbook

THIRD EDITION

Preface

Using English is puzzling work, but this book assumes that it is less puzzling than it has sometimes been made to seem and that it becomes least puzzling when studied by principles rooted in language habits. Our book, therefore, is based on the following beliefs:

(1) Writing is the use of language for expression and for communication; much attempted writing fails because the writer begins writing before he has something to say.

(2) Good writing—as manifested in word choice, in sentence structure, and in the broader aspects of composition—must be based upon clear thinking.

(3) A mastery of writing can be acquired most quickly and thoroughly through improvement rather than correction; so-called errors disappear only when the writer learns to construct a sentence well.

(4) A study of any grammar promotes skill in the use of language, but to be most helpful, the grammar studied should describe the language to which it is peculiar. The student of English derives the greatest benefit from the study of *English* grammar, not the grammar of another language —not even that of one so excellent as Latin.

(5) Usage is the basis of idiom, and hence eventually the basis of language. It determines standards; but the varying degree of respect paid to tradition at various language levels is a part of usage, and different sorts of language have different effects. Students should be aware of the importance of language differences and able to use standard English.

(6) The native language is worth studying for itself; a knowledge of the working of man's greatest invention promotes his use of it. No great immediate results can be expected from pure language study, but such study provides a foundation for continued improvement in writing and speaking.

To the authors, this approach has seemed successful. Students are aware that they are studying something important, something not to be dismissed as "just commas." They improve faster under this system than under some others because they are learning to write, not merely to "correct" weak sentences, which will remain weak after they are corrected. This method helps the teacher, too, because the student who learns to think will outgrow many infelicities and require less correction. To promote these ends, we have given more than usual attention to such subjects as development and predication.

On the other hand, our presentation of materials does not reflect a disregard for established practice. We have preserved the conventionally accepted grammatical terms and the more tenable of the common grammatical concepts, even though the resulting mixture may occasionally seem inconsistent. Similarly, we have restricted our discussion and our examples mainly to standard written English.

Among those to whom we are grateful for many helpful criticisms and suggestions are Nathaniel M. Caffee, Louisiana State University; William Card, Chicago Teachers College; Muriel J. Hughes, University of Vermont; Robert L. Kellogg, University of Virginia; Eleanor Prosser, San Jose State College; Edgar V. Roberts, Hunter College, New York City; and John C. Sherwood, University of Oregon. We thank the staff of Prentice-Hall, Inc., for constant guidance and careful editing. Those who have been concerned with the present edition most intimately are Paul O'Connell, John Beasley, and Harry Rinehart, designer of the book. Our colleagues at the University of Nevada have given us innumerable helpful suggestions. From several generations of students we have gained good as well as horrible examples, but, more important, we have had occasional evidence that the teaching of English is not entirely futile. To our wives, Johnnie Belle Gorrell and Helene Laird, we are grateful for patience and for practical assistance; we had need for both.

ROBERT M. GORRELL
CHARLTON LAIRD

The Third Edition
and the Reference System

The present-day course in English composition almost inevitably requires alternative approaches. The student needs information about his language and positive counsel on rhetoric to help him use it; at the same time he needs to have his writing criticized precisely and understandably. In the original edition of *Modern English Handbook* we attempted a rhetoric-handbook somewhat different from other available texts in its reconciliation of these alternative approaches. We tried to discuss what seemed to us essential principles of rhetoric and important information about the workings of language, as well as to provide exercises and suggestions for practice. In each section a Guide to Revision gave the teacher a quick and economical way to criticize writing. We devised a reference system flexible enough that teachers could use it for various purposes—detailed enough to permit marking papers with considerable exactitude, yet sufficiently simple so that a busy teacher could indicate routine revisions in a routine way, particularly for students needing only a reminder of what they already know. A second edition provided an opportunity to tighten the book for consistency. We hope that in the third edition we have been able to bring the volume still closer to the book we originally envisaged. We have revised mainly along two lines; we have tried to strengthen positive portions of the book, and we have tried to simplify the portions especially concerned with revision.

In strengthening the positive discussions of the book, we have, first of all, reorganized, working toward a more logical arrangement of sections and also combining some subjects to provide more workable sections for class assignments. We have also expanded both the rhetorical and the linguistic discussions. Section 11 on style and tone is essentially new, as is Section 24 on the nature of language and the growth of English. We have expanded the sections on rhetoric of the sentence—especially those dealing with such topics as predication, the choice of the sentence subject, and the choice of sentence patterns. Additional material on the paragraph appears in the first part of the book, and fuller treatments of the *précis* and summary are part of the expanded sections on the research paper, although they can be treated as individual topics if the instructor wishes. Sections on language have been revised, sometimes to include frequently neglected topics such as Indo-European bases.

Along with these changes, we have reworked the reference system, hoping to retain its flexibility and precision and at the same time to make it simpler and easier for both student and instructor to manage. The total number of reference symbols has been reduced for convenience; for example, a single number now suffices for all punctuation errors. Also, a few common blunders in student writing have been moved to new sections of the book where they can perhaps more easily be found; the comma fault, for example, is now discussed as a punctuation error, and a single number refers to all errors in agreement or concord. Since, however, the reference system remains suitable for various kinds of marking, the following observations may help the teacher adapt the text to his course and his system of recommending revisions.

(1) Although the book attempts a logical sequence of subjects, sections are relatively independent and are provided with cross references; thus subjects may be considered in any order.

(2) Section 33 discusses uses of the reference system; the teacher may wish to assign it early in the course, perhaps when the first marked papers are returned.

(3) Three systems of symbols can be used independently or in conjunction: (a) reference to sections by numbers charted on the front endpapers; (b) reference by copyreading symbols and abbreviations charted on the front endpapers and listed alphabetically on the back endpapers; (c) reference by numbers to rhetorical discussions charted in the box on the front endpapers.

(4) Brief and direct instructions for revision appear as the second part of most sections, unless, as in Section 24 on language, discussions of revision are inappropriate. The instructor may wish to call the students' attention to the distinctions between the reference and rhetorical sections.

(5) The instructor may use the different sets of symbols in various ways to suit his needs or his methods of correction. He may, for example, mark a failure to set off a non-restrictive modifier with "27," directing the student to the reference portion of the section on punctuation, where he can find his error described with suggestions for revision. Or he may wish to direct the student more specifically by using "27e." On the other hand, he may wish to use the symbol "P," or he may wish to specify the error by "P4." If he feels that the student may profitably study something of the nature of English punctuation he can direct the student to the positive discussion in the rhetorical section, with "27-2."

(6) The book includes reference symbols for a number of infelicities of writing not usually classified in handbooks; the instructor can often avoid the need for a lengthy comment by using symbols to refer to rhetorical revisions—for example, "3–4" for coherence within the paragraph, "13–4" for predication with the verb *to be,* "17–3" for appropriate use of the passive voice, "10–5" for a discussion of introductions.

(7) The teacher can often save time in correction by encircling an expression included in the Glossary, 34, and by instructing students to look up circled expressions in the Glossary.

Acknowledgments

The authors are grateful to the following for the illustrative material reproduced in this handbook:

Appleton-Century-Crofts, Inc.: the selection from *A History of the English Language,* 2nd ed., by Albert C. Baugh, used by permission of Appleton-Century-Crofts, Inc.

The Atlantic Monthly: the selections from Jacques Barzun, "What Is Teaching?" 174 (December, 1944); James B. Conant, "Force and Freedom," 183 (January, 1949); David L. Cohn, "Who Will Do the Dirty Work?" 183 (May, 1959); and "Moonlight and Poison Ivy," 183 (January, 1949); Hilary St. George Saunders, "Can France Come Back?" 183 (March, 1949). Used by permission of *The Atlantic Monthly.*

Bobbs-Merrill Co., Inc.: the selection from *Company Manners* by Louis Kronenberger, used by permission of Bobbs-Merrill Co., Inc.

Cornell University Press: the selection from *Runaway Star* by Robert A. Hume, used by permission of the Cornell University Press.

Dodd, Mead & Company: the selection from *Life and Literature* by Lafcadio Hearn, copyright, 1917, by Mitchell McDonald, and used by permission of Dodd, Mead & Company.

Doubleday & Company, Inc.: the selection from *Rain* by W. Somerset Maugham, used by permission of Doubleday & Company, Inc.

E. P. Dutton & Co., Inc.: the selections from *The World of Washington Irving* by Van Wyck Brooks, Everyman's Library, used by permission of E. P. Dutton & Co., Inc.

Farrar, Strauss & Cudahy, New York, Cassell and Company, Ltd., London, and Robert Graves: the selection from *Occupation Writer* by Robert Graves, copyright, 1950, by Robert Graves, and used by permission of the above.

Harcourt, Brace and World, Inc.: the selection from *Book of Bays* by William Beebe, copyright, 1942, by Harcourt, Brace and Company, the selection from

Abraham Lincoln: The Prairie Years by Carl Sandburg, copyright, 1926, by Harcourt, Brace and Company, the selection from *Language: An Introduction to the Study of Speech* by Edward Sapir, copyright, 1921, by Harcourt, Brace & World, Inc.; renewed, 1949, by Jean Sapir. Reprinted by permission of the publishers.

Harper's Magazine: the selection from Russell Lynes, "Highbrow, Lowbrow, Middlebrow," (February, 1949), used by permission of the author.

Harvard University Press: the selection from *Philosophy in a New Key* by Susanne K. Langer, copyright, 1942, 1951, and used by permission of the Harvard University Press.

Holt, Rinehart & Winston, Inc.: the selection from *Three Keys to Language* by Robert M. Estrick and Hans Sperber, used by permission of Holt, Rinehart & Winston, Inc.

Houghton Mifflin Company: the selection from *Letters of Henry Adams* by Worthington C. Ford, the selection from *Convention and Revolt in Poetry* by John Livingstone Lowes, the selections from *Patterns of Culture* by Ruth Benedict, used by permission of the Houghton Mifflin Company.

Indiana University Press: the selection from *The Old Northwest: Pioneer Period, 1815–1840* by R. Carlyle Buley, copyright, 1951, and used by permission of the Indiana University Press.

John Lane The Bodley Head Limited: the selection from *Heretics* by G. K. Chesterton, used by permission of John Lane The Bodley Head Limited, London.

Alfred A. Knopf, Inc.: the selection from *Hieroglyphics: A Note Upon Ecstacy in Literature* by Arthur Machen, used by permission of Alfred A. Knopf, Inc.

The Macmillan Company: the selection from *Science and the Modern World* by A. N. Whitehead, the selection from *The Mind of Primitive Man* by Franz Boas, the selection from *Men of Destiny* by Walter Lippmann, the selection from "Misspelling in the Twelfth Grade" *(Teachers Service Bulletin in English)* by Thomas Clark Pollock, the selection from *Modern English and Its Heritage* by Margaret Bryant, used by permission of The Macmillan Company.

The New Yorker: the selection from John Updike, "On the Sidewalk," (February 21, 1959). Used by permission of *The New Yorker.*

Oxford University Press: the selection from *Man: A History of the Human Body* by Sir Arthur Keith, copyright, 1912, and used by permission of Oxford University Press; the selections from *The Classical Tradition* by Gilbert Highet, copyright, 1949, and used by permission of Oxford University Press; the selection from *Under the Sea Wind* by Rachel L. Carson, copyright, 1941, by Rachel L. Carson, and used by permission of Oxford University Press.

Penguin Books, Inc.: the selection from *Our Language* by Simeon Potter, used by permission of Penguin Books, Inc.

Philosophical Library: the selection from the preface written by George Bernard Shaw to *The Miraculous Birth of Language* by Richard Albert Wilson, used by permission of the Philosophical Library.

Prentice-Hall, Inc.: the selection from *Thinking Straight: A Guide for Readers and Writers* by Monroe C. Beardsley, copyright, 1950, 1956, and used by permission of Prentice-Hall, Inc.

Charles Scribner's Sons: the selection from *Of Time and the River* by Thomas Wolfe, used by permission of Charles Scribner's Sons; the selection from *How to Write Short Stories* by Ring Lardner, used by permission of Charles Scribner's Sons.

Viking Press, Inc.: the selection from *On The Road* by Jack Kerouac, copyright, 1957, by Jack Kerouac, reprinted by permission of The Viking Press, Inc.; the selection from *Sea of Cortez* by John Steinbeck and Edward F. Ricketts, copyright, 1941, and used by permission of The Viking Press, Inc.; the selection from *Winesburg, Ohio* by Sherwood Anderson, copyright, 1919, and used by permission of The Viking Press, Inc.

Wright, Louis B.: the selection from *The Colonial Civilization of North America* by Louis B. Wright, used by permission of the author.

Contents

6

EVIDENCE: INDUCTIVE REASONING, page 88

7

LOGIC: DEDUCTIVE REASONING, page 104

Organization and Style SECTIONS 8–11

8

ANALYSIS AND CLASSIFICATION, page 125

9

ORGANIZATION; THE OUTLINE, page 136

10

TRANSITIONS, INTRODUCTIONS, CONCLUSIONS, page 157

11

STYLE AND TONE, page 176

15

SUBORDINATION; MODIFICATION, page 247

16

CONTROLLING SECONDARY PATTERNS; INCOMPLETE PATTERNS, page 274

17

EMPHASIS: USING THE PATTERNS OF ENGLISH, page 284

21

AGREEMENT OR CONCORD, page 359

21 Agr

22

FORMS OF MODIFIERS, page 369

22 Adj; Adv

23

FUNCTION WORDS, page 379

23 FW

Mechanics SECTIONS **27–29**

27

PUNCTUATION, page 465

28

THE MANUSCRIPT, page 497

29

SPELLING, page 508

The Research Paper SECTIONS 30–32

30

THE PRÉCIS AND SUMMARY; TAKING NOTES; PLAGIARISM, page 537

31

COLLECTING MATERIAL, page 552

32

WRITING A RESEARCH REPORT, page 576

Appendix: Ready Aids To Revision SECTIONS 33–34

33

REVISING AND CORRECTING THE THEME, page 601

Modern English Handbook

Getting Started—
the Paragraph

First catch the rabbit . . .

The old recipe for rabbit stew begins with the obvious, but it begins wisely. The rabbit is essential, and the essential must not be overlooked just because it is obvious. Any advice about writing must begin: "First have something to say."

But ideas are more elusive than rabbits, and writing is more complicated than rabbit stew. Writing requires thinking, and thinking is always complicated and hard. Writing is complicated also because the writer needs to do everything at once, and the student of writing needs to study everything at once. A writer produces words, sentences, paragraphs, and extended compositions all at the same time; words must be spelled, sentences punctuated, and paragraphs unified. A writer may be studying the meanings of words, but to practice what he is learning he must at the same time use sentences and paragraphs. Thus there is no one right place to begin the study of writing. But the student must start; one sure way not to learn to write is not to start. This book opens with discussions of main ideas and of some of the uses of main ideas in brief compositions and paragraphs—discussions of rabbits and rabbit traps and a few basic recipes.

Section 1 attempts to clear away some of the barriers to writing by encouraging disciplined thinking. The student sitting among his sharpened pencils, staring with mounting desperation at the clock or his blank paper, waiting for inspiration to strike, may get started best by directing his thinking. Finding something to write about, getting "an idea" for a theme, is not so difficult as it often seems, if the student recognizes what he is trying to do. Section 1, therefore, suggests some ways of thinking about a subject, of narrowing a general subject to something specific enough so that it can be significantly discussed in a relatively short paper, by selecting aspects of a subject which fit the writer's interests and knowledge. A subject, however, even a fairly specific one, is not "an idea" for a paper. The writer must do more than find a tractable topic; he must think *about* the topic. The "idea" for a theme is usually what the writer thinks about a topic—particularly, what he concludes about it. Isolating, expressing, and developing such an idea is, of course, not simple. In one sense, getting started involves most of the materials in the early sections of this book— generalizing from evidence, for example, or analyzing a subject. That is, the main idea involves the writer's attitudes about a subject and his purpose in writing, and it may shift as the writing progresses. The first section, therefore, proceeds from a discussion of topics for writing to consideration of the main idea for a paper.

An idea, something to write about, is a logical enough starting place for a discussion of writing, but it is only a start. The idea must be controlled, expanded, and built into some kind of meaningful statement; and since this is intended to be a practical book, we proceed in the second and third sections to the kind of writing problem which the student is likely to face at the beginning: the writing of a paragraph. Section 2 carries the discussion of the main idea to an immediate practical application in the paragraph, where a main idea often appears as a topic sentence. Principles of unity and of focusing material on a central topic are essential to the writing of paragraphs and can be applied also to longer compositions. Section 3 centers on methods of holding a paragraph together, on coherence.

Obviously, these discussions do not complete the student's knowledge of how the paragraph works; but later sections on developing and controlling an idea and on organization all add pertinent information. The paragraph is a place to begin; the student who has learned to focus on a main idea in a unified paragraph has progressed a long way toward clear and forceful composition.

1

The Topic;
The Main Idea

For Guide to Revision, see page 13

Writing animates a purpose; it develops something the writer has to say about a specific topic.

Friends gather after midnight in a dormitory room. Most of the group have something to say, and much of the time they interest one another. A student home from a play rehearsal starts to tell what happened. Before he has finished, someone else has thought of a high school play rehearsal and has his anecdote ready. Others pick up the thread. But one student with no story to tell says that dramatics is a waste of time and should not be allowed to divert students from the more serious business of studying chemistry. Someone calls on his experience for a story which he thinks justifies the value of plays. Someone else quotes his psychology book on the values of recreation. Someone describes a very bad high school production to show that amateur plays threaten the future of drama. The argument turns into a discussion of the idiosyncrasies of various dramatic coaches and finally drifts off into enthusiastic if unreasoned views of the heroine in a current moving picture.

The discussion probably produces no conversational triumphs. In the cold permanence of ink and paper, many of the comments would seem feeble; but the stuff of writing is there, as it is in the experience and interests of almost every student. The writer has experience, opinions, and knowledge which give him a purpose for writing; he draws on them, supplements them with further thought and further reading, and gives them form and order to turn them into prose.

1-1 AN "IDEA FOR A THEME"

The writer relies on experience and knowledge for his materials, but he must select from them in an orderly way before he can produce good writing. He may appropriately begin with what students often refer to as "an idea for a theme." This sort of idea, properly refined, gives the writing its individuality, its reason for existence. Dozens of sportsmen have written essays on fishing, for example—some good, some bad; but the writing is not necessarily repetitious, because each writer can narrow the general subject to a topic which interests him and he can write about this restricted topic for his own purposes, focusing on his own idea. The college theme may be an artificial exercise in some ways, but in most ways, such as its dependence on a main idea, it is like most other writing. A letter or a newspaper editorial or a report on a business inspection trip or a political speech or a legal brief may have its subject dictated by orders or circumstances; but it gets its distinction and has its impact because it focuses on main ideas, because it has a purpose. The deadlines of the world are at least as rigorous as those of the classroom, and editors or juries or vice presidents are more ruthless critics than are instructors.

An "idea for a theme" can develop in many ways, even in a sudden flash of insight. Usually, however, it requires effort and thought. The student can simplify the effort, or at least make it more fruitful, by directing his thinking in two ways: (1) by narrowing or restricting his topic and (2) by deciding as specifically as he can what he wants to say about his topic.

1-2 LIMITING THE TOPIC

To have something to say the writer may take a subject which interests him, or which has been assigned, and narrow it systematically. For example, a student recalls that he has been thinking about extracurricular activities in college and decides to write on the subject. He realizes that "Extracurricular Activities in College" is too broad for a 750-word paper, so he decides to narrow the topic by considering one activity. He breaks the general subject into athletics, music, drama, social affairs, campus politics. He might, of course, have thought of more subtopics, but he knows something of campus politics. "Campus

Politics," however, is not specific enough for a relatively short paper. The student considers various aspects of campus politics: graft in campus politics, relations of campus politics to academic work, methods for succeeding in campus politics, the value of campus politics. He decides on the last, but as he considers ways in which campus politics is valuable, he discovers that he still has more to say than he can put into one paper, and he sees he must break down his topic again. Re-examining his ideas, he finds that he considers campus politics valuable to the nation as training in democracy, valuable to the school, and valuable to the individual student. He sees that these sub-topics partially overlap, but he also sees the advantage of separating them and selecting one for his paper. Because he feels he is best able to discuss the value of politics to the student, he works down to a topic specific enough so that he can hope to do something with it: "Campus Politics as Education." The process, then, whereby a specific topic can be drawn from a general subject is roughly pictured in the following chart:

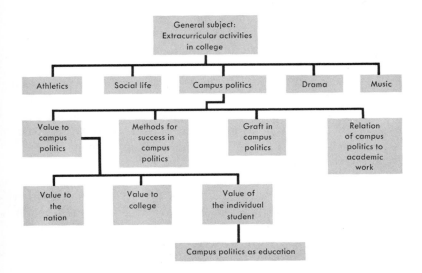

The process is essentially that of analysis (see Section 8), breaking a subject into its parts in an orderly manner and then selecting a specific part to be discussed in detail.

Even when a topic is assigned, the writer can usually improve his paper by narrowing the topic. Assignments for student writing frequently grow from reading assigned in the composition course. After class study of an essay on language—such as those by Sir Arthur Quiller-Couch or George Orwell or H. L. Mencken, which often appear in freshman readers—the instructor might ask for a paper recording some of the student's observations or attitudes on language. The student would need to restrict the subject for his individual purposes. He might ask himself questions and rule out some large portions of the subject, such as the history of English, comparison of different languages, or changes in modern studies of grammar, as too complicated or outside his knowledge and interest; he might decide that he would write on some aspect of modern usage in language. Again he could think of various narrower possibilities: some dialect peculiarities, modern "errors" in usage, current slang, for example. He could pick any one of these and narrow it; modern "errors" in usage might be restricted to current attitudes toward *like* and *as* or *lie* and *lay*. Or current slang might be narrowed as the student remembers his experiences with a dance orchestra, decides to write about musicians' slang, and then realizes that he can restrict still further and write about musician's slang for naming instruments. With his topic restricted he can recall pertinent details from his experience, fill in by reading, and write an interesting paper. Or he might turn the assignment in a quite different way. He might recall that dictionaries provide all sorts of exciting information and decide to use them to do something on word history or word origins. He could then start working toward something specific and develop a good paper on meaning variations in a single word—"Do You *Dig?*" or "*Nice* Was Not Always Nice."

A final title may differ from the descriptive topic that a writer selects for his own guidance. But a writer can help himself greatly by restricting his thinking to a topic narrow enough to be manageable and descriptive enough to serve as a guide. He need not, of course, proceed as formally as the chart above suggests, but he needs to ask himself questions until he can focus on a topic in which he is interested, about which he has some knowledge, and which he can develop in the space allotted.

1-3 A MAIN IDEA

A topic alone is not sufficient basis for starting to write a paper. In fact, a writer seldom settles on a restricted topic without thinking, at the same time, about his main idea; the topic and the main idea develop together. A student may be told to write a paper on Milton's *Paradise Lost.* He may narrow his subject to something about religious attitudes in the poem and then, further, to puritanism in the poem. But he has something to say, an idea for a paper, only after he decides from his study of the poem that Milton does not sound like the puritan he is called by the introduction in his text. He then has something to say about his topic. Or a student may experience a month of college social life and find he wants to talk about it—describe it, criticize it, suggest changes, praise it. If he narrows a topic to some manageable aspect of college social life and then decides from his month of experience what he thinks about it, he has an idea for a theme, something to say. An idea for a paper may come from long-held convictions of the writer, from study and research, from questions the writer asks himself about his experiences, from all sorts of sources, and even from prejudices. It may grow or change as actual writing progresses, but a main idea is essential in writing that has purpose and unity.

Almost any unit of writing, from a sentence to a book, focuses on a main idea. The main idea may be a highly important interpretive statement or a highly personal point of view. Frederick Jackson Turner in his influential essay on *The Significance of the Frontier in American History* marshals evidence to support the view that:

> . . . the existence of an area of free land, its continuous recession, and the advance of American settlement westward, explain American development.

Well-known facts of history are seen in a new light when interpreted on the basis of this central idea. On the other hand, Robert Louis Stevenson in an entirely different kind of essay, *Walking Tours,* offers no profound conclusions; he holds his facts together with a central theme that walking tours, well conducted, are a source of genuine delight and satisfaction. But both essays give clear evidence that the writers had thought about the central meaning of what they had to say, and had selected and organized their material with a main idea or purpose in mind.

Usually student writing will center on main ideas that are less ambitious than those which govern the full-length essays mentioned above. In fact, this book suggests that the student can best begin by working to unify a very brief composition about a main idea stated in a topic sentence (see Section 2).

1-4 STATING THE MAIN IDEA

Even for a brief composition, however, the student trying to improve his writing can develop no better habit than that of *writing down his main idea in a complete sentence* as part of his planning. The sentence need not appear in the finished paragraph or composition, but writing it is one of the most useful steps in planning a paper.

This statement of the main idea—which might be called a theme sentence or thesis sentence—is usually in a writer's mind as he narrows his topic. Narrowing the topic and narrowing the main idea are parts of the same thinking processes; stating the main idea is a way of focusing still more precisely. For example, if a student had decided to write on "Campus Politics as Education," he would have had reasons for his selection. He would have thought about his attitude toward the subject and his purpose in writing the paper; he would have thought about his main idea. He would then need to sharpen his thinking to confine it in a clear sentence. He might adopt a controversial point of view and phrase his main idea as:

> Campus politics provides the opportunities for practical education that are lacking in formal courses in political science.

Another student might phrase his main idea as:

> Campus politics, because it deals with artificial situations and insignificant problems, has no place in an educational institution.

A third student might decide that he could take no controversial stand, that he wanted to describe, not argue; but he would still need to state his main idea as a guide to his planning:

> Campus politics is sometimes educational and sometimes a waste of time, but it is almost always exciting for the participating student.

Even these statements, however, suggest a paper of considerable proportions. For the kind of paper usually required in college classes, the student would need to limit his main idea further. The first student, for example, might think of specific opportunities for education in campus politics, using a process of dividing and selecting like that outlined above for limiting a topic. His statement could become one of the following, more specific and more workable:

> Campus politics teaches students the psychological principles of political campaigning.
>
> Campus politics is a practical way of teaching a student public speaking.
>
> Campus politics teaches the methods of organizing a large group of people and directing their efforts toward a single goal.
>
> Campus politics gives students practice in operating the machinery of government.
>
> Campus politics tests the student's integrity because it often requires him to choose between his selfish interests and the general good.

As he writes, the student may, of course, change his mind or collect new evidence which will result in a modification of his main idea; but until he can tie himself down to some tentative view, he has not thought enough. Before he starts he should be able to make a statement of the main idea which has the following qualities:

> (1) It should be a complete sentence. The statement should not be merely a wordier version of the topic.
>
> (2) It should be specific, the more specific the better. "This paper describes a house I knew in my childhood" only postpones the necessary thinking. "An old house had an important influence on my childhood" is better. "An old house in our block, because it reminded me of the man in the Charles Addams cartoons, gave me a horror of dark rooms" is still better.
>
> (3) It should be exact; an inexact statement usually results from cloudy thinking. For instance, the first topic mentioned above might have been phrased as follows: "Campus politics provides more opportunities for practical education than all the formal courses in political science in the university." This is a possible subject, but the student probably has no intention of writing on it. Has he taken "all the formal courses in political science"? Probably not, and even if he has he probably has no intention of contrasting them systematically with what a student can learn from campus politics.

1-5 IDEAS FOR WRITING; A JOURNAL

One good way to collect ideas for writing is to keep a thoughtful journal. The student who takes a little time every night to ask and answer the following question is never at a loss for a subject: What was the most interesting thing I did, heard, thought, read, observed, or experienced today? He may answer to himself: "For the first time today I understood what *calculus* means"; "I am beginning to observe that my roommate is a complex person"; "Lunch in the dining hall is unpleasant, even though the food is good, because the constant noise and confusion make conversation impossible"; "Looking about this afternoon, I noticed that I can detect about three generations of style in the campus architecture"; "What Professor Whitsmall said today about Freud's theory of the unconscious seems to me to contradict what he said day before yesterday"; "I cannot study efficiently and watch television at the same time." If the student can tell himself in some detail what he means by one of these generalizations and can collect evidence or illustrations to develop it, he has most of the raw material he needs to write a brief composition. The instructor may control assigned material in composition more or less rigidly, but the student who is thrown on his own need never lack for something to write about if he keeps a tolerably full journal.

1-6 MAIN IDEA AND UNITY

A motion picture camera man photographing a crowd faces a problem like the writer's. He attempts to present a large number of details in such a way that they will make a unified impression. He often provides views from a distance which give a general over-all impression of the large scene, then turns his camera to details, to pictures of individual characters and smaller scenes; and almost always he helps his audience to keep these more concentrated scenes in order by focusing attention on some central object. A tree or a building or an important character becomes a focal point, and the camera swings back to it and then away from it so that the audience can keep the great mass of details in order by relating them to this point of focus. Similarly, the skillful writer keeps his reader's attention turned toward a main idea or to central objects which he can use as focal points.

These focal points are important in every stage of the writing, from planning to proofreading. Any alert mind constantly receives new suggestions and continually sees new implications in familiar material; but not all suggestions, however enticing they may be, are useful when they appear. A student may decide to write a paper arguing that fraternities often harm campus politics by using the methods of machine politicians. He remembers that one of the finest men on the campus had been defeated for office because he refused to join a fraternity; several fraternities had combined to elect an inferior candidate. He begins his paper with this story. Then he remembers that the fraternity machine had triumphed partly because it could afford to plaster the campus with advertising. He writes a paragraph on campaign posters. Next he remembers that his group in high school once elected Jimmie Good over Henry Maibie by using on its posters the slogan, "We want a Good president, and we don't mean Maibie." But this slogan, he recalls, had been based on a pun in his mathematics class, and accordingly the student turns to a discussion of the witty remarks of the mathematics teacher—and is by this time completely off the subject. He has failed to concentrate on his main idea, his controlling purpose.

1-7 DEVICES FOR UNITY

Usually the main idea or central propostion becomes the focal point of the paper, the unifying device. A student writing a theme on the educational value of student self-government might take as his theme sentence a statement that student government provides experience in democracy. He could then unify his paper by relating subsidiary facts and arguments to this thesis.

Often, however, other devices help to keep the reader's attention in focus, as in Thomas Henry Huxley's famous essay *On a Piece of Chalk*. The main idea of the essay is that the earth "has been the theatre of a series of changes," that physical characteristics and living inhabitants of the earth have been affected by evolution. The essay is unified around a specific example, around the story of the changes embodied in a piece of chalk.

Similarly, Esmé Wingfield Stratford labels a chapter of his *History of British Civilization* "Gothic Christianity." He wishes to describe the particular qualities of the growth of religious ardor in England about the thirteenth century. To unify his chapter he relates his ideas to the development of the Gothic architecture which distinguished English cathedrals built during the period. These cathedrals become a symbol for the thesis of the chapter.

A student theme on the value of student self-government uses a similar device for unity. Its central thesis is that student government improves efficiency and justice in handling student affairs. Its title, however, is *The Bookstore,* and the arguments in the paper are unified about a story of how a student government acquired a university bookstore and improved its service and management. The paper makes such general points as these: students are better aware of their own needs than are other groups; they are capable of sensible management; they are stimulated by the challenge of the problems of regulating their own affairs. The paper connects all these by relating them to the specific instance of the development of the bookstore.

Unity can be furthered by keeping the reader's attention focused. A textbook explanation of the working of a gasoline engine provides a good example. The explanation follows the fuel from the storage tank through the carburetor into the cylinders and finally, as waste, out the exhaust. By explaining the working of each part of the engine in terms of its effect on the fuel, the writer makes a clear and unified explanation. An account of the workings of the houses of Congress gains unity by centering attention on the progress of a bill from its original drafting through readings and committee reports and votes and conferences to its final signing.

Some devices for unity are more artificial than these, invented solely to hold the composition together. A bridge game unifies one mystery novel, for instance; it has no relation to the plot of the story, but ties it together. The murder takes place during a bridge game, and subsequent events are talked about, sometimes whimsically, as if they were parts of a game. A chapter in which the women characters do some expert investigating is called "Queens are Trumps"; the device gets mixed in a chapter called "One-eyed Jacks Wild," but the book returns to the original game and concludes with "The Last Trick." Even so contrived a device as this may unify writing.

1 Top; MI

THE TOPIC;
THE MAIN IDEA

Guide to Revision

Consider your purposes in the paper and frame a statement of the main idea, limiting the topic if necessary; then rewrite to focus attention on the main idea.

A sufficiently restricted topic and a significant main idea for a paper usually develop together; the topic limits itself as the main idea emerges more sharply. Usually, therefore, the paper that attempts to discuss a broad subject can be improved by some attention to a main idea.

1a   THE TOPIC   Top

Many student themes are doomed at the outset; a workable main idea is almost impossible because the themes attempt too much. Students try to discuss in 500 words "The Culture of the Middle West"; they strive in a page or two to analyze "America's Foreign Policy" or "University Education in America." These are, of course, worthy general subjects, but they are topics for books or series of books, not for short essays. A theme on any one of them would be only a string of unsubstantiated generalities.

The writer must limit himself, must focus on the aspect of his general subject to which he can make an individual contribution. He might, for example, narrow a subject like "The Culture of the Middle West" geographically, restricting his topic to the culture of one state or further to the culture of a city or a section of a city. He might narrow the subject still more to various aspects of culture—the literature or the religion or the art of a restricted area. Religion could then be restricted to some attitude toward religion. A possible working topic might be "Fundamentalism in Religion in Midtown, Michigan."

ORIGINAL	REVISION
Fishing	How to Tie a Fly
Interesting People I Have Known	My Temperamental Music Teacher
Athletics	How to Play First Base
Photography	Photographing Against the Sun
Newspapers in the United States	The Editorial Attitude of *The Daily News* Toward Expansion of the School System
War Between the States	A Problem in Tactics at the Battle of Bull Run

Preliminary restriction of the topic can prevent the theme from rambling. The writer can break a larger topic into its parts, select the one on which he wants to concentrate, and eliminate the others from his discussion in a single sentence of his introduction.

ORIGINAL

The accomplished skier has many means of negotiating steep country. The beginner, of course, cannot hope to learn them all at once, and he does not need to, although they are all worth learning, and anyone who loves to ski will keep learning new ones. Some maneuvers are important for safety, even though they are not much used by experts interested in speed.

[*The writer is forced into generalities because he has not broken the broad subject of skiing maneuvers into its parts and selected the one he wants to write about.*]

REVISION

The accomplished skier learns many means of negotiating steep country, but for the beginner the snow plow is the most useful. With this simple skill even a novice can come down any slope without breaking his neck.

[*More or less consciously the writer has divided maneuvers into those suitable for experts and those for beginners, then divided the latter group again and selected the snow plow for his topic.*]

1b   THE MAIN IDEA   MI

A paper without a main idea is almost certain to become a purposeless jumble. Clarity of organization depends on a unifying central idea; materials introduced for development and expansion can be relevant only if they can be related to a central idea.

ORIGINAL

Reading

It is said that we learn to read in order to learn l reading. And because reading is the greatest individual means of acquiring knowl-

REVISION

Reading to Learn

There are so many reasons for reading that we sometimes overlook the obvious one—that reading is our most important single means of acquiring

ORIGINAL (*Cont.*)

edge, it is easy to understand why the person who lets himself hang back in the shadows of illiteracy can never attain anything in life worth shouting about.

Many of the happiest hours of my childhood were passed in reading. I can remember when I found my father's discarded stories of Frank Merriwell in a box in the garage and found them more exciting than the batch of comic books I had acquired. It was from those books that I learned how much fun reading could be. I used to push myself back into a corner of the garage and sit for hours while Frank Merriwell struck out the entire Harvard team or rescued Elsie from the head-hunters.

Many people I know say that they do not like to read. I do not understand their point of view, because most of the knowledge of the world can be acquired from reading. In some countries of the world today people are not so fortunate, because there is no freedom of the press and they cannot acquire knowledge so easily. In America we need only to read in order to become educated.

A reader should not be content to read something he is already an authority on, but he should tackle books about subjects of which he is relatively ignorant. It is true that a good book can teach you a lesson, one which you can profit from, if you will stop and think how pleasant and easy it is to read. . . .

[*The paper continues generally in the same vein. Much is wrong with it, but at the bottom of most of the trouble is the absence of a main idea. One cannot say that the paper wanders from the point; there just is no point. To begin with, the title is too broad; it needs to be narrowed. Then the writer needs to decide what he wants to say about reading and start over.*]

REVISION (*Cont.*)

knowledge. We talk nostalgically of childhood hours spent with Frank Merriwell among the head-hunters, or we cite the emotional power of a great poem, and we forget some of the more pedestrian uses of printed language.

Even our most common day-to-day activities require some ability in reading. The worker has to read signs to drive his car to the plant in the morning. The careful shopper reads labels as she compares the quality of the products she is considering. Telegrams, memoranda, letters are read every second, and important matters turn on the communication they carry. Lives often depend on the ability of a military officer to read orders accurately. Our daily lives turn on communication, much of which requires skillful reading.

Almost equally important is our use of reading to acquire more general but equally practical information. We read to find out how to bake a cake or make a model airplane or identify a horned lark. Words describe the cast of a play, tell us when and where to find a meeting, help us order a meal or catch a train. More complex reading can make a student an expert in chemistry or philosophy. And in a very real sense, reading can make a democracy work. Only reading can create an informed electorate in a world as complex as ours.

In still another way, however, reading is the route to valuable information. By reading literature we begin to learn what life is about. . . .

[*With a main idea—that reading is necessary because it is our most important means of acquiring knowledge —the theme makes more sense. The topic is still too broad, but the writer can collect illustrative details because he knows what he is trying to illustrate.*]

ORIGINAL (*Cont.*)

I like Walt Kelly's comic strip, *Pogo.* One of my favorite characters is Albert the Alligator; good old lazy Albert is somewhat of a big, conceited show-off. And of course everybody loves Pogo. As for Deacon Muskrat and the Buzzard, they are anything but lovable, though they are not so short-tempered as Albert, who though he is loyal to his friends and even sentimental on occasion will sometimes throw a towering tantrum. His friend, Churchy La Femme. . . .

[*At the beginning this composition threatens to become confused because it lacks any unifying main idea.*]

REVISION (*Cont.*)

Walt Kelly's comic strip, *Pogo,* gains part of its charm from the fact that each of the swamp creatures becomes a satire on some recognizable type of human being. Albert the Alligator is an irresponsible but genial ne'er-do-well, a lazy, rather cowardly show-off, short-tempered enough to throw a towering tantrum, but loyal to his friends and even, on occasion, sentimental. Deacon Muskrat, on the other hand. . . .

[*With the unifying idea that each of Walt Kelly's creatures can be equated with a human type, the writer can give order and unity to his composition.*]

EXERCISE 1

A. Criticize the following topics and statements of main ideas; which are suitable for student themes?

1. TOPIC: Large and Small Schools.
   MAIN IDEA: Advantages and disadvantages of both large and small schools.
2. TOPIC: Learning American History from Stamps.
   MAIN IDEA: Collecting American stamps is a painless but profitable way to learn the facts of American history.
3. TOPIC: The Two-Party System.
   MAIN IDEA: The two-party system has many advantages over political systems which are split into many parties.
4. TOPIC: Building Your Own Boat.
   MAIN IDEA: How to build your own boat, the different kinds of boats available, the methods, and all the fun and also all the disappointments involved.
5. TOPIC: Making Your Own Drapes.
   MAIN IDEA: Making drapes for your room requires consideration of texture and color in choosing material, selection of a suitable and practical style, patience, and a sense of humor.
6. TOPIC: Woodchucks as Game Animals.
   MAIN IDEA: Hunting woodchucks provides good sport; woodchucks are plentiful and never out of season, and properly dressed the flesh is excellent food.

7. TOPIC: Sutphen's Mansion.
   MAIN IDEA: An hour wandering through the ruins of the old
                 mansion makes one feel a sense of loss for a way of
                 life that has disappeared from the South.
8. TOPIC: Orientation.
   MAIN IDEA: This theme will show various problems of the fresh-
                 man at a large university and how his courses are
                 different from his high school work and something
                 should be done to remedy the situation.
9. TOPIC: Yellow Creek.
   MAIN IDEA: A description of Yellow Creek as it wanders through
                 rich fields and thick woods to the swimming hole
                 where I spent many happy hours.
10. TOPIC: Dormitory Life.
    MAIN IDEA: To show what life is like in a dormitory.
11. TOPIC: Ballet.
    MAIN IDEA: I would expect to give a brief sketch of the invention,
                 history, and development of ballet, say something
                 about the recent popularity of ballet in this country,
                 the leading ballet companies, stars, choreographers,
                 new ballets like *Age of Anxiety,* movies like *The Red
                 Shoes,* writers like Agnes de Mille, etc., and give
                 some of my own opinions of ballet as an art, based
                 on my lessons in ballet.
12. TOPIC: Becky Thatcher's Home.
    MAIN IDEA: When we visited Hannibal, Mo., we went to see it.
13. TOPIC: Sweaters.
    MAIN IDEA: Uses of sweaters in a girl's wardrobe. Many kinds.
                 Sizes, colors, styles, etc. What will go with what?
                 How many should a girl have? Styles. Goods from
                 which made.
14. TOPIC: Future of Mexico.
    MAIN IDEA: Although Mexico has great natural resources, the Re-
                 public is so backward that in a world dominated by
                 technology she can have no promising future without
                 closer ties with the United States or with some other
                 modern power.
15. TOPIC: Improving Bus Service.
    MAIN IDEA: Bus service in my city could be made better, and even
                 profitable, if the bus company would change some of
                 the routes to fit shifts in population, adjust schedules
                 to popular need, and teach drivers some common
                 courtesy.

B. From the list below, select five general subjects. Then, (a) narrow
each of the five to a topic which might be managed in a theme of

about 500 words, (b) for each restricted topic write a sentence stating a main idea which you might develop if you were to write a theme on the topic, and (c) for each restricted topic write a still more specific statement which might serve as the main idea of a single paragraph of 100–200 words within the longer paper.

1. Advertising
2. Television programs
3. Magazines
4. Desserts
5. Regional prejudices
6. College sports
7. Snobs
8. International tensions
9. Southern hospitality
10. Farming

C. The following is part of a paragraph from Van Wyck Brooks, *The World of Washington Irving,* concerning David Crockett, a picturesque frontier figure who got himself elected to Congress, partly by his outrageously tall tales.

. . . He [Crockett] was quite willing to have it known that he had waded the Mississippi and whipped his weight in wildcats and leaped over the Ohio, that he salted his bear-steaks with hail and peppered them with buckshot and broiled them with a flash of lightning, after riding on it. He had hugged a bear out of breath and caught and tamed an alligator and set him up beside his cabin and used him as a bench, and even wrote the story of his life, in which a friend helped him to "classify the matter." He liked the kind of real life that made a book "jump out of the press like a new dollar fresh from a mint-hopper," he said; and this *Narrative,* with its fresh images and homespun style, at once became, and remained, a frontier classic.

Obviously, Brooks has set limits to this piece of writing; it is about Crockett, and furthermore, it is about a certain aspect of Crockett. Discuss each of the following as a theme sentence which will make clear the limitations that Brooks has imposed upon this passage:

1. Crockett had his own means of attracting attention.
2. Crockett had a language of his own, a mixture of fantasy, poetry, and backwoods wit.
3. Crockett had quite a career, and even got himself elected to Congress.
4. Crockett, son of a tavern keeper, was hunter, trapper, scout, and itinerant farmer.
5. Crockett never tired of recounting his truly remarkable exploits.

D. Select an essay from a reader used in your course or an article from a magazine like *Harper's* or *The Atlantic* or *The Reporter* and state in a sentence what seems to you to be its main idea. Then choose a topic for a paper which you might write, suggested by the article, and write a statement of the main idea of the paper.

E. From the following list of subjects select those appropriate for treatment in a theme 500 to 1000 words long:

1. Ideal Communities in New York State in the Nineteenth Century
2. My First Lost Tooth
3. Should Medicine Be Socialized?
4. How to Poison Coyotes
5. How to Ride a Subway
6. The Monroe Doctrine
7. A Major Weakness of the Sales Tax
8. Prejudice in a Small Town
9. Making a Coal Mine Safe
10. Clam Chowder

F. All American libraries use some system of breaking down subjects into smaller compartments so that books can be arranged according to subject. Many American libraries use the Dewey Decimal System, which breaks the subjects of the world into ten main fields, each of these into ten fields, and so forth. Your library uses this or a similar system and has a chart describing it posted for your convenience. The following exercise assumes that your library uses the Dewey system, but it can be adapted to whatever system your library uses:

Find out the ten fields of knowledge recognized in the ten main divisions of the Dewey system. Select one subdivision under each of these main divisions; that is, select ten in all. Then narrow each of these subdivisions until it would be suitable for a theme of 500 to 1000 words.

2

Unity and the
Standard Paragraph

For Guide to Revision, see page 32

Develop paragraphs as planned units of writing, brief compositions, to reveal a main idea.

Ideas for writing vary, and so do the purposes for expressing them. One friend asks another, "What have you been doing?" and receives the reply, "Nothing much." In the circumstances, for the casual conversation to which neither friend is paying much attention, the answer is adequate and presumably more or less accurate. The friend might have taken the question more seriously and answered in a sentence rather than two words, "As I get older, I seem to accomplish less and less, becoming steadily slower to protest, more contented, and more lazy." The sentence does more with the idea, making the answer more specific, more precise, more nearly accurate. Other circumstances might require a still more fully developed answer. Robert Louis Stevenson, for example, wrote an extended essay called *An Apology for Idlers*. Or, the idea might become the basis for an organized paragraph in a friendly letter.

2-1 THE STANDARD EXPOSITORY PARAGRAPH

The paragraph is the conventional working unit for developing an idea with more detail and more precision than a sentence allows. It is indicated by indentation, usually about half an inch in script and five spaces on the typewriter. But, except for a few special uses, as in newspapers or in dialogue, the paragraph is not merely a mechanical device for breaking up a page. It is not any set number of words or sentences. A few types of paragraphs provide guides for the reader, transitions, introductions, or conclusions. Most paragraphs, however, are units of composition, organized discussions of one topic or one part of a larger topic.

Paragraphs can be written in many ways, with different methods of development and organization. They cannot be constructed by formula. But the paragraph is so important to successful composition that the student writer can profit from consciously practicing a few common patterns. The basic pattern, one which occurs with variations time after time in any writing, is so useful that we are calling it the *standard expository paragraph.*

This standard paragraph, which might be called the "workhorse paragraph," often has only two or three parts, and these may not be sharply distinguished. The standard paragraph usually includes (1) some topical material introducing the subject and (2) development, which may break into divisions and even subdivisions, and (3) sometimes a conclusion. Of these, the first, the topical material, is usually brief; it may consist only of a topic sentence, often the first sentence in a paragraph, which sometimes is supported by restatement or amplifying comments at various points throughout the paragraph. The development is likely to comprise the bulk of an expository or argumentative paragraph. In very informal or unsophisticated prose it may comprise only a sentence or two presenting relatively few details in support of the topic sentence, but most closely reasoned or adequately developed paragraphs are likely to include a hundred or perhaps several hundred words of development. The conclusion, if one is required, is almost always brief, and often is merely implied in the topical material opening the next paragraph.

2-2 SIMPLE PARAGRAPH STRUCTURE

The succeeding sections of this book consider a number of complicated problems of developing and controlling an idea and organizing a composition, the basic problems of building paragraphs. But the student can begin at once practicing a few varieties of the standard paragraph. Perhaps the simplest pattern—and one of the most useful—begins with a topic sentence and then presents a series of details that illustrate that topic. For example, if the friend mentioned above wanted to answer a question like "What have you been doing?" with greater accuracy, and perhaps some humor and grace, he would need more than a word or a sentence. His answer might be a paragraph in a friendly letter, like the following:

> I am no better than a procrastinating cuss, and since being married I do less than ever before. Here is another winter gone and I am again nursing nasturtiums and feeding mosquitoes. I am going on to thirty-eight years old, the yawning gulf of middle-age. Another, the fifth, year of professordom is expiring this week. I am balder, duller, more pedantic, and more lazy than ever. I have lost my love of travel. My fits of wrath and rebellion against the weaknesses and shortcomings of mankind are less violent than they were, though grumbling has become my favorite occupation. I have ceased to grow rapidly either in public esteem or in mental development. One year resembles another, and if it weren't for occasional disturbing dreams of decay, disaster, or collapse, I should consider myself as having attained as much of Nirwana as a man of my race and temperament can expect to do.

The paragraph is from a letter by Henry Adams, one of America's most cogent writers. For other purposes and more subtle ideas, Adams often wrote more complicated paragraphs. Here he needs only to announce a subject, develop it with a series of details having no expressed order, and finish with a more general illustration of the topic which serves as a conclusion.

The following paragraph is another illustration of the same simple pattern:

> His folks talked like other folks in the neighborhood. They called themselves "pore" people. A man learned in books was "eddicated." What was certain was "sartin." The syllables came through the nose; "joints" were "j'ints"; fruit "spiled" instead of spoiling; in corn-planting time they "drapped" the seeds. They went on errands and "brung" things back. Their dogs "follered" the coons. Flannel was "flannen," a bandanna a "banddanner," a chimney a "chimbly," a shadow a "shadder," and mosquitoes plain "skeeters." They "gethered" crops. A creek was a "crick," a cover a "kiver."
>
> —CARL SANDBURG, *Abe Lincoln: The Prairie Years*

The paragraph begins by summarizing the main idea. The remainder of the paragraph lists particular instances to illustrate and support the opening statement. No conclusion is needed.

In some paragraphs the two or three parts are not sharply distinct, and the organization of the development may be rather loose. In brief paragraphs, particularly those that are quasi-narrative, little organization may be needed. The details may be in chronological order, for example, and the author may be endeavoring to record no more than the details and their order. Notice the following consecutive paragraphs from Robert A. Hume's *Runaway Star,* a study of Henry Adams as an intellectual and artistic figure.

Henry Adam's first venture into published scholarly writing was an essay entitled "Captain John Smith," appearing in the January, 1867, issue of the *North American Review,* then edited by Charles Eliot Norton. As candidly admitted in *The Education,* the young man was eager "to make a position for himself," and such an article seemed calculated for an effect, since it struck at the Pocahontas legend, particularly precious to self-conscious exemplars of Virginian chivalry. Adams had done some research on Smith as early as 1861, after hints obtained in conversation from John Gorham Palfrey, author of *A History of New England,* but he owed most to Charles Deane, whose edition of Wingfield's *Discourse of Virginia* contained notes casting doubt on Captain John Smith's veracity. Adams finished a draft of his study in 1862 but laid it aside until 1866, when at Palfrey's urging he revised and sent it to the *North American.*

In essence the article virtually establishes that the famous story of Smith's rescue by Pocahontas is not history but hoax, invented by Smith in his later years, presumably to call attention to himself so that he might mend his tattered fortunes. At least it is highly suspicious that Smith's first account of the incident was that in his *General Historie of Virginia,* published in 1624, seven years after the death of the Indian maiden who was said to have laid her head upon his when the clubs of her father's warriors were about to fall. In his *True Relation* (1608) and subsequent writings, published before 1624, Smith had not mentioned the episode.

Here Hume is attempting nothing very complicated; in the first paragraph he is recounting the details of the publication of an article, and in the second he is summarizing the import of the article. He is laying the groundwork for more serious writing to come; the material is not difficult, and much of it is narrative with chronology making the order clear. He needs no elaborate organization; as a matter of fact the organizations of the two paragraphs are similar, although as usual this basic similarity does not seem repetitious because it is obscured by minor differences. In each paragraph the topic is announced at once, in the first part of the first sentence, but the topical material is brief enough so that the author can use part of the sentence to add details. Thereafter more details are presented in a few sentences and the details are kept in order by chronology, in the first paragraph through the chronology of the writing, revising, and printing of the article, in the second paragraph through the chronology of Smith's published works. Neither paragraph has a clear conclusion. The first paragraph has a sort of conclusion; it starts with the implication that the paragraph is to concern the publication of an article, and the last sentence sees the study published. The second paragraph has nothing much that can be called conclusion; the topic sentence had made the subject quite precise, that the Pocahontas legend was "not history but hoax." Hume then presents the evidence, and presumably assumes that in so brief a paragraph he need not remind his reader of the subject, particularly since this is all background as far as Hume's book is concerned, and whether Smith was or was not a genial liar makes little difference in his discussion.

Elsewhere, Hume feels he must make points more precisely. Consider the following:

> A man's birth is indispensable to his physical existence but is intellectually unimportant, belonging on the same level with his conception about nine months earlier, or with his taking successive breaths and imbibing maternal milk. It is difficult, therefore, to identify the author of *The Education of Henry Adams* with a certain helpless, presumably intractable male brat that appeared on February 18, 1838, in Boston, Massachusetts, to be promptly designated the fourth child and third son of Charles Francis Adams, who was the son of John Quincy Adams, who was the son of John Adams. That complicated entity Henry Brooks Adams—diffident, contemptuous; energetic, indolent; rebellious, tradition-conscious; eye-twinkling, dour—did not indubitably emerge for a number of years, just how many it is hard to say.

The structure is still relatively simple. Again, the topical element is in the first part of the first sentence—birth is physically indispensable but not intellectually important. The remainder of the first sentence and the second sentence provide development of this idea, that for a time Adams was more brat than brain. The final sentence pins down the conclusion rather sharply, that Adams as an entity did not emerge for some time. The one-two-three sequence that we have noticed above is here sharper, but not much complicated.

2-3 MORE COMPLICATED PARAGRAPHS

Not all paragraphs are so simple in structure. Many main ideas fall naturally into parts, and the development accordingly breaks into enough parts so that each has its own unity as the development of a sub-idea. Such a paragraph may be organized as follows:

I. Topical material, often a topic sentence, which may contain transitional material referring to an earlier paragraph

II. Development
   A. First main subdivision
      1. Sub-topical element, a sentence, a clause, phrase, or even a word
      2. Development of A1; this development may itself break into parts
   B. Second main subdivision
      1. Sub-topical element for second part of main idea
      2. Development of B1

(This may continue through IIC, IID, or any appropriate number of divisions which in turn may have subdivisions.)

III. Conclusion, often a sentence, or III may be omitted if the conclusion is obvious or the paragraph is sufficiently linked by a transition at the beginning of the next paragraph.

In the following paragraph, well along in Hume's book, the author uses a moderately complicated structure composed of a topic sentence, two main divisions themselves somewhat complicated, and no conclusion. (The numbers are not in the original.)

> (1) He [Adams] knew, surely, what any competent scientist is aware of: that no one method or set of experiments can be regarded as final. (2) The scientist works not in terms of certain, ultimate cause (though in the name of human dignity he holds this forever before him as an ideal), but in terms of probability. (3) Probability arises from the findings in one experiment. (4) If the findings in a second experiment are at least roughly equivalent, the probability becomes stronger. (5) It becomes still stronger with similar findings in a third experiment, and so on. (6) If findings in continual and repeated experiments all point to the same end, the scientist gains confidence in his original hypothesis and eventually may cease to

regard it as a mere hypothesis but as something so strongly impregnated with probability that it can be adopted for convenience as a workable fact. (7) But the scientist, if he be worthy of his name, will never quite lose sight of the lurking latency of error. (8) He will be sufficiently a philosopher to feel the force of David Hume's contention that causation is never established in a manner answerable to logic. (9) To invoke the humdrum instance, although the sun has punctually risen on a hundred thousand successive days, it may not rise tomorrow.

The main idea of this paragraph, that Adams understood that probability can become a workable "fact" but never an absolute fact, breaks naturally into two parts: first, that degress of probability can be increased until the probability approximates certainty, and second, that the scientific worker will insist upon and respect the theoretical difference between certainty and even the highest degree of probability. Accordingly, Hume's paragraph, although it has a clearly conceived main idea and this idea is developed and controlled with a unified purpose, breaks into two parts in accordance with the natural divisions of this main idea, somewhat as follows:

I. Topical material, here a topic sentence—(1)
II. Development
    A. 1. Sub-topical element—(2)
       2. Development of IIA, 1—(3, 4, 5)
       3. Conclusion of IIA—(6)
    B. 1. Sub-topical element—(7)
       2. Development of IIB, 1—(8, 9)

The paragraph is sufficiently orderly so that it requires no conclusion beyond that implied in (9).

A later paragraph in Hume's book follows a similar plan, varying mainly in the addition of a concluding summary sentence. (The numbers are not in the original.)

(1) It is dangerously easy to overstress the near-tragic quality of the aging scholar, caught as never before in the impingement of beauty but knowing, too, the final ineffectuality of its comfort for one whose mind insisted on discovering monstrosity and chaos on every side. (2) He still was one to relish good food and drink, to enjoy the company of handsome women and vigorous men and stimulate them by questions and banter. (3) He was by no means

the bitter, broken prophet that many critics, gullibly misreading his own account, have pronounced him to be. (4) He had asserted in *The Education,* with rather ponderous irony, that he had failed in various specific efforts—to be a teacher, an editor, a historian—but he never attached the term of failure to his whole being. (5) The distinction here is important, constituting, as S. I. Hayakawa has urged, the difference between sanity and self-destruction. (6) Nevertheless, one comprehends Adams most clearly as a man who to the last felt and not quite successfully defied the personal and universal disorder encroaching upon a sensitive dweller in the nineteenth and twentieth centuries. (7) His dilemma was at once individual and typical.

As frequently, the topical element is in the first sentence, especially in the first part of it; Hume insists that it is easy to "overstress the near-tragic quality" in Adams and explains why in the remainder of the sentence. The bulk of the paragraph breaks into two parts, sentences 2, 3, and 4, and sentences 5 and 6. The first sequence (2, 3, 4) gives three evidences that Adams's tragedy can readily be mistaken or exaggerated. The second main division (5, 6) provides two attempts at a juster estimate, one through Hayakawa, one by the author. Then comes sentence 7, to drive home the conclusion in a few words, "His dilemma was at once individual and typical."

Obviously, paragraphs reflect many varieties upon the standard or-organization, even deviations from it, but the standard paragraph is so much the most orderly form of presenting expository or argumentative material that many of the best writers use it for ninety per cent or more of their paragraphs. Variations upon it are so numerous and subtle that only close students of prose appreciate how pervasive this structure can become in closely knit writing (see also 3).

2-4 THE TOPIC SENTENCE

We have already observed that writing turns about a central purpose and a main idea (see 1). In no unit of writing is a main idea more important than in a paragraph; in fact, the main idea of a paragraph is usually stated in what is called the *topic sentence.* Although paragraphs are sometimes successfully written without an expressed topic sentence, the standard paragraph described above almost always turns about a topic sentence.

Notice, for example, the opening sentence of another paragraph from Hume's *Runaway Star:*

> Once more, then, Henry Adams was not an unalloyed pessimist.

The sentence is a topic sentence. It begins with a reference to earlier material, with a *transition* (see also 10); the first three words of the sentence show that this section of the writing is related to earlier discussions and is essentially parallel with them. The remainder makes an assertion about Henry Adams, that he was "not an unalloyed pessimist." The statement is clear enough and complete, but it is the kind of assertion that obviously needs further explanation; in fact, it mentions two subjects that need explanation: the pessimism and the fact that it was "alloyed." It suggests, in other words, the kind of two-part organization for the paragraph that we have observed in other examples. The paragraph develops as the topic sentence suggests. The first half summarizes what has apparently been mentioned earlier, that Adams was pessimistic. Then the writer supplements the topic sentence with an introduction to his second division, an explanation of the assertion that the pessimism was "alloyed": "He [Adams] never gave up." This statement, which might be considered a sub-topic sentence, introduces the second section of the development of the paragraph.

To demonstrate that this example is not unique we need only look at the first sentence of Hume's next paragraph, which reads:

> For Henry Adams, with all his typically human limitations and his unheroic idiosyncrasies, had an unmistakable Socratic greatness.

Here, again, the transitional material comes first, linking this paragraph both to the previous paragraph and to earlier discussions; then we have the continuing subject, Henry Adams, and the assertion that he had "an unmistakable Socratic greatness." But what is "Socratic greatness"? All of us can make rough guesses, but none of us may know very exactly what this means in relationship to Adams. As would be expected, Hume proceeds to show in detail after detail how at least some of the characteristics associated with Socrates can be observed in Adams.

2-5 CHARACTERISTICS OF A TOPIC SENTENCE

The examples above illustrate such characteristics of a good topic sentence as the following:

1. It lets the reader know the main idea of the paragraph, focusing his attention on it. That is, it introduces and may summarize the content of the paragraph.
2. It usually provides a transition, relates the paragraph to other parts of the composition.
3. It may indicate the organization of the paragraph.
4. It is often brief, even terse, but it presents the main idea as specifically as possible.

We have already observed how the topic sentences from Hume mentioned above have the first three of these characteristics; they also demonstrate the fourth one. The sentences, especially the parts that introduce the new materials of the paragraphs, are brief, but they introduce specifically and accurately. For either sentence Hume might have written something like the following:

> We must now consider another aspect of Adam's character, one that we have not as yet treated, but one which we surely should not ignore in any extensive treatment of our subject's character.

This sentence is not bad; it would serve. But it postpones the decision as to what is to be said in each paragraph. It gets much less done than Hume's brief but precisely thought and carefully worded statement.

That is, although a topic sentence may contain some routine transitional material, its excellence is likely to reflect clear thinking, to rest on definition in the etymological sense of that word, thereby setting up boundaries. A good topic sentence blocks out enough space for the paragraph and sets limits to it. It is general enough to provide scope for the idea in the paragraph, but it should restrict the subject so as to exclude other materials.

For variety, we might consider a paragraph from Gilbert Highet's *The Classical Tradition:*

Nineteenth-century writers admired this culture for two chief reasons: because it was beautiful, and because it was not Christian.
They saw their own civilization as squalid and greedy; they praised
the Greeks and Romans as noble and spiritual. They felt contemporary Christianity to be mean, ugly, and repressive; they admired the
cults of antiquity as free, strong, and graceful. Looking at the soot-
laden sky, pierced by factory chimneys and neo-Gothic steeples, they
exclaimed

Great God! I'd rather be
A Pagan suckled in a creed outworn.

Highet wishes to say that nineteenth-century writers admired the
Greek and Roman culture for two reasons, "it was beautiful" and "it
was not Christian," and his topic sentence restricts the discussion to
just these subjects, although he carries them parallel through the paragraph. He might have written:

In this connection it is interesting to note that earlier periods ex-
erted a certain charm over many of the more sensitive spirits of the
nineteenth century and that among the reasons for this charm were
the differences between theirs and an earlier day. They saw in their
own civilization. . . .

As a topic sentence this could have been worse. It would have permitted the writer to say almost anything he pleased; but it is clearly
a worse topic sentence than Highet's, partly because it is less exact,
less precise. It tells the reader too little of what he should know; it
does not restrict the paragraph to just that material which is to be its
content.

Similarly, Highet might have begun his paragraph in this manner:

Nineteenth-century writers resented living under a soot-laden sky.
They resented the growing ugliness of an industrial society. They
disliked the factory chimneys that thrust up everywhere, and not
only the factories but the neo-Gothic spires, which suggested that
the Christianity of the day, like the industry, was ugly. They saw in
their own civilization. . . .

Again, he did not, and the reason is obvious. He would have been
starting with material so specific that it provides no proper introduction to the whole.

That is, any good paragraph is likely to contain two sorts of material, neither sharply definable in itself but each distinguishable from the other. One is more general, more abstract; the other is more concrete, more specific. Neither term, general or specific, can be sharply defined, but their characteristics are clear when the two are contrasted, and on the whole their uses, also, can be contrasted. The more general material is suited to the topic sentence and to other topical material; the more concrete and specific matter is best suited to development. Now we should make one more observation. Although the topic sentence should be general enough to comprise the paragraph, within this limitation, the more specific it is, the more precise it is, the better.

Topic sentences may appear anywhere, or even be omitted. For any of a number of reasons the writer may wish to have the topic sentence at the end; for example, he may wish to develop a paragraph inductively, doing no more than hint at the subject until he has developed it, and summarizing it when it is developed. Or the topic sentence may be pivotal, somewhere about the middle of the paragraph, with details developing toward it and conclusions drawn from it. Some paragraphs have nothing that can clearly be called topic sentences, particularly in rather chatty writing on a light subject broken into small units. Such writing may ramble on without much organization and be none the worse for its loose-jointed manner, but most modern, carefully constructed prose rests on standard paragraphs, most of which have topic sentences to open them. The student will do well to write one standard paragraph after another until he can produce them easily, inevitably, and naturally before he experiments with variations and before he tries to write without the discipline of drafting standard paragraphs carefully.

2 U; ¶

UNITY AND THE STANDARD PARAGRAPH

Guide to Revision

Unify paragraphs by focusing on a main idea, usually expressed in a topic sentence.

Paragraph structure is fundamental to good writing; difficulty with it, therefore, is usually symptomatic of a number of weaknesses. One good way to overcome such difficulty is to revise wobbly paragraphs according to the standard pattern, unifying them under topic sentences.

2a UNITY UNDER A TOPIC   U a; ¶ a

Paragraphs that lack unity usually need to be rewritten, often reconceived; revision may appropriately start with the construction of a good topic sentence.

ORIGINAL

A teacher must be interested in his subject. A teacher must also be able to understand his pupils and reach them on their own level. I had a number of teachers who could do this. I did not consider them stupid or below a mental age of fifteen. They were intelligent and well-educated people. My mathematics teacher in junior high school had a Master's degree from a good university. He knew mathematics. He was vitally interested in his subject. He could also relate mathematics to what I was interested in. He could show us how we could use mathematics in building our cars for

REVISION

A teacher need not have a mental age below fifteen in order to reach pupils on their own level. I had a number of teachers who were intelligent and well-educated and who could sense my interests and abilities. My mathematics teacher in junior high school, for example, had a Master's degree from a good university and a vital interest in his subject, but he could relate mathematics to what I understood. He could show me how to use mathematics in building a car for the soap-box derby or keeping my allowance straight. I think that it was partly because he was intelligent that

ORIGINAL (*Cont.*)

the soap-box derby or in keeping our allowances straight. I think that it was partly because he was intelligent that he could approach us on our own level.

[*The paragraph is repetitious, badly organized, and choppy, but a central weakness is its lack of a topic sentence.*]

There was an oval mirror on one wall with a heavy black frame containing fat angels carved into the wood. I have never much cared for representations of angels. The insipid ones on Sunday-school cards seemed to me dull even when I was a child, and fat ones are not very attractive, to say the least. There was a faint tinge of violet perfume hanging over the room. A bad print of a Rosa Bonheur picture was hanging on the wall over the high walnut bed. Faded lace curtains bordered the high, narrow windows, which contrasted with a mantel that had been recently dusted; they were rather dirty. Some books sat on the table.

[*Presumably the details are accurately recorded, but they produce no unified effect because they are set down one after the other with no apparent main idea controlling the selection.*]

REVISION (*Cont.*)

he could approach pupils at their own level.

[*The sentence structure has been improved, and by opening with a topic sentence, the writer has some basis for organizing the material, selecting the details which are relevant, and centering attention on a main point.*]

The contents of the room seemed to exhale the faint scent of violet that hung over it. The oval mirror, framed heavily with fat angels carved into blackened wood, the silver brush and comb on the massive walnut dresser, the faded lace curtains, the high walnut bed, the bad print of a Rosa Bonheur picture all seemed part of the odor of the mildly sickening perfume. A few volumes, propped between bookends painted with roses, were slim and gold-lettered; one sensed that they concerned well-dressed gentlemen, very properly courting demure but willing ladies in crinoline.

[*The writer has focused upon a main idea, which he announces in a topic sentence. He has furthered unity by rearranging his materials, removing the irrelevant comment on his personal reaction to angels, and, by closer observation, describing the details to show how they relate to the main idea.*]

2b ADEQUATE TOPIC SENTENCE   U b; ¶ b; TS

Inaccurate expression of the main idea misleads the reader and even confuses the writer, because a clumsily phrased statement usually reflects careless thinking. Often a main idea is obscure because the writer allows minor issues, which he never intends to develop, to appear as if they were main propositions of the paper.

ORIGINAL

(1) *The success of the American educational system can be traced directly to freedom of speech.* American instructors are not mouthpieces for the government. (2) Their job is to teach a sound doctrine, one not influenced by a person or group of persons. (3) And what about the students? (4) Very few students have ever been condemned for expressing their ideas in the classroom. (5) *In Germany, when Hitler was dictator, the fellow who dared criticize the system of government was promptly executed or rushed to a concentration camp.* (6) It is not like that in this great land of ours. (7) The man in the street is granted by constitutional law the privilege of saying what he pleases without fear of prosecution. (8) Newspapers in the United States are at liberty to present their readers with local, national, and world news without dictation from the government. (9) Radio broadcasting, though censored to a certain degree by the Federal Communications Commission, is another example of freedom of speech in this country.

[*This paragraph fails, partly because it does not fulfill what the first sentence seems to promise. The reader assumes he will learn how freedom of speech has caused the success of education. He learns something else. Probably the writer did not intend this sentence as a proposition, but he has written as if he did; (5) does not fit here.*]

REVISION

America, unlike Hitler's Germany, enjoys freedom of speech. The man in the street is granted by constitutional law the privilege of saying what he pleases without fear of prosecution. Education is generally free from censorship. Instructors in America are not mouthpieces for the government. Their job is to teach a sound doctrine, one not influenced by a person or group. And very few students have ever been condemned for expressing their ideas in the classroom. Newspapers in the United States are at liberty to present their readers with local, national, and world news without dictation from the government. Radio broadcasting, though censored to a certain degree by the Federal Communications Commission, provides another example of freedom of speech.

[*The writer's selection of details suggests that he probably intended the paragraph's main purpose to be the presentation of evidence that freedom of speech exists in America. Perhaps in another place he intends to show also that this freedom distinguishes America from other nations, such as Hitler's Germany. The revision supplies a proposition which seems to be the one intended, and then lists the details, which were already available in the paragraph to support the proposition; (5) and (6) of the original are reduced to parts of the opening sentence.*]

Topic sentences may be more or less adequate to the paragraphs they serve.

ORIGINAL

I shall always remember an experience I had last summer; it was the most exciting thing that has ever happened to me.

REVISION

Last summer, while I was trying out my new skin-diving equipment, I blacked out and nearly drowned.

[*This sentence, although it may*

ORIGINAL (*Cont.*)

[*This has the earmarks of a poor topic sentence. The writer probably does not intend to demonstrate that he will remember this incident while forgetting others, or to make a comprehensive study of his exciting moments.*]

REVISION (*Cont.*)

have no great virtues as a topic sentence, says something, and what it says is to the point. It is briefer than the original, does not mislead the reader, and introduces with some exactness what the writer apparently expects to say.]

A topic sentence may fail to provide sufficient evidence of the relationship of the paragraph to other paragraphs or to the whole composition.

ORIGINAL

. . . My mother's graduation present was tied up in two neatly ironed strips of gingham, which I recognized as her apron strings.

I got the job I had applied for, and I also received a letter saying I had been admitted to the University.

[*The lack of transition leaves the reader wondering where the account is going.*]

REVISION

. . . My mother's graduation present was tied up in two neatly ironed strips of gingham, which I recognized as her apron strings.

These apron strings soon became a symbol for the new life which, I discovered, I was now beginning to lead.

[*Not all topic sentences require repetition of words but most of them require some transitional material.*]

2c   CHOPPY PARAGRAPHING   ¶ c

For reasons unrelated to the logical development of a paragraph—reasons of appearance and quick readability—newspaper writers customarily start a new paragraph every few lines, often at the end of every sentence. In writing which does not follow the special forms of journalism, however, choppy paragraphing is usually a symptom of poor organization or a lack of continuity. Indentations every sentence or two do no more to help the reader than the period that ends each sentence. A series of short, choppy paragraphs is often symptomatic of either lack of organization or lack of development; either the writer has not planned his composition and is writing from one sentence to the next, or he is writing down one topic sentence after another without developing them.

ORIGINAL

(1) In the suburbs and on the highways of many large American cities,

REVISION

On the highways in and around many large American cities, young

ORIGINAL (*Cont.*)

young men are killing themselves by the thousands.

(2) Many of the accidents could be avoided if a little common sense were used. When a boy gets behind the steering wheel of a car, the first thing he thinks of is how fast he can go.

(3) Speed is the reason for so many deaths. The teen-ager does not seem to realize that his car is dangerous if it is not used sensibly.

(4) There is another reason for a large number of teen-age automobile accidents.

(5) This is the playing of games with cars. These senseless games kill hundreds of teen-agers every year.

(6) The most popular game is "Ditch 'Em." Two or more cars. . . .

[*The body of the theme concerns the game mentioned in paragraph 6, but the preceding matter is broken into what appear as five paragraphs. This introduction is not well planned or closely knit, but such plan as it has is obscured by the meaningless indentations.*]

REVISION (*Cont.*)

men are killing themselves by the thousands in automobile accidents which could be avoided by the use of a little common sense. First, young drivers must learn to be sensible about speed. When a boy gets behind a steering wheel, the first thing he thinks of is how fast he can go. He does not seem to realize that his car is dangerous if it is not used sensibly. Second, young drivers must learn some sense about the senseless games played with cars which kill hundreds of teen-agers each year.

The most popular game is "Ditch 'Em." Two or more cars. . . .

[*The first five paragraphs have been combined into a single introductory paragraph, but the revision has involved more than removing the indentations. For example, the first two sentences have become a single sentence, with elements subordinated. The three sentences of paragraphs 4 and 5 have become a single sentence. Sentences have been reworked to provide continuity between them, and the remark of the original about common sense has been exploited to provide unity.*]

2d DIALOGUE PARAGRAPHS   ¶ d

In order to help the reader identify speakers, writers of dialogue, especially in fiction, have adopted the convention of beginning a new paragraph whenever the speaker changes, as indicated in the version on the right below.

"Good evening. It's a cold night," said Holmes. The salesman nodded, and shot a questioning glance at my companion. "Sold out of geese, I see," continued Holmes, pointing at the bare slabs of marble. "Let you have 500 tomorrow morning." "That's no good."

"Good evening. It's a cold night," said Holmes.

The salesman nodded, and shot a questioning glance at my companion.

"Sold out of geese, I see," continued Holmes, pointing at the bare slabs of marble.

"Let you have 500 tomorrow morning."

"That's no good."

EXERCISE 2

A. The following paragraphs are different sorts of examples of the standard paragraph described in the chapter. Analyze each, indicating the
topic sentence, and any material later in the paragraph that supplements the topic sentence, and describing how the development of the
topic works.

As a matter of fact, we are all of us original in our expression until
our wings are clipped. I know a three-year-old boy who calls an automobile a "cadeúga." It is, both to him and in point of fact, an ex-
cellently descriptive term, based, like many a word in the pristine days
of speech, on the sound the thing makes. But you can't go to the
telephone and ask for a "cadeúga" with any valid hope of seeing it
appear. And since the world with which the young adventurer must
communicate prefers to call the affair a motor, or a car, or a machine
(incomparably less exact and fitting terms), he will infallibly drop
his own fresh and vivid coinage, and conform. The tangential energy
of the individual beats its wings in vain against the centripetal force
of the community, and every infant anarchist in speech yields at last
to the usage of that world by which, if he is to live, he must be understood.

—JOHN LIVINGSTON LOWES, *Convention and Revolt in Poetry*

The Yellow or Silver Pine is more frequently overturned than any
other tree on the Sierra, because its leaves and branches form the
largest mass in proportion to its height, while in many places it is
planted sparsely, leaving long, open lanes, through which storms may
enter with full force. Furthermore, because it is distributed along the
lower portion of the range, which was the first to be left bare on the
breaking up of the ice-sheet at the close of the glacial winter, the
soil it is growing upon has been longer exposed to post-glacial weather-
ing, and consequently is in a more crumbling, decayed condition than
the fresher soils farther up the range, and therefore offers a less secure
anchorage for the roots.

—JOHN MUIR, *The Passes of the Sierra*

Proud of his wonderful achievements, civilized man looks down
upon the humbler members of mankind. He has conquered the forces
of nature and compelled them to serve him. He has transformed in-
hospitable forests into fertile fields. The mountain fastnesses are yield-
ing their treasures to his demands. The fierce animals which are ob-
structing his progress are being exterminated, while others which are
useful to him are made to increase a thousand-fold. The waves of the
ocean carry him from land to land, and towering mountain-ranges set

him no bounds. His genius has moulded inert matter into powerful machines which await a touch of his hand to serve his manifold demands.

—FRANZ BOAS, *The Mind of Primitive Men*

If you subtract from this book the personality of H. L. Mencken, if you attempt to restate his ideas in simple unexcited prose, there remains only a collection of trite and somewhat confused ideas. To discuss it as one might discuss the ideas of first rate thinkers like Russell, Dewey, Whitehead, or Santayana would be to destroy the book and to miss its importance. Though it purports to be the outline of a social philosophy, it is really the highly rhetorical expression of a mood which has often in the past and may again in the future be translated into thought. In the best sense of the word the book is subrational: it is addressed to those vital preferences which lie deeper than coherent thinking.

—WALTER LIPPMANN, *Men of Destiny*

B. Discuss each of the following as a topic sentence for a paragraph in context. Assume that the paragraph will contain approximately 150 words.

1. There are many things about the university which I do not like.
2. In consideration of these factors, there are several aspects in the case which seem to be basic for a fundamental understanding of the circumstances.
3. In spite of my many objections to fraternity life, I found that I enjoyed my days in Upsilon Delta, mainly because I liked the easy camaraderie among the men.
4. I also recall my great-grandfather, partly because of the intense, blinking way he had when he looked at me over his spectacles.
5. In selecting the brick with which to line the fireplace, you should consider color, size and shape, and resistance to heat.
6. The most important thing for a girl to consider in college is the preparation for her future life.
7. Basketball is an excellent sport because it can be enjoyed by players and spectators alike, comes at a season when there are few outdoor sports, and can be played by a few players, making it suitable for the small high school.
8. Weaving as though driven by a drunken driver, a red convertible roared down the highway toward me, traveling at least ninety miles an hour.
9. Now, I want to tell you all about it.
10. So then I thought it all over, and that is something I often do, thinking things all over.

C. Consider the following topic sentences:

1. Mrs. Jones was even stingier than her daughter.
2. Mrs. Jones was the stingiest woman I ever knew.
3. Mrs. Jones's name was a synonym for *stingy* in our town, and everybody had some anecdote to tell about her.

Each of these sentences might serve as a topic sentence, but each implies a different paragraph. The first implies that the daughter's stinginess has been discussed in a previous paragraph. The second seems to imply that Mrs. Jones is to be compared with all other stingy women the writer has known; probably he has no such intention, and the reader would probably assume that these words mean no more than "Mrs. Jones was very stingy," but the writer would do well to say what he means. The last sentence could suitably introduce a paragraph of tales told about Mrs. Jones. Now examine the following groups of possible topic sentences and distinguish the implications of each.

1. (a) Janet is the most tiresome salesgirl I ever dealt with in my whole life.
   (b) I do not like Janet as a salesgirl.
   (c) Obviously, Janet is a poor salesgirl.
   (d) Janet is a poor salesgirl because she wants to do all the talking.
   (e) Janet is a poor salesgirl because she has never learned to let the customer do a little healthy griping.
   (f) Janet is the worst salesgirl in the store.
   (g) Janet would be a better salesgirl if she would cultivate a little interest in her customers.
   (h) Janet would be a better salesgirl if she were a kind and sympathetic person who could take a natural interest in her customer's wishes.
   (i) Janet might be a better salesgirl if she would read a book on selling.
   (j) Janet would not be such a bad salesgirl if she would remember what she was told in her course in salesmanship.

2. (a) The French attitude toward South Asian affairs is wholly wrong.
   (b) The French attitude toward South Asian affairs seems to me wrong.
   (c) The French attitude toward South Asian affairs seems to me unrealistic.
   (d) The French attitude toward South Asian affairs seems to me shrewd but dangerous.

(e) The French do not understand the Pakistan problem.

(f) If the French understand the Pakistan problem, their recent moves do not reveal the fact.

(g) The French may or may not understand Pakistan problems, but they are endeavoring to give the impression of knowledge, not to say clairvoyance.

(h) The French cannot be expected to reveal their Pakistan proposals until they have studied the reactions of London and Washington.

(i) The French attitude toward Pakistan is uncertain and probably unimportant.

(j) Barring unexpected developments in the French attitude toward Pakistan, at least one trend in South Asian affairs would seem certain.

3. (a) All that I can now remember learning in high school I gained from playing basketball.

(b) Until I started playing basketball, I had no interest in high school.

(c) Chemistry is now my major interest, but I got started in chemistry only through my high school basketball coach.

(d) For me, basketball was a bridge between bumming around town and studying chemistry.

(e) If I ever become a chemical engineer, one reason is to be sought in a tricky backhand shot I have, which brought me to the coach's attention.

(f) I think basketball should be a required course for every student.

(g) Basketball is an American invention, and the more people live in cities where there is no room for baseball diamonds the more basketball becomes our national sport, and that was my experience, that it changed my life.

(h) The lessons learned on the basketball court are the factors which make for success in the classroom and in the world of today.

(i) For all-around fun and character building, give me basketball.

(j) Basketball, so called because the first games were played with a peach basket with the bottom knocked out, provided a turning point in my life.

D. The paragraphs below lack unity because they have inadequate statements of their main ideas; that is, they lack topic sentences. Revise the paragraphs, beginning each with a clear topic sentence.

1. There are many dictionaries on the market, and some of these are reprints of older dictionaries. Some are good and some are bad. Some of these reprints reproduce books which were badly prepared when they were new, and some of them are reprints of books which were once good, but are now out of date. Many of them carry the name *Webster* on the title page. In fact, more than 140 dictionaries have that name on the cover, and the word *Webster* has been declared by the Supreme Court as part of eminent domain. Thus anyone can now use the word if he wants to, although anyone who uses it must be able to show that he follows principles laid down by Noah Webster. This, however, is not hard, and thus the word *Webster* does not tell much about what is inside a dictionary.

2. Although it is far from the largest museum in New York, the Cloisters is one of the most interesting for its size in the city, well arranged and well managed. It provides ready and revealing insight into the Middle Ages. Here, within a few miles of the greatest industrial concentration in the world, is a little bit of the Middle Ages. A thirteenth-century French cloister, with its ancient stonework from corbels to statues, has been taken down stone by stone and re-erected here.

3. The electric saw is certainly one invention which has helped the modern carpenter. With an electric saw a carpenter can cut the frame for a small house in a few hours. Or with an electric drill an electrician can drill the frame for wiring in a short time. In the old days cutting framing timbers by hand was a long and tedious job, in spite of a sharp saw. Today few people are alive who know how to sharpen a saw properly. And drilling was always a long and hard job. In the same manner the sanding and finishing of hardwood floors has been simplified by electrical tools.

E. The following paragraph—minus its topic sentence—is taken from a letter from an officer in the Second Iowa Regiment describing what he saw and heard of the Battle of Shiloh, April 6, 1862. Endeavor to construct topic and closing sentences which taken together will give the paragraph unity.

"What was the plan of the battle, General?" asked Gen. Buell of Acting Brig. Gen. Tuttle. "By God, sir, I don't know!" he replied. Gen. Sweeney on our right said he gave all his orders on his own hook, and so of many others. The army was scattered over about twenty miles. The greenest regiments were on the outposts, and not a shovel full of dirt thrown up to protect them until they could be reinforced from the interior of the camp. As a natural consequence, they were panic stricken and retreated in, reporting their regiments "all cut to pieces." Col. Peabody's brigade, on the left, had none but green regiments, viz.: the 12th Michigan, 16th Wisconsin, and the 23d and 25th Missouri. They lost both their batteries, which soon were turned upon us. Sherman's regiments on the right and Prentiss in the centre had few troops that had ever seen a fight.

F. A rather ignorant and illogical woman visited the Comstock Lode during the mining boom and wrote a description of the mines. It reads in part as follows:

In many of the mines the miners cannot strike the pick more than three blows before they have to go to the cooling station and stay double the time they are at work.

The cooling stations are where they have a free circulation of air. These stations are on every level. They have large tanks or reservoirs to hold the water that is pumped from one level to another. These vats are often full of boiling water. In many of the mines the water is so hot that if a person slips into one of these tanks, he is generally scalded to death before he can be rescued.

If he is rescued alive, it is only to linger a few days, suffering the most intense agony, till death relieves him of his sufferings. He is often so completely cooked in the scalding vats that the flesh drops from the bones while taking him out. His suffering and agony are terrible to witness.

The heat of the mines is very great. In some mines it is almost unendurable. In such mines it is almost impossible to work, while in others they can work without such excessive heat.

Miners are brought to the surface almost daily from overheat.

There is scarcely a day in the year that there is not from one to two funerals among the miners; and I have known of there being five in one day.

There are a great many different causes of death. Sometimes death is caused by the caving in of rock, or by falling into the scalding tanks, or by a misstep, by falling hundreds of feet down the shafts or inclines.

—MRS. M. M. MATHEWS, *Ten Years in Nevada,*
or Life on the Pacific Coast

This writing is not without promise. It contains concrete observation and some significant generalization, but the whole is jotted down in a scatter-brained way. Try to make a good paragraph of this material, expressing a central idea in a topic sentence, developing the paragraph in accordance with some orderly plan, and omitting extraneous matter.

G. Select three of the possible topic sentences below and develop each into a standard paragraph. Then write a brief analysis of each paragraph, describing the general pattern and pointing out the relationships of each sentence to the whole paragraph.

1. I could not always predict how the professor would react.
2. A college cafeteria can do some remarkable things to food.
3. One class was more puzzling to me than any of the others.
4. If there were no God, it would be necessary to invent one.
5. For me registration day was only a series of confusions.
6. The campus was unified about the main quadrangle.
7. A little learning is a dangerous thing.
8. There are certain qualities which a student expects to find in a good classroom lecture.
9. A student union building should serve students.
10. Human beings do not always seem wiser than animals.
11. Even scientists have sometimes been wrong.
12. A few snatches of my childhood reading still stick in my mind.
13. Students have developed a variety of techniques to conceal inadequate study from their teachers.
14. The educational value of college social life is greatly overrated.
15. A campus newspaper reflects the interests of the student body.

3

Coherence and
the Paragraph

For Guide to Revision, see page 50

Good paragraphs have continuity; the parts cohere.

Obviously, as indicated in Section 2, all paragraphs are not what we have called standard paragraphs. But all good paragraphs need coherence; the parts must stick together, and the reader must be able to see how the parts fit. Or, to put it another way, a paragraph must have continuity; the reader must be able to follow easily from one idea to the next and to see how the parts of the whole are related.

Consider, for example, the following remarks about the American opossum.

> The opossum has survived in definitely hostile surroundings for 70 million years.
> The opossum is small; it can easily find hiding places.
> The opossum can always find a little food, where big animals starve.
> The individual opossum is not very delicate; it can stand severe punishment.
> It "plays 'possum" when it gets into trouble.
> It can go without food for a long time.
> Many different things are food to an opossum.
> Traits of the opossum have a high survival value.
> The opossum is a survivor from the Age of Reptiles.

These ideas are abstracted from a single paragraph; they appear in the order of the original. But merely removing the indentations would not reproduce the original, would not produce a good paragraph. The material would be there, and it would even have a kind of unity because the details all refer to the same topic, the opossum, but the whole lacks coherence. Compare the original:

> The reasons our opossum has survived in definitely hostile surroundings for 70 million years are evident. One is his small size: small animals always find hiding places, they always find a little food, where the big ones starve. Another of its assets was its astounding fecundity: if local catastrophes left only a few survivors, it did not take long to re-establish a thriving population. Also the individual opossum is not exactly delicate: it can stand severe punishment—during which it "plays 'possum" and then scampers away—and it can go without food for a considerable time. Finally, a great many different things are "food" to an opossum. Each of these traits has a high survival value, and their combination has presented the United States with a survivor from the Age of Reptiles.
>
> —WILLY LEY, *The Lungfish and the Unicorn*

The paragraph differs from the list of ideas largely because it has continuity and coherence. The coherence results primarily, of course, from the new unity of the paragraph; the paragraph has what we have called a standard expository pattern, with a topic sentence, development, and a conclusion. It gains coherence as the writer provides guides to reveal the plan of the whole. It also gains coherence in other ways—through transitional words and phrases, through the repetition of words and ideas, and through word order.

3-1 REVEALING THE PLAN OF THE PARAGRAPH

If the reader is to follow the path of the writer's thoughts, he must have clear directions. He must know where he is going; he must understand the plan of each paragraph. As indicated in Section 2, revealing the plan of the paragraph is one of the most useful functions of the topic sentence. Notice, for example, the difference between the first sentence in the list above and the topic sentence of the original paragraph.

> The opossum has survived in definitely hostile surroundings for 70 million years.
>
> The reasons our opossum has survived in definitely hostile surroundings for 70 million years are evident.

The additions in the second topic sentence reveal the purpose of the paragraph, show the reader what its plan will be, and prepare him to look for apparent reasons. As he then proceeds to the list of facts about the opossum, the reader knows how he is expected to interpret them, how they fit into the plan of the paragraph. The concluding sentence reinforces the plan of the whole by explaining why the facts are reasons—each represents a trait that has high survival value.

When paragraphs fall into parts, as extensive expository paragraphs often do, the reader must see the divisions and must be able to relate them. A paragraph might begin, "These results can be accounted for in any of three ways." The writer will then treat the three ways one after the other, and will indicate when the first stops and the second begins; he may even label them, *first, second, third*. He may feel no occasion to be so pedestrian; but if he is a careful, orderly writer he will still keep his three parts separate and will let his reader know when he passes from one to the other, as the author does in the following description of a neighboring genial maniac whom he had known as a child.

> One of Mrs. Sedley's inner convictions was that she was the nymph of the spring in the valley which provided our drinking water. This conviction usually smote her in the evening shortly after sundown. Once she had been smitten, Mrs. Sedley got into a white nightgown, let down her stringy gray hair, and walked to the spring. She then washed her feet in the water and sang original little songs as she dabbled about the rim of the pool. If anyone came near her, she called a cheery greeting and said: "I am the nymph of this spring. Won't you be a nymph too?" No one ever accepted her invitation, but that didn't trouble Mrs. Sedley. She stuck a few flowers in her hair, sang another song, and went on being the nymph of the spring until someone from her house missed her and sent a servant down to lead her home. There were rumors afloat that if the servant didn't get to the spring soon enough, Mrs. Sedley was smitten by a conviction that a nymph wore no clothes, but my sister and I, though we watched her a number of evenings, never saw anything to confirm this.
>
> —JOHN J. ESPEY, *Minor Heresies*

The paragraph runs so smoothly that it can be read with no more than a vague awareness of its organization, but it is developed in three parts as carefully controlled as though Espey had marked them, *first, second, third*. The first sentence is clearly the topic sentence, after which the first portion begins with "This conviction," the second with "If anyone came near," and the third with "There were rumors afloat." If the paragraph dealt with difficult material, such easy-going indications of plan would probably be insufficient; the writer might well feel that he needed what would amount to three minor paragraphs within his paragraph, each with its own clear topic sentence, perhaps each with its own conclusion. The organization should be adapted to the material, but all careful writing should have plan, and within the paragraph it should contain sufficient evidence of this plan, the subject matter and the reader being what and who they are.

3-2 WORDS OF TRANSITION

The guides in the topical material of a sentence are usually supplemented by transitional words, words which identify the relationships between the parts of a paragraph and improve continuity. Notice, for example, the use of the words *also* and *finally* in the paragraph on the opossum. The following are some of the most useful transitional words:

(a) To mark an addition: *and, furthermore, next, moreover, in addition, again, also, likewise, similarly, finally, second*

(b) To introduce or emphasize a contrast or alternative: *but, or, nor, still, however, nevertheless, on the contrary, on the other hand, conversely*

(c) To mark a conclusion: *therefore, thus, then, in conclusion, consequently, as a result, in other words, accordingly*

(d) To introduce an illustration or example: *thus, for example, for instance, that is, namely*

Others indicate shifts of time or introduce clauses; almost all connectives can provide transitions. Overuse of transitional expressions makes stiff prose; careful use of them helps make clear prose.

3-3 REPETITION OF WORDS AND IDEAS

Almost every sentence in clear prose is linked with the sentences around it by direct or implied references. Sometimes pronouns in one sentence refer to words in the sentence before. Sometimes an idea of one sentence is briefly rephrased in another. Repeated references to the central idea of the paragraph may serve to bind sentences together. These central ideas echoing through the composition, along with transitional expressions, make the parts of the writing cohere and draw the reader effortlessly along the trail of the writer's thoughts. The following passage indicates how parts of clear writing are linked together.

A driver doesn't have to look at his road map once he starts on a highway, as long as he doesn't come to any intersections. He doesn't have to worry about which way to go if he has no choice about it. But when he comes to a crossroads, with signs pointing in various directions— then he can't just let the road decide where he is to go; he has to make up his mind. He has to stop and think.

—MONROE C. BEARDSLEY, *Thinking Straight*

The passage carries through a single subject, *driver,* designated by the pronoun *he* after the first mention. Sentences cohere, also, by the repetition of patterns like *doesn't have to* and *has to, intersections* and *crossroads;* the connective *but* holds the two main parts of the paragraph together, marking the contrast between them.

Another passage relies on different echoes of meaning and pattern.

In time of peace in the modern world, if one is thoughtful and careful, it is rather more difficult to be killed or maimed in the outland places of the globe than it is in the streets of our great cities, but the atavistic urge toward danger persists and its satisfaction is called adventure. However, your adventurer feels no gratification in crossing Market Street in San Francisco against the traffic. Instead he will go to a good deal of trouble and expense to get himself killed in the South Seas. (In reputedly rough water, he will go in a canoe; he will expose his tolerant and uninoculated blood to strange viruses.) This is adventure. It is possible that his ancestor, wearying of the humdrum attacks of the saber-tooth, longed for the good old days of pterodactyl and triceratops.

—JOHN STEINBECK and EDWARD F. RICKETTS, *Sea of Cortez*

A pronoun subject, standing for *adventurer,* carries through, but references to adventure and danger also hold the paragraph together. *However* and *instead* mark shifts in the thought.

3-4 CONTINUITY AND WORD ORDER

Most of the devices mentioned above succeed because they rely upon the word order in the sentence (see 12-1 to 12-3).

Repetitions of sentence patterns emphasize parallels or contrasts in ideas and help the reader to move smoothly from paragraph to paragraph, from sentence to sentence. In both the paragraphs above, the sentence subjects link one sentence to the next mainly because each sentence repeats the order of the preceding one. The following two sentences are linked, even though the subjects differ, because the subjects appear in the same relative place in each:

> An old man stood in front of the monkey cage excitedly throwing peanuts at a score of begging arms. A small boy only a few feet away sat with his face buried in a comic book.

The repetition of sentence order sharpens the contrast between the two main actions, and the contrast helps link the sentences. On the other hand, variations from usual word order may provide bridges, carrying special emphasis from one sentence to another.

> In front of the monkey cage stood an old man, excitedly throwing peanuts at a score of begging arms. A few feet away sat a small boy, his face buried in a comic book.

The shift in order throws emphasis on the location, heightens the contrast in the actions by stressing the nearness of the two persons, and helps link the sentences through the repetition of the reversed pattern. There is some loss of continuity when the word order pattern is not repeated, as in the following:

> In front of the monkey cage stood an old man, excitedly throwing peanuts at a score of begging arms. A small boy only a few feet away sat with his face buried in a comic book.

3 Coh

COHERENCE AND
THE PARAGRAPH

Guide to Revision

Revise for coherence by revealing the plan of the paragraph in the topic sentence or through transitional devices.

Each word or sentence of a paragraph must lead clearly to the next, and the parts of a composition must stick together—must cohere.

3a REVEALING THE PLAN OF THE PARAGRAPH   Coh a

A paragraph should be built upon a conscious plan, and this plan should be apparent to the reader. There are many methods of making a plan clear; the most common employ a topic sentence, supplemented with other transitional material at various points through the paragraph.

ORIGINAL

Gail McDermott is likely to win the election as president of the Associated Students. He is both a quarterback and an actor, and has support from organizations all over the campus. Meanwhile, some candidates for offices are running unopposed or are opposed by candidates who have little support. The widest interest in the election is being drawn by the races for the three vacant seats in the Student Senate. Many campaigners believe that the election of so many as one candidate for the Senate supported by the Associated Resident Halls Party, known as The Barbs, will assure the decline or abolishment of football at State University. The reasons for this belief are complicated and will later require some analysis. Meanwhile, Nancy Jenkins and Doro-

REVISION

Interest in the State University student elections this year centers in the race for the three vacant seats in the Student Senate. The other contests are likely to be side-shows. Gail McDermott, known as both an actor and a quarterback, has support from so many organizations that his election as president of the Associated Students is practically conceded. Some of the class officers are running unopposed, and other races are attracting little attention. None of the freshman candidates, for instance, is well known or widely supported. For the presidency of AWS Nancy Jenkins and Dorothy Cochran are leading a lively field of candidates, but the race is attracting no attention off the campus, and relatively little on the campus. The election of three members to the Senate,

ORIGINAL *(Cont.)*

thy Cochran are leading a lively field of candidates for the presidency of AWS. That race is attracting no attention off the campus, and very little on the campus, though the question of who is to be elected to the Student Senate has become a statewide issue. The other contests, except for the race for the Student Senate, are side-shows. None of the freshman candidates, for instance, is well known or widely supported. But the Senate race has raised questions of such interest and has stimulated so much electioneering that billboard space is getting scarce on the campus, with placards plastered all the way from the President's gate to the back door of the Aggie Greenhouse. [*Much of the effect of this paper is lost because there is no apparent plan. The topic sentence is inadequate as an introduction, and although the nature of the material suggests division into two or more parts, these parts do not become readily clear. Furthermore, since this is the first paragraph of a theme, it should lead naturally to the next paragraph, which it does not.*]

REVISION *(Cont.)*

on the other hand, has become a question of interest throughout the state and has led to so much electioneering that placards are plastered all the way from the President's gate to the back door of the Aggie Greenhouse. The issue, of course, is the future of football at State University, and many campaigners believe that the election of so many as one candidate from the Associated Resident Halls Party, known as The Barbs, will assure the decline or the abolishment of football at State University. The reasons for this belief are complicated, and will require some analysis. [*The paragraph now has a clear plan. The topic sentence announces the purpose. A subtopic sentence introduces the campaigns of minor interest. The discussion of candidates is tied together by synonyms. The second half of the paragraph is introduced by "The election of three members to the Senate, on the other hand. . . ." It leads to a conclusion and a transition to the succeeding paragraph.*]

3b   COHERENCE THROUGH WORDS AND CONSTRUCTIONS   Coh b

Especially within paragraphs, the repetition of words, of ideas through synonyms, and of grammatical structures promotes coherence.

ORIGINAL

(1) A fraternity pledge finds life during the week preceding his initiation complex and not very pleasant. (2) This week is commonly known as hell week, and there are many good reasons for the name. (3) The pledge cannot speak to any person without first begging for permission in a long and difficult set oration. (4) Any number can make the pledge do his bidding. (5) He can make him shine anybody's shoes, and the pledge must

REVISION

(1) For a week preceding his initiation a fraternity pledge finds life complex and not very pleasant. (2) The week is commonly known as hell week, and there are good reasons for the name. (3) For seven days the pledge cannot speak to any person without first begging for permission in a long and difficult set oration. (4) He

ORIGINAL *(Cont.)*

sing, dance, and generally entertain at all meals and sleep under the dining room tables at night. (6) An infraction of any of the rules brings any number of swats from the members' paddles. (7) The swats are not administered gently and are by no means soothing to the receiver. (8) Why it is called hell week is a question never asked by any pledge. (9) Since it is the last test and marks the end of months of trial, most freshmen look forward to it.

[*Some of the weaknesses of this paragraph result from failure to subordinate secondary ideas (see 15); (6) and (7), for instance, might be combined. The choppiness, however, is evidence that sentences are not arranged and linked so that continuity is smooth. For example, (4) and (5) might be recast so as to continue the subject in (3); with some transition and recasting, (7) could be constructed so as to carry on the subject of earlier sentences.*]

REVISION *(Cont.)*

must do the bidding of any member; shine the shoes of anybody a member designates; sing, dance, and generally entertain at all meals; and sleep under the dining room tables at night. (5) An infraction of any of these rules brings swats from the members' paddles, not administered gently and by no means soothing to the receiver. (6) No pledge ever asks why the week is called hell week. (7) Nevertheless, most pledges look forward to it as their last test and the end of months of trial.

[*Suggested changes have been made; (1) has been revised, and a transition has been prefixed to (3) so that week holds the three sentences together. These rules in (5) refers to the two preceding sentences.*]

Clumsy repetition produces awkward, wordy writing. Useless repetition of the same idea produces only redundancy (see 26f). Skillful repetition, however, particularly skillful use of synonyms, will give writing a coherence which can be obtained in no other way.

ORIGINAL

Modern scholars now agree that the ancestor of the Romance languages is not now much taught in our schools. It was Vulgar Latin, which is usually taught today only in the graduate schools. The kind of language that was written by Virgil and Cicero is the kind that is usually taught both in high school and in college, but that is not the kind from which French or any other language of that sort has come. In English we have words from the language of the Romans, and some of those words did

REVISION

The modern Romance languages descended from Latin, but not from the Latin usually taught in the schools. There are several Latins, notably Classical Latin, Church Latin, and Vulgar Latin. Of these three divisions of the Latin language, Classical Latin is taught almost exclusively. Church Latin is still spoken but is seldom taught to undergraduates. Vulgar Latin is taught only in a few graduate schools. Yet Vulgar Latin is the ancestor of all modern Romance languages—Italian, French, Spanish, Por-

ORIGINAL *(Cont.)*

come from the language written by the famous Romans. However, what are called Romance languages did not. The working men were the ones who determined the language in the various countries which had been conquered by Caesar and the other classical generals. Church Latin is still spoken but is not much taught. Vulgar Latin is made up of words spoken by the common people, or *vulgus.*

[This paragraph is confused, partly because the order of material is faulty, but partly also because sentences are not linked by synonyms and repeated words. Three ideas run parallel in the paragraph: the kinds of Latin, the descent of the Romance languages, the teaching of Latin in the schools. These ideas should be distinct, but should also be tied together.]

REVISION *(Cont.)*

tuguese, and Romanic. Classical Latin has accounted for words borrowed into these languages, as it accounted for words borrowed into English, but all scholars now agree that the Romance languages did not come from the classical speech of Virgil and Cicero. French and Italian and Spanish came from the Latin speakers who were working in France and Italy and Spain, the soldiers, the merchants, the laboring men, that is, the *vulgus* whose speech is known as Vulgar Latin.

[The three ideas are carried through the paragraph by repetition of words like Latin, *and the generous use of synonyms and partial synonyms like* Vulgar Latin *and* the classical speech of Virgil and Cicero.]*

Similar constructions in consecutive sentences help to tie a paragraph together.

ORIGINAL

Most co-eds at State University did not come here to get married, though the president did make a joke something like that. We didn't come to get dates, either, at least not mainly, though the Dean kind of hinted that. And I suppose the profs think we are just being nice to them to get good grades without working.

[This paragraph is not completely incoherent, but the reader is given little help in moving through it.]

REVISION

Whatever the administration may imply, the co-eds at State University have not come here mainly to get married. Whatever the Dean of Women may say, they have not come mainly to get dates. And whatever the faculty may think, they have not come mainly to get good grades by flashing their smiles at professors.

[With sentences having similar constructions and similar or contrasting words, the paragraph moves to a cumulative effect.]

Especially within a paragraph, material can be cemented by a subject continued from sentence to sentence.

ORIGINAL

I can remember when tires were quite different from what they are today. Twenty to thirty thousand miles

REVISION

To anyone who knew touring in the old days, the modern automobile tire is a marvel and a joy. It will run, with

ORIGINAL (*Cont.*)

is not now considered unusual tire mileage, provided tires are kept at proper inflation and are not run at excessive speeds. Also, anybody can change a tire with ease now. The modern tire is a marvel and a joy. A good tire, when it is new, will turn most nails and almost any old tire ought to zip through broken glass from milk bottles without a scratch. You can buy tires in nonskid, high-speed, and antisnow types.

[*The reader is needlessly confused because the subject shifts from sentence to sentence.*]

REVISION (*Cont.*)

proper care, twenty to thirty thousand miles. It will zip through smashed milk bottles without a scratch. When new, it will turn most tacks and nails. At reasonable speeds and with proper pressure, it is almost blowout-proof. It is available in nonskid, high-speed, and antisnow types. Best of all, it can be changed in a few minutes.

The ancestor of the modern tire, however, was quite different. . . .

[*The paragraph gains coherence because the subject of discussion, modern tires, has become the grammatical subject of the individual sentences.*]

EXERCISE 3

A. Describe the methods used in the following paragraphs to gain continuity, and point out specific examples of each method:

1. The doctrine of energy has to do with the notion of quantitative permanence underlying change. The doctrine of evolution has to do with the emergence of novel organisms as the outcome of chance. The theory of energy lies in the province of physics. The theory of evolution lies mainly in the province of biology, although it had previously been touched upon by Kant and LaPlace in connection with the formation of suns and planets.

—A. N. WHITEHEAD, *Science and the Modern World*

2. I have already given you a summary account of the manner in which young misses are educated in this country. They are all sent early to school; where they are taught to spell, and read, and write. From parochial schools, many of them are transferred to boarding-schools and academies. Here they learn to understand arithmetic, which indeed is usually taught them in parochial schools, and study English grammar, geography, history to some extent, criticism, and composition. In a few instances they are taught moral science, and in some ascend to higher branches of mathematics, the Latin and French languages. To these are added embroidery, drawing, and music.

—TIMOTHY DWIGHT, *Travels in New England and New York*

3. Twenty-four hours have elapsed since writing the foregoing. I have just returned from the haymow, charged more and more with love

and admiration of Hawthorne. For I have just been gleaning through the Mosses, picking up many things here and there that had previously escaped me. And I found that but to glean after this man, is better than to be at the harvest of others. To be frank (though, perhaps, rather foolish) notwithstanding what I wrote yesterday of these Mosses, I had not then culled them all; but had, nevertheless, been sufficiently sensible of the subtle essence in them, as to write as I did. To what infinite height of loving wonder and admiration I may yet be borne, when by repeatedly banqueting on these Mosses I shall have thoroughly incorporated their whole stuff into my being,—that, I cannot tell. But already I feel that this Hawthorne has dropped germinous seeds into my soul. He expands and deepens down, the more I contemplate him; and further and further, shoots his strong New England roots into the hot soil of my Southern soul.

—HERMAN MELVILLE, *Hawthorne and His Mosses*

4. I am therefore led to my final assumption, that the admission of a principle of relativity and uncertainty should not be simply depressing. It does not destroy all possibility of knowledge and judgment. Rather, it is the outcome of comprehensive knowledge, and the means to further knowledge of man's history. It enables a higher objectivity, a fuller understanding of present and past. It enables wiser choices among the possibilities open to us—among goods that are no less real because they are relative, and that are more relevant than arbitrary absolutes. Above all, this principle encourages a positive faith in positive values: of liberality, of breadth of spirit, hospitality to new ideas, willingness to adventure, humility in admitting one's own fallibility and the limitations of the human mind—of the tolerance that is indispensable for the pursuit of truth, for social harmony, and for simple humanity. If these are not the highest values, none are more essential to the hopes of world order and peace.

—HERBERT J. MULLER, *The Uses of the Past*

B. Analyze the following paragraphs carefully for organization and continuity. Identify topic sentences or other topical material. Describe the plan of the paragraph. How is this plan made clear to the reader? Does the paragraph break naturally into parts? If so, what are they, what does each concern, and how are they marked off for the reader? Do any main divisions have subdivisions? How are they indicated? What other devices are used for continuity? If there is a conclusion, identify it. What material is apparently intended to link this paragraph to other paragraphs? The numbers are not in the originals, but are intended for use in discussion.

1. (1) Their sufferings, they told him, were too great to be endured. (2) All the men had received one, most of them two or three wounds. (3) More than fifty had perished, in one way or another, since leaving Vera Cruz. (4) There was no beast of burden but led a life preferable to theirs. (5) For when the night came, the former could rest from his labors; but they, fighting or watching, had no rest, day or night.

   —WILLIAM H. PRESCOTT, *Conquest of Mexico*

2. (1) There are, however, one or two minor points in Rabelais that may be worth notice. (2) I might, you know, analyze it as I attempted to analyze *Don Quixote.* (3) There is in *Gargantua* and *Pantagruel* that same complexity of thought and construction: you may note, first of all, the great essence which is common to these masterpieces as to all literature—ecstasy, expressed in the one case under the similitude of knight-errantry, in the other by the symbol of the vine. (4) Then, in Rabelais you have another symbolism of ecstasy—the shape of *gauloiserie,* of gross, exuberant gaiety, expressing itself by outrageous tales, outrageous words, by a very cataract of obscenity, if you please, if only you will notice how the obscenity of Rabelais transcends the obscenity of common life; how grossness is poured out in a sort of mad torrent, in a frenzy, a very passion of the unspeakable. (5) Then, thirdly, there is the impression one collects from the book: a transfigured picture of that wonderful age; there is the note of the vast, interminable argument of the schools, and for a respond, the clear, enchanted voice of Plato; there is the vision, there is the mystery of the vast, far-lifted Gothic quire; and those fair, ornate, and smiling *chateaux* rise smiling from the rich banks of the Loire and the Vienne. (6) The old tales told in the farmhouse kitchens in the Chinonais, the exultation of the new learning, of lost beauty recovered, the joy of the vintage, the old legends, the ancient turns of speech, the new style and manner of speaking: so too the old world answers the new. (7) Then one has the satire of clergy and lawyers—the criticism of life—analogous, as I said, with much that is in Cervantes, and so from divers elements you see how a literary masterpiece is made into a whole.   —ARTHUR MACHEN, *Hieroglyphics: A Note Upon Ecstasy in Literature*

3. (1) Conscience, Elizabeth never wearied of proclaiming, was unmolested; every English subject might think what he pleased. (2) No Inquisition examined into the secrets of opinion; and before the rebellion no questions were asked as to what worship or what teaching might be heard within the walls of private houses. (3) The Protestant fanatics, who had from time to time attempted prosecutions, were always checked and discouraged; and unless the laws

were ostentatiously violated, the Government was wilfully blind. (4) Toleration was the universal practice in the widest sense which the nature of the experiment permitted; and if it was now found necessary to draw the cords more tightly, the fault was not with Elizabeth or her ministers, but with the singular and uncontrollable frenzy of theology, which regards the exclusive supremacy of a peculiar doctrine as of more importance than the Decalogue.

—JAMES ANTHONY FROUDE, *History of England*

4. (1) As for our brand of humor, the tall tale of the nineteenth century, being the expression of a young, healthy, hell-raising frontier people, gave something new and exhilarating to the humor of the world. (2) Our contributions in the twentieth century—the gag, the wisecrack, the comeback, the nifty, the clincher—are nowhere so good. (3) As long as it was expertly used—indeed, scrupulously stylized—in old vaudeville routine; as long, too, as it represented a second stage of the American humor, a kind of retort on the tall tale's boastfulness, the American gag had its real virtues. (4) But we have turned the gag into a mechanical, ubiquitous, incessant national tool so brassy as to be vulgar, so unchanging as to be dull. (5) As for the comeback, though fond of it, we have never been very good at it; in terms of cussing and repartee alike, our truck drivers are mere duffers by comparison with even the average cockney. (6) After all, the essence of a good comeback is a certain delayed sting, a certain perfection of surface politeness. (7) Two Frenchmen who had been brilliant and bitterly hostile rivals at school went on to become a famous general and a distinguished cardinal. (8) The cardinal, seeing the general, after many years, on a railway platform, approached him haughtily and said, "Mr. Stationmaster, when does the next train leave for Bordeaux?" (9) The general paused, smiled, and said, "At half past two, madame." (10) By comparison, how very American at bottom is the most famous of modern comebacks; how lacking in all subtlety and in any final wit is Whistler's "You will, Oscar, you will."

—LOUIS KRONENBERGER, *Company Manners*

5. (1) The planter-aristocrats of Virginia and South Carolina have been often compared and the pride of both became a byword. (2) The description of lowly North Carolina as the valley of humiliation between the two mountains of conceit, Virginia and South Carolina, is traditional. (3) But the two aristocracies were significantly different. (4) The Virginia planters, living in relative isolation, were more nearly imitative of the English county families. (5) Furthermore, their inheritance of ideology from the early seventeenth century gave them a traceable connection with the

great tradition of the English Renaissance that was less apparent in South Carolina. (6) The South Carolina planter-aristocrats were a far more compact society than their counterparts in Virginia. (7) They also were more urban in characteristics. (8) Though they might live during most of the winter months on their river planta-tions, they gathered together in Charles Town for definite social reasons and enjoyed the benefits of a cultivated city life. (9) In-stead of Renaissance thought, South Carolinians found the essays and admonitions of Addison and Steele congenial to their tastes. (10) Instead of reflecting old-fashioned notions of the obligations and responsibilities of the country gentleman as revealed in the seventeenth-century treatises of Peacham and Braithwaite, South Carolinians imitated the urbane life of Pope's London.

—LOUIS P. WRIGHT, *The Colonial Civilization of North America*

6. (1) The development of language is the history of the gradual ac-cumulation and elaboration of verbal symbols. (2) By means of this phenomenon, man's whole behavior-pattern has undergone an immense change from the simple biological scheme, and his men-tality has expanded to such a degree that it is no longer com-parable to the minds of animals. (3) Instead of a direct trans-mitter of coded signals, we have a system that has sometimes been likened to a telephone-exchange, wherein messages may be relayed, stored up if a line is busy, answered by proxy, perhaps sent over a line that did not exist when they were first given, *noted down and kept* if the desired number gives no answer. (4) Words are the plugs in this super-switchboard; they connect impressions and let them function together; sometimes they cause lines to become crossed in funny or disastrous ways.

—SUSANNE K. LANGER, *Philosophy in a New Key*

7. (1) Among medieval and modern philosophers, anxious to estab-lish the religious significance of God, an unfortunate habit has pre-vailed of paying to Him metaphysical compliments. (2) He has been conceived as the foundation of the metaphysical situation with its ultimate activity. (3) If this conception be adhered to, there can be no alternative except to discern in Him the origin of all evil as well as of all good. (4) He is then the supreme author of the play, and to Him must therefore be ascribed its shortcomings as well as its success. (5) If He be conceived as the supreme ground for limitation, it stands in His very nature to divide the Good from the Evil, and to establish Reason "within her domina-tion supreme."

—A. N. WHITEHEAD, *Science and the Modern World*

C. Below are paragraphs from student themes which are faulty because they lack plan, fail to turn about a topic sentence, include irrelevant material, or lack continuity. Criticize each paragraph; then supply a plausible topic sentence for each and rewrite it into a coherent unit.

1. In his story *The Devil and Daniel Webster,* Stephen Vincent Benét uses the Devil, or Mr. Scratch, to stand for evil. There is entirely too much evil in this world of ours. Mainly the story teaches a very important rule, that evil can win over almost anything but not over goodness. This appears at the end of the story. Daniel Webster has been losing almost all the time in the trial, because he is not dealing with a fair judge or a fair opponent. In the beginning of the trial a legal battle is fought between Mr. Scratch and Daniel Webster, with Webster trying to argue fine legal points with the Devil. Finally Daniel Webster realized that he could not fight his opponents with their own weapons. You cannot win fighting evil with evil. The tactics of Daniel Webster were changed, and a long speech about the good things in the world was the next order of business. "The simple things that everybody's known and felt" were what he talked about. The rule has been taught to society in many ways, but this method of teaching it through fiction is one of the most effective. Evil cannot conquer goodness is the rule which is the main theme of the story.

2. For one thing, cotton had to be picked by hand in the eighteenth century. The pickers had to spend long hours working with the cotton if they were to get anywhere. Cotton is an example of how the Industrial Revolution developed in the eighteenth century. From the fields the cotton went to the home. Here seeds were removed from the cotton by hand. This job required a considerable amount of time and patience. Then the cotton was spun into thread and woven into cloth. Men finally became tired of slow and tedious manual labor, and they began to seek new methods of producing cotton textiles. It was about the middle of the century when a number of inventions appeared which tended to shift the cotton industry from the home to the factory. Hundreds of workers could be replaced by the new machinery. Factories were built in order to house this machinery.

3. She has native aptitude as a literary critic, or at least as a critic of current magazines. Unless restrained, she literally devours *The Atlantic,* concentrating on the front and back covers, if she can stuff them into her mouth. My young brother attributes this preference for *The Atlantic* to the whisky advertisements on the back page, but I am convinced she genuinely has taste for a good thing, something solid enough so that she can get her teeth into it. This

theory of mine gains support from her other tastes. She prefers the woodpulp of *The New York Times* to that of the local paper, and I confess that I prefer the *Times,* also, to read as well as to swat flies. She will have none of the sleazy magazine digests. She throws them on the floor with a squawk of disgust. The *Saturday Evening Post* and Mother's home-building magazine intrigue her for short periods—she likes to chew the square binding at the back, for there is a certain four-square practicality in Barbara— but not for long. I gather she finds them jargonic and repetitious, lacking in the sort of body required by a young woman with three teeth. *The New Yorker* she toys with, but never consumes. I suspect that it is too brittle for her taste, caviar to the nursery. Mother, I am happy to report, encourages Barbara in her literary leanings; Mother approves of *The Atlantic,* partly because the covers are so tough that Barbara can seldom chew anything loose. Think what might happen to her taste and her stomach if she were some day to swallow a chunk of a true confession magazine.

Developing and Controlling an Idea

It is not growing like a tree, in bulk, doth make man better be. . . .
—Ben Jonson

Students often excuse the infrequency of their letters home by protesting that they have nothing to say. Then they prove their point:

> Most of my courses are very good, but some are better than others. The house is old but very pleasant. It is enjoyable, especially because of the many good friends I have made. Studying is encouraged at the house, and the study table every night is valuable for me. Everything is fine, although I am not sure my allowance will be enough for the rest of the month.

Even a mother might yawn over this. The passage has achieved a certain length—it has grown in bulk—but it is not very interesting; it does not say much. The difficulty can be looked at from two directions. First, the paragraph does not focus on any central topic. The writer has not selected any central idea; he has simply jotted down random thoughts. He has, in fact, introduced a number of topics which might serve to unify a paragraph, but he has not settled on any of them. The paragraph has no governing topic sentence.

Furthermore, the writer has not developed any ideas. He has mentioned half a dozen topics—opinions or generalizations—but he starts them and drops them. To develop an idea, the writer thinks about it, raises questions a reader may want answered, and answers them. He searches in his experience or in the library to substantiate or illustrate a main idea. To make a letter from the generalities above, the writer could ask himself why some courses are better than others; from his answers he could develop a paragraph—or probably two or three—by mentioning characteristics of particular courses, describing specific things that happened in them. Or he might recall details describing the house, characterize his new friends, or tell how the "study table" operates. He might even gain practically by citing the inadequacies of his allowance.

Writing, like thinking, explores the limitless links and lapses, connections and separations, affinities and repulsions, similarities and opposites in the world. It therefore involves constantly the interplay in the mind of man between things and the relations among them. Writing at once records and stimulates this activity of the mind. It exploits the relations among facts and the judgments one can make about facts, among details and general statements that the facts can illustrate, among generalizations and evidence, among broad ideas and their applications. The stuff of writing can be thought of as being of two sorts: records of facts, what has happened or what exists or what can be imagined, and thoughts about facts, what they mean, how they are related, what they demonstrate. *Moby Dick* is a collection of facts about whales, of specific happenings on a ship, of details from the lives of a number of men, of specific things men have said or done or felt. But it is also a complex exploration of how all these details are related, of their significance, of what they mean. Any paragraph—even any sentence—or any two-volume book, is essentially this sort of thing—some kind of combination of details plus some kind of observation about how these details are related to one another.

We can, therefore, look at the process of writing in two ways. We can consider questions that involve the broad general expressions of relationships, of significances. And we can consider the facts or details that these general comments describe. But when we write we consider both of these at the same time. If we wish to make a general observation, "Dogs are a nuisance at vacation time," for example, we do so because some complex of experiences—information, books, hearsay, or other knowledge—has led us to such a conclusion. If we want to write the statement so that it will be clear and convincing, we record some of the details that stimulated it. These may help the reader to understand us. Writing and thinking work together in a kind of two-way process—generalizing from details and using details to explain or support generalizations.

In Sections 1–3 of this book we have already looked briefly at how this process works, especially in a paragraph. We have emphasized the importance of having a central idea, a central theme, and a topic sentence, toward which supporting information can be directed. In this part of the book we consider the whole question of development—the difference between a generalization and supporting detail, the inductive process in development and the validity of evidence, the question of the relevance of details to the main point or the topic sentence, methods of illustration, and problems of preserving a logical approach and using the methods of deduction.

4

Definition

For Guide to Revision, see page 68

Definition may both control and develop an idea.

The Romans were great extenders of boundaries. They found that boundaries have at least two uses: they keep something out and they provide an area for development within. Boundaries have these same uses in writing; in fact, we have adopted the Latin word for setting up limits, *definire,* for one important process in writing, definition. That is, definition in writing can set limits to an idea, even the main idea of a composition; and such limitation as this often becomes a way of developing or controlling an idea. For purposes of writing, then, definition is often more than the kind of formal delineation of a term to be found in a dictionary or in a science handbook. A definition of a university or of relativity may become a book.

4-1 DEFINITION AND DEVELOPMENT

We have already observed that writing can be looked on as two essential—and inseparable—processes: establishing a main idea or central purpose and then controlling and developing it. Definition is useful in both. Notice, for example, the way in which Eldridge Colby describes the purpose of his book *Army Talk: a Familiar Dictionary of Soldier Speech.* The first sentence of the preface reads:

> This is an attempt to put in a book the language that lives on the lips of fighting men in the army of the United States.

This is a statement of the book's purpose, but it is mainly a definition, a clarification of what the writer means by *Army Talk* in the title.

The definition limits his subject, specifying that he will include in his book only words used orally, words used by men who did the fighting, words common enough so that they "lived on the lips." That is, he will eliminate words used by officers in making reports, words used in a spectacular way by one individual, and technical words not common in speech. Definition also extends beyond the opening sentence, to govern the development of the entire opening paragraph. The development of the paragraph, in fact, is mainly an extension of the definition, with specific examples of what he will include as army talk. He explains that "A 'recoil spring rod' and a 'magazine floor plate' do not enter conversation unless a man is talking shop." He points out that he includes slang, but not all slang: "To be army slang, a phrase must either have originated in or be peculiar to the army."

Or consider the following paragraph in which definition controls and develops the main idea:

> It is this association of culture with every aspect of daily life, from the design of his razor to the shape of the bottle that holds his sleeping pills, that distinguishes the highbrow from the middlebrow or the lowbrow. Spiritually and intellectually the highbrow inhabits a precinct well up the slopes of Parnassus, and his view of the cultural scene is from above. His vision pinpoints certain lakes and quarries upon which his special affections are concentrated—a perturbed lake called Rilke or a deserted quarry called Kierkegaard —but he believes that he sees them, as he sees the functional design of his razor, always in relation to the broader cultural scene. There is a certain air of omniscience about the highbrow, though that air is in many cases the thin variety encountered on the tops of high mountains from which the view is extensive but the details are lost.
> RUSSELL LYNES, *Highbrow, Lowbrow, Middlebrow*

The writer uses definition, telling what something is, as the basis of the topic sentence, the main idea, of his paragraph. His purpose is to "distinguish" the highbrow from others, and the distinguishing characteristic to be discussed in this paragraph is his "association of culture with every aspect of daily life." Definition provides the purpose, the point of focus, for the paragraph. It also suggests the material for development. The writer builds his paragraph by reporting some of the specific ways in which the highbrow associates culture with daily life; each sentence contributes something toward clarifying the writer's definition of his concept of the highbrow, so that the entire essay becomes an extended definition or series of definitions.

W. H. Auden organizes a discussion of detective stories by various sorts of definition:

> The vulgar definition, "a Whodunit," is correct. The basic formula is this: a murder occurs; many are suspected; all but one suspect, who is the murderer, are eliminated; the murdered is arrested or dies.
>
> This definition excludes:
>
> (1) studies of murderers whose guilt is known, e.g., *Malice Aforethought*. There are borderline cases in which the murderer is known and there are no false suspects, but the proof is lacking, e.g., many of the stories of Freeman Wills Crofts. Most of these are permissible.
>
> (2) thrillers, spy stories, stories of master crooks, etc., when the identification of the criminal is subordinate to the defeat of his criminal designs.
>
> The interest in the thriller is the ethical and eristic conflict between good and evil, between Us and Them. The interest in the study of a murderer is the observation, by the innocent many, of the sufferings of the guilty one. The interest in the detective story is the dialectic of innocence and guilt.
>
> As in the Aristotelian description of tragedy, there is Concealment. . . .
>
> —*The Guilty Vicarage*

The writer is not attempting to establish a scientifically accurate definition of the detective story; he is defining rhetorically, using devices of definition to develop. In the passage above he uses a synonym, lists basic characteristics identifying his subject, excludes things which might be confused with his subjects, and then moves on to discuss the basis of interest in the detective story. The essay is much more than a definition, but definition directs both its organization and its development. Similarly, when Cardinal Newman became rector of the new Dublin University, he needed a statement of purpose under which he, his faculty, and his students could work together. He prepared a series of lectures now called *The Idea of a University Defined,* in which he tried to determine what a university should do by asking himself what education is. He found that he could explain and even persuade by defining. Structurally, the work is an extended definition.

4-2 METHODS OF DEFINITION

As indicated above, definitions may have different purposes. They may be needed to limit a term so that it can be used with absolute precision in a scientific discussion. Formal or logical definitions often have this purpose. Or they may be what are often called rhetorical definitions, which a writer may use to clarify or explain or develop or even amuse. In the essay mentioned above, Russell Lynes quotes A. P. Herbert's definition of a highbrow:

> A highbrow is the kind of person who looks at a sausage and thinks of Picasso.

The statement is not a scientifically precise definition, but it makes its point; it is useful rhetorically. The following are some of the most useful kinds of definition for both logical and rhetorical purposes.

(1) *Logical or Formal Definition.* This method, specified by logicians since Aristotle, places a term in a general class and distinguishes it from others within the class. Man can be classified as an animal, and distinguished from other animals by his reason.

> Man is a rational animal. A triangle is a plane figure with three sides. Materialism is a philosophical theory which holds that the existence and nature of matter sufficiently account for the universe.

This is the most precise type of definition, but not always the most readily understood. Carelessly used it can become what is called circular definition which leads the reader back in a circle, defining a concept in terms of itself. "A washing machine is a machine that washes," does little to inform the reader.

(2) *Definition by description.* Some terms can be defined by relating them to other known things: telling how something works, how it looks, what it is made of, what it does, where it is, or how it is used. Often this sort of definition is less conclusive than logical definition because it does not distinguish a term from all others in its class. "Red is the usual color for firetrucks" might help someone to understand *red,* but it does not define adequately. An old definition of gold as "the most precious metal" is no longer adequate. Other descriptive definitions are more precise:

> A circle is the figure covered by a line fixed at one end and moving in a plane.

(3) *Definition by example.* Often examples help to clarify, and hence to define. Children learn meanings of words by repeated examples, but the method does not usually provide a complete definition.

> Epics are poems like *The Iliad, Beowulf,* and *The Song of Roland.*

(4) *Definition by synonyms.* Some terms can be defined with synonyms, that is, with other words which have similar meanings.

> *Hund* in German means *dog* in English. Osculation is kissing. To define is to distinguish.

This type of definition has the virtue of brevity. Inevitably, most definitions are longer than the words they define, but a synonym may be only one word. Definition by synonyms has its limitation, however, since no two synonyms ever have exactly the same meaning; hence the definition can be no more than approximate, and often it is not even that.

(5) *Comparative and Metaphorical Definition.* Figures of speech, metaphors, similes, or analogies (see 25-7) may help to define. Of course, comparisons can never be exact, and consequently definitions by comparison cannot be exact, but they may be revealing. If we say that a girl is catty we may be suggesting that she has some of the characteristics of a cat, but we are not suggesting that she has four legs or long whiskers. More extensively, if we define slang as "language that takes off its coat, spits on its hands, and goes to work," we may reveal one aspect of slang in a picturesque way. If we add that "slang is to language what an elevator is to a stair; it may get you there quickly and easily but it exercises neither your mind nor your legs," we may reveal another aspect of slang, but we are not so defining it that a reader can tell when *dig* is or is not slang. But, used for clarity and not for restrictive definition, metaphors can be extremely useful.

(6) *Definition by Contrast or Negation.* Defining something by telling what it is not can seldom be exact or adequate because it cannot be exhaustive, but it may be revealing. Consider the problem of defining a word like *bobbysoxer.* "A female who wears bobbysox" will not do; some wearers of short sox would not be recognized by other bobbysoxers as one of them, and a genuine bobbysoxer may put on something else for a party. For similar reasons, "an American

female teenager" will not suffice. Neither will the following statement define adequately, but it helps: "a bobbysoxer is a girl who is no longer young enough to act like a child but is not yet old enough to take more than a fluttery interest in the opposite sex." It does not define in any exact sense, but it tells us something about what a bobbysoxer is by telling us what she is not.

(7) *Definition by Origin, Process, or Growth.* A two-cycle motor can be distinguished from a four-cycle motor by describing the process by which one motor achieves an explosion for each revolution of the crankshaft, whereas the other requires two complete revolutions for one explosion. Like definitions involving comparisons or contrasts, definitions which account for something by telling how it came to be or how it works may be unusually useful in defining a complicated or difficult subject. For example, what is a *wool hat politician?* To say that he is a politician who represents one of the more rural and economically backward parts of the deep South may be tolerably accurate, but it may not mean much until the statement is supplemented with some explanation of how these areas have developed in contrast with some other areas. The definition would need to consider the aftermath of military defeat and carpetbag rule, the conflict between the white and Negro peoples, the declining role of agriculture in society, trends in education, the impacts of certain religious beliefs, and the like. The wool hat politician can be defined revealingly if not exactly by the society that has helped to culture his ideals and his prejudices.

4 **Def**

DEFINITION

Guide to Revision

Supply or revise definitions, to control the main idea, to clarify unfamiliar terms, or to provide development.

Writing can be vague, confusing, or inadequate because a writer has not defined key terms or taken advantage of an opportunity to develop by definition. A statement, for example, like "The United States is not a democracy," can be intelligently discussed only in the light of some agreement about a meaning for *democracy*. Such a definition might serve to clarify a main idea and also to provide material for development. Definition, however, is useful only if it is clear and accurate enough to serve the purposes for which it is intended. If the writer is using definition rhetorically, primarily to describe or clarify, he does not require complete logical accuracy. But if he pretends to valid logical definition, he should provide it. Circular definition, for example a statement that has the form of definition but only repeats itself, taking the reader in a circle, does not define:

A clothes drier is a drier to dry damp clothes.

And a definition by inadequate synonyms neither defines nor clarifies:

Democracy refers to the American way of life as we all conceive it.

The statement merely substitutes one confusion for another.

ORIGINAL

In the true sense of the word, a conservative is the person who really keeps our society from disaster. He is the man we should honor as the preserver of our traditions, not vilify as a foe to progress. . . .

[*The opening sentence appears to define, but does not. The remainder of the paper suffers because the reader does not understand a key term in the writer's special sense.*]

College football is no longer a sport. Coaches are hired for their ability to win games. Players are hired from whatever coal mines develop the biggest muscles, and stadiums are built or not built depending upon whether or not they will "pay off." Rooters go to the games as they would go to the movies, to see a hired actor put on a show. And collegiate sport promotes school spirit, but commercialized athletics does not.

REVISION

If we consider a conservative as the person who is reluctant to change until he is convinced that the new is better than the old, we can see that the conservative keeps our society from disaster. He is . . .

[*A definition, distinguishing the term conservative as a type of person, clarifies the remainder of the discussion. The reader may not agree, but he at least understands.*]

College football is no longer a sport, at least not in the sense that a sport is an activity engaged in for the fun of the activity. Coaches are hired for their ability to win games. Players are hired. . . .

[*The original paragraph is unclear; most of what it says would apply, for instance, to professional baseball, which is usually called a sport. The addition of a definition, specifying the particular sense in which the word* sport *is used, makes the paragraph clearer.*]

4 Def

ORIGINAL (*Cont.*)

We may define luxury commodities as those commodities which are not necessary. Necessary commodities are those which are not luxuries.

[*The definition is circular, defining with the terms to be defined.*]

REVISION (*Cont.*)

We may define luxury commodities as those articles of commerce which are unnecessary to life and health.

[*A logical definition helps the reader to understand an essential term.*]

EXERCISE 4

A. Indicate which of the methods of definition described above (4-2) are used in each of the following statements:

1. Rhetoric is speech designed to persuade.
2. Persuasion involves choice, will; it is directed to a man only insofar as he is *free*.—KENNETH BURKE
3. A narcotic is a drug which in moderate doses allays sensibility, relieves pain, and produces profound sleep, but in poisonous doses produces stupor, coma, or convulsions.
4. A chocolate éclair is like a cream puff stretched oblong and frosted or glazed with chocolate.
5. A concierge is a doorkeeper.
6. Religion is what is involved in Buddhism, Mohammedanism, and Christianity.
7. A hammer is what you use to drive nails or break rocks or beat smooth the dented fender of a car.
8. In a democratic government, the citizens, or their representatives, act freely and according to established forms to appoint or recall officers and to enact or revoke the laws by which the society is to be governed.
9. An example of a palindrome is *Able was I ere I saw Elba.*
10. In other words, education is the instruction of the intellect in the laws of Nature, under which name I include not merely things and their forces, but men and their ways; and the fashioning of the affections and of the will into an earnest and loving desire to move in harmony with those laws.—THOMAS HENRY HUXLEY
11. For the first quarter of my life I was nothing but a parrot at whom other parrots chattered.—VOLTAIRE
12. Moreover, man is the sole possessor of language. It is true that a certain degree of power of communication, sufficient for the infinitely restricted needs of their intercourse, is exhibited also by some of the lower animals. Thus, the dog's bark and howl signify

by their difference, and each by its various style and tone, very different things; the domestic fowl has a song of quiet enjoyment of life, a clutter of excitement and alarm, a cluck of maternal anticipation or care, a cry of warning—and so on. But these are not only greatly inferior in their degree to human language; they are also so radically diverse in kind from it, that the same name cannot justly be applied to both.

—WILLIAM DWIGHT WHITNEY, *The Life and Growth of Language*

13. ANCHOR BEND . . . is especially useful when attaching or bending a line or rope to a ring, as for example the ring on an anchor. It is equally secure when used on a spar or timber. It is made by passing the two round turns around the object and passing the fall over the standing part and between the object and the turns, then finishing the bend with a half hitch around the standing part.

—CHARLES D. WHITE, *Handbook of Sailing*

14. Aircraft carriers are the backbone of a Naval task force. They are slower than planes, but, of course, faster than fixed land installation.—U.S. Navy pamphlet

15. Mental agility is not necessarily jumping at conclusions.

B. Consider the adequacy as definitions of the statements below. Describe any fault you find in them.

1. A highbrow is a man who has found something more interesting than women.—EDGAR WALLACE

2. A tie rack is a rack for holding ties.

3. A fallacious argument is an argument used by somebody else to prove a conclusion you do not agree with.

4. Life is but an empty dream.

5. A good book is the precious lifeblood of a master spirit embalmed and treasured upon purpose to a life beyond life.

6. A genealogist is one who traces your family back as far as your money will go.

7. *Toves* are something like badgers—they're something like lizards—and they're something like corkscrews.

8. A straight line is the shortest distance between two points.

9. Network: anything reticulated or decussated at equal intervals, with interstices between the intersections.

10. Liberty is the right to do anything which does not interfere with the liberty of others.

11. A man's house is his castle.

12. History is the lengthened shadow of one man.

13. History is philosophy teaching by examples.

14. A clank is a sharp, brief, ringing sound, duller than a clang and deeper and stronger than a clink.

15. Knowledge is power.

C. Define each of the following terms by putting it into a class and then adding characteristics which differentiate it from other members of the class.

1. river	4. revolver	7. botany
2. basketball	5. sonnet	8. rectangle
3. pan	6. asphalt	9. chuckle

5

Adequate Development

For Guide to Revision, see page 80

Facts support judgments; details clarify generalizations.

We have all heard the kind of fruitless conversation which is a string of vociferously maintained opinions:

> "Modern music is no good. It isn't worth listening to. You have to go back to the old masters if you want to hear something."
>
> "You don't know what you're talking about. There's a lot of good modern music."
>
> "Oh, no, there isn't. The moderns just turn out popularized tripe."
>
> "Oh, no, they don't. It's the long-hairs that turn out tripe."

This kind of dialogue, obviously unproductive as communication, can only exaggerate confusion or lead to a fist fight. But much bad writing fails because it consists mainly of unsubstantiated judgments or opinions like those in the dialogue.

Fundamental to the process of writing is a balance between generalization, judgment, and opinion on the one hand and fact, detail, illustration, and evidence on the other. That is, the writer must be able to draw conclusions from what he knows or can discover about a subject (see 1 and 6); but he also must support or clarify each conclusion with samples of the thinking behind it. A bald statement of preference for either modern or classical music will interest only a poll taker; such a statement supported with details or reasons may develop into a readable composition. As an early step in developing skill in composition, a writer must learn to distinguish between fact and judgment.

5-1 DISTINGUISHING FACT AND JUDGMENT

Compare the following sets of statements:

JUDGMENT: Martha is a bad girl.
FACT: Martha took two pieces of candy without asking.

JUDGMENT: Snidhart is a murderer.
FACT: Two witnesses saw Snidhart shoot twice at the cashier who died in the hospital this morning.

JUDGMENT: Smith's dog kills sheep.
FACT: I saw Smith's dog kill a sheep.

JUDGMENT: College football is on the way out.
FACT: In many major universities football costs are increasing more rapidly than gate receipts.

The judgments are opinions, decisions, pronouncements. They characterize or classify; they express approval or disapproval; they make a general statement. Their truth or falsity cannot finally be demonstrated. The facts report what has happened or exists; they result from observation or measurement or calculation; they can be tested or verified.

Most statements, however, cannot be distinguished so sharply as these examples. A comment like "I believe that Martha is a bad girl" can be called fact—presumably the writer knows what he believes— but it obviously includes a judgment. Or a primarily factual statement like "We saw the murderer Snidhart shoot the cashier" includes a judgment in the label *murderer*. Furthermore, judgments are not always so nearly final as those above. They often are plausible opinions which provoke thought or lead to factual development:

A little learning is a dangerous thing.
Athletics are a valuable part of an educational program.

Many statements are somewhere between, seemingly factual but not clearly verifiable. They often introduce substantiating evidence or illustrative fact.

The trouble with youth is that it belongs to those who are too young to enjoy it.
College football has ceased to have any relation to education.

Obviously, not all statements can be clearly classified, but fact and judgment can generally be distinguished as products of different kinds of thinking with different uses in writing.

5-2 GENERAL AND SPECIFIC

One distinction is that judgments are almost always more general than facts. A general statement refers to the whole or a class, a type, a group. A specific statement refers to a particular. Practically, however, *general* and *specific* are relative terms: they refer to a relationship and do not describe an absolute characteristic. One statement is more or less specific than another. For instance, *man* is more specific than *living being; American citizen* is more specific than *man; John Jones* is more specific than *American citizen.* Or compare the following examples:

> College activities are bad.
> Extracurricular activities in college are harmful to the student.
> Extracurricular activities in college prevent good academic work.
> Bill Jones failed chemistry because he spent too much time in dramatics.

Clearly each statement is more specific than the one preceding it. And each statement is nearer than the one preceding it to expressing fact rather than judgment.

5-3 DISCIPLINING GENERALIZATIONS AND DETAILS

Judgments are deceptively easy to come by. We hear them all about us, and often, especially if we think uncritically, we accept them because other people do. When we need to put words on paper, judgments and opinions often occur to us first, but they impair writing unless they introduce factual material. Facts are harder to collect than judgments, but judgments are useless without them.

Furthermore, accepted at face value, judgments impede the writer because they tend to bring his thinking to a dead end. In serious writing, judgments as nearly final as those cited above leave the reader only two choices: agreement or denial. Confronted by "John is a fool" a reader can only agree or say, "He is not." The judgment opens no further discussion. It begins by settling the matter. Such a judgment, in other words, is so sweeping that it cannot be substantiated, even by evidence that John behaved foolishly. The writer can only reassert his opinion, and repetition does not convince. The successful writer, therefore, recognizes the limited usefulness of judgments, preferring statements which he can develop with facts.

Specific details are harder to collect than judgments or general pronouncements; they require thinking and often reading or other investigation. But any writer who has a judgment or generalization worth stating can find specific details with which to develop it. If, for example, the participants in the conversation above about music wanted to become serious and write a composition on their views, they could ask themselves questions about specific composers, specific compositions, or observable characteristics of the music, such as instrumentation, complexity of harmony, or range of subject matter. If they know enough even to justify the judgments they have been making, the answers to such questions will give them specific details with which they can develop their ideas.

Furthermore, such questions, the search for developing details, help the reader to clarify and discipline his generalizations. If the two disputants about music were to force themselves toward the specific, they would probably find their pronouncements altering to fit the facts they could muster. "Modern music is no good" might become something which the speaker could hope to support: "The rhythms of modern music are less subtle than those of Beethoven" or "Modern music does not develop clear melodies." If they cannot find details to support their judgments about music, they will obviously do better writing about something else about which they do have information.

Both judgments and facts, then, generalizations and specific details, help composition. They work together, usually with writing developing as it does in the following, by moving from the general to the more specific:

> Like most of the American Indians, except those of the Southwest pueblos, the tribes of the Northwest Coast were Dionysian. In their religious ceremonies the final thing they strove for was ecstasy. The chief dancer, at least at the high point of his performance, should lose normal control of himself and be rapt into another state of existence. He should froth at the mouth, tremble violently and abnormally, do deeds which would be terrible in a normal state. . . .
>
> —RUTH BENEDICT, *Patterns of Culture*

The paragraph begins with a general statement. The second sentence explains the first, and the term *Dionysian,* with a statement a little more specific. The third illustrates the second and the meaning of *ecstasy.* The fourth becomes more specific still in illustrating the third. The writing becomes more vivid as it becomes more specific.

The paragraph illustrates the dual fundamental process of writing: centering on a main idea—topic sentence in a paragraph—which evolves from detailed information about the topic; then citing relevant information as a way of supporting, clarifying, and illustrating the main idea. This procedure is basic to writing, and the possible variations on it are numberless. The following include only a few of the more useful variations.

5-4 CITING PARTICULARS

We can describe a man or a house or a scene by giving the reader particulars which will add up to a clear idea. The following paragraph lists a selection of details to set a scene and establish a mood:

> It was early evening of a day in the late fall and the Winesburg County Fair had brought crowds of country people into town. The day had been clear and the night came on warm and pleasant. On the Trunion Pike, where the road after it left town stretched away between berry fields now covered with dry brown leaves, the dust from passing wagons arose in clouds. Children, curled into little balls, slept on the straw scattered on wagon beds. Their hair was full of dust and their fingers black and sticky. The dust rolled away over the fields and the departing sun set it ablaze with colors.
>
> —SHERWOOD ANDERSON, *Winesburg, Ohio*

5-5 EXAMPLES OR INSTANCES

"Give me an example" is a common request of anyone wanting to understand. The writer who wants to be understood complies; he clarifies with examples or specific instances. Consider the following paragraphs.

> Many naturalists are of opinion that the animals which we commonly consider as mute have the power of imparting their thoughts to one another. That they can express general sensations is very certain; every being that can utter sounds has a different voice for pleasure and for pain. The hound informs his fellows when he scents

his game; the hen calls her chickens to their food by her cluck, and drives them from danger by her scream.

Birds have the greatest variety of notes; . . .

—SAMUEL JOHNSON, *The Idler*

Johnson works toward specific instances—the hound, the hen, birds— in order to illustrate his general statement. The following paragraph develops in a similar way.

But, indeed, the dictum that truth always triumphs over persecu- tion is one of those pleasant falsehoods which men repeat after one another till they pass into commonplaces, but which all experience refutes. History teems with instances of truth put down by persecu- tions. If not suppressed forever, it may be thrown back for centuries. To speak only of religious opinions: the Reformation broke out at least twenty times before Luther, and was put down. Arnold of Brescia was put down. Fra Dolcino was put down. Savonarola was put down. The Lollards were put down. The Hussites were put down.

—JOHN STUART MILL, *On Liberty*

The paragraph progresses from general statements toward specific in- stances or examples.

5-6   INCIDENT

Sometimes a writer can illustrate most effectively by telling a story to show what he means. Ruth Benedict, wishing to say that the social customs of a people are fundamental to their happiness, begins her book *Patterns of Culture* by recounting her conversations with a chief of the Digger Indians of California. The old man expresses his de- spair as he sees a way of life disappear; his comments illustrate the writer's point vividly and feelingly.

In the following passage the historian James Anthony Froude uses a story to illustrate a point and incidentally reveals something of the differences between money values in the 1870's and now:

Will you have an example of what may be done by an ordinary man with no special talents or opportunity? A Yorkshireman, an agricultural labourer, that I knew, went to Natal twelve years ago. I suppose at first he had to work for wages; and I will tell you what the wages are in that country. I stayed myself with a settler on the borders there. He had two labourers with him, an Irishman and an Englishman. They lived in his house; they fed at his own table. To the Irishman, who knew something of farming, he was paying fourteen pounds a month; to the Englishman he was paying ten; and every penny of this they were able to save.

With such wages as these, a year or two of work will bring money enough to buy a handsome property. My Yorkshireman purchased two hundred and fifty acres of wild land outside Maritzburg. He enclosed it; he carried water over it. He planted his fences with the fast-growing eucalyptus, the Australian gum-tree. In that soil and in that climate, everything will flourish, from pineapples to strawberries, from the coffee-plant and the olive to wheat and Indian corn, from oranges and bananas to figs, apples, peaches, and apricots. Now at the end of ten years the mere gum-trees which I saw on that man's land could be sold for two thousand pounds, and he is making a rapid fortune by supplying fruit and vegetables to the market at Maritzburg.

—*On the Uses of a Landed Gentry*

5-7 ANALOGY

To explain or illustrate the unfamiliar to the reader, a writer can speak in similar but more familiar terms. That is, he can develop ideas by analogy. The device is familiar; to explain the rotation of the earth to a child, we are likely to speak in terms of a rubber ball or a top. Victor Hugo describes the Battle of Waterloo as a giant letter *A*. Thomas Henry Huxley in a famous analogy says that life is like a game of chess. Sir James Jeans cites Rutherford's description of the structure of the atom:

Rutherford supposed the atom to be constructed like the solar system, the heavy central nucleus playing the part of the sun and the electrons acting the parts of the planets.

—*The Universe Around Us*

5 Dev

ADEQUATE DEVELOPMENT

Guide to Revision

Rewrite, eliminating repetitious or undeveloped judgments or supplying adequate development with facts and specific details.

Often the writer who cannot finish a paper because "he has said everything he knows" is partly right; he has stated every conclusion, every judgment or opinion, that he can relate to his topic. In another sense, the writer is stalled because he has not really started; he is repeating judgments but has not thought of anything to say about them, to develop them. Writing which lacks adequate development, which is too exclusively a series of unsupported general statements, requires two types of revision.

First, the generalizations need to be reconsidered—limited or revised so that they can be supported (see also 1). Often the trouble is that the generalizations are too inclusive, so sweeping that they cannot be illustrated. The writer who begins by saying "American teachers are uneducated" may shock his readers into interest, but he also makes logical development of his paper almost impossible. How can he obtain convincing data on all teachers? Unless he wishes merely to repeat judgments, he must modify his assertion by suggesting that he means "many teachers" and "inadequately educated"; and when he modifies in this way, only a rather obvious comment remains. If he makes his general statement more specific—for instance, "Many American teachers have not been trained for the jobs they are required to do"—he opens the way for illustration.

Second, the generalizations need to be developed—not merely restated or repeated. The writer must marshal the facts he knows or look up new material in order to clarify or illustrate what he has asserted. With his more specific statement on teachers, for instance, the writer mentioned above might cite examples of teachers he has known who have been put into jobs for which they have not been prepared. Such illustrations would not prove the generalization, but they would show the reader more specifically what the generalization means. Or the writer might find statistics about teacher training, the numbers who are not teaching the subject of their college major, for example.

ORIGINAL

College education is much too expensive in America, and it is getting worse every day. Many deserving students either have to postpone college indefinitely or work so much of the time that they neglect their studies. If democracy is to survive, the government must provide some method for enabling more capable students to get college educations. Scholarship awards are unfair because they put a premium on memory and mental ability and not on character and need. If our country is to survive, something must be done about this problem.

[*It is no wonder that this paper stopped short of the required number of words; except for the second sentence, the paragraph is made up of judgments, none of them substantiated or illustrated. Furthermore, the judgments are so broad that they discourage development. The writer should begin by abandoning the unnecessary judgments.*]

The old Union Building at Winnemac University must be replaced. We must have a modern building which will be worthy of an institution like Winnemac. The present building is a disgrace and a shame, far from providing any beneficial college atmosphere. Both inside and out the building is inadequate. It does not, even in the most elementary way, fulfill the needs of student body and faculty. The building stands out on the campus like a sore thumb.

[*The writer of this paper also had trouble finishing, probably because*

REVISION

The cost of a college education in the United States has almost doubled in the last fifteen years. It is no longer easy for a young man to save enough from his paper route and a job in the soda fountain on Saturdays to see him through four years at a university. Tuition costs in many private institutions have doubled, and many state universities have had to increase fees substantially. The textbook that cost $5.00 a few years ago is likely to be $10.00 or $12.00 now. Inflated food prices have affected college cafeterias, and even the soft drink or cup of coffee which used to provide a couple of hours of afternoon recreation for a nickel is now ten or fifteen cents. . . .

[*The revision narrows the scope of the paragraph; instead of broad judgments, it uses a general factual statement which can be illustrated. It leaves the writer with a chance to develop his topic.*]

The old Union Building at Winnemac University is not meeting the needs of the student body. There are now about 8,000 students in residence, but the cafeteria seats only 75 at a time. The dance floor is so small that a hundred couples crowd it; as a result Union dances are becoming more and more unpopular. The bookstore is so crowded that it cannot keep texts in stock. Furthermore, many important activities are entirely neglected. No rooms are available for meetings of student or faculty groups. There is no space for accommodation of guests of

ORIGINAL (*Cont.*)

there seemed to be a limit to the number of times he could say the same thing in different words. The paper fails to be convincing or clear because no idea is developed; it is a series of judgments—or repetitions of one judgment.]

Obviously, the theater was everything that a university theater should be. It had all the qualities that one wants to find in a campus playhouse. In size and equipment it was almost perfect. It is no wonder that drama was so popular on the campus and that plays were so well attended. We should attempt to get something like it for our university. And the responsibility for action rests in part with the students themselves.

[*Like most examples of inadequate development, this passage from a student theme is general rather than specific; it repeats judgments; it includes in one short paragraph material which could be developed into a long theme. The writer gets into trouble at the very beginning by failing to illustrate what he means. The writer may be willing to make his obvious statement on the basis of his knowledge, but the reader does not have enough information to accept it.*]

More than one American statesman has revealed aptitude in fields quite unrelated to politics and diplomacy. It is possible to find men in our history who were capable of all sorts of tasks, ranging from manual labor to technical science. Many men were not only skillful in political affairs but really achieved a great deal in such occupations as printing, medicine, science, agriculture, finance. Among the men with broad interests in addition to their interests in affairs of state were Washington, Jefferson, Franklin, and

REVISION (*Cont.*)

the University. There is no theater, no auditorium, no office space for publications or other activities.

[*The addition of some facts makes the judgments more plausible.*]

The theater was everything that a university theater should be. It was small and intimate, holding only about 250, and you could hear and see from every seat. The seats were comfortable but not new, and an occasional rip in the leather gave the place an atmosphere of permanence; it did not have the kind of polish that makes you expect to smell fresh paint when you walk in. There was no revolving stage or other complex machinery, but the stage was large and there was plenty of room to get around backstage. There was enough equipment to make possible all kinds of experiments— good and bad—but there was not enough to keep the stage crew from using ingenuity.

[*The first sentence of the original can be developed into a paragraph. If the other general statements of the original are to remain, they need similar illustration.*]

More than one American statesman has revealed aptitude in fields quite unrelated to politics and diplomacy. There was Jefferson, for example. An astute politician, he was also an important political philosopher, developing in his writing his theories that government should rest in the hands of the producing class. His interest in science was practical as well as theoretical; he is credited with a mathematical formula that still governs the shape of plowshares, with the invention of the swivel chair, and with the

ORIGINAL *(Cont.)*

others. Many such men were always doing things not directly connected with national or foreign affairs.

[*The paragraph begins to develop at times, but it remains general and repetitious. Even a single well-developed example would illustrate better than do these general statements.*]

REVISION *(Cont.)*

design of a leather buggy top. He contributed to the University of Virginia not only his knowledge as an educator but also the plans for the campus, one of the most beautifully arranged in America. He studied language, and was one of the first Americans to learn Anglo-Saxon. His was the kind of inquisitive mind that found interest and new ideas in many subjects.

EXERCISE 5

A. Which of the following statements are mainly fact and which mainly judgment? Some may be considered relatively more or less factual, depending upon the circumstances. For instance, if an entomologist says, "That is a golden-eyed fly," he may be identifying a tabanid of the genus Chrysopa, but if a five-year-old child makes the same remark he may be implying much less fact.

1. Water freezes at 32 degrees Fahrenheit.
2. The early bird catches the worm.
3. The road was a ribbon of moonlight across the purple moor.
4. Patriotism is the last refuge of a scoundrel.
5. If a man in some one else's house calls another a perjurer or accosts him insultingly with scandalous words, he shall pay 1s. to the householder, 6s. to the man whom he insulted, and 12s. to the king.—Anglo-Saxon Law, 685–86 A.D.
6. In the seventeenth century, although three hundred crimes in English law were punishable by death, the Massachusetts Body of Liberties listed only ten, and in some of the other states there were fewer.
7. Being in a ship is being in a jail—with the chance of being drowned.
8. We cannot continue to support the nations of Europe forever.
9. Parallel lines will never meet, no matter how far extended.
10. William James, elder brother of Henry James and one of America's most significant philosophers, was born in 1842 and died in 1910.

B. Study the following student theme and determine· which statements are primarily judgment and which primarily fact. Then select two of the judgments which interest you, rewrite them as generalizations limited enough to permit illustration, and make a list of facts which you might use in a paragraph illustrating each of your generalizations.

A good campus newspaper can be a great asset to any college or university. However, it must be truly a campus paper, and it should be very outstanding. Many campus papers are more concerned about national or international news than about the affairs right on the campus. They are ill-advised. It is much more desirable for a campus paper to concentrate its efforts on local matters and leave major news stories to larger papers, which have the advantages of a huge staff and expensive news services.

Local news is just as important as the events that make the head-lines in the large dailies. Students are often more interested in the campus prom queen election than in the election of a representative to Congress. Interest in local affairs is highly desirable. Everyone should be interested in what goes on in his immediate surroundings.

A paper which is primarily concerned with campus events also pro-vides better training for budding journalists. This country, and every country in the world today, has need for good journalists. Journalism has much to do with the formation of public opinion, and in a de-mocracy public opinion is very important. It is therefore of the greatest significance for a country like ours that papers should train the best type of journalist.

A local paper is also more interesting because it does not pretend to be something more important than it is. Any pretension is always unpleasant. We can, however, really be interested in a campus paper which tells us the things we want to hear about.

For these reasons I believe that a campus newspaper should be con-centrated on reporting campus news.

C. The following selections concern change in language. Which contain broad judgments? Which judgments are buttressed by fact?

1. The worst vulgarism in English speech is a habit of prefixing a neutral vowel . . . to all the vowels and diphthongs. . . . When I pass an elementary school and hear the children repeating the alphabet in unison, and chanting unrebuked "Ah-yee, Be-yee, Ce-yee, De-yee," I am restrained from going in and shooting the teacher only by the fact that I do not carry a gun and by my fear of the police.

   —GEORGE BERNARD SHAW, *The Miraculous Birth of Language*

2. A happier expedient than the use of discarded meanings by mod-ern writers would appear to be functional shift, which also figures largely in the creation of words and has been a source of fine poetic effects in the work of our greatest poets, including Shake-speare and Keats. Since poetry may frequently be called "double

talk," that is, saying one thing in terms of another, a poetic image, the change in word usage which is called functional shift would appear to have it merits.

—MARGARET BRYANT, *Modern English and Its Heritage*

3. All languages being imperfect, it does not follow that one should change them. One must adhere absolutely to the manner in which the good authors have spoken them; and when one has a sufficient number of approved authors, a language is fixed.

—VOLTAIRE, *Philosophical Dictionary*

4. As used in the title of this work, "Americanism" means a word or expression that originated in the United States. The term includes: outright coinages, as *appendicitis, hydrant, tularemia;* such words as *adobe, campus, gorilla,* which first became English in the United States; and terms such as *faculty, fraternity, refrigerator,* when used in senses first given them in American usage.

—MITFORD M. MATHEWS, *A Dictionary of Americanisms*

5. The mechanism of the English language would also be improved by the adoption or invention of some indefinite pronoun other than *one* to correspond in meaning and usage to French *on,* deriving from Latin *homo, hominem* "man," and to German *man,* which is readily distinguishable from *der Mann* both in speech (because, like *man* in the Scandinavian languages and like *men* in Dutch, it is pronounced with weaker stress and with reduced vowel) and in writing (since it has one final *n* and no initial capital).

—SIMEON POTTER, *Our Language*

D. Rewrite each of the following in specific terms, inventing specific details to develop the general statements:

EXAMPLE: Later Milly and her mother were sitting outside looking as usual at the flowers.

After lunch Milly and her mother were sitting as usual on the balcony beyond the salon, admiring for the five-hundredth time the stocks, the roses, the small, bright grass beneath the palm, and the oranges against a wavy line of blue.

—KATHERINE MANSFIELD, *The Dove's Nest*

1. When we rose in the morning, we could see all over the streets the signs of the storm of the night.

2. Mary was always doing the kind of thing which gave her the reputation of being a girl you could not trust.

3. The shelves were packed with books of a great many kinds and varieties.

   4. The pond was bordered by very beautiful patches of lovely flowers and shrubs.

   5. The kitchen was well equipped with all the modern conveniences.

   6. The white tablecloth was almost invisible because it was so thoroughly covered with so many good things to eat.

   7. The children came to the Hallow'een party in the many kinds of costumes customary to such celebrations of an old holiday.

   8. The desk was piled in high confusion with numerous evidences of Wendy's varied interests.

   9. When Sue sat down to study, she always found her thoughts wandering off to many unrelated subjects.

   10. Before he started in college, Phil had not realized that he would constantly be needing money for a variety of incidental and miscellaneous expenses.

E. List fifteen specific details which you might use in describing any three of the list below. Make the details concrete; prefer "the soiled brown chair with protruding springs" to "the furniture in the room."

   1. A college room
   2. A favorite restaurant
   3. A teacher I know
   4. A classroom
   5. The lake front
   6. A campus politician

List specific details which you might use to illustrate each of the following statements:

   1. A university provides wide opportunities for wasting time.

   2. Drugstores have become more than places that sell drugs.

   3. The modern automobile has developed with concern for the comfort of driver and passengers.

   4. Members of theater audiences are guilty of a variety of discourtesies.

   5. Comic books are not designed exclusively for children.

Describe a specific instance which might be used to illustrate any five of the following statements:

   1. Abraham Lincoln had great respect for the feelings of others.

   2. Incidents of childhood may have profound effects on human beings.

   3. The most beautiful places in America have not all been discovered by tourists.

   4. Athletes are not necessarily poor students.

   5. Proverbs are not always applicable.

   6. Pets can be nuisances.

7. Emergency measures sometimes become permanent parts of a social system.

8. Economy does not always pay.

9. Newspaper columnists are not always right in their prophecies.

10. Individuals may profit from a war.

F. If you wish to discuss the fact that the lever action of a typewriter forces the typewriter key to travel at considerable speed, you might make your meaning clear by giving the ratio of the lever action in a specific typewriter and estimating the speed a key might attain under normal touch. That is, you might give an example. Or you might try to explain the lever action and its effect by comparing the typewriter key assembly to the human forearm. That is, you might use an analogy. For each of the following statements supply (a) a possible example, and (b) a possible analogy.

1. As modern furniture becomes more popular, prices are likely to drop.

2. A rocket attains its great speed through the propulsive powers of discharging gas.

3. The central portion of the United States is a great, shallow bowl.

4. An end run can be a deceptive play.

5. A personnel manager should have training as well as experience.

6. Animals can be taught more with kindness than with whipping.

7. Race prejudice should be discouraged in the public schools.

8. This year's automobiles are designed more to sell cars than to improve transportation.

6

Evidence:

Inductive Reasoning

For Guide to Revision, see page 93

Support generalizations with sound, adequate, appropriate evidence, or avoid the generalizations.

Writing records thinking; the preceding discussions of approaches to writing have all presumed reasoning—the kind of thinking employed constantly in life, by the doctor diagnosing an illness and prescribing possible remedies, by the lawyer preparing and arguing a case, by the scientist generalizing from experiments and then applying his generalization to particular instances. This kind of thinking can be considered in two parts: induction, the process of generalizing from specific data, and deduction (see 7), the process of applying generalizations, like those produced by induction, to particular instances. Both of these are involved in the writing processes we have been considering—settling on a main idea on which to focus information and recording sufficient information to develop this main idea.

6-1 INDUCTION

A city council in the Midwest recently considered continuing government controls on rents. Representatives of landlords protested that they could not meet their bills and asserted that there was no real housing shortage. A hastily organized committee of renters appeared at the next meeting declaring that renters could not meet their bills either and asserting that there was a severe housing shortage in the area. The council, understandably, was puzzled. Finally an astute newspaperman took a list of all the apartments, real estate offices, and rental agencies in the city and started telephoning, pretending he had just arrived in the city and needed a place to live. After three hours he located only two available apartments, both at rents well above prescribed limits. His story was instrumental in the council's decision to continue rent controls. It was convincing; it was "logical"; it was based on evidence.

The newspaperman's process was inductive. He collected data which led to a generalization. He proceeded from specific instances to a general conclusion.

6-2 TYPES OF INDUCTION; GENERALIZATION, HYPOTHESIS

We use induction every day, to reach conclusions, to determine causation, to make decisions. We must work with varying kinds of evidence; as a result our conclusions vary in reliability and in usefulness. For example, a man goes out in the yard on a cool morning in spring wondering whether a frost the night before has killed the cherries. He examines a dozen blossoms in different parts of his tree and finds black spots in the center of each where the fruit should be forming. A neighbor's tree shows similar black spots. He believes that he has found enough specific instances to warrant the generalization that there has been a killing frost. He has noticed a number of unharmed cherries on a small tree partially protected by an overhanging porch roof, but he rejects these because they are not typical examples. The generalization is reliable because it is induced from a sufficient number of typical relevant instances.

Other generalizations develop in much the same way, but less directly. For example, we can generalize that if we flip a light switch the light will turn on, even though we are aware that current is sometimes off and bulbs burn out. The generalization rests on evidence of a pattern of occurrences; it is, strictly, a prediction, a statement of probability, but it is practically useful. With less assurance, but on the same basis, we can generalize that if we pull a cat's tail we shall provoke some kind of noise.

Similarly we can generalize from statistical probability. If statistics record 542 traffic deaths during the Fourth of July holiday last year and reveal that holiday traffic deaths have tended to increase annually, we can predict with some assurance that there will be more than 542 traffic deaths over the holiday this year. But statistical evidence is likely to be dubious, subject to many variables. The political candidate who relaxes in his campaign when he discovers that 58 per cent of the voters are registered in his party may be surprised.

Analogy provides another type of evidence for inductive generalization. We may conclude, for example, that the chukkar partridge will flourish in Western American semi-deserts because it lives in parts of India which have similar climate. The generalization may be useful if the two areas are sufficiently similar. That is, analogy is reliable as evidence if the instances compared are similar in all important respects and if any differences between them can be explained. Most often, it serves best to illustrate or clarify (see 4), not as evidence.

Arguments involving causation are also inductive. Usually they lead to hypotheses which are useful but require further testing. For example, a girl comes into her dormitory room late at night and finds her roommate's clothes spread about. She sees an empty flower box on the dresser. She finds a new bottle of perfume open. She remembers that is the night of a formal dance. She discovers that her roommate's new gown is missing from the closet. She forms a hypothesis to explain the facts she has observed: that her roommate received a last-minute invitation and has gone to the dance. A hypothesis is usable if it is a better explanation for all known facts than any alternative; but it is only a tentative explanation, requiring verification from the observation of more data.

6-3 INDUCTION IN WRITING

The writer is likely to use as the main idea of a composition or as the topic sentence of a paragraph a generalization based on his observation of a body of evidence. He may develop this idea by citing evidence for the generalization. For example, Ruth Benedict, in *Patterns of Culture,* suggests that among cultures there is wide diversity in social habits and attitudes, but she does not leave the statement as an unsubstantiated judgment. She examines various cultures in terms of customs concerning adulthood, warfare, and marriage. The facts gathered lead to conclusions which lead in turn to a main idea. The whole structure might be described as a pyramid, a pyramid which is solid and convincing because its foundation is factual. Specific details support each general statement, and the analysis could be carried down to even smaller units of composition, supported by even more specific details. The lower left block of the pyramid below, for example, is the paragraph which follows it.

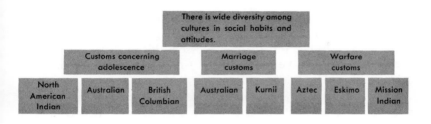

Adulthood in central North America means warfare. Honour in it is the great goal of all men. The constantly recurring theme of the youth's coming-of-age, as also of preparation for the warpath at any age, is a magic ritual for success in war. They torture not one another, but themselves; they cut strips of skin from their arms and legs, they strike off their fingers, they drag heavy weights pinned to their chests or leg muscles. Their reward is enhanced prowess in deeds of warfare.

The paragraph also resembles a pyramid, with details supporting statements which support another more general statement.

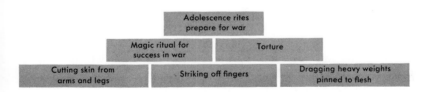

In the scheme of the whole chapter, however, as shown above, the apex of this pyramid becomes another statement which the writer uses to document further conclusions.

6-4 TESTS OF EVIDENCE

To be reliable, evidence must be adequate, relevant, typical, and accurate. If the man examining his cherry trees had looked at only one blossom, he might have seen one damaged by the neighbor boy's baseball; his evidence would have been inadequate. If he had considered only the size or color of the blossoms, or even whether the petals had dropped off, his evidence would have been irrelevant to his conclusion. If he had looked at only the tree protected from frost, he would not have seen typical instances. If the man had taken his information from the testimony of a near-sighted neighbor, who had mistaken a dead bee for a frozen blossom, his evidence would have been inaccurate. To be useful to the writer in developing his ideas, evidence should be able to withstand tests of its authority:

(1) *Is the evidence adequate?* A generalization that all cows are black and white, made by a city boy after his first visit to a farm specializing in Holstein-Frisian cattle is not reliable; it is based on too few instances. A visitor's "first-hand account" of the attitude of the Japanese toward the United States, based on a two-day guided tour of Tokyo, is not trustworthy; his evidence is inadequate.

(2) *Is the evidence relevant?* A writer who uses statistics about football gate receipts as evidence that football builds character is not convincing; his evidence is not relevant to his generalization. It might be pertinent to some other proposition—that football helps finance college athletic programs, for instance. Testimony of a large number of students that examinations should be abolished is not evidence for the proposition that examinations are not fair tests of knowledge.

(3) *Is the evidence typical?* A poll of its subscribers conducted by a business magazine is not likely to provide reliable evidence on the attitudes of Americans toward taxing corporations. The instances considered would not be typical. The kind of student paper which begins "Cats can never be trusted. I once had a cat which . . ." is probably unconvincing both because the instance he cites is not typical and because the evidence is inadequate.

(4) *Is the evidence accurate?* A biography commissioned by a political party as part of the campaign of its candidate for office is suspect as evidence. It is likely to be prejudiced as evidence. A probable partner in crime is not a reliable character witness for an alleged criminal. Neither is outdated evidence accurate. The Battle of Bull Run does not necessarily provide evidence for current military strategy. And evidence is trustworthy only if it has been provided by a competent observer. If a nine-year-old boy reports that his neighbor

is a political spy, his evidence must be discounted because of his limited knowledge and experience.

6 Ev; Rel

EVIDENCE:
INDUCTIVE REASONING

Guide to Revision

Supply adequate evidence for generalizations or modify the generalizations.

Development of an idea in composition always must be clear, adequate, and reliable; but especially when it should provide evidence for a generalization, it must be sound as inductive reasoning. The writer who says that he thinks Swedes are stubborn, or policemen have big feet, or coyotes are cowardly, and then assumes that he can *prove* such statements by citing one incident from his experience, is not likely to convince anyone whose mind is working. Unsupported generalizations are unconvincing.

6a EVIDENCE   Ev a; Rel

To be convincing, evidence must be adequate, relevant, typical, and accurate.

Human beings readily jump to conclusions without adequate evidence. A mother, quite innocently, indulges in what is known as "wishful thinking" to select only a small part of the evidence and conclude that her child has been grossly wronged by a teacher. Reporters from newspapers of rival political parties, perhaps not innocently, make different generalizations by selecting only part of the facts in their report of a mass meeting. Even statistics, if not completely analyzed, easily lead to false conclusions. A campus newspaper once reported, quite accurately, that during the year fifty per cent of the women in one college of the university had married their instructors. Hasty but vociferous conclusions, based on the accurate figure but still on inadequate evidence, had to be withdrawn when it was revealed that the college was the engineering college and the total number of women students for that year was two.

ORIGINAL

Purebred dogs are essentially stupid. When I was a child, I had a fine pedigreed Dalmatian. I tried for months to teach him to shake hands. I succeeded only in encouraging him to jump up and wipe his front feet on anyone who came in sight. An expensive spaniel which succeeded him was no better. I tried to teach him to bring in the newspaper; he learned only to chew the paper to bits.

REVISION

I never expect to own another purebred dog; my experiences have prejudiced me thoroughly in favor of curs. When I was a child. . . .

[*The sweeping pronouncement about dogs in the original is unjustified and also unnecessary. With an opening like that in the revision, the writer can use his details as illustrations, avoid the problem of proof, and write a convincing paragraph.*]

Even material that has emotional appeal or some other sort of first-glance attraction works as evidence only if it is relevant to the generalization it pretends to support. Name-calling is one variety. Slipping in a clever—but irrelevant—comment or slogan is another. Advertising relies heavily on information that pretends dramatically to relevance and significance but often is quite beside the point. The number of ingredients in a headache tablet is not necessarily relevant to the efficacy of the medication. Neither the absence nor presence of suds guarantees that a soap cleanses well. Charming girls in bathing suits are not relevant evidence for the virtues of cigars, beer, or automobiles. Juries are cautioned to avoid such irrelevancies as the diction of the defense attorney or the dress worn by the defendant. Irrelevant statements in writing are not adequate to support generalizations.

ORIGINAL

The Windhover is obviously not a good poem. I read it twice and was unable to make any sense at all of it. Many of the words were unclear to me, and some of them are run together in unusual ways. I do not see any reason for this kind of writing. . . .

REVISION

The diction of Hopkins in *The Windhover* causes much of the poem's complexity. For example, the word *wimpling* used to describe the falcon's wing is unusual because it combines effects of meaning, sound, and a slightly archaic flavor. Or the compounded *dapple-dawn-drawn*. . . .

ORIGINAL (*Cont.*)

[*The comments following the opening sentence are not relevant to the topic introduced. They are pertinent only to some kind of confession by the writer about his difficulties in reading; they tell nothing of the quality or excellence of the poem.*]

Statistics show that everyone in the office is making enough money to live comfortably. The average salary, computed on certified figures for last year, was a little more than $6,000 per year per employee.

[*The statistics cited are not relevant to the first statement, although they may, at first glance, seem to be.*]

(1) Early in the morning they began chanting prayers and dancing around a large fire in the clearing. (2) The monotonous beat of the drums and the rhythm of the voices were punctuated by loud whoops. (3) The sound of the women beating sticks together, keeping time with the drums, blended with the barking of the dogs and the yelling of the children. (4) *This celebration is carried on much as it was centuries ago.* (5) *They dance from morning until late at night.* (6) The bright feathers of the war-bonnets made weird shadows on the trees.

REVISION (*Cont.*)

[*The writer should try to collect evidence relevant to the topic, not merely to his own feelings, or he should revise his topic sentence so that it becomes more specific and more susceptible to proof with relevant evidence.*]

Although the average salary for workers in the office last year was more than $6,000, many employees were not making a living wage. Only three salaries, those of executives at $30,000, were as high as the average figure; whereas two clerks received $1800 per year and three others $1950.

[*Completed statistics require a different generalization.*]

Early in the morning they began chanting prayers and dancing around a large fire in the clearing. The monotonous beat of the drums and the rhythm of the voices were punctuated by loud whoops. The sound of the women beating sticks together, keeping time with the drums, blended with the barking of the dogs and the yelling of the children. The bright feathers of the war-bonnets made weird shadows on the trees.

[*Sentences (4) and (5) are irrelevant and have been omitted, perhaps to be worked in somewhere else in the composition.*]

If we take a room in a city's best hotel, spend a week looking out the window, and then conclude from our observations that the city has no slums and no poverty, we are likely to be wrong. We have looked at some evidence, but it has not been typical. Or if we conclude from a vote of fraternity members that weekly all-campus dances in the Union Building should be discontinued we have not examined typical evidence.

ORIGINAL

Required physical education courses tend to improve study habits and raise grade point averages for college students. A poll of physical education majors at State College reveals that more than 90 per cent testified that they studied better and made better grades while they were taking the required physical education courses.

[*Obviously the evidence is not typical, and the conclusion is not justified.*]

REVISION

Physical education majors at State College believe that the required physical education courses improve their study habits and help their grade averages, according to a recent poll. More than ninety per cent . . .

[*The most likely revision is to change the topic sentence to something factual. The generalization might be maintained with sufficient evidence.*]

To be reliable, evidence must be based on facts. Hearsay, legend, opinion, or speculation is not sufficient to support a generalization.

ORIGINAL

Some of the most important discoveries of modern times have been the result of accidents. For instance, according to the story, the great strike at Goldfield, which uncovered more than three billion dollars in gold and silver, resulted from the random kick of a bad-tempered jackass. Old Jim, while he was prospecting the area, had made camp, and was boiling his nightly coffee. The coffee pot tipped over, and splashed some boiling water on the jackass, which kicked at the pot, missed, but hit a ledge of rock instead. Old Jim stood staring, and with good reason. The sharp little hoof of the jackass had knocked loose a chunk of high-grade gold ore.

[*The writer admits that his story, improbable on the face of it, has no reliable authority; yet he proceeds to use it as evidence.*]

REVISION

In spite of the great advance in science, individual curiosity and even pure luck still play a part in important discoveries. As a matter of course the so-called "miracle drugs" have in the main resulted from careful planning, deliberate search, and vast technical knowledge. But even here, chance observations have helped make pharmaceutical history and save lives. Consider, for instance, penicillin. . . .

[*To substantiate his serious generalization about important discoveries, the writer needs a more reliable instance than the kind of folk legend which can be given no more authority than "according to the story." If he knows the interesting story of the development of penicillin, he can proceed to write a convincing paper, with authoritative support for his generalization.*]

6b CAUSATION   Ev b

A person dealing with causes is especially tempted to generalize quickly, or to admit as evidence material which is not properly evidence at all. He sits in a draft Monday night, wakes up with a cold Tuesday morning, and concludes, too readily, that the draft "caused" the cold. It may, of course, have caused it or helped to cause it, but a little reflection shows that the evidence does not warrant the conclusion. He plays with a toad on Monday and discovers a wart on his finger on Friday. He finds a horseshoe at ten o'clock, throws it over his left shoulder at 10:02, and finds a $10 bill at noon. If he concludes that playing with the toad caused his wart or that finding the horseshoe was responsible for his good luck, he is making the error known as the *post hoc ergo propter hoc* fallacy, "after this therefore because of this." It is not a sound method of determining cause. Day comes after night, but night does not cause day. The fact that banks failed after the election of Herbert Hoover does not prove that Hoover caused the depression.

ORIGINAL

Governor Jones was elected two years ago. Since that time constant examples of corruption and subversion in government have been unearthed. It is time we got rid of the man responsible for this kind of corrupt government.

[*The assumption that Governor Jones caused the corruption exemplifies the* post hoc *fallacy.*]

REVISION

Governor Jones was elected two years ago. Since that time frequent examples of corruption and subversion in government have been unearthed. It is time to see whether a new administration can clean up the government.

[*The revision is equally sweeping in its assertions, but it avoids the illogical causal conclusion.*]

6c ANALOGY Ev c

Analogy is a useful device for development, often illustrating or explaining vividly (see 5-7). The writer, however, must be aware of the limitations of analogy; it is usually not valid as evidence, as proof. A writer trying to explain the breeds of horses to city children might wish to say that just as racing automobiles have light wheels and chassis, and trucks have very heavy running gear, racing horses are relatively light and draft horses very heavy. This is an analogy. But a horse is not a machine, and an automobile is not an organism, even though the two have common use and some common qualities. The writer cannot prove anything about a horse by evidence from an automobile, but he may be able to promote understanding of the structure of the horse by noting similarities. An analogy can be a useful device, but it should not be misused.

ORIGINAL

The modern corporate businessman, in his use of ingenuity, is like the Indians of western Canada. Needing light during their foggy winters, they discovered a new use for the candlefish, which had long been a staple of their diets. This fish is so fat when it swims inland to spawn in the spring that the Indian has only to stick a rush into the fish's back and light it. The fish will then burn like a candle. It is evident, therefore, that modern business owes its success to the ability of Americans to take advantage of their natural resources.

[*The comparison of the ingenuity of the businessman with that of the Indian may make a useful analogy, but it does not warrant the conclusion of the final sentence.*]

REVISION

The modern businessman, in his use of American natural resources, has often shown ingenuity, comparable to that of the Indians of western Canada. The Indians had long included in their diet a fatty smelt called the candlefish. Finding that they had too little light through the foggy winter, they discovered that they could stick rushes in the backs of the oily fish and burn them like candles. Similarly the great oil companies have found more uses for oil than to furnish fuel for power and heat. From petroleum they have developed many kinds of synthetic rubbers, and plastics by the hundred.

[*Used as an analogy, not as a proof, the story of the candlefish aids explanation.*]

EXERCISE 6

A. The passages given below contain generalizations which are illustrated or supported by evidence. Comment on the reliability of each generalization, indicating whether it is merely illustrated or is supported by evidence and pointing out especially instances of inadequate or unreliable evidence, of misused analogies, or of faulty causation. Examine each passage in light of the requirements listed in 6-4.

1. During the past month living costs in America have risen 3.4 per cent. This figure is based on statistics compiled by governmental bureaus through sampling prices of selected commodities, and on rents in important areas throughout the United States. It does not take any account of changes in federal or state taxes.

2. A woman preaching is like a dog's walking on his hind legs. It is not done well, but you are surprised to find it done at all.

3. There is no doubt that the students at State University want football to be continued. The campus newspaper in a recent issue invited letters showing why the present sports program should be continued, and more than 200 students replied. Every letter favored retention of football.

4. The enclosed manuscript contains about 22,000 words. In order to arrive at this figure I counted the words on ten typical pages,

computed from this total the average number of words per page, and multiplied this average by the number of pages.

5. If the Jews are legally or morally entitled to Palestine, then Mussolini would have been entitled to claim Britain as a colony of the ancient Roman Empire.

6. Although there are more than a hundred quadrillion stars, space is less crowded with stars than the air of Europe would be if it were populated by three wasps.

7. On every occasion in which major tests of atomic bombs have been made, serious storms have been reported in various parts of the United States. It is evident that these tests must be stopped unless we wish to change the entire weather pattern of our country.

8. Some people think there is nothing in spiritualism, but they have never seen any of the proofs. I was convinced last year when a friend of mine told me what he had actually seen. He had been to a meeting where a woman went into a trance, and then pretty soon people all over the room started trying to talk with spirits out of the other world. It couldn't have been faked, because the spirits knew the people they were talking to and could remember things that happened a long time ago. And a couple of the spirits even materialized and floated around the room. They didn't look much like the real people, of course, because they were spirits, but you could see them so plainly there was no doubt about them.

9. The newspapers are full of nothing but stories about sex and crime. In last night's paper, for instance, there were five crime stories on the first page.

10. The learned man will say, for instance, "The natives of Mumbo-jumbo Land believe that the dead man can eat and will require food upon his journey to the other world. This is attested by the fact that they place food in the grave, and that any family not complying with this rite is the object of the anger of the priests and the tribe." To anyone acquainted with humanity this way of talking is topsy-turvy. It is like saying, "The English in the twentieth century believed that a dead man could smell. This is attested by the fact that they always covered his grave with lilies, violets, or other flowers."—G. K. CHESTERTON, *Heretics*

11. Clearly Mr. B cannot be guilty of using his business offices to disguise the headquarters of a world-wide syndicate distributing illegal drugs. Two of his business partners testify without reservation to his honesty and good character.

12. The Roman Empire collapsed when Rome became too prosperous. We should be sure to avoid too much prosperity for the United States.

13. "There's more evidence to come yet, please your Majesty," said the White Rabbit, jumping up in a great hurry; "this paper has just been picked up."

"What's in it?" said the Queen.

"I haven't opened it yet," said the White Rabbit, "but it seems to be a letter, written by the prisoner to—to somebody." . . . He unfolded the paper as he spoke, and added, "It isn't a letter after all: it's a set of verses."

"Are they in the prisoner's handwriting?" asked another of the jurymen.

"No, they're not," said the White Rabbit, "and that's the queerest thing about it." (The jury all looked puzzled.)

"He must have imitated somebody else's hand," said the King. (The jury all brightened up again.)

"Please, your Majesty," said the Knave, "I didn't write it, and they can't prove I did: there's no name signed at the end."

"If you didn't sign it," said the King, "that only makes the matter worse. You *must* have meant some mischief, or else you'd have signed your name like an honest man. . . ."

"That *proves* his guilt," said the Queen.

—LEWIS CARROLL, *Alice in Wonderland*

14. The Japanese people are completely in accord with American democratic principles. This is the conclusion of Mr. J who has just returned after spending a week in Tokyo visiting his son who has been in Japan for some time as the American representative of a large corporation. Mr. J reports that in spite of his handicap in not knowing the Japanese language he was able to collect many favorable opinions about this country in his conversations.

15. "People of discrimination smoke Foggs," says beautiful debutante Debbie Dune, "because scientific tests have proved that they are easier on the throat."

B. Select any three of the following generalizations and list various sorts of evidence which might be used in support of each:

1. Extracurricular activities in college require a great deal of the student's time.
2. Fraternities and sororities are valuable parts of college life.
3. Fraternities and sororities foster snobbishness.
4. Radio advertising is often misleading.
5. Lobbies may discourage honest legislation.
6. Convenience does not dictate fashions.
7. Comic books encourage juvenile delinquency.
8. Television is a handicap to education.

C. The following table gives statistics on school-age population, school enrollments, and numbers and average salaries of teachers. Using inductive reasoning, draft three generalizations based upon the table.

School Year Ended in	Population 5 to 17 Years	Pupils Enrolled	Male Teachers*	Female Teachers*	Average Salary† per Member
1900	21,404,322	15,503,110	126,588	296,474	$ 325
1910	24,239,948	17,813,852	110,481	412,729	485
1920	27,728,788	21,578,316	95,654	583,648	871
1930	31,571,322	25,678,015	141,771	712,492	1,420
1940	29,805,259	25,433,542	194,725	680,752	1,441
1945	. . .	23,225,784	127,102	699,271	. . .
1950	30,788,000	25,111,427	194,968	718,703	3,010
1956	37,262,000	31,162,843	294,170	838,923	4,156
1958	40,164,000	33,538,591	331,826	906,023	4,702
1959 ‡	41,728,000	34,758,000	352,900	938,100	4,940

* Prior to 1954, includes other nonsupervisory instructional staff (librarians and guidance and psychological personnel).

† Average annual salary per member of instructional staff.

‡ Estimated.

SOURCE: U.S. Office of Education; Salaries cover supervisors, principals, and teachers.

D. What evidence would be required to establish the following assertions?

1. Taxes are high because of corruption in government.
2. Lanolin makes the skin softer and smoother.
3. Interpretive dancing has a great future on television.
4. Knute Rockne was the greatest football coach of all time.
5. The Mississippi and Missouri drain the world's largest river basin.
6. International treaties can be relied upon.
7. Lemmings march by hordes to drown themselves in the sea.
8. The airplane was invented, not by the Wright Brothers, but by Samuel P. Langley.
9. The Dodgers will win the next world championship.
10. There are 5,280 feet in a mile.

E. Assume that you are to write an essay on each of the following subjects: (a) "Television Supplants Radio," (b) "Radio Around the World," (c) "An American Is a Man with a Receiving Set," (d) "Radio-Television: Big Business," (e) "Two Decades of Radio." Which of the following facts would be relevant to which essays?

1. Radio sets in the U.S.S.R., 1950—8,000,000.
2. Value of radio and television tubes manufactured in the United States, 1930—$50,000,000.
3. Radio sets in Europe, 1960—95,500,000.
4. Sets manufactured in the United States, 1959—radio, 15,500,000; television, 6,400,000.
5. Frequency modulation stations in the United States, 1950—760; 1960—690.
6. States having the largest number of broadcasting stations—Texas, 222; California, 219.
7. In 1950 Transjordania, Northern Rhodesia, and French Somaliland each had only a few hundred receiving sets.
8. Value of radio and television tubes manufactured, 1950—$550,-000,000; 1959—$850,000,000.
9. Radio and television sets in Asia, 1950—12,000,000; 1960—24,-700,000.
10. Sets manufactured in the United States, 1950—radio, 14,000,000; television, 6,500,000.
11. Television broadcast stations, 1950—New York, 13; Ohio, 12; California, 11.
12. Total sets of all kinds in the United States, 1950—103,000,000.
13. Replacement tubes in the United States, 1950—100,000,000; value, $160,000,000.
14. In 1930 practically no auto sets were in use; by 1960 Americans were using 41,500,000 sets.
15. Total sets of all kinds outside the United States, 1960—178,600,-000.
16. By 1950, radio and television sets in Italy numbered 2,204,580; in Spain, 557,794.
17. Television sets in use in the United States—close of 1949, 3,250,-000; close of 1950, 9,800,000; close of 1960, 54,000,000.
18. By 1950, the annual bill of the United States for radio and television had passed $4,450,000,000.
19. Retail value of sets manufactured in the United States, 1950—radio, $650,000,000; television, $2,000,000,000.
20. Frequency modulation resulted in part from the discoveries of Dr. E. H. Armstrong.
21. In 1960 in the United States there were radios in 54,500,000 homes; there were also 41,500,000 automobile radios.
22. By 1950, there were 1,500 radio, television, and record manufacturers in the United States, doing an annual gross business of

$1,500,000,000, and unnumbered distributors doing an annual gross business of $2,500,000,000.

F. Each of the following generalizations is followed by four other statements, some of which might be relevant as supporting evidence for the generalization, some of which would not. Comment on the suitability of each of the proposed supporting statements as relevant evidence.

1. In the half century preceding World War I, the United States came of age.

   (a) In fifty years it was transformed from a rural republic to an urban state.

   (b) Woodrow Wilson, who brought the Democrats into power at the end of the period, after three Republican administrations, was a native of Virginia.

   (c) Great factories, steel mills, and railroad systems, developed throughout the land.

   (d) The Civil War, according to one writer, "cut a great white gash through the land."

2. The first quarter of the twentieth century in America brought a flood of important inventions.

   (a) The principle of the dynamo was developed as early as 1831 and held great interest for Henry Adams.

   (b) The first successful motor-driven airplane was invented in 1903 by the Wright brothers.

   (c) Nearly a million patents were issued in the United States between 1900 and 1925.

   (d) The x-ray tube was invented in the United States in 1916.

3. After the first rush of gold mining in the West, cattle raising developed as a major industry in many states.

   (a) Between 1866 and 1888 some six million cattle were driven from Texas to winter on the high plains of Colorado, Montana, and Wyoming.

   (b) In the late 1860's and 1870's cattle raising spread from Texas throughout much of the western territory, and herds moved annually on the "long drive" to shipping points in Kansas.

   (c) Theodore Roosevelt, twenty-fifth President of the United States, worked on a cattle ranch in the Dakota territory.

   (d) The cowboy was one of the most picturesque figures of American life in the nineteenth century.

7

Logic:

Deductive Reasoning

For Guide to Revision, see page 113

If writing pretends to develop an idea logically, the reasoning should be sound.

> "To begin with," said the Cat, "a dog's not mad. You grant that?"
> "I suppose so," said Alice.
> "Well, then," the Cat went on, "you see a dog growls when it's angry, and wags its tail when it's pleased. Now *I* growl when I'm pleased, and wag my tail when I'm angry. Therefore, I'm mad."

The logic of the Cheshire Cat could hardly be expected to fool anyone outside Wonderland. The absurdity more than the validity of his argument suggests his madness. But consider this:

> Nobody would accuse American industry of communistic tendencies. American business traditionally supports the Republican party and the interests of investors. On the other hand, labor traditionally supports the Democratic party and seeks the welfare of the worker rather than the prosperity of the investor. Naturally, therefore labor tends toward communism.

The paragraph is not obviously silly. Some persons reading it might agree with the final controversial statement. But they could not have formed their opinion on the basis of the argument presented in the paragraph. The information does no more to establish that labor tends toward communism than the argument above does to prove that the Cheshire Cat is mad. The illogicalness in both examples involves the same sort of faulty deduction.

7-1 INDUCTION AND DEDUCTION

Thinking almost always combines more than one process. For example, the man described in 6-2 recognizing a frost in the blossoms of his cherry tree could not have reached his conclusion by induction alone. He could observe that the blossoms had turned black in the center, but he could interpret this change in color only with the aid of another process. He had to call on his experience or his knowledge to give him inductively a generalization; that blossoms which have turned black in the center may have been frozen. Then he could apply this generalization to the facts he saw on his trees and reach the hypothesis that the blossoms he had examined had been frozen. Testing this hypothesis by his knowledge of recent weather and his further investigation, he could generalize that there had been a killing frost. The process by which he interpreted the meaning of the blackened blossoms is deduction, carrying understanding farther by applying generalizations to specific cases in order to learn more about the specific cases.

Thinking, in other words, progresses by chain reaction, in which induction and deduction constantly work together. By induction we examine specific instances until we are justified in making a generalization. Then we can apply this generalization to specific instances and understand the instances more fully. By induction we learn that all students in the college of arts and sciences must enroll for a course in basic science; we discover that Bill Jones is enrolled in the college of arts and sciences. By deduction, applying our general principle to the case of Bill Jones, we know that Bill Jones is enrolled for a science.

A lawyer building a case to prove that Elbridge Dangerfield is guilty of murder uses inductive reasoning to collect evidence which will lead to a generalization. He reasons inductively: a victim was shot through the heart; Mr. Dangerfield was found in the victim's room just after the shooting with a smoking revolver in his hand; the bullet taken from the victim's body was fired from the gun Mr. Dangerfield was holding; the victim had been blackmailing Mr. Dangerfield; therefore Mr. Dangerfield is probably guilty of murder. But an insurance agent sitting in the courtroom as the jury announces its verdict uses deduction to conclude that Elbridge Dangerfield is a bad insurance risk.

7-2 DEDUCTION

Fully understood, deduction is a complicated process, but viewed simply it consists in putting two and two together. It applies generalizations—the results of induction, or general principles, or laws, or even definitions—to specific cases. The reasoning of the insurance agent making a professional estimate of Mr. Dangerfield might be formalized as follows, in a series of patterns known as syllogisms.

MAJOR PREMISE: Any man judged guilty of murder has an excellent chance of hanging.

MINOR PREMISE: Elbridge Dangerfield has been judged guilty of murder.

CONCLUSION: Elbridge Dangerfield has an excellent chance of hanging.

MAJOR PREMISE: Any man who has an excellent chance of hanging is a bad insurance risk.

MINOR PREMISE: Elbridge Dangerfield has an excellent chance of hanging.

CONCLUSION: Elbridge Dangerfield is a bad insurance risk.

The insurance man has seen the relationship between generalizations he knows about and has been able to reach a valid conclusion.

Deduction operates by putting together ideas or statements with a common term, called in logic *the middle term*. In the first group of statements above, the element common to each premise is *has been judged guilty of murder;* in the second group each premise contains *has an excellent chance of hanging.* Oversimplified, then, deduction is sometimes like the algebraic formula: if *a* equals *b* and *b* equals *c*, then *a* equals *c*. Two terms *a* and *c* can be related on the basis of the common term *b*. If John is the same age as Bill and Bill is the same age as George, then John is the same age as George. Or, we know that Sir Philip Sidney was killed in the Battle of Zutphen, and we know that the Battle of Zutphen occurred in 1586. We know the date of Sidney's death. We know that all students who do not have medical excuses must take physical education. We know that John Atlas is a student and does not have a medical excuse. We know that he must take physical education. Or we know that no student with a medical excuse needs to take physical education. We know that Wilfred Atlas is a student who has a medical excuse. We know that he does not have to take physical education.

We can look at deduction in another way by thinking of it as a process of relating groups or classes. The statement *Daisy, as she is a cow, is a ruminant,* involves three elements or terms, which might be represented by three circles varying in size according to the relative sizes of the classes they name.

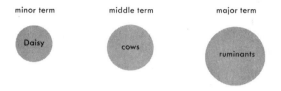

minor term   middle term   major term

The minor term indicates the small class, the major term the large class, and the middle term the class somewhere between the other two in size. When the statement about the terms is put into its logical steps, it reads:

MAJOR PREMISE: All cows are ruminants.
MINOR PREMISE: Daisy is a cow.
CONCLUSION: Daisy is a ruminant.

The statements say something about how the terms are related or, if we think of the terms as circles, about which term includes the others. By the authority of the major premise, the middle circle can go into the larger one; but the minor premise puts the small circle into the middle one. Necessarily, therefore, the small circle must also be included in the large one.

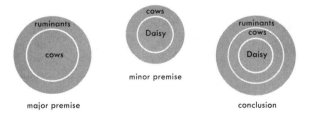

major premise   minor premise   conclusion

Clearly Daisy belongs among the class of ruminants; the conclusion is *valid* because it follows logically from the premises stated. It is *true* if the premises are true.

7-3 CONTROLLING THE MIDDLE TERM

Reasoning turns about a middle term; if conclusions are to be valid, the middle term must be clear and stable. It must have the same meaning each time it appears. *Cow,* the middle term of the statements above, refers to the same thing in both the major and the minor premise. But consider the following:

> All acts which threaten the American way of life are treasonable.
>
> The new bill on socialized medicine threatens the American way of life.
>
> The new bill on socialized medicine is treasonable.

The common element, *threatens the American way of life,* is vague to begin with, and its meaning changes from one sentence to the next. When Mark Twain says, "It is easy to give up smoking. I have done it thousands of times," he is shifting the meaning of *give up.* The effect is humorous but not logical.

The middle term must also be "distributed" at least once in any valid logical statement. A term which is distributed includes or excludes all members of the class it denotes; *all cows* or *no cows* is a distributed term. That is, in *all cows are ruminants, cow*s is distributed, made by *all* to embrace an entire class. Similarly, in the following syllogism *no cows* is distributed: *no cows read books; this female student is reading a book; this student is not a cow.* The following syllogism would not be valid because the middle term is not distributed: *cows have horns; this animal has horns; this horned toad is a cow.* The middle term is not distributed; it is not true either that all cows have horns nor that all animals that have horns are cows. In any logical pattern, one premise must say something about all members of a class or no members of a class.

To be valid, then, a syllogism must contain a firm middle term distributed at least once. To be true, a syllogism must be valid and contain premises that are true. The following is valid, though not necessarily true.

> All communists read Karl Marx.
>
> Mr. Jones is a communist.
>
> Mr. Jones reads Karl Marx.

The middle term, *communists,* is distributed in the first statement. Or *reads Karl Marx* could be distributed once and used as the middle term.

> Anyone who reads Karl Marx is a communist.
> Mr. Jones reads Karl Marx.
> Mr. Jones is a communist.

Reads Karl Marx, the middle term, is distributed in the major premise. The conclusion is valid, though untrue; but it would not be valid if the middle term were undistributed.

> All communists read Karl Marx.
> Mr. Jones reads Karl Marx.
> Mr. Jones is a communist.

One term, *all communists,* is distributed, but it is not the middle term. The middle term, *read(s) Karl Marx,* is not distributed, and the conclusion is not valid. Although arguments like the above are often accepted—especially when there are emotional reasons for liking the conclusion—they are no more valid than the following:

> All chickens have feathers.
> This canary has feathers.
> This canary is a chicken.

7-4 USING DEDUCTIVE REASONING

Most of us do not spend our time consciously forming major and minor premises, but we use deduction constantly, usually without knowing that we do so. No thinking of any sort from constructing a formula for relativity to deciding to drink a milk shake is possible without deductive logic, though the process is so familiar to us that we perform deduction without ever considering that we are doing anything so formal as thinking logically. We perform deductions so naturally that we even hop over several pairs of premises at once.

For instance, a student is aware of an unpleasant feeling in his stomach only a few minutes before his next class. He turns to the soda-fountain attendant and says, "Chocolate shake." He is probably unaware that he has thought at all. If you were to ask him why he ordered the chocolate milk shake he would probably say that he "felt like one." Actually, his reasoning is much more complex and is mainly deductive. It may have gone something like the following: I feel a little strange inside; previously, when I have felt this way I have been hungry (major and minor premise reversed); therefore, I must be hungry. Anybody who is hungry should get something to eat; I am hungry; therefore, I should get something to eat. Anyone who must get something to eat in a hurry should get something which can be prepared and eaten quickly; therefore, a chocolate milk shake is a good thing for me to order if I am in a hurry. Anyone who should be in class in seven minutes is in a hurry; I am due at Economics 106 in seven minutes; therefore, I am in a hurry. Chocolate milk shakes are available at soda fountains; this is a soda fountain; therefore, chocolate milk shakes are available here. Chocolate milk shakes can be purchased if the purchaser has the money; I have the money; therefore, I can buy a chocolate milk shake. And so on, and on, and on. The process of buying a milk shake, considered with any care, becomes such an elaborate chain of deductive patterns that any student who started to analyze his thoughts probably would never be on time at Economics 106, to say nothing of drinking his milk shake. We are all familiar with deduction as a simple process. Only when it becomes complicated, as it often does in writing, does deduction lead to faulty reasoning.

7-5 DEVELOPMENT BY DEDUCTION

If every statement in writing had to be analyzed into logical patterns like those above, writing would be both wordy and dull. Deductive patterns, however, are basic to writing, even though they are not labeled premises and conclusions. The following sentences, for example, develop mainly by deductive reasoning.

> As enemy territory becomes more thoroughly protected by fighter planes during daylight hours, it becomes increasingly difficult to take the desired reconnaissance photographs each day. Therefore, the trend is toward more night photography, when darkness lends to planes increased safety from antiaircraft fire and aerial pursuit.
> —GEORGE RUSSELL HARRISON, *Atoms in Action*

The logic behind the development of the passage might be put as follows:

> MAJOR PREMISE: Pictures cannot be safely taken over areas protected by fighter planes.

| MINOR PREMISE: | In daylight, areas are protected by fighter planes. |
| CONCLUSION: | Pictures cannot be safely taken in daylight. |

MAJOR PREMISE:	The trend is toward photography in periods of increased safety.
MINOR PREMISE:	Darkness is a period of increased safety.
CONCLUSION:	The trend is toward photography in darkness.

The reasoning could be described in other ways and broken down more completely, but clearly the paragraph develops as a series of syllogisms.

7-6 ASSUMPTIONS; MAJOR PREMISES

These syllogisms, however, are not formally expressed. In fact, the major premises are not stated at all. They are assumed by the writer, and if the reader is to accept the ideas of the paragraph he must accept these assumed premises. In actual practice—in development in writing or in everyday thinking (see 7-4)—deduction usually works in this way. Assumptions which are not formally expressed are used as the major premises of the reasoning. Both the writer and the reader, therefore, need to be able to distinguish assumptions from the discussion based on them.

Assumptions lie behind almost everything we do or say. We plan tomorrow and next week on the assumption that the sun will continue to rise, that there will be a tomorrow, that the earth will not burst into a shower of meteorites. This is a tolerably safe assumption. Students go to class on the assumption that the instructor will be there. This assumption is somewhat less certain, and is more or less reliable depending upon a number of conditions, including the instructor's health. Formerly, everybody assumed that if a line looked straight it was, for all practical purposes, straight. Then Einstein demonstrated that all lines curve. Now we have two assumptions. Philosophically we assume that all lines curve. Meanwhile, carpenters work on the assumption that a plumb bob or a square will provide a straight line.

Often assumptions in writing are as reliable and acceptable as that of the carpenter. An editorial writer states: "Police records prove that the old pool hall on Jones Street is encouraging juvenile delinquency; it should be closed." He is assuming, as a major premise, that anything that encourages juvenile delinquency is bad. Probably most readers will accept his assumption and therefore his argument. Or a writer states: "The sight-seeing tour into the mountains should begin at five so that it can be completed before dark." His assumption that sight-seeing is better in daylight than darkness will probably not meet serious opposition.

Suppose, however, that a student writes a theme recommending geology as a liberal arts subject because it promotes an understanding of the world in which we live. He is making many assumptions, among them that knowing about the physical world is so good that it is helpful to everybody. A reader says, "Yes, but geology casts doubt on the truth of Genesis, and anyone who does not believe every word of the Bible will be damned. Saving our souls is the only purpose in life, and thus geology does more harm than good." The reader has not accepted the assumption. The discussion proposed by the theme is not adequate for this reader, and if discussion with him is to continue, the earlier assumption—that knowledge of the physical world is absolutely good—must become not the assumption but the subject for discussion. Or a writer comments, "The man had been on relief for three years; he was obviously lazy." His assumption, the major premise of his argument, that only lazy men are on relief, is questionable, and therefore his argument is questionable.

Clearly, the writer needs to be aware of the assumptions on which he is basing his statements. He needs to change his argument if the assumed major premise is untenable. Or sometimes he needs to state his assumption so that the reader can judge its acceptability. By 1946, a writer on military tactics could assume, perhaps without comment, that the *blitzkrieg* would be part of any subsequent war; but if he was to assume, also, that atomic weapons would determine strategy, he had to say so in order to make the basis of his discussion clear. By 1962, the writer could assume silently that subsequent weapons would be atomic; but if he assumed that an aggressor nation would attack from a space platform, he would need to state his assumption. Sometimes a writer may even adopt an unreal assumption for the sake of discussion. A writer on child psychology, for instance, might begin an article: "Let us assume that you are only three months old."

Stated or not, however, assumptions are the basis of deduction, and therefore of much of our thinking and writing. Both writer and reader need to be aware of them, to distinguish the assumptions from the discussion based on them.

7 **Log**

LOGIC:
DEDUCTIVE REASONING

Guide to Revision
Writing should be logical in its whole plan and in its parts.

Even though a writer may not employ the formal terminology of logic, his work should be logical. Since writing is always complicated, being logical in expression involves many reasoning processes, but much of logic can be comprised within the general process of deduction. Some of the troublesome aspects of deduction are considered here.

7a ASSUMPTIONS; TENABLE PREMISES   Log a

Since reasoning seldom appears in the neat formal patterns of the syllogism, assumptions behind statements are not always apparent. The methods of deduction can be used to reveal and test assumptions.

Consider, for instance, the following from a student theme:

> Although there have been a few highly publicized instances of serious injury, football is not really harmful to students and should be retained as part of every university program.

The statement appears in valid form, and some readers might accept it without question. When, however, the basic assumption of the statement appears as the major premise in a syllogism, it is absurd:

> Anything not harmful should be on a university program.
> Football is not harmful.
> Football should be part of every university program.

The syllogism is valid, but it is not true because it is based on an untenable major premise; even the writer probably would not maintain that anything harmless—eating a cream puff, for instance—belongs on all university programs. Consider another statement of the same type:

> It is difficult to take your eyes off this magnificent lamp since it is a hundred years old.

Faced with a bald statement of his assumption—that anything a hundred years old must be worth attention—the writer would probably be less positive. Or consider a less obvious example:

> He found himself actually enjoying the plays of Shakespeare.

The statement does not explicitly state a logical proposition, but behind it is the assumption that Shakespeare's plays are dull.

A logical statement is true only if its premises are true, and reader and writer must be aware of the assumptions on which statements depend.

ORIGINAL

A liberal arts course is a waste of time because it trains for no profession.
[*The assumption is that any course which does not train for a profession is a waste of time, a more doubtful statement, perhaps, than the writer realized.*]

Fraternities are obviously valuable parts of college life. Consider how long they have existed.
[*Is the implied reason one the writer would try to maintain? Gangs of hoodlums also have a long history.*]

REVISION

1. A liberal arts course trains for no profession.
2. A liberal arts course is a waste of time.
[*The writer should select one of the two statements combined in the original, or perhaps drop the whole idea.*]

1. Fraternities contribute to college life.
2. Fraternities have been a valuable part of college life for many years.
[*The writer can find means of supporting his generalization if he restates it.*]

7b DISTRIBUTING AND STABILIZING THE MIDDLE TERM   Log b

A conclusion is invalid if it is deduced from statements in which the middle term is undistributed (see 7-3). Attempts to establish "guilt by association" are among the most common examples of the fallacy of the undistributed middle: Communists oppose anti-strike legislation; Mr. M opposes anti-strike legislation; therefore, Mr. M is a communist. The middle term, *opposes anti-strike legislation,* is not distributed, not made to include a class or group with the words *all* or *no*. If the middle term were distributed—Everyone who opposes anti-strike legislation is a communist; Mr. M opposes anti-strike legislation; Mr. M is a communist—the conclusion would be valid; but it would obviously not be true because the major premise is not true. The fallaciousness of an argument with an undistributed middle term should be apparent, but often emotional reaction to the conclusion tends to hide its invalidity. Compare the following:

> All the students cheating lived in Miss Goodge's rooming house.
> Walter lived in Miss Goodge's rooming house.
> Walter must have been cheating.

> All goats have beards.
> Santa Claus has a beard.
> Santa Claus is a goat.

Conclusions like that in the first argument are accepted every day; whereas the absurdity of the second is obvious. Actually, the argument of the second is just as good as that of the first; in both patterns the middle term is undistributed.

ORIGINAL

All the gangs of juvenile delinquents in our part of the city had a kind of uniform—a leather jacket and dark trousers. The boy on the corner, with his black leather jacket hanging open, was obviously from one of the gangs.
[*The argument exhibits the fallacy of the undistributed middle:*
All juvenile delinquents wear leather jackets.
The boy on the corner is wearing a leather jacket.
The boy is a juvenile delinquent.]

REVISION

The boy on the corner wore a black leather jacket, like those that were part of the uniform of the gangs of juvenile delinquents in our part of the city.
[*The original does not distribute the common term,* wear leather jackets, *and the argument is invalid. The revision, even though it still has dubious implications, avoids the invalid conclusion. Distributing the middle term would have required the writer to reveal his untenable premise:* All wearers of leather jackets are juvenile delinquents.]

Great poetry becomes richer on successive reading. This must be a great

Only great poetry becomes richer on successive reading. This must be a

ORIGINAL *(Cont.)*

poem, since it has revealed so much more to me on each reading.

[*The argument implied is:*

Great poetry becomes richer on successive readings.

This poem becomes richer on successive readings.

This poem is a great poem.

The statement does not exclude the possibility that bad poems also become richer on successive readings and that this is a bad poem.]

REVISION *(Cont.)*

great poem because it has revealed more to me on each reading.

[*The addition of* only *distributes the middle term in the major premise and makes the conclusion valid. There is, of course, a question about the truth of the major premise and therefore of the conclusion.*]

An argument is fallacious if it uses the same term with different meanings. The difficulty with this fallacy, often called equivocation, is that it seldom appears in a single sentence or even paragraph; it is likely to develop over the course of a longer composition. Especially susceptible are abstract terms like *democracy* or *freedom* or *moral,* which sometimes are used in one way at the beginning of a paper and in another way later on. For example, a paper which starts out as a criticism of *liberal* education and then uses the term to refer to political *liberals* in his argument is making a bad pun rather than an argument. Popular affection for equivocation was probably partly behind the decision some years ago to change the name of the Cincinnati Reds baseball team.

ORIGINAL

The things which have real educational value should obviously be the core of a college curriculum. Nobody who has ever tried to get a job will deny that typing is valuable. Certainly, then, all students should be required to take typing.

[*The terms, especially the middle term* value, *shift and slide.*

Courses of value should be required.

Typing has value.

Typing should be required.

The term value, *as it is used in the passage, changes from a vague general idea to a more specific practical idea.*]

REVISION

I think that typing, because of its practical value, should be a required course in the college curriculum.

[*There is probably no way in which the writer can make his conclusions both true and valid. Revised so that the middle term is tied down, the statement is logical:*

All courses with practical value should be required.

Typing has practical value.

Typing should be required.

But the major premise—and thus the truth of the conclusion—is now in doubt. Few college curricula ·could find room for every subject having practical value.]

7c CONSISTENCY   Log c

If a writer states in the first paragraph of a paper that freedom of speech is a basic tenet of our democracy and must be preserved and then in the fourth paragraph insists that an opposition newspaper must stop criticizing the administration, he is obviously inconsistent. He is applying principles only when they suit his convenience. Statements are logically incompatible when one implies that the other is false. If a writer believes that all criminals are stupid, he cannot logically believe that one criminal he knows is clever and intelligent. He must modify one of his beliefs to preserve logical consistency.

ORIGINAL

Democracy can succeed only with an educated citizenry. It is of the greatest importance that our schools be as good as possible and that teachers' salaries be high enough to attract our best citizens.

The city of B has always been proud of its schools, which have stood high in comparison with those of other communities. The city has also been proud of its financial record, its freedom from debt and its willingness to live within its means. It is regrettable, therefore, that the school board in its meeting last night should have seen fit to authorize a bond issue for the sake of expanding our school system and increasing salary scales. . . .

[*The writer of the editorial is trying to support two incompatible propositions at the same time; he cannot logically do it. He cannot at once support the extension of education and object to the extension of education.*]

REVISION

Democracy can succeed only with an educated citizenry. Our schools must be as good as possible and teachers' salaries must be high enough to attract our best citizens.

The city of B has always been proud of its schools, but the city has also been proud of its financial record, its freedom from debt and its willingness to live within its means. The school board, therefore, should not have authorized a bond issue in its meeting last night but should have found ways to meet the educational needs of the city through taxation and more efficient use of funds. We must expand our school system and increase salary scales, but we must pay for it as we go.

[*The revision shifts the ground of the argument in a manner which the original writer would probably not accept, but if he is to be logical, he must change one of his basic attitudes or shift the basis of his complaint.*]

7d ARGUING IN A CIRCLE   Log d

A circular argument assumes or implies whatever it purports to prove. The reader remains no wiser than he was at the beginning, except in his knowledge of the unreliability of the writer.

ORIGINAL

There is a kind of basic sense or voice within everyone which tells him to be careful and resist when a possible act is wrong. Cheating is that kind of act. Therefore cheating is wrong, because our consciences tell us so.

[*The statement purports to be an argument, but merely turns in a circle, going no place.*]

REVISION

Cheating is one of the acts which our consciences tell us are wrong.

[*There was no material for a logical conclusion in the original, but with a general statement which says what he wishes to say, the writer can then try to substantiate his main idea with other facts or arguments.*]

7e INCLUDING STEPS IN THE ARGUMENT   Log e

Writers sometimes fail to carry the reader with them through all the steps of their argument, either because the argument is confused in their own minds or because they forget the need for showing the reader their reasoning processes.

ORIGINAL

When clarinets are not playing, a band sounds dull, because the notes of the clarinet are so high and shrill.

[*The sentence makes no sense as it stands, although the reader can guess that the writer had some logical notion in mind. The reader cannot see how highness and shrillness prevent the band from being dull.*]

Apparently the *Titanic* had been built very well, for the crew did not know the lifeboat assignments.

[*The ignorance of the crew about lifeboat assignments is not conceivably a reason for believing that the ship had been well built. The writer has jumped so many steps that his thinking seems confused.*]

REVISION

The high and shrill tones of the clarinets are needed in a band to give it life and color. Therefore, when the clarinets are not playing, a band sounds dull.

[*With all the steps of the argument stated, the conclusion is valid, although many readers might reject the premise, and hence the conclusion.*]

Everyone on the ship considered the *Titanic* so well built that she was unsinkable. Members of the crew were so confident of the ship's safety that they had not even learned their lifeboat assignments.

[*With steps in the thinking filled in, the relationship between the building of the ship and the lifeboat assignments appears.*]

EXERCISE 7

A. Indicate which of the sets of premises and conclusions given below are valid and which are true. Give the reasons for your decisions.

1. All athletes eat Crumples for breakfast.
   Jerry is an athlete.
   Jerry eats Crumples for breakfast.

2. Men of distinction drink Old Overshoe.
   I drink Old Overshoe.
   I am a man of distinction.

3. All cats have nine lives.
   Tabby is a cat.
   Tabby has nine lives.

4. All good citizens vote.
   Al Capone voted.
   Al Capone was a good citizen.

5. Money is the root of all evil.
   Time is money.
   Time is the root of all evil.

6. No tigers have wings.
   This creature has wings.
   This creature is not a tiger.

7. Sixty men require one-sixtieth the time required by one man.
   One man can remove an automobile tire in sixty seconds.
   Sixty men can remove the same tire in one second.

8. No cat has eight tails.
   One cat has one more tail than no cat.
   One cat has nine tails.

9. Any golfer who makes a hole in one is lucky.
   Francis made a hole in one.
   Francis was lucky.

10. Man is the only creature capable of reason.
    Mary is not a mán.
    Therefore Mary is incapable of reason.

B. Discuss the logical truth and validity of the reasoning in the following passages:

1. Students, like all young people with active minds, are easily susceptible to any idea like communism, which seems to be advanced

and at first glance may hold out hope for the impractical idealist. It is easy to see why our colleges should be shot through with communism.

2. People who are poor lack ambition; if they did not lack ambition they would not be poor.

3. The editorial in the last student newspaper says that only a student can understand the need for a better intramural program on the campus. Well, I am a student, and I certainly think that the program we now have is all anyone could ask for. The editorial writer should be more logical about what he says.

4. The money was taken between 11 o'clock and noon from the desk in this room. Nobody has left the room since eleven o'clock. One of the persons who have been present in the room must have taken the money. John was in the room. Obviously, he took the money.

5. All governments, for reasons of security, must deceive the public from time to time. This bulletin, therefore, issued by the government, must be false.

6. Houses with shallow foundations should be avoided at all costs; but since this house has an unusually deep, reinforced foundation, you can have no reason for rejecting it.

7. It was plain as a pikestaff. Anyone traveling on the African mail boat would be three days late. Mr. Sims was three days late. Therefore he must be on the mail boat from Africa.

8. We ought to be guided by the opinion of our ancestors, for old age is wiser than youth.

9. Of course, art is dying. The capacity of one man among ten million to create, whether in art or thought, whether in science or invention, is the hallmark of men's inequality, so that democracies which aim at equality have neither reward nor honor to offer to genius.

10. Man has so few distinct and characteristic marks which hold true of all his species, that philosophers in all ages have found it a task of infinite difficulty to give him a definition. Hence one has defined him to be a *featherless biped,* a definition which is equally applicable to an unfledged fowl: another, to be an animal *which forms opinions,* than which nothing can be more inaccurate, for a very small number of the species form opinions, and the remainder take them upon trust, without investigation or inquiry.
—THOMAS LOVE PEACOCK

C. Each of the statements below assumes a major premise which is not stated. Supply the assumption behind each statement.

1. She must be intelligent if she is on the honor roll.

2. All high school students should have courses in driver education; careful driving is something they should know about.

3. The people next door go to church regularly; they will want to make a contribution to the Red Cross.

4. Many comic books are bad for children as they deal with wild and improbable adventures.

5. It is ridiculous to suppose that we can ever get rid of anything that has existed in our society as long as nationalism has.

6. He cannot be expected to be in sympathy with American ideas of democracy; he was born in Europe.

7. It should be a good dress; it cost more than any dress in the store.

8. You could tell she was a gossip because she criticized some of the most important clubwomen in town.

9. General B is certain to make a good university president; look how successful he was during the war.

10. Socialists really support the American system of government, for they believe in government by the people.

D. In this selection from *Macbeth,* Lady Macbeth is berating her husband because, having proposed murdering the king, he now prefers not to do so. Upon what general assumptions (major premises) is Lady Macbeth relying, even though she does not express all of them, but assumes their truth?

Lady M.   Was the hope drunk
Wherein you dressed yourself? and hath it slept since?
And wakes it now, to look so green and pale
At what it did so freely? From this time
Such I account thy love. Art thou afeard
To be the same in thine own act and valour
As thou art in desire? Wouldst thou have that
Which thou esteems the ornament of life,
And live a coward in thine own esteem,
Letting "I dare not" wait upon "I would,"
Like the poor cat i' the adage?

Macb.   Prithee, peace:
I dare do all that may become a man;
Who dares do more is none.

Lady M.   What beast was't then,
That made you break this enterprise to me?
When you durst do it, then you were a man;
And, to be more than what you were, you would
Be so much more the man.

Organization and Style

Order is Heaven's first law.

—*Alexander Pope*

The ancient world had a pleasant if erroneous idea that divine order regulated the entire universe. Planets, stars, angels, men, animals, or stones all fit set places, and each of these had order within it. The pattern for order was established and clear, and it fitted man or beast or the heavens. The great world, for example, the *macrocosm—macro-* meaning great and *cosmus* a universe—comprised the earth and heavens with all the stars and planets. Man, the microcosm, was a little universe, supposed by early thinkers to be like the physical universe in nature and organization, with some necessary variations for size. Arteries and veins, they observed, were like the rivers of the greater world; the seven openings in man's head—two eyes, two ears, two nostrils, and a mouth—corresponded to the seven planets. While this order was preserved, all went well. When it was violated, in any part, chaos prevailed.

As a scientific explanation, this elaborate analogy has long been abandoned; there are differences between blood and river water. As a description of expository composition, the old system is still at least interesting, both for its insistence on the importance of order and for its enthusiasm for correspondences in patterns.

For composition is, in essence, a process of imposing order, of organization. All writers have the same words at their disposal. The problem is to put them into patterns—sentences, paragraphs, chapters, books. "To write," says Jean Cocteau, "is to disarrange the dictionary." Furthermore, in expository prose, at least, the writer does not invent material or make up facts; rather he finds them and puts them in order. It is the new order he gives them, their particular organization to suit his particular purposes, that gives his writing its individuality or originality or significance. Hundreds of books can be written about the Elizabethan theatre or the French Revolution because the material can be ordered in almost infinite ways to suit the purposes and main ideas of different writers.

There is, of course, no single plan of organization; the Almighty was not so systematic about composition as the ancients thought He was about the universe. But the old analogy between the small and great worlds can be applied to composition in another way, to a correspondence in general patterns of order between small and larger units of composition. The same general principles of ordering ideas to show how they are related apply to sentences, to paragraphs, and to longer units. In particular, one can think of the paragraph as a kind of "micro-composition," reflecting in miniature the same sorts of order which govern longer pieces of writing. The student, therefore, approaching problems of organization discussed in the following section of the book, has already learned much of what he needs to know from his study of the paragraph (see 2 and 3).

In the first place, like the paragraph, a longer composition is unified about main ideas, governed by specific purposes (see 1). The main idea may be simple or complex, clearly stated or left for the reader to infer, but it is almost inevitably clear in the writer's mind. Moreover, in the longer composition the writer orders paragraphs into a pattern much as he orders sentences to focus on the topic sentence of a paragraph. And just as the writer seeks coherence in a paragraph, he uses transitions and other topical devices to give his longer paper continuity and coherence.

Most of the discussions of this part of the book, then, extend and elaborate methods and procedures already considered in connection with the paragraph, devices for order especially pertinent to composition beyond a single paragraph. First, there are some principles for finding the parts of a topic and then putting the parts in order—analysis and classification. There follows a discussion of some of the practical machinery which can be useful in organization, particularly the outline. Section 10 presents further practical devices of organization, those with which the writer can make his plan clear, start the reader in the right direction, lead him easily from point to point, and bring him to a satisfactory conclusion.

As mentioned above, the ordering of material has much to do with the individuality of any composition. In sentences, paragraphs, or the entire paper, order reveals relationships; and the particular relationships and emphases of a composition distinguish it from others. As a summary of this part, then—as well as of those that precede and of much that follows—Section 11 discusses the distinguishing qualities of any writing—its style.

8

Analysis and Classification

For Guide to Revision, see page 131

Organization of a composition develops from analysis and classification of materials.

Analysis and classification can make order out of chaos. To oversimplify, they work even in so ordinary an activity as cleaning up a student room after a Saturday night party. The student can analyze the mess and break it up into its elements or parts; he discovers clothes, books and papers, food, dirty dishes, trash. Then he considers each of these parts of the mess as if it labeled a class, and classifies individual items under one or another head—clothes in a pile for the closet, dishes in another pile for the kitchen, trash in the wastebasket, and so on.

These processes—actually different ways of looking at the same process—constantly work together. By analysis, wholes are divided into parts—directions into north, east, south, and west; colors into primary and secondary, and then primary colors into red, yellow, and blue. By classification we may attain the same result by a reverse process, by bringing like things together. Given a number of colors we can assort them on the basis of one of their characteristics into primary and secondary. These two approaches supplement each other, and both are useful in writing. The process described in Section 1, for example, for limiting a topic or a main idea is primarily analysis. Both processes are important in developing an idea. But analysis and classification are especially important in organizing material, in arranging material while planning a composition.

8-1   SCIENTIFIC AND LITERARY ANALYSIS

Roughly speaking, analysis is of two sorts: scientific or formal, and literary or informal. The first, scientific analysis, attempts to be complete and exact. A biologist, for instance, endeavors to make an analysis account for every sort of bird, plant, fish, animal, or reptile. He establishes the families, the subfamilies, the genuses, and the species, and continues his subdivisions until every known sort of creature is accounted for. For example, the Canadian lynx, which clearly belongs in the cat family or Felidae, is placed within the genus Lynx and becomes *Lynx canadensis* to distinguish it from *Lynx rufus,* the bay lynx. If a new sort of lynx were now to be discovered, a Canadian lynx but different from previous known lynxes of the species, a new category within *Lynx canadensis* would be required to differentiate it from the first. This sort of analysis is useful in bringing permanent order into a complex subject, but it is necessarily exacting and time consuming.

Literary or informal analysis, being less exacting, is usually used for practical and relatively immediate ends. The same ornithologist who spends his lifetime endeavoring to correct and complete the classification of Pacific Ocean birds may open a lecture as follows: "Birds which frequent the Hawaiian Islands represent several aquatic species in such families and subfamilies as the Sternidae, the Pelecanidae, the Sulidae, but I am concerned this morning with only *Pterodroma phaeopygia sandwichensis,* the Hawaiian race of the dark-rumped petrel." He is using literary analysis. He feels no obligation to enumerate all the main categories of Pacific birds or to pursue any category to its final subdivision. He has said enough to indicate that there are a number of sorts of birds and to center attention upon the subject of his lecture. A lecturer in history may say, "Land fighting in the War Between the States divides roughly into campaigns in the East and those in the West. The western campaigns were important, but by the very nature of Southern population distribution they could never be decisive." He has been systematic so far as he has gone, but he will certainly feel no obligation to analyze either campaign to the last skirmish—he would have few students left if he did—and he has provided, in his word *roughly,* for the fact that he has ignored minor actions like raids into the North and Indian action in the far West. Furthermore, some subjects are not amenable to scientific analysis. A lecturer on recent American literature, for instance, might mention the Southern school of novelists, the Midwestern regionalists, the proletarian novelists, the psychological novelists, the novelists concerned with race problems. This rough, informal analysis would be adequate for his purposes, but it is not, because of the nature of the material, a scientific analysis. What would the lecturer do, for instance, about a novel written by a Southern writer and concerned with psychological problems of a Negro steel worker? Literary or informal analysis is not so detailed or so systematic as scientific analysis, but it is much more common, and for most purposes, more useful. In this book we shall be concerned with some common types of literary or informal analysis.

8-2 LOGICAL ANALYSIS

A writer analyzing the government of the United States could begin by considering three branches: legislative, executive, and judiciary. In a section treating each of these branches he could analyze further, perhaps dividing the discussion of the executive branch into chapters on the President, the cabinet, and executive bureaus. Or a student explaining a printing press might discuss in turn the feeding device, the inking mechanism, and the impression mechanism. A writer discusses the weather by dividing his topic into discussions of each of the "seven American airs." Another discussing jet-propulsion units breaks his topic down by discussing each of four types of power units. A historian approaches his problem by analysis, titling a chapter "The Three Great Divisions of Christendom at the Close of the Sixteenth Century." Or a writer discusses how a teacher conducts a class:

> Let me explain. The three basic ways are the lecture, the discussion group, and the tutorial hour. In a lecture, a silent class is addressed, more or less like a public meeting. In a discussion group, comprising from five or six to not more than thirty students, the members of the class speak freely, putting or answering questions on points which the teacher organizes so as to form a coherent account of some topic. It may be that for this purpose discussion by the class is broken at intervals by lecturettes from him. In a tutorial hour, the instructor is really holding a conversation, usually with one student, certainly with not more than three or four. This is in the best sense a free-for-all and it presupposes a good stock of knowledge on the part of the students.
> —JACQUES BARZUN, *What Is Teaching?*

Here the writer analyzes the topic, breaking it into three basic methods.

8-3 THE BASIS OF CLASSIFICATION

Classification relies on similarities and differences. For example, considering all living things on earth, we could observe that some are similar in that they have four feet. We could group them as quadrupeds. But within this class, brought together because of a particular similarity, we would also find differences, and distinguish cows, horses, sheep, pigs, and lions. Furthermore, each of these subclasses could again be subdivided—cows into Guernseys, Jerseys, Holsteins, Herefords.

The same items may also be grouped in a number of ways by using different points of similarity as the basis of classification. Consider the following items: fire truck, bluebird, violet, yellow convertible, goldfinch, poinsettia, sunflower, blue bicycle, cardinal. They can obviously be classified by kinds, as follows.

Vehicles	*Birds*	*Flowers*
fire truck	bluebird	violet
yellow convertible	goldfinch	poinsettia
blue bicycle	cardinal	sunflower

But a painter might very well classify them by colors:

Red	*Blue*	*Yellow*
fire truck	blue bicycle	yellow convertible
cardinal	bluebird	goldfinch
poinsettia	violet	sunflower

The students in a classroom may be classified by the registrar as freshmen, sophomores, juniors, and seniors; by a minister as Baptists, Catholics, Episcopalians, Methodists; by the instructor as A students, B students, C students; by the football coach as potential spectators, potential halfbacks, potential linemen; by a boy in the back row as men and potential "dates." The important consideration is that *material can be classified on only one basis at one time.* The women in a class may be classified by the color of their hair as blondes, brunettes, and redheads. The redheads can be reclassified on the basis of their grades, and the B-student redheads can be classified into Pan

Hellenics, members of local sororities, and independents. They cannot be classified on any two of these bases at one time, since some students would belong to both classes and some to neither.

The interests of the classifier determine the basis for the classification. There is an old story of a college dean who had to deal with a parrot that had become a nuisance in a dormitory, even though its presence did not violate any existing rule. "I suggest," he told the owner of the offending bird, "that you dispose of your parrot before I am forced to classify it as a dog or a radio."

8-4 CO-ORDINATION AND SUBORDINATION IN CLASSIFICATION

Classification reveals or establishes two basic relationships between ideas: co-ordination and subordination. When the chemist lists under the heading *elements* aluminum, argon, arsenic, calcium, chromium, copper, oxygen, nitrogen, and zinc, he implies that all of these items are equal or parallel in some way and that they are also secondary in some way to the general concept, element. In other words, the individual elements are co-ordinate, but they are all subordinate to the general idea of elements.

Co-ordination, then, is the process of putting items into the same class, showing them to be equal or parallel or similar in some way and to possess certain common qualities (see also 14).

Subordination is the process of relegating some items to a secondary position, showing them to be dependent on some larger concept or to be aspects of it (see also 15). Usually subordination indicates specification—that is, a subordinate item is a specific example of what it depends on. Thus, in a classification, zinc and copper might be subordinated to metals, as more specific than metals.

8-5 ANALYSIS AND CLASSIFICATION IN PLANNING A COMPOSITION

Orderly thinking and orderly writing require analysis and classification, conscious or unconscious, and in planning a composition most good writers employ the processes consciously (see also 9-5). For example, in the paragraph in 8-2 above, Barzun analyzes the conduct of a class into three types. Then he classifies details under each of these types to get his material into order. Consider the following, which concerns the career of Henry Plantagenet, son of Henry II of England:

His career had been wild and criminal. He had rebelled against his father again and again; again and again he had been forgiven. In a fit of remorse he had taken the cross, and intended to go to Jerusalem. He forgot Jerusalem in the next temptation. He joined himself to Lewis of France, broke once more into his last and worst revolt, and carried fire and sword into Normandy. He had hoped to bring the nobles to his side; he succeeded only in burning towns and churches, stripping shrines, and bringing general hatred on himself. Finding, we are told, that he could not injure his father as much as he had hoped to do, he chafed himself into a fever, and the fever killed him.

—JAMES ANTHONY FROUDE, *Life and Times of Thomas Becket*

A series of details are classified together as evidence and made subordinate to the idea that the prince is "wild and criminal."

The "career" of Henry II, however, is a subordinate idea in the essay in which it appears, a part of a general view of the temper of twelfth-century England which has been distinguished by analysis. In such a longer composition, analysis and classification have varied uses. For example, a historian trying to find out why Lee's army lost at Gettysburg considers Longstreet's failure to move as he was ordered, Stuart's failure to arrive until the battle was essentially over, the questionable tactic of Lee in ordering Pickett to charge, and a number of other factors, and decides to consider the question of the unexpected effectiveness of the Union artillery. He has now narrowed his subject by analysis, but he is not done. He has now to ask himself why the Union batteries wrought such havoc. Another analysis suggests that the key reason was that Brigadier General Henry J. Hunt had managed to trick the Confederate command into believing he was out of ammunition, although he was not. How did he manage to do this? Of all the artillery actions, of all the evidence from spies and skirmishers, which will be significant and which will not be significant for this question? Now the job becomes one of classification; evidence must be sorted, rejected if it is not pertinent, and grouped with other like evidence if it is pertinent. This process may become complicated, with new analysis of minor questions, new categories into which evidence must be classified, and with the historian moving as his evidence and his interpretation of this evidence lead him. Through it all he will be using analysis and classification, sometimes one, sometimes the other, and often both of them.

8 An; Class

ANALYSIS AND CLASSIFICATION

Guide to Revision

Use analysis and classification to provide clear organization for a composition.

The writer who merely records material in the order in which it occurs to him usually reveals more about his own mental processes than about his subject. Analysis and classification are twin processes which can bring order to disorganized material.

ORIGINAL

What is a hot rod? Ask this question of the average person. It is almost a certainty that he will picture it as an old vintage roadster less fenders and paint. Furthermore, he will think that the driver is incompetent. In reality, the hot rod has changed tremendously during the past decade, even if the public's conception of it has not.

The public is unaware that the present-day hot rod is really a complex mechanism, involving a good deal of hard work on the part of the boy constructing it. It is really a complete rebuilding of many of the most important parts of a car, not just a heap of junk put in temporary running order.

Such things as the body and engine are thoroughly overhauled and put into shape for greater speed and better lines. The car, therefore, is made lighter and more compact. Moreover, the engine is a better engine than the original car because it has greater

REVISION

What is a hot rod? Most people would answer this question by describing an old-vintage roadster, lacking fenders, paint, and a competent driver. Actually a modern hot rod is a complex automobile, embodying a series of improvements over the ordinary stock car.

A hot rod varies most obviously from an ordinary car in the structure of its body. The body of a hot rod is likely to begin as that of a discarded light car; this body is first rebuilt so that it sits several inches down over the chassis and lowers the center of gravity of the car. Then excess parts of the body, especially chrome ornaments, are removed, and the doors are welded shut and smoothed in to fit the lines of the rest of the body.

More important to the actual running of the car, however, are the extensive changes in the running gear. The hot rod builder improves wheels, axles, brakes, and differential assembly

ORIGINAL *(Cont.)*

horsepower. The hot rod does not look like an ordinary car, but it does not look like a dilapidated car either. Hot rods often resemble more nearly the custom-built sport cars that one sometimes sees.

It is a mistake to look on the hot rod as a dangerous toy for careless boys, because it is not that. It is really good training for young men to work with hot rods, because they can feel pride in accomplishing a good job of remodeling.

[*The weaknesses of this theme can be described in many ways: the main idea is forgotten as the paper wanders from point to point; there are too many unsubstantiated judgments; statements are general and not specific. Analysis and classification provide one way of avoiding most of those difficulties. If the writer would break his subject into parts, he would give his paper some order and would probably find that he could classify specific material to substantiate his judgments.*]

REVISION *(Cont.)*

as extensively as his pocketbook will allow; safety requires some changes. He must, for example, change the size of the wheels and use regulation high-speed tires. He must install modern brakes, either hydraulic or disc type. He may lower the center of gravity by dropping the front axle, and he may change the differential to an assembly with a lower ratio.

Changes in the engine vary with the ingenuity and patience of the builder, but they provide the extra speed characteristic of the modern hot rod. They may be as fundamental as a modernized carburetor or as nonessential as chrome plate on the exhaust manifold, but improvements in the engine increase the power of the average motor by thirty-five to fifty horsepower.

Changes like these, rather than those the public imagines, distinguish the modern hot rod.

[*By analyzing the hot rod, breaking the subject into three main groups, the writer finds something to say.*]

Even in informal analysis the basis of the analysis should be clear to the reader, and the writer may need to indicate what items have been eliminated and on what basis the analysis was made.

ORIGINAL

Prior to the Communist occupation there were more than four million Christians of all denominations in China. Matthew Ricci, S.J., who arrived in the sixteenth century was one of them. . . .

[*The writer has used analysis, although not in an orderly manner, and he has not made the basis of his analysis clear.*]

REVISION

Christianity has been introduced into China three times, but the missionary ventures of the seventh and thirteenth centuries proved abortive. Not until Matthew Ricci, S.J., arrived in 1582 to replant the faith of the West did Christianity play a leading part in Chinese life. . . .

[*The chronological analysis is now clear to the reader.*]

Items in each rank must be classified on a single basis. Otherwise classes overlap, and the material of the paper is confused rather than organized. Apples cannot be classified as green, yellow, red, small, winter; the bases for classifications differ—color, size, time of ripening—and the classes overlap. Small apples may be green, winter apples may be red, and yellow apples may be small.

ORIGINAL

During the period 1932–1936, the government of the United States created a large number of temporary bureaus and agencies. In this paper I shall be concerned with the question of why some of the supposedly temporary agencies were accepted permanently. I shall consider four groups of agencies: agricultural agencies, financial agencies, agencies established after 1936, and agencies that exist today. . . .

[*The classification is unsatisfactory because classes have been established on different bases. The first two depend on matter the agencies dealt with; the third is based on time of establishment of the agency, and the fourth on permanence of the agency. The material needs to be reclassified on a consistent basis—probably a basis indicated by the central purpose of the paper.*]

REVISION

During the period 1932–1936, the government of the United States created a large number of temporary bureaus and agencies. In this paper I shall be concerned primarily with the question of why some agencies were accepted permanently whereas others were soon abandoned. I shall consider the agencies in four groups: those abandoned after a short trial, those replaced by other agencies, those abandoned because their purpose was accomplished, and those still in existence.

[*The classification of the final sentence is changed to one which depends on a single principle—the permanence of the agencies. The basis for classification in the revision is the one suggested by the paragraph's statement of the purpose of the paper.*]

EXERCISE 8

A. Select any five of the following topics and list parts, types, or elements of each revealed by structural analysis:

1. A university
2. A newspaper
3. A football team
4. A gasoline engine
5. A corporation
6. A radio program
7. The gland system of human beings

8. Socialism
9. Snobbishness
10. Fashion
11. A cement mixer
12. A garden
13. A farm
14. Tolerance
15. Courtesy

B. Select any three of the following topics and list stages or steps in each revealed by chronological analysis:

<table>
<tr><td>1. The beginning of the War Between the States</td><td>8. Setting up an experiment</td></tr>
</table>

1. The beginning of the War Between the States	8. Setting up an experiment
2. Getting a newspaper ready for the press	9. Harvest day
3. Making camp	10. Learning to swim
4. Building a tree house	11. Refinishing a boat
5. Preparing for a test	12. Planning a campaign for a school election
6. Organizing a party	13. Registration day
7. A storm	14. Fraternity or sorority pledging
	15. Decorating for a dance

C. Make two separate classifications for the items in each of the following groups, classifying each time on a different basis (Be sure to classify on only one basis at a time):

1. canned peas, frozen pears, canned peaches, a can of wax, a dozen clothes pins, 10 pounds of potatoes, a dozen oranges, frozen peaches, a can of kitchen cleanser.

2. baseball, tennis, swimming, basketball, diving, skiing.

3. advanced economics, freshman chemistry, beginning history, physics seminar, beginning German, first-year Italian, freshman biology, senior French.

D. Indicate one item in each of the following classifications which is inconsistent because it has not been classified on the same basis as the other items:

1. Books *into* novels, collections of poems, collections of short stories, leather-bound books, collections of plays, histories, textbooks.

2. Shoes *into* leather shoes, canvas shoes, horse shoes.

3. Dresses *into* evening dresses, afternoon dresses, sports dresses, cotton dresses, dinner dresses.

4. Criminals *into* burglars, murderers, incorrigibles, arsonists, embezzlers.

5. Literature *into* novels, poetry, drama, pastorals, short fiction.

E. Consider the following subjects; obviously they are much too broad for brief papers. Limit these subjects by analysis, and then write a theme sentence for each in which you announce the subject of the proposed essay and give sufficient indication of the basis on which the analysis was made. Review of Section 1 will help.

1. Political tension in Asia	6. Juvenile delinquency
2. The teacher shortage	7. The farmer in the modern world
3. A recent political campaign	
4. The problem of imperialism in Africa	8. Picking the right college
	9. Summer vacations
5. Automation and the labor problem	10. Modern music

F. The following paragraph is confused for a number of reasons, but it can be put in order if it is revised after clear analysis of the problem. What light do our presidents throw on the question of humor as an asset in politics? Analyze the problem, classify the evidence on the basis of your analysis, and rewrite the paragraph with a central idea and clear evidence of organization.

Neither Richard Nixon nor John F. Kennedy was devoid of a sense of humor, but neither was notable for it; Kennedy's victory seems to provide little evidence one way or the other. Calvin Coolidge did have a sense of humor, a salty Vermont wit. Very few people liked it much. George Washington was a great general and a great president. He had dignity, but apparently not much sense of humor. William Howard Taft is said to have been a very genial man in private, but he was also a very heavy man, and thus in public life he was more frequently the butt of humor than the creator of it. Most of our presidents, if they do not illustrate the assertion, "The people expect their statesmen to be solemn asses," give us little reason to suppose that a sense of humor is a political asset. Woodrow Wilson had a sense of humor, which he used in his scholarly writing and in the privacy of his home. John Adams and John Quincy Adams were men of subtle mind, but they seem not to have enjoyed laughing. Adlai Stevenson, who convulsed his audiences when he was campaigning against Dwight D. Eisenhower, was defeated twice, whether because of his humor or in spite of it. Of the early presidents, only Thomas Jefferson seems to have enjoyed a joke, a very quiet joke well screened from public view. Theodore Roosevelt was perhaps not subtle enough to have much humor; as Professor T. V. Smith has said, "He exclaimed 'bully' from the larynx more often than he laughed from the belly." Franklin Roosevelt used his humor sparingly and for calculated effects. When Peter Cartwright, a frontier evangelist, was campaigning against Lincoln for Congress, he accused Lincoln of not knowing where he wanted to go because he would stand neither with those who were certain they would go to heaven nor with those who expected to go to hell. "I aim, of course, to go to Congress," Lincoln drawled. Presidents like Zachary Taylor and Andrew Jackson were blunt, almost humorless men, but they were triumphant vote getters and popular presidents. Even Madison and Monroe were notably solemn. Abraham Lincoln, whose sense of humor became legend, offers the only notable exception to the general rule that our presidents have not been characterized by their sense of humor. Some presidents seem to have had some sense of humor, but hesitated to use it in politics, or in any connection suggestive of state affairs. Harding probably lacked the liveliness of mind either to engender or to appreciate much humor.

9

Organization;

the Outline

For Guide to Revision, see page 147

Organization, planned in the outline, reveals the relationships among ideas, the essentials of the composition.

The arrangement of material defines relationships. The positions of paragraphs, sentences, and words convey meaning. In the sentence, order is the basic device for indicating grammatical relationships. In larger units of composition, material can be ordered, after analysis and classification, on the basis of a main idea, to reveal relationships which can be classified generally as chronological, spatial, and logical.

9-1 CHRONOLOGICAL ORGANIZATION

In the following sentences, order shows a chronological relationship:

> A yellow convertible flashed by the billboard and screamed around the curve. A traffic policeman wheeled his motorcycle from its hiding place and roared into the highway.

Because one sentence precedes the other, the reader assumes that the event it describes precedes the other event. Reversing the order of the sentences would reverse the order of events and save a fine for the driver of the convertible.

Any record of happenings can almost always be planned around related times—often by the simple procedure of putting first things first. The following description of Mary Stuart's preparation for execution is organized in this way:

She laid her crucifix on her chair. The chief executioner took it as a perquisite, but was ordered instantly to lay it down. The lawn veil was lifted carefully off, not to disturb the hair, and was hung upon the rail. The black robe was next removed. Below it was a petticoat of crimson velvet. The black jacket followed, and under the jacket was a bodice of crimson satin. One of her ladies handed her a pair of crimson sleeves, with which she hastily covered her arms; and thus she stood on the black scaffold with the black figures all around her, blood-red from head to foot.

—JAMES ANTHONY FROUDE, *History of England*

9-2 SPATIAL ORGANIZATION

Order can show relationship in space as well as in time. To help the reader picture relative positions, the writer reflects spatial arrangement by the arrangement of his sentences. For example, a writer describing a scene can arrange details in the order in which they meet his eye.

The ship turned sharply and steamed slowly in. It was a great landlocked harbour big enough to hold a fleet of battleships; and all around it rose, high and steep, the green hills. Near the entrance, getting such breeze as blew from the sea, stood the governor's house in a garden. The Stars and Stripes dangled languidly from a flag staff.

—SOMERSET MAUGHAM, *Rain*

Even though the writer's purpose may be to set a scene and center attention on a particular object, the method may be by spatial arrangement, as in the following, where the relationship words are notably those of space—*on, among, removed, near, above, under, where,* and the like.

On the shelving bank of the river, among the slimy stones of a causeway—not the special causeway of the Six Jolly Fellowships, which had a landing place of its own, but another, a little removed, and very near to the old windmill which was the denounced man's dwelling-place—were a few boats; some, moored and already beginning to float; others, hauled up above the reach of the tide. Under one of these latter Eugene's companion disappeared. And when Eugene had observed its position with reference to the other boats, and had made sure that he could not miss it, he turned his eyes upon the building, where, as he had been told, the lonely girl with the dark hair sat by the fire.

—CHARLES DICKENS, *Our Mutual Friend*

9-3   LOGICAL ORGANIZATION

Material may be ordered in various ways which roughly can be called "logical." Sometimes organization is logical in relatively strict senses; Commander X receives unexpected reinforcements just at the time the river freezes over between him and his enemy and his scouts report that the opposing forces have been decimated by a plague. Commander X decides to attack; the organization of a description of this decision is clearly that of cause to effect. Conversely, consider the situation of a householder who discovers water leaking into his living room. The leak is an effect; what is the cause? He checks the flashing of the chimney, the calking around essential nails, the flue, and the concrete cap on the chimney. All seem to be in order. Then he remembers that although the chimney is built of porous blocks it was never waterproofed. He concludes that the chimney needs waterproofing. The order here is clearly that of effect back to cause. But most writing is essentially logical if only loosely so. Consider the following, in which Thomas Jefferson is writing to a young student friend of his, urging him to examine objectively the claims of truth made by different religions.

> For example, in the book of Joshua, we are told, the sun stood still several hours. Were we to read that fact in Livy or Tacitus, we should class it with their showers of blood, speaking of statues, beasts, etc. But it is said, that the writer of that book was inspired. Examine, therefore, candidly, what evidence there is of his having been inspired. The pretension is entitled to inquiry, because millions believe it. On the other hand, you are astronomer enough to know how contrary it is to the law of nature that a body revolving on its axis, as the earth does, should have stopped, should not, by that sudden stoppage, have prostrated animals, trees, buildings, and should after a certain time have resumed its revolutions, and that without a second general prostration. Is this arrest of the earth's motion, or the evidence which affirms it, most within the law of probabilities?
>
> —THOMAS JEFFERSON, *Letter to Peter Carr*

Jefferson is presenting a problem logically, and he orders his material with a respect to logic, stating a proposition, breaking it into parts, presenting evidence, moving toward a conclusion.

The following paragraph is essentially logical, but less strictly so because the logical requirements are less rigid. The authors have said that language grows, and in this paragraph they are providing an example; their presentation of an example, however, differs from Jefferson's in that they are presenting evidence, not balancing one set of evidence against another set.

The history of *torpedo* offers a good illustration. It was originally the name of a fish of the ray family (*torpedinidae*), capable of emitting electric discharges. The name is derived from Latin *torpere,* "to be numb or stiff." There existed in English names for this fish, as for instance, *cramp-fish, cramp-ray,* and *numb-fish,* which, however, were early superseded by the Latin term. The fish's curious electric power provided an atmosphere of mystery to a people who knew nothing of electricity. Naturally they regarded it as venomous and thought of it with horror. The *Oxford Dictionary* illustrates the use of the word in the sixteenth century with the quotation (1589), "like the fish Torpedo, which being towchd sends her venime alongst line and angle rod, till it cease on the finger, and so mar a fisher for euer." The traditionally dangerous nature of the fish made it early a suitable source of metaphor. Christopher Marlowe applied it to a dangerous human being:

Fair queen, forbear to angle for the fish
Which, being caught, strikes him that takes it dead;
I mean that vile torpedo, Galveston,
That now I hope floats on the Irish seas.

Another metaphorical use is illustrated by Dr. Johnsons's remark, "Tom Birch is as brisk as a bee in conversation; but no sooner does he take a pen in his hand, than it becomes a torpedo to him, and benumbs all his faculties."
—ROBERT M. ESTRICK and HANS SPERBER, *Three Keys to Language*

The organization of the material is to a degree chronological, but mainly logical, telling how the word came from Latin, how it acquired new implications by superstition, and then how it developed metaphorical uses.

9-4 THE OUTLINE

For the word, for the paragraph, for the whole composition, various devices are available which can be used to show classifications and relationships. For an extensive composition, the most useful tool for these purposes is the outline. With it, the writer can organize his material, co-ordinating it, subordinating it, arranging it. With the outline he can also test the results of his organization.

Student writers often resist the suggestion that they should write from an outline. An outline, they insist, is too limiting; it "stifles inspiration." Usually such students either have the wrong notion of what an outline should be or have found that outlining requires clear thinking, and they do not want to think. Actually, an outline provides the easiest method of doing preliminary thinking well, and good writing requires clear thinking. An outline is a means of saving time—provided the writer is trying to write well.

All writing not formless and unconvincing requires some plan, even in its smallest units, and the outline is essentially a memorandum of that plan. For a single paragraph or a short theme, one may keep his plan in mind without a written record, and an experienced writer knows basic patterns so well that he can compose still larger units without a written outline. A skilled carpenter can put together sets of bookshelves without a blueprint. But a contractor is not likely to start construction on a house without a set of carefully worked-out plans. A writer working seriously on an extensive piece of writing will not proceed without an outline.

The outline is a means to an end, not an end in itself. It is practical. It should therefore have the most useful form the writer can devise. For a paragraph or two or for an answer to an essay question on an examination, a few scribbled headings may be sufficient. For longer compositions, however, the writer should follow the procedures described below because they will produce the kind of outline which will help most in writing.

9-5 CLASSIFICATION, CO-ORDINATION, AND SUBORDINATION IN THE OUTLINE

A statement of the main idea (see 1) is the first stage in the construction of an outline. It provides the basis for classification, and guides the co-ordinating and subordinating of details. It should constitute a complete sentence. The writer thinking through a possible theme on "Women at State University" tentatively decides that he wants to show that "At State University women do not have rights and privileges equal to those of the men." He begins his outline with this statement.

He then jots down ideas; let us assume that he produces something like the following:

1. Rules requiring women to live in dormitories
2. Rules regulating hours women must come in at night
3. The paragraph in the University Catalogue concerning equal rights for all students
4. Women in student-body offices
5. Men's lounge in Union Building, but no women's lounge
6. As many girls on campus as men
7. Women not willing to assert their rights
8. Rules requiring women to eat in dining hall
9. Swimming pool privileges
10. Rules on leaving campus
11. Intercollegiate athletics
12. College women just as responsible as college men
13. Attitudes of parents
14. The time Anne Wilkins was expelled but the boy who was equally guilty was not
15. Girls not interested in student government
16. Gymnasium and athletic facilities
17. Modern women taking equal responsibilities in the world
18. Military service of women

The list is a beginning, a record of random thoughts about a subject; it is not a record of organized thinking. To organize his material, the writer needs to analyze his subject and classify his details.

He may do so in a more or less systematic way. He may ask himself: What are the principal parts or aspects of the life of women on the campus, and which of these do I wish to consider? That is, he may start by analyzing his subject and stating a main idea which can be used as the basis of classification. Or, he can start by examining his jottings to see whether he can observe any general groups and by classifying material under general headings. He can check his findings later by asking himself whether the headings he gets do or do not constitute an adequate analysis. As a matter of practice, of course, most writers use analysis and classification pretty much unconsciously as twin means of restricting a subject, ordering it, and developing it.

The student may now appropriately look over his jottings. If he is to write on discriminations against women at State University, some material is obviously inappropriate and can be thrown out, items 4 and 17, for instance. On the other hand, items 1 and 2 begin a list of discriminatory rules. Items 5 and 9 suggest a class of inequalities in university facilities. Items 3 and 6 might suggest reasons for equality. Item 7 might suggest a class which would require new material, reasons for inequalities. Some items would seem inappropriate to the main idea and should therefore be stricken out. The list, then, could be rearranged and expanded by classification somewhat as follows:

Rules that discriminate against women

1. Rules requiring women to live in dormitories
2. Rules regulating hours women must come in at night
8. Rules requiring women to eat in dining hall
10. Rules on leaving campus
14. Expulsion of Anne Wilkins (Might fit here as example of use of rules)
   Rules for sororities stricter than those for fraternities (The writer thinks of a new point as he is making the classification.)

Inequalities in university facilities

5. Men's lounge in Union Building
9. Swimming pool privileges
11. Intercollegiate athletics
16. Gymnasium and athletic facilities

Reasons why there should be equality

3. The statement of the University Catalogue
6. As many girls on campus as men
12. College women just as responsible as college men
17. Modern women taking equal responsibilities in the world
18. Military service of women

Causes for inequalities

7. Women not willing to assert their rights
15. Girls not interested in student government
   Tradition in colleges and world
   Prevalence of men in administration and on faculties
   Old prejudices against educating women
   (The writer adds new items.)

Such classification is the beginning of an outline, but the writer must still give the outline form by considering the classes in terms of the main idea and in terms of the proposed length of his paper. Strictly speaking, only the first two of the classes listed above apply to the proposed subject. Reasons for equality and causes of inequalities could be incorporated, but they would expand the paper beyond manageable length. The writer therefore limits his main headings to:

I. Rules that discriminate against women
II. Inequalities in University facilities

He then subordinates details to these main headings, thinks of further details to support his ideas, and chooses an order for his topics.

The writer should never hesitate to add to his outline any kind of note that may help him later. Often as he works he has useful ideas for a transition, for a striking introduction, for an incident for illustration, for an apt phrase. He can jot them down on his outline so that he will not forget to use them in the appropriate places.

The degrees of subordination are conventionally indicated in an outline by indenting and by labeling subdivisions alternately with numbers and letters. The standard form is shown below.

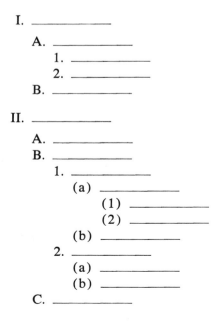

I. _____
   A. _____
      1. _____
      2. _____
   B. _____

II. _____
   A. _____
   B. _____
      1. _____
         (a) _____
            (1) _____
            (2) _____
         (b) _____
      2. _____
         (a) _____
         (b) _____
   C. _____

9-6 THE COMPLETE OUTLINE

The final outline, then, includes a statement of the main idea, a note on the introduction and conclusion, and a summary of the main topics to be discussed in the body of the paper, with relationships between them indicated by numbers and indentation. The following outline might be developed from the materials collected above for a paper on "Women in State University."

Outline

STATEMENT OF MAIN IDEA: At State University, women do not have rights and privileges equal to those of the men.

INTRODUCTION: Use the statement in the University Catalogue that all students have equal rights and privileges and point out that the paper will show the statement to be false.

[A detail that the writer recalled when first thinking about the topic seems to provide a possible introduction. The writer gives himself a reminder.]

I. Rules that discriminate against women
  A. Dormitory rules (begin paragraph with story of expulsion of Anne Wilkins)
    1. Rules requiring women to live in dormitories
    2. Rules on hours
    3. Registration and signout system
    4. Rules forbidding leaving dormitory and campus
  B. Sorority rules — regulations stricter than those for fraternities
  C. Rules requiring women to eat in dining hall
    1. Expense of dining hall
    2. Quality of food

[Again the writer sees a place to use a detail and makes a note.]

[The writer sees need for classification more detailed than in preliminary organization.]

[The expansion of point B is not illogically made a single subdivision.]

II. Inequalities in University facilities. (Possible transition pointing out that above rules can be justified on ground that they are for students' "own good" but that other inequalities cannot.)

[A lengthy note for future use records an idea that occurs to the writer as he makes the outline.]

A. Social facilities
  1. Lack of meeting places for women's organizations
  2. Lack of a room comparable to the Men's lounge in the Union Building
B. Athletic facilities
  1. Lack of women's activity comparable to men's intercollegiate athletic program
  2. Lack of equal swimming-pool privileges
  3. Restriction on women's use of gymnasium

[Co-ordination of topics is indicated by parallel form.]

CONCLUSION: Use idea that there are as many women on the campus as men, that they will have equal responsibilities in the world, and that they should have equal rights and privileges in college.

[A possible conclusion is suggested by another of the groups of details rejected in preparing the body of the outline.]

The outline is a working guide. It should be used but should not be followed slavishly. Obviously a writer cannot visualize a paper perfectly. He will change his mind as he works out paragraphs and sentences, and he will think of new material. He should use his outline as a preliminary sketch, constantly subject to revision and expansion as the writing proceeds.

9-7 THE SENTENCE OUTLINE

Many writers prefer a sentence outline, which differs from the sample outline above only in that it employs sentences rather than topics. The outline above, put in the form of a sentence outline, would start as something like the following:

MAIN IDEA—At State University, women do not have rights and privileges equal to those of the men.

INTRODUCTION—The University catalogue includes the statement that all students have equal rights, but this statement is not true, either in light of the regulations or the interpretation of regulations.
I. University rules discriminate against women.
  A. Dormitory rules discriminate against women, as is apparent in the case of Anne Wilkins.
    1. Rules require that all freshmen women live in dormitories, sororities, or private dwellings approved by the Dean.

A respect for form and parallelism in an outline requires either that all headings in the outline be sentences or that none of them be, and certainly any outline used for itself should use one form or the other consistently. An outline, however, is usually practical; when the paper is written the outline has become useless, and many a competent writer pays little attention to whether his headings are parallel or not. The extra thinking required to make items parallel certainly does no harm, and most writers find it useful, even for a strictly utilitarian outline.

9-8 UTILIZING THE OUTLINE TO CHECK LOGIC

Obviously, an outline provides an orderly guide to writing, but it can have other uses as well. We have already noticed that it encourages thinking prior to writing; it also encourages continuity in thinking and in collecting material. Weeks, months, or even years may elapse during the preparation of an extensive piece of writing, but if the author has prepared a good outline with which to refresh his memory he can always return to his original plan. More immediately, the writer can use his outline to check the adequacy and logic of his planning.

Since an outline is a chart of the skeleton of a prospective piece of writing, any disproportion or gap in the bony structure becomes apparent at once. The writer has only to examine his outline comparatively and critically. If the introduction comprises half the outline, something is wrong. The writer may have failed to analyse his subject fully, to develop adequate plans for central portions of his paper. He may have failed to restrict his subject, and having fallen victim to that fatal desire to discuss everything on earth has tried to drag impertinent material into his introduction. In any event, any portion of the outline disproportionately large or small becomes a danger signal; something is wrong with the writer's planning, and he had better investigate before he spends needless hours or days preparing material that will have to be replanned or discarded.

Similarly, with an outline the writer can test the validity of his logic, the adequacy of his analysis, the consistency of his classification. He can do this by comparing the various degrees of his subordination and checking to be sure that they total the heading of which they are ostensibly subdivisions. For example, in an essay drafted in accordance with the form given in 9-5 above, all of the heads labeled with Roman numerals (I, II, III) should be roughly parallel in nature and importance, and they should add up to the main idea. Likewise, all the headings labelled with capital letters should be at least roughly parallel and they should add up to the heading with a Roman numeral; that is the first A and B should total I, and the second A, B, and C should total II. Similarly, 1 and 2 should add up to A, or the capital letter of which they are subdivisions. If subdivisions do not total the headings of which they are supposedly the parts, something is wrong with the analysis or the classification (see 8, especially 8-4 and 8-5).

9 **Org**

ORGANIZATION;
THE OUTLINE

Guide to Revision

Rewrite to improve organization. Usually revision of the outline is a first step.

Faulty organization almost always results from a combination of difficulties, including faulty classification (see 8), lack of proper subordination (see 8-4), inadequate development (see 5), and lack of a main idea (see 1). Usually the writer should go back to the outline stage and reorganize and rewrite the entire paper.

9a CLEAR PLANNING   Org a

Every piece of writing should have a clear, orderly plan.

ORIGINAL	REVISION
A word not only indicates an object but can also suggest an emotional meaning. The essence of poetry de-	A word not only "means"; it conveys emotion. If we refer to a dog as a *mongrel,* we objectively define his

ORIGINAL *(Cont.)*

pends upon words that arouse the emotions of the reader. An experiment may be conducted to prove how much words mean in poetry. Replace the emotionally filled words with neutral ones, and all the poetic value will be knocked out of the poem by the change. Politicians are apt at changing the public's opinion merely by the use of words. "Bolshevik," "Fascist," "reactionary," "revolutionary" are examples of emotional words used by politicians. Emotional words find their place in poetry but are out of place in modern science where exact thinking is required. The scientist wants only the facts. He does not want to be swayed by words, only facts. This type of straight scientific thinking results in new discoveries. Science has worked hard ridding their books and discussions of emotional words; politics should do the same. The use of emotional words makes it hard for us to think straight in national and social problems. If clear unemotional words were used by people in the government, it would benefit our civilization. People would then be able to form their opinions by facts, not words.

Emotion-filled words are used not only by politicians but also by critics. By the use of words a critic can sway the public opinion against a writer, simply because he does not like the work.

We need to be careful not to form opinions on emotionally filled words.

[The student theme printed above contains many inaccuracies in writing; as a review exercise, the student might profitably see how many errors he can find in it. Worse, the paper lacks any clear plan. An attempt to outline the theme reveals its weakness, for a meaningful outline proves to be almost impossible. An attempt might look like this:

REVISION *(Cont.)*

pedigree, but we also reveal an attitude toward the dog.

The emotional meanings of words are useful, especially if the writer's purpose is to sway opinion. Poetry, for example, depends on words that arouse the emotions of the reader, as anyone may demonstrate if he will replace the emotion-filled words of a poem with neutral ones; all the poetic value will be knocked out of the poem by the change.

Emotional words have their place in poetry, but they are misleading when we are concerned with facts and not with attitudes. The scientist, for example, wants facts; he does not want to be swayed by words. He has worked to rid his books and discussion of emotional words, and by straight scientific thinking has made important discoveries. Politicians have not done the same. They are apt at changing the public's opinion merely by the use of such emotional words as *Bolshevik, Fascist, reactionary,* or *revolutionary.* They prevent straight thinking about national and social problems. If people in the government would use clear, unemotional words, we could form opinions on facts, not words, and society would benefit.

Emotional words can present a danger as well as an advantage, and we need to be careful not to form opinions on emotion-filled words.

[The theme is still undeveloped, in spite of the addition of an illustration or two. But it does come nearer than the original to showing how ideas are related. The revision involved first of all a new outline:

STATEMENT OF MAIN IDEA: *Emotion-filled words are a handicap to scientific thinking.*

INTRODUCTION: *Words not only "mean"; they convey emotions.*

ORIGINAL *(Cont.)*

INTRODUCTION: *Words have emotional as well as denotative meaning.*

  I. Importance of emotional words to poetry
 II. Use of emotional words by politicians
III. Avoidance of emotional words by scientists
IV. Dangers of emotional words in politics
 V. Use of emotional words by critics

CONCLUSION: *We need to be careful in using emotion-filled words.*

Topic II is out of order. The outline reveals the lack of classification of material and the failure to subordinate minor to major topics.]

REVISION *(Cont.)*

 I. Usefulness of emotional words
    A. Usefulness in swaying opinions
    B. Usefulness in poetry
II. Dangers of emotional words
    A. Use in science
    B. Use in politics

CONCLUSION: *We should avoid emotion-filled words to form opinions.*

The new outline classifies topics under two main headings and organizes the paper around a central idea. It changes the illogical order revealed by the original outline. The writing follows the outline, corrects the obvious errors in accuracy, revises many of the sentences, and leaves out the undeveloped and nonessential example of the critic.]

9b PROPORTION   Org b

Inadequate planning leads to badly proportioned compositions. The writer who puts words on paper without a good outline may find that he has used half his space without reaching the center of his topic. He may become so much interested in a single example that he has no space for other topics. A writer must apportion his space so that secondary matters do not steal space needed for main ideas. The following outline of a 2,000-word investigative paper reveals the difficulty:

ORIGINAL

Marijuana and Juvenile Delinquency

STATEMENT OF MAIN IDEA: Marijuana is not an important cause of juvenile delinquency in our society.

  I. The history of marijuana
     A. American Indians
     B. Europe
     C. The United States
 II. Methods of growth and preparation of marijuana

REVISION

Marijuana and Juvenile Delinquency

STATEMENT OF MAIN IDEA: Marijuana is not an important cause of juvenile delinquency in our society.

INTRODUCTION: Current concern about use of marijuana by juveniles and widespread opinion that it is a major cause of juvenile delinquency

  I. Use of drugs by juveniles

ORIGINAL (*Cont.*)

   A. Growth of the hemp plant
     1. Ease of cultivation
     2. Extent of cultivation
   B. Extraction of the drug
   C. Commercial uses of the plant
III. Use and effects of marijuana
   A. Methods of taking drug
   B. Characteristic behavior of users
   C. Question of habit formation
IV. Use of drugs by juveniles
   A. Methods of distribution of marijuana
   B. Control of distribution
   C. Marijuana and music
   D. Studies of extent and use
     1. Government statistics
     2. Recent studies of New York schools

CONCLUSION: Marijuana is not one of the major causes of juvenile delinquency in the United States today.

[*The outline suggests a superficial discussion of questions not pertinent to the main idea. Sections I, II, and III are out of proportion. Part IV is the central part of the paper, and should be built up. The remainder should be omitted or reduced.*]

REVISION (*Cont.*)

   A. Methods of distribution of marijuana
     1. Distribution by amateurs
     2. Professional dope rings
   B. Marijuana and music
   C. Control of distribution
     1. Control by schools and welfare groups
     2. Law enforcement
   D. Cost of drugs to juveniles
   E. Studies of extent of use
     1. Government statistics
     2. Recent studies of New York schools
II. Effects of marijuana on juveniles
   A. Characteristic behavior of users of drug
     1. Actions while under influence of drug
     2. After effects
   B. Habit formation
   C. Limited use of the drug
     1. Numbers of addicts in recent years
     2. Improved methods of restricting use
     3. Areas in which drug is used

CONCLUSION: Marijuana is not one of the major causes of juvenile delinquency in the United States today.

[*The revised outline needs further development, but at least it improves proportions, omitting the first two sections of the original and suggesting development of the sections pertinent to the main idea.*]

9c   INDIVIDUAL ITEMS IN THE OUTLINE   Org c

    Individual items in the outline should be specific enough to be useful, should be parallel in form, should be arranged with due consideration for co-ordination and subordination, and, taken with other items, should approximate the item of which they are subdivisions.

    Items should be as specific as the treatment of the subject allows. Notice the following:

Getting a Deer

I. Planning the hunt
  A. Reasons
  B. Methods
II. Finding the deer
  A. Methods
  B. Incidents
III. The kill
  A. Incidents
  B. Results

[*The writer has done almost nothing to plan his paper beyond deciding on what is apparently a chronological arrangement in three main stages. There is no main idea. And none of the material has been classified or arranged. One suspects that the writer has just not thought much about what the "methods" and "incidents" are.*]

The handling of the items in an outline permit the writer to record his thinking as the basis of writing and to assure himself that his plan is adequate and orderly. Consider the following, which is the first part of a sentence outline.

TOPIC: Satire in Washington Irving's *Knickerbocker's History of New York.*

MAIN IDEA: The character of the satire in the Knickerbocker History changed as the work progressed and as the author matured, from genial persiflage and parody in the earlier section chapters, to salty high comedy toward the middle, and to trenchant, even bitter satire after the death of Irving's fiancée.

INTRODUCTION: Writing is inevitably associated with the writer; Irving's *History* seems to provide a good example, reflecting the changing emotions of a brilliant but disturbed young man.
I. The early chapters reflect Irving as an impudent young litterateur in a provincial city.
  A. In the early years of the nineteenth century, Irving was one of a group who wrote gay, witty articles.
    1. The pieces were intended to poke good-natured fun at the stodgy burghers and to flaunt a zeal for the arts.
      a. The pieces were published as the *Salmagundi Papers.*
        (1) A salmagundi is a sort of stew.

[*The outline starts well; clearly, the author has thought his subject through. He has a main idea and he has phrased it with some care.*]

[*After the introductory material an outline should not be read chronologically but by levels of subordination and co-ordination. That is, I should be read with* II *and* III, *which should approximate the whole of the main idea. In this outline they will, if* III *reads something like the following:*
III. The latter chapters, written after the shock which followed his fiancée's death, are feverish, bitter, and a little sad.]

[*Similarly,* A *and* B *should approximate* I.]

[*Obviously* a *and* (1) *are illogical; nothing can be subdivided into fewer than two. If there is no* b, *that is, if there was no second group of published papers,* a *can be incorporated within* 1. *Certainly* (1) *can be incorporated, if it is not so trivial as to be omitted.*]

2. Irving and his bachelor friends had gay parties in which they planned the next "paper" and laughed hilariously at the effect it would have.

    a. They delighted in listening to the lively speculation as to who the authors were.

    b. The authors obviously belonged to socially prominent families because they knew all the important gossip, but they wrote under pseudonyms.

    c. Irving and his friends like James K. Pauling thought these satirical pieces great good fun.

B. The earlier chapters of the History read like an extended *Salmagundi* paper.

    1. There is a tendency to try to be funny by using learned words to say nothing and to parody local history writers.

    2. The content is similar; here we find the same twitting of important people, especially venerated Dutchmen.

    3. Style.

        a. Irving seems to be trying to show off and to be funny—even when he is funny.

        b. Irving one of great American writers.

II. The body of the work reflects Irving as an unwilling law student, who took out some of his hatred of law by satirizing the foibles of officialdom.

[*Clearly, something is wrong here; 1 and 2 do not add up to A. Furthermore, a, b, and c do not add up to 2. Examination of the entries will reveal that the difficulty arises from the handling of what is now 2. If what is now 2 is made subordinate as* c, *and what is now* c *is made co-ordinate with 1 as 2, the whole will become relatively logical.*]

[*Again, something is wrong. A and B do add up roughly to I, but 1, 2, and 3 do not add up to B. The trouble is that B should apparently have two parts, one for content, one for style. The present 1 is not parallel with the present 2 and 3, which should become 1 and 2. Then the present 1 will find its appropriate place along with the present* a *under 3. The present* b *probably has no business in the outline, at least not here. Number 3 should be rewritten; it is not a sentence and hence not parallel with the other sentences.*]

[*The last two thirds of the outline are omitted. To round it out, II should be developed and III should read something like the proposed heading above.*]

EXERCISE 9

A. Comment on the weaknesses of the following outlines.

TOPIC: Satire in Moving Picture Cartoons

STATEMENT OF MAIN IDEA: The satire in cartoons which appear today on the moving picture screen.

   I. Introduction
     A. Increasing tendency toward satire in the cartoons
  II. Caricatures of human beings
     A. Caricatures of types
       1. The man who loses his temper
         (a) Donald Duck
       2. The pedant
         (a) Examples
       3. Sentimental lovers
         (a) Examples
     B. Particular individuals may appear in cartoons
 III. Satire on situations in life
     A. Domestic life
     B. National affairs
 IV. Conclusion
     A. General quality of satire
     B. Conforms to attitudes already present in most people

TOPIC: Success in the American University

STATEMENT OF MAIN IDEA: To write about success at the university.

   I. Introduction
     A. The purpose of a university
       1. Details of the purpose
       2. Further details
     B. The organization of a university
       1. Schools and colleges
       2. The campus
       3. The administration
       4. Registrar's office, comptroller, etc.
       5. Fraternities and sororities
     C. Types of students in a university
       1. Men
       2. Women
       3. Foreign students
       4. Negro students
       5. "Barbs"
       6. Alumni organizations

II. Methods of attaining success in a university
    A. Attaining social success
        1. Fraternities and sororities
        2. Dances
        3. Games and athletic events
        4. Snack bars, soda fountains, etc.
            1. Make new friends, get dates, etc.
        5. The library
        6. Contacts which will be valuable in afterlife
    B. Athletic successes
        1. Major sports
        2. Minor sports
        3. Passing your courses
            1. Choosing courses you can pass
            (a) Advice about choosing courses
III. Conclusion
    A. Success in college and social activity

B. Below are preliminary notes for a theme on *Education for Women Today.* They are not complete and are not necessarily pertinent or sufficiently specific. Using the list as a start, select a main idea for a possible theme and then construct an outline for it, using the notes which are pertinent. You will probably need to eliminate some notes, revise others, and add new ones to fit your main purpose.

  1. Beauty shop apprenticeship
  2. Teacher-training courses
  3. Liberal arts training
  4. Special course for social workers
  5. Nurses' training
  6. Laboratory technology for women
  7. Preparation for life
  8. Home economics
  9. Courses in preparation for marriage
10. General culture
11. Business courses
12. The importance of English composition for the secretary
13. Number of women in college last year
14. Adult education
15. Music and dancing schools
16. Business colleges
17. The old-fashioned finishing school
18. Women in industry

C. Below are numbered sentences which might be arranged into a short essay describing the group of sea animals which includes squids and octopuses. Make an outline which arranges the sentences in the order they might have in a theme. Do not copy the statements; refer to them by number.

1. Among the animal's most interesting characteristics is its system of jet propulsion.

2. With this jet engine the cephalopod attains extraordinary speed.

3. They are octopuses, cuttlefish, and squids, and they are remarkable organisms in a variety of ways.

4. Among the thousands of creatures that inhabit the oceans of the world none is more interesting than those known as *Cephalopoda* or "head-footed ones."

5. The cephalopod can protect itself not only with its speed and remarkable strength for its size; it also has two physical properties with which it can become almost invisible.

6. Some of the tiny, slim varieties streak through the water as fast as flies move through the air.

7. They can leap from the water and dart by so fast that the eye cannot follow them.

8. Cephalopods may not live up to all the fantastic yarns about them told by ancient mariners, but they are certainly among the most interesting of the animals of the sea.

9. First, it has developed the technique of the smoke screen long before modern navies.

10. The cephalopod is encased in a long, slim cloak, with a muscular collar that rings its neck and a funnel that sticks up in front.

11. Larger varieties, it is estimated, move over the surface of the ocean faster than the fastest speedboat.

12. The cephalopods have little ink sacs which manufacture and store ink, and they can squirt sepia cloud screens to shield them from their enemies.

13. It can then close the collar and squeeze its body suddenly and violently.

14. Swimming on its belly, the octopus or squid can pump water into its body cavity through the space between this collar and its neck.

15. They also can hide themselves because of their chameleon-like ability to change colors.

16. The water shoots out the funnel, propelling the animal backward.

17. The propulsion system of the squid or octopus is no more remarkable than its special devices for defense.

18. They can turn purple when annoyed, or on white sand they can pale to near invisibility.

D. Use the following as a main idea: "The story of the letter *A* reflects the history of the alphabet." Construct a suitable outline by classifying, co-ordinating, and subordinating. Reject any material not pertinent, and note any main divisions which need to be further divided or developed, and any details which have no general heading. To do this exercise the student should remember that Greek and Roman times are often referred to as *classical,* that the Egyptians, Babylonians, and Semites were pre-classical peoples, and that the period between classical and modern times is often called the Middle Ages, for which the adjective is *medieval.*

Changes in Latin
Sounds of the various letters
Early known forms of *A*
Introduction—story of how I learned letter *A*
Changes during the Middle Ages leading to modern upper-case *A*
Lost Greek forms of *A*
Greek reversal of the letter
Development of North Semite *A* into Phoenician *A*
The North Semites and the earliest known form of *A*
Modern upper-case *A* from the medieval book hand
Difference between *a* and *an*
Contributions of medieval Irish scribes to modern upper case *A*
Changes in Greek
Interesting details about *U* and *V*
Medieval and modern forms of the letter
Influence of Greek "boustrophedon" writing on *A*
Symbol for Egyptian sacred bull as possible ancestor of *A*
Contributions of medieval French scribes to modern upper-case *A*
Hypothetical origins of *A*
Modern upper-case *A* from medieval court hand
Developments in classical times
Babylonian aleph as possible ancestor of *A*
Pre-classical history of *A*

10

Transitions, Introductions,
Conclusions

For Guide to Revision, see page 166

Transitions, introductions, and conclusions reveal the organization of a composition.

A reader can be compared to a person following a trail through a strange land, and the writer is the guide who must show where the trail leads. If the trail is long, the guide must break the journey into stages, so that those who follow the trail do not become exhausted, but have places to stop for rest or food. If there are obstacles in the trail, the guide must provide methods for coping with them—with rivers, mountains, or swamps. There must be a plan in the whole route, and a plan in the parts. Similarly, the writer must give adequate instructions at the start and must give warning every time there is a turn in the trail. He should even give occasional assurance that the reader is still on the trail, just as the markers of highways occasionally put up a sign, *U.S. 30,* even though there has been little opportunity to get off the road.

Devices for guiding the reader, for marking the trail, give continuity and coherence. They show how the thought continues from one element to another and how the parts cohere, stick together. Coherence depends in great measure on devices within the paragraph—transitional words, repetition of words and ideas, word order (see 3). The longer composition, however, often requires more elaborate machinery to reveal its plan and outline—transitional sentences or paragraphs, introductions, conclusions.

10-1 REVEALING THE MAIN OUTLINE

A writer should give the reader signposts or indications of the main plan of the composition. Without necessarily relying on the formal "first, second, and third," he can naturally and directly keep the reader aware of where the discourse is headed. Following, for example, are guides included by Sir Arthur Keith in an essay on studying the human body.

In all the medical schools of London a notice is posted over the door leading to the dissecting room forbidding strangers to enter. I propose, however, to push the door open and ask the reader to accompany me within. . . . We propose to watch them [the students] at work. Each student is at his allotted part, and if we observe them in turn we shall, in an hour or less, obtain an idea of the main tissues and structures which enter into the composition of the human body.

[These passages appear in the opening paragraph and show the reader the over-all purpose of the essay and the writer's plan for achieving it—by observing the students as they dissect.]

By good fortune a dissection is in progress in front of the wrist, which displays, amongst other structures, the radial artery. . . .

[The second paragraph locates the reader near the first student.]

Lying side by side with the sinews of the wrist there is another cord. . . . It is the median nerve. . . .

[The third paragraph tells the reader that the essay is turning to another aspect of the wrist dissection.]

We propose to observe the dissector as he traces the radial artery to the heart. . . .

[The reader is guided to a further observation.]

Before leaving the dissection we have been surveying it will be well to see one of those marvelously contrived structures known as a joint. . . .

[The reader is led to another aspect of this dissection and is also warned of a change to come.]

We have surveyed the anatomy at the wrist in some detail and with a very distinct purpose. . . .

[A summary or transitional paragraph marks the end of this episode; the reader is led to a turn in the trail.]

We now propose to transfer our attention for a short time to two students who are uncovering the parts in front of the neck between the chin and breastbone or sternum. . . .

[The writer indicates a major shift to a new dissection.]

Our time with the students in the dissection room has almost expired; there remains only a moment to glance

[The writer marks another turn and also prepares the reader for the end of the trail.]

ORIGINAL (*Cont.*)

at a dissection which is exposing the important organs which are enclosed within the thorax and abdomen. . . .

Our cursory visit to the dissecting room has not been in vain if the reader has realized how complex the structure of the human body really is, and how necessary it is that those who have to cure its disorders should try to understand the intricacy of its mechanism. . . .

—*Man: A History of the Human Body*

REVISION (*Cont.*)

[*The conclusion reminds the reader of the purpose of the discussion.*]

The essay includes even more guides to its general pattern than have been excerpted here, but these samples, most of them opening sentences of paragraphs, illustrate the importance of such aids. These passages outline the complete essay:

> TOPIC STATEMENT: A visit to the dissecting room reveals the complexity of the human body and the importance of studying it.
>   I. The anatomy at the wrist: the first dissection
>   A. The radial artery
>   B. The median nerve
>   C. Tracing the radial artery to the heart
>   D. The joint
> II. The parts in front of the neck
> III. Organs within the thorax and abdomen

The reader can follow clearly and easily because the writer has revealed his outline step by step.

10-2 TOPIC SENTENCES AS TRANSITIONS

As the selections above indicate, the topic sentence (see 2-3) is the most useful guide from paragraph to paragraph. It introduces the topic of its own paragraph, but it can also link its paragraph with preceding material, providing a transition. Consider, for example, the following three topic sentences, taken at random from a discussion of the formation of a national government in America:

> This solution was achieved under the Articles of Confederation, a formal agreement which had loosely unified the colonies since 1781. . . .
> Thus a new colonial policy based upon the principle of equality was inaugurated. . . .

> Unfortunately, however, in the solution of other problems the Articles of Confederation proved disappointing.

In the first of the topic sentences, *This solution* refers directly to what has preceded; then the sentence goes on to introduce the Articles of Confederation as the topic of its paragraph. The second sentence refers with the word *Thus,* but it provides continuity also because it summarizes the entire preceding paragraph, putting the material into new terms which emphasize the new aspect of the topic to be considered, the use of equality as a basis of the policy. The third provides a transition in two ways, by echoing the word *solution* from the first sentence and by referring to previous material with *other problems.*

Frequently, in order to clarify a transition, a writer uses two sentences, making his transition in the first sentence of the paragraph and stating his topic in the second. For example, DeWitt H. Parker moves to a new section of an essay on aesthetics as follows:

> In our discussion thus far, we have been assuming the possibility of aesthetic theory. But what shall we say in answer to the mystic who tells us that beauty is indefinable? . . .

The first sentence summarizes what has preceded. The second introduces the topic of the paragraph, the possibilities of defining beauty.

10-3 TRANSITIONAL PARAGRAPHS

For brief papers, well-written topic sentences can supply all the transitional material necessary. Longer compositions, however, sometimes are broken into large divisions containing several paragraphs, and transitions are important enough to require a brief transitional paragraph. Thomas Henry Huxley needs an entire paragraph for a relatively formal transition in an essay on the method of scientific investigation. He moves from a series of examples of how we behave "scientifically" in everyday life to a more serious discussion of causal relationships.

> So much, then, by way of proof that the method of establishing laws in science is exactly the same as that pursued in common life. Let us now turn to another matter (though really it is but another phase of the same question), and that is, the method by which, from the relations of certain phenomena, we prove that some stand in the position of causes toward the others.
>
> —*Darwiniana*

The paragraph has the qualities of a good topic sentence used transitionally, although it is developed more fully. Its first sentence summarizes what has preceded; the second tells us precisely and directly what is to follow.

10-4 USES OF THE INTRODUCTION

"I think," Anton Chekhov is reported as saying, "that when one has finished writing a short story one should delete the beginning and the end. That's where we fiction writers mostly go wrong." Student themes also are often weighed down by heavy, obscure introductions or conclusions, but all compositions must start and stop. Beginnings and endings are important.

Introductions vary. A long paper usually requires more introduction than a short one. Special circumstances demand that the introduction do special jobs, but, in general, introductions do the following:

(1) The introduction must introduce. It must lead directly into the paper.

(2) Usually, the introduction must tell, directly and simply, what the composition concerns. That is, it usually states the main idea of the composition; and if not, a statement of purpose should usually follow the introduction, as a sort of second introduction.

(3) It may provide necessary preliminary information.

(4) It may provide background concerning the writing of the paper, the validity of the material, and the like.

(5) It may be used to attract the reader's attention.

(6) It usually sets the tone of the paper.

A good introduction is likely to do several of these at once. The most important, of course, are the first two. Whatever else it does, the introduction must tell the reader what the paper is about and lead him gracefully into the body of the discussion. It must not be so long that it is out of proportion to the rest of the paper; usually a student theme requires only two or three sentences. There are no recipes for introductions; various approaches may serve well. Furthermore, the writer may change his introduction half a dozen times before he finishes the final draft. He may prepare a very formal introduction which he knows he will discard, go on to complete the writing, and then return to work out a final introduction. Or he may hit upon a telling idea for an introduction when he is first thinking about the subject.

10-5 TYPES OF INTRODUCTIONS

The introduction may say directly what the paper concerns; it starts the reader properly and indicates the subsequent plan. It need not be so cumbersome as: "In this paper I am going to show. . . ." or "These pages are intended to prove. . . ." Still, it should direct the reader without doubt as to the subject.

Force and Freedom

Can there be a moral basis for freedom in a world of force? This is one of the ugly questions which disturb many intelligent people at this moment. Can we reconcile the doctrine of military force—the idea of killing men in war—with a moral purpose? As a matter of history, freedom has often emerged from the successful use of force; yet we abominate war as intensely as we love freedom. How are we to resolve this paradox?
—JAMES BRYANT CONANT

[*The opening paragraph uses a series of questions to lead to the basic problem of the paper: the relationship between force and freedom. The first question is the main question the writer will try to answer. This type of introduction is often effective, although an unskilled writer may make a series of questions seem overoratorical and affected.*]

An introduction by direct statement may be more formal; for instance, it may analyze the subject:

Juvenile delinquency is one of the most pressing problems in the city of C, and it can be solved only after more careful study than the heated and usually uninformed letters that have been appearing in the newspapers or the irate and accusing speeches in recent P.T.A. meetings. A first step will require examination of at least three related matters: the adequacy of recreational facilities in the city, the methods of the police in dealing with juvenile delinquency, and the question of the relations between juvenile delinquency and problems of home life.

[*A paper like the student investigative paper from which this introduction is taken often profits from an introduction which maps out the course to be followed. The introduction here summarizes the analysis which is to be developed.*]

An effective variation upon this standard beginning opens with a statement the writer expects to oppose. He describes a popular opinion which he believes is erroneous; he comments on earlier writing with which he expects to disagree; he mentions a person with whom he differs. By this device the writer can gain the interest that always attaches to an argument, and at the same time define his own stand by its opposite.

Roosevelt and the Far East

Even the most friendly of the many Roosevelt biographers have a tendency to imply that the President gave little thought to foreign affairs before 1939. The impression created is far from accurate.

—SUMNER WELLES

[*The introduction moves the writer —and the reader—quickly into the main matter of the essay: a discussion of Roosevelt's understanding of foreign policy, which the writer wishes to defend.*]

A writer may work logically into his subject by summarizing events or attitudes on which his new comments are based. Historical or political commentaries frequently follow this pattern, leading to discussions of current situations by brief outlines of what is behind them. Such discussions can take a dramatic form.

The Pittsburgh Story

Six years ago, insiders were wondering if Pittsburgh was a used-up community. For a variety of reasons, the oldest, biggest, and most powerful center of heavy industry, the leading steelmaker for all the world, was shriveling away. . . .
Then, suddenly, something happened.

—KARL SCHRIFTGIESSER

[*The essay describing the plan on which a city is being developed begins by describing the situation which stimulated development of the new plan.*]

Subjects sometimes require that the writer make clear what right he has to discuss particular material. He may have been an eye-witness to an important event; he may have done exhaustive research; he may have conducted controlled experiments. Research papers often require some statement of this sort so that the reader may judge the validity of the material presented.

Thomas Couture

My first meeting with Couture, who became one of my best and dearest friends, was odd and characteristic. It was in 1834; I was not yet one and twenty, and had just arrived from the United States, well provided for in the way of courage and determination, with a stock of youthful illusions, and very little besides.

—GEORGE P. A. HEALY

[The introduction has the easy grace of familiar narration, but it also lets the reader know that the writer is speaking on the basis of long and intimate acquaintance with his subject.]

To gain the attention of readers, writers may begin with a sample of their most striking illustrations, with pertinent facts that are dramatized into conversation, or with a record of an event that demonstrates the importance or interest of the discussion.

Can France Come Back?

Some time ago Monsieur Schuman, French Foreign Minister, was taking an early morning walk in the gardens of his official residence on the Quai d'Orsay. In the course of it he met an elderly gardener at work upon a flower bed. "Be off with you," said the gardener, "the public are not allowed in these gardens." "But I am the Minister." The gardener gazed distastefully at Monsieur Schuman. "Oh, well," he said at last, "if you're the Minister . . ." and turning his back, went on with his work.

Such an attitude may betoken. . . .

—HILARY ST. GEORGE SAUNDERS

[An amusing anecdote which illustrates an attitude important to the theme catches the interest of the reader. Note that the second paragraph proceeds at once to explain the significance of the incident for the purposes of the essay and to lead the reader from it into the main matter to be discussed.]

10-6 USES OF THE CONCLUSION

Since the final position is emphatic, the conclusion offers an opportunity for the writer to press whatever points he wishes his reader to remember most. In a short paper, the writer may need no formal conclusion, but he will still choose carefully the idea with which he closes. Whether a full summary or a brief final statement, a conclusion has the following functions:

(1) The conclusion must close the paper, and make the reader

feel that the writer stopped because he completed what he had to say—not because a bell rang or he came to the bottom of a page.

(2) The conclusion must recall the *whole* composition, the central idea. It should help the reader see what the paper has accomplished.

(3) The conclusion offers an opportunity for any final suggestion or warning the writer wants to add.

10-7 TYPES OF CONCLUSIONS

Probably the most common type of ending in essays in current magazines is a statement—usually a restatement—of the main idea, of what the writer wants the reader to remember. It may be brief. One essay on the development of the city of Pittsburgh ends with a three-word paragraph: "Meanwhile, Pittsburgh booms." It may be a fully developed conclusion.

Who Will Do the Dirty Work?

"When two men ride a horse, one must go in the front," said Thomas Hobbes. The time has come when Americans must consider whether their countrymen will be long content to ride on the mare's rump.
—DAVID L. COHN

[*The essay enlarges on the main idea that the United States is developing a national discontent because most people "must content themselves with becoming, at best, skilled workers." The final two sentences restate the main idea.*]

To emphasize the theme, the writer may close with a dramatic incident, a striking example or illustration, or a telling quotation. The method has the advantage of making a point objectively and strongly, and is especially useful in an essay that is mainly a record of facts or incidents.

The Private Eyes

As one professional private detective, admitting a personal fondness for whodunits, put it recently, "I read that stuff just to get my mind off my work."
—WILLIAM S. FAIRFIELD and CHARLES CLIFT

[*The exposé of private detectives is composed of four sections, each of which ends with a dramatic incident or telling quotation. This section concerns the ruthless but pedestrian competence of some private detectives.*]

The writer concludes by adding to his main idea a plea for action. He suggests that the reader do something specific, that he heed a warning, that he accept a point of view.

Moonlight and Poison Ivy

Better marriage relations in this country await an extensive revaluation of our attitude towards life and living. If our values are shabby and our attitudes adolescent, how can American marriage, made in our image, be anything but a monumental failure?

—DAVID L. COHN

[*An essay on the weaknesses of our attitudes toward marriage ends by suggesting that we change and by pointing out the necessity for change.*]

The conclusion, then, is designed chiefly to make sure that the reader leaves the essay with its main point clearly in mind. It helps the reader recall the pattern of ideas the essay has followed; and it may make a final effort to show him the special significance of the whole.

10 Trans; Intro; Conc

TRANSITIONS, INTRODUCTIONS, CONCLUSIONS

Guide to Revision

Rewrite the introduction, transition, or conclusion so that it contributes to the interest and coherence of the writing as a whole.

Topical materials, whether in long or short compositions, should be adequate and so co-ordinated that they become a frame for the development of the ideas in the composition. Topical material within the paragraph is usually brief (see 3). For longer compositions topical material must be more extensive, and may require paragraphs or whole chapters as introductions, as transitions within the composition, and as conclusions.

10a   TRANSITIONS   Trans

All writing of any extent requires transitions, and clumsy or inadequate transitions impede clear, smooth writing.

ORIGINAL

Derring-do is an example of a meaning that has developed from misunderstanding, the original being something like, "He was one of few daring do it."

Edward Sapir, in his book, *Language,* makes use of the English word *foot, feet* to illustrate linguistic change, what he calls *drift.*

[*This transition is clumsy; concluding and topic sentences would smooth it out, but since this is a turning point in the discussion, a transitional paragraph may be in order. The writer is discussing two books on language. In the section with which the passage above opens, he has said that the first of the two books is mainly concerned with telling amusing stories about odd words. He is now ready to turn to a more penetrating book by Sapir.*]

REVISION

Derring-do is an example of a meaning that has developed from misunderstanding, the original being something like, "He was one of few daring do it."

Thus, the first of the two books under discussion is mainly concerned with telling engaging stories about the origin or growth of odd words. The second, Edward Sapir's *Language* is quite different; Sapir studies words—common words more than odd ones—to try to understand the nature and working of language.

Take, for example, his illustrations for his theory of linguistic change of the sort he calls *drift.* He starts with the common English words *foot* and *feet,* and by tracing these to such early forms as *foti* in Gothic. . .

[*A transitional paragraph warns the reader that the composition is taking a new direction.*]

10b INTRODUCTION THAT INTRODUCES   Intro

Perhaps the most common weakness of beginnings in student papers is that they fail to show the reader what the paper is to be about—they do not introduce. The introduction should present the subject. Sometimes the opening paragraph can best be omitted.

ORIGINAL

Proper Feeding of Cattle

I have always been interested in cattle, and I have noticed the growing importance of the cattle industry in all parts of the country. Not only has the quality of American beef improved in recent years, but the raising of beef cattle has spread throughout the nation.

The first requirement of proper feeding for beef cattle is. . . .

[*The main idea of the paper is that scientific feeding of cattle has improved the entire beef industry.*]

REVISION

Proper Feeding of Cattle

The American beef industry has shown important developments in recent years. Not only has cattle raising been introduced in areas formerly thought unsuitable; at the same time the quality of beef has improved. The progress is due primarily to the introduction of scientific feeding.

The first requirement of. . . .

[*The revised introduction omits superfluous, confusing material and tells the reader what the paper is to be about; it introduces the subject.*]

Often an introduction fails because the writer does not show how it is related to the main body of the discussion. The writer sees the connection, but he forgets that the reader may not see it unless he is shown how to see it.

ORIGINAL

College Humor

Last week four mechanical engineering students dismantled a Model-T Ford, carried the parts quietly up the back stairs of the dormitory one night, and reassembled the car in the third-floor hall. It was an interesting example of college humor, of the practical variety, as it exists in colleges today.

[*The incident attracts the reader's attention and makes an effective opening. But the second sentence does not relate it to the main idea of the paper, that practical joking in college has remained about the same for many years.*]

REVISION

College Humor

Last week four mechanical engineering students dismantled a Model-T Ford, carried the parts quietly up the back stairs of the dormitory one night, and reassembled the car in the third-floor hall. Undergraduates admired, janitors were puzzled, and the incident made the national news reports, but it was only a repetition of a pattern that has characterized practical jokes in college for many years.

[*The new transitional sentence interprets the introduction in terms of the main idea of the paper.*]

The introduction should be independent of the title, partly because the title may be changed or may be dropped from a paper submitted for publication. Especially, a pronoun or adjective like *this* or *these* referring to the title should not begin the paper.

ORIGINAL

Freedom of Speech

This subject is basic to the survival of democracy in America.

[*The reference to the title weakens the introduction by destroying its independence and betrays the writer into using imprecise diction.* Freedom, *not* the subject, *is basic.*]

REVISION

Freedom of Speech

Freedom of speech is basic to the survival of democracy in America.

[*Repetition of the title makes the introduction independent, and also more accurate.*]

Better be dull than confusing or misleading. A reader will usually forgive dullness in an introduction or a conclusion if the writing is clear and direct, especially in very practical writing, but a skillful writer can be at once interesting and exact. In many kinds of writing an interesting introduction is imperative. Many an article is made or ruined by the introduction. An introduction can prepare the reader to go on with a zestful sense of anticipation, or it can make him toss the article away. Similarly, an interesting conclusion can enforce a discussion at its most crucial point.

ORIGINAL

I am going to tell you what happened the last time I went out with our truck. It was quite a rainy day, and we live quite a ways out in the country, and I had a big load of hogs to haul.

[*After a fashion this introduces, though not very exactly. We do not yet know that anything interesting is to happen, and the wordy way in which the passage is written leads us to believe it will not.*]

REVISION

It was stuck, hub down in the black gumbo, a great hulking five-ton truck, loaded with a couple of dozen grunting, squealing sows. I was alone. I was still weak from influenza. And I had lost a chain, somewhere back in the sea of mud.

[*The introduction has become dramatic, and we know that the driver, in a very unpleasant situation, must somehow try to get out of it.*]

10c THE ADEQUATE CONCLUSION   Conc

The paper that seems to stop in the middle of things is usually less effective than one that stops because the writer has completed his job. Usually a single sentence is enough to conclude a theme.

ORIGINAL

. . . All too frequently scholastic standards have been subordinated to football. I know of one instance in which an important player was allowed to take a final examination over twice, for no reason except that it took him that long to pass it. All of us have heard of exceptions to entrance requirements made for athletes.

[*The paper attempts to show that football is a business in this student's university. The final sentences concern only one aspect of this theme; they do not return the reader to the main idea.*]

REVISION

I may be condemned for lack of school spirit or for idealism or for something worse, but I cannot help hoping that some day football in State University may become a sport instead of a business.

[*The addition of a concluding paragraph which returns to the central topic rounds out the composition. It suggests that the writer has concluded, not just stopped. The conclusion here presents the point of view which the writer has explained by the evidence already submitted.*]

A conclusion is illogical if it makes a statement not justified by the body of the paper. The trouble may lie in the paper itself; difficulty in finding a logical conclusion suggests that the writer has not proved his case.

ORIGINAL

[*The body of the paper presents reasons to justify the heavy expenditures on modern college football.*]

On Saturday afternoon in the crowded stadium twenty-two young men are fighting for the kinds of ideals that have made this country great. May the best team win!

[*The conclusion is a string of stock statements that happen to fit football, but it has no intimate relationship with the point of the paper.*]

REVISION

Football may have become big business, but it is a business worth preserving because its aims are the aims of education.

[*When the writer starts thinking about what he has said—not just vaguely putting together sentences that happen to get associated in his mind with the subject of football—he finds that he can make a general statement that sums up his main argument and effectively concludes his theme.*]

10d   **PROPORTION IN INTRODUCTION OR CONCLUSION**   Intro; Conc

Most student themes are so short that they require little introduction or conclusion; the writer is wise to start what he wants to say as quickly as he can and to stop when he is finished. An introduction that uses, say, 200 words of a 500-word paper is obviously out of proportion (see 9b); often it merely multiplies judgments or generalities (see 5-1) and postpones development of the writer's ideas. A rambling, repetitious ending is no better.

ORIGINAL

Decorating a Living Room

As a hobby, I draw house plans, one of which I hope to have blueprinted and built in the near future. I have been working on various plans for many years, and I find the hobby fascinating. It is instructive as well as pleasant, and I have learned many things from my experiments. My first plans were amateurish and impractical. The plans I draw now are more detailed and more concerned with functional requirements. I have been especially interested in plans for decorating living rooms because actually the living room sets the theme for the rest of the house.

REVISION

Decorating a Living Room

Decorating the living room is the most important step in decorating a house, since the living room sets the theme for all the other rooms. . . .

[*The introduction was obviously too long for a paper of 300 words. The solution, as usually, is to omit material not relevant to the main purpose of the paper. The omission makes the paper more direct as well as better proportioned. The student might appropriately write, on another occasion, a paper detailing his experiences as an amateur architect, but the material is not appropriate here.*]

10e   APOLOGETIC INTRODUCTION OR CONCLUSION   Intro; Conc

Out of what may be commendable motives of modesty, a writer is sometimes tempted to begin or conclude by protesting his own inability to deal with his topic or by apologizing for the topic itself. Such apologies should be avoided. The reader sees that if the apologetic writer means what he says, he should have kept his pen in his pocket. If he does not mean it, and is being falsely modest, the reader sees the deception.

ORIGINAL

Illegal Gambling

I have no first-hand knowledge of illegal gambling, and perhaps I should not write about it. But I do have some opinions . . .

[*One suspects that the writer's first impulse was right; he should have changed his topic.*]

The only hope for peace in our time lies in world federation.

Although this is a brief and inadequate treatment of so complex a subject, it perhaps serves to give some idea of my feelings.

[*The qualification may be honest and may even be useful elsewhere, but it should not weaken the beginning or ending of the theme.*]

REVISION OF INTRODUCTION

Illegal Gambling

Illegal gambling is dangerous to our society mainly because of the other crimes which accompany it.

[*The writer has thought of the "opinion," which is what he planned to discuss, and he has used it to start the paper.*]

REVISION OF CONCLUSION

The only hope for peace in our time lies in world federation.

[*Omission of the final apology, or inclusion of a shortened form of it somewhere in the body of the theme, concludes the paper with a strong and pertinent statement.*]

EXERCISE 10

A. Of the following sentences, assume that *a* is the concluding sentence of one paragraph and that *b* is the topic sentence of the next paragraph. Consider the following pair:

(a) Thus a thunder shower saved us from losing the first baseball game of the season, and gave us another week in which to tighten our team play.

(b) A week later our pitchers were in better condition.

This is not a good transition. The opening of the second sentence, *a week later,* does something by setting the time; but the end of the preceding paragraph had seemed to promise some account of the practice during the week to develop team work, and sentence (*b*) does not fulfill the promise. Something like the following would be better:

(c) The next Monday afternoon the coach started a series of drills intended to show us how to work together.

Now consider the following sequences of sentences. Which provide good transitions? Which are inadequate, and why?

1. (a) The pool to assess student sentiment showed overwhelming enthusiasm for the proposed Student Union Association.
   (b) They decided I should be chairman of the membership drive committee.

2. (a) Here with a view of the mountains on three sides and the tiny creek near the center of the area was a perfect site for the new school.
   (b) The site was nearly fifty miles from a sizable town. Supplies and help would be a problem. Building costs would be high.

3. (a) Everybody had left by midnight, and we went to bed.
   (b) I put the coffee on and started to mix batter for pancakes.

4. (a) Interpreting local news, therefore, is perhaps the most important single function of the college newspaper.
   (b) National affairs should be of interest to college students and college journalists.

5. (a) In such ways are college traditions useful as laws or regulations which help students to live together.
   (b) The tradition of fraternity hazing does not, it seems to me, have any reason for continued existence.

6. (a) Late that afternoon we arrived at Quahog Beach, ready for two glorious weeks of sun, sand, and sea.
   (b) After the storm and the big waves of the previous week, there was nothing left of the cottage but the piling, sticking up through the rock-strewn shore.

7. (a) Thus for a century or two, the natives of southeast Asia have associated extortion, brutality, and bad manners with white men.
   (b) They are making white men pay—all white men, from whatever country they come and whatever their previous connection with Asia—for the mistakes and crimes of a few.

B. The following topic sentences of paragraphs selected from various essays provide transitions. Study each one and try to determine ·what has preceded the sentence and what is to follow. Some reveal more than others.

1. The distribution of the three techniques between the three departments of study is, however, less watertight than might be supposed. . . .

2. What is true of Heinrich Hertz working quietly and unnoticed in a corner of Helmholtz's laboratory in the later years of the nineteenth century may be said of scientists and mathematicians the world over for several centuries past.

3. The impact of such lawless novelties upon the more staid English of the motherland is terrific.

4. This knowledge of nature reacted on the conception of human life.

5. Meantime, there occurred an equally notable expansion of the time frame of reference.

C. Rewrite the following paragraphs from student themes, attempting to improve the continuity from sentence to sentence (see 3):

1. The mythology and folkways of a primitive people are the basis of their society. Wise men and priests explain the mysteries of the universe. Folkways are learned by the young by imitation and under the pressure of authority. Traditions of a different society are sometimes imposed on a primitive group, and then the old folkways are submerged and covered by superficial acquired habits. The dress and language of the new society are adopted. You have to probe beneath the surface to find the old beliefs persisting.

2. What to wear was a very important problem to me. Blue was the color which my mother considered most flattering to me, but I liked red. I was only in the seventh grade. It was very hard for me to find a formal that fit me. Dress designers apparently did not take sufficient account of the special problems of seventh-graders. Many dresses, both blue and red, were presented. I did not seem to have curves in the right places. When I did find a suitable dress, the alterations turned out to be more complicated than making the dress could have been.

D. Select a paragraph from a theme you have written. Using the paragraphs in 3-3 as models, draw lines tracing the continuity from key word to key word. Then revise the paragraph, attempting to improve its continuity, and draw lines on the revision to test whether more ideas carry from sentence to sentence.

E. Below are beginning paragraphs, with the sentences that follow them, taken from papers discussing the general subject of fraternities and sororities in college. Comment specifically on the effectiveness of each as an introduction.

1.   College fraternities obviously fail in a number of ways, but I believe that they are essentially valuable to our educational system

because they contribute to the social development of the individual student.

First of all, they help the student learn how to get along with other human beings. . . .

2.   Fraternities have long been an essential part of the educational system of the United States. Most major colleges and universities now have many chapters on their campuses.

The first reason that they should be retained is that they provide living quarters for many students. . . .

3.   When Bill Jones came to college he was one of my closest friends, the kind of person everybody liked. Then he joined a fraternity. Now he hardly speaks to his old friends.

This is just one of the reasons for abolishing fraternities and sororities. . . .

4.   Birds of a feather flock together. In the same way those who want to join sororities join, and those who do not stay out.

It is obvious, therefore, that there is no reason for changing the sorority system on our campuses. . . .

5.   Not being a member of a fraternity, this is a subject about which I have little information, but I will write about it as well as I can.

I am sure, however, that there needs to be a drastic change in the way fraternities operate on this campus. . . .

6.   I have been a pledge to a national sorority for nearly three months, and I am sure that most of the criticisms that one hears about sororities are not true. These criticisms that sororities are snobbish and that they do not encourage study certainly do not apply to my sorority.

The first advantage of sororities which I want to consider is . . .

7.   When I first proudly attached my fraternity pledge pin to my lapel, I dreamed happily of the days the rushing chairman had described for me—days of scholarly companionship, of good food and superior lodging, of brotherly love, of the cultural benefits of sophisticated social life. After three months of waxing floors and reaching for my toes my dreams are the same, but they are no longer connected with the fraternity.

I dream, for instance, of the scholarly companionship, but I have not found it. . . .

8.   In this theme I shall consider fraternities and sororities.

There are both disadvantages and advantages to fraternities and sororities. . . .

F. Below are concluding paragraphs taken from papers discussing the general subject of fraternities and sororities in college. Comment specifically on the effectiveness of each as a conclusion.

1. [*The paper cites instances from the writer's experience which seem to him to show disadvantages of living in a fraternity.*]

    It took me only three months as a pledge to learn that there is a wide difference between the stories pledges hear during rush week and the realities of life in a fraternity house.

2. [*The paper cites evidence intended to show that living in a sorority is really no more expensive than living in a dormitory and that one gets more for her money in the sorority.*]

    Sororities, therefore, should be encouraged on our campuses in America. They give a girl the kind of college life which prepares her for real-life situations.

3. [*The paper maintains that sororities aid education because they provide necessary supplements to academic work.*]

    My sorority includes the nicest group of girls I have ever known. It is a pleasure and an honor to be associated with them.

4. [*The paper maintains that fraternities are undemocratic in their methods of selecting members and should therefore be banned from campuses of state institutions.*]

    Instances like those I have presented could be multiplied to show that fraternities discriminate against certain races and religions. I believe that such organizations should not be recognized by colleges and universities in a democratic country.

5. [*The paper presents a logical argument to establish the idea that democracy is based on individual freedom and that any organization should be given freedom to choose its members as it pleases.*]

    Of course, there may be other arguments, and this is a big subject which requires further investigation, but I see no reason for discriminating against fraternities.

G. Select one of your previous themes and rewrite the beginning and the ending in three ways. Try to use a different approach for each pair. For instance, if you used a direct statement of purpose in your original theme, you might try to phrase this statement more briefly and picturesquely; you might begin with a question or series of questions, or you might make use of an incident or a quotation. Try one set in which your approach is inductive and one in which it is deductive.

11

Style and Tone

For Guide to Revision, see page 189

Style is the man himself.
A good style must, first of all, be clear.
A good style must have an air of novelty, while concealing its art.
For a man to write well, there are required three necessaries; to read the best authors, observe the best speakers, and much exercise his own style.
He that will write well in any tongue . . . must speak as the common people do, but think as the wise men do.
Let your matter run before your words.
A man's style is as much a part of him as his face, his figure, or the rhythm of his pulse.
All styles are good save the boresome kind.
The style of an author should be the image of his mind, but the choice and command of language is the fruit of exercise.
Style is the physiognomy of the mind.
There is no way of writing well and also writing easily.
I confess to you I love a nobility and amplitude of style, provided it never sweeps beyond its subject.
The secret of the style of the great Greek and Roman authors is that it is the perfection of good sense.
A man's style in any art should be like his dress—it should attract as little attention as possible.

Since the dawn of sophisticated culture men have been talking about style in writing; the first two quotations above are from Aristotle and most of them are more than a century old. The quotations suggest that thinkers have offered various solutions to the problem of style, but they suggest, also, some general agreement about the nature of style in writing. Style is the name we give to the particular combination of characteristics that gives any piece of writing its distinction, that differentiates it from other writing. Style is the "character" of writing. Style therefore includes almost everything that we have discussed in this book and most of what is to be discussed later—especially the material on language in Sections 18–23. It is partly as a kind of summary, then, that we here look at some of the general topics that a writer must consider as he develops a style.

11-1 CHARACTERISTICS OF STYLE

Parodies provide a ready means of studying style, since parodies are verbal caricatures which criticize a style by exaggerating, often to absurdity, some of its qualities. Of the following paragraphs, the first provides an example of a distinctive, though not necessarily distinguished, modern style, and the second is a critical parody of it.

> . . . They rushed down the street together, digging everything in the early way they had, which later became so much sadder and perceptive and blank. But then they danced down the streets like dingle-dodies, and I shambled after as I've been doing all my life after people who interest me, because the only people for me are the mad ones, the ones who are mad to live, mad to talk, mad to be saved, desirous of everything at the same time, the ones who never yawn or say a commonplace thing, but burn, burn, burn like fabulous yellow roman candles exploding like spiders across the stars and in the middle you see the blue centerlight pop and everybody goes "awww." What did they call such young people in Goethe's Germany? Wanting dearly to learn how to write like Carlo, the first thing you know, Dean was attacking him with a great amorous soul such as only a con-man can have. "Now, Carlo, let *me* speak— here's what *I'm* saying . . ." I didn't see them for about two weeks, during which time they cemented their relationship to fiendish allday-allnight-talk proportions.
>
> —JACK KEROUAC, *On the Road*

> I was just thinking around in my sad backyard, looking at those little drab careless starshape clumps of crabgrass and beautiful chunks of some old bicycle crying out without words of the American Noon and half a newspaper with an ad about a lotion for people with dry skins and dry souls, when my mother opened our frantic banging screendoor and shouted, "Gogi Himmelman's here." She might have shouted the Archangel Gabriel was here, or Captain Easy or Baron Charlus in Proust's great book: Gogi Himmelman of the tattered old greenasgrass knickers and wild teeth and the vastiest, most vortical, most insatiable wonderfilled eyes I have ever known. "Let's go, Lee," he sang out, and rubbed raw by a cheap handkerchief and a dreary Bandaid unravelling off his thumb. "I know the WAY!" That was Gogi's inimitable unintellectual method of putting it that he was on fire with the esoteric paradoxical mood.

I said, "I'm going, Mom," and she said "O.K.," and when I looked back at her hesitant in the pearly mystical UnitedStateshome light I felt absolutely sad, thinking of all the times she had vacuumed the same carpets.

                                                —JOHN UPDIKE, *On the Sidewalk*

This style does not follow the advice of the final quotation above, by Samuel Butler; it does not "attract as little attention as possible." The style is so obtrusive that parody is relatively easy. But the parody reveals, in what it selects to ridicule, characteristics of Kerouac's style.

The parody, even though it does not refer specifically to the paragraph of the original, concentrates on the subject matter—the preoccupation of the original with "madness" for life or a "great amorous soul." But the parody also makes fun of the attitude of the original toward this abstract subject matter, its tone. By exaggerating at the same time the excessive enthusiasm of discussion and the triviality of what is discussed, the parody implies that the tone is inappropriate. In the absurdity of the "beautiful chunks of some old bicycle crying out without words of the American Noon" the parody indicates that the actual facts of the original do not justify the frenzied manner in which they are described. In many small details also the parody has picked up characteristics of style—tricks like the compounded adjectives, the self-conscious images, or the pretentious and vague literary allusions. The parody is also skillful in catching the rhythm of the original.

Aspects of style such as those mentioned above can seldom be separated from one another. Attitude and tone develop from content; sincerity is partly a matter of word choice; directness often grows from a knowledge of sentence patterns. But a few of the qualities of good style can be isolated for purposes of discussion.

11-2 STYLE AS MIND

One of the statements quoted at the beginning of this chapter is Arthur Schopenhauer's "Style is the physiognomy of the mind." Although it cannot be taken too literally, the statement emphasizes the central characteristic of a good style: it has something to say. Fundamental in style are content, matter, meaning, information; obviously, to some degree, style is the man. For this reason, many intelligent, mentally alert, well educated people write interestingly, even brilliantly, without ever having studied language or composition formally. The habits of mind that produce clear thinking also produce a good writing style. Many a scientist writes well, not so much because he has studied writing as because he has studied bugs or atoms. For the student, therefore, the preceding chapters of this book are almost all fundamental to the cultivation of a good style, because they are concerned mainly with the handling of content—finding a theme idea, collecting information to develop it, thinking logically about it, and so on. But some scientists who know much about bugs or atoms also write abominably. A good style requires knowledge of a subject; it also requires knowledge of language—what it is, how it works, how it can be used. Style is the man, but a good style is the wise man using words and sentences so that they reveal him faithfully.

11-3 READING, IMITATION, ORIGINALITY

A writing style develops, of course, in many ways, but especially from reading. Renaissance writers like John Lyly acquired much of their ornate styles from reading Latin; nineteenth century writers often reveal their early reading in the Bible. Probably the best single thing a student can do to improve his writing is to read. In fact, he can profitably read writers whom he admires and make a conscious attempt to learn from them, analyzing their sentences, their diction, their tone. Writers often learn by direct imitation, learning what they can from another writer and then going on to create their own styles. Chaucer, for instance, as a young man admired the French poets of his day and imitated them until he could do as well as they in their own manner—in fact, the French poets like Machaud whom he imitated are now mainly remembered because they influenced Chaucer. Then he found out about the great Italians of his time, Boccaccio and Petrarch, and imitated them. But he did not become truly himself until he had outgrown both his French and Italian teachers and had begun to write in his own style. Robert Louis Stevenson describes how he "played the sedulous ape"; that is, he imitated writer after writer, deliberately, until he had mastered their ways of writing. "That," Stevenson concludes, "is the way to learn to write . . . Before he can tell what cadences he truly prefers, the student should have tried all that are possible; before he can choose and preserve a fitting key of words, he should long have practiced the literary scales."

"Perhaps," Stevenson goes on, "I hear someone cry out: But this is not the way to be original! It is not; nor is there any way but to be born so." Originality is a virtue much admired in writing, but a student cannot write originally by imitating what seems clever in some other writer. Trying to make characters talk like those of Damon Runyan or Hemingway will not in itself produce originality, nor will attempts to reproduce the superficial characteristics of. an unusual style—to omit periods or capital letters, to write in incomplete sentences, to affect nonstandard diction. Originality is not mere novelty or trickery. Especially unimpressive are old favorites of student writing such as the character sketch of "my best friend" which turns out in the end to be a description of a dog or a horse, or the theme that spends five hundred words telling why the writer could not find a topic, or the narrative that ends with the revelation "and then I woke up." Most students, however, are born with originality, at least with individuality. The originality emerges in writing when the student thinks and learns enough about his topic to make the ideas he presents his own. Tricks and devices are likely to be less original than clearly conceived material presented with sincerity, directness, and simplicity.

11-4 TONE—ATTITUDE TOWARD MATERIAL AND AUDIENCE

From one very important point of view, then, style is the man. From another, style, especially in its variations, is tone.

Tone is a useful term, but it is almost as difficult to define as *style*. It is metaphorical in its meanings, used in reference to all the arts but basically connected with sound. That is, the tone of a paragraph has much the same importance as the tone of voice in which something is spoken. "Yes," spoken in different tones, can have a wide variety of effects—questioning, skeptical, affirming, hesitant, doubtful. In the same way, a composition, from the way in which it is written, from its style, has different effects, expresses different attitudes. *Tone* is used here to refer to the quality of a piece of writing which reveals the attitude of the writer toward his subject matter and toward his audience.

Compare the following passages from two student themes, written about the same central idea—that some types of advertising should be discontinued.

The general public has great faith in the printed word. People tend to believe what they read in supposedly reputable newspapers and magazines. Advertising, therefore, which makes false claims about the values of a product or the consequences of failing to use it may cause real hardship and may eventually even harm the standing of the company.

In the living room I found my mother in tears; she had been snubbed by the Tuesday Afternoon Bridge Club. Sadly I watched her fingering the white blouse in which tattle-tale gray persisted in spite of the new soap. My sister was revising the second paragraph of her suicide note; she had not had a date for a week in spite of using all the proper soaps and toothpastes and mouthwashes. Shc faced the question why romance had passed her by, and there were no more answers in the advertisements.

The first theme is serious and objective, an attempt to make a reasoned, logical statement; the second is ironic, exaggerated; it employs ridicule, reducing to absurdity the kind of advertising its author resents. The themes differ in *tone*—that is, in the attitude the writer takes toward his material and toward his reader.

11-5 VARIETIES OF TONE

Since tone reflects attitudes, it can vary almost infinitely. Compare, for example, the following brief passages on the same general topic—the weather.

What happens in this particular case—and it accounts for half our winter days—is simply that the cool ground of the wintry continent chills this moist, warm air mass—chills it just a little, not enough to change its fundamental character, and not all the way up into its upper levels, but in its bottommost layer and that only just enough to make it condense out some of its abundant moisture in the form of visible clouds; it is quite similar to the effect of a cold window pane on the air of a well-heated, comfortable room—there is wetness and cooling right at the window, but the bulk of the room's air is not affected.

—WOLFGANG LANGEWIESCHE, *What Makes the Weather*

And spring? Ah! there is no spring in the Delta, no sense of refreshment and renewal in things. One is plunged out of winter into: wax effigy or a summer too hot to breathe. But here, at least, in Alexandria, the sea-breaths save us from the tideless weight of summer nothingness, creeping over the bar among the warships, to flutter the striped awnings of the cafes upon the Grande Corniche.

—LAWRENCE DURRELL, *Balthazar*

Clearly the pieces differ in tone. Partly, of course, the differences grow from the content, but the content, the selection of materials, is partly determined by the attitude taken in each passage. The first is informal and familiar, but its tone is mainly objective; its purpose is to inform the reader of facts. The second is concerned more to convey an impression, a "feeling" about the day, and its style and tone are different, more "poetic," more dependent on images.

Precise description of the varieties of tone is almost impossible. The writer may approach his material and his audience seriously, or he may adopt a joking or whimsical manner or both. He may promote confidence with a judicial calm, or he may stimulate action with exaggerated enthusiasm. He may be objective, formal, informal, ironic, jovial, confidential, flattering, wheedling, belligerent, conciliatory. Aristotle describes tragedy as written in "lofty language," and the impact of poetic drama depends greatly on the formalized, non-conversational quality of verse. An encyclopedia article normally attempts an impersonal tone. The following are only a few of the more obvious approaches which may determine tone:

(1) *Objective.* A telephone directory or a compilation of statutes reveals little of the opinions or prejudices of its writer, but it has tone; that is, it assumes an objective, noncommittal attitude toward its material and its readers. Many other types of writing approach a similar tone, offering material as impartially as possible. Scientific works, textbooks, histories, newspaper accounts, factual magazine articles, or informative bulletins are likely to be primarily objective in tone.

(2) *Formal.* Serious writing often, though not always, promotes a formal author-reader relationship, the writing acquiring a dignity and decorum dictated more by literary tradition than by the habits of ordinary speech. Consider the following selection from Emerson's essay, *Self-Reliance:*

> Trust thyself: every heart vibrates to that iron string. Accept the place the divine providence has found for you, the society of your contemporaries, the connection of events. Great men have always done so, and confided themselves childlike to the genius of their age, betraying their perception that the absolutely trustworthy was seated at their heart, working through their hands, predominating all their being.

The tone of planned, formal expression appears in the vocabulary, in the patterned, balanced rhythm, in the elevated manner. The tone suits Emerson's subject and purposes; a similar manner would be embarrassingly inappropriate for a student theme pleading for softer seats in the gymnasium.

(3) *Informal.* Much modern writing gains the allegiance of the reader by an intimate, genial manner. Charles Lamb's essay, *Old China,* establishes an informal tone at once:

> I have an almost feminine partiality for old china. When I go to see a great house, I inquire for the china-closet and next for the picture-gallery. I cannot defend the order of preference, but by saying that we have all some taste or other, of too ancient a date to admit of our remembering distinctly that it was an acquired one.

Lamb chats with his reader, observing neither forms nor ceremony. His essay may have a serious purpose, but it remains friendly, informal.

(4) *Emphatic, enthusiastic.* Especially in fiction, writers may heighten style and overstate for emphasis. Observe an emotional scene in Charles Dickens' *Bleak House:*

> I saw before me, lying on the step, the mother of the dead child. She lay there, with one arm creeping round a bar of the iron gate, and seeming to embrace it. She lay there, who had so lately spoken to my mother. She lay there, a distressed, a sheltered, senseless creature.

The context may justify the highly rhetorical, figurative style, although out of context the passage sounds inflated. Such a tone conveys emotion, but unjustified, it rings false.

(5) *Understated.* Another description of death, from Ernest Hemingway's story, *My Old Man,* describes the death of the narrator's father in a different tone:

> Then Gilford rolled over to one side off my old man and got up and started to run on three legs with his off hoof dangling and there was my old man laying there on the grass flat out with his face up and blood all over the side of his head. I ran down the stand and bumped into a jam of people and got to the rail and a cop grabbed me and held me and two big stretcher-bearers were going out after my old man and around on the other side of the course I saw three horses, strung way out, coming out of the trees and taking the jump.

In contrast to the heightened style of Dickens, the passage from Hemingway describes the same sort of scene with almost exaggerated restraint, using colloquial language, emphasizing facts rather than describing emotions. Modern writers, especially, use understatement, letting the facts rather than the style convey the desired emotion.

(6) *Ironical.* Compare with the above excerpt from Dickens another passage by the same writer, this from *Pickwick Papers:*

> Rising rage and extreme bewilderment had swelled the noble breast of Mr. Pickwick, almost to the bursting of his waistcoat, during the delivery of the above defiance. He stood transfixed to the spot, gazing on vacancy. The closing of the door recalled him to himself. He rushed forward with fury in his looks, and fire in his eye.

The two passages by Dickens differ in tone. In *Bleak House* the tone is dramatic and tense, in keeping with the narrator's discovery of the dead mother. In *Pickwick* the scene shows a humorous character reacting to a belligerent little doctor who has just said, "I would have pulled your nose, sir." The incident is dramatic but not tragic, and the tone is ironic. That is, the reader understands from the context that he is not to interpret words literally—that the breast of Mr. Pickwick is more "noble" in size than in courage, that the "fury" in Mr. Pickwick's look or the "fire in his eye" is more ludicrous than frightening. Irony may vary from this sort of tolerably subtle whimsy to bitter sarcasm. It may be the tone of a sentence like a young man's "Aren't you afraid we'll be early?" to a girl who has kept him waiting in the dormitory hall until the play is half over. It may be the tone of an entire essay like Swift's famous *A Modest Proposal,* suggesting that if Irish children are to be starved they had as well be butchered. Writing may be ironic whenever a statement in its context suggests a sense different from—often opposite to—its literal meaning.

The possible variations on these or other approaches are infinite; good writing requires a tone which is appropriate to the writer, his material, and the reader. Usually what seems most "natural" to the writer works best, but once the tone is established it should be maintained.

11-6 APPROPRIATENESS OF STYLE AND TONE

Although the same material may be treated in different ways, some styles are obviously more appropriate for certain situations than others. A writer adjusts his style and tone to be appropriate both to his subject and to his audience—to the circumstances in which he is writing. The style of a columnist ridiculing the foibles of bargain-hunting shoppers differs from that of a sociologist trying to explain why a juvenile delinquent may kill for fun. An editorial writer for a college newspaper may discuss a post-game invasion of the girls' dormitory as a serious blow to the school's reputation, or he may take an ironic or serious approach; a writer for the audience of a metropolitan paper is more likely to treat the subject lightly. Neither writer, however, would be likely to comment humorously on a large-scale violation of a national border that carried threats of war. An economist would use quite different approaches in a paper prepared for a learned society analyzing the financial structure of a beach community, in a report to a corporation on the same community as a site for a shopping center, and in a letter to his wife suggesting that the community would be a pleasant place for a vacation. Situations and purposes for writing vary so much that any "rules" for appropriateness are dubious, but the following observations may be useful to the student writer.

(1) *Suitability.* Creative writing may reflect only the author's sense for significance, but most expository and argumentative writing must be suited to the audience. Much writing should be understandable by all adults, most newspaper writing, for example. The writer of popular works should avoid rare words and complex constructions, and even in semi-popular writing he should explain any terms not in common use. But popular writing is not the only kind of useful writing. Most good writing for children will bore intelligent adults. Conversely, a theoretical physicist would be justifiably irked if, in reading a learned paper on his speciality, he was constantly interrupted by explanations of matters familiar to every graduate of Physics 1—but not to every layman. Good professional music criticism is likely to be incomprehensible to even a learned reader who does not know music; much good philosophy written for philosophers will inevitably be unreadable for many of us. Most writing should be guided by the audience for which it is intended; usually, student writing is directed toward a semi-popular audience, but the student should learn, also, to do more specialized writing upon occasion. Many college students are preparing for careers in which their most important writing will be specialized or technical.

(2) *Maturity and taste.* One of the problems of the student writer is to remove himself far enough from his subject matter to view it objectively, with some perspective. The student who adopts a tone of high seriousness and an ornate style to describe the value of his contribution of a touchdown run in the final game of the high school football season is writing with neither taste nor maturity. The student whose theme describes with a straight face the glories of a 4-H fair— "the most important moment of my life—" is often unintentionally humorous.

(3) *Sincerity and simplicity.* Usually conscious efforts to adopt a style are unsuccessful. They sound insincere or affected. They may produce mere pompousness. The kind of sports writing, for example, which relies on always calling a baseball a pill or the old apple is likely to sound false and weary, not clever and racy. The theme that tries to be impressive by always referring to Shakespeare as the bard or the swan of Avon is likely to sound trite and juvenile. Sinclair Lewis in *Babbitt* burlesques the affected high style of some society-page prose:

> 'Twixt the original and Oriental decorations, the strange and delicious food, and the personalities both of the distinguished guests, the charming hostess and the noted host, never has Zenith seen a more recherche affair than the Ceylon dinner-dance given last evening by Mr. and Mrs. Charles McKelvey to Sir Gerald Doak. Methought as we—fortunate one!—were privileged to view that fairy and foreign scene, nothing at Monte Carlo or the choicest ambassadorial sets of foreign capitals could be more lovely. It is not for nothing that Zenith is in matters social rapidly becoming known as the choosiest inland city in the country.

Or for a sample of a style that is perhaps more subtly bad, consider the following from a contemporary mystery novel:

> The black gabardine suit she wore instead of the electric-blue gown seemed to have been stroked to her form by a sensitive young sculptor who fell in love with his creation and let his sensual imagination run wild. She walked toward him with slow grace, and he saw the tautness that made her red mouth seem completely imperious, in the firm mold that some mistake for courage.
>
> And for a moment he was trapped again, like a small boy looking at the grandest, most sparkling and magnificent red wagon he

has ever seen. She was the chrome and polished enamel, the speed and the powerful promise of the low-slung car shining through the window from the plush interior of the showroom.

—WILLIAM L. ROHDE, *Murder on the Line*

The effort in the writing shows; neither the prose nor the lady is as seductive as the writer apparently intended; the description does not ring true.

For most purposes the student writer does best to write sincerely, naturally, simply, directly.

(4) *Objectivity and emotion.* Directness and sincerity become a virtue of style and tone especially when the writer is trying to convey emotion. Just as in life the depth of grief is not measured by buckets of tears, so in writing sincerity of emotion is not measured by excessive protests and multiple superlatives. The sob-story in the Sunday supplement seldom evokes the tears its style seems to seek. A student theme is no more successful in communicating sincerity of emotion when it attempts to force feeling with lines from old motion pictures: "Little did I know that I would never see that fluffy little ball of fur alive again."

If emotion is there, it will be conveyed best by a straight and objective presentation of the material. Writing that tries to milk more emotion than the facts warrant is *sentimental*—false in its emotion.

(5) *Humor.* Humor is likely to be most successful in writing when it is presented with a straight face. Notice, for example, the style of the following brief excerpt from James Thurber's well-known reminiscences about university days:

> One day General Littlefield picked our company out of the whole regiment and tried to get it mixed up by putting it through one movement after another as fast as we could execute them: squads right, squads left, squads on right into line, squads right about, squads left front into line, etc. In about three minutes one hundred and nine men were marching in one direction and I was marching away from them at an angle of forty-five degrees, all alone. "Company, halt!" shouted General Littlefield. "That man is the only man who has it right!" I was made a corporal for my achievement.
>
> —*My Life and Hard Times*

The writer lets the humor grow from the facts.

(6) *Rhythm.* Good prose moves with subtle and varied rhythms; in fact, prose is partly distinguished from verse by its rhythmic variety

and subtlety. Careless writers mostly ignore rhythm, and even skillful writers may proceed mostly by "feel." They like, or do not like, the way a sentence or a sequence of sentences sounds to them. President John F. Kennedy, addressing the Canadian Parliament, probably did not analyse the rhythms in the following very carefully, but he certainly knew what he was doing:

> Geography has made us neighbors. History has made us friends. Economics has made us partners. And necessity has made us allies. Those whom nature hath so joined together, let no man put asunder.

Obviously, there are two sorts of rhythm here. The first four sentences are short, blunt, and highly parallel. Ordinarily so skillful a writer as Mr. Kennedy would never use four childishly simple sentences one after the other, but here he had a purpose. He wanted those four salient facts to strike his hearers like blows, and probably he wanted the rhythm to become just a bit monotonous before he changed it. When he does change the rhythm the effect is dramatic, and partly because the new rhythm is a parody of the marriage ceremony, as though he were the officiating priest solemnizing the sacrament joining two great nations.

The next day Mr. Kennedy said essentially the same thing again, but he said it in a different way and with different rhythms.

> In the effort to build a continent of economic growth and solidarity, in an effort to build a hemisphere of freedom and hope, in an effort to build an Atlantic community of strength and unity of purpose, and in an effort to build a world of lasting peace and justice, Canada and the United States must be found, and I am certain will be found, standing where they have always stood, together.

In a sense this sentence is like the earlier passage; the four parallel clauses beginning with *in* suggest the four staccato sentences, but here instead of establishing something the rhythm seems to suggest that the speaker is building up to something. He is; the final word, *together,* climaxes and clinches the whole.

Detailed study of rhythm, an aspect of rhetoric, is too elaborate and difficult for the present book, but even a beginning writer can be aware that rhythm is important in prose and can train his ear to be sensitive to the cadences of good writing.

11 St

STYLE AND TONE

Guide to Revision

Revise the composition for appropriateness or consistency in style and tone.

As a larger problem the development of an interesting and adaptable style involves long study and practice, but limited immediate results can be obtained by revising to make the style suitable to the subject and the occasion and by promoting consistency of style within a composition.

11a   APPROPRIATENESS IN STYLE   St a

An appropriate style fits its subject matter and its reader. A student who writes in sober ecstasy of the world-shaking importance of a home-run he hit to win a junior-league baseball game is likely to create more unintentional humor than genuine respect for his batting eye. The lecturer who takes a tone of patronizing condescension to a group of college students misjudges his audience by treating them as children and annoys more than he informs. The writer who offers commonplace or trivial ideas in a formal, rhetorical manner is likely to appear more pompous than wise. An appropriate tone should be established and maintained.

ORIGINAL

Graduation from high school is a very important event, often shaping much of a person's future career in life. It is a time of commencement, not of ending. But it also is a time when a person realizes the importance of the hard struggle that has carried him successfully through four years of heartbreaks and triumphs. When those

REVISION

To the high school graduate, commencement may seem the most important event in life. The parade in white dresses and blue suits or caps and gowns, the music with all the ringing discords of which a nervous school orchestra is capable, the grim, freshly-scrubbed faces, the earnest platitudes of the student orations, all convince

ORIGINAL (*Cont.*)

wonderful words of congratulation ring out after the awarding of diplomas, every graduate knows a thrill which he will never forget. It is truly a wonderful moment.

[*The tone of overstatement and high seriousness is not justified by the occasion, and the passage does more to reveal the immaturity of the writer than to convince a reader.*]

REVISION (*Cont.*)

the graduate that this is the real turning point of his life. He leaves certain that he will never forget a moment of what has occurred, and a year later he may actually remember something of it.

[*A lighter tone, with factual details replacing the overstatement, leads to a less naïve paragraph. Other approaches, of course, would have been possible.*]

Not uncommonly, inappropriate style results from a heavy-footed attempt to be funny. Humor may be the salt of society, but its savor is delicate; a remark that produces a laugh or a smile in one reader elicits bewilderment in another and something approaching nausea in a third. A joke which sends Junior into hysterics may make his parents hope only that someday Junior will grow up. Non-professional attempts at humor often fail because the writer relies exclusively on overworked devices of style—stale quips or slang intended to suggest a blasé style, attempts at exaggerated, thesaurus-inspired high style (*In elucidating that toothsome phenomenon characterized among the ranks of the intelligentsia as granulated cow . . .*), or irony with a question mark to explain the joke (*The instructor started his clever? lecture*). These devices can be, and have been, successfully used, but they usually amuse the writer more than the reader.

ORIGINAL

When the light of day next osmosed through our hero's casement it discovered the would-be Romeo and mighty guzzler with a disturbance in that portion of his anatomy known as the cranium that was so perceptible that it resembled nothing so much as the activities of a jack-hammer. In short, he was, to use the vernacular, hanging over.

[*Some readers may find this mildly amusing the first time through, but a discerning person is likely to be disgusted at a cheap attempt to show off.*]

REVISION

Jeffrey was half awake with the pain throbbing in his temples. He fought his way under the covers, but he could not escape the sense of smothering. He tried with his right hand to block off the sun from the window, but he could not get things quite right. His head kept pounding, and his eyes hurt.

[*The revision is not very funny, but it is not disgusting, and it says much more than did the original.*]

11b CONSISTENCY IN STYLE   St b

Some variety in style and tone is inevitable, even desirable, but in general a writer should adopt a tone suited to his subject and maintain it. A writer or speaker may assume an easy, conversational manner to introduce his subject and become more terse, more dramatic, more persuasive as he moves into the body of his composition. A conclusion may differ somewhat in tone from the evidence that has preceded it. A violent shift in tone may be deliberate and striking, but skillful writers generally avoid sharp shifts of tone, and they never shift tone without good reason.

. . . Tying flies requires patience, practice, and skill, but there is a special thrill in hooking a trout with a fly you have made yourself.

And now if you are not completely bored by my lesson on how to tie a fly, let us go on, dear reader, to what the flies are to be used for. Fly-fishing. . . .

[*After a straightforward discussion, the writer shifts to what is perhaps an attempt at mild humor or "lightening" the paper.*]

. . . Tying flies requires patience, practice, and skill, but there is a special thrill in hooking a trout with a fly you have made yourself.

Catching a trout, however, requires not only a well-made lure but a good deal of skill in using it. Fly-fishing. . . .

[*A more direct transition introduces the new topic equally well and avoids the awkward shift in tone.*]

EXERCISE 11

A. Following are two paragraphs, the first a selection from a novel and the second a selection from a parody of the style of the novelist. Write a discussion of the parody as a representation or criticism of the novelist's style. Is the parody fair? What specific qualities of the novelist's style does the parody exaggerate?

1. Sight of the old gilt clock had made Arthur Winner think of his father—indeed, the room was full of such mementos. A little-disturbed museum, its collection, informal and unassuming, preserved evidences of that many-sided mind, of the grasp and scope of interests, of perceptions so unobtrusive as to be nearly private, of quiet amusements and quiet enjoyments. Seeking Arthur Winner Senior's monument, you could look around you. You could ask yourself, for example, how many lawyers—or, to give the point proper force, how many small-town lawyers, born and brought up in a fairly-to-be-called rural county seat like Brocton—would, fifty

or more years ago, have had the interest—let alone, the taste, the
eye—to pick over, unaffected by then current ideas of what was
fine or beautiful, of what was rare or valuable, the then next thing
to junk—the secondhand, the old-fashioned, the discarded—and
select, exchanging a few dollars for them, exactly the items that
the antique trade (at that time hardly born) was going to look on
as prizes half a century later. Would you guess one in a thousand,
or one in ten thousand?

—JAMES GOULD COZZENS, *By Love Possessed*

2. Author Winner sat serenely contemplating his novel. His legs, not
ill-formed for his years, yet concealing the faint cyanic marbling
of incipient varicosity under grey socks of the finest lisle, were
crossed. He was settled in the fine, solidly-built, cannily (yet never
parsimoniously, never niggardly) bargained-for chair that had been
his father's, a chair that Author Winner himself was only beginning to think that, in the fullness of time, hope he reasonably might
that he would be able (be possessed of the breadth and the depth)
to fill. Hitching up the trousers that had been made for his father
(tailored from a fabric woven to endure, with a hundred and sixty
threads to the inch), he felt a twinge of the sciatica that had been
his father's and had come down to him through the jeans. Author
Winner was grateful for any resemblance; his father had been a
man of unusual qualities; loyal, helpful, friendly, courteous, kind,
obedient, cheerful, thrifty, brave, clean and reverent; in the simplest
of terms: a man of *dharma*.

—FELICIA LAMPORT, *James Gould Cozzens by Henry James Cozened*

B. Following are selections from varied types of prose, taken from their
contexts. Describe what seems to you to be the tone of each selection
and point out how the tone is revealed. You may wish to look at the
whole compositions from which some of the selections have been
taken in order to check your judgments.

1. Although I had been baffled in my attempts to learn the origin of
the Feast of Calabashes, yet it seemed very plain to me that it was
principally, if not wholly, of a religious nature. As a religious
solemnity, however, it had not at all corresponded with the horrible
descriptions of Polynesian worship which we have received in some
published narratives, and especially in those accounts of the evange-
lized islands with which the missionaries have favoured us. Did
not the sacred character of these persons render the purity of their
intentions unquestionable, I should certainly be led to suppose that
they had exaggerated the evils of Paganism, in order to enhance
the merits of their own disinterested labours.

—HERMAN MELVILLE, *Typee,* Chapter XXIV

2. In taking up the clue of an inquiry, not intermitted for nearly ten years, it may be well to do as a traveller would, who had to recommence an interrupted journey in a guideless country; and, ascending, as it were, some little hill beside our road, note how far we have already advanced, and what pleasantest ways we may choose for further progress.

—JOHN RUSKIN, *Modern Painters*

3. Of recent years there has been a noticeable decline of swearing and foul language in England; and this, except at centres of industrial depression, shows every sign of continuing indefinitely, until a new shock to our national nervous system—such as war, pestilence, revolution, fire from Heaven, or whatever you please—revives the habit of swearing, together with that of praying. Taking advantage of the lull, I propose to make a short enquiry into the nature and necessity of foul language: a difficult theme and one seldom treated with detachment.

—ROBERT GRAVES, *Lars Porsena*

4. "And who is this? Is this my old nurse?" said the child, regarding with a radiant smile a figure coming in.

Yes, yes. No other stranger would have shed those tears at sight of him, and called him her dear boy, her pretty boy, her own poor blighted child. No other woman would have stooped down by his bed, and taken up his wasted hand, and put it to her lips and breast, as one who had some right to fondle it. No other woman would have so forgotten everybody there but him and Floy, and been so full of tenderness and pity.

—CHARLES DICKENS, *Dombey and Son,* Chapter XVI

5. THE KING? There he was. Beefeaters were before the august box; the Marquis of Steyne (Lord of the Powder Closet) and other great officers of state were behind the chair on which he sate. *He* sate— florid of face, portly of person, covered with orders, and in a rich curling head of hair. How we sang, God save him! How the house rocked and shouted with that magnificent music. How they cheered, and cried, and waved handkerchiefs. Ladies wept; mothers clasped their children; some fainted with emotion. People were suffocated in the pit, shrieks and groans rising up amidst the writhing and shouting mass there of his people who were, and indeed showed themselves almost to be, ready to die for him. Yes we saw him. Fate cannot deprive us of *that* . . . that we saw George the Good, the Magnificent, the Great.

—WILLIAM MAKEPEACE THACKERAY, *Vanity Fair,* Chapter XLVIII

6. I suppose you could call it a frame. But it wasn't like no frame that was ever pulled before. They's been plenty where one guy

was paid to lay down. This is the first I heard of where a guy had to be bribed to win. And it's the first where a bird was bribed and didn't know it.

—RING LARDNER, *A Frame-up*

7. John B. Smith takes the stand.

Q. Mr. Smith, are you familiar with the clichés used in football?

A. Naturally, as a football fan. . . .

Q. Mr. Smith, as an expert, what lesson do you draw from the game of football?

A. Life is a game of football, Mr. Sullivan, and we the players. Some of us are elusive quarterbacks, some of us are only cheer leaders. Some of us are coaches and some of us are old grads, slightly the worse for wear, up in the stands. Some of us thump the people in front of us on the head in our excitement, some of us are the people who always get thumped. But the important thing to remember is—Play the game!

Q. How true!

—FRANK SULLIVAN, *Football is King*

8. Animals talk to each other, of course. There can be no question about that; but I suppose there are very few people who can understand them. I never knew but one man who could. I knew he could, however, because he told me so himself. He was a middle-aged, simple-hearted miner who had lived in a lonely corner of California, among the woods and mountains, a good many years, and had studied the ways of his only neighbors, the beasts and the birds, until he believed he could accurately translate any remark which they made.

—MARK TWAIN, *Jim Baker's Blue-Jay Yarn*

9. It is true to nature, although it be expressed in a figurative form, that a mother is both the morning and the evening star of life. The light of her eye is always the first to rise, and often the last to set upon man's day of trial. She wields a power more decisive far than syllogisms in argument, or courts of last appeal in authority. Nay, in cases not a few, where there has been no fear of God before the eyes of the young—where His love has been unfelt and His law outraged, a mother's affection or her tremulous tenderness has held transgressors by the heart-strings, and been the means of leading them back to virtue and to God.

—T. L. HAINES and L. W. YAGGY, *The Royal Path of Life*

C. In the 19th century, two contemporaries wrote philosophies of clothes. One, ecstatic, philosophical, and violent, was the work of Thomas Carlyle. The other, moral, pedantic, doctrinaire, was an editorial by Louis A. Godey, editor of *Godey's Lady's Book*. The "paragraph" below has been made by mixing selections from these two accounts. Naturally, the tones of the two are quite different. Judging by the tone, try to sort out the sentences so that you get two consistent accounts. The sentences occur in the same order they had in the original versions. The following might be used as a topic sentence for the matter from Carlyle: "Man's earthly interests are all hooked and buttoned together, and held up, by Clothes." The following would serve as a topic sentence for the passages from Godey: "The Bible, as our readers well know, is the standard of authority by which we test the right or the wrong of ideas and usages; nor can we comprehend the full import of clothing or its advantages unless we look at the evil results that follow neglect of or disobedience to this law of necessity for the human race, ever since 'the Lord God clothed' the first man and woman before sending them out of Eden."

(1) Clothing has nine distinct phases of teaching the philosophy of its usefulness. (2) It gives covering, comfort, comeliness; it marks custom, condition, character, and civilization; it symbolizes Redemption through Christ, and the holiness of the saints in Heaven. (3) Society sails through the Infinitude on cloth, as on a Faust's mantle. (4) Strange enough, it strikes me, is this same fact of there being Tailors and tailored. (5) The Horse I ride has his own whole fell; the noble creature is his own sempster, and weaver, and spinner. (6) A clothing of rags symbolizes wretchedness, wickedness, ignorance, imposture, or imbecility. (7) While I—good Heaven—have thatched myself over with the dead fleeces of sheep, the bark of vegetables, the entrails of worms, the hides of oxen and seals, the felt of furred beasts. (8) Nakedness is savagery, or shameless sin, or extreme misery. (9) Heathenism has no darker shadow on its Godforsaken horizon than the half nude millions on millions of its worshipers; until these people are clothed, neither China nor India can become Christian countries. (10) Day after Day I must thatch myself anew; day after day this despicable thatch must lose some film of its thickness, till by degree the whole has been brushed thither, and I, the dust-making, patent Rag-grinder, get new material to grind on. O subter-brutish! vile! most vile! (11) Wherever Christian civilization prevails, as in Europe and America, dirt and disorder in a household or in dress are proofs of ill-conditioned or ill-trained people. (12) For have not I too a compact all-enclosing Skin, whiter or dingier? Am I a botched mass of tailors' and cobblers' shreds, then; or a tightly-articulated, homogeneous little Figure, automatic, alive? (13) The dress must be decent before we can have confidence in the character of any person. (14) For my own part, these considerations, of our Clothes-thatch, and how, reaching inwards even to our heart of hearts, it tailorizes and demoralizes us, fill me with a certain horror at myself, and mankind. (15) We feel and judge thus intuitively, because the

instincts of humanity tell us that without decent clothing there cannot be real delicacy of feeling or true dignity of mind, unless the 'miserable' suffers from the sins of others. (16) And this does not weaken the force of our moral of dress—that there is or has been wrong doing wherever we see people badly or indecently clothed. (17) There is something great in the moment when a man first strips himself of adventitious wrappages; and sees indeed that he is naked, and, as Swift has it, 'a forked straddling animal with bandy legs'; yet also a Spirit and unutterable Mystery of Mysteries.

D. Biblical scholars recognize that the Old Testament we know is made up of several older versions edited into one by breaking up the earlier accounts and running them together. Two of these versions are called *P* and *JE*, *P* standing for a version which we suppose to have been the Priests' Code, and *JE* for a more popular account which combined two versions, in one of which the Lord is called Javeh, and in the other Elohim. Thus, whatever the reason for the Bible's appearing in this form, many of the Old Testament stories are told twice, and naturally the style differs in the two versions. For example, here are two accounts of early days in the Garden of Eden in the King James version, but with modern punctuation and paragraphing. The first is from JE.

Now, the serpent was more subtil than any beast of the field which the Lord God had made, and he said unto the woman, "Yea, God hath said, 'Ye shall not eat of every tree of the garden?'"

And the woman said unto the serpent, "We may eat of the fruit of the trees of the garden, but of the fruit of the tree which is in the midst of the garden, God hath said, 'Ye shall not eat of it, neither shall ye touch it, lest ye die.'"

And the serpent said unto the woman, "Ye shall not surely die."

Now try to describe this passage. For what sort of reader does it seem to be intended? What is the content? How would you characterize the style? Next, study the following passage from *P*.

This is the book of the generations of Adam. In the day that God created man, in the likeness of God made he him, male and female created he them, and called their name Adam, in the day when they were created. And Adam lived an hundred and thirty years, and begat a son in his own likeness, after his image, and called his name Seth. And the days of Adam after he had begotten Seth were eight hundred years, and he begat sons and daughters.

Now try to describe the audience, the content, and the style of this passage and contrast it with that from *JE*.

The following is a continuous passage from Chapter Eleven of Genesis, which contains material from both *P* and *JE*. Identify the passages from each and determine where the break or breaks come. Enumerate as many differences in style as you can with which you distinguish the two versions.

And the whole earth was of one language, and of one speech, and it came to pass, as they journeyed from the east, that they found a plain in the land of Shinar, and they dwelt there.

And they said one to another, "Go to, let us make brick, and burn them thoroughly," and they had brick for stone, and slime they had for mortar. And they said, "Go to, let us build us a city and a tower, whose top may reach unto heaven, and let us make us a name lest we be scattered abroad upon the face of the whole earth.

And the Lord came down to see the city and the tower, which the children of men had builded, and the Lord said, "Behold, the people is one, and they have all one language, and this they begin to do. And now nothing will be restrained from them, which they have imagined to do. Go to! Let us go down and there confound their language, that they may not understand one another's speech."

So the Lord scattered them abroad from thence upon the face of all the earth, and they left off to build the city. Therefor is the name of it called Babel, because the Lord did there confound the language of all the earth, and from thence did the Lord scatter them abroad upon the face of all the earth.

These are the generations of Shem: Shem was an hundred years old, and begat Arphaxad two years after the flood. And Shem lived after he begat Arphaxad five hundred years, and begat sons and daughters. And Arphaxad lived five and thirty years, and begat Salah, and Arphaxad lived after he begat Salah four hundred and three years, and begat sons and daughters.

If you wish to check the accuracy of your guess, the break comes between the ninth and tenth verses in the King James numbering. If you care to pursue this study and make a more elaborate distinction between the styles of P and JE, the following include suitable passages in the King James numbering; the Douay version differs slightly: Genesis 5:1-28 (P); 5:29 (JE); 5:30-32 (P); 6:1-8 (JE); 6:9-22 (P); 7:1-5 (JE); 7:6 (P); 7:7-24 (JE); 8:1-5 (P); 8:6-12 (JE); 8:13-20 (P); 8:21-22 (JE); 9:1-17 (P); 9:18-27 (JE); 9:28-29, 10:1-7 (P); 10:8-19 (JE); 10:20 (P); 10:21 (JE); 10:22-23 (P); 10:24-30 (JE); 10:31-32 (P).

English
Sentence Patterns

The congruent and harmonious fitting of parts in a sentence hath almost the fastning and force of knitting and connexion: As in stones
well squar'd, which will rise strong a great way without mortar.

—Ben Jonson

"Language is the armory of the human mind," Samuel Taylor Cole-
ridge wrote; "and at once contains the trophies of its past, and the
weapons of its future conquests." From the earliest civilized times, man
has seen that these trophies in the "armory of the mind" are worth studying for themselves, and that they help us forge mental weapons for the
future. The Egyptian and Chinese systems of education were founded
upon the study of the use of language; and others, like the Classical Greek
and Roman and the Continental European and British systems, have
made much of language study.

All languages are composed of units of various sizes, most frequently
of three sorts: small units of meaning—conventionally in English they
are called words—extended compositions, and intermediate combinations
of words or other semantic units. In English these intermediate groups
are called sentences; they are the subject of Sections 12–17. On the whole
they can be studied in two ways: the way they are made and the way
they work, a study which we call *grammar,* or the way they may be appropriately used to suit the needs of speaker or writer, a study which we
call *rhetoric.*

Actually, we have already been studying rhetoric, as it applies to extended compositions, in considering such questions as unity, organization,
and development in Sections 1–11. The principles of rhetoric can be observed working also in sentences; but since the rhetorical value of a sen-

tence depends in part on its structure or grammar, rhetoric and grammar cannot always be distinguished. Nor do we usually need to distinguish, provided we understand both rhetoric and grammar. The principles expounded in Sections 1–11 will be presumed in the following discussion of sentences, of rhetoric but also of grammar.

Stated briefly, grammar is the way language works, and its devices reveal the relationships of words within sentences. These devices of grammar are not universal; they are different for different languages, and the modern student must recognize that scholars have as yet devised no single, universally accepted and entirely satisfactory grammatical description of English. Some kind of grammar, of course, is taught in the schools, and has been for many years—although the word *grammar* has often been used to designate what is more properly called usage. Elementary schools are still often called grammar schools. But many recent studies seem to suggest that whatever is being taught under the heading of grammar in many schools and colleges has almost no impact, for better or for worse, upon students, except to make them groan. This traditional grammatical description depended on classifying words on the basis of meaning and function into parts of speech. It made great use of the Latin parts of speech and the few inflections that have survived in English. It provided a vocabulary of terms like *noun* and *verb* and *preposition* which are well known to all educated users of English. The system is useful, but modern grammarians no longer find it an adequate statement about current English. They point out, for example, that the parts of speech seem to have only limited application in English, and that when all words in a sentence have been ticketed with names, we still do not know much about how the language is working. They find concepts like subject and complement more useful than categories like noun and gerund. In other words, modern students of language agree that better grammatical descriptions are needed, but language study has progressed so rapidly during the present century that no single descriptive statement has become standard. Of special importance to grammar has been the work of the *structuralists* or *structural linguists*.

The structuralists try to be as scientific about the study of language as possible; and they accordingly reject meaning and function as bases for a grammatical statement, because they can find no accurate way of measuring or defining meaning and function and they deny that a scientifically sound grammar can be built upon concepts which cannot be accurately measured. First, they point out that the basis of language is oral, that languages existed as oral speech long before they became written language, and that the original grammar was made and continues to be made through oral use of the language. Therefore, the study of grammar should be essentially the study of oral grammar, with the study of written grammar only secondary. Furthermore, sound can be measured and described, and hence provides a scientific basis for the study of language. The structuralist would point out, for example, that the grammatical differences in the following two sentences are revealed primarily by sound, only inadequately by the comma which is the only written difference between them.

He called me first lady.
He called me first, lady.

The differences between the sentences are many and subtle, but among them are these: there is a longer pause after *first* in the second sentence. The primary stress in the first sentence falls on the beginning syllable of *lady;* the primary stress in the second sentence falls on *first.* And there are other distinctions and other problems; for example, what happens to meaning if *me* is accented in either sentence? And how can the writer distinguish grammatically between two possible meanings of the second sentence: that the speaker is telling the lady that he was the first one to be called or that he is telling her he has been called the winner of first place.

Utilizing sound and starting with the spoken language, the structuralists have worked out new ways of describing the language, based on what is called the phoneme rather than on the word, which they find unadaptable to scientific definition. The two following chapters of this book do not attempt to elucidate structural study of English nor to adapt the results of structural study wholeheartedly to English grammar and sentence structure. Nor does the statement employ structural terminology, since structural concepts require definition beyond the scope of this book; and no single structuralist system has as yet become standard. The statement does, however, endeavor to profit from modern linguistic studies, including those of the structuralists, and in particular to be based on the following principles:

(1) *The grammar of a language is inherent in the language, and hence a grammatical statement about English should be derived from English, and should be as objective and descriptive as may be practicable.* A grammatical statement should not be merely an adaptation of the grammar of another language not even of an excellent language like Latin or Greek. It must recognize that English is a dynamic, constantly changing language and that change is not necessarily deterioration. Grammar is a valuable study for its own sake, an important part of the information essential to any basic education. It also helps the writer and speaker to improve his use of his native language.

(2) *More than one kind of grammatical description may be possible and useful.* We have observed above something of the structuralist's approach in using sound to describe the two sentences involving *first* and *first lady.* The analysis by sound reveals certain distinctions that other approaches miss, but it does not work to distinguish two possible meanings of the second sentence. A more traditional observation does distinguish—that *first* can be considered as a modifier of *called* in one sense

or as an objective complement in another. An explanation substituting other words to clarify meaning might point the distinction even more clearly:

> He called me earlier, lady.
> He called me the winner, lady.

Furthermore, although language does develop and grow as speech rather than writing, the grammar of the written language has special practical importance and is the grammar primarily considered in this book on written composition.

(3) *Objective grammatical description is distinct from decisions about usage. Observing changes is not judging them.* Deciding which of two locutions to choose is a separate problem, although it may be affected by knowledge of language. One can observe objectively that in English grammar *who* is becoming more and more common than *whom* when it begins a sentence, even though it is the object of a verb or a preposition. He may still, quite consistently, insist on "Whom do you wish to see" as the dialect he wishes to adopt.

(4) *English grammar is mainly distributive—revealed primarily through word order, secondarily through function words and inflections.* The signs of grammar differ in different languages. Some languages rely primarily on inflectional endings or changes in the forms of words to reveal grammar. Latin, for example, indicates which word is the subject and which the complement in a sentence by the endings of the words. *Puella agricolam amat* says that the girl loves the farmer. A simple change in endings alters meaning considerably. *Puellam agricola amat* says that the farmer loves the girl. Changing the order would have no effect on the meaning; changing the endings changes the grammatical relationships. A grammar which is revealed mainly in this way is called an *inflectional* or *synthetic* grammar. Classical Greek and Latin had primarily inflectional grammars; like them, Anglo-Saxon, the ancestor of modern English, was strongly inflected.

English, however, has now a different kind of grammar. We could use endings with a group of three words like *farmer girl love*. We could, for example, put an *s* on *love* and make it *loves*. But we would still not know who loves whom, and we have no endings for *farmer* or *girl* which would tell us. We could tell, however, if we put the words into a different order: *farmer loves girl*. We do not have a conventional sentence, but the words make a kind of pidgin-English sense, at least. The essential relationships, who does the acting and what he does, are clear. English, in other words, expresses its basic grammatical ideas not mainly by inflection but by word order.

English grammar employs another important device to reveal relationships: function words, words which may convey little meaning in themselves but indicate how more meaningful words are related. For example, if the Latin sentence above were changed to *Puella agricolam amaverat,* it would mean *The girl had loved the farmer.* In Latin the new sentence requires only a slight change in the ending of the verb, *amaverat* instead of *amat;* but in English, we must change *loves* to *loved,* and also add a word, *had.* Now this word *had* is here clearly not a verb in the ordinary sense. *Had* can be a verb in *Johnny had the measles* or *Dad had a bald spot,* but here it has no such meaning and merely indicates that the loving took place prior to a time that is already in the past. As a matter of fact, another word in the sentence serves a similar purpose; *the* does not mean much except that it indicates that the girl is a particular girl, that the farmer is not just anybody who lives by agriculture, and that a word like *girl*—a noun in common parlance—is to appear shortly. That is, *the* and *had* as they appear in the sentence, *The girl had loved the farmer,* are relationship or function words. Function words can be even more important in English if more subtle distinctions of meaning are attempted: for example, *The girl must have been about to fall in love with the farmer.*

A grammar which mainly uses function words and changes in word order to indicate relationships is called a *distributing, isolating,* or *analytic* grammar. In it the signals of grammar and the signals of meaning tend to become separated. Clearly, English, although it retains some inflectional endings, is mainly distributive. Many modern students of language would say that the distinctions indicated in the terms inflectional and distributive do not adequately distinguish languages like Latin and English; they are, of course, right, but the distinction is useful for practical purposes.

(5) *A study of English grammar should focus on basic patterns of the sentence.* Because word order is so important in revealing basic grammatical relationships, the main patterns assumed by English sentences have central importance in any consideration of grammar. Actually only a very few core patterns characterize the bulk of English sentences, subject-verb and subject-verb-complement combinations. The uses and development of these structures, however, can be very complex, and the patterns seem not to be simplifying. As we have already seen, English grammar began subtly to change, probably more than fifteen hundred years ago. Changes in language take place over long periods of time, centuries or even millenia, and we cannot assume because changes started long ago that they have necessarily worked themselves out. Some changes probably have; English sounds are shifting less rapidly than they used to. The grammar, on the other hand, seems still to be developing, rather rapidly as grammatical changes go. We are devising phrasal verbs, for example, in such structures as He *could not get out of* his difficulties; A modern doctor *must try to keep up on* his subject.

An examination of the history of the English language reveals that the sorts of changes in grammar that started at least as far back as Old English have continued, and they are probably still at work. Early Old English verbs tended to be single words—roots with endings to indicate tense, person, number, mood, and the like. Complements tended to be simple and well defined. The modern English verb is likely to require more than one word, sometimes more than a half dozen. For example, Old English had no formal future at all, but used the present to suggest the future. Modern English has dozens of future structures, most of them phrasal, and many seem to involve complements within them. We delight in such future combinations as *We cannot expect to be able to teach* them much; They *are considering making a start toward paying* their bills; He *may get around to doing* something; You *ought to get somebody to fix* that loose connection. Fortunately for our understanding, however, developments like these are only variations on the basic English sentence pattern, and even within the variations we may observe secondary patterns.

Sections 12–17 of this book, therefore, consider in considerable detail the handling of English sentence patterns, describing them grammatically and also discussing them rhetorically—that is, considering relative strength, clarity, directness, or appropriateness of various patterns. Rhetorically, these sections will recall principles such as unity, coherence, emphasis, subordination, and co-ordination discussed in earlier Sections. It will apply these, however, along with grammatical analyses, particularly to the structure of the English sentence.

12

The Complete Sentence;

The Fragment

For Guide to Revision, see page 215

A complete sentence says something about something.

We have seen in the introduction to these sections that the grammar of English is unlike that of many European languages—Latin, Greek, and Russian, for example, and to a lesser degree French, German, and Spanish—because it is more nearly distributive. This fact has large implications for English sentence structure and warrants further examination before we ask how English sentences are built and how better English sentences can be built.

12-1 DISTRIBUTION REPLACES INFLECTION IN ENGLISH

English is a direct descendant, along with the other languages mentioned above, of an ancient tongue known as Indo-European, which was spoken, presumably in east central Europe, perhaps about seven to eight thousand years ago. No examples of Indo-European exist today, but scholars have been able to reconstruct it from a study of its descendants. It was a highly inflected language, having fourteen to sixteen declensions of the noun, about as many conjugations of the verb, three declensions of the adjective, more than a dozen cases, and so on. Most of the languages that have descended from Indo-European have been dropping these inflectional characteristics, most suffixes, and some prefixes and internal changes; English has gone farthest of the Indo-European languages and has jettisoned most of the old inflectional forms.

The change was already far advanced in Anglo-Saxon, or Old English—the earliest written form of English, preserved in poems which we believe to be nearly thirteen hundred years old—but enough of the Indo-European inflection had survived to identify the key grammatical parts of a sentence. Notice the two following sentences, which an Anglo-Saxon might have written in prose:

> Biteth thone monnan se hund.
> Biteth se monn thone hundan.

The words and their order are the same in both sentences, but the sentences have different meanings because the inflected articles and the inflectional endings on the key words indicate different relationships. The words, without their articles, are *bite, man,* and *dog,* in that order. The first sentence means what a reader would expect, that the dog bites the man, because the inflected article *se* indicates that the word which comes after it, *hund* or *dog,* does the biting. In the second sentence, with the declined articles and the *-an* ending the *hund* receives the action; the whole sentence becomes the bromidic definition of news, and the dog, not the man needs the bandage. That is, in *Biteth thone monnan se hund* a reader of Old English knew who was the biter and who was bitten by inflection; but in *The man bites the dog* we know in other ways who did the biting, partly at least because *man* comes before the verb and *dog* comes after it.

12-2 PATTERNS IN ENGLISH

How do we know who bites whom or what in a sentence? Clearly, communication goes on without speaker or reader reminding himself that *man* precedes *bites* and that the man is accordingly the aggressor. True, in the simple sentences *The man bites the dog* and *The dog bites the man* the obvious difference is that the words *man* and *dog* are reversed, but the statement may be too simple. We know much more than this about the sentence. For example, as soon as we encounter the word *the,* we know that soon a word like *man* or *dog* will come along; we assume, also, that the next word will not be one like *of, and,* or *his.* We assume that if the next word is *fly* it will be used to name a small winged insect, not what the insect can do with its wings. We assume that if the next word is *excuse,* the word will be understood as one that has as its final sound that of *s,* not of *z.* We assume that if *the man* is followed by a comma in writing or by a pause and a change of tone in speaking, the next word will not be one like *bites,* but will be something descriptive of the man, perhaps *one of several in the psychopathic ward.* Similarly, as soon as we encounter the word *of* in this context—but not in some others—we know that soon we shall have a word or words like *those, several,* or *the inmates.* That is, as we learn English we learn to recognize various patterns into which words fall. When we recognize a word, we associate it automatically with certain patterns into which it customarily fits.

The patterns into which the two million or so named meanings in English can or cannot fall must be almost infinite, and nobody has ever learned all of them; but neither has anybody learned to use the language well until he has learned a large number of them. Some patterns are so common that they appear in almost every sentence, and almost any child of five or six is likely to control the most important ones like *dog bites man* or *I like bubblegum.* Some important patterns, however, remain unfamiliar even to adults. College students who have difficulty reading or writing serious prose often have never learned adult sentence patterns because they have not heard much sophisticated speech or read much adult writing. Skill in sentence structure requires a knowledge of sentence patterns, the understanding to select appropriate patterns and the ability to use them deftly and precisely.

12-3 THE BASIC SENTENCE PATTERN IN ENGLISH

Every language has its own grammar, that is, its own way of working; and this way is likely to become the way the minds of the speakers of the language work, for although minds make languages, languages also influence minds. Users of Latin, as observed in the introduction above, had to recognize patterns of words distinguished by endings, such as *-at, -am, -a,* in *Amat agricolam puella* or *The girl loves the farmer.* For an American Indian this knowledge would not be very useful. The American Indians developed many languages, but most of them did not work much like either Latin or English. Some were what we call *incorporating;* that is, they incorporated into one long phrase the ideas which we would put into a subject, a verb, and a complement. An idea like "The man is standing over there" might have appeared as something like "Object, man-type, upright, distant but not very." Such languages may be quite terse; usually a passage written in an American Indian's language requires considerably less space than an English translation of it. But like it or not—and there is no reason we should not like it—speakers of English do not use their language this way. To use English well we must command English grammatical patterns.

On the whole, minds that use English choose a subject and make an observation about it; they modify, develop, restrict, refine or somehow alter the concept involved in this subject. The core of the English sentence then is a subject plus something said about it, a *subject* and *predicate*. Such a pattern comprises all the words in the sentence *Fish swim; fish* is the subject, and *swim,* the verb, is the predicate. Consider another sentence, *Fish contain vitamins.* Here, again, *fish* is the subject, but *Fish contain* is not the complete subject-predicate pattern; it is not a sentence at all, for it has no meaning. To make a predicate of *contain* we must add something to complete it, like *vitamins.* The subject is a single unit, but the predicate often is composed of two main parts, the first part a *verb* (*swim, contain*) and the second a *complement* (*vitamins*), whatever is necessary to complete the functioning of the verb. All these parts of the basic sentence may become complicated, even so interrelated as to be almost indistinguishable, but the basic pattern remains: *subject-predicate,* which may be either *subject-verb* or *subject-verb-complement.* On the basis of its meaning, this pattern is often called the *actor-action-goal* pattern.

12-4 THE SUBJECT

The starting point of the basic pattern is the subject. Speakers of English think and say something like one of the following:

The girl | smiles.
         | is putting up her hair.
         | is happy.
         | is the only redhead in the class.
         | told me she had a date when she did not.

This is so much the pattern of English that we recognize it even without anything that can be called words, as in the following:

The quigquig obled a biscum.

We know at once that *quigquig* must be a symbol like the word *girl,* and that it is the subject, not a word like *off.* That is, in English a word of the sort that can be a subject is likely to become one if it appears before any other such word in the sentence. For example, the first nonsense "word" in the following "sentences" is clearly not the subject:

> Before the next boofoo, the quigquig obled a biscum.
> Mip, the quigquig will oble a biscum.
> While skugling his kim, the quigquig should oble his biscum.

How do we know that *boofoo, mip,* and *skugling* are not subjects? Partly, we recognize signals which warn us that although anything like *boofoo* could be a subject, once we have a word like *before* we must have a word that could be a subject but is not; that is, we expect something like, *Before the next class, the girl* . . . Similarly, when we see *mip* with a comma after it in writing, or a pause and change of tone in speaking, we suspect that it stands for an idea like that in *tomorrow* or *obviously,* and that the subject is still to come. Likewise *while* warns us that something other than the main subject will come next. Accordingly, we can now lay down a fundamental principle in English sentence structure: *The first word in an English sentence which can function as a subject is likely to become the subject, unless the structure provides clear warning that it is not the subject.* This would not be true in Latin; it would not be true in Hopi, but, except for a few modification patterns and inverted patterns (see 17-1 to 17-3), it is true in English, and writers of English must take it into account, consciously or unconsciously, if they are to write good sentences.

12-5 VERBS AND COMPLEMENTS

Neither verbs nor complements are easy to define, and they can become so intermingled that even experts may argue as to where one stops and the other begins; but fortunately most natives can learn to handle verbs and complements without being able to define them exactly. Approximate definition may, however, be useful. In general, verbs are like the italicized words in the following sentences: Motors *sputter.* Twelve daughters *are* enough. I *should have loved to spank* him. In general we may say that a verb predicates, that it shows that the subject exists, acts, has certain characteristics, or is linked to another subject or quality; it indicates that the subject is or does something. A verb which links the subject to something in the predicate, like *are* in the sentence above, is known as a *copulative* or *linking verb*. Complements are of several kinds, but they can all be divided into two main categories, subject complements and object complements.

The *subject complement* completes the verb but elaborates or modifies the idea expressed in the subject. It may give another name for the subject, mention a class which includes the subject, or include the subject in a group and sharpen our understanding of it.

> Tam O'Shanter was a *Scotsman*.
> He was an old *soak*.

The student may already be familiar with this type of complement under the name *predicate noun* or *predicate nominative,* since it is the name of something and it appears in the predicate. The subject complement may also give a characteristic or quality of the subject.

> Tam seemed *thirsty*.
> He was *drunk* every Saturday night.

The student may know this type of complement under such names as *predicate adjective, predicate attribute,* or *attribute complement.*

The *object complement* completes the verb by introducing the name of something which is not the subject and which receives the predication of the verb.

> Tam saw a *witch*.
> He admired her short *skirt*.
> The devil was going to roast *him*.
> His wife was nursing her *wrath* to keep it warm.

These object complements are highly varied, and a complete analysis of them is not easy. For instance, in the sentences *Mary made a cake* and *The cake made Jimmie sick,* the cake, clearly, did not make Jimmie in the same sense that Mary made the cake. Fortunately, however, the student need not be able to distinguish all the different sorts of object complements in order to understand fundamental English sentence structure, or to write correct and vigorous sentences. He may already have learned to recognize object complements like those above under the name *direct object.* Two other types of object may be worth identifying. One is called the *indirect object* and is most frequently encountered in sentences declaring that something (the direct object) is given to something or somebody else (the indirect object).

> Tam gave his *nag* (indirect object) a *dig* (direct object) in the ribs.
> Tam's wife gave *him* (indirect object) a *scolding* (direct object).
> She told *him* (indirect object) the *truth* (direct object).

If in doubt the student can identify an indirect object by recasting the sentence so that the indirect object appears in a phrase introduced by *to: Tam's wife gave a scolding to him.* Without the *to,* the indirect object comes before the direct object; with the *to* it follows the direct object.

A similar complement is sometimes called an *objective complement,* since it provides another name for the object or otherwise completes the statement as it affects the object. It comes after the direct object.

> Tam's wife called *him* (direct object) a *blithering blellum* (objective complement).
> The devil wanted to make Tam's *wife* (direct object) a *widow* (objective complement).

12-6 DEVELOPING BASIC PATTERNS

The three basic patterns of the English sentence can be summarized as follows:

(1) SUBJECT | VERB

Something	*does* or *is done*
Blue	fades.
Sopranos	sing.
The book	was printed.

(2) SUBJECT | VERB | OBJECT COMPLEMENT

Something	*does*	*something.*
Tam	sang	a sonnet.
The voters	made	him an ex-president.
Jack	threw	Evelyn the orchid.

(3) SUBJECT | VERB | SUBJECT COMPLEMENT

Something	*is*	*something.*
Life	is	real.
The moon	was	a ship.
The coat	felt	warm.

These patterns control most sentences in English, but adult users of the language seldom employ examples so simple as these. Rather than *Fish swim,* a modern sentence is likely to read more like the following:

> Most fish of which we have any record, either contemporary or geologic, swim with the digestive organs downward.

The core pattern, *fish swim,* is still there, but it has been developed to reveal more precise grammatical relationships.

In general, basic patterns are developed into the complicated sentences of ordinary speaking and writing in three ways:

1. Groups of words rather than single words function as one of the main parts of the pattern, especially the complement.

> Jack hated *washing the car.*
> Jerry learned *how to retouch the photographs.*
> The new boss promised *that nobody would be fired.*
> *Where you find the parrot* is not my concern.

In the first three the italicized word group is a complement, in the last the subject.

2. Words or groups of words can be combined or co-ordinated to serve as any of the main parts of the pattern (see 14).

> *Music* and *poetry* can open *hearts* but not *purses.*
> The children *ran out the door* and *jumped on their bicycles.*
> They knew *what they wanted* and *what they could get.*

In the first example *music* and *poetry* are joined by *and* as the subject and *hearts* and *purses* are joined as compound object complements. In the second, two predicates, verb-complement combinations, are joined by *and.* In the third, two word groups are joined as object complements. Furthermore, complete patterns can be joined to develop complicated sentences.

> Tam sang a sonnet, but his wife made him change his tune.

Almost infinite combinations of patterns and parts of patterns are possible.

3. Any part of the pattern may be modified by a word or group of words subordinated to it (see 15).

When it is exposed to strong sunlight, blue often fades into a dull gray.

The basic pattern is *blue fades;* the beginning word group modifies the whole pattern and *often* and *into a dull gray* modify the verb *fades.*

Most sentences in English, even the longest and most complicated, are constructed in this way; main subject-predicate frameworks, basic patterns, are developed by these three processes. The basic pattern reveals the most important grammatical relationship of English, predication; the development reveals secondary grammatical relationships, co-ordination and subordination. The following sections discuss each of these in more detail.

12-7 THE BASIC SENTENCE PATTERN IN MINOR CONSTRUCTIONS: CLAUSES

We have noticed that groups of words may serve instead of a single word in any of the parts of the basic sentence pattern. We must now add that some of these groups of words follow the basic pattern, although with slight variations from it. That is, they fall into the subject-verb or subject-verb-complement pattern, but they are not themselves the single core of a sentence; they are called *clauses.* The sentences above provide several examples; in *Where you find the parrot is not my concern,* the clause, *where you find the parrot,* serves as subject. In the sentence *They knew what they wanted and what they could get,* two clauses, *what they wanted* and *what they could get,* serve as complement. Kinds of clauses and their uses will be discussed in more detail in Sections 14 and 15.

12-8 THE INCOMPLETE SENTENCE

Often in conversation and sometimes in writing, some parts of the basic sentence are not expressed; they are understood from the context. They are incomplete in form, but they can stand independently in their contexts and are punctuated as sentences. Among the most common are exclamations, like *Oh, wonderful!* or *Incredible!* or *Good morning,* and replies to questions, like *No, Yes,* or *Of course.* Also used in both speaking and writing is the command, in which no subject is expressed: *Go wash the dishes* or *Let sleeping dogs lie.* Our feeling for usual word order is so firm, moreover, that other types of incomplete sentences can make complete statements in context. *How old are you?* might be answered by the complete sentence *I am twenty years old,* but the incomplete sentence *Twenty* is more. likely. *Years old* can be omitted because we habitually state ages in years (we would specify *two decades*), and *I am* can be omitted because it is so obvious a part of the regular word order that the question implies it. The following from Dickens's *Pickwick Papers* concludes with a properly independent incomplete sentence:

> But bless our editorial heart, what a long chapter we have been betrayed into. We had quite forgotten all such petty restrictions as chapters, we solemnly declare. So here goes, to give the goblin a fair start in a new one. A clear stage, and no favour for the goblins, ladies and gentlemen, if you please.

A paragraph from Wolfe's *Of Time and the River* illustrates a modern writer's use of the incomplete sentence, punctuated like a complete sentence and making a statement.

> The coming on of the great earth, the new lands, the enchanted city, the approach, so smoky, blind and stifled, to the ancient web, the old grimed thrilling barricades of Boston. The streets and buildings that slid past that day with such a haunting strange familiarity, the mighty engine steaming to its halt, and the great trainshed dense with smoke and acrid with its smell and full of the slow pantings of a dozen engines, now passive as great cats, the mighty station with the ceaseless throngings of its illimitable life, and all of the murmurous, remote and mighty sounds of time forever held there in the station, together with a tart and nasal voice, a hand'sbreath off that said: "There's hahdly time, but try it if you want."

Such sentences are incomplete as grammatical units because they omit one of the essential elements, subject or verb. They are often successful, as they are above, because basic word order has become standard in English. We anticipate missing elements, and in successful incomplete sentences we automatically supply them. The writer establishes a pattern in his style which helps the reader perceive unexpressed thoughts. The incomplete sentences in the Wolfe paragraph above are subjects; the reader can understand what the writer means to say about these subjects—that they were observed or were part of his experience. Most writers, however, use the incomplete sentence sparingly, except in reports of conversation. It is a special device, to be used for special effects. In the hands of anyone but an expert, it is usually unsuccessful because basic patterns have not been established, and missing ideas cannot be supplied.

Quite different are the incomplete sentences which result from carelessness or ignorance of the English sentence pattern. For instance, the writer who intends to write an independent complete sentence confuses his reader if he begins with a word which signals that the subsequent material is subordinate to something else. *We were eating dinner* is a complete and independent sentence, but *When we were eating dinner* is not. Such unsuccessful incomplete sentences, sentence fragments, are common; and they are serious, partly because they impede communication and partly because they are commonly looked upon as evidence of ignorance or stupidity.

12 Frag

THE COMPLETE SENTENCE;
THE FRAGMENT

Guide to Revision

Complete an incomplete sentence mistakenly used as complete, or join it to another sentence.

Incomplete sentences are useful in English, especially in spoken English. The student writer may need them for reporting conversation or, occasionally, for other special types of writing. But for most student prose the only safe rule is: *Be sure that every group of words punctuated as a sentence contains at least one independent basic sentence pattern with a subject and verb.* Almost all standard writing is done in sentences, and the fragment is a serious error, resulting from carelessness or from confusion about the very basis of English communication, the sentence pattern. Usually, in fact, the fragment is a symptom of a more fundamental weakness in writing, failure to relate ideas logically. As in the examples below, most fragments should not be corrected simply by supplying missing elements; they need to be combined with other sentences to show how ideas work together.

The English verb is often made up of a series of words (see 20-2) centering about one key verb; *was going, was planning to begin, should have been preparing.* These combinations do the work of the verb only when they are complete; omission of a part of them is omission of a crucial part of the sentence. A form customarily used only as part of a verb ceases to function as a verb when it is used by itself; it takes the character of a subject or complement (see 18-2) or modifier (see 22-2).

ORIGINAL

A communistic government attempts to distribute the products of industry equally. It often restricts individual liberty, however. The system requiring careful control of the means of production.

[*The final group of words contains no verb.* Requiring *could work as part of a combination of verbs,* is requiring *or* had been requiring, *but alone it is not a verb. Here it seems only a modifier of* system. *The final group of words is only a name; it does not say something about the system. The error can be corrected, as the revisions show, by making the fragment dependent (1); changing the part of a verb to a verb (2); making the fragment a modifying phrase (3).*]

REVISION

(1) A communistic government attempts to distribute the products of industry equally, but since the system requires careful state control of the means of production, it often restricts individual liberty.

[*Often this method of revision is best, since it clarifies relationships of ideas although it may require, as does this sentence, that the author rethink his statement and subordinate some of it.*]

(2) The system requires careful control of the means of production.

(3) It often restricts individual liberty, however, requiring careful state control of the means of production.

ORIGINAL

The actor had to strap his ankle to his thigh. In this manner giving the impression that he had only one leg.

REVISION

The actor had to strap his ankle to his thigh in order to give the impression that he had only one leg.

A fragment may lack any of the essential portions of the basic sentence pattern, usually the subject or the verb, or both.

ORIGINAL

He failed the course in physics. Either because of laziness or because of stupidity.

[*The final group of words fills no basic sentence pattern. The writer probably only mispunctuated, having meant something like (1). He could*

REVISION

(1) He failed the course in physics, either because of laziness or because of stupidity.

(2) He failed the course in physics. Either laziness or stupidity was his trouble.

(3) Because of either laziness or

ORIGINAL *(Cont.)*

revise also by adding a verb (2) or by making the subordination clearer (3), which is often preferable.]

With the knowledge that, although the documents have been stolen, they have not yet been seen by a foreign agent.
[*The group of words can add information to something else, but it cannot stand alone as a sentence.*]

REVISION *(Cont.)*

stupidity, he failed the course in physics.

We know that, although the documents have been stolen, they have not yet been seen by a foreign agent.
[*The revision adds a subject and verb to make the fragment a sentence.*]

Even an expression containing all elements of a basic pattern cannot stand independently if a subordinating word signals its dependence.

ORIGINAL

In the morning Thoreau was released from jail. Although he still refused to pay the tax.
[*Although labels the second group of words as dependent, incapable of standing as an independent sentence. The fragment can be joined to the independent clause it depends upon (1); or it can be made independent by removing* although *(2).*]

REVISION

(1) Although he still refused to pay the tax, Thoreau was released from jail in the morning.
(2) In the morning Thoreau was released from jail, but he still refused to pay the tax.
[*The second revision alters the meaning, but the meaning of the fragment itself is uncertain—just because it is a fragment.*]

Names may be mistaken for sentences.

ORIGINAL

Looking out toward the horizon, she saw only the old cabin in which Mary had been born. A single cottonwood that had escaped the drought. The apparently boundless expanse of sunburned prairie.
[*The last two groups are actually additional objects of* saw; *they name and do not tell anything about* what *they name. They are not complete. They can be placed in the usual word order as complements (1), or they can be made sentences by adding verbs (2).*]

REVISION

(1) Looking out toward the horizon, she saw only the old cabin in which Mary had been born, a single cottonwood that had escaped the drought, and the apparently boundless expanse of sunburned prairie.
(2) Looking out toward the horizon, she saw only the old cabin in which Mary had been born. A single cottonwood that had escaped the drought stood near it. The apparently boundless expanse of sunburned prairie spread into the distance.

EXERCISE 12

A. Choose at random any passage of English prose 200–300 words long. Select it from one of your texts or any other book easily available. Analyze the structure of the sentences, pointing out the subjects, verbs, and complements in each. Observe the word order and copy any sentences which deviate from the usual actor-action pattern. Can you see reasons for the deviation?

B. Analyze a theme you have written, underlining subjects, verbs, and complements in each sentence. Mark any sentences which deviate from usual word order; revise these sentences so that they fit the actor-action pattern, and judge whether the new or old version is more effective.

C. Point out subjects, verbs, and complements in the sentences in the following paragraph:

> We have another neighbor, whose name is Bates; he keeps cows. This year our gate has been fixed; but my young peach trees near the fence are accessible from the road; and Bates's cows walk along that road morning and evening. The sound of a cow-bell is pleasant in the twilight. Sometimes, after dark, we hear the mysterious curfew tolling along the road, and then with a louder peal it stops before our fence and again tolls itself off in the distance. The result is my peach trees are as bare as bean-poles.
>
> —FREDERICK S. COZZENS, *Living in the Country*

D. The passage below contains a number of fragments used as sentences. Revise the passage, using methods outlined above, to make the fragments complete sentences or combine them with other sentences.

> (1) Catherine II, called Catherine the Great, came to the throne of Russia in 1762. (2) Her reign being the most notable of those which followed the long rule of Peter the Great. (3) Although she was actually not a Russian by birth, Catherine remained on the Russian throne for thirty-four years. (4) Since she was a German princess whose marriage to Peter III had been arranged by Frederick the Great. (5) Peter III being half-insane when he took the throne.
>
> (6) Catherine, a despot who wished to be regarded as an "enlight-ened" despot like Frederick II of Prussia, more concerned actually with maintaining prestige than spreading culture through her country. (7) She continued some of the work of Peter the Great, ruling the country firmly, and strengthening the central authority by administrative reorganization. (8) Divisions of the government under appointed governors and vice-governors, all responsible to the tsa-

rina. (9) A church dependent for its property and power on the desires of the central authority. (10) By maintaining a strong foreign policy and striking her rivals when they were weak, she established the international position of the Russian empire. (11) A war against the Ottoman Empire, 1768–1774, was highly successful. (12) Which led to navigation rights for Russian ships and added considerably to Russian territory. (13) Poland, weakened by internal strife, and easily preyed upon by surrounding empires. (14) By 1795 Poland had virtually ceased to exist as an independent state. (15) Her territory partitioned among Austria, Prussia, and Russia. (16) With Catherine getting the lion's share.

(17) Catherine's internal policies did bring about a number of reforms. (18) The establishment, for example, of schools and academies. (19) Reform, however, being carefully regulated. (20) In order to prevent genuine enlightenment of the masses which might weaken the position of the aristocracy.

E. In the passages below, identify fragments (a) which do not have subjects, (b) those which do not have predicates, and (c) those which have neither subjects nor predicates. Revise the passage so that all fragments necessary to the composition become parts of sentences.

(1) Aunt Agnes, who was one of the gentlest women I have ever known, although that was not the reason she was my favorite aunt. (2) She being quite a nuisance to her husband at times, Uncle Joe, who was kind enough but did not believe in carrying things too far. (3) Just one of those things. (4) Uncle Joe being a very good shot, and there being a turkey shoot that year at the factory where Uncle Joe worked, where, in fact, he was the oldest workman in point of service. (5) Down by the levee, just north of the railroad tracks. (6) Uncle Joe brought home a turkey, a fine big gobbler, and chained up in the back yard to get fat for Thanksgiving. (7) Aunt Agnes, who had the notion that turkeys ate only wild rice, and that got pretty expensive, considering what wild rice costs. (8) She doted on that turkey. (9) Got it to eat out of her hand, and would stand by the half hour looking at it. (10) Called it pet names, Little Turkey-urkey, and the like. (11) And occasionally, as though she were joking—and especially when Uncle Joe had just eaten a big dinner and was feeling good—as though she did not really mean that they should not eat Little Turkey-urkey, but that was what she suggested. (12) Nonsense. (13) Uncle Joe said.

(14) Then it was the day before Thanksgiving, and Uncle Joe brought home a hand axe from the shop in the factory. (15) Aunt Agnes, meeting him at the door, telling him he must not kill the turkey, and she would not cook it if he did, and she would gag on it if she tried to take a bite. (16) Please, she begged, could they not buy a turkcy? And buy one they did. (17) Aunt Agnes all this time

very grateful to Uncle Joe for being so understanding, and promising that they would keep the turkey just a little while. (18) Before Christmas, trade it for another turkey, and then she would not mind the turkey they traded for being killed.

(19) Then the day after Thanksgiving, and Aunt Agnes feeding Little Turkey-urkey, thinking surely he looked sad, sad enough to die. (20) She was sure he was getting thinner. (21) Thinner every day. (22) Obviously being lonesome, and why would he not be lonesome without any woman turkey? (23) Accordingly, the next day, which was of course Saturday. (24) Uncle Joe had to drive out to a turkey farm and buy a turkey hen. (25) Christmas came and passed. (26) Then New Year's. (27) And Turkey-urkey and his hen sitting peaceful in Aunt Agnes' back yard, getting fatter and fatter. (28) Eating wild rice at two dollars a pound. (29) In those days wild rice being only two dollars a pound. (30) Never did eat those turkeys and both drowned in a flood the next spring.

13

Predication; Controlling the Basic Pattern

For Guide to Revision, see page 226

For clarity and precision all parts of the basic sentence pattern must interact clearly and logically.

Since the basic sentence pattern is the core of expression and communication in English, all parts of the sentence must be so chosen that they can work together and must be so handled that they do.

13-1 MAKING THE PARTS FIT

The following sentence has the structure of the basic pattern, but it does not communicate.

> Any person would have meant the failure.

We know the meanings of the words and can see how they are related grammatically, but the ideas for which the words stand do not make sense when put into this pattern. Now observe the sentence from which the above basic pattern was taken:

> Any person ill on the day of that first performance would have meant the failure of the entire summer theater.

Some kind of meaning can be extracted, but the sentence seems obscure and confused because the basic subject-verb-complement pattern is the nonsense sentence quoted above. The reader can guess what the writer meant to say, but, strictly, the writer produced only nonsense. Specifically, the writer did not express as his subject the threat he wanted to talk about, illness. He probably meant:

> The illness of any member of the cast on the day of that first performance would have caused the failure of the entire summer theater.

The sentence remains awkward, however, and in most contexts the following would be better:

> The entire summer theater would probably have failed if any member of the cast had been ill on the day of that first performance.

A better subject allows the use of a more vigorous verb, and permits a more vigorous sentence. Or consider another sentence:

> The basis for the continuing unrest, which was partly misunderstanding and partly understanding too well what our motives were, held little hope among our representatives for success in negotiating new treaties.

The words seem at first glance to communicate; they sound like a sentence. But they communicate only confusion because the basic pattern is confused: *The basis held little hope.* The subject, verb, and complement do not make sense together, even though the length of the sentence momentarily obscures the confusion. With a new subject and verb the sentence comes nearer sense:

> Our representatives had little hope of negotiating new treaties because of the continuing unrest, based partly on misunderstanding our motives and partly on understanding them too well.

As a first essential to clear communication, then, the writer should concentrate on his central predication, the basic sentence pattern. He must not allow the development of the sentence, compounds or modifiers, to obscure the main pattern and betray him into meaningless predication. He must select subjects, verbs, and complements that will work logically together, being especially suspicious of abstract or general terms.

13-2   CHOOSING SUBJECTS

As the sentences above illustrate, the choice of subject usually directs the remainder of the predication. Obviously subjects should be chosen with care, but often they are not. For example, a student decides to write a theme about his decision to come to college. He writes down the first words that come into his head: "The reason . . ." With the words, although he may not realize it, he has committed himself to the pattern of his opening sentence. He has chosen a subject for the sentence, because in English the first word that can be a subject usually becomes one. Aware that he has not yet said much, the student goes on: "The reason why I came to college. . . ." At this stage, his instinct for the basic English sentence pattern tells him that he needs a verb, but not many verbs will go with reason and make much sense; accordingly, he turns to a verb that does not commit him to much of anything and to an old formula: "The reason why I came to college is because. . . ." He is getting more and more involved, but he does not turn back: "The reason why I came to college is because, there being a law you have to have a degree for a license in the field of embalming in this state . . ." He has not yet written a sentence, but the string of words is getting long and he finishes off with ". . . which is my goal in life." The result is badly written in a variety of ways, but the trouble began with an unfortunate choice of subject, which led the writer into a meaningless predication: "The reason is. . . ." The predication requires a complement, and no workable complement has been provided. Suppose, however, that while the student was struggling with his sentence his roommate had come in and asked, "Say, Jim, why did you decide to come to college?" He might have replied with something like, "I want to be a mortician, and to get a license you have to have a degree." This is no literary triumph, but it is a successful sentence, largely because the student started with a concrete subject, *I,* instead of an abstract word like *reason,* which could not be much involved in action.

To control predication, then, the writer should start by choosing an appropriate subject; the following practical suggestions can save student writers from many verbal quagmires.

1. On the whole, make the subject the actor if there is one; or use as the grammatical subject the actual subject, what the sentence is mainly about.

2. Whenever possible, prefer concrete, specific subjects to abstract or general ones. Especially treacherous are abstract words which usually must be followed by *is* or *was—reason, explanation, conclusion, situation, attitude,* and so on. Often, of course, a

context demands a sentence beginning with such a subject, but more often a better sentence emerges when such subjects are avoided.

3. If a sentence causes trouble, try finding a new subject and starting over. Often you can ask yourself, "What am I trying to say?" and make the simplest answer you can. The subject in your answer often makes the best subject for the sentence you are trying to write.

13-3   THE PREDICATE—VERBS AND COMPLEMENTS

The subject establishes the basic pattern of a sentence, but the verb and complement carry the action, do the predicating. In the modern sentence most of what the sentence has to say is likely to appear in the predicate, which may be a verb and complement or a verb with modifiers which act very much like complements. For example, *Those boys are lying* may be said to have no complement if *are lying* is considered the verb. The sentence indicates that the boys are telling lies, but the following probably makes no comment about their truthfulness: *Those boys are lying on the beach.* Conventionally, *on the beach* would be called a modifier of the verb, but it serves the function of a complement because it is needed to complete, to determine the meaning of the verb. The sentence could be analyzed by calling *are lying on* the verb and *the beach* an object complement after it. Just to complicate matters, notice also that different complements or modifiers have different effects: *Those boys are lying in their teeth.*

Perhaps this is part of what having a distributive grammar means, that our words work together with no very clear grammatical distinctions between them; but however we analyze this and other English sentences, the fact remains that modern English predicates are often complex and often carry the burden of the meaning of the sentence. Sentences like the following appear frequently in modern prose:

> The painting gave me the impression that an artist had waked up on a foggy morning after a dream-filled night and hurriedly recorded on his canvas details from several of his nightmares, which had apparently been populated mainly by withered tulips throwing poached eggs at one another.

The subject and verb open the sentence and establish its pattern, the subject-verb-complement pattern most common in English. All the remainder of the sentence, the part that carries most of the meaning, is an elaborate complement, an indirect object, *me,* and a direct object, *impression,* followed by a string of interlocking modifiers explaining the object. Users of English usually handle such complex complements with little difficulty.

13-4   PREDICATION WITH *TO BE*

Difficulty with predicates may develop, however, when the writer selects for his basic pattern a verb which carries little meaning. Most verbs do stand for an idea; their meaning can be described in the dictionary. A few, however, often do not mean; they rather serve as function words (see 23), as connectives which do not mean but specify how other words are related grammatically. Of these, the handiest, and also the most troublesome, is the verb *to be,* which appears most frequently as *am, is, was, were,* or as *been* in combinations like *has been.* The verb may carry some meaning (*To be or not to be; Whatever is, is right*); it means, as the dictionary points out, to exist. Often, however, it has other uses. It may imply definition or classification (*Music is an art*), supply a name (*This is John*), connect a subject with a modifier (*The apple is ripe*), or act as part of another verb (*The picture is being made now*). In all these the "meaning" of the verb is relatively insignificant; the verb mainly joins or links other meanings. Used in this way, to link a subject and a complement, the verb *to be* almost always implies some kind of identity between subject and complement. Compare the following:

> The coat is in the closet.
> Happiness is where you find it.
> Happiness is oblivion.
> Two and two are four.
> My sister is a trained nurse.
> Alcoholism is the root of his trouble.
> Beauty is truth.
> Life is a dream.

In the first two examples the verb is modified by *in the closet* and *where you find it;* it retains much of the meaning of *exists* and does not link the subject with a complement. In the other sentences, however, the verb *to be* resembles the equals sign in mathematics; the sentences form a kind of equation. Whatever comes before the verb is conceived to be equal, from at least one point of view, with what comes after it.

13 **Pred**

PREDICATION; CONTROLLING
THE BASIC PATTERN

Guide to Revision

Examine the subject, verb, and complement basic to the sentence and revise so that their meanings work together to make sense.

13a   FITTING SUBJECT TO VERB TO COMPLEMENT   Pred a

The meaning of the subject must fit logically with the verb and the complement. Often when sentences are not clear, the writer has not chosen the subject he intends to talk about or has buried the real subject in a modifier.

ORIGINAL

My mother being unable to resist installment buying meant the difference between a comfortable existence and constant fear of poverty.
[Mother *makes no sense as a subject for* meant. *The subject probably intended is buried as a modifier.*]

The cowboy's job seems about to be replaced in many areas by helicopters and jeeps.
[*Not the job but the cowboy is being replaced.*]

The setting of this picturesque little town was filled with a colorful history.

REVISION

My mother's inability to resist installment buying meant the difference between a comfortable existence and constant fear of poverty.
[*Not* mother, *but* mother's weakness *was probably intended as the subject.*]

The cowboy seems about to be replaced in many areas by helicopters and jeeps.

This picturesque little town had a colorful history.

ORIGINAL (*Cont.*)

[*The setting was not filled. The writer should pick an appropriate subject and start over.*]

The lack of a proper diet and work as heavy as lumbering demanded a man with a strong body.
[*The second part of the compound subject fits logically with the verb, but the first does not.*]

REVISION (*Cont.*)

[*The writer may have meant this or something else, but the revision at least makes sense.*]

Work as heavy as lumbering, carried on without a proper diet, demanded a man with a strong body.
[*The main subject is selected and the inappropriate idea becomes a modifier.*]

The verb must not stand for some action which the subject is logically incapable of performing. Errors of this sort may result from careless diction (see 25).

ORIGINAL

They should not have allowed such tragedies to exist in their community.
[*Tragedies* do not *exist.*]

REVISION

(1) They should not have allowed conditions in their community which further such tragedies.
(2) They should not have allowed such tragedies to occur in their community.

Mr. Johnson's disagreement with Wilde was apparently done after a good deal of thought.
[*A disagreement is not* done. *The writer should be careful of the verb,* to do, *which is often misused.*]

(1) Mr. Johnson's disagreement with Wilde was apparently entered into after a good deal of thought.
(2) Apparently, Mr. Johnson broke with Wilde only after a good deal of thought.

The central idea of the poem shows how in youth all is beautiful.

The central idea of the poem is that in youth all is beautiful.

Especially when verbs refer to subjects in another clause, the writer must be careful that they do not represent actions inappropriate for the remainder of the sentence.

ORIGINAL

Perhaps there are omissions which should have been included.
[*Even though the verb* should have been included *is in a subordinate clause, it must make sense with* omissions, *represented by* which.

REVISION

(1) Perhaps there are omissions which should have been remedied.
(2) Perhaps material has been omitted which should have been included.
[*The second revision is more thorough and clearer.*]

A complement must have a meaning which makes it logically capable of receiving the action of the verb.

ORIGINAL

He managed during his life to defy all the traditional qualities of an outstanding politician.
[To defy qualities *makes no sense. The basic sentence is not logical.*]

Economists are still piecing together the over-all situation.
[*One cannot piece together a situation. If the writer insists on the trite metaphor, he must carry it through.*]

REVISION

He managed during his life to defy all the traditions associated with success in politics.

(1) Economists are still piecing together a picture of the period.
(2) Economists do not yet understand all that occurred.

13b   EQUATIONS WITH VERB *TO BE*   Pred b; Eq

Sentences with the verb *to be* have many important uses in English (see 13-4), but they may intrude so frequently into writing that they weaken it (see 17-1 to 17-3), especially when they link a subject and complement carelessly. Equations in writing, of course, do not have to be mathematically accurate; life obviously is not a dream. But the equation must link ideas that can plausibly be equated. Abstractions in such patterns are especially treacherous.

Ranching is an idea that has always attracted me.

Ranching is not an idea; the implausible equation spoils the sentence. It could be made accurate.

Ranching is a profession that has always attracted me.

But even this better equation does little but add words; the sentence is clearer without the equation:

Ranching has always attracted me.

When a sentence implies an equation with *to be,* the equation should be plausible. Eliminating the equation often improves the sentence.

ORIGINAL

The only knowledge I have had about horses is living on a farm and raising them.
[Knowledge *is not* living.]

REVISION

The only knowledge I have of horses comes from living on a farm and raising them.
[*Changing the verb makes the sentence logical.*]

ORIGINAL *(Cont.)*

Perhaps the most important action regarding the teacher's technique of adjusting behavior problems in the classroom is her attitude toward the problem child.

[*An* action *is not an* attitude, *and the sentence is further complicated by other inexact constructions. Various revisions are possible.*]

REVISION *(Cont.)*

(1) Perhaps the most important decisions for the teacher facing problems of classroom behavior grow out of her attitude toward the problem child.

(2) The teacher who wishes to solve her problems of classroom behavior should be careful of the attitude she adopts toward the problem child.

When a sentence is so constructed that a form of *to be* seems to be leading to a complement, the complement must appear and must be in some way equal to the subject or must be a quality of the subject. Often the substitution of another verb for *to be* improves the sentence.

ORIGINAL

The only uniform I have been issued was in camp last August.

[*The sentence is unclear because* was *links no complement with* uniform. *Either supply a complement* (*1*) *or change the verb* (*2*).]

The process of cutting hay in the early days was by means of the scythe, which was manipulated by hand.

REVISION

(1) The only uniform I have been issued is the one I received in camp last August.

(2) I have been issued only one uniform, which I received in camp last August.

(1) In the early days hay was cut by hand with a scythe.

(2) Pioneers mowed with a scythe.

Sentences are usually awkward if they contain plural and singular expressions carelessly equated.

ORIGINAL

The trouble was the many difficulties which complicated the sending of the invitations.

[*Trouble is singular and* difficulties *plural. As a result the meaning is not precise.*]

REVISION

(1) The trouble was that many difficulties complicated the sending of the invitations.

(2) The trouble grew out of complications in sending the invitations.

13c   *IS-BECAUSE, IS-WHERE, IS-WHEN* PATTERNS   Pred c

A clause specifying place or time and following the verb *to be* may cause trouble.

This is where we are going.
The mathematics class is where I catch up on my reading.
Tuesday is when I go to the doctor.

These are clear enough and might be useful in some contexts, although the last two are roundabout and would be stronger with the actor as subject:

I catch up on my reading in the mathematics class.
I go to the doctor Tuesday.

Consider, however, the following:

Radicalism is when you jump to conclusions.
The study of mathematics is where I get my lowest grades.

These assume different relationships between subject and complement, and the equations are not plausible. Whatever radicalism may be, it is not time, and study is not place. The sentences need rethinking, to make the equation plausible or avoid it:

Radicalism usually involves jumping to conclusions.
I get my lowest grades in mathematics.

Some constructions of this sort are not entirely illogical; notice the following:

The reason Johnson wrote *Rasselas* was because he needed money for his mother's funeral.

The clause beginning with *because* does supply the reason, and good writers have occasionally had recourse to a construction like this in complicated structures; but such equations are often confusing because the sentence pattern at first suggests that *because* is the complement rather than a signal for the clause which is the complement. At best such constructions may be needlessly wordy. In most contexts the sentence above would be better if revised to something like *Johnson wrote* Rasselas *because he needed money for his mother's funeral.*

ORIGINAL

A syllogism *is where* you use a major and minor premise to get a logical answer.
[*A syllogism is not a place.*]

REVISION

In a syllogism, you use a major and minor premise to obtain a logical answer.

ORIGINAL (*Cont.*)

The reason I do not like herring *is because* they taste so fishy.

Probation *is when* you are not eligible for competition.

REVISION (*Cont.*)

I do not like herring because they taste fishy.

On probation you are not eligible for competition.

13d   SHIFTS IN STRUCTURE   Pred d; Shift

Among the most confusing disruptions of the subject-verb-complement relationship are those which result from careless shifting of the structure or some part of it. The same sort of forgetfulness probably causes unnecessary shifts in patterns from one clause to the succeeding one. (See also 14 for shifts violating parallelism, 20c for shifts in time, and 18 for shifts in person.)

ORIGINAL

For information concerning almost any happening which is too minor to be found in periodical articles may be located through *The New York Times Index.*
[*The writer starts with one construction and shifts to another; thus the "sentence" never acquires a subject.*]

Any passage that pleased him he tried to write something in the same style.
[*What promises to be the subject,* passage, *becomes a new subject,* he.]

REVISION

(1) For information concerning almost any happening which is too minor to be found in periodical articles the research worker may use *The New York Times Index.*
(2) *The New York Times Index* will serve to locate information concerning almost any happening too minor to be reported in periodicals.

(1) Any passage which pleased him was likely to become the model for a passage in the same style.
(2) He would imitate any passage which pleased him.

Shifts from one pattern to another in successive clauses or from one subject to another can be confusing.

ORIGINAL

I looked out over the pines toward the tiny lake a thousand feet below us. You could hardly see the cabin where we had spent the night.

After the textbook had been mastered, he had no trouble with chemistry.
[*The impersonal passive construction shifts awkwardly to the active with the subject* he.]

REVISION

I looked out over the pines toward the tiny lake a thousand feet below us. I could hardly see the cabin where we had spent the night.

After he had mastered the textbook, he had no trouble with chemistry.

A. The sentences below contain faulty predication; that is, the basic sentence in each is illogical. Analyze subject-verb-complement relationships, and revise each sentence so that the subject, verb, and complement make sense together.

1. Roads covered with gravel or ice double the stopping distance.

2. A parrot can be stroked on the chest, but anywhere else usually costs the admirer a sore finger.

3. Her mental attitude is disturbed and may not return for several hours.

4. Abraham learned that necessities come by dint of hard labor.

5. For a person to not obey the Duke's wishes would mean the person's death.

6. The friends that you make often result from your manners.

7. A girl may have some classes after lunch, but if there isn't she may study.

8. All the people in the novel seemed to have a very good evaluation of themselves.

9. This method took as long as three days to plant three hundred acres.

10. Poor people are often impressed by the material evidences which they see which can be purchased with money.

11. For a rifle team to become a success, many points must be accomplished.

12. The amount of money lost by both the strikers and the employers took a matter of years in order to regain them.

13. The main idea of Donne's *Song* seems to be about a man who has been jilted by his mistress.

14. Before we can criticize the essay, fundamentalists in the sense they were used in the essay must be explained.

15. These are basic traits of character which I hope to attain.

16. The setting of the play takes place in Athens.

17. Many citizens practiced an anti-Christian cult during the period.

18. It does not seem plausible that God makes him victorious as much as the confidence the man has in himself.

19. Constant experimentation with different techniques of painting increased her versatility and incidentally her composition.

20. Any person that annoyed him he tried to make the person uncomfortable by sarcastic remarks.

21. In two years in the club she managed to break every situation required by the rules.

22. As soon as they are corrected these disadvantages will improve the club a great deal.

23. The theme of the *Tempest* is set in two places.

24. A people needing food and insecure in their jobs ultimately causes revolution.

25. Pineridge is my grandmother's house in which so many happy days took place.

B. The sentences below contain inaccurate equations linked by forms of the verb *to be*. Identify subjects and complements in each sentence. Then revise each sentence, either by using a more expressive verb than *to be* or by changing subject or complement so that they work together. Make any other necessary alterations.

1. The most dominant characteristic of Spanish architecture is in the element of contrast.

2. Liberalism has always been a pleasing connotation to Americans.

3. The plans of a log cabin should be very compact and not too roomy.

4. The value of this book, in my opinion, was in the fact that it showed more than one cause of juvenile delinquency.

5. The story is where a group of men find themselves the sole survivors of a civilization destroyed by war.

6. The reason I was nervous is because I used to stutter.

7. A fireplace planned from a diagram is the best clue to a comfortable living room.

8. A person's education is a very important task and one that may decide his whole future.

9. The purpose of a Geiger counter is with it you can find uranium.

10. The subject of *The Washerwoman's Day* is about the situation in which a girl finds herself.

11. One other example of Shakespeare's humor being portrayed in his characters was Bottom.

12. A basic method of binding books is the use of cords to which each signature is stitched.

13. Listening to good records is where I get real enjoyment.

14. The primary purpose of colleges was intended to be an institution of higher learning.

15. The most outstanding of their rivalries were over a woman.

16. A follower and a leader are both qualities he must possess to enable him to achieve his goals.

17. Journalism is not a romantic life as some books play it up to be, and as some people believe; it is a hard job for anyone to undertake.

18. It can clearly be seen from the story that the desire to return Cassio to her husband's favor was because she honestly felt that it was best for him.

19. The most important reason for the growth of the Diesel locomotive is its many advantages over steam locomotives.

20. The source of my material is from two books.

21. A logical grammar for modern Americans would be to teach them the present system that we now have.

22. A tragedy is when all the main characters die at the end.

23. College spirit is an experience long remembered after school is over.

24. The only halt for undemocratic ideas is through the education of the masses.

25. In the play, the weavers' situation, which in broad terms is a people born into a society where they must struggle to develop in all ways, is a basic problem of humanity.

C. Recall the suggestions in 13-2 for choosing subjects. Then examine the two sorts of words below, one marked S, as potential subjects, the other V, as potential verbs. Then from the group marked S choose one of the likely and the least likely subjects. Using one of the verbs, write a sentence using each subject. Then compare the two sentences for the economy of structure and for the amount you get said in each sentence.

1. S—reason, I, deal, intentions, Randy; V—work(s), am(is).

2. S—circumstances, fish, pickerel, conditions, sharks; V—were, leap, feed, appear.

3. S—superiority, characteristics, character, students, men, women; V—are, reveal, grow, show, reflect.

4. S—he, she, problem, difficulty, Ronald; V—presents, studies, experiments, searches, tries to discover.

5. S—Egypt, international affairs, difficulties, problems, solution, secretary of state; V—reveal(s), explain(s), is, fights.

6. S—tendency, development, Picasso, Michelangelo, modern art, reason; V—is, develops, indicates, continues.

7. S—rockets, developments, indications, expectations, Harry, Senator Smith; V—argued, exceeded, was (were), beat, appeared.

8. S—dancing, entertainment, we, Jane and I, opportunity; V—danced, learned, whirled, struggled, found.

9. S—acceleration, transportation, newness, sports car, Sandra, he; V—screeched, rolled, was, missed, hit, swerved, appeared.

10. S—play, *Hamlet,* dramatic entertainment, enjoyable evening, actor; V—was, reveled, produced, provided, charmed, made.

D. Identify subjects of the sentences in the passage below. Then, substitute for each subject some other word in the passage, or another word of your own which is not a synonym for the subject, and change the construction to make sense. Which version is briefer, yours or Hardy's? Which is more effective?

The lamb, revived by the warmth, began to bleat, and the sound entered Gabriel's ears and brain with an instant meaning, as expected sounds will. Passing from the profoundest sleep to the most alert wakefulness with the same ease that had accompanied the reverse operation, he looked at his watch, found that the hour hand had shifted again, put on his hat, took the lamb in his arms, and carried it into the darkness. After placing the little creature with its mother, he stood and carefully examined the sky, to ascertain the time of night from the altitudes of the stars.

The Dog-star and Aldebaran, pointing to the restless Pleiades, were half way up the Southern sky, and between them hung Orion, which gorgeous constellation never burnt more vividly than now, as it swung itself forth above the rim of the landscape. Castor and Pollux with their quiet shine were on the meridian; the barren and gloomy Square of Pegasus was creeping round to the north-west; far away through the plantation, Vega sparkled like a lamp suspended amid the leafless trees, and Cassiopeia's chair stood daintily poised on the uppermost boughs.

"One o'clock" said Gabriel.

                                    —THOMAS HARDY, *Far from the Madding Crowd*

E. Select four passages 100 to 150 words in length, one from a current newspaper, one from a current novel, one from a magazine like *Harper's,* the *Atlantic Monthly,* or *The Reporter,* and one from a textbook. Count the number of forms of the verb *to be* in each, and the number of verbs not forms of *to be.* Study the styles of the four works, and make any observations you can as to the effectiveness of the four writers, as writers, and what effect their use of the verb *to be* has upon their writing. Report your findings in a written statement, giving the facts and your conclusions.

14

Co-ordination

and Parallelism

For Guide to Revision, see page 242

For most purposes the basic sentence pattern requires development; co-ordination, revealed in parallel structure, provides means to develop complicated ideas.

"I see the kitty" is a sentence, and within its uses nothing is wrong with it, but few writers who have progressed beyond nursery school are likely to have much use for it. Modern life is sophisticated and complicated, and communication must be, also. Even relatively simple situations usually require a somewhat varied use of the basic sentence pattern, and modern life is not usually simple. Particularly, the kind of intellectual life for which students are presumably preparing is not simple; it requires close and exact reading of and listening to difficult and often abstruse matter. It requires the ability to draft sophisticated prose adequate to complicated subject matter. Usually, adult prose, if it is to be adequate and yet economical, must employ at least some moderately long sentences with elaborate and varied structures. Learning to write such sentences and to deal with them effortlessly when others use them in speaking or writing provides part of the essential equipment of any modern cultured person. Thus, although the basic sentence pattern in English is relatively simple, working English sentences mostly are not (see 12), and much of the secret to clear and vigorous writing is to be sought in the developing and controlling of the basic pattern.

14-1 CO-ORDINATION FOR DEVELOPMENT

Developing the basic sentence pattern requires secondary patterns, of which the two most useful types can be distinguished as co-ordination and subordination, co-ordination being the simpler. In its simplest form the pattern is no more complicated than *John and Mary, ham and eggs*. This pattern is so elemental that any child can handle it as soon as he has acquired the basic sentence pattern. In fact, childish talk is likely to be a combination of the basic and the co-ordinational sentence patterns—"I took my fish pole, and I took Rover, and I took my Daddy, and I went down to the fish pond." That is, *co-ordination* is bringing like things together, combining them; *parallelism* is a term often used to indicate the patterns which reveal co-ordination. Naturally, they are not all as simple and easy to handle as *ham and eggs*. The author of the following was a New York newspaper man, and presumably a practiced writer; he certainly knew the patterns of co-ordination, but he here failed to use them carefully:

> Among the items in the collection are the only known document bearing the signatures of Queen Elizabeth and Sir Walter Raleigh and a cigar-store Indian.

By fitting his words inappropriately into the pattern, the writer attributed more skill to the Indian than he probably intended. Co-ordination can be used for development with most important elements of the sentence; the various patterns and their adaptations warrant study.

14-2 CO-ORDINATION OF CLAUSES

Among the grammatical groups which can be co-ordinated within the sentence are varieties of the basic sentence pattern itself. Consider the following:

> The sun had set. A cool breeze was blowing across the lake. The tiny cabin was still too warm to be comfortable.

Here are three sentences; each can be considered as independent. One concerns the sun, one the breeze, and one the cabin. But more revealingly, there is only one idea here, that in spite of certain cooling agents the cabin was still too hot. Obviously, the three sentences had better become one, somewhat as follows:

> Although the sun had set and a cool breeze was blowing across the lake, the tiny cabin was still too warm to be comfortable.

The actor-action-goal patterns of the three short sentences are preserved here, but the patterns work together to make a single sentence with a larger purpose than any of the sentences had separately. As we have seen in 12-7, these groups of words which complete the sentence pattern but which are themselves parts of a sentence are called *clauses.* Clauses of like nature can be co-ordinated; consider the following:

> Marriage and hanging go by destiny. Matches are made in heaven.
> Marriage and hanging go by destiny; matches are made in heaven.
> Marriage and hanging go by destiny, but matches are made in heaven.

In the first version, the two ideas stand as independent sentences, although they are obviously to be taken together. In the second version the ideas are still independent—neither relies on the other—but their inter-relation is emphasized by their being joined into one sentence with a semicolon between them. What were formerly sentences have become independent clauses. Robert Burton understandably preferred the idea in this form. The third version also contains two clauses which could serve as independent sentences, with the contrast between them emphasized by the signal word, *but.* For the punctuation of such sentences see 27c.

Not all clauses can be co-ordinated because they are not all of like nature; that is, they have different uses and follow different clause patterns. Conventionally, clauses are divided into two sorts, *independent* and *dependent.* Grammatically, the distinction is not very sharp in English; but of course independent clauses can co-ordinate only with other clauses like themselves, independent with independent, dependent with dependent. For purposes of sentence structure the distinction is sharp enough, since we recognize like patterns. For working purposes we can say that clauses like those above, concerning marriage and matches, are *independent clauses;* as they stand they could be independent sentences. Dependent clauses employ the subject-verb-complement pattern, but the position of the clause in the sentence or a relationship word indicates that the clause in its present form could not stand as a sentence. Notice the following witticism, attributed to Fred Allen:

> He is so narrow-minded that, if he fell on a pin, it would blind him in both eyes.

The clauses *he fell on a pin* and *it would blind him in both eyes* are here dependent; their dependence is signaled by the reference words *that* and *if*. Distinctions between clauses can better be considered in connection with subordination (see 15); here we need only notice that clauses which are co-ordinate in use should be parallel in form.

14-3 CO-ORDINATING LESSER SENTENCE ELEMENTS

Sentence elements lesser than clauses can be co-ordinated, and often ideas which might be expressed in a sentence or a clause may be reduced to a phrase or a word co-ordinated with another phrase or word. Consider the following:

> In the Indian Parliament a member may call his colleague a simian. In the Indian Parliament a member may not call his colleague a baboon.

Obviously, the sentences are alike except for one part of the complement. The whole can be said with one sentence having a co-ordinate complement:

> In the Indian Parliament a member may call his colleague a simian, but not a baboon.

Buffon was using a similar sort of co-ordination, although he co-ordinated more parallel complements, when he wrote:

> The human race excepted, the elephant is the most respected of animals. . . . We allow him the judgment of the beaver, the dexterity of the monkey, the sentiment of the dog, and the advantages of strength, size, and longevity.

Using a sentence for each of the elephant's virtues would expand the statement to a paragraph. In these sentences, only the complements are co-ordinated, but most elements of a sentence can be used co-ordinately, and most sentences of any complexity have more than one sort of co-ordination. For instance, H. L. Mencken recorded his disapproval of zoos as follows, without, of course, italicizing his co-ordinate elements:

> The sort of man who likes to spend his time watching *a cage of monkeys chase one another,* or *a lion gnaw its tail,* or *a lizard catch flies,* is precisely the sort of man whose mental weakness should be *combated* at the public expense, not *fostered.*

14-4 CO-ORDINATION AND PARALLEL STRUCTURE

Co-ordination can be more or less elaborate. When a zoo keeper remarked that "We need good, strong cages to protect the animals from the public," he was using co-ordination very simply to join the words *good* and *strong.* On the other hand, the same device can be used to knit together extremely complicated structures; for instance, in the sixteenth century, balanced and contrasted constructions became a fad, and when John Lyly wrote the following he was gaining a number of effects, along with having fun with language:

> This young gallant, of more wit than wealth, and yet of more wealth than wisdom, seeing himself inferior to none in pleasant conceits, thought himself superior to all in honest conditions, insomuch that he deemed himself so apt to all things that he gave himself almost to nothing but practicing of those things commonly which are incident to these sharp wits, fine phrases, smooth quipping, merry taunting, using jesting without mean, and abusing mirth without measure.
>
> *—Euphues*

The style is exaggerated, but the passage illustrates how intricately words, phrases, and clauses can be balanced against one another in writing.

However complicated or simple the co-ordination may be, the pattern of the sentence should be clear; that is, the co-ordinated elements should be sufficiently parallel so that their relationship is certain. As a minimum, the co-ordinated elements should be alike grammatically. In the phrase *good, strong cages,* only the most common grammatical devices are required. *Good* and *strong* are words of similar type; they both describe the cage. They have the order of words in a series; that is, they stand side by side. The comma between them indicates that they are a series. No more parallelism is needed to assure us of their co-ordinate meaning.

More complicated co-ordinate ideas may require more complicated structures. In the quotation from Mencken, for example, the first series of clauses is made coherent by the repetition of *or.* In the quotation from Lyly this device is carried further. Lyly might have written *of more wit than wealth, and yet more wealth than wisdom.* These phrases would be understandable, but the reader might hesitate as to which of the elements the word *and* co-ordinates. As Lyly did write the sentence, repeating the word *of,* misunderstanding is scarcely possible. Such use of signal words supplements grammatical parallelism.

Word order also helps to support co-ordination. Signal words especially need to be placed carefully. Compare:

> You are either *late* or *early.*
> Either *you are late* or *I am early.*
> You are either *late* or *I am early.*

The first two sentences are clear because the signal words *either* and *or* appear just before the two expressions to be co-ordinated. The third is not clear because *either* is out of position. The following howler from a student paper illustrates a similar danger.

> To be polite he first poured some of the wine into his glass so that he would get the cork and not the lady.

The intention of the writer is clear enough; in speech he could have made himself understood by emphasis. In writing he would need to put the parts of his compound subject together.

> To be polite he first poured some of the wine into his glass so that he, and not the lady, would get the cork.

The requirements of handling co-ordinate material may be summarized as follows:

(1) Co-ordinate elements must usually be in parallel grammatical form, independent clauses with independent clauses, subjects with subjects, complements with like complements.

(2) Co-ordinate elements must appear in the proper order, usually in series, with appropriate punctuation.

(3) Co-ordinate elements should often be joined with signal words indicating co-ordination: *and, but, or, nor, yet,* and some correlative groups like *either . . . or, neither . . . nor.* The signal words need to be placed so that the elements to be parallel are clearly distinguished.

(4) If necessary to indicate co-ordination, other kinds of signal words (*of, the, in, to,* for instance) should be repeated in parallel structures.

14 Paral

CO-ORDINATION
AND PARALLELISM

Guide to Revision

Revise to make appropriate use of co-ordination or to put co-ordinate elements in parallel form.

Co-ordination—especially within sentences—can strengthen, enliven, and clarify prose, giving it at once economy and order. Beginning writers, especially, often make too little use of co-ordination, writing consecutive simple sentences or clauses which could be combined as co-ordinated subjects, verbs, complements, or modifiers. But the patterns of co-ordination must be kept clear. Consider the following sentence:

> The play was lively, witty, and the audience responsive though not very many of them.

A diagram reveals at once that the co-ordinated elements are not parallel:

The play was	(1) lively	
	(2) witty	
	(3) the audience	(1) responsive
		(2) not very many of them

Audience is not parallel with *lively* and *witty;* nor are the co-ordinated modifiers of *audience* parallel. The writer probably intended a pattern like the following:

(1) The play was	(1) lively	
	(2) witty	
(2) The audience was	(1) responsive	
	(2) small	

> The play was lively and witty, and the audience was responsive though small.

Parallelism is effective only when the balanced expressions correspond in form. When two or more words are joined by *and, or, nor, but,* or *for,* or are in a series, they should, in general, all be the same parts of speech or words of the same class (for grammatical forms, see Sections 18–23). Balanced phrases or clauses should correspond in structure.

ORIGINAL

Today a secretary has to be *attractive* in appearance and a high *intelligence.*
[*Attractive is here a modifier,* intelligence *a noun. Revise by making both modifiers (1) or both nouns (2).*]

REVISION

(1) Today a secretary must be *attractive* and *intelligent.*
(2) Today a secretary must have an attractive *appearance* and high *intelligence.*

Buffalo Bill could *ride like the wind* and *who shot a bottle cap thrown into the air.*

Buffalo Bill could *ride like the wind* and *shoot a bottle cap thrown into the air.*

When items occupy parallel positions in a series, they should have consistent forms, even though the series is long.

ORIGINAL

Mary enrolled for *painting, harmony, music appreciation,* and *to study art history.*
[*The final item of the series is not parallel.*]

REVISION

Mary enrolled for *painting, harmony, music appreciation,* and *art history.*
[*The final item appears as the name of a course, like the others.*]

Often parallelism will be apparent if similar structures are placed side by side, but in more complicated sentences words which signal similarities should be repeated. A student wrote the following excellent sentence:

> Bacon's "idols" dwell in the minds of men, but their temples are in London, in Moscow, and in Washington, for in these world capitals clouded thinking is condoned, perpetuated, and to some extent originated.

The signal is wisely repeated to make the parallelism certain.

ORIGINAL

I told him that he should have an agreement about his situation at home, he needed a room to himself with a good light, and specified hours when he could have freedom to study.
[*Failure to repeat the signal word* that *leaves the sentence confused. The reader starts to read* he needed *without understanding that he has begun the second of three things* I told him.]

REVISION

I told him that he should have an agreement about his situation at home, that he needed a room to himself with a good light, and that he should be allotted specified hours when he could have freedom to study.
[*The three clauses which follow* I told him *are now marked off by the repeated signal word* that.]

ORIGINAL

The only enemies of the sloth are *the eagles, jaguars,* and *the large boas.*
[*Inconsistency in the use of articles in a series is not always confusing, but it breaks the rhythm of the sentence and destroys the parallel structure.*]

REVISION

(1) The only enemies of the sloth are *the* eagles, jaguars, and large boas.
[*The first* the *is understood for all items of the series.*]
(2) The only enemies of the sloth are *the* eagles, *the* jaguars, and *the* large boas.

14b MISLEADING PARALLELISM   Paral b

Expressions not parallel in sense should not appear in a pattern suggesting parallel structure. Difficulty arises especially when parallel passages are woven together in a sentence and not kept separate.

ORIGINAL

On the first day we visited the *Metropolitan Museum,* the *Planetarium,* and *rode* the ferry to Staten Island.
[*Museum, Planetarium, and* rode *are not parallel in meaning, and should not appear in parallel form. The first two are logically parallel, but* rode *should parallel* visited.]

REVISION

On the first day we *visited* the *Metropolitan Museum* and the *Planetarium* and *rode* the ferry to Staten Island.
[*Insertion of* and *in place of the first comma breaks up the illogical series and makes the parallels clear.*]

ORIGINAL

Penicillin was found to cure most diseases *more quickly, effectively,* and *less dangerously* than did the sulfa drugs.
[*Again the series is not a series as it stands. The sentence can be revised either to avoid the illogical series or to make it logical.*]

REVISION

(1) Penicillin was found to cure most diseases *more quickly* and *effectively* and *less dangerously* than did the sulfa drugs.
(2) Penicillin was found to cure most diseases *more quickly, more effectively,* and *less dangerously* than did the sulfa drugs.

ORIGINAL

New Orleans is exciting, surprising, and which I should like to visit again.

REVISION

New Orleans is exciting and surprising, and I should like to visit it again.

A. Each of the sentences below violates parallelism. Recast the sentences so that ideas and forms are parallel, or remove unwarranted parallel structure.

1. On the shelf were sets of the novels of Dickens, Thackeray, and an old volume of Jonson's plays.

2. We found worms in the corn, tomatoes and the broccoli.

3. To survive without a guide in the north woods one has to be well trained as a woodsman as well as excellent physical condition.

4. She told her mother she wanted either a wedding in a church with flower girls, organ music, long trains, or a quick elopement to a justice of the peace.

5. I much prefer listening to concerts on the radio rather than to sit in the heat and discomfort of our auditorium.

6. His career, unlike most people who played a musical instrument, ended when he left school.

7. His job consisted mostly of planning and constructing roads, bridges, and various forms of surveying.

8. From the air the stream looked languid, twisted, and flowed on its course like some giant caterpillar en route to its cocoon.

9. She dreamed that she had gone to the concert wearing a scarlet bathrobe, black riding boots, and carrying a silver fox muff.

10. He accused the senator of being a fool and too stupid to know the real issues.

11. The professional players were more skillful, accurate, but less enthusiastic than their amateur opponents.

12. The dean told Alice that she should find a better place to study, she needed to spend less time at the movies, and ought to attend class more frequently.

13. She seemed pretty, clever, perceptive, and the courtesy required of an airline hostess.

14. We found the two gamblers in the dressing room and talking to the captain of the team.

15. Elaine, the first girl elected president of the student council, was attractive, popular, capable, but placed in a position of special difficulty.

B. Combine the materials of each of the following groups of sentences into a single sentence using parallel structure.

1. The battle proved the courage of the recruits. They behaved just as courageously as the seasoned veterans.

2. Seated on the steps were a tan spaniel and brindle boxer. Angela, the Manx cat, was also there.

3. A good nurse possesses a willingness to do more than her required tasks. She is also constantly alert to guess her patient's wishes.

4. The brown pup seemed to possess intelligence. None of the other dogs in the litter seemed so intelligent.

5. A nationalistic rather than a sectionalistic attitude developed in the West. This was partly because the West needed a national government to protect it from the Indians. It also looked toward the national government to provide aid in the development of transportation facilities. Furthermore, foreign affairs could be handled by a strong national government.

6. Without the mariner's compass, Columbus could not have discovered America. Neither could Vasco da Gama's trip to find a sea route to India have occurred. Magellan's sailing around the world would not have taken place without it, either.

7. Jean spent an hour with the tea committee. After it she knew that she had never before known how intricate planning a tea could be. She did not believe that the event was worth the trouble it took. She would never be on another tea committee, she was sure.

8. A course of study in music may prepare a student for concert performances. It may also provide preparation for a career in teaching. And many students gain preparation for occasional recreational activity through their entire lives.

9. Upon the chair hung a neatly folded suit. Over it was a crumpled red tie. A crushed gardenia was also on the chair.

10. Every person in the tournament knew bridge thoroughly. Each one was intelligent in his playing. A firm determination to win was in every player.

15

Subordination;

Modification

For Guide to Revision, see page 255

Subordination, which works mainly through modification, can promote terse, clear, vigorous writing.

A child, with two or three strokes of a crayon, can draw a recognizable picture of a man, but his creation is not a finished portrait. It does not, for example, present a particular impression of a particular person. It distinguishes a man from a horse, but it does not distinguish one man from other men. As the child grows older, he may make more complicated drawings: the lines for the hat brim may lengthen, and the picture represents a cowboy; or the head enlarges to a globe-like helmet, and the picture represents a space man. The skillful portrait painter does more than the child with his few lines. He makes his outline more accurately; he adds details which distinguish his sitter from others, but notably he heightens certain effects by subduing others—anyone who endeavors to emphasize everything ends by emphasizing nothing. That is, the artist not only selects his detail but he subordinates some of it.

He may use a great variety of devices for subordination, obscuring the outlines, subduing the color, reducing the size through perspective. He may even use position; some experimental painters like Picasso have achieved an effect by putting an eye where no anatomist would ever expect to find one, and have subordinated all other details by putting them in less dominant positions. A painter gets part of his effects by eliminating details, but always he must use details which he subordinates. Similarly, the writer must select details, but most of those which he does not eliminate he must subordinate, and like the painter he has at his disposal a vast and subtle array of devices with which to obtain varied effects in subordination.

15-1 PATTERNS OF SUBORDINATION

Subordination describes the innumerable ways in which words or groups of words are attached as grammatical dependents to the basic sentence pattern or parts of it. *The writer, like the painter, chooses subordinate positions for some of his details.* By subordination the writer specifies relationships more precisely, and often more economically. He might, for example have the following ideas in mind:

> We are offered a penny for our thoughts.
> We consider what we have been thinking.
> Many things have been in our minds.
> From these many things we can select a few.
> The things we select do not compromise us too nakedly.

These ideas could be set down as separate sentences, as they are above, or they could be strung together with *and* into a rambling coordinate sentence. But the skillful writer would subordinate some of the ideas, picking out the idea he wanted to stress and subordinating the others to it. He might end with something like the following sentence, from which the above ideas were taken:

> When we are offered a penny for our thoughts we always find that we have recently had so many things in mind that we can easily make a selection which will not compromise us too nakedly.
>   —JAMES HARVEY ROBINSON, *Mind in the Making*

Most of the subordination in this sentence has been achieved through the use of *subordinate* or *dependent clauses*. In 12-7 we saw that a basic sentence pattern—subject-verb or subject-verb-complement—is called a clause when it is a section of a sentence. In 14-2 we saw that an independent clause makes an independent assertion, does not depend on any other part of the sentence. The independent clause in Robinson's sentence is *we find* plus the elaborate complement that comprises the remainder of the sentence. At the beginning of the sentence and within the complement, however, are four dependent clauses, beginning respectively with *when, that, that,* and *which,* connectives which signal that the clauses are dependent. The four dependent clauses actually do most of the work of the sentence. The material could have been subordinated in other patterns, without the use of dependent clauses:

> Offered a penny for our thoughts, we always find that, having recently had many things in mind, we can easily make a selection not too nakedly compromising.

Instead of three of the dependent clauses of the original, this sentence uses three modifying phrases, gaining something in economy and perhaps losing in clarity.

In other words, subordinated material may appear as single and dependent words or as word groups of many sorts. Most sentences in English have modifiers of several sorts, as does the following:

> The various forms of intellectual activity, which together make up the culture of an age, move for the most part from different starting points and by unconnected roads.

The simple statement of the sentence is *forms move,* but twenty-five other words tell what forms move in what ways.

15-2 WORD ORDER OF MODIFIERS

Like other parts of the sentence, modifiers assume their meaning in the sentence and their grammatical relationship to it mainly because of their position. In a sentence like

> The maid guided the old gentleman through the dark hall, turning suddenly at the end of the passage to a heavy door.

we know that the gentleman, not the maid, is old, because of the positions of the words. We know that it was the turning which was sudden and the hall which was dark. When the order of words changes, the application and meaning of the modifiers changes.

> The old maid suddenly guided the heavy dark gentleman through the hall, turning at the end of the passage to a door.

In general, modifiers are understood to modify the eligible expressions nearest them. Modifiers, however, are extremely adaptable, and the language has developed numerous arrangements for them which seem to follow these general principles:

(1) Modifiers which apply clearly and specifically to particular expressions in the sentence are in fixed positions, usually immediately before or after the expressions they modify.

(2) Modifiers which do not apply to particular expressions but modify more generally may occupy different positions.

(3) Variations in the positions of modifiers produce variations in meaning and emphasis.

15-3   FIXED MODIFIERS

Modifiers of specific expressions, especially of nouns (see 18), normally appear in fixed positions according to the following word-order patterns:

(1) Single-word modifiers of nouns usually precede the expressions they modify.

> *The bright red* convertible pulled into *the filling* station.

Since this word order is standard, variations from it turn special emphasis on the modifier and are useful devices in writing and speaking. Sometimes single-word adjectives are given prominence in a position immediately after the expression they modify.

> The convertible, *bright red,* looked like a fire engine.

Appositive modifiers, which repeat in different words the expressions they modify, conventionally follow what they modify.

> My brother, a former private *detective,* took charge of the investigation.

In this shifted position, single-word modifiers are usually set off by commas, which mark the change from normal word order. Or consider the changes in meaning and emphasis in the following:

> They found the *deserted* village.
> They found the village *deserted.*

The sentences have different meanings, imply different contexts.

(2) Modifiers used as complements take the complement position after the verb.

> Grass is *green.*

Reversals of the order gives special emphasis to the modifier.

> *Gay* were our hearts.

(3) Normally, phrases and clauses immediately follow the expressions they modify.

He walked *with a slight limp.*

The captain *of the ship* set out to find the boat *which had broken from its moorings.*

I was the first person *the board interviewed.*

(4) Modifiers of other modifiers immediately precede the expressions they modify.

They supplied *too* little *too* late.

Very quickly we were *thoroughly* disgusted.

(5) Certain limiting modifiers (*only, nearly, just, almost, merely, ever, hardly, scarcely, quite*) often modify most clearly when placed immediately before the expressions they modify. Compare:

Only Williams could hope to win the hundred dollars.
Williams could *only* hope to win the hundred dollars.
Williams could hope to win *only* the hundred dollars.

(6) Modifiers of verbs may appear in any of several positions, sometimes without much shift in meaning or emphasis. They occur most frequently directly after the verb (*He drove* slowly *down the street*). They may appear within complex verbs (*She was* always *losing her gloves*). Many one-word modifiers can occur immediately before the verb (*I* soon *recovered;* but not, *I* into the street *fell*). Some modifiers, especially those of direction, regularly appear after the verb but either before or after the complement. (*Take* back *what you said;* but usually *Take that* back). Sometimes one position is obligatory, or almost so (*Set the clock* ahead; but usually not *Set* ahead *the clock*).

Many modifiers have become so closely associated with verbs that they are best thought of as parts of verbs (see 20-1). They usually appear before or after the complement, often with little difference in meaning or emphasis (*Turn* off *the light;* or *Turn the light* off).

15-4   SENTENCE AND CLAUSE MODIFIERS

Fitted into such word-order patterns, modifiers tend to limit specific expressions. Some modifiers, however, are not intended to modify a single word; they modify all of an actor-action pattern and do not function in fixed positions. They are best considered as sentence modifiers.

> *Before lunch,* he read two novels.
> He, *before lunch,* read two novels.
> He read, *before lunch,* two novels.
> He read two novels *before lunch.*

Since it modifies the entire action of the sentence, *before lunch* can occur in various positions, although it is least awkward at the beginning or end. Such sentence or clause modifiers are movable, relating to the entire sentence pattern and not to individual words.

Sentence modifiers, however, are movable only within limits. Consider the following:

> *Walking in the park* the man found a mushroom.
> The man *walking in the park* found a mushroom.
> The man found a mushroom *walking in the park.*

In the first sentence, *walking in the park* modifies the action of the entire sentence. In the second, however, the phrase identifies the man. In the third, it has moved into the position of a fixed modifier of *mushroom* and causes either awkwardness or absurdity. Sentence or clause modifiers do not usually occupy fixed positions, but there are relatively few points at which they can appear without ruining or altering the sentence. Often they work best at the beginning of the sentence, where they do not interrupt the subject-verb-complement pattern or fall into fixed positions for modifiers of specific expressions.

15-5   SUBORDINATION AND STYLE

Economy and terseness as well as clarity in relationships require extensive use and deft handling of subordination. Notice, for example, the obvious immaturity of writing like the following:

> Beechwood is a park. It is in my home town and is a cool, shady park. I knew it as a child. Then I went on many picnics there.

The repetitions indicate that all four sentences would combine into one.

> When I was a child, I went on many picnics to Beechwood, a cool, shady park in my home town.

The final sentence becomes the basis of the new sentence, and all the other sentences are subordinated as short modifiers.

Now consider the following sentences:

> Calling a spouse vile names is grounds for divorce, *and this is true if the names are put into language composed only of signs.*
>
> Calling a spouse vile names *which are couched in the language of signs* is grounds for divorce.
>
> Calling a spouse vile names *by using the language of signs* is grounds for divorce.
>
> Calling a spouse vile names *in sign language* is grounds for divorce.

Notice what has happened to the idea of using signs for marital epithets. In the first sentence, this idea requires all the words after the function word *and;* that is, it is an independent clause and a rather complicated one. In the second sentence the idea has been reduced to the italicized dependent clause. In the third sentence this idea has been subordinated still further to the italicized group of words introduced by *by*. In the last sentence the idea has become *in sign language*. The groups of words which express this idea in the last three sentences can all be thought of as modifiers; they all show subordination, but the subordination is progressive. Naturally, the Spokane court which made this ruling preferred the last sentence, in which the modifiers show the greatest evidence of subordination.

Deciding what to subordinate in what patterns is one of the most complicated and difficult tasks of writing. Compare the following, all of them descriptions of the same phenomena:

The girl in the green hat.   The green hat on the girl.
The girl wearing a green hat.   The girl's green hat.
The girl who wears a green hat.   The green hat which the girl is wearing.

The two things being considered, the girl and the green hat, appear in all the expressions, with the same physical relationship maintaining; the hat presumably remains on the girl's head. But in those on the left the hat is grammatically subordinate to the girl; in the others the girl is subordinate to the hat. That is, either the girl or the hat can be selected as the thing to be talked about and the other can be subordinated to it. The writer makes his choice not because either item is necessarily more important than the other, but because for his immediate writing purposes he wants to relate the items grammatically in a certain way. He wishes to say something about the girl and uses the hat to distinguish her, to point out which girl he means, even to suggest what kind of girl she is. Or he wishes to say something about the hat and to use the girl to specify which hat. In other words, the relationships which the writer wants to reveal determine which items he subordinates. In the following the subordination differs; so does the meaning:

> The green hat is ugly.
> The green on the hat is ugly.

Contexts, then, and the author's desire for particular emphases and meanings determine what should be subordinated; for certain purposes almost any idea can be placed in a subordinate position.

Some sorts of details, however, are more likely to profit from subordination than are some others.

> That night in a drafty hall at Red Lion Square, having escaped from an importunate hostess who wanted me to meet her niece, I heard a little, greying old man, England's leading living novelist, Thomas Hardy, read Greek poetry with an understanding and love that bespoke a lifelong devotion to the classics.

One might notice the sorts of material that are here subordinated; they include the following: time (*that night*), place (*in a drafty hall at Red Lion Square*), incidental information (*having escaped . . .*), details of description (*little, greying old*), identification or apposition (*England's leading living novelist, Thomas Hardy*). Such details are usually best subordinated; they provide attendant circumstances, offer explanations, fill in minor bits, and keep the relationships of the main predication clear in light of other predications. Of course, a very minor notion may provide the sentence's grammatical framework.

> Not until long after my vacation was over, and I had returned to my studies at Oxford, did I realize that the quiet, little gray man whom I would occasionally overhear as he trudged the hedgerowed lanes muttering Greek poetry was England's leading novelist, Thomas Hardy.

The main pattern of the sentence is *I did realize* plus a long subordinate clause used as the complement and carrying most of the meaning of the sentence.

Choosing the appropriate details to subordinate requires taste and long practice, but all good writers have learned to do it. The most obvious marks of immature writing appear in independent clauses strung together, with complete predications required to present details of identification, location, and description. Subordination provides the cure.

15 Sub; Mod

SUBORDINATION;

MODIFICATION

Guide to Revision

Subordinate to correct an immature sentence style; when subordinate materials modify, make them modify clearly.

15a ADEQUATE SUBORDINATION   Sub

Inadequate subordination characterizes the kind of writing sometimes called "primer English" because it suggests a schoolboy's reader. Strings of short sentences, excessive use of *and* and *so* to join clauses, clumsy repetitions and repeated use of *this* and *that* as subjects are usually symptoms of inadequate subordination.

ORIGINAL

Margot Macomber must have been a very beautiful woman. She had everything except wealth. When she married Francis Macomber she acquired this wealth. Although she was married to Francis, she was very untrue to him.

One day they went on a hunting expedition to Africa. They took a white man as a guide. His name was Wilson.

REVISION

Margot Macomber was a very beautiful woman who had everything except wealth. When she married Francis Macomber, she acquired that. Although she married Francis, she was untrue to him, and during a hunting expedition to Africa, she sought the attention of their white guide, Wilson. Although Francis felt very sorry for himself, he knew his wealth

ORIGINAL *(Cont.)*

Of course, Margot had to have his attention, and she did. Francis felt very sorry for himself. He knew that she would never leave him because of his wealth. He would never divorce her because of her beauty.

One day Francis and Wilson went out hunting lions. They came upon one and wounded it. It ran into the brush and hid. Getting the lion out would be a very dangerous job. Wilson and Francis began moving into the brush looking for the lion. All of a sudden, the lion jumped out of the brush. Macomber became frightened. He turned and ran. Wilson stood his ground and shot the lion, killing it. Francis knew that he would be the laughing stock of the party.

Some time later, they went on a buffalo hunt. They came upon a herd of buffalo. A buffalo was wounded and ran into the brush. Previous incidents seemed to be repeating themselves. Francis saw a chance to redeem himself. He began going through the brush. All this time, his wife had been watching him from a distance. All of a sudden, the buffalo jumped up and charged Francis. Francis held his ground and aimed at the animal's nose. In the meantime, Margot saw the animal charge too. She brought a heavy rifle to her shoulder. Then there was the sound of two shots. Francis and the buffalo both toppled to the ground dead. When she saw that Francis was dead, she became hysterical. She began to realize that Francis was really the man she loved.

[*The theme above deserved the* F *it received—in spite of its lack of grammatical errors. The style is that of a small child telling the story of* Red Riding Hood *in his own words.*]

REVISION *(Cont.)*

would keep Margot from leaving him and that her beauty would keep him from divorcing her.

One day while Francis and Wilson were out hunting, they wounded a lion and let it get away to hide in the brush. They moved into the brush after him, although getting him out was dangerous. Suddenly the lion jumped out. Macomber, frightened, turned and ran. Wilson stood his ground and killed the lion. Francis knew he would be the laughing stock of the party.

Some time later they went after buffalo, found a herd, and wounded one, losing him in the brush. As the earlier situation re-occurred, Francis saw a chance to redeem himself and began to go into the brush. Suddenly the buffalo jumped up and charged Francis. He held his ground and aimed at the buffalo's nose. Margot, who had been watching from a distance, saw the charge, too, and raised a heavy rifle to her shoulder. Two shots sounded. Francis and the buffalo both toppled to the ground dead. When Margot saw that Francis was dead, she became hysterical, realizing that Francis was really the man she loved.

[*The theme purported to be a character sketch of Margot Macomber, but turned out to be merely a plot sketch revealing some curious misinterpretations of Hemingway's story. The revision is still a naïve misreading of the story, but it illustrates how much the style can be improved and clarified simply by subordinating some elements to others. For the most part the revision does nothing beyond reducing independent sentences to dependent clauses, phrases, or single words.*]

Perhaps the most frequent sign of inadequate subordination is the repeated subject, especially the word *this* needlessly and often vaguely carrying on as the subject of a new sentence (see 19a). Usually the two sentences should be joined.

ORIGINAL

When Lord Byron was at Cambridge, he published *Hours of Idleness.* This was in 1807. The volume was Byron's first book of poems.

[*The repetition of subjects—this and* volume—*suggests inadequate subordination.*]

REVISION

In 1807, when Lord Byron was at Cambridge, he published his first book of poems, *Hours of Idleness.*

[*The combination says everything in the original more clearly and more economically.*]

ORIGINAL

Dramatics develops assurance. This is very valuable.

REVISION

Dramatics develops valuable assurance.

Some sentences wind on and on, held together by connectives like *so* and *and.* Almost always they can be improved by selecting one part of the sentence as a main clause and subordinating other elements to it.

ORIGINAL

Louise was tired of listening to the concert and it was dark enough that her grandmother could not see her and so she slipped out into the lobby.

[*The relationships between the three clauses are not accurately marked for the reader by linking them with* and *and* so.]

REVISION

Since Louise was tired of listening to the concert, she slipped past her grandmother in the dark into the lobby.

[*With ideas subordinated to a main subject-verb framework—*she slipped *—the sentence is clearer and more economical.*]

ORIGINAL

There was a garage just around the corner and nobody wanted to be responsible for the keys so we took out our luggage and put the car in the garage.

REVISION

Since nobody wanted to be responsible for the keys, we removed our luggage and put the car in a garage just around the corner.

Indirect questions follow a regular pattern of subordination in which the question appears as a noun clause complement (see 18-1). Compare:

Direct: Paul asked, "Are the others ready?"

Indirect: Paul asked whether the others were ready.

Direct: The question is: "Can enough qualified students be found?"

Indirect: The question is whether enough qualified students can be found.

The indirect question usually converts the question to a clause using regular order, introduced by *whether* or *if* or an interrogative word.

ORIGINAL

The issue is can television replace the teacher.

He asked was I coming.

REVISION

The issue is whether television can replace the teacher.

He asked whether I was coming.

A minor detail may assume the main position in the sentence so awkwardly that the subordination seems illogical or upside-down. Often a shift in subordination may make the sentence fit its context more logically.

ORIGINAL

Andrea stepped confidently into the hall. Joe pulled the rug out from under her, when she fell down.
[*Either reversed subordination (1) or co-ordination (2) seems more likely in the context.*]

REVISION

(1) Andrea stepped confidently into the hall. When Joe pulled the rug out from under, she fell down.
(2) Andrea stepped confidently into the hall. Joe pulled the rug out from under her, and she fell down.

Shifting adverbial modifiers can be so misplaced that they apply with equal ease in more than one way. They "squint," seeming to look in more than one direction at once. The difficulty arises when an adverbial modifier follows a word which it would normally modify but also precedes another word which it can modify.

ORIGINAL

The person who lies frequently gets caught.
[Frequently *can be taken to modify either what precedes it or what follows it; it "squints." If* frequently *modifies the whole sentence, it should precede it (1). Sentences (2) and (3) are possible if they convey the writer's meaning. The sentence might well be recast (4).*]

REVISION

(1) *Frequently,* the person who lies gets caught.
(2) The person who lies gets caught *frequently.*
(3) The person who *frequently* lies gets caught.
(4) Anybody who lies *frequently* is likely to get caught.

She told me *as soon as the dance was over* she would marry me.

(1) *As soon as the dance was over,* she told me she would marry me.
(2) She told me she would marry me *as soon as the dance was over.*

15b POSITION OF MODIFIERS   Mod

Usually, fixed modifiers can appear in only one position for a given purpose. In any other position they have a different meaning or become ludicrous.

ORIGINAL

He gave the book to his father *that was bound in leather.*
[*The final clause should modify* the book, *but it does not appear in the usual fixed position immediately after what it modifies. Moreover, the word* father *intervenes, and thus the man rather than the book seems to have the leather binding. The word order can be changed (1, 2), or the sentence revised (3, 4). Usually misplaced modifiers are symptoms of wordiness; the cure is cutting and revising.*]

In order to understand the importance of the magazines, we investigated *their* sources of popularity.
[*The sense of the sentence suggests that* their *was probably intended to modify* popularity.]

The youngest girl only thought of new clothes.
[*The context might make the sentence clear, but a reader could be temporarily misled to take* only *as a modifier of* thought—*suggesting that the girl only* thought *of clothes, did not, for instance, buy any.*]

She *nearly* saved half her allowance.

REVISION

(1) He gave the book *that was bound in leather* to his father.
(2) He gave his father the book *that was bound in leather.*
(3) He gave the *leather-bound* book to his father.
(4) He gave his father the *leather-bound* book.
[*The sentence is revised; modifiers are reduced so that they can be more easily applied. Obviously the last two revisions are preferable to the longer versions above.*]

In order to understand the importance of the magazines, we investigated the sources of *their* popularity.
[*The single adjective is placed in its fixed position before the word it modifies.*]

The youngest girl thought only of new clothes.
[*In some colloquial idioms* only *appears before the verb even though it modifies the complement:* He only paid me a quarter. *Here the sentence is clearer with the modifier in its usual position.*]

She saved *nearly* half her allowance.

Since the same words or groups of words can be used as either fixed or movable modifiers, the reader must depend on word order to see how they apply and what they mean. He interprets according to his expectations of word order patterns. From the sentence

The man *in the boat* was a tyrant.

the reader understands automatically that *in the boat,* in a fixed position, is a modifier specifically locating the man. If the phrase is moved, the reader interprets it as a movable modifier which applies to the entire sentence, and he understands the sentence differently.

> *In the boat,* the man was a tyrant.

The first sentence makes clear that the man was a tyrant, presumably all the time. The second preserves a little respect for him, limiting his tyranny to the time during which he was in the boat. So long as the sentence modifier is kept out of a fixed position, it may be moved, with changes in emphasis but no alteration of essential meaning.

> *In the boat,* the man was a tyrant.
> The man was a tyrant *in the boat.*

The writer must be sure that modifiers intended to apply generally are not put where they apply to a specific word. Compare:

> *At first* he thought that the detective would believe him.
> He thought that the detective would believe him *at first.*

In the first version, the modifier does not attach clearly to any particular expression and applies to the entire action. In the second, *at first* becomes part of the dependent clause rather than the entire sentence and modifies its action; the meaning of the sentence changes.

Negative sentences especially cause trouble. Compare:

> Nobody was ever punished *because the camp was run so carelessly.*
> *Because the camp was run so carelessly,* nobody was ever punished.

With the clause at the end, the sentence is ambiguous; it can mean either what the second version says or that the careless management of the camp brought no punishment.

ORIGINAL

He fired three shots at the lion *with a smile of triumph on his face.*

[*Often a sentence modifier may appear at either the beginning or the end, but at the end it may fall into a fixed position. In this sentence the reader has trouble locating the smile.*]

REVISION

With a smile of triumph on his face, he fired three shots at the lion.

[*The modifier is moved so that it applies to the action of the sentence and does not seem to be a fixed modifier describing the lion.*]

ORIGINAL (*Cont.*)

I didn't know whether the planes would find me *on the first day.*

[*In this position the modifier becomes part of the dependent clause and seems to modify* find.]

Closed accounts are not to be deleted in order that numerical sequence will be preserved.

[*The reader cannot be sure whether deleting or keeping the closed accounts will preserve numerical sequence.*]

REVISION (*Cont.*)

On the first day, I didn't know whether the planes would find me.

[*The modifier is shifted from the end of the sentence so that it clearly modifies the entire predication.*]

So that numerical sequence will be preserved, all closed accounts are to be retained.

[*Changing the negative sentence to positive clarifies at least one possible meaning.*]

Modifying words which serve also as connectives [*however, therefore, moreover, consequently,* sometimes called *conjunctive adverbs* (see 23-5)], appear at the beginning of a clause when they modify its entire action; placed within a clause they throw stress on the words they follow. Preceding clauses or sentences usually indicate which sentence parts need emphasis and therefore indicate where conjunctive modifiers should be placed.

> John was afraid to look at me; *however* he was eager to look at Alice.
>
> John was afraid to look at me; he was eager, *however,* to look at Alice.

The position of *however* in the second sentence stresses *eager* and accents the contrast between *eager* and *afraid.* The following sentences illustrate a related problem in emphasis:

> I had no desire to listen to another hour of boasting; *therefore* I determined to try to slip out of the lecture.
>
> I had no desire to listen to another hour of boasting; I determined, *therefore,* to try to slip out of the lecture.

Even though *determined* requires no emphasis, the second sentence would usually be preferable because it avoids special stress on an unimportant modifier like *therefore.* In the first version, *therefore* gains undue accent at the beginning of the second clause.

ORIGINAL

He ate baseball, slept baseball, and dreamed baseball; and when he

REVISION

He ate baseball, slept baseball, and dreamed baseball; and when he

ORIGINAL *(Cont.)*

thought he thought baseball. *Therefore,* a mere football game could hardly make him blink an eye.

[*Therefore has stress at the beginning of the sentence, which it probably does not deserve, and in its present position, it fails to emphasize a significant contrast.*]

REVISION *(Cont.)*

thought he thought baseball. A mere football game, *therefore,* could hardly make him blink an eye.

[*Placed as it is here,* therefore *emphasizes* football game *and the contrast between football and baseball which is crucial for the sentence.*]

15c   "DANGLING" MODIFIERS   DM

Some sentence modifiers, especially verbal phrases, do not contain subjects in themselves. Even though they modify the sentence as a whole and appear at the beginning or end, they tend to depend on the subject or on the noun nearest them in the main sentence to clarify their meaning. Compare:

> *Eating lunch on the lawn,* the children were amused by the speeding cars.
>
> *Eating lunch on the lawn,* the speeding cars amused the children.

The first is clear, but the second is ludicrous because the subject, *speeding cars,* cannot logically supply the sense of a subject for the verbal *eating*—cannot tell what was eating. Similarly, the modifier that opens the following sentence dangles:

> *Sitting on the bridge,* the huge steeple looked like part of a toy village.

The subject, *steeple,* seems to govern *sitting,* but the huge steeple could scarcely be sitting on the bridge. The sentence can be revised by using as a subject whatever was sitting on the bridge (*Sitting on the bridge,* we *could see* . . .). The sentence can be revised, also, by providing the modifier with a subject of its own (*As we* sat on the bridge, the huge steeple . . .), or by changing the modifier in some other way so that it does not rely on anything in the main clause (*From our position on the bridge, the huge steeple* . . .).

Since introductory modifiers readily refer to the subject, confusion may result if the subject is postponed or the sentence is passive (see 17-1 to 17-3). Notice the following:

> *Finding something important,* there are complete details to be recorded by the secretary.
>
> *When finding something important,* complete details were recorded by the secretary.

The modifiers make sense only if the reader can tell who was doing the finding. Usually the name of the actor used as the subject of the sentence, in the position just after the modifier, supplies such information. In sentences like the above, therefore, in which the actor is not the subject, the modifiers dangle. Compare:

> *When the staff found something important,* the secretary recorded complete details.
> *When they found something important,* the staff dictated complete details to the secretary.

These revisions name the actor in the normal position in the actor-action pattern. In English the feeling for this pattern is sufficiently strong so that it will work even though the subject is only implied, as in a command:

> To avoid a cold, wear a piece of red flannel around your neck.

If normal order is not followed, the modifier dangles:

> To avoid a cold, a piece of red flannel may be worn around the neck.

The initial modifying phrase is so common in the pattern of the English sentence that an introductory modifier without its own subject may still seem relatively clear in itself and be useful because it is economical.

> *Talking with* students, the same questions arise time after time.

Since *talking* is so nearly complete in its meaning—like *fishing* or *swimming*—that it relies but little on the subject, *question,* the sentence is reasonably clear. Or consider:

> *When lunching at the Union,* conversation must be sacrificed for speed.

The conversation is not lunching, of course, but the sentence is not confusing, and the use of an impersonal *one* or *a person* would not improve it.

ORIGINAL

Having rotted in the damp cellar, my brother was unable to sell any of the potatoes.
[*The modifier applies automatically to the main action as it is expressed,*

REVISION

(1) Having rotted in the damp cellar, my brother's potatoes were unfit for sale.
[*Word order is changed so that the subject referred to by the modifier be-*

ORIGINAL *(Cont.)*

to the subject-verb of the sentence. The result is the absurdly unsanitary state of the decomposing brother. The modifier should apply to an actor-action pattern of which potatoes *is the subject, but* potatoes *is not in the subject position.*]

Convinced that people of the state were not well-informed about the university, pamphlets were printed describing the postwar educational program.
[*The sentence is not obviously absurd, but it is unclear because the reader needs to know who was convinced, and* pamphlets *does not tell him accurately. A subject to complete* convinced *may be supplied in the sentence (1) or in the modifier (2).*]

At the age of ten, cowboys and Indians were my main interest.
[*The modifier concerns the writer, not the age of a group of youthful cowboys and Indians; the sentence is imprecise.*]

Brought up among many advantages, it was only natural that Florence should show distaste for a life of poverty.
[*The reader can see easily the application of the modifier to* Florence, *but he could understand more easily if* Florence *were the subject of the main clause, not a dependent clause. The real problem is the unnecessary postponement of the logical subject,* Florence.]

REVISION *(Cont.)*

comes the subject of the sentence.]
(2) Since the potatoes had rotted in the damp cellar, my brother was unable to sell any of them.
[*The modifier is changed to a clause, which can include its subject,* potatoes.]

(1) Convinced that people of the state were not well-informed about the university, the committee published pamphlets describing the postwar educational program.
(2) Since the committee was convinced that people of the state were not well-informed about the university, it published pamphlets describing the postwar educational program.

(1) When I was ten, cowboys and Indians were my main interest.
(2) At the age of ten, I was interested mainly in cowboys and Indians.

(1) Brought up among many advantages, Florence naturally showed distaste for a life of poverty.
[*With* Florence *as subject of the main clause, modification is clearer, and the sentence is more concise.*]
(2) Since Florence had been brought up among many advantages, it was only natural that she should show distaste for a life of poverty.

Concluding verbal phrases, like introductory ones, often depend on the main sentence, usually on the name of the actor, to complete their meaning. If the word to be understood as a subject for the verbal is not expressed or is obscured in a passive construction, the modifier dangles.

ORIGINAL

The grain fields had been burned by the invaders, *thus causing suffering in the valley.*

[*The sentence seems to say that the fields caused the suffering; the intention obviously was to say that* the burning of the fields, *not expressed in the sentence, caused it.* Invaders *cannot complete the meaning of* causing *because it is put into a dependent position in the passive sentence. The sentence is logically unbalanced; the main idea is subordinated in the modifier.*]

He hit a home run in the eighth inning, *resulting in the winning of the game.*

[*The modifier has nothing to modify, but the confusion arises from obscuring the predication* He won the game *in the modifier.*]

REVISION

(1) Because the invaders had burned the grain fields, there was suffering in the valley.

[*The dangling expression, since it is really the most important idea of the sentence, is made the main clause.*]

(2) By burning the grain fields, the invaders caused suffering in the valley.

(3) The inhabitants of the valley suffered because the invaders had burned the grain fields.

(1) His home run in the eighth inning won the game.

(2) By hitting a home run in the eighth inning, he won the game.

(3) He won the game with a home run in the eighth inning.

15d   "SPLIT" CONSTRUCTIONS   Split

Normally modifiers should not be allowed to split constructions by separating closely related sentence elements, particularly if the separating element is long or complicated, although sometimes separation is unavoidable or is desirable for special effects. Subject and verb, parts of the verb, verb and complement, parts of a verbal, or elements of a series should be separated only with caution.

We may, if the weather clears, go to Birmingham.

Separation of parts of the verb *may go* might be desirable to put special emphasis on *may,* but usually the modifier, *if the weather clears,* would appear at the beginning of the sentence. Or consider the following in which subject and verb or subject and modifier are separated by long modifiers:

The *driver,* confused by the snow balling upon his windshield wiper and the tires skidding on the ice and his wife yanking at his elbow, *yelled.*

I *asked* the *conductor,* because at home we have breakfast in bed and I always get a headache unless I have some coffee before I do another thing, *if there was a diner on the train.*

The unnecesary division of the basic pattern obscures meaning.

ORIGINAL

I, every Saturday afternoon I got the chance, would take the subway to Coney Island.
[*Subject and verb are needlessly separated.*]

He expected that they would *in the shortest possible time* agree to our terms.
[*The long modifier obscures the main word order pattern of the sentence by separating words that logically belong together.*]

REVISION

Every Saturday afternoon I got the chance, I would take the subway to Coney Island.

He expected that they would agree to our terms *in the shortest possible time.*
[*The modifier should be placed where it does not interrupt the main sentence movement.*]

Similarly, placing a modifier between *to* and the remainder of an infinitive may falsify emphasis.

He promised to *firmly* hold our position.

The meaning is clear, and *firmly* would "squint" before *to,* but the sentence gains strength if *firmly* is moved.

He promised to hold our position *firmly.*

On the other hand, a split infinitive sometimes becomes almost a necessity. Herman Melville in *The Confidence Man* prefers to split an infinitive for the sake of clarity in modification.

The sick man seemed to have *just* made an impatiently querulous answer.

Placed either before *to* or after *made* the modifier *just* would change meaning, carrying something of the sense of *only.* Usually, however, the split infinitive should be regarded as a deviation from normal word order, warranted only by special circumstances.

ORIGINAL

I expected to *quickly* remove my incomplete, and to *never again for any cause whatever* get another.
[*Revision of the first split infinitive is advisable and revision of the second is imperative.*]

REVISION

I expect to remove my incomplete *quickly* and *never again* to get another *for any cause whatever.*
[*Revision of both split infinitives tightens the sentence structure and promotes ready comprehension.*]

A. Combine each of the following groups of sentences into a single sentence:

1. *Charley's Aunt* is still a popular play. It was first presented, however, in 1892. And it is implausible and farcical.

2. Many flowers come out in the spring. They include violets, anemones, bloodroot, and trilliums. This is in the Middle West. These flowers appear about May. They cover the ground in woods and parks.

3. Henry Purcell was a composer. He was English. He lived in the seventeenth century.

4. Many of the new dance steps are difficult. Anyone can learn them, however. That is, anyone can learn them if he has a good sense of rhythm.

5. I am not a very good swimmer. This is because I have always been afraid of the water. I have spent many hours on the beach, however.

6. In *Jane Eyre* Charlotte Brontë describes abuses of education. These were in a real school. Miss Brontë had once attended the school, and it was at Cowan Bridge.

7. The oboe is a difficult instrument. This is because it has a double reed. This is hard to blow.

8. First all the girls in the camp had to take exercises. Then all the girls had breakfast and had to clean up the bunks. Then all the girls of the camp reported for swimming. I liked swimming better than any other activity.

9. In 1864 Atlanta was one of the most important cities of the South. This was so for the reason that the Confederacy had developed it as an important railroad center. It was also developed as a manufacturing center. This was done in the belief that it was far from the center of military activity. It would therefore be safe.

10. I grew up in a small town. It was in the South. I have not visited this town for many years. To be exact, I have not been there for eight years. It is still, however, the place I think of as home.

B. Revise any sentences among the following which you think might be improved by subordinating different elements. Be able to explain the effect of any changes you make.

1. Since I am majoring in automotive design, I am interested in aeroplane motors, especially jet propulsion units.

2. We moved from Charleston to Durham, North Carolina, in which I found the customs about having dates were very different.

3. I was still very young, although I thought it was getting to be time for me to make up my mind about whether I wanted to be a teacher or a librarian or an airline stewardess.

4. Although we had been warned against hiking over the rocky slope in the dark, we started before daylight. The sun peeped over the horizon just as I fell and sprained my ankle.

5. After three months of haunting casting offices and leaving her phone number with producers, Jane decided to go back to St. Louis. The telephone rang when she was almost too disgusted with New York to answer it.

6. Jack was seven years old, although he had never seen grass growing. He had never been outside the area about four blocks square which surrounded the dingy apartment house.

7. When he finally decided to work, he had no trouble finding a job. But when he had trouble keeping it was after he had taken a job.

8. By midnight all of us in the car were sure that we could get to Santa Fe in time for the plane. Then we just rounded a curve and saw the lights of the city when a tire blew out.

9. The man who was peeping in the window and who was immediately noticed by me, was on the outside.

10. Abraham Lincoln was the man that was the leader of the Union cause and Jefferson Davis was the president of the Confederate states, although there are reasons to think of Robert E. Lee as the true leader of the South, and there were generals in the Northern armies, of whom one was to become famous as General Ulysses S. Grant.

C. Rewrite the following selection from a student theme, improving its style in any way you can and paying particular attention to opportunities for clarifying relations between ideas by subordination:

On the night of the flood four of us drove across the river away from home to see what damage had been done. We drove around on the other side for about an hour and a half. We finally decided to start home. We came back to the bridge. There was about three feet of water over the road. We had to get across for classes the next day, so we had to find some way to cross to the other side. After considerable debate we decided to drive across. We had gone about a fourth of the way and the ignition got wet. The car stalled in about two feet of water. The water started pouring in under the doors. The heat of the engine dried the ignition, and the car started again. We went about half way and stalled again. This time we were in about three feet of water. The water poured in. We talked about pushing the car across. The three boys got out and pushed. I steered. The water was deep, and so they could not push the car. They got back in. I thought maybe the water would get deeper. It was very exciting. The water was swift. Finally a large truck came in behind us. He pushed us across. We still could not start the car, and so we had to leave it. The water was still rising. We came back the next day. The car was still there and the water had not come to it again. We tried to start it. It would not start. We pushed the car for three or four blocks. It did not fire at all. We pushed it to a garage, and the mechanic said the carburetor was full of mud. The river water was very muddy in the flood. We left the car at the garage to be cleaned.

D. The sentences below probably do not say what their writer intended. Revise them, paying particular attention to modification.

1. The player who breaks the rules in the end hurts his own team.

2. No one is allowed to dump anything along this road except a city official.

3. *The Secret Life of Walter Mitty* by James Thurber is the typical story of a daydreamer.

4. A person in the assembly line only worked eight hours a day five days a week except for foremen.

5. After two days in an open boat we began to get frightened with only a little water and a few biscuits.

6. He knew that the boat had been sunk because he had seen the battle.

7. My home is a good place for a boy who likes horses to grow up in the United States.

8. The old man was not arrested because he had befriended the natives.

9. Explain and demonstrate the various positions of the foot on which words of command are given, first in slow time, then in quick time.

10. Clarity was their basis of effectiveness.

11. Joan decided that she would not marry him at the last possible moment.

12. They should not move the old road so that the trees will shade travelers.

13. The nurse brought in Robert, Jr., to see his father in his bassinet.

14. I do not believe that the pterodactyl was able to catch fish for several reasons.

15. The truck's bumper was bent and twisted when it struck several logs enroute to San Francisco.

E. Revise the following sentences so that modification is clear and logical:

1. When hardly more than a baby, a gang of older boys threw me into the creek and told me to sink or swim.

2. Being very dark, we were unable to find our way about the cellar.

3. Knowing that the whole future of the club was at stake, the investigation found us reluctant to say a word.

4. At the age of nine my father's interest in languages was already developing.

5. Every promise had been broken by the new governor, causing widespread dissatisfaction.

6. On approaching the village the gold spire was the only evidence of civilization that we could see.

7. Although only pretending to shoot, the gun suddenly went off with a loud roar.

8. Having had no sleep for two nights, the dirty haystack actually seemed inviting.

9. Being afraid of his own shadow, we were not much disturbed by his threats.

10. Trying to climb in the dormitory window at night, the Dean of Women caught her and recommended her suspension.

F. Revise the following sentences by reducing italicized expressions to shorter modifiers, by making clauses into phrases or phrases into shorter phrases or single words:

1. *Smoking when a person is in bed* is prohibited.

2. He avoided tall girls *because of the fact that he was only five feet two in height.*

3. He did not believe *in the factor of hereditary influences.*

4. Hybrids are formed by crossing two species *which are pure before they are crossed.*

5. I confess *in a spirit of freedom and willingness.*

6. The will, *which can never be conquered,* sustains the rebel.

7. He was not merely a chip *which had been cut from the old block,* but the old block itself.

8. *When twelve o'clock had rolled around,* I was ready to eat.

9. *When I was a child,* I learned to respect nature.

10. *Since the potatoes had rotted in the damp cellar,* my brother was unable to sell any of them.

11. They looked at the cow *whose horn had been crumpled.*

12. *When breakfast had been finished,* the boys got out their fishing tackle.
13. The children's voices rang out *in loud tones.*
14. She was *the kind of girl that is a blonde type.*
15. She specializes in answers *that are in the negative.*

G. Combine the sentences below with the *introductory modifier* suggested for each, leaving the modifiers as they are but revising the sentences so that the combinations are clear and logical. Notice that the sentences as they now stand have passive verbs. Most of the sentences join logically with the modifiers if you make the verb active.

   1. To prove that there were no hard feelings. A dinner was given for us by the winning team.
   2. Working without rest for two afternoons. The cabin was finally cleaned by the Boy Scouts.
   3. While trailing his line carelessly beside the boat. A five-pound bass was caught by Jim.
   4. Having turned off the light. Ominous shadows were seen by Marie lurking in every corner.
   5. After walking for an hour. The old cabin was finally seen by our leader.
   6. After watching for an hour. The rare birds were finally seen by us.
   7. Unable to get materials. A new product was put on the market by my father's company.
   8. Playing the last ten minutes with a broken finger. The game was finally won by Jack with a free throw.
   9. While flying a kite in a storm. Information about electricity was discovered by Benjamin Franklin.
   10. While raking the yard. Her left knee was twisted.

H. Below are groups of slightly varied sentences. Comment on distinctions in emphasis or meaning you can discern among the versions in each group.

   1. a. With the field glasses the girl found the dog.
      b. The girl with the field glasses found the dog.
      c. The girl found the dog with the field glasses.
   2. a. Suddenly the clown jumped up and slapped the acrobat.
      b. The clown suddenly jumped up and slapped the acrobat.
      c. The clown jumped up and suddenly slapped the acrobat.
   3. a. The past, at least, is secure.
      b. The past is secure, at least.
      c. At least the past is secure.

4. a. The Duke still lives that Henry shall depose.
   b. The Duke still lives that shall depose Henry.
   c. The Duke that Henry shall depose still lives.

5. a. Hope springs eternal in the human breast.
   b. Hope springs eternally in the human breast.
   c. Eternal hope springs in the human breast.

6. a. The law smiles in your face while it picks your pocket.
   b. While it picks your pocket, the law smiles in your face.
   c. While the law smiles in your face, it picks your pocket.

7. a. In the long run, we are sure to lose.
   b. We are sure to lose in the long run.
   c. We are, in the long run, sure to lose.

8. a. This was a better way of making a living.
   b. This was a way of making a better living.
   c. This was a way of making a living better.

9. a. Just before noon we decided that the program was too long.
   b. We decided that the program was too long just before noon.
   c. We decided that the program just before noon was too long.

10. a. Although he hated everyone there, John stayed at the party.
    b. John stayed at the party, although he hated everyone there.

I. Revise each of the sentences below, moving the italicized modifier to a different position. Then explain any changes in meaning or emphasis effected by the shift in word order.

1. The girl *with the broken arm* grabbed the new doll.
2. The children promised to *carefully* chew every bite.
3. She *nearly* threw away all her diamonds.
4. *In complete confusion* the speaker finally found his audience.
5. *Happily* the old man watched the children singing.
6. One girl *I know* is in love with you.
7. The hill is not really pretty *because of the big rocks on it*.
8. We found the girl *breaking into the back room*.
9. He ordered them *at once* to dump the ammunition into the sea.
10. *In a few minutes* the new bridge was built.
11. I decided I would get up *when my roommate threw a glass of water on me*.
12. The room looked filthier than any stable I had ever seen *by daylight*.
13. He decided that working was a way of making a *better* living.
14. He decided to fight *because he disliked the color of Bill's hair*.

15. He guessed that *only* about half the new troops were fully equipped.
16. The boy *climbing the rope* threw his knife at the old sailor.
17. *Wishing he had never heard of sloe gin,* he opened the door and saw his uncle.
18. *For two days* I wondered what my brother had been doing.
19. Tennyson looked like a lion *with his mane parted in the middle.*
20. I am certain the Smiths can come; I am not sure, *however,* about the Joneses.

16

Controlling Secondary Patterns;
Incomplete Patterns

For Guide to Revision, see page 277

Controlling secondary sentence patterns permits economy with clarity.

A small boy, developing his feeling for sentence structure more rapidly than his knowledge of natural history, heard someone remark that "he was hungry as a bear." The pattern was attractive, and for some months the child was regularly "tired as a bear, sleepy as a bear, cold as a bear, happy as a bear, scared as a bear." Even though the meanings of the words were not especially appropriate, the intention of the child was clear, because his word-order pattern is standard in English. That is, many secondary patterns appear in English sentences and, like the basic sentence pattern, reveal easily recognized grammatical relationships. If the child had heard an adult say, "I was blink as a blunk," he would have encountered no grammatical difficulty with the sentence; he would have needed only to know what *blink* and *blunk* mean. In fact, these patterns become so much a part of the way speakers of English talk and think that parts of them can sometimes be omitted for still further economy.

16-1 FIXED AND REDUCIBLE SENTENCE PATTERNS

Many sentence patterns in English, particularly secondary patterns, are so fixed that they can be changed little or none, and they cannot be abbreviated without altering structure and meaning. Consider the familiar pattern "the (a, an) _____ _____." This is the commonest pattern of a modified noun, and might be filled in to read *the sudden death* or *an owl-eyed Phi Beta Kappa*. In some ways this pattern is completely rigid; we can not say *death sudden the,* and not without setting up quite a different pattern with a different effect can we make such a change as that in *How sudden the death*. That is, the order of the words is fixed. Something can be done with the first element in the pattern, for *the* we may substitute *a* or *an* or nothing at all, but if we do so we alter the effect of the pattern. For example, we can say, "The sudden death of my aunt cut short our vacation." For certain purposes we can even truncate this pattern and say, "Death waits for no man," but we can not say "The death waits for no man," and "A death waits for no man" would alter the meaning. That is, many of the very numerous secondary patterns in English are fixed; or if they can be altered or abbreviated, they can be varied only for particular effects and meanings.

Many patterns, however, can be abbreviated for economy without change of meaning, and if the constructions are used judiciously, without loss of clarity. The writer can leave out passages which would repeat meanings, allowing the reader to fill in missing elements from what has preceded. Even so common a device as using co-ordinate sentence parts (see 14) saves words by combining two simple sentences into one.

> He knew the rules and (*he knew the*) regulations.

The italicized repetition is understood easily and need not be expressed. The pressure of word order allows many such short cuts. For example, verbs or parts of them can often be omitted in parallel sentences.

> We knew that we would soon have to stop using paper plates and (*we knew that we would soon have to*) start washing dishes.

The opening words automatically carry over to their position in the parallel structure. Or, in a comparison, we do not write:

> Plants grow more rapidly in California than (*plants grow rapidly*) in New York.

We sometimes substitute shorter expressions whose meaning is clear because they occupy the same relative positions as the words they stand for.

> Plants grow more rapidly in California than *they do* in New York.

Or we omit the repeated expressions and allow the pressure of word order to carry the meaning.

> Plants grow more rapidly in California than in New York.
> She was treated more politely than he (*was treated*).

Connectives can sometimes be omitted from parallel structures and subordinate expressions.

> He was afraid of no man and (*of*) no rule.
> Philo knew (*that*) he was being followed.

Word order is sufficient to indicate relationships without the help of the connectives.

Even when a repeated idea is not expressed in the required form, it can sometimes be omitted. Sentences like the following are common, especially in informal English:

> He ran as fast as he could (*run*).

Usually, however, such omissions are clear only if other words in the sentence give the reader the exact information needed to fill in missing parts of the patterns. Constructions may become obscure whenever the "understood" expressions cannot repeat previous expressions exactly.

16-2 PATTERNS OF COMPARISON

One kind of relatively fixed pattern expresses comparisons. These have been set fairly rigidly and provide some economy; the child does not have to say that "he was as hungry as a bear was hungry." But the patterns do require that the items being compared appear in parallel forms and that essential elements are not omitted. Notice the following:

> The *joke* was as old as the *hills*.
> *George* looked like his *mother*.
> *My cousin* was older than *any other freshman*.
> It is easier *for a camel to go through the eye of a needle* than *for a rich man to enter into the kingdom of God*.

In each sentence, the italicized expressions are put into parallel forms and are comparable in meaning. These sentence patterns work in English so long as expressions in parallel positions have parallel form and compatible meanings.

16 Inc; Comp

CONTROLLING SECONDARY PATTERNS;
INCOMPLETE PATTERNS

Guide to Revision

Supply missing sentence elements or revise sentences so as to complete patterns consistently.

Often words can profitably be omitted, even words which fill out the sentence pattern. Notice the following: *I heard him admit that he was a vegetarian.* The meaning would be instantly and certainly clear without the word *that,* even though it signals a familiar sentence pattern. Sometimes such connectives are better omitted; but often they are necessary to complete the pattern, and omitting them causes confusion.

16a   COMPLETING SECONDARY PATTERNS   Inc

ORIGINAL

The liquor was confiscated and the barrels dumped into the sea.

[*The reader is expected to be able to supply a verb between* barrels *and* dumped, *but the verb suggested by word order is* was, *which does not fit the plural* barrels.]

Many of the soldiers saw only what hundreds of tourists always had and always will be seeing.

The water cask was nearly empty by noon and drained for evening rations.

[Drained *must be preceded by* was *understood, but the* was *after* cask *is a complete verb; it cannot be understood as part of the verb* was drained.]

REVISION

(1) The liquor was confiscated, and the barrels *were* dumped into the sea.

(2) The liquor was confiscated and the bootlegger arrested.

Many of the soldiers saw only what hundreds of tourists always had *seen* and always will be seeing.

(1) The water cask was nearly empty by noon and was drained for evening rations.

(2) The water cask was nearly empty by noon; we drained it for evening rations.

277

The preposition can be omitted in parallel passages only when the expressed preposition fits logically into the place where it is to be understood (see also 14a). The preposition should not be carelessly omitted from clauses in which it is separated from the verb.

ORIGINAL

REVISION

D'Artagnan was interested and skillful at fencing.
[*No connective follows* interested; at, *which does not make sense, is the only word available.*]

(1) D'Artagnan was interested *in* and skillful at fencing.
(2) D'Artagnan was interested in fencing and skillful at it.

My mother objected to the people which I associated.
[*The writer has forgotten a necessary preposition.*]

My mother objected to the people with whom I associated.

Word order often makes subordination clear without the use of introductory words like *that, who,* or *which.*

Everybody knew (*that*) he had failed.

None of the books (*which*) I had studied clarified the question.

Before a dependent clause used as a subject, object, or other complement, however, omission of the connective is often confusing.

ORIGINAL

REVISION

Mr. Chamberlain forgot the umbrella had been torn.
[*The reader is momentarily misled into interpreting* the umbrella *as the object of* forgot *rather than the beginning of a clause.*]

Mr. Chamberlain forgot *that* the umbrella had been torn.
[*The connective is supplied, and the reader can no longer suppose that Mr. Chamberlain left the umbrella behind.*]

The trouble was the janitor had forgotten to lock the doors.
[*A clause used as a subjective complement is seldom clear without the connective.*]

(1) The trouble was *that* the janitor had forgotten to lock the doors.
(2) The trouble arose because the janitor had forgotten to lock the doors.

In the introduction the author proposed nothing happens.

In the introduction *which* the author proposed, nothing happens.

16b PATTERNS IN COMPARISONS   Comp

Comparisons frequently fit a word-order pattern so well fixed that parallel elements need not be completely repeated, and when a shorter construction becomes established, it, too, provides a pattern and the basis for further economy. Consider the following:

It was easier to take a cab *than it was easy to take* a bus.

It was easier to take a cab *than to take* a bus.

It was easier to take a cab *than* a bus.

One idiomatic pattern in English involves a special problem. Sentences like the following are common colloquially:

That night the team was as good if not better *than* any other team in the league.

But the connective *than* cannot be logically understood after *good,* where *as* is required. Standard English, therefore, requires some kind of completion of comparisons of this sort.

In another colloquial pattern which sometimes causes trouble in writing, expressions like *so beautiful, most wonderful, biggest, finest, prettiest* appear as vague indications of enthusiasm.

It was *such* a lovely party.

He was the *nicest* man.

These expressions begin a comparison, and in standard written English either the comparison should be finished or modifiers should be used which do not imply a comparison.

ORIGINAL

I knew her better than Mary.
[*With parts of the comparison omitted, two meanings are possible.*]

The people had been as kind if not kinder than my own family.
[*Than cannot serve both comparisons. Revision (2) is accurate, though stiff; (1) lacks logical connectives, but follows a familiar pattern.*]

The heroine was so charming.
[*The writer probably did not intend a comparison but added the intensifier under the impression that it made his statement more convincing.*

Albert was such a kind man.

REVISION

(1) I knew her better than Mary did.
(2) I knew her better than I knew Mary.

(1) The people had been as kind as my own family, if not kinder.
(2) The people had been as kind as, if not kinder than, my own family.

(1) The heroine was charming.
(2) The heroine was so charming that I paid no attention to the other characters.
[*If the writer has a comparison in mind, he should complete it.*]

Albert was a kind man.
Albert was a very kind man.

Patterns in comparison which appear complete may be incomplete in fact because they have been completed with a word which cannot logically work with the words in the remainder of the comparison.

ORIGINAL

During the war the *value* of the Negro troops was found to be on a par with white service *forces.*

[*The sentence compares* value *and* forces, *which are not logically comparable. The writer probably intended to compare the value of one force with the value of the other, or to compare the two forces.*]

The foreman insisted that his job was harder than a common laborer.

[*Job* and laborer *are not comparable.*]

His ears were longer than a jack rabbit.

But the *battle* against eating pumpkin seeds in school continued, as *gum chewing* does in most American schools.

[*The words put into parallel positions,* battle *and* gum chewing, *are not comparable.*]

Cyrano is more popular than *any* of Rostand's plays.

[Cyrano *cannot be more popular than itself, and* any of Rostand's plays *includes* Cyrano.]

REVISION

(1) During the war the Negro *troops* were found to be on a par with white service *forces.*
(2) During the war the Negro *troops* were as valuable as the white forces.

[Troops *and* forces *can be logically compared. The idea of value can be retained by making it the basis for comparison.*]

(1) The foreman insisted that his job was harder than a common laborer's.
(2) The foreman insisted that his job was harder than that of a common laborer.

His ears were longer than a jack rabbit's.

(1) But the *battle* against eating pumpkin seeds in school continued, as does the *battle* against gum chewing in most American schools.
(2) But the eating of pumpkin seeds in school continued, as gum chewing does in most American schools.

Cyrano is more popular than any *other* of Rostand's plays.

[Cyrano *can logically be compared with the* other *plays of Rostand.*]

EXERCISE 16

A. In the sentences below, supply any words needed for clarity. The meaning of some sentences is immediately and certainly clear; indicate that these sentences are correct as they stand.

1. Her insistence her son should become a doctor ruined his health.
2. Chiffon is as hard to sew on a sewing machine or harder than burlap.
3. The only answer I could give the dean was my preparation in Latin was inadequate.
4. When I looked into the cell I disliked Dandy Jack as much as the police officer.
5. Drama is the poetry of conduct, romance the poetry of circumstance.
6. He did not consider the team would be able. to take a united stand.
7. He learned respect and obedience to the new officers.
8. She soon became aware living with her husband was impossible.
9. I don't believe that churches are increasing people's belief and trust in God. They are changing from the way they used to.
10. People say that reading a book a week increases your vocabulary and your manner of speaking.
11. The girls found the cabin so beautiful, and Aubrey was such a handsome man.
12. Her gray hair adds rather than detracts from her appearance.
13. There were great scientific advances, but precious little chance to use them until government regulations had been removed.
14. Some cruelties still pass for service done in her honor: no thumbscrew is used, no iron boot, no scorching of flesh; but plenty of controversial bruising, laceration, and even lifelong maiming.
15. I have and will continue to be a defender of liberty.
16. She looked as old or older than Methuselah.
17. After an hour of this conversation, I decided that I disliked Mary's cousin as much as Mary.
18. At the same time he was afraid and fascinated by the eyes of the tiger.
19. He promised the people food and medical supplies would be flown into all the flood areas.
20. It is one of the cruxes of history, the Celts having captured Rome, did not keep it.

B. In the following sentences complete any incomplete patterns of comparison, either by adding the appropriate material or by revising any words which illogically complete the pattern.

1. She liked Picasso better than any painter.
2. You can't imagine. She is the nicest girl.

3. Because cars are so well built, the driver drives much faster than he can safely handle the car.

4. The lecturer compared his life with a medieval peasant.

5. His arms dangled down longer than a baboon.

6. Wordsworth's *Prelude* was written, not like Rousseau wrote his *Confessions,* to reveal himself, but for the happiness and moral betterment of men.

7. The vampire leered at the little girl, showing teeth as white and sharp as a wolf.

8. Olive much preferred making her own clothes than to buy them in the shops.

9. His career was more brilliant than any musician who had graduated in his class.

10. Geology, unlike most professional men, seems to have entered into a period of shrinkage in job opportunities.

C. As the sense for sentence patterns has become strong in English, that is, as the language has become more distributive, writers can use the patterns to write with more economy. The following, from Chapter 2 of Exodus in the King James Version of the Bible, is the famous story of the birth of Moses, which followed the order by Pharaoh that all male Hebrew children should be killed. The writing represents good English prose of about 350 years ago. Retell the story as best you can in modern English. Then compare the versions, noticing where you have been able to be briefer and terser than the original by omitting parts of constructions which the authors of the King James Version thought essential.

1   And there went a man of the house of Levi, and took to wife a daughter of Levi.

2   And the woman conceived, and bare a son: and when she saw him that he was a goodly child, she hid him three months.

3   And when she could not longer hide him, she took for him an ark of bulrushes, and daubed it with slime and with pitch, and put the child therein; and she laid it in the flags by the river's brink.

4   And his sister stood afar off, to wit what would be done to him.

5   And the daughter of Pharaoh came down to wash herself at the river; and her maidens walked along by the river's side: and when she saw the ark among the flags, she sent her maid to fetch it.

6   And when she had opened it, she saw the child: and, behold, the babe wept. And she had compassion on him, and said, This is one of the Hebrews' children.

7   Then said his sister to Pharaoh's daughter, Shall I go and

call to thee a nurse of the Hebrew women, that she may nurse the child for thee?

8   And Pharaoh's daughter said to her, Go. And the maid went and called the child's mother.

9   And Pharaoh's daughter said unto her, Take this child away, and nurse it for me, and I will give thee thy wages. And the woman took the child, and nursed it.

10   And the child grew, and she brought him unto Pharaoh's daughter, and he became her son. And she called his name Moses: and she said, Because I drew him out of the water.

11   And it came to pass in those days, when Moses was grown, that he went out unto his brethren, and looked on their burdens: and he spied an Egyptian smiting a Hebrew, one of his brethren.

12   And he looked this way and that way, and when he saw that there was no man, he slew the Egyptian, and hid him in the sand.

13   And when he went out the second day, behold, two men of the Hebrews strove together: and he said to him that did the wrong, Wherefore smitest thou thy fellow?

14   And he said, Who made thee a prince and a judge over us? intendest thou to kill me, as thou Killedst the Egyptian? And Moses feared, and said, Surely this thing is known.

15   Now when Pharaoh heard this thing, he sought to slay Moses. But Moses fled from the face of Pharaoh, and dwelt in the land of Midian: and he sat down by a well.

16   Now the priest of Midian had seven daughters: and they came and drew water, and filled the troughs to water their father's flock.

17   And the shepherds came and drove them away: but Moses stood up and helped them, and watered their flock.

18   And when they came to Reuel their father, he said, How is it that ye are come so soon to-day?

19   And they said, An Egyptian delivered us out of the hand of the shepherds, and also drew water enough for us, and watered the flock.

20   And he said unto his daughters, And where is he? why is it that ye have left the man? call him, that he may eat bread.

21   And Moses was content to dwell with the man: and he gave Moses Zipporah his daughter.

17

Emphasis: Using the Patterns of English

For Guide to Revision, see page 294

Variations on the subject-verb-complement pattern can provide emphasis for special purposes.

Exploding bombs are notably emphatic, but they do little of the work of the world and they produce little of lasting beauty. Good writing seldom requires bombs. Variations from usual word order patterns can produce special meaning or special emphasis—and also special weakness. Commenting on the style of *Time, The New Yorker* quips, "Backward ran the sentences until reeled the mind."

Some variations are like counterpoint or variations on a theme in music, which depend for their effect on recollections of the original or basic pattern. Other deviations are emphatic; a word shifted from its usual position gains emphasis, as a man in a bathing suit would gain attention at a formal dinner party. Still other deviations are mistakes; proverbially carts do not work well before horses, and in English grammar, some words do not work well in front of some others.

Since the subject-verb-complement pattern is the core of expression in English, it provides the soundest structural basis for emphasis. As we have seen in Section 13, it throws emphasis upon the subject, where most sentences require it. Often, however, the writer needs special sorts of emphasis, and this chapter is intended to survey some stylistic devices, particularly patterns which deviate from normal word order: the postponed subject, the substitute subject, the passive pattern, and inverted patterns.

17-1 THE POSTPONED SUBJECT

The words *it* and *there* can introduce a sentence so that the subject is postponed. These introductory words, called expletives, are signals, reminders to the reader that a subject is coming in an unusual position. Usually the construction combines with some form of the verb *to be* to assert only the existence of the subject; and since the subject with its modifiers is the core of the sentence, unusual word order provides appropriate emphasis.

Introductory Word	Verb	Subject	Modifier
There	are	two reasons	for doubting his word.
There	will be	time	for a hundred questions.

Notice that in these examples we would never use usual word order and say *Two reasons for doubting his word are* or *Time for a hundred questions will be* (although we might say *Two reasons for doubting his word exist*). Often, however, usual word order would be possible but would change emphasis.

> There are two men in the boat. (Compare *Two men are in the boat.*)
> It was heavy artillery which finally stopped us. (Compare *The heavy artillery finally stopped us.*)
> It is John who should be blamed. (Compare *John should be blamed.*)

This construction is perhaps most useful when the writer has a long and complicated subject but wishes only to say that it exists—not to say more about it. Consider:

> But there was a class of residents which appears to be perennial in that University, composed out of the younger masters; a class of men who, defective alike in age, in wisdom, or in knowledge, were distinguished by a species of theoretic High Church fanaticism; who, until they received their natural correction from advancing age, required from time to time to be protected against their own extravagance by some form of external pressure.
> —JAMES ANTHONY FROUDE

If the subject, *class,* were to appear in its usual position at the beginning of the sentence it would be separated from the verb by more than fifty words of elaborate modification; and when the verb finally appeared it would be only *was* or perhaps some such wordy device as *was in existence.* The expletive construction allows the subject to come after the verb but near it; *there was,* in effect introduces the subject and then allows it to have the major emphasis of the sentence.

17-2 THE SUBSTITUTE SUBJECT WITH LINKING VERB

In the typical English sentence, the grammatical subject names what the sentence is about, usually the actor. Sometimes, however, to provide a transition from preceding sentences or to give a word special emphasis in the subject position, the writer prefers a framework with the verb *to be,* the linking verb (see 20-1). For example, in the usual pattern one might write

John studied only his algebra course that year.

The sentence is about John; John is the actor. In some contexts, however, *algebra* might require special emphasis:

Algebra was the only course John studied that year.

The goal of the basic pattern, *algebra,* becomes the grammatical subject with the verb *was,* and the actor has a secondary position in a dependent clause. A subject displaces the actor so that it gains special prominence. Or consider the following:

The sound of her voice was all he could remember.
Bankruptcy seemed the only course open to him.
This quarrel with his son was now his chief regret.

Each of these is weakened by its dependence on a linking verb, but the construction has enabled the writer to start with special emphasis on *the sound of her voice, bankruptcy,* and *this quarrel.* The more usual actor-action pattern would have given the verb more to do:

He could remember only the sound of her voice.
He saw no course open to him but bankruptcy.
He chiefly regretted this quarrel with his son.

17-3 THE PASSIVE

Usually the agent or actor needs to be mentioned first in a sentence, so that we know what we are talking about. But sometimes the agent or actor is less important than the action or the result; sometimes the actor is unknown, or should not be mentioned. By changing the form of the verb (see 20) and varying word order, we can shift emphasis away from the actor. The actor is either omitted or relegated to a subordinate position in the sentence. The verb is made passive. The goal or receiver of the action—which would be a complement in a sentence following standard order—becomes the grammatical subject.

Compare the following:

> In June somebody completed the new road.
> The new road was completed in June.

The first sentence follows the actor-action pattern, but forces the indefinite *somebody* into the subject position. The second sentence omits mention of the actor and uses the complement of the first as its subject.

Passive constructions are frequently misused, but they have good uses. Sometimes the actor is unimportant. Suppose, for example, we wish to mention the publication of a book in 1623, but we have no reason to name the publisher. We want the publishing to be the main action, but if we use the usual actor-action pattern, we are faced with something like this:

> A person or persons whom we do not wish to mention just now published the book in 1623.

In this sentence, the receiver of the action, *book,* is more important than the missing actor. We therefore solve the problem by putting *book* into the subject position and using a passive form of the verb.

> The book was published in 1623.

For a statement as simple as this, however, a separate sentence is usually inappropriate; the writer might better reduce the idea embodied in this sentence to a modifier and go on to another idea.

> The book, *published in 1623,* has provided the basis for all subsequent editions of Shakespeare's works.

Sometimes circumstances make the passive construction convenient, or even imperative. The actor may be known, but there may be reasons for not mentioning him. A newspaper reporter might be telling the truth if he were to write:

> John A. Scrogum murdered Joseph Meek at 7:45 this morning in the Hot Spot Lunch.

This statement is libelous; the reporter and the newspaper which publishes the sentence can be sued for accusing a man of murder who has not been legally convicted. Accordingly, the reporter would probably write something like the following:

> Joseph Meek was shot and killed at 7:45 this morning in the Hot Spot Lunch.

The actor has now been removed, and the statement is legally publishable.

Or the actor or agent may not be known. A historian writes:

> The world of St. Paul was steeped in guilt and wretchedness.

He does not know who steeped it; the agent, even if it could be determined, would be much too complicated for expression in a single sentence. Or consider:

> Nations which have lost their moral self-respect are easily conquered.

This sentence is a generalization which does not depend at all on who conquers these nations; no one actor could be specified. Occasionally, a passive construction is desirable for stylistic reasons; for instance, a writer may wish to avoid inserting complicated material between the subject and verb. Compare the following

> The hearing was opened by the chairman of the committee, who was known for his ruthlessness in smirching the reputation of innocent witnesses and for his cleverness in beclouding the issue by his own witticisms and innuendoes.
>
> The chairman of the committee, who was known for his ruthlessness in smirching the reputations of innocent witnesses and for his cleverness in beclouding the issue by his own witticisms and innuendoes, opened the hearing.

The first version, although it employs the passive, has the advantage of keeping subject and verb together. A verb in a dependent clause may be thrown into the passive in order to continue the subject of the main clause, as in the following:

> Carlo, although he was known to have communist leanings, maintained his position because he always met his payrolls.

The passive, then, has very definite uses. It is properly used when

(1) The subject is not known;
(2) The subject is known, but for some good reason cannot, or had better not, be mentioned;
(3) The receiver of the action is so much more important than the actor that emphasis properly belongs on the receiver.
(4) One of the elements of the actor-action pattern must be moved from its normal position for stylistic reasons.

Except in these special situations, the passive usually weakens English prose. Consider the following passage, in which most of the verbs are passive:

> Zoroaster's spirit was rapidly caught by the Persians. A voice which was recognized by them as speaking truth was responded to eagerly by a people uncorrupted by luxury. They have been called the Puritans of the Old World. Never, it is said, was idolatry hated by any people as it was by them, and for the simple reason that lies were hated by them.

Compare this passage with the following written by James Anthony Froude.

> The Persians caught rapidly Zoroaster's spirit. Uncorrupted by luxury, they responded eagerly to a voice which they recognized as speaking truth to them. They have been called the Puritans of the Old World. Never any people, it is said, hated idolatry as they hated it, and for the simple reason that they hated lies.

Froude's version keeps the actor-action pattern everywhere but in the third sentence and the parenthetical *it is said* of the fourth—in which the actual subjects of the action are unknown. Obviously, his paragraph is more direct, more economical, and more effective.

17-4   EMPHASIS BY POSITION; THE PERIODIC SENTENCE

Certain positions in the sentence are inevitably emphatic, notably the beginning and the end, and accordingly in languages which make little or no use of position for grammar, emphatic words can be moved freely into these positions. Roman and Greek rhetoricians recommended this practice, and accordingly many Latin sentences have the subject and the verb the first and last words. English makes so much use of position in the sentence as a grammatical device that complicated sentences having the Latinate pattern are rare, although somewhat similar effects are obtained through the basic sentence pattern, which puts the subject and its modifiers first, the complement and its modifiers last. The effect of these Latinate sentences has been cultivated in what is called the *periodic sentence,* that is, a sentence in which a period cannot be placed prior to the end of the sentence. Notice the following:

> That Boswell was a hunter after notabilities, that he loved such, and longed, and even crept and crawled to be near them; that he first (in old Touchwood Auchlinlek's phraseology) "took on with Paoli"; and then being off with "the Corsican landlouper," took on with a schoolmaster, "ane that keeped a schule, and ca'd it an academy"; that he did all this, and could not help doing it, we account a very singular merit.
>
> —THOMAS CARLYLE

This is a telling sentence; it amasses the evidence in a series of dependent clauses and builds up the striking if somewhat sarcastic conclusion implied in "a very singular merit." Such sentences are now somewhat out of fashion; they sound rather too formal in the context of modern prose, which is characterized by easy fluidity, but they still have their uses. More common in modern prose is an approximation of the periodic sentence, in which at least some of the modifiers, especially the sentence modifiers which provide such incidental information as time, place, cause, and attendant circumstances, appear at the beginning of the sentence. The reader thus has the qualifying details in hand when he approaches the main statement. The following is from Samuel Butler's *Erewhon.*

> When I talked about originality and genius to some gentlemen whom I met at a supper party given by Mr. Thims in my honor, and said that original thought ought to be encouraged, I had to eat my words at once.

This sentence is almost periodic, and has much of the strength of the periodic sentence, but it retains the relaxed quality of the *loose sentence.*

Since words in an English sentence appear usually in regular patterns, they can be emphasized by being drawn out of the regular pattern to appear in an unusual position. The device works well if it is not overworked, and is often especially justified by the context in which the sentence appears. Standing alone, for example, the following sentence seems unnecessarily backward:

> This heifer they sold in despair.

When the sentence is put into its context, however, the reasons for the irregular order are clear.

> One heifer refused to stay in the farm close. This heifer they sold in despair.

Or consider the following, which at first seems an unjustifiable inversion:

> The ashes Daniel spread over the floor.

Compare the sentence in its context:

> The servant brought a gleaming torch and a sack of ashes. He set the torch in a bracket on the wall. The ashes Daniel spread over the floor.

One sentence, or group of sentences, suggests by its meaning and its emphasis the prinicipal idea of the subsequent sentence.

17-5 SUBORDINATION AND EMPHASIS

Like many devices of sentence structure, subordination allows the writer to show relationships and to shift emphasis. The purposes of the writer determine which ideas are subordinated and the manner of their subordination. Consider, for example, various ways of combining the following relatively simple ideas:

> I was twelve years old.
> I got my first long pants.
> I took the girl next door to the movies.

Most obviously, perhaps the first idea might be subordinated to the others as an indication of the time; the last two ideas share equally the stress of the sentence.

> When I was twelve years old, I got my first long pants and took the girl next door to the movies.

A change in the subordinating word (see 23-4), however, would vary the meaning and emphasis considerably.

> Although I was only twelve years old, I got my first long pants and took the girl next door to the movies.

Or both the first two ideas might be subordinated.

> When I was twelve years old and in my first long pants, I took the girl next door to the movies.

The trip to the movies becomes the event which the writer wants primarily to talk about, and the acquisition of the pants drops out.

Subordination should vary with the sentences which precede and follow. The last version above, for example, might be appropriate in a paragraph narrating a story about the friendship of a boy and girl. The context might suggest even wider variations in the pattern of subordination. Consider:

> When I had my first long pants and had taken the girl next door to the movies, I was twelve years old.

This unusual emphasis might be logical if the preceding sentence had read:

> The actual date of my twelfth birthday meant nothing to me.

Or a different preceding sentence might suggest the wisdom of a parallel pattern of subordination following it.

> At the age of eleven, I tore my knickers trying to catch a toad with which I hoped to frighten the girls at the Sunday School picnic. At twelve, I wore my first long pants to take the girl next door to the movies.

The second sentence fits the pattern of the first, draws the contrast between the events, and enforces the continuity (see 3-4).

17-6   EMPHASIS BY REPETITION OF WORD-ORDER PATTERNS

Consider the uses of variation to stress parallel ideas:

> By foreign hands thy dying eyes were clos'd,
> By foreign hands thy decent limbs compos'd,
> By foreign hands thy humble grave adorn'd,
> By strangers honoured, and by strangers mourn'd!

Usual order is changed in each clause in a curious way so that each involves a kind of double inversion. The usual pattern would be:

Subject	*Verb*	*Complement*
Foreign hands	closed	thy dying eyes.

The poet, Alexander Pope, has followed two procedures for varying word order. He has reversed subject and object, making the verb passive:

Thy dying eyes were closed by foreign hands.

Then he has gone a step further and moved the modifier, which would have been the subject of the action in a conventional sentence, into the position of emphasis at the beginning. The result is stress on the initiator of the action, *foreign hands*—even more stress than normal word order would provide.

Repetitions of this pattern throughout the clauses multiply the stress. The first three clauses build on the importance of *by foreign hands* so that the meaning of *by strangers* is sharp and clear. The result is that the reader remembers most vividly, even in the presence of death itself, the circumstance that only strangers were present at the death.

Less spectacularly, but equally importantly, repetitions in word order affect meaning and emphasis in ordinary prose. Repetition of the standard actor-action pattern to introduce each of the following sentences reinforces the parallel in the ideas presented:

> *Dr. Woods looked* his *creed* more decidedly, perhaps, than any of the professors. *He* had the firm *fibre* of a theological athlete, and *lived* to be old without ever mellowing, I think, into a kind of half-heterodoxy, as old ministers of stern creed are said to do now and then,—just as old doctors grow to be sparing of the more exasperating drugs in their later days. *He had manipulated* the *mysteries* of the Infinite so long and so exhaustively that he would have seemed more at home among the mediaeval schoolmen than amidst the working clergy of our own time.
>
> —OLIVER WENDELL HOLMES, *The Autocrat of the Breakfast Table*

This paragraph is more typical of writing in English than is the passage of poetry above. In it the pattern of the ideas forces the sentences into the actor-action order. Continuity of thought in a paragraph usually demands this normal order. The writer should be sure, therefore, that the context of his sentences justifies a variation before he deviates from standard order.

17 **Em**

EMPHASIS: USING THE
PATTERNS OF ENGLISH

Guide to Revision

Revise word order or omit words in order to clarify meaning and make emphasis appropriate to the sentence in its context.

Variations from usual word order patterns often provide needed special emphasis, but sometimes variations falsify emphasis and obscure meaning.

17a POSTPONED SUBJECTS   Em a

We need the reverse gears of an automobile in order to back into a parking place; but we do not, after we have discovered how to shift into reverse, go backward down the highway just because the reverse gears are available. We need the construction with *it* and *there* in English to delay expression of the subject in certain special situations, but we should not use the device just because it exists. Overuse of the postponed subject is one of the sins of student writing. The construction is by its nature roundabout; often it is wordy, and it obscures the parts of the sentence which are potentially strongest, the subject and the main verb. Many a page of weak writing is weak because sentence after sentence, which should begin with the name of some concrete thing, begins with *it* or *there*. Consider the following:

> It is a fact that it is hard to get people to see that there is a lot of sport in skiing.

Several weaknesses mar this sentence, but the needlessly postponed subjects cause most of them. The writer might better have said

> Skiing can be a good sport, though few people know it.

A writer who finds himself beginning many sentences with *it* or *there* can appropriately ask himself: have I any good reason for not beginning this sentence with its logical subject?

ORIGINAL

It was after a long argument that we decided to push on. It was soon agreed among us, however, that we had made a mistake. Within an hour there were two sharp attacks which scattered our rear guard. It was obvious that we should have stayed at the fort.

[*Postponed subjects became troublesome when successive sentences are needlessly inverted. One inverted sentence may add variety; a dozen make writing indirect and wordy.*]

His escape set England again on fire. There were Llewelyn wasting the border, the Cinque Ports holding the sea, the garrison of Kenilworth pushing their raids as far as Oxford.

[*Postponement of the subject weakens the second sentence and blocks the continuity of ideas from one sentence to the next.*]

REVISION

After a long argument we decided to push on. Soon, however, we agreed that we had made a mistake. Within an hour two sharp attacks scattered our rear guard. Obviously, we should have stayed at the fort.

[*Normal order strengthens and shortens the passage. For variety some writers might prefer to leave the last sentence:* It was obvious that we should have stayed at the fort.]

His escape set England again on fire. Llewelyn wasted the border; the Cinque Ports held the sea; the garrison of Kenilworth pushed their raids as far as Oxford.

[*With normal order restored, the reader can see that the second sentence develops the general idea of the first; parallel patterns clarify further relationships.*]

17b   SUBSTITUTE SUBJECTS WITH LINKING VERB   Em b

Unjustified use of a framework with a linking verb and with a subject other than the name of the actor often leads to awkward, roundabout writing.

ORIGINAL

The way in which Mary wore her clothes was with an air of sophistication.

[*The actor in the sentence is Mary, but* way *is used as the subject.*]

Every morning in his eight-o'clock English class is the time Harry studies his French.

The reason Alice wants a new dress is because there is a dance Friday that is to be her first formal.

REVISION

Mary wore her clothes with an air of sophistication.

[*The framework is useless; the actor-action-goal sentence is clearer, more direct.*]

Harry studies his French every morning in his eight-o'clock English class.

Alice wants a new dress for her first formal dance Friday.

17c PASSIVE SENTENCES

Usually a statement tells who or what acts (the subject) and what it does (the verb). Inversion through use of the passive verb throws stress on the receiver of the action and draws attention away from the actor-action pattern. It makes the receiver of the action the subject and the center of attention. This type of inversion, therefore, is justified only in special circumstances. Used indiscriminately it weakens writing; a sentence like the following is painfully awkward.

> The lake where the meetings of our gang are held is reached by an old road that was found by me when I was hidden out there by the kidnappers.

Less cluttered sentences may be equally harmful to direct communication, especially when they occur frequently and do not provide special emphasis warranted by the context. Needless passive constructions weaken a writing style. A student writer can find few better ways to improve his style than to practice using active instead of passive verbs, to hesitate every time he finds himself using a passive form, to ask himself whether the passive form is justified, and if not, to try recasting the sentence in actor-action order.

ORIGINAL

That there were many difficulties whereby women were unable to use the new union lounge was the attitude which was stated by the first speaker. It was her contention that women were resented in the lounge by the men students and that this resentment was clearly made known by the men in their actions. A different point of view was introduced by the second speaker, by whom it was stated that the reason for the inability of the women to make full use of the lounge was caused by the attitude of the women themselves. The views which were expressed by this speaker were the objects of sharp criticism from the other members of the panel.

REVISION

The first speaker insisted that women were unable to use the new union lounge because men students resented having women there and made their resentment clearly known. The second speaker introduced a new point of view, that women were unable to make full use of the lounge because of their own attitude. The other members of the panel sharply criticized the views of this speaker.

[*The original has many weaknesses, but basic to most of its difficulties is overuse of unwarranted passive sentences. The revision still needs development, but it improves the passage, mainly by recasting sentences in the actor-action pattern.*]

ORIGINAL *(Cont.)*

The trouble was caused by John's insistence that he begin.

[*Nothing here warrants departing from normal order. The actor-action elements are present and important; they should appear in normal order.*]

REVISION *(Cont.)*

(1) John's insistence that he begin caused the trouble.

(2) John caused the trouble by insisting that he begin.

[*More thorough revision, reducing part of the subject to a modifier, clarifies the sentence.*]

17d INVERTED SENTENCES   Em d

Shifting subject, verb, or complement from its usual position can achieve special effects, but unless these effects are justified, normal word order should remain. Inverted sentences not required by the context or warranted by special intentions of the writer make writing confusing, falsely rhetorical, or affected.

ORIGINAL

We were never happy about the climate in New York. Cold were the winters; hot were the summers.

[*This inversion, unless the writer is attempting some kind of half-humorous exaggeration, sounds absurd.*]

I was only a child, inexperienced and trusting. Little did I know what was in store for me.

[*The second sentence is trite, but the staleness is obvious because the inversion is unwarranted. The unusual word order makes the sentence overdramatic.*]

REVISION

We were never happy about the climate in New York. The winters were cold, the summers hot.

[*Usual order is more direct, and there is no artificially induced special emphasis.*]

I was only an inexperienced and trusting child, unaware of what was in store for me.

[*Restoration of usual word order removes most of the affectation from the sentences, although the reader is still suspicious of the significance attached to the facts.*]

17e EMPHASIS THROUGH VERBS   Em e

Sometimes linking verbs can be very effective.

Although he *looks* gentle, he *is* the notorious hatchet murderer.

Part of the impact of the sentence depends on the slight difference in meaning between *looks* and *is*. Usually, however, the linking verb has little meaning; and since the verb in good prose carries much of the meaning, a writer who uses excessive linking verbs dilutes his prose and introduces needless, childish predications. Usually excessive use of linking verbs, especially of forms of *to be,* betrays the writer's lazy thinking or faulty structure. The overuse of *to be* often reveals inadequate subordination (see 15) or illogical relationships between ideas. Often linking verbs usurp places better filled by more vigorous verbs.

ORIGINAL

The conversion of the pottery craft into what is now a highly ramified industry is due to a long series of improvements, as well as to the methods which are now in use in distribution and marketing. The first step toward the better manufacture of pottery was the use of common salt. When the pot was red hot in the oven, the attendant was ready to pour salt through the top of the furnace. This method was the factor which put a smooth, colorless glaze on the earthenware. It was one hundred years later when Enoch Booth was the introducer of the double-firing process to improve glazes. . . .

REVISION

A series of improvements in manufacturing, distributing, and marketing turned the craft of pottery making into a highly ramified modern industry. Salt provided the first improvement. Cast into the furnace when the earthenware glowed red hot, it fused to form a colorless glaze. A hundred years later, Enoch Booth improved glazes with a method of double firing which permitted the use of colors. . . .

[*The original is cumbersome because misused forms of the verb* to be *require awkward, roundabout sentences. Removing the inappropriate linking verbs shortens and strengthens the paragraph.*]

17f MINOR WORDS IN EMPHATIC POSITIONS Em f

ORIGINAL

This nation must return to the ideals which inspired its founding. *Yes,* we must re-examine our goals.

[*The frequent insertion of words like* Yes, indeed, well, now, *borrowed from speech, can emphasize insignificant parts of the sentence.*]

Well, first I thought I ought to see what was in the cave. *Now* I was not really afraid to look, but I decided there was no hurry.

[*The italicized words would be useful only if the writer was trying to reproduce the effect of some kind of speaking.*]

REVISION

This nation must return to the ideals which inspired its founding. We must re-examine our goals.

[*Even with the* yes *omitted, the sentence is oratorical enough in its tone.*]

(1) First I thought I ought to see what was in the cave. I was not really afraid to look, but I thought there was no hurry.

[*Omission of the introductory words removes the false emphasis, but weakens the connection between the sentences.*]

(2) I thought I should first see what was in the cave, but, although I was not really afraid to look, I decided there was no hurry.

17g RHETORICAL QUESTIONS   Em g

The rhetorical question is an inversion of regular sentence order for the sake of emphasis, a statement in question form. Sometimes the answer is assumed to be so obvious that the reader will supply it automatically and will be convinced of the entire implied statement. Sometimes the writer supplies the answer. In either instance the device—another favorite in oratory—provides strong emphasis and should be used only when the situation warrants unusual stress.

ORIGINAL

There are five reasons for joining a sorority in college. *What are those reasons?* The first is . . .

[*The question dramatizes a prosaic statement, which should be clear enough without repetition in inverted order.*]

REVISION

There are five reasons for joining a sorority in college, of which the first is . . .

[*Omission of the rhetorical question makes the emphasis more appropriate to the meaning.*]

EXERCISE 17

A. Write a paragraph in which you avoid all use of the passive verb and do not postpone subjects with *it* or *there*.

B. Mark every sentence in one of your themes in which you vary from usual word order. Then revise these sentences to the actor-action pattern and judge whether or not the change improves the theme.

C. The sentences below vary word order by having the receiver of the action at the beginning and by using a passive verb. Revise the sentences so that they follow usual word order with active verbs.

1. Blue taffeta dresses were worn by all the girls in the class.

2. The introduction of the speaker was made by the past president of the club.

3. Undeterred by the stories in the papers, a trip around the lake after midnight was contemplated by Jane and her roommate.

4. At the end of the passage our progress was arrested by a pile of huge boulders.

5. Tickets were bought by Mr. Sims from a scalper for twice their value.

6. A small shop was opened on Fifth Avenue by two of my class-

mates where clothes could be designed by them to suit both the figure and the purse of the average girl working in an office.

7. A very rigid censorship was imposed by the commanding officer on war news.

8. For the first time officeholders could be criticized by the people.

9. By using a spectroscope it is possible for many metals to be identified by a laboratory technician.

10. The man in the street is granted by the Constitution the right to say what he pleases without fear of prosecution.

11. A moral is conveyed to the reader by many kinds of stories.

12. Important information about military matters should not be revealed by the newspapers.

13. After working for fifteen minutes, the ground was finally cleared and leveled by the men enough for the sleeping bags.

14. Provisional governments were set up by the military forces as soon as an area had been conquered.

15. Citizens of the United States were guaranteed freedom of speech by the first ten amendments to the Constitution.

16. If the petition is signed by enough people, it will be considered by the assembly.

17. Drifting down the river out of control, a series of dangerous rapids was approached by the boat.

18. The enemy was driven into the sea by our reinforcements.

19. Although still eager to write a great epic, many prose pamphlets had to be turned out by Milton.

20. The ball was thrown accurately by the first baseman, but it was missed by the catcher, and the runner was waved home by the third-base coach.

D. Revise the following sentences by making more extensive use of the actor-action pattern:

1. There was quite a lot of commotion because of there being a live mole in my roommate's bed.

2. There were two chaperons in attendance at the dance, but still the uninvited guests soon outnumbered the invited ones.

3. It was because so many students had forgotten to register for the examination that there were new rules passed by the academic council.

4. There was a tall white stallion standing all alone at the edge of the cliff.

5. It is obvious that there should be more courses in fine arts taken by the average student.

6. There were two points of basic disagreement which prevented successful negotiation.

7. It is in his book *The Diary of a Writer* that Dostoevsky describes how a mother hen defended her chickens from a brutal and sadistic boy.

8. If there is the desire to help, there are always lots of ways for a father to be saved money by the student.

9. It was when I was waiting in a registration line and I was talking with a graduate student that the realization came to me of how complicated a university is.

10. That was the time when there was an opportunity for me to buy my first colony of bees.

E. Revise for emphasis and clarify the faulty sentences in the following student theme; often sentences can appropriately be combined.

(1) When our Constitution was written, the thing foremost in the people's mind was to have freedom of speech. (2) People were tired of listening to the government tell them what to say and what not to say. (3) They had come over here to escape from a society where there were always government agents, and the people could be persecuted by them. (4) Town meetings were broken up unless the speakers were told by a government official exactly what to say.

(5) After the Constitution took effect, freedom of speech began to be used by the people in its true meaning. (6) Opinions could be voiced by anyone on any subject. (7) No longer did a person have to be afraid of landing in jail or getting deported from the United States. (8) Often there were soap-box speakers, and they stood on boxes in the streets or in the city squares and gave speeches. (9) Sometimes public officials were attacked by these speeches. (10) These speeches were finished without punishment by the speakers.

(11) It seems that nowadays nothing can be said by a citizen, or he will be in danger of being thrown in jail by the government. (12) If a person talks against our government or any high official in it, he may be labelled a Communist. (13) I wish a different system could be found by the Government to enforce its laws. (14) Yes, what people say should not be used as evidence against them. (15) If it were not, there would be for us more of the kind of freedom of speech we used to have.

Parts
of Speech

The textbooks mostly used for grammar are sixpennyworth of horror calculated to make a lad loathe his own tongue.

—J. Runciman

The notion of grammar as an instrument of torture has grown in great measure from misconceptions about the nature and importance of parts of speech. Grammar in the schools often degenerates into a kind of game, frustrating to the student because the rules are difficult or changing. The game is to contrive definitions for classes of words and then try to put each word in any given passage into the appropriate class. Traditional definitions seem not to work very well, but the game causes serious trouble because it tends to monopolize the time available for the study of grammar. Grammar has, unfortunately, become popularly identified with mere labeling, deciding whether a given word is noun, adverb, preposition, or conjunction. The schoolboy, impatient with grammatical concepts which seem not to help much when he tries to understand or make himself understood, emerges with a large share of justice on his side. The unwarranted enthusiasm for mere identification has both distracted students from more important topics in grammar and obscured any importance a study of parts of speech may have.

Classification of words into parts of speech does have some practical importance, largely in connection with the use of function words and inflectional changes as grammatical devices in English. As we have seen, three devices enunciate most of the grammatical relationships in English (see Sections 12–17): word order, function words, and changes in form or inflectional changes. Of the three, word order certainly reveals the most important relationships, especially those concerned with the subject-verb-complement pattern. English grammar is mainly distributive, and when word order does not provide adequate signals of grammar, function words or relationship words usually serve.

To see how function words work, consider three meaningful units, *Bill Sikes, dangled,* and *a rope.* In this order they make sense, but if they are to describe a familiar scene in *Oliver Twist,* something must be added to change the relationships, as in *Bill Sikes dangled from a rope.* In a distributive grammar, relationship words like *from* supplement word order.

English, however, has not always been a distributive language. Like most European languages, it descended from a very early language known as Indo-European, which relied upon a third device, *inflection.* That is, Indo-European indicated relationships mainly by changing the forms of words. This device was still prevalent in Old English, the ancestor of English, and in 12-1 we saw that by inflecting the Old English words for *man* and *dog* we could change the actor to the goal, the biter to the bitten, without changing the order of the words.

Inflection remains as a device in modern English, although for many purposes inflections have been supplanted by function words. An Anglo-Saxon chronicler, for instance, when he believed that the Lord had intervened on behalf of his people, could write *Godes thonkes,* putting our words *God* and *thank* into the genitive case. We would say something like *by the grace of God,* using three function words instead of two endings. According to a poem inserted in the *Chronicle,* King Athelstan and his brother gained fame *sweorda ecgum.* Here *ecgum* is the word *ecg* (our *edge*) with the ending *-um,* which indicates that the word is a plural in the intrumental case, that is, it is a means of doing something. *Sweorda* is our word *sword* with a genitive plural ending, and the two words with these endings mean "with the edges of their swords." Even for surviving endings such as the *-s* for the plural and the *-'s* for the possessive we have alternative constructions using function words: *a hundred boys* but *dozens of people, my father's head* but *the head of the house.*

Form changes and inflections, then, cause some trouble for modern users of the language, largely because they are disappearing. For most purposes the language tends to do without them and to rely on word order instead. Changes in the form of the verb to designate the subjunctive mood, for example, are seemingly disappearing, especially from spoken English. Even when changes in form persist, confusion develops because of the pressure of word order, a device so prevalent that the ordinary user of the language automatically gives it preference. Personal pronouns retain form changes which indicate their use; *I* is used as a subject, *me* as an object. The tradition of form changes requires the subjective form in the sentence *It is I* because *I* is a subject complement and therefore should be in the subjective form. But according to the principles of word order, the pronoun is in the position usually occupied by the object. As a result *It is me* is becoming more and more common, at least in spoken English.

Form changes as grammatical devices, then, must be given special attention, not because they are prevalent in English grammar but because they are exceptional. Furthermore, the writer of standard English must often preserve even distinctions which are disappearing from speech. Language changes constantly, and change is healthy in language. By changing, language fills our changing needs, but if language changes so rapidly that users of the language have difficulty understanding one another, or the language of one user seems markedly strange and out of place to other users, both language and communication suffer. Thus the makers of dictionaries and handbooks of usage, and the teachers who endeavor to apply these books, very properly discourage rapid change in grammatical usage, as they discourage rapid change in word usage. Our grammar has undergone a revolution; our language is probably the better for the change, but only because the revolution proceeded through many hundreds of years. Grammatical devices, whether sentence patterns or forms of words, can function only because they have currency, and currency is destroyed by rapid change.

Classification of words into parts of speech clarifies both inflectional changes and the varying uses of function words. In the first place, only certain groups of words are involved in the few inflectional changes remaining in the language. They can be profitably considered as classes of words. Furthermore, some words are more or less restricted to function as one part of the sentence and not another, as subject, verb, complement, modifier, or function word. *Village* can be used as a subject or complement but not as a verb, but it might be used as a modifier in *village idiot. Necessity* could be a subject or complement, but it would not be used as a modifier; *necessary* is available as a modifier.

Classification, however, is not easy. English, being a distributive language, does not readily fit into the classifications of parts of speech which have been borrowed from Latin grammar. Furthermore, in English *functional shift* is relatively easy; that is, in English many words are readily shifted from one use in the sentence to another. *Cow,* for example, is usually used as a noun. But consider the following:

The principal thought he could *cow* the rebellious students.

The road to the old mine was little more than a *cow* path.

In the first sentence *cow* is a verb, in the second a modifier. Or the word *fast* can be thought of as any of several parts of speech.

It was a *fast* trip.   We *fast* during Lent.

He ran *fast.*   *They* broke their *fast* on Easter Sunday.

Classification, therefore, does not justify our saying categorically that any word *is* any part of speech. We cannot say *cow* is always a noun. We can say that in the sentence

The *cow* was chewing her cud

cow is a noun. Or we can say *cow* may be used as a noun or verb or modifier. To complicate matters still further, the traditional definitions of the parts of speech do not define very clearly, and they involve classifications made on differing bases. They thus defy the fundamental principle of classification, that material can be classified on only one basis at a time. A noun, for example, is conventionally classified on the basis of its meaning as the name of a person, place, or thing, an adjective—"a word that modifies a noun or pronoun"—on the basis of its function. Accordingly, in phrases like *asphalt paving, asphalt* can be called a noun because it is the name of something or an adjective because it modifies *paving.* Or, if we accept the conventional definition of a verb as a word which expresses action, how do we classify words like *explosion* or *collision,* which certainly "express action"? Another kind of definition, used by most modern grammarians, classifies words on the basis of their form —"A noun is a word that can add an *–s* to become plural or *–'s* to become possessive." Structural linguists, keeping attention on the spoken language, describe also the stress and positional patterns which various types of words fill. Definitions of this sort are likely to be more accurate than others, but they also must become very complicated if they are to account for all exceptions and if they are to describe the language completely. In other words, no entirely satisfactory classification into parts of speech has been developed for English.

This lack need not be very disturbing for our purposes. We are not concerned with classification for its own sake; we are not concerned to label each word in a sentence. We are rather concerned to observe distinctions among words which illuminate the structure of the sentence, which help us to talk more directly about sentence patterns, about inflection, and about uses of function words. Most educated users of the language already have a fairly good notion of general meanings for the names of the traditional parts of speech. They would not call *collision* a verb, even though it fits the definition for a verb that they know. They have learned, as we learn a great many things about language, by examples. One way, in other words, to define a noun is to say that it is a word like *blackbird, hair, mother's,* or *head* in the following sentence:

The blackbird pulled hair from my mother's head.

The following descriptions of categories are more nearly complete than this, but they are not intended as scientifically accurate ways of classifying words in the language. They are rather working guides to using terms in the discussions in the following chapters.

Noun. A few nouns cannot be readily identified by form, but most of them can become plural with an *–s* ending, can become possessive with an *–'s* ending, and can be introduced by *a, an,* or *the.* In its meaning a noun is usually a name. By function, a noun can be identified through its use as a subject, a complement, or part of a modifier connected to the sentence by a preposition.

Pronoun. Pronouns are probably most accurately defined just by listing the relatively small number of words that constitute the class (*he, she, it, who, someone,* and so on). Also they differ from nouns in not having the *–s* plural and in not being used with *a, an,* and *the.* In meaning they are hard to distinguish, since they derive their meaning from the nouns they refer to. They function in the same positions as nouns, acting as subjects, complements, or objects of prepositions.

Verb. Verbs have certain formal characteristics, but not all verbs have all of them. Most verbs have an *–s* ending to mark the third person singular present: *I walk, he walks; I try, she tries. May, can, shall,* and *ought* are exceptions. The usual definition of a verb by its meaning, that it expresses action or state of being, may be helpful though it is inadequate. The definition by function, that a verb makes an assertion about a subject, is useful if we understand subjects. Probably verbs are most often recognized from position, from learning basic sentence patterns. We know which are verbs in the following from word order:

> Annie pickles peels.
> Annie peels pickles.

But an inflectional change would allow us to identify a verb even in an unusual position.

> Annie pickles peeled.

Many verbs are complex, being composed of one or more verbal forms and one or more auxiliaries:

> He may be trying to find us.

Adjective. Adjectives can be distinguished in their form as words that can be compared (*high, higher, highest; lovely, lovelier, loveliest*). They can also be distinguished as words that can be modified by adverbs (*the brilliantly red dress*). Even when a noun modifies, it does not take an adverb modifier; we would not say *the brilliantly cloth dress.* Definitions by meaning clarify some adjectives—that an adjective describes, limits, or restricts. The most common definition is functional: an adjective is a word that modifies a noun or pronoun. It works, except that some words, especially nouns, also modify nouns and pronouns (*wood fence, garage door*).

Adverb. Adverbs, as they are conventionally recognized, are not very readily described as a group, partly because they include at least three subclasses. In the sentence, *Obviously* he was driving *very slow,* the italicized words are usually called adverbs, but they differ in form, meaning, and function. Many adverbs can be distinguished by form, since they end in *–ly;* exceptions include adverbs like *not, very, little, well* and *hard,* which do not end in *–ly* and other parts of speech like *homely, likely,* and *Molly* which do. Meaning identifies many adverbs, but omits many others—an adverb tells where, when, how, or how much. The functional definition serves for most purposes; an adverb modifies a verb, an adjective, another adverb, the predicate, or an entire predication.

Preposition. Function words can hardly be defined by meaning, since some, like *of,* have very little meaning; others, like *on,* have more. The usual definitions are functional, that a preposition relates a noun or pronoun, its object, to some part of the sentence. The preposition combined with its object functions as a modifier (*the book on the table; the end of the road*). Some words commonly identified as prepositions seem not to fit this definition very well. In *dozens of geese, dozens* seems to modify *geese,* and *geese* seems not to modify *dozens.* In *The host turned on the barbeque spit,* if *on* is a preposition the guests may anticipate a grisly meal.

Conjunction. Conjunctions are also function words and are usually defined as words that connect words or groups of words in sentences. They do not refer to antecedents as do relative pronouns (*who, which*).

Particles. Various sorts of words which constitute small classes can be conveniently grouped as particles. They include *interjections,* indications of emotion or strong feeling like *ouch* and *oh!,* which are but little involved in structure. The articles *a, an,* and *the* might be included here; they are often called adjectives, although they are classifiers, not modifiers. Some grammarians would include intensifiers like *very* here rather than among the adverbs.

These definitions, of course, apply only to words in use; the same word may function in various ways.

> The glove cushions the blows.
> The wind blows the cushions.

Obviously *cushions* is a verb in the first and a noun in the second, and *blows* is a noun in the first and a verb in the second. Furthermore, these are not the only plausible explanations that could be made. Presumably like all grammars, the grammar of English is shifting and works on more than one principle; thus for most locutions more than one explanation is possible, and choice among the alternatives may not be easy. Consider the following: *He tried to fly.* By the conventional grammatical statement *tried* is the verb, and *to fly* is an infinitive functioning as the direct object of the verb. On the other hand, *fly* seems to involve the idea of the verb; if so, *tried* becomes an auxiliary, as *is going* becomes an auxiliary in *He is going to fly.* We have tried to avoid such uncertainties unless they are involved in the practical need of the writer or speaker, and to prefer the conventional statement if it is tolerably workable. In any event, the definitions or descriptions given here are not intended as directions for labelling, and they will not provide the basis for an adequate description of modern English grammar. They are intended to introduce the following chapters which discuss mainly problems of rhetoric and usage that accompany inflectional changes and the use of function words in English.

18

Nouns

and Pronouns

For Guide to Revision, see page 315

Substantives, including nouns and pronouns, are used as subjects, complements, and objects of prepositions.

The term *substantive* is used to include nouns and pronouns and any other words or word groups which function as equivalents to them. That is, substantives function as subjects or complements—except modifiers used as complements (see 12-5)—and as objects of prepositions. The italicized words in the following sentences are all substantives used as subjects or complements.

The *boy* speared the *fish*.
They knew *what they wanted*.
She was the only *contestant who* could play *Mozart*.

As objects of prepositions, nouns are linked to the sentence or some part of it by a function word, a preposition.

Most *of the passengers* were staring *out the window*.

The preposition *of* relates *passengers* to *most* so that *passengers* completes the idea of the subject, functioning as part of it. Similarly, *out* links *window* to the verb, so that *window* completes the idea carried forward through *were staring*. Thus a noun can become a modifier by means of a preposition, by being what is called the object of the preposition.

18-1 TYPES OF SUBSTANTIVES

Nouns, single-word substantives, are sometimes grouped as *proper* or *common* nouns, with capital letters marking the proper nouns (see

28a). A few nouns are also distinguished as *collective nouns,* words which name groups rather than individuals, words like *squad, committee, flock, swarm, family, group, herd.* This classification of nouns is important mainly in questions of agreement (see 21).

Pronouns are distinguishd from nouns in form, in their lack of independent meaning, and in their dependence on *antecedents* (see 19-1), the substantives to which they refer.

Verbal Nouns and Verb Phrases also function as substantives. English retains some multiple-purpose forms, among which are the verbals, so called because they come from verbs and like verbs can take a subject or complement, but function also as nouns or modifiers (see 22-2). They include verbal nouns, which function not as complete verbs but as substantives.

> The Joneses always *go* to the moving pictures.　(*verb*)
> The Joneses *are going* to the moving pictures.　(*verb*)
> *Going* to the moving pictures amuses them.　(*verbal*)
> His ambition was *to go* to the moving pictures.　(*verbal*)

The verbs *go* and *are going,* with their accompanying subject, complements, and modifiers, make complete assertions. The verbals *going* and *to go* do not make complete assertions.

Two types of verbals are used as nouns: the *infinitive,* usually characterized by its sign, *to,* preceding it (*to see, to be lost, to have found*), and the *gerund,* identifiable because some part of it always ends in *-ing* (*seeing, being seen, having been seen*).

Verbal nouns are useful because they can name an action for which no regular name exists in the language. Even when a noun for the action exists, the verbal noun sometimes allows special distinctions in meaning. Compare:

> The mad hatter liked *conversation* at the tea table.
> The mad hatter liked *to converse* at the tea table.
> The mad hatter liked *conversing* at the tea table.

Verbal nouns may have any of the usual functions of noun expressions:

> *Infinitive as subject: To understand* his decision was impossible.
> *Gerund as subject: Knowing* German got him a new job.
> *Infinitive as postponed subject:* It was impossible *to understand* his decision.

Gerund as subject and subject complement: Seeing is *believing.*
Infinitive as object of verb: I told him *to adjust* the carburetor.
Gerund as object of preposition: He replied by *hitting* George in the left eye.

Noun Clauses, considered dependent or subordinate clauses (see 15-1), are usually marked by introductory function words, which include *that, which, who, whose, where, whoever, what, whatever, how, whether,* and *if.* Occasionally, however, the clause appears without an introductory word: *I think you know the answer; I believe you can do it.* They can be used in any position in the sentence in which a noun might appear, even within another dependent clause, as in *I wonder how you knew what I was going to do.* Compare the following patterns:

My vacation *plans* are my business.
Planning my vacation is my business.
Where I expect to spend my vacation is my business.

In the first a noun is subject, in the second a verbal with its object, and in the third a clause; the clause provides a way to express a more complex or more specific subject. Or compare the following with substantives in other uses:

He asked a *question.*
He asked *whether we would ever reach the top of the hill.*
The officer gave *them* the directions.
The officer gave *whoever was there* the directions.
This is *the place.*
This is *where we will build our homes.*
Anticipating *your answer,* I ordered an attack.
Anticipating *what you would say,* I ordered an attack.
You may speak to *anyone.*
You may speak to *whomever you like.*

Clauses appear in the sentences as direct object, indirect object, subject complement, object of a verbal, and object of a preposition. In each pair, the clause makes the substantive more precise or more detailed.

18-2 FORMS OF SUBSTANTIVES

Although an elaborate system of endings distinguished nouns in Old English, only two endings are used with most nouns in modern

English: *—s* or *—es* to indicate the plural, and *—'s* (or *—s'*) to indicate the possessive. Since these forms are easily identified, they are considered below as problems in spelling (see 29a, 29c).

Pronouns, however, have preserved more of the Old English form changes than any other group of words. Some of them change form to indicate the person speaking, the number of the antecedent, the gender, and the use of the pronoun as subject, object, or possessive.

A pronoun conforms in number, person, and gender with its antecedent (see 21).

A pronoun's case (that is, whether it has the subjective, objective, or possessive form) derives from its use as a substantive in its own clause.

Consider the following sentence:

> Jean asked the florist whether *he* had made up the corsage of faded carnations *which* Jack had sent *her.*

He, which, and *her* are pronouns, each with a different antecedent. *He* refers to its antecedent, *florist; which* to *corsage,* and *her* to *Jean.* The selection of each pronoun depends upon its use and its antecedent. *He,* for example, is the subjective form because it is used as the subject of its clause; it is masculine and singular to conform with its antecedent. *Her* is the objective form because it is the indirect object of the verb *sent;* it is feminine and singular because it refers to *Jean.* On this basis pronouns can be selected from varying forms in the following lists of pronouns.

Personal pronouns distinguish the speaker (first person), the person spoken to (second person), and the person spoken of (third person). They are preserved in three cases, as follows:

SUBJECTIVE (NOMINATIVE)

	First Person	*Second Person*	*Third Person*
Singular	I	you, thou	he, she, it
Plural	we	you	they

These forms are used for subjects of clauses and sentences and for subject complements after linking verbs.

OBJECTIVE (ACCUSATIVE)

Singular	me	you, thee	him, her, it
Plural	us	you	them

These forms are used for all objects and complements, except subject complements, both of verbs and prepositions, and for the subjects of infinitives.

POSSESSIVE (GENITIVE): FORMS USED AS MODIFIERS

Singular	my	your, thy	his, her, its
Plural	our	your	their

These forms are used as modifiers to show possession (see 22-3).

Your nose has *its* own shape.

They also indicate a wide variety of intimate relationships which cannot be classified as indicating possession. Consider the following sentence:

Our representative in *your* territory will be glad to call at *your* office.

The word *our* does not indicate possession; the company hires this representative but does not own him. Nor does the first *your* indicate possession; the prospect merely does business in the territory. Whether it be New York City or the state of Louisiana, he does not own it. The third *your* may indicate possession; the prospect may own his office, but it is more likely that he rents it or that it has been assigned him by his employer. For possessive forms with the gerund, see 22c.

POSSESSIVE (GENITIVE): FORMS USED AS SUBJECTS OR COMPLEMENTS

Singular	mine	yours, thine	his, hers, its
Plural	ours	yours	theirs

These forms are used as subjects or objects, but most frequently as subject complements.

The book is *mine*.   My daughter is *yours*.   *Yours* is *mine*.

The alternate forms given here for the second personal singular are no longer in use, except for special purposes, notably in addresses to the deity, in the speech of certain sects, and for archaic diction.

Relative pronouns are function words which join a dependent clause to the remainder of the sentence, but they act also as noun expressions within the clause.

Grandmother, *who* wore spit curls to her dying day, arrived sprouting curlicues like a squid.

Who relates the clause to the main predication but serves also as the subject of the dependent clause, *who wore spit curls to her dying day.* The relative pronouns *who* and *whoever* are declined as follows: *who, whoever* (subjective); *whom, whomever* (objective); *whose, whosever* (possessive). These forms are used for persons. *Which, whichever, what, whatever* are used for inanimate objects, and usually for animals. The forms for persons are also sometimes used for animals. *That* is used for either persons or things. Relative pronouns other than *who* and *whoever* are not declined; the other relative pronouns use the same form for the subjective and objective, and *whose* for the possessive. Some writers prefer *that* for a restrictive clause, *which* and *who* for a nonrestrictive. For punctuation of restrictive and nonrestrictive clauses, see 27e.

The relative pronoun can be readily confused with the relative or subordinating conjunction, the more because some of the forms are the same. A relative pronoun can be distinguished because it serves as a noun in the grammar of its clause. The relative conjunction has no grammatical function within the clause. In

> I tried to buy Fido, *who* had just swallowed a twenty-dollar bill.

who is the subject of a clause and is thus a pronoun. In

> I tried to buy *whichever puppy* had swallowed the twenty-dollar bill.

puppy is the subject of the clause, and *whichever* does not function as a noun. It is a modifying relative conjunction (see 23-4).

Interrogative pronouns, which signal a question, have the same form changes as relative pronouns:

> *Who* is he? *Whom* do you see? *Whose* book is it?

Intensive pronouns and *reflexive pronouns* have forms developed from personal pronouns: *myself, yourself, himself, herself, itself, ourselves, yourselves, themselves* (not *theirselves*). Their names distinguish only their use; intensive pronouns emphasize; reflexive pronouns redirect the predication to the subject. Compare:

> *Intensive:* I cut the rope *myself.*
> *Reflexive:* I cut *myself.*

Indefinite pronouns (words like *anyone, everyone, anybody, everybody, anything, everything, each, any,* and *all*) and *demonstrative pronouns* (*this, that, these, those, such*) do not change form to show their use in their clauses. They are pronouns when they function as substantives; often the same words are modifiers. Compare:

Pronoun: Any of you may taste the jam.
Modifier: Any person here may taste the jam.
Pronoun: That is the man I saw through the window.
Modifier: I saw *that* man through the window.

18 Pron

NOUNS

AND PRONOUNS

Guide to Revision

Use the subjective form for a pronoun subject, the objective form for a pronoun object.

Whether a pronoun is subjective or objective in form depends on the pronoun's use in its own clause—not on the use of its antecedent.

18a   PERSONAL PRONOUN SUBJECTS   Pron a

The subjective form should be used as the subject of a sentence or a clause.

ORIGINAL

Jim and *me* made the first team as forwards.
[*The double subject should not obscure the use.*]

Since I was not hungry, I told them that *him* and Mary could divide the lunch.
[*Though they follow the main verb* told, *the words* him and Mary *comprise the subject of* could divide the lunch.]

REVISION

Jim and *I* made the first team as forwards.
[*Test by dropping out the noun portion of the compound,* Jim and.]

Since I was not hungry, I told them that *he* and Mary could divide the lunch.
[*The objective form* him *has been changed to the subjective form* he.]

As a courtesy, *I* and *we* usually are last in a sequence; other pronouns usually appear first.

ORIGINAL	REVISION
I and Evelyn won the doubles.	Evelyn and I won the doubles.

18b   PERSONAL PRONOUNS AFTER LINKING VERBS   Pron b

If we follow the practices of inflected grammar, a linking verb (see 20-1) should be followed by the subjective form, since the verb links a following complement to the subject. The subject-verb-object sentence pattern is so prevalent, however, that users of English tend to use the objective form whenever it appears after the verb.

There is a legend that the late Professor George Lyman Kittredge, one of the world authorities on language, was working late in his office one night when an alert student janitor became suspicious that robbers might be ransacking the professor's office.

"Hey, who's in there?" the student yelled.

"It's all right," Professor Kittredge replied. "It's me. Kittredge."

"The devil it is," the student retorted. "Kittredge'd say, 'It is I.' "

Whether or not this story is apocryphal, there is a growing tendency to use the objective form after *it is,* especially in colloquial speech—*It's me, It's her.* Careful speakers still preserve logic under formal circumstances, however, and say *It is I, It is she.* If, for instance, the student janitor had gone down the hall and telephoned, Professor Kittredge might have said, "It is I."

ORIGINAL	REVISION
"May I speak to Dr. Jordan, please?" "This is *him*."	"May I speak to Dr. Jordan, please?" "This is *he*."

18c   OBJECTIVE FORM OF PERSONAL PRONOUNS   Pron c

Use the objective case for an object complement (direct or indirect object), for the principal word of a prepositional phrase (object of a preposition), or for the subject or object of an infinitive (see 18-1).

ORIGINAL	REVISION
We never liked the Broadnicks, neither *she* nor her husband. [*She is in apposition to* Broadnicks *and is thus part of the object complement.*]	We never liked the Broadnicks, neither *her* nor her husband. [*The objective* her *has replaced the subjective* she.]

ORIGINAL (*Cont.*)

  It was impossible for Mary and *I* to hand in our papers Friday.
[*The subject of an infinitive has the objective form.*]

  Just between *you* and *I,* no hair ever got that color naturally.

  The manager promised my wife and *I* the new apartment.

  The manager promised *we* girls the new apartment.

REVISION (*Cont.*)

  It was impossible for Mary and *me* to hand in our papers Friday.
[*The objective* me *replaces the subjective* I.]

  Just between *you* and *me,* no hair ever got that color naturally.

  The manager promised my wife and *me* the new apartment.

  The manager promised *us* girls the new apartment.

18d RELATIVE OR INTERROGATIVE PRONOUN   Pron d

Like other pronouns, a relative or interrogative pronoun takes its number and gender from its antecedent, and takes its form from its function in its clause. This duality causes some difficulty. Since interrogative and relative pronouns are function words, they must be placed so that they show relationships within the sentence. As pronouns, they are often either subjects or complements; but since they acquire their position as function words, the normal order of actor-action-complement may be disturbed. The result is pressure to choose a pronoun form which would fit the order, not the logic of the sentence.

  I asked him *who* he thought he was hitting.
  I asked him *whom* he thought he was hitting.

In these sentences *who* and *whom* function as object complements of *was hitting.* Logically, the correct form is *whom.* The word is the first word in its clause, however, and since it occupies the subject position, speakers naturally say *who.* The English language seems here to be in transition, *whom* preserving a detail of our declined grammar, *who* being natural to a distributive grammar. Many careful writers would still insist upon *whom* in this example, but more liberal authorities would sanction *who,* especially in colloquial use. Similarly, the pressure of word order has made sentences like *I knew* who *you wanted* common colloquially, even though the logic of inflection requires *I knew* whom *you wanted.* Interrogative pronouns particularly, since they always appear at the beginning of the sentence in the subject position, tend to have the subjective form in all but the most formal situations (Who *do you mean?* Who *did Tom invite?*). Occasionally writers who have been corrected for using *who* in sentences of this sort become fearful and use *whom* whenever they are in doubt, even in sentences like *Whom does he think he is?*, which can scarcely be justified on any ground.

ORIGINAL

I asked him *whom* he was.
[Whom *is not the object of asked, but the subject complement of* was.]

I met the girl *whom*, everyone said, was going to win the beauty contest.
[Whom *is not the object of said, but the subject of* was.]

She will ask *whoever* she can find.
[Whoever *is the object complement of* can find.]

Who are you calling?
[*Common in most situations.*]

We wondered *who* he would take to the party.

REVISION

I asked him *who* he was.
[*The subjective form has been substituted.*]

I met the girl *who*, everyone said, was going to win the beauty contest.
[*The subjective form has been substituted.*]

She will ask *whomever* she can find.
[*The objective form,* whomever, *has been substituted.*]

Whom are you calling?
[*Appropriate formally.*]

We wondered *whom* he would take to the party.

English no longer has a possessive form to correspond to *which*. Most writers now use *whose* freely for this purpose, but some authorities object to using a form of *who* to refer to inanimate objects. The usage can be avoided by a change in structure.

ORIGINAL

I do not like a ring whose setting reminds me of Grandmother's day.
[*Usually acceptable and more economical than the revision.*]

REVISION

(1) I do not like a ring with a setting which reminds me of Grandmother's day.
(2) I do not like a ring the setting of which reminds me of Grandmother's day.

18e REFLEXIVE PRONOUNS USED FOR PERSONAL PRONOUNS Pron e

Perhaps in an effort to avoid the choice between *I* or *me,* or from a sense of modesty, speakers now frequently use the reflexive or intensive form of the pronoun which traditionally called for a personal pronoun. The usual personal pronoun is preferred in most writing.

ORIGINAL

Henry and *myself* started to make a "hot-rod" car.
[Myself *is part of the subject.*]

They invited Anne and *myself* to the Sigma Nu formal dance.

REVISION

Henry and *I* started to make a "hot-rod" car.
[*The subjective form has been substituted.*]

They invited Anne and *me* to the Sigma Nu formal dance.

EXERCISE 18

A. Revise each of the following sentences making a noun clause rather than a noun the complement; you may, of course, have to invent material to fill out the pattern of your clause, and you may wish to change the subject or the verb. Be able to discuss the effect of the change.

1. This is his desire.
2. Nobody knows the method he used for opening the window.
3. Stanley did not know his destination.
4. The accident was the thing expected by my father from the moment I got the car.
5. They will elect any person able to understand parliamentary procedures.

Change the complements of the following sentences from clauses to nouns; the nouns, of course, may be modified. Does the change improve or weaken the sentences?

1. The new director promised that there would be an immediate change in camp regulations.
2. No one had really studied what had been the accomplishments made by the non-professional investigators.
3. Orville could not find where there was any evidence to prove his innocence.
4. Herman could not see that any possibility of making up the quarrel existed.
5. He could not see why he should pay the check.

B. Choose the appropriate pronoun form in the following sentences, and give the reason for your choice.

1. Ask Mary. Mother said it was (she, her) who took the cake.
2. Everybody thought Uncle Angus was stingy, but he left (we, us) girls a beautiful house.

3. The bartender told my cousin and (I, me) that we should go get a few years older.
4. When she had the ingredients jumbled in the pan, she stood staring as though she did not dare ask what (we, us) girls would have done.
5. Ask the patrolman (who, whom) he thinks he is arresting.
6. The quarrel between my sister and (I, me, myself) began when I was a child.
7. Mother promised a glass of lemonade to (whoever, whomever) could get back from the store first.
8. I cannot help wondering (who, whom) he thinks he is.
9. Aunt Amy asked Ethel and (I, me, myself) out for the weekend.
10. He was afraid to ask (who, whom) would be playing the piano accompaniment.
11. We heard voices coming over the water, and we knew it was (they, them).
12. The trouble between my roommate and (I, me) all began when she started chewing bubble gum.
13. (Who, whom) do you expect to find buried under the cellar steps?
14. You may nominate (whoever, whomever) you please.
15. Harry kept complaining about the rain, but after a while we agreed that (he, him) and (I, me) would start out.
16. When Father cooks, nobody feels sorry for (he, his, him) sweating over a hot stove.
17. He stabbed in the dark, without knowing (who, whom) he might hit.
18. The janitor was always nice to (we, us) girls.
19. (Who, whom) do you think will be the new basketball coach?
20. The stupidity of both Hester and (she, her) was remarkable.

19

Reference

For Guide to Revision, see page 324

Clear reference provides economy and coherence within the sentence and between sentences.

Nouns frequently and pronouns regularly work by what may be called reference; that is, they repeat or echo some part of the meaning of other words. Coherence within the sentence and between sentences depends extensively on reference (see 3). With pronouns, as already observed, the word a pronoun refers to is called its antecedent.

"Reference" works in various ways. In the following sentence, for example, a noun summarizes meanings that have preceded it.

He annoyed many people by his smugness and intolerance, attitudes which developed from his early training.

Attitudes can be said to refer to *smugness* and *intolerance*. It restates them in order to develop the sentence. To observe the importance of selecting words so that such reference is clear, consider the following:

He annoyed many people by being smug and intolerant, attitudes which developed from his early training.

In this sentence, reference is not clear; *attitudes* does not logically repeat the meaning of *smug* and *intolerant,* which are modifiers and not names for attitudes or anything else. Or consider another sentence.

People in America believe that everyone should share the good and the bad, but this principle does not apply here.

The sentence turns on the reference of the word *principle* to the clause *that everyone should share the good and the bad.* The sentence is clear. But compare the sentence from a student theme from which the above was revised:

> Our country's democracy believes in everyone's sharing the good and the bad, and in this case the assumption would not hold true.

The words mean something as individual words, but they do not combine to make a clear sentence. Part of the trouble is that subjects, verbs, and complements do not work sensibly together, but further trouble arises from the key word, *assumption,* which does not logically refer to any previous idea—no assumption has been made.

19-1 PRONOUNS AND REFERENCE

Pronouns, of course, are reference words by their very nature; their meaning depends on that of an antecedent. Obviously, then, a reader must be able immediately to relate a pronoun to its antecedent. In English, two kinds of signals help him: word order and word forms or inflections.

Word order has assumed major importance in patterns of reference in English as inflections have tended to disappear. Clear reference in modern English follows mainly from clear order. The pronoun, however, retains considerable remnants of earlier form changes, and these work also as signals of reference. That is, the writer can make reference clear both by word order and by selecting pronoun forms which agree in person, number, and gender with their antecedents (see 21).

Often choice of proper forms, along with attention to meaning, is enough to establish reference. The following sentence, for example, is clear:

> John showed *his* sister *his* copy of the book which *she* had written.

Since *she* is feminine in form it must refer to sister; the authorship is clear.

Notice, however, the difference if John had met his brother.

> John showed *his* brother *his* copy of the book which *he* had written.

Because of meaning and order we could probably guess whose copy is involved, but we cannot even guess who wrote the book. Form distinctions are not enough to establish reference.

To insure clarity, then, the writer can profitably observe the following rule:

Be sure that every reference word has a clear antecedent, and be sure that the form of the reference word and the order of words in the sentence make the reference immediately certain.

19-2 PATTERNS OF REFERENCE

Often we must rely on word order to establish reference relationships, and the patterns of reference in English sentences are variable enough to make vague and inaccurate references a hazard for the writer. There is no simple, universally applicable rule, but in general the following principles apply:

(1) The subject, as the most important noun or pronoun in a clause, and especially the subject of a main clause, tends to become an antecedent of a personal pronoun. Consider:

> Shakespeare was two months younger than Marlowe; a record of his baptism April 26, 1564, has been preserved.

Even though *his* could apply sensibly to either *Shakespeare* or *Marlowe,* and even though *Marlowe* is much nearer *his* in the sentence, the reader knows that *Shakespeare,* the subject, is the antecedent of *his.*

(2) If the subject is obviously impossible as the antecedent of a personal pronoun, a complement tends to be the next choice.

> She took the rooster out of the sack and put a rock in *its* place.

Its cannot refer to the subject, but it does refer to *rooster.* Notice that while the meaning helps clarify reference, the order is essential here. We could change the fate of the rooster by transposing *rock* and *rooster.*

(3) The less important the position of the word in a sentence, the greater is the difficulty of making the word an antecedent. Modifiers and other words in subordinate uses, however, often work as antecedents of pronouns used in parallel ways.

> I visited the library and spent an hour looking through the book. I found nothing in *it.*

It refers to *book;* pronoun and antecedent have parallel uses and positions.

(4) A noun expression immediately before a relative pronoun

tends to be its antecedent. Notice what happens when a relative pronoun is used in the sentence above.

> Shakespeare was two months younger than Marlowe, a record of whose baptism in February, 1564, has been preserved.

The relative pronoun *whose* refers to *Marlowe,* and the date has to be changed to keep the sentence accurate.

19 **Ref**

REFERENCE

Guide to Revision

Select and arrange all reference words so that they refer clearly and logically to antecedents.

To promote the clarity and economy possible through reference the writer must provide an antecedent that is immediately and certainly identifiable, or he must build up his expression so that its reference to an idea not briefly expressed becomes clear.

19a GENERAL REFERENCE   Ref a

Pronouns like *this, that, it,* and *which* are sometimes used, especially colloquially, to refer to a general idea.

> I had thrown a loaf of bread at the Marquis, which hit him on the cheek, and *that* made me feel good.
>
> —ROBERT GRAVES

No particular noun can be labelled as the antecedent of *that,* but the meaning is clear, with *that* referring to the entire action which is described in the first part of the sentence. This use of the pronoun, however, is subject to considerable abuse, especially in student writing. Too often the construction disguises sloppy thinking; the pronoun is used to stand for an idea which the writer assumes the reader understands, but which he has not made clear to the reader and may not have made clear to himself. Too often, also, the device is a symptom

REFERENCE

5a). Before using a pronoun to refer
to a general idea, the writer must be sure that the reference is not
vague and that the sentence would not be clearer with a different
construction.

ORIGINAL

Some critics have accused Chaucer
of Frenchifying English, which has
been disproved.
[Which *has no certain antecedent.*]

The constant reminder of Norway
and home made Beret become nostalgic, which was one of the causes
of her insanity.
[*The antecedent is only implied; the
sentence would be clearer with an expressed antecedent.*]

REVISION

Some critics have accused Chaucer
of Frenchifying English, but the accu-
sation has been disproved.
[*No antecedent is necessary.*]

(1) The constant reminder of Norway and home made Beret become
nostalgic, and her nostalgia provided
one cause of her insanity.
(2) The constant reminder of Norway and home caused Beret's nostalgia, which promoted her insanity.

Sentences sometimes begin with a dependent clause followed by a
pronoun referring to a noun in the clause.

If this article makes a few people take democracy seriously, it will
have served its purpose.

It is a clear restatement of *article*. This construction has perhaps led
to the colloquial popularity of a similar pattern in which the pronoun
lacks an antecedent and in which the vague reference handicaps the
reader. Compare:

If this article makes a few people take democracy seriously, it means
that some progress has been made.

It has no clear antecedent. The sentence is weak because the main
clause has no clear subject.

ORIGINAL

If they are taken into the army, it
means they will not graduate.
[It *lacks an antecedent. Even the
loose idea which the reader might
supply for* it, *their induction into the
army, does not make a good subject
for the main clause.*]

REVISION

If they are taken into the army, they
will not graduate.
[*Usually, as here, vague reference is
a symptom of roundabout writing.
The vague pronoun usurps the position of the real subject of the sentence,*
they.]

325

ORIGINAL (*Cont.*)

If there were some way to get all people to use the same dialect, it would be much simpler.
[*Not even a vague idea can be supplied as an antecedent for* it.]

REVISION (*Cont.*)

If there were some way to get all people to use the same dialect, communication would be much simpler.
[*Revision supplies a subject to replace the vague* it.]

Impersonal constructions become ambiguous when the sign of the impersonal construction can be mistaken for a personal pronoun. *It,* used for either purpose, readily becomes ambiguous.

ORIGINAL

My Chevrolet has a Mercury motor which makes it hard to shift gears.
[*The second* it *should be impersonal, but it appears at first to be a personal pronoun with* Chevrolet *as its antecedent.*]

The building of the Mississippi River jetties should be a good research topic, but it is going to be hard to find the technical details of construction.
[It *is impersonal, but seems to refer to* building.]

REVISION

(1) My Chevrolet has a Mercury motor; with this combination I have trouble shifting gears.
(2) I have trouble shifting gears because my Chevrolet has a Mercury motor.

The building of the Mississippi River jetties should be a good research topic, but I expect trouble when I try to find the technical details of construction.

Colloquially *they* and *it* are used as indefinite pronouns to refer generally to "people" or "society." Except in reference to weather (It *is cold today*), this indefinite use is often indirect and vague and is inappropriate in serious writing.

ORIGINAL

In the paper it says the weather will change.
[*Nobody knows who* it *is.*]

While she was in the hospital her hair turned white, and now *they* say she dyes it.

REVISION

The paper says that the weather will change.
[*Omission of the vague pronoun often is the solution.*]

While she was in the hospital, her hair turned white, and now, apparently, she dyes it.

19b   REFERENCE AND POSITION OF ANTECEDENTS   **Ref b**

Unless pronoun forms clarify reference, a pronoun usually refers clearly only to a noun expression in an important position in the sentence or in a use parallel to its own. If the word order does not clarify the reference, the sentence must be revised or an antecedent provided.

ORIGINAL

I should like to find out how authors were affected during the depression and how it changed their styles of writing.
[*Presumably* depression *is the antecedent of* it, *but this relationship is not at once apparent, because* depression *is not the subject, does not occur immediately before the pronoun, and is not in parallel structure.*]

REVISION

(1) I should like to find out how authors were affected during the depression years, and how the depression changed their styles of writing.
(2) I should like to find out how the depression affected authors, and how it changed their styles of writing.
[*In (1),* it *has been removed in favor of a noun; in (2) it refers to* depression *because that word has become the subject of a preceding clause.*]

In Hemingway's book *For Whom the Bell Tolls,* he tells about an American teacher in the Spanish Civil War.
[He *must refer to a person, but* Hemingway's *is not a person. It helps identify* book.]

In his book *For Whom the Bell Tolls,* Hemingway tells about an American teacher in the Spanish Civil War.
[*With the pronoun in the dependent position and the noun,* Hemingway, *as the subject, the reference of* his *is clear.*]

Novelists gave biographers help. They set the example by showing them the value of records of life.
[*Since* novelists *is the subject and* biographers *comes shortly before* they, *the reader must hesitate before he is sure who is helping whom.*]

Novelists helped biographers by showing them the value of records of life.
[They *has been removed, and* them *is sufficiently near to being* parallel *with* biographers *so that the relationship is clear.*]

19c WORD REFERENCE   Ref c

Word reference may become inaccurate when specific terms are restated by a general word or when general terms are broken into more specific parts. The writer, as he moves forward in the sentence, becomes careless of the exact terms he has used and refers to them by a word that applies only inexactly. Consider, for instance, the following sentence from a student theme.

I don't know just what I was expecting, but the faces were friendly, self-confident, individual, and interesting, not the featureless automatons I had read about.

By the time the writer wants to refer to the faces of the early part of the sentence, he has forgotten the words he used; and thinking of the people who have the faces, he refers to *faces* as *automatons*. Whenever ideas are repeated or referred to more than once in the progress of a sentence, the writer must be sure that he uses terms which can logically work together.

ORIGINAL

The field of interior decorating holds vast opportunities for the women who want to apply themselves to the task.
[*A* field *is not a* task, *and the repetition helps make the sentence ambiguous.*]

A good teacher must be patient, and I do not fall into that category.
[Category *cannot logically refer to* patient *or to anything else in the sentence.*]

Of all the regulations for women, I hated most being in by nine o'clock.
[Being in *is not a regulation; the general term does not logically include the specific one.*]

REVISION

(1) Interior decorating holds vast opportunities for women who **want to** apply themselves.
(2) Women who become interior decorators have vast opportunities.
[*Here, as often, confusion can best be cured by deletion.*]

A good teacher must be patient, but I am not.

I hated most the regulation for women requiring us to be in by nine o'clock.
[*The restatement is avoided.*]

Modifiers and the words to which they refer must be compatible in meaning. When they are not, the modifier should be changed or a more appropriate word supplied for it to modify.

ORIGINAL

He started out as a senior economist, very difficult for a person without much experience.
[*The writer probably did not mean to say that the economist was difficult, but that his work was.*]

When she applied the next time, she was appointed head dietician, vacated only the day before by a sudden resignation.
[Vacated *requires something to modify;* dietician *will not serve. The*

REVISION

He started out as a senior economist, doing work very difficult for a person without much experience.
[Work *provides a plausible idea for* difficult *to modify.*]

(1) When she applied the next time, she was appointed to the position of head dietician, vacated only the day before by a sudden resignation.
(2) When she applied the next

ORIGINAL *(Cont.)*

*position, not the dietician, was va-
cated.]*

REVISION *(Cont.)*

time, she was appointed head dietician,
filling a position vacated only the day
before by a sudden resignation.

Writing sometimes becomes confused when modifiers patterned to
restate an idea reveal a shift in the writer's attitude rather than the
notion he intended. For example, in

The common bi-valve, the oyster, is originally a French word.

The writer has shifted his notion of the meaning of *oyster* he intends;
the reference is therefore confused.

ORIGINAL

Bowling Green, the name of my
home town, is in the southern part of
Kentucky.
[Bowling Green *can be either a
name or a town, but the town, not the
name, is in Kentucky.*]

REVISION

Bowling Green, my home town, is
in the southern part of Kentucky.

Some modifiers resemble pronouns in that they refer to an antecedent at the same time that they serve their own grammatical function. Words of this sort include *the* and *such, there, here, other,
another, this, that, these,* and *those,* when they are used as modifiers.

ORIGINAL

He meant no harm by his pranks,
but this result did not always come of
his mischief. Such result came from
one affair.
[*Both* this *and* such *require antecedents but do not have them.*]

China's unceasing wars are just one
symptom of her decadence. In such
a country corruption is common.

I feel that harbor dredging will be
a very interesting subject. Since I have
lived there for fifteen years, I am well
acquainted with it.
[There *has no antecedent.*]

REVISION

He meant no harm; his pranks were
only mischievous, but they sometimes
ended unhappily.
[*The sentence has been recast and
the awkward construction removed by
simplified word order.*]

China's unceasing wars are only one
symptom of her decadence, and in a
decadent country corruption is common.

I feel that harbor dredging will be
a very interesting subject, and I am
well acquainted with it, since for fifteen years I have lived where I could
observe operations.

ORIGINAL (*Cont.*)

We saw a little adobe house and rode over. The man and his wife greeted us pleasantly.
[The *suggests a man who has been mentioned before, but presumably he has not.*]

REVISION (*Cont.*)

We saw a little adobe house and rode over. A man and his wife greeted us pleasantly.
[A *indicates that the man is being introduced; the false reference disappears.*]

A substitute verb or verbal (see 20-7), usually some combination with *to do,* must refer clearly and logically to another verb.

ORIGINAL

He expresses the revolt against bondage and the desire to be free. His argument centers around the possibility to do so.
[*There is no verb in the first sentence which could work as an antecedent for* to do so *except* expresses, *and reference to it does not make sense.*]

REVISION

He speaks of revolting against bondage and being free. His argument assumes the possibility of doing so.
[*The original is so unclear that accurate revision is difficult, but the rearrangement provides parallel antecedents in* revolting *and* being.]

If he has any time for fooling around after class he will do so.
[*He cannot* do *fooling around.*]

If he has any time to fool around after class, he will.
[*With the form changed, no substitute is necessary.*]

EXERCISE 19

A. Revise the following sentences, correcting any examples of illogical word reference:

1. His long punts and accurate passes, qualities which made him feared by all opponents, helped us to win the championship.
2. He was always boasting about his conquests in love, and I have never admired this characteristic.
3. He applied for the position of office manager, much too ambitious for a beginner.
4. The girls decided to restrict membership in the club to members of sororities, an attitude which seemed to me undemocratic.
5. Girls who are friendly lead happy lives, and I am glad I share this quality.
6. Of all the people in our neighborhood, the sadness of one case affected me most.

7. The field of chemistry is exciting for anyone who undertakes this great adventure into science.

8. All the men were looked on as a brother in the camp.

9. An important part of a student's life, especially a man, is activity in student government.

10. College, the word dreamed about by so many high school students, was not what I had expected it to be.

11. The other secretaries all conspired to give me the most unpleasant jobs, aspects I had not anticipated.

12. Several incidents occurred while I was learning to operate a switchboard, but I remember best my many conversations with the chief operator.

13. I believe that Hoover Dam, which is the topic for my paper, is one of the greatest sources of power in the world.

14. On inspecting the engineering field you will find that not only are improvements made but inventions are brought forth by these gallant young explorers.

15. Although there are many faults in the unicameral system of legislation, there are not enough to make it an unprofitable change.

16. Since all of my friends play bridge, I am glad that I come under that class.

17. They are taught to be agreeable and sociable with their companions, an advancement toward friendly relations.

18. Gordo, the name of my dog, chased the rabbit into the woodpile.

19. If the state chose to give money to public and parochial schools alike, nobody could criticize it for this affair.

20. Some feel that they do not have the ability to study, and others feel that they have better things to do. The latter include marriage, traveling, or work.

B. Correct the faulty references in the following passage:

Our outfit, which was among the toughest men in the infantry, had several Texans on its roll call. Not all Texans I have known are the boaster type, but one of these men thought Texas had the biggest of everything. I suppose he even thought they had bigger modesty than anybody else, but he certainly was not in that category. We called him Fort Worth, because that town was always in his mouth. Our sergeant, who came from Pennsylvania—a pretty capable collection of boasters, too—did not like Fort Worth, I suppose because they were both too much of a boaster. Fort Worth would get the better of the sergeant boasting, and the sergeant would get even with Fort Worth by putting him on latrine duty or giving him some other menial task. This went on and on, with the enlisted men siding with

Fort Worth so often that the sergeant even threatened to charge him with insubordination, a condition which is a very serious offense in the army. Finally, the German lines gave way a little, a movement that is very hard to follow in rough mountains, but we surged forward to a ridge, and from being there we could see Vesuvius over to our left, rolling up smoke, and at night a dull red glow.

"Hey, Fort Worth," the sergeant called, indicating the spectacle which every school child knows is practically a synonym for *marvel,* "you got any a' them volcanoes hotter 'n that one in Texas?"

The Texan looked at the fiery mountain as though he were trying to recall himself from the scenes of battle to the details of Texas terrain, and then he said, "No, we ain't. But in Fort Worth we sure got a fire department could put her out."

C. Most faulty sentences can be improved with any of several means of strengthening structure. Most of the sentences in Exercise 13B can be most readily improved by substituting a more expressive verb for *to be,* but many of them could be strengthened in other ways. Try to revise each sentence in 13B by keeping a form of the verb *to be* but clarifying word reference. For which of the sentences do you consider the revision satisfactory?

D. Revise the following sentences so that all pronouns or other reference words refer clearly to logical antecedents:

1. If clear, unemotional words were used by people in the government, it would benefit the world greatly.
2. While dialects do not help the standards of speech, they do not hinder it too greatly.
3. Charles lacked refinements, which annoyed her.
4. Before the depression people might have gone on vacations or patronized community amusements, but now this was impossible.
5. Television requires little mental activity, and in my opinion this is what we need.
6. When Admetis discovered that the veiled woman was his wife, it certainly had a significant effect on his thoughts.
7. Some of Cortez's horses were so outstanding in battle that it caused the Indians to consider them gods.
8. In the pterodactyl the hind legs were poorly developed, and thus we do not see any of them walking or crawling around on land.
9. If anything wrong has been done, I hope they put them in jail.
10. In the time of Shakespeare there existed much anti-Jewish prejudice and their religion set them apart from the rest of the people.
11. The chest had been her mother's, and she remembered the sorrow she had felt when she left for America.

12. The only used trailers we found for sale had been lived in by families with children which had been all scratched up.

13. At the club they said that all matches had been postponed.

14. The children had scattered small pieces of bread among the ducks which they had been eating all afternoon.

15. Later several experimenters added more keys to the clarinet to give it range, and this is why its popularity increased.

16. Glass-making flourished in very early times; it was made and used by the Egyptians before 1400 B.C.

17. In the first chapter of Miss Langer's book she talks about symbols.

18. Too often people make the mistake of thinking that education is not as valuable as experience, and that is why I am in school.

19. If the minister can really influence people with his sermons, it will do a lot more good.

20. Macbeth fears that Banquo knows that he has killed Duncan, the king, and this necessitated his death.

E. Notice carefully the occurrences of *this* in the paragraph below, and revise so as to remove any vague reference.

Acetylene is usually only mildly poisonous and it is commonly available; this makes it a handy way of getting rid of vermin. It has other properties aside from being poisonous and convenient, and this is not always remembered. A Swedish garage owner recently provided an example of this. While he was driving to work, he became aware that a rat was chewing the cushion of the rear seat of his car, and hearing this, he stopped to kill the rat. This did not help much, because the rat scrambled under the back of the seat, which could not be removed although the seat could have been. Knowing this, the garage owner drove to his place of business, determined to poison or to smoke out the rat. This was sensible, and the garage owner got out his acetylene welding kit with a good fresh tank of gas, thinking this would kill the rat or get him out. It got him out. Shortly after the car was filled with gas, the garage owner saw his roof flying seventy-five feet into the air, this presumably being due to a short circuit in the automobile which had ignited the acetylene. Along with the roof went much of the owner's automobile, and parts of five others. This was not the only damage the owner saw around him. Six men had to be hospitalized because this was so unexpected that people stood still in the street staring while pieces of garage fell on them. The rat has not been seen since. Neither has the cushion. In spite of this, the garage owner is not taking out a patent on his rat exterminator.

F. Use the facts given below for a brief composition. Subordinate as many of the details as the material warrants, using reference words and being sure your reference words have clear antecedents. If the present phrasing does not supply these antecedents, insert them.

Alice Marriott wrote an article.

The article is called "Beowulf in South Dakota."

Alice Marriott is an ethnologist.

Alice Marriott studies American Indian tales.

The New Yorker published the article.

The New Yorker is a sophisticated magazine.

The author was collecting stories from an old Indian.

The Indian lived in South Dakota.

One day the old Indian was bored and restless.

The Indian looked as though he did not want to tell more stories.

The Indian asked a question.

The Indian wanted to know why the white people wanted his stories.

The Indian wanted to know if the white people had no stories of their own.

The author said she wanted to compare the stories of the Indians with the stories of the white people.

The old Indian became interested.

He acted pleased.

The Indian said that the author's idea was a good idea.

The Indian said he wanted the author to tell him one of the white people's stories.

The author retold the story of *Beowulf*.

The author used Indian terms and Indian concepts.

The author made Beowulf a great war chief.

Beowulf gathered the young men of the tribe around him.

Beowulf and the young men went on a war party.

Beowulf and the young men attacked the Witch of the Water and her son.

The Witch of the Water lived under a great stone in a rushing, dangerous river.

A great fight took place under the water.

There was blood welling up through the water.

The water was as red as the sun rising.

Beowulf killed the Witch of the Water and her son.

The Indian liked the story.

The author had to tell it over and over.

The Indian told it to his friends and the friends talked about it.

The Indians talked about Beowulf.

The Indians sounded like a seminar in literature.

The Indian did not tell any more stories that day.

The author had to go home and wait until the Indians recovered from *Beowulf.*

The old man told the author many stories.

The storytelling continued for weeks.

Another ethnologist was trying to get the old Indian to tell him stories.

Ethnologists have methods of working and standardized ethical practices.

An ethnologist who tries to use another ethnologist's information is unethical.

Two ethnologists are likely to confuse an informant.

A confused informant gives unsatisfactory evidence to both scientists.

The old Indian said he liked the author.

The author was the friend of the old Indian.

The Indian offered not to tell the other ethnologist Indian stories.

The author went back to her university.

The author heard that the other ethnologist wanted to question the old Indian.

Two or three years passed.

The author was reading a learned journal.

The author found an article signed by the other ethnologist.

The article was called "Occurrence of a Beowulf-like Myth among North American Indians."

The author wondered whether or not she should tell what she knew.

(If you want to see what Alice Marriott did with the story, you will find the reference in 31-10.)

20

Verbs

For Guide to Revision, see page 347

The English verb, the central part of the basic sentence pattern, promotes both vigor and exactness.

The English verb, and especially the American verb, is so intricate, delicate, and varied that very few people not native to the language ever master it. Having said so much, one can add that the difficult parts of the verb cause native speakers little trouble. Natives learn verbs naturally and are usually unaware that they are doing something difficult with great ease. Most of our elaborate verbs rely upon order, and we handle order in grammar easily. The conjugated forms, however, give us trouble. Fortunately, they are relatively few and not difficult to master.

To see how our verbs work, consider the following sentences:

> I should have liked to be with you.
> I should have liked to be able to be with you.
> I should have liked to have been able to be with you.
> I should have like to have been able to have been with you.

All of these verbs are complicated, and they carry delicate gradations of meaning. These complicated forms fit the usual patterns of a distributive grammar, and hence cause little trouble for native speakers, even for those who may have trouble choosing between *lie* or *lay,* or *blown* and a dialect form like *blowed.*

20-1 TYPES OF ENGLISH VERBS

Compare the following sentences:

INTRANSITIVE: The tide turned.

336

INTRANSITIVE: The car turned over.
LINKING: The milk turned sour.
LINKING: The book turned up missing.
TRANSITIVE: The car turned the corner.
TRANSITIVE: The cook turned on the gas.

The same verb appears in each sentence, but its meaning alters in its three different uses: (1) as an *intransitive* verb, which completes a predication without a complement but may be modified; (2) as a *linking* verb, which links a subject and a subject complement; or (3) as a *transitive* verb, which is completed by an object complement. Furthermore, meanings alter within each use as verbs combine with suffixes (*over, up, on*).

Intransitive verbs. When a verb has no complement it is called *intransitive.* That is, it does not *transfer* or *transmit* meaning to a complement. In sentences like *She lives, She sings, She used to sing, She was singing,* all the words except the pronoun subject *she* are intransitive verbs or parts of intransitive verbs. Or an intransitive verb may be the core of a long sentence.

> In spite of her incipient laryngitis, the drafty old barn in which she was asked to perform, and the handicap of a foreign audience, she *sang* very well, reaching high C with scarcely a suggestion of a squeak.

The subject is *she* and the verb is *sang,* used intransitively, without a complement. Some verbs in English are appropriate in only intransitive uses (*exist, occur, belong, subside, faint, depart,* for example), but many verbs, like *turned* above, fit more than one use.

Linking verbs or copulas. Linking verbs seldom have much meaning and serve mainly to link a subject with a subject complement (see also 12-5).

> Life *is* real, life *is* earnest.   Life *is* a shadow.

Is links the subject *life* with words which describe it, *real* and *earnest,* or it links *life* with another noun, *shadow,* which tells something about the subject by restating it in different terms. Forms of *to be* (*am, is, are, was, were*) are the most common linking verbs and seldom appear except as linking verbs or function words. Other verbs which are frequently used transitively or intransitively may become linking verbs with special meanings when used with a subject complement. Among the most common of them are *seem, appear, look, get, become, feel, taste, smell,* and *sound.* Compare:

> You look tired.   You look at the apple.
> The rose smelled good. He smelled the rose. The dog smelled.
> The task proved impossible. The exception proves the rule.

In the first of each group, a verb is used with a subject complement as a linking verb; in the other uses each verb has different meanings. Note that the last sentence is ambiguous; *proves* can be interpreted as either a linking verb or a transitive verb, to mean either *becomes* or *tests.* For questions of pronouns and modifiers with linking verbs, see 18b and 22a.

Transitive verbs. When it takes a complement which does not merely describe or repeat some aspect of the subject, a verb is called *transitive.* The relationships in meaning between verb and complement vary. Consider the following sentences:

> God made a green apple.
> Johnny saw the apple.
> Johnny wanted the apple.
> Johnny ate the apple.
> Thereafter Johnny disliked green apples.

In each sentence, *apple* is the object complement, but its relationship with the rest of the sentence varies. It does not always "receive action" from the verb, but it does complete the meaning of the verb. If, for example, the object were dropped from the fourth sentence, the meaning would change.

Verbs and separable suffixes. The variety of verbs in English is constantly growing as users of the language combine words to function as verbs. Consider the following sentences:

> Johnny looked at the apple.
> Johnny picked up the apple.
> Johnny broke off the stem.

Superficially, these sentences look different from those above. It is possible to say that in the first sentence *looked* is the verb and that this verb is modified by *at the apple*. This does not, however, make very good sense. Johnny did not just *look,* his look being modified by the direction of his looking, *at the apple.* He was scrutinizing the apple, deciding what to do next, as becomes clear in the following sentences:

Subject	Verb	Complement
Johnny	examined	the apple.
Johnny	looked at	the apple.

Clearly *examined* is the grammatical equivalent of *looked at,* and *apple* is most logically thought of as the complement of both verbs. Similar analysis is needed to explain the other sentences, especially the third, where it is clear that Johnny did not *break* in any particular way, but that he *broke off* something.

Similarly, words are combined to function as intransitive verbs.

The airplane blew up.

What does *up* mean here? Obviously not *up* in the sense of away from the earth. The plane, or what was left of it, came down. Nor does *blew* in this sentence mean *blew.* The two words, *blew up,* mean *exploded.* That is, two words have lost their original meanings and have become a new word with a meaning of its own. There are many such, as in *hold up a train, get up a subject, call up a girl. Up* is not the only word so used; hundreds of combinations employ *at, by, in, on, of, off, out, to,* and the like. Constructions of this sort are often called *verb-adverb combinations,* since the element which was not a verb was probably formerly an adverbial modifier; they are also called *fused verbs* and *separable-suffix verbs.*

These verbs are peculiar in that the second element must often be separated from the verb and placed after the complement or at the end of the clause or sentence.

You can *count* me *out.*
How are we going to *find* that *out?*

In some sentences the second element can be separated, or need not be.

Look these words *up.*
Look up these words.

These combination verbs are multiplying rapidly in the language, and many have developed so recently that they lack currency or have been accepted only as colloquial or vulgate.

20-2 COMPOSITION OF VERB FORMS

We use two devices to make verbs: (1) we change the form of a single word (*I am, he is; I go, he goes; I speak, I spoke*); or (2) we put several words together to make a verb (*I expect to be able to go; I should have liked to go*). Many verbs combine these devices. The result is that modern English affords a richness and accuracy in verb choice which has quite possibly never been paralleled in any other language. Our verb is an extremely exact and useful tool; but anything complicated requires some discretion in its use, and the verb is no exception.

On the whole, changes in individual words come down to us from an earlier stage of the language; verbs made by placing words side by side are of more recent development. On the whole, also, native speakers have little trouble with verbs which are constructed by placing words side by side—that kind of grammar, apparently, Americans find easy. Fortunately, most of our verbs are of this sort. On the other hand, Americans often have difficulty with the single words which change in form, perhaps just because they are so few that we do not learn them as part of our familiar speech pattern. They require special attention.

The modern verb is too complicated to permit giving a synopsis of it here. The groups of forms below include only the most common, and those most likely to give trouble. Verbs can be variously classified. They may be *active* or *passive* (see 17-3). They may indicate the speaker's concept of the sentence, that is, the *mood*. Common moods include the following: the *indicative,* which presents material as fact; the *conditional,* which provides conditions; the *subjunctive,* which indicates varying degrees of doubt, desire, uncertainty; the *interrogative,* which asks a question; and the *imperative,* which gives a command. Verbs may represent the *aspect* from which the action is viewed; for instance, *I go to school* implies that the action is customary; *I keep making that same mistake* implies that an action repeats itself; *I am about to start payments* implies that an action is to begin.

Verbs can represent *person* and *number*. English formerly had an elaborate inflectional system to designate these, but only a few endings remain. In general, *-s* or *-es* is added to the infinitive or first person form in the third person present singular. Other forms have no ending. (The second person singular, which adds *-t, -st, -est* is now almost unused.) For the agreement of subject and verb in person and number, see 21. The verb *to be,* since it preserves forms from four old verbs, is irregular; for its forms, see the lists below. *Have* has the third person singular *has.* Verbs can be divided, also, on the basis of the time to which they refer, that is, on the basis of *tense: I will go, I am going, I have gone, I had gone.*

20-3 PRINCIPAL PARTS OF VERBS

For convenience in distinguishing verb forms, we recognize *principal parts,* which users of the language need to know. The task is easier than it sounds, since the principal parts of most verbs follow a rule. Most of the others fall into recognizable patterns.

We use three principal parts, as follows: (1) the infinitive, which (except for *to be* with *I am*) is the same as the present form used with *I* (*go, see, jump, mimeograph*); (2) the past form (*went, saw, jumped, mimeographed*); (3) the past participle (*gone, seen, jumped, mimeographed*). For most verbs, these three forms are reduced to two. Every verb now being made and every verb made during the last thousand years have had two principal parts, the infinitive, and the infinitive plus *-d* or *-ed,* which serves for both past and past participle (*sew, sewed; dance, danced*). Verbs of this type, for no good reason, are called *weak verbs.* In a very early ancestor of English, verbs had principal parts which expressed a change of sound (and accordingly a change of spelling) within the verb itself. Most of these old verbs have disappeared from the language or have become weak verbs, but some have preserved their early forms and are usually called *strong verbs.* They often seem irregular, although usually they are not. There were once many classes of these verbs, each with a different sequence of changes, and since only a few verbs have survived from each class, strong verbs now seem irregular. Patterns can be observed, however, in verbs like the following: *sing, sang, sung; ring, rang, rung; ride, rode, ridden; write, wrote, written.* Past participles formerly ended in *-n,* and some still do.

Many of these old verbs are among the most common and important in the language. Thus they require special attention. The list below of principal parts includes the verbs which most commonly give trouble. A writer should be sure he knows them.

Infinitive	*Past*	*Participle*
awake	awaked, awoke	awaked
be	was, were	been
bear	bore	borne
begin	began	begun
blow	blew	blown
break	broke	broken
burst	burst	burst
catch	caught	caught
choose	chose	chosen
cling	clung	clung
come	came	come
dive	dived, dove	dived
do	did	done
drag	dragged	dragged
draw	drew	drawn
drink	drank	drunk
eat	ate	eaten
fall	fell	fallen
give	gave	given
go	went	gone
grow	grew	grown
have	had	had
know	knew	known
lay	laid	laid
lead	led	led
lend	lent	lent
lie	lay	lain
lose	lost	lost
pay	paid	paid
prove	proved	proved, proven
put	put	put
ride	rode	ridden
rise	rose	risen
run	ran	run
see	saw	seen
set	set	set
shine	shone	shone
sit	sat	sat

Infinitive	Past	Participle
speak	spoke	spoken
steal	stole	stolen
swim	swam	swum
swing	swung	swung
take	took	taken
teach	taught	taught
throw	threw	thrown
wake	woke, waked	woke, waked
wear	wore	worn

20-4 PRESENT TENSE

Simple present
I prove
  I prove the theorem this way.
  I go to class at eight.

Often called the simple present, but not usually used for this purpose. Used most commonly to indicate a customary action.

Familiarity breeds contempt.
Antonio is a good man.

Often used for generalizations.

He cudgels his brains, fills reams of paper with strange marks, and proves the binomial theorem.

Used sometimes as the so-called historical present.

Progressive or continuous
I am proving
  I am trying to help you.
  I am living in Eastwood.

Uncommon in English until the eighteenth century, progressive verbs are now probably the most common for expressing the simple present.

What are you doing now? I am going to college.

Particularly suited to actions begun in the past and continuing into the present.

Emphatic
I do prove

Do, characteristically used in interrogative forms, also makes an emphatic form.

Interrogative
Do I prove?
  Do you find the city pleasant?
  Are you happy here?

Inversion can make almost any form interrogative, but *do* makes an interrogative form of the simple present.

Passive
It is proved
  Examinations are given on Tuesdays.
  Nothing can be done about it.

To be is used as an auxiliary in verbs which allow the receiver of the action to take the place of the subject.

Variations in mood and aspect
Life can be difficult.
I may be staying all night.
I keep remembering her face.
I should be working now.
I must try to improve.
This must be the place.
He would sing if he were able to.
Would this watch be yours?

Through the use of various function words, the English verb expresses a remarkable variety of ideas such as hope, wish, probability, obligation, conceivability, and the like.

20-5 PAST TENSE

Simple past
I proved
  We won the first set easily.

He returned Tuesday.
Just then the storm began.

More limited than other past tense verbs, almost always refers to action completed in past.

Usually used with modifiers which specify the time.

We played tennis every day.

Can indicate continuous action completed in past.

Present perfect
I have proved
  I have finished my lessons.
  Someone has broken the gate.
  We have all eaten breakfast.

I have always hated turnips.

I have just spent my last dollar.

Probably most common of past forms, usually indicates action carried out before the present, with emphasis on fact that it is completed or "perfected" at the present.

Can indicate action begun in past and continuing in present.

Can, with modifiers, indicate past action without emphasis on present state.

Past perfect or pluperfect
I had proved
  By Wednesday we had finished.
  Before the guests came, John had prepared lunch.

Related to past time as present perfect to present; that is, it indicates action as completed by some past time which is usually specified in the sentence.

Progressive or continuous
I was proving
I have been proving
I had been proving
  At six o'clock the sun was shining.
  We have been talking about you.
  He had been smiling while I talked.

Widely used in all past tenses, especially for action continuing at specified times in the past; can be used for past actions which continue into the present.

Emphatic
I did prove

Interrogative
Did I prove?

Passive
It was proved
It has been proved
It had been proved

Used in all past tenses, with *to be* as function word.

Variations in mood and aspect
We used to skip rope after school.
Then we would usually go swimming.
He must have seen her.
It could have happened.
He may have told his father.
He might have told his mother.
He should have telephoned.
Had it been possible, he would have come.

Function words vary mood and aspect widely when used with the above tense forms. They can suggest completion or continuation of action, habitual action, doubt, uncertainty, possibility, obligation, and various other modal ideas.

20-6 FUTURE TENSE

Shall-will future
I shall (will) prove
He will make up the test tomorrow.
Nobody will understand.

Shall or *will* is used in what is traditionally called the "simple" future, although the form carries a sense of modality and other forms frequently express simple futurity. For distinctions between *shall* and *will*, see 20b.

I'll prove

Contracted form.

I prove
He makes up the test tomorrow.
I go to Chicago next week and I get home on the first.

The same form used for the present often serves for the simple future when modifiers specify the future time.

I am to prove
I am to arrive at the airport in two hours.

Can be used for most future situations.

Immediate future
I am going to prove
Are you going to invite the teacher?
Who is going to be first?
He is going to make up the test soon.

Currently the most common future form, especially colloquially.

Future perfect
I shall have proved
By Monday he will have learned his lines.

Refers to an action which is imagined as completed at some indicated time in the future.

Progressive or continuous
I shall be proving
I am proving
   They will be driving by in a minute.
   I am taking the next train.

With *will* and *be* as function words or with the usual present tense form, progressive verbs are useful to express the future.

Passive
It will be proved

Passive versions of the forms above use *to be* as a function word.

It is going to be proved
It will have been proved

Variations in mood and aspect.
   When you arrive, call me.
   He could finish if he would try.
   I must see you at once.
   I should write some letters.
   I can meet you at nine.
   I have to be ready in an hour.
   I could meet you at the library.
   Let us try again next week.
   You may go when you have finished.
   It would be fun to go.

Since the future is always uncertain, almost all future verbs are to a degree conditional, some more than others. English is uncommonly rich in ways of expressing in verbs various degrees of such uncertainty. The sentences here represent only a few of the more common variations in mood and aspect in verbs suggesting future time.

20-7   VERBALS

Two types of verb forms may have special uses, retaining enough of their characteristics as verbs to take subjects and objects but functioning generally as nouns or modifiers. The two types are those usually characterized by the separable prefix *to* and those with the endings *-ing* or *-d* or *-ed*. They appear frequently in the lists above in combination with function words; such combinations predicate as complete verbs. Outside these combinations, however, these forms are not complete verbs and are called *verbals.* Compare:

> *Verb:* They *are going to prove* the theorem.
> *Verbal:* We asked the students *to prove* the theorem.
> *Verb:* Somebody *has been proving* the theorem.
> *Verbal: Proving* the theorem was their assignment.

The first of these forms is the *infinitive,* one of the principal parts of the verb and usually distinguishable by its sign, *to,* and it may be used as a verbal noun (see 18-1) or sometimes as a verbal modifier (see 22-2). The following six forms are relatively common in modern English:

	Active	Passive	Progressive active
Present	to lose	to be lost	to be losing
Past	to have lost	to have been lost	to have been losing

The second type of verbal is called a *gerund* when it is used as a verbal noun and a *participle* when it is a verbal modifier. The most common forms of this verbal are:

	Active	Passive
Present	proving	being proved
Past	proved, having proved	having been proved

The simple past form *proved* is common for the participle but is not used for the gerund.

20 Vb

VERBS

Guide to Revision

Select an appropriate verb and express it in the standard form for the tense and mood the sentence requires.

Verb forms in English can be complex, but most of the difficulties with them come from a relatively few problems in usage of common verbs—for example, the shifting uses of *lie* and *lay* or the confusion of standard and dialect principal parts of certain verbs. Other errors result from carelessness, such as forgetting the relative time of the action described and shifting the tense.

20a CHOICE OF VERBS   Vb a

Three pairs of similar verbs have been so thoroughly confused in dialect and vulgate usage that many people have trouble distinguishing between them in meaning and spelling, particularly in their uses with separable suffixes.

Lie (*lay, lain*), intransitive, but usually modified or combined with a suffix like *down,* indicates that the subject occupies a position.

The book *lies* on the table.
The book *lay* on the table yesterday.
The book *has lain* on the table in the past.

Lay (laid, laid), transitive except for a few special uses (*The hens
lay well. Lay on, Macduff*), means *place* or *put* and now appears
mainly in a variety of special contexts (see dictionary).

He *lays* brick in his spare time.
The men *laid* their plans carefully.
The soldiers *have laid* down their arms.

Sit (sat, sat), intransitive except for a few uses, especially with suffixes like *out* or *with* (*She sat out the dance. She sits a horse gracefully.*), indicates that the subject occupies a place or seat or is in a
sitting position.

He *sits* by the window.
He *sat* by the window last week.
He *has sat* there for a year.

Set (set, set), transitive except for a few uses (*The sun sets in the
west. The hens are setting.*), means *place* or *put*, often varied in combinations with words like *off, up, by.*

He *sets* the lamp on the table.
They *set up* the new organization yesterday.
Finally they *have set out* on their journey.

Rise (rose, risen), intransitive, often combined with suffixes like
up, indicates that the subject moves.

He *rises* before dawn.
He *rose* before dawn yesterday.
He *has never risen* before dawn in his life.

Raise (raised, raised), usually transitive (but *John opened the bet-
ting, and Tom raised.*), indicates that the subject acts on something,
making it rise or appear.

He *raises* his hand when he wants to talk.
The committee *raised* a new issue.
His salary *has* not *been raised* for a year.

ORIGINAL

Her clothes were *laying* on the bed.
[*A mistaken notion that* lie *refers only to animate things sometimes leads to this error.* Lay *needs an object to complete it.*]

We decided just to *lay* around on the beach.
[To lay on *means* to place another object upon.]

He *laid* on the sofa.
[*This sentence—if the feat were possible—would mean that he laid an egg on the sofa.*]

When the preacher *raised* his hands, and we all *raised* up, Ma just *set*.
[*Raised is a transitive form; the first use is therefore correct, the second incorrect.* Set *is a transitive verb except in the meaning "to endeavor to hatch eggs."* The sun sets *is an exception sanctioned by usage.*]

REVISION

Her clothes were *lying* on the bed.
[To lie *indicates that the subject occupies a position.*]

We decided just to *lie* around on the beach.
[To lie on *means* to place oneself upon.]

He *lay* on the sofa.
[*In verbs meaning to place oneself or rest,* lie *appears as* lie, lies *in the present,* lay *in the past, and* lain *in the past participle. In verbs meaning to place another object,* lay *appears as* lay *or* lays *in the present, and* laid *in the past and past participle.*]

When the preacher *raised* his hands, and we all *rose*, Ma just *sat*.
[*The intransitive* rose, *the past form of* rise, *has replaced the incorrect use of* raise. Sat, *the past form of* sit, *has replaced* set.]

20b SHALL AND WILL   Vb b

The verbs *shall* and *will* are troublesome because they have a troubled background. In Anglo-Saxon *shall* and *will* were not signs of the future; the word for *shall* meant *ought to* and the word for *will* meant *willing to, to be about to.* These meanings have been preserved in *should,* which implies obligation, and *would* which implies willingness. But *shall* and *will* became indications of the future, just as words with the same meaning today (*I am about to go; I have to go*) are becoming future forms. For hundreds of years little effort was made to distinguish between *shall* and *will* as auxiliaries, and users of English apparently never have had any deep-rooted feeling for a distinction between them—a fact which may account for the distinction's being difficult.

In the eighteenth century, a popular grammarian laid down rules for the use of *shall* and *will,* and most handbooks of usage since then have repeated his rules—though a few have turned them exactly backwards. At present, most people, especially in America, pay little attention to these rules. Partly because contractions (*I'll, we'll*) are so common in speech, *will* is used in all persons in most informal situations. A few people, however, attach great importance to the arbitrary distinction between the words, and the following rule is still observed in some formal English.

In the first person, use shall *to denote simple futurity,* will *to denote determination and purpose; in the second and third persons, use* will *to denote simple futurity,* shall *to denote determination and purpose.* In general, *should* and *would* also follow this rule, except when the use would interfere with the basic meaning of these two words, *should* implying duty, *would* implying willingness.

ORIGINAL

I *will* consider each of the arguments of my colleague.

[*Presumably the verb implies only simple futurity; the form* will *is common informally, but is often not accepted in formal English.*]

I predict that the people *shall* rise up in indignation.

[*Consciousness of a distinction sometimes leads writers to a mistaken preference for* shall *as an affectation of "correctness."*]

REVISION

I *shall* consider each of the arguments of my colleague.

[*According to rule,* shall *is used with the first person to indicate simple futurity,* will *with the second and third persons.*]

I predict that the people *will* rise up in indignation.

[*There is no need for the unusual form of the original.*]

20c TENSE

Tense must remain consistent. The writer assumes a position in time in relation to his subject; he must let the reader know his position, and he must not shift without warning. He may, of course, need to use different forms to express the varying times involved. For example, a term paper on Shakespeare could involve a variety of times which the writer would need to distinguish.

1. Shakespeare *was* thirty-eight years old when the first edition of *Hamlet* appeared in London.
2. He *had earned* a reputation as one of the leading dramatists of his day.

3. *Hamlet has been discussed* and *criticized* more than any of the other plays.
4. It *is* a favorite on the modern stage.
5. In the play Hamlet *is faced* with a decision which he *cannot* make.
6. Ironically the only course consistent with Hamlet's character and satisfactory to the audience *leads* to disaster.

The first sentence indicates the basic attitude of the writer; he is in the present writing of events in the past. The second mentions what has occurred *before* the past time of the first. The third concerns what has occurred continuously and indefinitely in the past. And the last three treat the play as it exists while the writer is discussing it.

ORIGINAL

The play begins with a scene on the castle walls of Elsinore. Horatio, a friend of Hamlet, met the soldiers who were on watch and learned from them about the ghost that had appeared. Then as the soldiers were talking, the ghost, dressed in full armor, appeared again.

[*The writer, as he proceeds, perhaps begins to think of his experience in reading or seeing the play rather than the play itself. After one sentence he writes as if he were describing actual events.*]

Finally Mr. B abducts Pamela and keeps her prisoner at a country estate. Mrs. Jewkes guards her day and night. Pamela made only one attempt to escape, and it failed.

[*The writer shifts, in the third sentence, from present to past forms.*]

REVISION

The play begins with a scene on the castle walls of Elsinore. Horatio, a friend of Hamlet, meets the soldiers who are on watch and learns from them about the ghost that has appeared. Then as the soldiers are talking, the ghost, dressed in full armor, appears again.

[*The revision consistently considers the play as a piece of literature still in existence which can therefore be referred to in present time.*]

Finally Mr. B abducts Pamela and keeps her a prisoner at a country estate. Mrs. Jewkes guards her day and night. Pamela makes only one attempt to escape, and it fails.

[*When makes and fails replace the past forms, the passage is consistent. All verbs might have past.*]

When the sense requires it, tenses should be changed. Particularly, when two or more times are distinguished within the sentence, the forms of the verbs should indicate which events come before and which after. Partly because many English verb forms can serve several functions, these distinctions require attention. In general, the relationships of the tenses can be suggested by a formula like the following:

The past perfect forms	are to	the other past forms
as the past forms	are to	the present forms
as the present forms		
and	are to	the other future forms.
the future perfect forms		

This works out somewhat as follows:

When the boss *had come* (past perfect form) I *received* (past form) my pay.

At noon, if the boss *has come* (past form) I *receive* (customary present form) my pay.

By noon, the boss *will have come* (future perfect form), and I *shall receive* (future form) my pay.

By noon, if the boss *comes* (present form), I *shall receive* (future form) my pay.

ORIGINAL

She *broke* the doll her mother *gave* her for her birthday.
[*The doll had been given before it was broken.*]

When he *wrapped* and *addressed* the package, he *took* it to the post office.
[*He did not do the wrapping on the way.*]

When you *wrap* the package, be sure you *sealed* the ends.
[*The actions are to be simultaneous, and the tenses should be the same.*]

REVISION

She *broke* the doll her mother *had given* her for her birthday.
[*The past perfect,* had given, *makes the sequence of time clear.*]

When he *had wrapped* and *addressed* the package, he *took* it to the post office.
[Wrapped *has been changed to* had wrapped.]

When you *wrap* the package, be sure you *seal* the ends.

When a direct quotation is reported as an indirect question, the word order shifts and the time is sometimes pushed back. Patterns are not consistent; in the following the tense does not change:

DIRECT: He asked, "Was Caroline on time?"
INDIRECT: He asked whether Caroline was on time.

ORIGINAL

DIRECT DISCOURSE: "I don't want that junky old car parked in front of my house," the old lady yelled at me.

INDIRECT DISCOURSE: The old lady yelled at me that she *does* not want my junky old car parked in front of her house.

[*The verb has been changed from first to third person, but the time has not been changed.*]

DIRECT DISCOURSE: "You were wrong," he said.

INDIRECT DISCOURSE: He said I *was* wrong.

REVISION

DIRECT DISCOURSE: "I don't want that junky old car parked in front of my house," the old lady yelled at me.

INDIRECT DISCOURSE: The old lady yelled at me that she *did* not want my junky old car parked in front of her house.

[*The present form* don't want *of the direct discourse has become the past form* did not want.]

DIRECT DISCOURSE: "You were wrong," he said.

INDIRECT DISCOURSE: He said I *had been* wrong.

The tense of a verbal is determined by the relationship of the time of the action of the verbal to the time of the action of the main verb. The present verbal is most common and is used when the verbal and the main verb refer to action at the same time.

We expected him *to burn* the papers.

Both verb and verbal refer to the past; the verbal is therefore present in form.

Smiling at his discomfort, she looks at the photographs.

Verb and verbal both refer to the present and both forms are present. The present form is also used sometimes with a function word like *after* to suggest action preceding that of the main verb.

After *smiling* at his discomfort, she closed the photograph album.

The past forms regularly indicate action previous to the time of the main verb.

We expected him *to have burned* the papers.
Having smiled at his discomfort, she closed the photograph album.

The burning and the smiling preceded the expecting and the closing. The simple past participle often describes a state of affairs caused previously but existing at the same time as that of the main action.

Reconciled, he continued to praise the photographs.

ORIGINAL

I was pleased to have received your note.
[*This sentence implies that he became pleased some time after he had received the note.*]

REVISION

I was pleased to receive your note.
[*The pleasure is now simultaneous with the receiving of the note.*]

Hamlet found Claudius about to have prayed and spared him.

Hamlet found Claudius about to pray and spared him.

Now I am in college I know I am lucky to have a good teacher in high school.

Now I am in college I know I am lucky to have had a good teacher in high school.

20d   PRINCIPAL PARTS OF VERBS   Vb d; Prin

Standard principal parts, especially of strong verbs, should be used in the formation of verbs (see the list in 20-3).

ORIGINAL

I must have broke my glasses in the fall.
[*The third principal part, the participle, is required in the perfect form.*]

REVISION

I must have broken my glasses in the fall.
[Broken, *not* broke, *is the participle form.*]

By noon we had finished the digging and began to pour the concrete.
[Began *is parallel with* finished, *with* had *understood.*]

By noon we had finished the digging and begun to pour the concrete.
[Begun *is the proper principal part to be used in forming the pluperfect.*]

20e   MOODS   Vb e; Mood

The writer should choose a form for an appropriate mood: the indicative to state a fact, the interrogative to ask a question, the imperative to issue a command, the conditional for conditions, and the subjunctive for situations involving uncertainty, suppositions, or desire. Of these moods, the subjunctive occasions the greatest difficulty because a few uses requiring special forms survive, and these are disappearing except in formal usage.

The main situations in which the special forms are still used are: (1) in main clauses to express a wish (*The Lord be with you*); (2) in *if*-clauses expressing a so-called "condition contrary to fact," that is, a supposition that is impossible or thought to be improbable (*If I were he, I would quit*); (3) in *that*-clauses expressing a wish, command, or request (*The major ordered that the prisoners be held for interrogation).* In formal uses the present subjunctive is sometimes used in if-clauses which are not contrary to fact (*If these data be verifiable, the hypothesis becomes untenable).*

The special forms for the subjunctive which survive are two: (1) the third person present subjunctive singular does not have the ending -*s* or -*es* (indicative, *he proves;* subjunctive, *if he prove);* (2) for the verb *to be,* the present singular subjunctive form is *be,* the past singular subjunctive form *were.*

ORIGINAL

If my brother *was* here, you would behave differently.
[*The clause states a condition contrary to fact but uses an indicative verb form according to common colloquial practice.*]

If I *was* you, I would tell him what I think of him.
[*Even colloquially the subjunctive is usual in this expression;* if I was you *is more characteristic of dialect or vulgate usage.*]

The President will refuse if the Senate demands that he discharges his secretary.
[*The* that-*clause expresses a command.*]

Is he live, or *is* he dead, I'll grind his bones to make my bread.
[*In archaic, very formal or oratorical practice, the subjunctive is often used in conditional clauses.*]

If I would (or had) have known you were coming, I would have cleaned the house.
[*In the past, a condition is usually referred to in past perfect tense.*]

REVISION

If my brother *were* here, you would behave differently.
[*Formally, the subjunctive form still appears in such clauses; the subjunctive* were *replaces indicative* was.]

If I *were* you, I would tell him what I think of him.
[*The subjunctive form has been substituted in the* if-*clause.*]

The President will refuse if the Senate demands that he *discharge* his secretary.
[*The subjunctive has been used in the* that-*clause.*]

Be he live, or *be* he dead, I'll grind his bones to make my bread.

If I had known you were coming, I would have cleaned the house.

EXERCISE 20

A. In the following sentences select the more appropriate of the verbs in parentheses and explain your choice.

1. While I (*lie, lay*) hidden behind the sofa, the other members of the family filed into the dining room and (*sit, set*) down to dinner.

2. He had been (*lie, lay*) on his back for three weeks, and he was so weak that he could not (*rise, raise*) his hand.

3. The coat still (*lie, lay*) where we had left it in the morning.

4. When the peasants finally (*rise, raise*) in rebellion, issues which had (*lie, lay*) dormant for years assumed new importance.

5. The sun (*rise, raise*) at 6:30 a.m. and (*sit, set*) at 5:50 p.m.

6. After I had eaten, I (*lie, lay*) down on the couch and (*sit, set*) the book on the stand in front of me.

7. All the children (*lie, lay*) in the tall grass watching the ducks (*rise, raise*) into the air and head south.

8. The pitcher should be (*sit, set*) wherever you (*sit, set*) it this morning.

9. He decided to (*lie, lay*) the difficult problems aside.

10. They let the injured man (*lie, lay*) in the middle of the highway until the ambulance arrived.

11. (*Lie, lay*) the slices of eggplant in a dish, (*lie, lay*) a weight on them, and allow them to (*sit, set*) there overnight.

12. He (*lie, lay*) the canceled check in the drawer, and presumably it (*lie, lay*) there yet.

13. I have (*lie, lay*) in bed all morning, and now you say I must (*lie, lay*) here all afternoon.

14. He had (*lie, lay*) emphasis on this fact, that the land (*lie, lay*) adjacent to the river.

15. He (*lie, lay*) a wager that the billfold would be found (*lie, lay*) on the dresser.

B. Distinguish different types and meanings of verbs in the following groups of sentences.

1. a. Gertrude turned up her nose.
   b. Her nose turned up at the end.
   c. The book turned up under the bed.
   d. The car turned up the hill.

2. a. He promised to look into the charges.
 . b. He tried to look into the microscope.

3. a. I ran across my roommate in the parking lot.
   b. I ran across the street.

4. a. The police broke up the fight.
   b. The party broke up in the early morning.
   c. The axle broke up in the mountains.

5. a. After the quarrel the children made up.
   b. Mary made up for the play in five minutes.
   c. Bill made up for lost time.
   d. Louise made up the entire story.
   e. Progress was being made up on the hill.
   f. The costumes were made up in New York.

C. For each blank in the following sentences select an appropriate form of the verb in parentheses:

1. If you are going fishing with me you _____ (be) quiet.
2. When I _____ (eat) my lunch, I took a short nap.
3. If you want to stay out after hours, you _____ (ask) permission.
4. While I was looking in the closet for my windbreaker, part of the ceiling _____ (fall) down.
5. Since you say you can see in the dark so well, why _____ you _____ (stumble)?
6. While I _____ (set) the table, you might put some water to boil.
7. Before you screw down the lid, be sure you _____ (check) the safety valve.
8. You _____ (prove) the theorem before you could have proved the corollary.
9. Mother told me that strange men _____ (be) not to be trusted.
10. When Uncle Joe came to dinner he always _____ (bring) us oranges.

D. For each blank in the following sentences select an appropriate form of the verb in parentheses:

1. If I _____ (be) you, I would take it back and get my money.
2. If it _____ (be) noon, I would go right now.
3. If the plant _____ (be) sitting on the piano, it must have left a mark in the dust.
4. If only Father _____ (be) here!
5. If anybody _____ (save) him, Dr. Worley would be the man.
6. If your father _____ (be) not carrying a gun, I would think him a religious man.
7. Mary, I often wish you _____ (be) smarter than you are.
8. John, I often wish you _____ (act) smarter than you do.
9. Children, _____ (can) you not keep from squabbling if you would try?
10. If those children _____ (can) keep from squabbling, I would let them play together.

E. Supply the verb forms missing in the following table:

Present form used with I	Past form	Past participle
1. pay	. . . .	. . . .
2.	caught	. . . .
3. run	. . . .	. . . .
4.	. . . .	chosen
5. drag	. . . .	. . . .
6. swing	. . . .	. . . .
7. swim	. . . .	. . . .
8.	. . . .	done
9.	. . . .	set
10. see	. . . .	. . . .
11. lay	. . . .	. . . .
12.	lay	. . . .
13. wear	. . . .	. . . .
14. wake	. . . .	. . . .
15. sit	. . . .	. . . .
16. steal	. . . .	. . . .

F. In the following sentences, select the appropriate forms of the verbal and explain the reason for your choice:

1. I was glad (to receive, to have received) your invitation.

2. It was the largest audience ever (to convene, to have convened) in Severing Hall.

3. When you get into the boat be sure (to fasten, to have fastened) your life belt.

4. The stairs are steep; be sure (to hold, to have held) the guard rail.

5. Father came along just when I was about (to be lost, to have been lost).

6. I was ashamed (to lose, to be losing, to have been losing) the game for our team.

7. If they were not doing their algebra, they ought (to be doing, to have been doing) it.

8. Those who were about (to die, to have died) took a last glance at each other.

9. She was unwilling (to undergo, to have undergone) the operation.

10. He expected (to be, to have been) elected house manager.

21

Agreement or Concord

For Guide to Revision, see page 361

Pronouns agree with their antecedents; subjects and verbs agree.

Agreement or concord refers to a correspondence in form between parts of a sentence. That is, two words which both have forms distinguishing the plural are said to agree in number. Or two words with forms restricted to the first person are said to agree in person.

In a highly inflected language like Latin, agreement can be complex and very important. An adjective, for example, has an ending to mark its agreement with the noun it modifies; *good* in Latin has one ending when it modifies *boy* (*puer bonus*), a different ending when it modifies *girl* (*puella bona*). The adjective agrees in gender. Without these signs of agreement, a Latin sentence would often be unintelligible; the reader could not tell what went with what.

In English, which has now lost most of its inflections, agreement applies to only a few grammatical relationships. Furthermore, clarity seldom requires distinctions of agreement. No one would miss the meaning of *The man walk to work,* even though the sentence sounds like pidgin English. Since agreement is not often essential for communication, it is often not observed in vulgate English; and in many constructions agreement is only partially observed in spoken English. Agreement is, however, characteristic of standard English, and writers need to know common practices.

The inflections in English involved in agreement are the following:

> The different forms of personal pronouns which distinguish person (*I, you, it*), number (*I, we*), and gender (*him, her, it*).

The ending on nouns, or sometimes the form change, which distinguishes the plural number.

The *–s* ending on the third person present singular of verbs which distinguishes person and number.

The form changes of the verb *to be* which distinguish number and person (*am, is, are*).

These forms affect mainly two relationships in English, between a pronoun and its antecedent and between a subject and verb. In general, two principles apply:

A pronoun agrees with its antecedent in gender, number, and person, but not in case. That is, if a pronoun refers to a feminine, singular antecedent (*woman* or *Evangeline*), a feminine, singular pronoun would be chosen (*she* or *her*).

A subject and its verb agree in number and person. That is, if a subject is third person and singular (*goat* or *salesmanship*), the inflected form of the verb is used (*is, does, works*).

One other relationship, that between two nouns, is sometimes important. In *The children washed their faces every morning, faces* is plural partly to agree with *children* and partly to make sense.

In most sentences, agreement causes difficulty only to the most inexperienced writers, but some constructions cause trouble because the number of the antecedent or the subject can not readily be determined. Is *committee* singular or plural? What of *everybody,* which is logically singular, but tends to carry a sense of the plural to most users of the language? And sometimes the sentence pattern is so obscured that the writer forgets or mistakes his antecedent or subject.

The dancer, with her ballet company, her orchestra, her stage crew, and her managers and directors, occupies the sixth floor.

Dancer, although separated from the verb by modifiers that are plural, is singular, and *occupies* is singular to agree.

For these special problems no single rule suffices, but surviving inflections give the writer an opportunity to specify number precisely. In general, modern English tends, in questionable instances, to determine the number of an antecedent or a subject according to the meaning intended, rather than according to set rules or "logic." If the sense of the subject is singular, the verb is singular; if the sense of the subject is plural, the verb is plural.

21 **Agr**

AGREEMENT OR CONCORD

Guide to Revision
Revise so that pronouns agree with their antecedents in person, number, and gender, or so that verbs agree with their subjects in person and number.

Errors of agreement usually occur because the writer fails to identify an antecedent or a subject, has trouble deciding on its number, or confuses it with its modifiers. Usually meaning determines the number.

> Two *hours* of his last twelve *were gone.*
> Two *hours is* a long time.

In the first sentence *hours* is plural, according to the sense of the sentence, but in the second sentence, in spite of its plural form, *two hours* specifies a singular unit of time and is therefore in agreement with a singular verb. Usually form and meaning are the same, and often when a subject plural in form is used in a singular sense it is imprecise. Consider

> Late *hours was* responsible for his illness.

The sense of the subject is singular, but revision would make the meaning more exact.

> *Keeping* late hours *brought on* his illness.

21a   AGREEMENT WITH INDEFINITE OR COLLECTIVE SUBJECTS   Agr a

Indefinite pronouns like *everybody, anybody, everyone, each, somebody* are traditionally considered singular, as specifying one of a group. They have been used so often, however, with a plural sense—to mean "all people," for example—that colloquially they have long been considered plural. Even in formal writing, *none* is used as either singular or plural, depending on the sense intended, and words like *everybody* are occasionally considered plural when they clearly have a plural sense. Generally, however, in serious writing such pronouns are considered singular; pronouns referring to them are singular in form and verbs of which they are subjects are also singular. Confusion becomes acute if the verb and pronoun do not interpret the subject in the same way—that is, if an indefinite pronoun is followed by a singular verb and then referred to by a plural pronoun.

ORIGINAL

When *everybody* has given *their* opinions, the committee can decide.
[Everybody *has a singular meaning here and is used with a singular verb. The pronoun referring to it should be singular.*]

Anybody knows it is to *their* advantage to have a college degree.

Each of the umpires *have* to have *their* eyes examined.
[Each *refers to only one of the umpires at a time; the plural* umpires *should not be allowed to obscure the singular* each.]

REVISION

When *everybody* has given *his* opinion, the committee can decide.
[*The singular* his *has replaced the plural* their.]

Anybody knows it is to *his* advantage to have a college degree.

(1) Each of the umpires *has* to have *his* eyes examined.
(2) The umpires ought to have their eyes examined.

In written American English, a collective noun is treated as singular unless the meaning clearly shows that the parts in the collection, not the collection as a whole, are being considered. Colloquially, however, plural verbs and pronouns are common even when the sense of the noun is not clearly plural (*The* team are *coming out of the dressing room*). Certainly, in writing, the verb and any pronouns referring to the subject should agree.

ORIGINAL

The *company* moves forward to *their* position in the line.
[*The company, thought of as a unit, is singular.*]

The company considers John one of *their* best men.

REVISION

The *company* moves forward to *its* position in the line.
[*The singular pronoun* its *has replaced the plural* their.]

(1) The company considers John one of *its* best men.

ORIGINAL *(Cont.)*

[Their *can be replaced with the singular form (1), or it can be given an antecedent (2).*]

The committee *have* voted to lay the motion on the table.
[*The committee acted as a body and is singular in meaning.*]

The committee *differs,* some supporting the motion, some opposing it, and some calling it irrelevant.
[*Here the various members of the committee are the subject, not the committee as a unit.*]

REVISION *(Cont.)*

(2) The managers of the company consider John one of *their* best men.

The committee *has* voted to lay the motion on the table.
[*The singular* has *replaces the plural* have.]

The committee *differ,* some supporting the motion, some opposing it, and some calling it irrelevant.
[*The plural* differ *indicates the plural sense of the committee.*]

21b   AGREEMENT WITH COMPOUND AND ALTERNATIVE SUBJECTS   Agr b

A compound subject usually is plural, even though its parts are singular. *Corn and lettuce* combine into a subject as clearly plural as a plural form like *vegetables*. The meaning of the subject, however, usually determines its number, and occasionally compound subjects join to form a noun expression whose sense is singular. Compare:

Ham and eggs are among his most profitable products.
Ham and eggs is a good dish.

The compound is plural in the first sentence, but in the second it names a single item for a menu.

ORIGINAL

Adrian and Harry *rides* the trolley to school and *walks* home.
[*Two people are riding, even though each part of the subject is singular.*]

A horde of little Mexicans and one lone donkey *was* trooping down the road.
[*Donkey is singular, but the horde and the donkey were trooping.*]

REVISION

Adrian and Harry *ride* the trolley to school and *walk* home.
[*The plural verbs* ride *and* walk *replace the singular so that subject and verbs agree.*]

A horde of little Mexicans and one lone donkey *were* trooping down the road.
[*Were* agrees with horde *and* donkey.]

Either, neither, or, nor, usually separate alternatives and do not combine elements as compounds. Logically alternative subjects govern verbs and pronouns individually: *Virtue or honesty is its own reward.* Colloquially, however, such subjects are not always regarded individually (*Neither of them were afraid*), and competent writers sometimes feel that the sense of alternative subjects is plural. Usually, if both alternates are singular, a singular verb or pronoun follows; if both are plural, verb and pronoun are plural. If one is singular and the other plural, usage varies. There is a tradition that the verb or pronoun agrees with the item nearest it:

> Either the boys or their father is going to help.
> Either the dog or the chickens were doomed.

Most writers, however, would avoid either sentence.

ORIGINAL

Either French dressing or mayonnaise *go* well with tomatoes.
[*The subject is singular,* dressing *or* mayonnaise, *not both.*]

Neither Columbus nor Henry Hudson achieved *their* ambitions.
[*The subject, being alternative, is singular.*]

Neither the captain nor the radar men *was* aware of the approaching bomber.

Neither processes of education nor force is likely to succeed.

REVISION

Either French dressing or mayonnaise *goes* well with tomatoes.
[*The singular* goes *has replaced the plural* go.]

Neither Columbus nor Henry Hudson achieved *his* ambition.
[*The singular* his *has replaced the plural* their.]

Neither the captain nor the radar men *were* aware of the approaching bomber.

Neither education nor force is likely to succeed.

21c AGREEMENT WHEN SUBJECT FOLLOWS VERB   Agr c

Subject-verb-complement order is so well-established in English that speakers may have trouble recognizing a subject that follows the verb and fail to make the verb agree with it. Colloquially, an introductory *there* or *it* is frequently taken for a singular subject and followed by a singular verb, even when the real subject is plural. In standard writing, however, the verb takes the number of its subject, even though the subject may follow it.

ORIGINAL

There *was* left only one seat in the balcony and one behind a post.

REVISION

There *were* left only one seat in the balcony and one behind a post.

ORIGINAL (*Cont.*)

[*The subject is compound and thus plural.*]

Behind the tree *was* two squirrels. [Squirrels *is the subject.*]

REVISION (*Cont.*)

[*The plural* were *has replaced the singular* was.]

Behind the tree *were* two squirrels.

A similar problem arises when the subject and complement of a linking verb differ in number; is the subject the word following or the word preceding the verb? Usually the basic word order pattern prevails, and the verb agrees with the word preceding it:

Oranges were his main product.
His main product was oranges.

ORIGINAL

The *answer* to our problems *are* well-trained soldiers.
[*The verb should agree with* answer. *This sentence will be awkward unless the linking verb is replaced* (*see* 13b).]

REVISION

(1) The *answer* to our problems *is* well-trained soldiers.
(2) We need well-trained soldiers.

21d   CONSISTENCY IN PRONOUNS   **Agr d**

Unnecessary shifts from one person to another (see 13d) can produce awkward constructions, especially in impersonal constructions, which do not develop gracefully in modern English. Constructions like *we find, they say,* and *you go* are common, but ambiguous. The indefinite *one* is less ambiguous but can become very awkward, especially when the possessive *one's* is required. For all but the most formal writing, however, *one* can be combined with *he* and *his*.

ORIGINAL

When *one* is abroad, you will almost always find somebody who can speak *your* language.
[*The shift from* one *to* you *is a shift of person.*]

I think everybody should be careful of *one's* grammar.

REVISION

When *one* is abroad, *he* will almost always find somebody who can speak *his* language.
[*The third person forms,* he *and* his, *are consistent with* one.]

I think everybody should be careful of *his* grammar.

21e   AGREEMENT IN DEPENDENT CLAUSES   **Agr e**

A clause or phrase used as a subject is considered singular and is followed by a singular verb.

What you are looking for is in the closet.
To know birth and death is to know life.

Within a clause the verb agrees with its subject, and when the subject is a relative pronoun its number may be hard to determine. The number of a relative pronoun is that of its antecedent. In a few types of sentences, therefore, the number of the verb form chosen may reflect different meanings in different contexts. Compare:

> The court is concerned mainly with the group of delinquent children responsible for the vandalism. John is one of those children, who *seems* unaffected by punishment.
>
> The courts have to deal with many different types of children. John is one of those children who *seem* unaffected by punishment.

The writer must be sure that the verb form reflects the intended meaning.

ORIGINAL

My father was one of the many businessmen who *was ruined* by the depression.
[*The subject of* was ruined *is* who, *which almost certainly is intended to refer to* businessmen *and thus is plural.*]

REVISION

My father was one of the many businessmen who *were ruined* by the depression.
[*The plural form* were *replaces the singular* was; *only in an unusual context would* one *be the antecedent of* who.]

21f   AGREEMENT WITH MODIFIED OR SEPARATED SUBJECTS   Agr f

When a subject is modified, a writer may carelessly mistake the modifier for part of a compound subject or may make the verb agree with the modifier rather than the subject. Colloquially, however, a subject modified by a prepositional phrase is sometimes used as a compound: *The captain with most of the crew were standing on deck.*

ORIGINAL

Orrie, with his little sister, were squatting in the middle of the puppy pen.
[*Orrie* is a singular subject, modified *by* with his little sister.]

Jim, as well as his brothers, *plan* to enter the university.

REVISION

Orrie, with his little sister, *was* squatting in the middle of the puppy pen.
[*The singular* was *has replaced the plural* were.]

Jim, as well as his brothers, *plans* to enter the university.

Sometimes the subject and verb are so widely separated by modifiers or other material, that the writer forgets the number of the subject.

The employer of all sorts of people, highly trained scientists, ignorant laborers, callow youths, and lovesick stenographers, *have* to have wide understanding of human nature.
[*The subject,* employer, *requires a singular verb.*]

The employer of all sorts of people, highly trained scientists, ignorant laborers, callow youths, and lovesick stenographers, *has* to have wide understanding of human nature.
[*The singular* has *has replaced the plural* have.]

21g AGREEMENT OF NOUNS IN NUMBER   Agr g

When one noun refers to another clarity requires that it agree with it in number.

ORIGINAL

Hundreds of soldiers threw their gun into the river and ran.

Women are treated as an equal, however, when they work in the fields.
[*Several women can scarcely be treated as one equal.*]

The men wear long robes, which somewhat resemble a dress.

REVISION

Hundreds of soldiers threw their guns into the river and ran.

Women are treated as equals, however, when they work in the fields.

The men wear long robes which somewhat resemble dresses.

EXERCISE 21

A. In the following sentences select for each blank the appropriate present tense form of the verb in parentheses:

1. A sales lot full of old cars, some with battered fenders and bashed grills, some badly needing paint, and some with broken glass and missing chrome, _____ (*resemble*) a portable junk yard.

2. Neither Darwin nor his critics today _____ (*understand*) the full implication of the theory of evolution.

3. In the United States, everyone who _____ (*want*) an education can have it.

4. Clarence is one of those men who never _____ (*do*) tomorrow what can be put off until next week.

5. Clark, with all his little brothers and sisters, _____ (*be*) trying to squeeze through the closing subway door.

6. A sundae, loaded with syrups, marshmallow and whipped cream toppings, nuts, and all the fixings _____ (*be*) always too much for Elaine's diet.

7. Each of them, in spite of the most stubborn resistance to education, _____ (*find*) that he cannot entirely escape learning something.

8. If either of you _____ (*like*) the sweater, you can have it.

9. If either Helen or Judy _____ (*like*) the sweater, I will give it up.

10. A parade, made up of a few children and a few horses, all the dogs in the neighborhood, and a home-talent rodeo, _____ (*be*) our annual Fourth of July celebration.

11. He was one of those lucky soldiers who _____ (*seem*) always to be where there is no battle.

12. There _____ (*be*), after all is said and done and your life has mostly run away, only two rewards which make life worth living.

13. The chairman of the committee, even the chairman of several committees, in spite of reams of advice and all the promises of help from committee members, usually _____ (*have*) to do most of the work.

14. What you are searching for and longing for _____ (*be*) not to be found in books.

15. Marjorie is one of those women who never _____ (*stop*) chattering.

B. In the following sentences choose a pronoun to agree in number with the collective noun which is its antecedent:

1. The herd of wild burros follows (its, their) path up the canyon.

2. The gang held (its, their) regular meeting Wednesday after school.

3. The Chamber of Commerce cast (its, their) ballots for various candidates for beauty queen.

4. The team took (its, their) positions about the field.

5. The Security Council will endeavor to reach (its, their) decision today.

6. The convention of nurses kept busy brushing (its, their) respective teeth.

7. The fraternity bowling team has just won (its, their) first victory.

8. The cordon of policemen tightened (its, their) net around the hideout.

9. The committee approved the minutes of (its, their) last meeting.

10. If one is in a national park (you, he, they) can find drinking water if (you, he, they) will ask a ranger.

22

Forms of
Modifiers

For Guide to Revision, see page 373

Form and usage distinguish some adverbs and adjectives and indicate the degree of modification.

In many languages the forms of modifiers are extremely difficult; elaborate systems of endings connect modifiers with expressions they modify. In English many modifiers are phrases or clauses, marked by function words, and single-word modifiers have lost most of their endings. *Red* can modify a girl's hair or a man's shirt, and if the red hair as subject is resting on the red shirt as object, the same form, *red* serves all purposes. The only surviving important form changes for modifiers serve to distinguish adverbs and adjectives and to indicate the degree of modification.

22-1 ADJECTIVE AND ADVERB

Many modifiers can be distinguished either as adjectives, which modify nouns and pronouns, or as adverbs, which modify other parts of the sentence. The distinction is important for single-word modifiers because certain words and forms are restricted by usage to function only as either adjective or adverb. *Satisfactory,* for example, can be used as an adjective to modify a noun, but not as an adverb; *satisfactorily* can be used as an adverb, but not as an adjective. The following statements describe certain characteristics of forms of modifiers:

(1) *Most single-word adverbs end in* -ly. Not all adverbs can be so distinguished, but most adverbs were formed by the addition of the word *like* to some other word, usually an adjective. When combinations such as *stormy-like* or *handsome-like* were shortened, they be-

came *stormily* or *handsomely*. We now make adverbs by adding *-ly* to almost any modifier. A few adjectives have been formed by adding *-ly* to a noun (*homely, leisurely*).

(2) Some adverbs existed in Anglo-Saxon and have survived in their early form; thus the ending *-ly* was not necessary to make adverbs of them (*well, however, down, ahead*).

(3) A few words function as either adverbs or adjectives (*better, early, fast, much, more, late*).

(4) A few words function informally or colloquially as either adverbs or adjectives, even though *-ly* adverb forms exist and are usually preferred in formal writing or speaking (*cheap* or *cheaply, close* or *closely, deep* or *deeply, even* or *evenly, loud* or *loudly, slow* or *slowly, tight* or *tightly*). Compare:

> It was a *slow* train.
> Go *slow* in this zone.
> You should proceed *slowly* with the reorganization.

(5) A few words are frequently confused because of similarities in spelling and meaning.

Adjectives	*Adverbs*
good (kind, agreeable, satisfactory)	*well* (satisfactorily, in a pleasing or desirable manner)
well (fortunate, fitting or proper, in good health)	
real (authentic, genuine)	*really* (actually, in a real manner)
sure (firm, secure, dependable)	*surely* (certainly)
some (in an indefinite amount)	*somewhat* (to a certain extent or degree)

22-2　VERBAL MODIFIERS

Verbals (see 20-7) may be used as modifiers as well as nouns (see 18-1). Like other verbals, verbal modifiers cannot serve as the complete verb in a clause (see 12), but they can take a complement. Both infinitives and participles serve as verbal modifiers, functioning either in fixed positions or as movable modifiers.

INFINITIVE AS SENTENCE MODIFIER: *To insure* delivery he sent the letter by registered air mail.

PARTICIPLE AS SENTENCE MODIFIER: *Relying* on our compass, we tried to keep a constant course through the underbrush.

PARTICIPLE MODIFYING NOUN: It was a *trying* experience.

PARTICIPLE AS MODIFYING SUBJECT COMPLEMENT: The experience was *trying.*

Notice that constructions with verbal modifiers are often much like constructions with complex verbs which use verbal forms in combination with function words.

VERB: He *was trying to forget* the experience.

22-3 OTHER TYPES OF MODIFIERS

A few other types of single-word modifiers need to be distinguished.

(1) *Appositive modifiers* are substantives used to modify; they usually follow nouns or pronouns (see 15), repeating an idea with a slightly different emphasis.

My *mother,* a very strong-minded *woman,* believed that a human back should never touch a chair back.

Woman, a word which usually works as a noun, is here called an appositive or said to be in apposition with *mother.*

(2) *Demonstrative adjectives* are function words which "point out" a noun expression: *these, those, this,* and *that* are most common. They are like pronouns in form (see 18) and like pronouns emphasize the reference between words in the sentence (see 19c).

(3) *Articles, a, an,* and *the,* are special function words which introduce noun expressions (see 23-7).

(4) *Possessive modifiers,* the possessive forms of nouns (see 29a) and pronouns (see 18), act as modifiers.

He put *his* head in the *lion's* mouth.

22-4 COMPARISON OF ADVERBS AND ADJECTIVES

We recognize three degrees of modifiers, as follows: Positive, implying no comparison (*fast car, beautifully landscaped*); comparative, implying that one exceeds another (*The boulevard is a faster street than the highway and more beautifully landscaped*); and the superlative, which implies the highest degree, at least within certain limitations (*The boulevard is the fastest road out of town, and the most beautifully landscaped*).

Modifiers are compared in two ways.

	Positive	*Comparative*	*Superlative*
Short adjectives	red	redder	reddest
	short	shorter	shortest
	greedy	greedier	greediest
	homely	homelier	homeliest
Long adjectives	beautiful	more beautiful	most beautiful
	superficial	more superficial	most superficial
Adverbs	slow	slower	slowest
	rapidly	more rapidly	most rapidly
	beautifully	more beautifully	most beautifully
	superficially	more superficially	most superficially

Short adjectives (all adjectives of one syllable and most adjectives of two syllables) and a few adverbs (especially those not ending in *-ly*) are compared by adding *-er* in the comparative and *-est* in the superlative. All long adjectives and most adverbs are compared by preceding the positive form with *more* and *most*. Adjectives of two syllables can be compared either way, and the distinctions are too subtle to be described by rule. The same person might say

He is *stupider* than an ox

but write

I never saw a *more stupid* boy.

A few modifiers retain irregular forms.

Positive	*Comparative*	*Superlative*
good	better	best
well	better	best
bad	worse	worst
little	less	least
much	more	most
many	more	most
far	farther	farthest
	further	furthest

22 Adj; Adv

FORMS OF
MODIFIERS

Guide to Revision

Substitute a form of the modifier appropriate in standard English for its use in the sentence.

Usage requires that some single-word modifiers be either adjectives or adverbs, and form changes enforce the distinction. Other form changes distinguish the degree of modifiers. Confusion of these forms is not acceptable in standard English.

22a   ADJECTIVES AND ADVERBS   Adj a; Adv a

Some words (see 22-1) are used as either adjective or adverb, but only colloquially as adverbs; others are restricted to only one of these uses.

ORIGINAL

Jack can *sure* sing.
[*Sure has developed a special meaning in this colloquial use.*]

When I called, they came *quick*.

She played her piece *real good*.

None of the work was done *satisfactory*.

REVISION

Jack can surely sing.
Jack can sing very well.
[*More formal expressions do not translate the original exactly*]

When I called, they came *quickly*.

She played her piece *very well*.

None of the work was done *satisfactorily*.

A modifier used as a subject complement after a linking verb should be an adjective, not an adverb. As a subject complement it modifies the subject, which is always a noun expression. Errors develop whenever the writer has trouble recognizing a linking verb, especially with

373

a verb which can be either transitive or linking. *Tastes,* for example, can be a transitive verb (*He tastes wine*) or a linking verb (*The wine tastes good*). *Good,* in the second sentence, is an adjective modifying *wine.* To say *The wine tastes well* would be nonsense. We cannot speak of the skill of wine in tasting. We could say *He tastes well* or *He tastes the wine well,* a compliment for a professional wine-taster. To say *He tastes good* implies cannibalism. As a kind of rough test, the writer can sometimes substitute a form of *to be* for the verb. If *to be* can be substituted without creating nonsense, the original verb is a linking verb and should be followed by a subject complement, not an adverb.

ORIGINAL

The dog smelled *badly.*
[*Unless the writer intends a reflection against the dog's ability as a bloodhound, he needs the adjective as a subject complement.*]

Tweed feels *roughly.*

He looked *timidly* standing all alone before the judge.
[COMPARE: He looked timidly about the room, *in which the adverbial form is properly used.*]

REVISION

The dog smelled *bad.*
[*Since is could be substituted for the verb without making nonsense,* smelled *acts as a linking verb.*]

Tweed feels *rough.*

He looked *timid* standing all alone before the judge.
[Timid *describes the man, not his way of looking;* was *could substitute for* looked.]

22b   COMPARATIVE AND SUPERLATIVE   Adj b; Adv b

Comparative and superlative forms are sometimes indicated by an ending, sometimes by a function word; but both signals are more than enough.

ORIGINAL

Stanley's singing was *more better* than his dancing.

REVISION

Stanley's singing was *better* than his dancing.

Extravagant superlatives may trap a writer into making statements he cannot substantiate and ultimately make his writing less strong and less convincing than more soberly qualified prose. Often overuse of superlatives leads to incomplete constructions (see 16).

ORIGINAL

The Rush Memorial represents Gutzon Borglum's *most* artistic achievement.

[*A judgment of this sort can be no more than an opinion and is likely to impress the reader as an unreliable opinion.*]

REVISION

(1) *Some critics consider* the Rush Memorial Gutzon Borglum's *most artistic* work.

(2) The Rush Memorial is impressive in its mass and artistic in its conception.

The Byington Parkway is the *most modern* highway in all the world.

The Byington Parkway embodies *many of the most recent developments* in highway construction.

Some modifiers have meanings which are not logically subject to comparison (*opposite, final, dead* in the sense of deceased, *waterproof, entirely, diametric,* for example). Strictly speaking, *fatal* cannot be thought of in degrees; a wound is fatal or not fatal. Colloquially, however, the function words indicating comparison (*most* and *more*) are often used to mean *more nearly* or *very* and are used with such words. Furthermore, colloquially many such words are losing their traditional meanings and assuming meanings which are comparable. Many of these new meanings have not been accepted for standard usage.

ORIGINAL

The new turbo-jet is a *most unique* advance in aeronautical science.

[Unique *originally meant* single *or* sole, *but it has come colloquially to be a rather vague—and overused— modifier meaning* extraordinary.]

REVISION

(1) The new turbo-jet is *unique*.

(2) The new turbo-jet represents a radical departure in engine design, since it relies upon a newly discovered principle of fuel consumption.

He was the *most outstanding* scholar in the school.

[*Although* outstanding *has developed a meaning like "excellent" or "distinguished," it often seems redundant when compared.*]

He was the *outstanding* scholar in the school.

[*Without* most, *the modifier is more economical and more forceful.*]

Although colloquial usage has never supported the distinction, formal practice restricts use of the superlative to comparisons among not fewer than three.

ORIGINAL

Between the flatboat and the spon-
son canoe, I should say that the flatboat offers the *best* chance of shooting
the rapids.

REVISION

Between the flatboat and the spon-
son canoe, I should say that the flatboat offers the *better* chance of shooting the rapids.

22c POSSESSIVES BEFORE GERUNDS   Adj c; Adv c

A distinction in precise meaning can sometimes be obtained by using the possessive of a noun to modify a gerund (see 18). Compare:

> He saw Alfred drinking sloe gin.
> He disapproved of Alfred's drinking.

In the first, the whole expression, *Alfred drinking sloe gin,* tells what
he saw; in the second it is the drinking that is disapproved and it is
identified as Alfred's.

ORIGINAL

The principal was not amused by
them playing poker in class.
[*Probably because it follows the
preposition* by, *the writer has used the
objective form* them. *But* playing, *not*
them, *is the word related to the sentence by* by.]

I was always surprised by my *father*
believing in ghosts.
[*Father did not surprise me; the belief did.*]

REVISION

The principal was not amused by
their playing poker in class.
[*With the possessive form, the
meaning of the sentence is clear; the
playing failed to amuse the principal.*]

I was always surprised by my
father's believing in ghosts.
[*Notice that if* belief *were substituted for* believing, *father's would be
used.*]

EXERCISE 22

A. In the following passage identify the verbal modifiers or participles
and parts of verbs which are identical in form with participles; indicate which are present and which past:

> I called the dog off; turning back into the thicket to hunt the other
> two [panthers], I heard him again running in full cry. I pursued
> them, and found by their tracks that he was pursuing the old one,
> which ran down a terribly steep hill toward the Savage River, and

into a thicket of laurel, when the dog came to bay. I went to him, and found him looking up a tree; but there was nothing on it. I examined, and found the scratches of her nails where she had climbed the tree; but as she was not there, I concluded that she had jumped off the tree before the dog had come in sight, and had run off. I looked around to see in what direction she had gone, but I could find no tracks in the snow. I then took a wider circle, and closed in; but still finding no track, I sat down on a log, and considered how it could be that she was gone, and no track left in the snow.

I reasoned with myself, that as she could not fly, she must have got on another tree, but there was no tree within her reach, though there were two large laurels standing in such a position that she could jump to them, and close by there were other laurels, so thick and strong that she might clamber on them. That was the last place I could see on which she could go without coming to the ground. But on looking down the hill, I observed, about twenty feet below, a leaning birch, which was so crooked that the top came within ten or fifteen feet, while the middle of it was perhaps twenty feet, from the ground. It had been so long crooked that two or three sprouts, about as thick as my thigh, had grown up from the main trunk; and between two of these sprouts lay the panther, lengthwise on the tree, with her long tail passed around one sprout, and crooked so as to lie on the trunk beyond the sprout next to her. I had passed directly under her, in circling around to find her tracks, and she was not more than fifteen or twenty feet above my head.

> —Slightly adapted from MESHAK BROWNING,
> *Forty-Four Years of the Life of a Hunter*

B. Supply for the blanks in the following sentences appropriate modifiers; some sentences may require modifiers of more than one word:

1. When the doctor arrived, the patient was looking very ————.
2. Both the tires are old, but put on the ———— of the two.
3. Neither cup is full, but yours is ———— than mine.
4. Alice's dress is unique, but mine is more ———— than hers.
5. He may not be simple-minded, but he always acts ————.
6. She came to our pledge party, but we decided that she was too ———— for us.
7. Walter Johnson was one of the ———— baseball pitchers this country ever produced.
8. The apartment was old and in a poor part of town, but it looked ————.
9. I watched both girls and decided the ———— one was probably a snob.
10. I ran to the window and looked ———— down into the street.

C. In the sentences below, decide whether each italicized modifier is appropriate or inappropriate. If it is inappropriate, select a better form.

1. Our "open-house" was the *most unique* party I can remember.

2. Your collie may be smart, but she looks *mean*.

3. The cougar clawed, and looked *meanly* from between the bars of its cage.

4. Before we were halfway down into the Grand Canyon my mule became *lame*.

5. The dog yipped, looked around as though for some protection, and ran *lame* toward his kennel.

6. Janice and Lorry lived in houses across the street from ours, but Janice's house was *more opposite* ours than Lorry's was.

7. Of the two sets, I should say that the *smallest* one has the *highest* fidelity.

8. When I was young I thought "The Song of the Lark" was the *beautifullest* picture I had ever seen.

9. When I saw that the cow moose had a calf with her I scrambled *lively* down the hill.

10. If I had had a shell in my gun, I could have shot that squirrel *easy*.

11. Mother was always an *easy* mark for any clever salesman.

12. Our old car did not have much power, but it rode *easy*.

13. The chair was deep, soft, and pitched back, so that it looked very *easily*.

14. Daniel Webster was the *most eloquent* orator whose voice ever rang through the halls of the Senate.

15. The old square in New Orleans is a *most unique* sight.

23

Function

Words

For Guide to Revision, see page 386

English grammar gains flexibility through function words.

English, as has already been observed (see pages 199–204 and pages 303–308), has developed a grammar which is primarily distributive. Its characteristics distinguish it from inflected languages; they appear in a comparison of three versions of the following passage from Boethius's *Consolation of Philosophy:*

Latin of Boethius:

Tandem,	"Vincimur,"	arbiter
At length	*"We are overcome,"*	*the judge*
Umbrarum	miserans	ait
Of Hades,	*pitying,*	*said;*
"Donamus	comitem	viro
"Let us give	*his consort*	*to the man;*
Emptam	carmine	conjugem."
He has bought	*with his song*	*his wife."*

Anglo-Saxon of King Alfred:

Tha cleopode se hellwara cyning,   ond cwæth   "Wuton
Then spoke the of Hell king   *and said:*   *"We ought*

agifan   thæm esne   his wif,   for thæm he hi hæfth
to give back   *to the husband*   *his wife,*   *because he her has*

gearnad mid his hearpunga.
earned with his harping.

Middle English of Chaucer:

> At the laste the lord and juge of soules was moevid to misericordes, and cryeded: "We been overcomen," quod he; "yeve we to Orpheus his wif to beren him compaignye; he hath wel y-bought hire by his faire song and his ditee."

A number of differences are apparent among the passages beyond those in vocabulary. Word order has replaced the endings of the Latin to reveal the actor-action grammatical pattern. The number of words has notably increased, twelve for Latin, twenty-two for Anglo-Saxon, and forty-two for Chaucer. Translation into modern English would require a few more words: *we been overcomen* would be *we have been overcome,* and *yeve we* would be *let us give.* The comparison illustrates a second characteristic of distributive grammar, that it sorts out and separates the signs of grammatical function from the signs of meaning. Whereas an inflected grammar, like that of Latin, puts the two kinds of signs into a single word, a distributive grammar, like that of modern English, tends to use one word to signal a grammatical relationship and another word to convey meaning.

Modern English, then, uses words in two ways, as signs of meaning and as signs of grammatical function. That is, the words in sentences can be roughly distinguished as *content words* and what we have called *function words.*

23-1 FUNCTION WORDS AND CONTENT WORDS

Partly because English is still in process of becoming a language with a distributive grammar, words cannot be sharply classified as either content words or function words, and such classification is not necessary. Distinction between the two kinds of uses, however, is possible. Compare the following groups of sentences:

> I *have* two apples.
> I *have* eaten two apples.
> The apple is *pretty.*
> The apple is *pretty* good.
> *Up* is the right direction.
> The balloon blew *up*
> He blew *up* the balloon.
> The wind blew the balloon *up* the road.
> What he says is not *so.*

The truth was not *so* easy to discover.
He left *so* that we could speak freely.

In the first sentence, *have* is clearly a content word, a sign of meaning; but in the second it is a function word, a sign of the tense of the verb. In the second group, *pretty* is a content word in the first sentence, but a function word in the second. In the third group, *up* appears in a variety of uses: first as a content word naming a direction, second as a part of a verb *blow up* which works as a sign of meaning, third as a part of the same verb representing a different meaning in its transitive use, and fourth as a function word joining *road* to the sentence. In the final example, *so* appears first as a content word and then as two different kinds of function word. Since most function words formerly had other uses, they are now multiple-purpose words which did not lose entirely their old uses when they began to fill new functions required by our changing language.

23-2 VARIETY OF FUNCTION WORDS

Function words have developed remarkable variety and adaptability. Charles Carpenter Fries distinguishes fifteen groups of function words and points out that function words constitute a third of the bulk of the extensive materials he has examined.[1] In the following sentence, nearly half the words, those in italics, act as function words.

> *Although the* room contained many women *who would have* died unhesitatingly *for their* children, *when a* mouse appeared, courageous mothers *who had been* sitting *on* chairs found *themselves* standing *on the* tops *of* piano benches *or* clinging *to* strange men *for* protection.

Although relates the words before the first comma to the rest of the sentence, but it also suggests that the clause it introduces presents a seeming contrast to the main assertion. *The* warns us that we are concerned with a specific room. *Who* relates the following words to the rest of the sentence, especially to *women,* and implies that the idea involved in *women* will serve as the subject of a dependent clause. *Would have* has little meaning but specifies the form of the verb. *For* is best thought of as part of the verb, but it shows the relationship of

[1] Charles Carpenter Fries, *The Structure of English* (New York: Harcourt, Brace & Company, Inc., 1952), pp. 87–109.

children to the remainder of the sentence. To see how hard it is to reduce some function words to a meaning, try to find a definition which will fit this *for* and the *for* toward the end of the sentence. *When* warns us that a dependent clause is coming and that the action in the clause determines the time of an event expressed elsewhere in the sentence. *A* introduces one particular mouse, but with the understanding that this mouse might as well have been any mouse. *In, of, on,* and *to,* like *for,* may be parts of the verb, but they also show how words like *tops, tables,* and *piano benches* are related to other parts of the sentence. *In* and *on* have meanings of their own; they modify our conceptions of space relationships. But what is the meaning of *of? And* and *or* join other words; *and* suggests that two words are to be taken together, *or* that there is an alternative between the ideas expressed in two words. And so on.

Function words, most of which we use without difficulty, specify grammatical ideas which cannot be observed from word order. For example, we can often know that we are dealing with a question only because certain words signal a question. Compare:

> Jack spoke.
> *Who* spoke?

Word order does not show that the second is a question; we must recognize *who* as a sign of a question. Similarly, function words identify the variation from the actor-action pattern in passive sentences (see 17-3). Compare:

> Jack *has* told a lie.
> Jack *was* told a lie.

Only the difference in the function words specifies whether Jack was actor or receiver. Accuracy in the use of function words as connectives is especially important: failure to understand the subordinating function of some connectives is frequently responsible for fragmentary sentences (see 12). Certain groups of function words are therefore considered in detail.

23-3 CLASSES OF FUNCTION WORDS

Function words are so shifting in their combination of meaning and grammatical function, and so varied in the functions they perform for complex modern sentence structures, that definitions and classifications are not exact. Many function words tell something about the meaning and application of another expression. *Have* or *shall* or *may* joined with a verb signals something about the use of the verb. *More* or *most* before an adverb or adjective indicates the degree of modification. Such function words are usually considered in this book in discussions of the expressions with which they are allied. Other function words have quite distinctive uses. *It* or *there,* for example, may be used to postpone a subject. Most commonly, perhaps, function words are used as connectives, relating various elements in the sentence. Considered here are four groups of function words, three of them of connectives, not considered elsewhere.

23-4 CONJUNCTIONS

Conjunctions join sentence elements and have no other grammatical function. Theoretically, a *co-ordinating conjunction* joins like and equal elements, a *subordinating (relative, dependent) conjunction* joins a dependent element to an independent element, although the distinction among them is not so sharp as most dictionaries and handbooks suggest. *And, but, for, or,* and *nor,* and often *so* and *yet* are conventionally recognized as co-ordinating conjunctions; they may join independent clauses or other sentence elements in parallel construction.

> I jumped into the car without trouble, *but* Mary slammed the door on her fingers.
> Although it was Sunday *and* although I knew I ought to get up for church, I turned over to take another nap.
> The pavement was icy *and* treacherous from a night of raining *and* freezing.

Subordinating conjunctions join dependent clauses to other sentence elements (see 15-1).

> *When* his watch disappeared, he immediately suspected me.
> He said *that* he did not know who took his watch.

The italicized words are subordinating conjunctions; the word *who* in the last sentence is a relative pronoun, not a conjunction, since it serves as subject of a clause (see 18-2).

The distinction between co-ordinating and subordinating conjunctions is not always sharp.

I struggled hard;	I could not get loose.
I struggled hard, but	I could not get loose.
Although I struggled hard,	I could not get loose.
I struggled hard; however,	I could not get loose.
I struggled hard, even though I could not get loose.	

By conventional statement *but* is a co-ordinating conjunction, and the two clauses in the second sentence are independent. *Although* is a subordinating conjunction, and the first clause in the third sentence is subordinate. *However* is a conjunctive adverb (23-5), and accordingly in the fourth sentence both clauses are independent. *Even though* is a subordinating conjunction, and accordingly the second clause in the fifth sentence is dependent. These differences in classification may seem too varied to account for the changes in the sentences, but the differences are the basis of our standardized punctuation of sentences of this sort, and the writer should know them.

Correlative conjunctions combine to show a relationship between sentence elements and are separated by one of these elements.

Either you stop complaining, *or* I leave.
Neither Mary *nor* Ruth knew what he was talking about.
If six is one factor, *then* the other factor must be five.

23-5   CONJUNCTIVE ADVERBS

Conjunctive adverbs join clauses and act as modifiers within their own clauses.

I wanted one of the then fashionable dirndls; *however,* I got Jinny's old plaid skirt.
She was in no mood to take advice. I was angry, *however,* and I told her what I thought of her leaving the party.

The second *however* links the sentence to a preceding sentence. Other conjunctive adverbs include the following: *thus, then, nevertheless, nonetheless, moreover, likewise, similarly, also, furthermore, consequently, therefore, hence,* and *besides.*

23-6 PREPOSITIONS

Prepositions show the relationship between noun expressions and other sentence elements.

> My uncle, a man *of* few ideas, built the company *by* patient industry.

Of permits *ideas,* a noun expression, to modify *man*. *By* relates *industry* to the rest of the sentence. The preposition is conventionally thought of as the first word of a prepositional phrase.

23-7 ARTICLES

The *articles* are sometimes classified as modifiers, sometimes as function words; like many function words they serve far more than one use. *The,* called the *definite article,* often refers to something previously mentioned.

> One evening Father remarked casually that we might soon go to see Niagara Falls. Thereafter, for days, all conversations led inevitably to a discussion of what we would do when we went to see *the* Falls.

The often identifies a particular object from others in its class. Compare:

> He lost his eye in *an* accident.
> He lost his eye in *the* accident I was telling you about.

The can replace a personal pronoun referring to part of the body.

> Take the bow in *your* left hand and the bowstring in *your* right.
> Take the bow in *the* left hand and the bowstring in *the* right.

The *indefinite articles a* and *an* have developed from the numeral *one* and retain some of their earlier meaning. Usually they have the force of *any*. *An* is used before words beginning with a vowel; *a* before words beginning with a consonant (*an* officer, *an* enlisted man, *a* private). Since speech usually determines language, words beginning with a vowel sound may require *an* even though the word is spelled with an initial consonant (an hour), and, conversely, a word beginning with a consonant sound may require *a* before a vowel (a European, a unit).

Many noun expressions require no article. Plural nouns including all members of a class usually require no article.

On the whole, *Americans* like *dogs, cats,* and *children.*

Abstract and general nouns usually require no article.

The history of your town is part of the study of *history.*
Evening came down and soon we could see thousands of *stars. The night* was clear and bright.

23 FW

FUNCTION
WORDS

Guide to Revision

Consider the exact implication of a function word, and choose carefully; if necessary consult a good dictionary or synonym book to be sure the word does just what you want it to.

Function words are pivotal words; one function word can change the whole tenor of a sentence.

Because I love you I must leave you.
Although I love you I must leave you.

Accordingly, function words should be chosen with unusual care.

23a CO-ORDINATING CONJUNCTIONS   FW a; Conj a

Be sure to use the most meaningful co-ordinating conjunction. *And* joins like elements of thought or adds a similar element; *but* emphasizes a contrast; *or* offers a choice.

ORIGINAL

The sea was like glass, *and* that was the last calm day we had at the beach.
[*Probably, a contrast is intended.*]

REVISION

The sea was like glass, *but* that was the last calm day we had at the beach.

ORIGINAL (*Cont.*)

You can play all sorts of games, *and* if you want to, you can spend the afternoon under a tree reading a book.

[*A choice seems intended.*]

REVISION (*Cont.*)

You can play all sorts of games, *or* if you want to you can spend the afternoon under a tree reading a book.

In order to avoid lengthy sentences modern writers sometimes put co-ordinate ideas in separate sentences, beginning the second sentence with a co-ordinating conjunction.

> The wolf is today what he was when he was hunted by Nimrod. But, while men are born with many of the characteristics of wolves, man is a wolf domesticated, who both transmits the arts by which he has been partially tamed and improves upon them.
> —R. H. TAWNEY, *Religion and the Rise of Capitalism*

Although the sentences might have been combined, the separation sharpens the contrast between ideas, because *but,* the sign of the contrast, is in the position of emphasis at the beginning of the sentence. This device, however, is easily overworked. It is useful only when the writer needs the special emphasis given to the co-ordinating conjunction by the initial position.

ORIGINAL

At first I thought I would decorate the table with flowers. But I found that the roses had gone to seed.

[*Opening the second sentence,* but *is unduly emphatic.*]

REVISION

At first I thought I would decorate the table with flowers, but I found that the roses had gone to seed.

[*As a conjunction within a compound sentence,* but *is appropriately inconspicuous.*]

23b   SUBORDINATING CONJUNCTIONS   FW b; Conj b

Subordinating conjunctions do more than indicate that one part of a sentence is dependent; they also specify the particular way in which it is dependent. Compare:

> *Although* she was his wife, she stayed at a hotel.
> *Because* she was his wife, she stayed at a hotel.
> *Before* she was his wife, she stayed at a hotel.
> *Until* she was his wife, she stayed at a hotel.
> *After* she was his wife, she stayed at a hotel.
> *While* she was his wife, she stayed at a hotel.
> *Whenever* she was his wife, she stayed at a hotel.

In each sentence, the conjunction indicates a different kind of relationship between the ideas in the two clauses and gives the sentence a different meaning. Subordinating conjunctions need to be chosen with care to define relationships precisely (see also 13c).

ORIGINAL

While Father did not approve of alcoholic beverages, he always had some in the house for guests.
[While *is loosely used as an equivalent of* although *or* because. *Strictly used it means that one event takes place at the same time as another. That is, this sentence suggests that Father eventually approved of alcoholic beverages and thereafter illogically refused liquor to his guests.*]

Since my mother was a little girl, she was not allowed to sit at the table.
[Since, *often, refers to time, but it has come also to be used in the sense of* because. *Here there is confusion.*]

I did not know *but what* she was afraid to come in.

He had heard *as how* anyone could make a living panning gold.

Marilyn preferred long hair which swept below her shoulders, *while* Louise liked to be able to run a comb through her short haircut and be ready for breakfast.

I washed my face *so as* I would be allowed to go in for dinner.

I arrived on time *so* I could leave early.

REVISION

Although Father did not approve of alcoholic beverages, he always had some in the house for guests.
[*The subordinate clause mentions a concession, and the concessive conjunction,* although, *has accordingly replaced* while, *which properly concerns simultaneous times.*]

Because she was only a little girl, my mother was not allowed to sit at the table.

I did not know *but that* she was afraid to come in.

He had heard *that* anyone could make a living panning gold.

Marilyn preferred long hair which swept below her shoulders; *whereas* Louise liked to be able to run a comb through her short haircut and be ready for breakfast.

I washed my face *so that* I would be allowed to go in for dinner.

I arrived on time *so that* I could leave early.

23c LIKE AND AS

FW c; Conj c

In standard English *like* is used only as a preposition (*He ran like a deer.*) and *as* and *as if* are conjunctions (*He ran as if he had seen a ghost.*) *As* is not used instead of *that* to introduce a noun clause. Colloquially, however, *like* is frequently used as a conjunction, and students, perhaps overcautious in avoiding errors with *like* in their writing, sometimes misuse *as* as a preposition. Notice the differences in meaning between *He slipped into the house as a thief* and *He slipped into the house like a thief,* or between *He cried as a baby* and *He cried like a baby.*

ORIGINAL	REVISION
He cried *like* his heart would break.	He cried *as if* his heart would break.
I do not know *as* I believe you.	I am not sure· *that* I believe you.
Like I said, there is no gas in the tank.	*As* I said, there is no gas in the tank.

23d CORRELATIVE CONJUNCTIONS   FW d; Conj d

A correlative conjunction should be completed with the proper word to fill the sentence pattern.

ORIGINAL	REVISION
Neither the socket wrench *or* my patented ratchet would reach the rear connecting rod bolt.	*Neither* the socket wrench *nor* my patented ratchet would reach the rear connecting rod bolt.

23e PREPOSITIONS   FW e; Prep

Prepositions determine many intimate relationships within the sentence; the writer should know the meaning of prepositions and should choose them with care. In addition, the use of certain prepositions with certain words and for particular usages has grown with custom; our usage of prepositions is not always based on apparent logic. It is what is often called *idiomatic,* but it is no less exact for that.

ORIGINAL	REVISION
He went *in* the house and stopped *at* the mirror.	He went *into* the house and stopped *before* the mirror.
I had never heard *about* him or *of* his famous rescue.	I had never heard *of* him or *about* his famous rescue.

Some prepositions must be composed of more than one word, but involved prepositions are to be avoided if a simpler construction will suffice.

ORIGINAL

I found the keys *in back of* the water pitcher.

He spoke *in regards to* the paving *of* the alleys.
[*When this is appropriate, the word is* regard, *not* regards.]

REVISION

I found the keys *behind* the water pitcher.

(1) He spoke *about* paving the alleys.
(2) He discussed paving the alleys.

23f CONJUNCTIVE ADVERBS   FW f; Conj Adv

Conjunctive adverbs are unusually useful to show relationships, but they must be chosen carefully and should not be used to excess. At the beginning or end of a sentence a conjunctive adverb is usually falsely emphatic (see 17f).

ORIGINAL

Clubs for girls can fill useful social functions. However, they should not take up all of a girl's time. Then, they merely interfere with a girl's achieving social maturity. Nevertheless, there is a time in a girl's life when a club can be helpful, and even exciting.
[*Childish sentences like these cannot be cured by merely removing excessive conjunctions.*]

REVISION

If a girl allows her clubs to consume all her time, they may only interfere with her achieving social maturity. Nevertheless, there is a period in a girl's life when a club can be helpful, even exciting.
[*The structure has been made simpler and more direct, and with the change several conjunctive adverbs have been dropped.*]

23g ARTICLES AND DEMONSTRATIVE ADJECTIVES   FW g; Art

The articles and demonstrative adjectives (see 22-3) carry little meaning as modifiers, but they cannot be used interchangeably. Failure to use articles which make the desired distinctions between the words they modify (see 23-7) makes unclear writing. Especially troublesome is the *generic singular,* in which a singular noun combines with *the* to imply all or most of the members of a class (*the man in the street, the average car buyer*). The generic singular should be used consistently, not interspersed with plurals.

ORIGINAL

When we first entered the park, it seemed almost deserted. *The* man was sitting alone on a bench, and a pigeon pecked at a paper cup. I saw no other signs of life.

[*Unless some missing part of the context has introduced* the man, *he is probably appearing here for the first time and should not be singled out by* the.]

REVISION

When we first entered the park, it seemed almost deserted. *A* man was sitting alone on a bench, and a pigeon pecked at a paper cup. I saw no other signs of life.

[*The more indefinite* a *serves to introduce the man.*]

On our way home from Sunday School, *this* man came up to me and took my hand, and then *this* fellow said. . . .

[*This* is sometimes overused, especially in narratives told by children, without any reference to what has preceded.]

On our way home from Sunday School, a man came up to me and took my hand, and then he said. . . .

[A *is preferable, since* this *is not designating any specific person but is acting only as a kind of vague and misleading intensive.*]

A good student keeps abreast of world affairs. Good students are always informed about current events.

[*The article appears in one of its common uses, to specify a singular as the type of a whole group, but in the next sentence the writer changes his device.*]

The good student keeps abreast of world affairs. He is always informed about current events.

[*The use of the article to specify an example of a group is common; compare the use of* the writer *in this book. But the device should be used consistently and not allowed to shift point of view.*]

EXERCISE 23

A. With each of the two pairs of clauses below make five sentences with five different meanings or shades of meaning by varying the conjunctions or conjunctive adverbs. You may change the order of the clauses if you wish.

1. I slid down the eaves spout I heard somebody scream upstairs

2. It is election day I go fishing

3. I have fast reaction time I like sports

4. I have to ride the subway to school I study the advertising on the car cards

5. The boat heeled over He worked at the sails

B. The sentences below contain some faulty usage in the italicized function words. If the function word is inappropriate, choose a better form, or revise the sentence.

1. *While* I do not like to complain about my guests, I do object to anybody who comes in with his shoes dripping mud.
2. I had expected to love Venice, *and* when I got there I could not stand the smell of the canals.
3. The weight-lifter came on the stage, *and* Jim would square his shoulders.
4. Extra-curricular activities is *where* you learn to make friends.
5. Mother always said that childhood is *when* you have the best time.
6. *While* I don't usually eat green onions, I sometimes do.
7. *While* I was trying to get the hook out of the pickerel, I jabbed it into my own thumb.
8. The reason I do not approve of federal aid for education is *because* we must protect our liberties.
9. We spent our vacation in the Big Smokies, *and* we knew it would be cool there.
10. The ore boats cannot come to Gary, *and afterward* the ice goes out.

C. Strengthen the following paragraph by adding and improving conjunctions and conjunctive adverbs; you may change the form of the verbs and the order of the clauses if necessary.

Time is very interesting. Our lives are made of time. Nobody knows what time is. You go in one direction and you gain time. You go in the other direction and you lose time. Airplanes now fly so fast that time stands still. A plane can fly as fast as the earth revolves past the sun. A baby born in a plane flying in the right direction could theoretically live its whole life of many years without living through one day. It would have a long birthday. Its whole life would be its birthday. Suppose the plane should fly faster. The baby would soon be minus-one day old. The plane flies still faster. The baby would be minus an old man. There is one place in the United States, and there time is different in every direction. The time belt follows the Snake River. The river makes an ox-bow bend. From within the ox-bow you shoot a long-range rifle north, east, south, or west. The bullet will land almost an hour before it was fired. The ox-bow is completely surrounded by another time belt. Time is all anyone has in the world. It is fluid. Nobody has ever found a good way of measuring it.

Words

Words are the most powerful drug used by mankind.
—*Rudyard Kipling*

Deliver not your words by number, but by weight.
—*H. G. Bohn, Handbook of Proverbs*

Ford Madox Ford tells us that when he heard of the death of Joseph Conrad, his long-time friend and collaborator, he saw again in his mind the two of them driving past "a ramshackle, commonplace farm building in an undistinguished country over slight hills on a flinty bye-road and heard Joseph Conrad saying to him, 'Well, Ford, *mon vieux,* how would you render that field of wheat?' " He goes on to recount that they had spent many hours through many years in that way, jolting through "a country of commonplace downlands," asking themselves how they would describe a field of wheat under the particular conditions of the moment. Should one say, "Fields of wheat that small winds ruffled into cat's paws"? No, that was too literary. But what ideas and what words should one use? Then there was that "ten-acre patch of blue-purple cabbage." What should one do about that?

Here we have the picture of two of the distinguished writers of our time, spending great chunks of their lives asking each other what words to use to describe a field of wheat or a patch of cabbages. Quite surely they were good writers partly because they were students of words and the power of words. Conrad said that his purpose was "above all things to make you see," but he understood that before he could make anyone else see, he had to see. Unless a writer sees sharply, he cannot make others see sharply. Unless he hears vividly, he cannot make others hear vividly. How does snow look when it falls in large flakes, widely spaced, in no wind? How do the brakes of a car sound when the driver jams them on suddenly to avoid a crash? What is the difference between the smell of roasting turkey and roasting goose? If one goes to his wardrobe in the dark and finds the particular garment he wants by feel, what is there about the texture of the cloth that makes him know it? What is the taste of Roquefort cheese?

A writer who will ask himself questions like these is likely to find that his writing improves because he has more to say. Granted that he has something to say, he needs words with which to say it; he needs vocabulary. The Anglo-Saxons had a revealing term for vocabulary; they called it a "word hoard," a treasury of words that each man owned and on which he could draw at any time he wanted to speak. They seem to have understood that if a man is to be rich intellectually, he needs a great store of words; the more words he has the richer he is. Modern psychologists agree with the Anglo-Saxons about this. They have found more direct relationship between the size and accuracy of vocabulary in one test, and general intelligence in another, than between general intelligence and anything else.

Certainly words are important, because they are the tools with which one speaks and writes. To express himself well, a writer must have a large number of words in his word hoard and must be able to select just the right word for each purpose. Let us postpone the question of selection and ask first how the writer can develop a rich treasury of words. The writer can learn words by many means, but perhaps most easily by listening to intelligent conversation and reading intelligent writing. We increase our vocabularies mainly by the same means with which we started them as children, by hearing, seeing, and using new words. Most people who have large vocabularies have learned the greater part of their words by reading, particularly by reading carefully and using a good dictionary. In the long run, nothing can help a student so much as the habit of reading widely and critically, and if he does not have the habit, he can acquire it.

Everyone builds some vocabulary in this way; he learns as he matures; the learning is mainly unconscious. But the process is slow, especially for someone who has not already developed good reading habits. The process can be speeded up, converted to conscious learning. A student can deliberately learn new words, and force himself to use them. Usually, the most satisfactory improvements in vocabulary come from increased interest in language and livelier knowledge of it. This section of the book is intended to help students learn language by learning about language; having fun with language can be a profitable occupation.

24

Language, the Means
of Being Human

Knowledge of language provides a sound foundation for the use of language.

Henry Ward Beecher once observed, "When we talk about ourselves we almost invariably use Latin words, and when we talk about our neighbors we use Saxon words." No doubt the witty divine was having fun, including fun with language, but he had a point. Many Latinate words are considered polite and even complimentary; many native English words seem salty, terse, even insulting. We use our language the way we do partly because languages grow their own nature into themselves, partly because they reflect the history and culture and mental processes of the people who have used the language, and partly because they reflect the history of the language itself. A user of language does well to know something of the nature of language and something of the history of his own language.

24-1 THE MIRACLE OF LANGUAGE

How does language work? Nobody knows exactly. Some things we know, things like the following: one of the authors of this book sits before a typewriter, thinking about language and what can best be said about it, and hitting the typewriter keys. A student sits before the book, looking at it, probably because he has been told to, possibly because he hopes the book will help him to write better, or at least to get a better grade in a course. If both the writer and the reader have done their jobs moderately well, ideas will appear in the student's mind which roughly approximate those that were in the writer's mind. Here, surely, is a marvel and a mystery, and this miracle can take place although the author writes on one continent and the reader studies on another; it can take place even if the writer has been dead for centuries. We do not know in detail how this marvel comes about, but we know whereof it takes place; it relies on language. For the marvel to work, the writer and the reader must know the same language, and the written form of it. If the marvel is to work well, both the writer and the reader must be so familiar with the necessary linguistic symbols that they use them unconsciously; the writer will seldom think about the words he is using, and the reader almost never will. To a degree this process can be described; the language contains symbols for meaning—whatever we mean by "meaning," and we shall have to ask that question—and ways of using these symbols. In English, although not in all languages, these symbols are what we call words, and the way we use the words is what we call grammar and rhetoric, and sometimes prosody. All users of a language have a sort of mutual agreement, an unwritten contract as it were, that certain linguistic symbols can be used in certain ways; given that mutual understanding and human minds, extensive and relatively precise communication can take place.

24-2   THE GROWTH OF LANGUAGE

No one knows who invented language, or when or how language was devised. The most nearly primitive peoples of whom we have any record have possessed languages already so developed that in some ways they have decayed. Guesses about the origin of language have been more contradictory than convincing; various learned thinkers have argued that language grew from cries of love and fear, from imitation of babies' prattlings, from mimicking the sounds of nature, from the accompaniments of gestures, from the love of naming things, and many more. No doubt all of these had effects, but the arguments about the origin of language became so varied and volatile that the whole discussion grew more humorous than enlightening, with people making up funny names for the theories: The Bow-Wow theory, the Mu-Mu theory, the Woo-Woo theory, the Whistle and Grunt. Of course somebody started language somewhere sometime; perhaps many people started in many places many times, and the "somebody" is more likely to have been plural than singular. Perhaps something like the following provides the best guess, and it must have some truth in it even though it lacks details: language is so complicated, varied, and subtle, that it probably was never "invented," in the way we use that word, in any one time and place. It is apparently so native to man that it began to spring up wherever vertebrates became human, and men were quite possibly not anything we would call human until they had some language; thus language and mankind grew simultaneously in a sort of hen-and-egg relationship. Animals, birds, bees, and perhaps earthworms can communicate in limited ways, but only man has a communications system that is sufficiently adequate to be called a language; apparently all man has language, and for all we know he has always had it, ever since he could be called human. Language and humanity may be only two aspects of the same thing; language may be a way of defining man.

24-3 THE ANCESTRY OF ENGLISH

Where did English come from? This is much easier to answer, although the answer has been known only relatively recently, and it has brought about a revolution in our thinking about language. A schoolgirl can now know fundamental principles of language that were not dreamed of by the most learned scholars two centuries ago. Of course learned men tried to study language; they could always try to describe languages in their own times, but, generally, they had too little knowledge of other languages, living and dead, to develop enough sound theories for the study of language. The ancient Greeks studied their contemporary native language and wrote excellent grammars of it—we have the conventional eight parts of speech from them—but the Greeks knew no languages from much earlier times. They knew only the languages that were geographically close to them, and they studied few of those. In the Hebraic tradition the notion seems to have been that Jehovah started talking with Adam as soon as He had made him; we are not told what language they used. Later we are told that the Lord, to keep people from building a tower to the sky, "confounded their languages" and scattered them abroad upon the face of the earth, sending their confounded languages with them. This account is now valued more for its theological than for its philological import, but even a man as late and learned as Noah Webster assumed that the diversity of modern languages stemmed from the dispersal at Babel. He guessed that western European languages came from a tongue spoken on the plains of Chaldee, and that this language was best represented in Celtic. We now know that both of these were bad guesses, and that a student of language needs to rely on only a few consecutive bad guesses to be fantastically wrong, but until about Webster's day nobody knew enough to be very right.

Some facts were known. Obviously, Latin had borrowed words from Greek, but Latin was a different language from Greek. On the other hand, French and Italian had grown from Latin. Latin had changed, subtly and slowly from Classical times, until it had become Italian in its native peninsula, and Latin as it was spoken in what had once been Gaul changed so much that it had become what was known as French; meanwhile, the Latin spoken in the Iberian Peninsula had changed still differently so that it became what is called Spanish and Portuguese. All this occurred in historic times, and the evidence has been sufficiently preserved in manuscripts so that no real doubt exists as to what, in general, happened. Scholars might have made something of this had they wished; after all, if Italian had Latin as its parent, did it not probably have a grandparent as well, the parent of Latin? And if so, might not all languages descend from a single parent language, as all men presumably descended from Adam and Eve, or from some group of arboreal apes?

Scholars might have so reasoned, but apparently they did not think much along these lines prior to the nineteenth century. Then new observations caused men to look closely at language; everybody knew that many English words resembled Latin words because English had borrowed words from Latin. Similarly, Latin words were like Greek words because Latin had borrowed from Greek. But now educated Englishmen found themselves in India in connection with the British government there; they knew Latin and Greek, of course, and they were struck with the fact that the ancient Indic tongue, Sanskrit, resembled Latin, Greek, and Old English in the verb *to be,* in the numerals, and in many other common words, far too many to be thought accidents. And yet, English and Latin had never had any contact with Sanskrit in historic times, and Greek had had too little to matter much. Why were these languages so much alike? Once this question had been asked the evidence started pouring in from all sorts of places. For example, here is a comparison put together by the great nineteenth-century American philologist, William Dwight Whitney:

English	Lithuanian	Celtic	Latin	Greek	Persian	Sanskrit
three	tri	tri	tres	treis	thri	tri
seven	septyni	secht	septem	hepta	hapta	sapta
me	manen	me	me	me	me	me
mother	moter	mathair	mater	meter	matar	matar
brother	brolis	brathair	frater	phrater		bhratar
night	naktis		noctis	nuktos		nakta

From evidence like this, the modern theory of the growth and descent of languages has been developed and made plausible. By examining evidence which has survived for languages living and dead, we have been able to reconstruct earlier languages, and from these. still earlier languages. For example, if we did not have records of Latin, we could reconstruct Latin at least approximately because we can guess about what the forms would have had to be to account for modern Romance languages. If we did not have the Latin word *oculis* (English *eye*), we should know that some such word must have been there to account for *oeil* in French, *ojo* in Spanish, and *occhio* in Italian. Similarly, we know some words that must have been in the ancestor language of English, Greek, and Sanskrit to account for the words that have come down to us. Of course this is only conjecture, but it is conjecture that can be worked out in such detail and such consistency that no person learned in languages doubts its essential truth. It has even found remarkable confirmation. By these methods scholars had reconstructed an ancient language, which they called Indo-European, which must have been spoken perhaps four or five thousand years before Christ, in what is now east central Europe. Meanwhile, among the languages that nobody knew how to read was one impressed into numerous clay tablets known to have come from the Hittites. Eventually, but only recently, scholars learned to read Hittite; when they could, they discovered that Hittite was closely related to Indo-European, and that the forms in Hittite confirmed the forms already obtained by reconstruction in Indo-European. Did Indo-European come from Hittite, or Hittite from Indo-European, or did they both have a common ancestor, Indo-Hittite? At the moment, the common-ancestor theory looks like the best one, but while the doctors are disagreeing we cannot make much of such theories in a general book; for our purposes we may accept Indo-European as the earliest known ancestor of English, at least the earliest ancestor which is well enough known so that we can work much with it.

24-4 INDO-EUROPEAN AND ITS DESCENDANTS

What do we know of these Indo-Europeans? Directly, nothing, or next to nothing; even their name is a modern name we have made up for them. History is no help; we have little history from before five thousand B.C., and none at all from then barbaric central Europe. Archaeology does not help much; presumably the Indo-Europeans were semi-nomadic and built no buildings that would endure. Their tools, if we have them, cannot be identified as theirs. Archaeology will help some when the relationships of the Indo-Europeans with the Hittites is worked out, because we know a good bit about the Hittites, but that is for the future. Written records do not help; presumably the Indo-Europeans could not write; at least no scrap of writing has survived from them. But we do have their language, at least approximately, and from language much can be inferred. We know, for example, that they had words for bears, wolves, and pine trees; they had no words for alligators, elephants, and palm trees. Accordingly, we assume that they lived in a cold climate. They had horses; they rode them, and drank their milk, but did not use them as draft animals. They had something with which to dig in the earth and promote growth, but they did not drag it like a plow. Accordingly, we assume they were semi-nomads with some herds, practicing a little dibble agriculture, but hunting and fishing, also. As we have mentioned earlier, they spoke a highly inflected language, with some sixteen case distinctions for nouns in more than a dozen classes, and many conjugations of verbs; even adjectives were declined in three ways.

During the half-dozen millenia before Christ they underwent a population explosion, and spread in almost all directions, although especially west, south, and southeast. Possibly their acquisition of the horse gave them a fighting advantage over their neighbors. Whatever the cause, they fought their way in all directions, in one of the great population movements of all time. Working east and southeast they account for a long-dead language, discovered among ruins in the Gobi desert in China, which we call Tocharian. Perhaps about 1500 B.C. they broke into the sub-continent of India, where they established the Indo-European language which we call Sanskrit, ancestor of modern Indic. Another branch, speaking what we call Iranian, has given us modern Persian. Armenian and a number of minor languages fit in here somewhere. Some barbaric Indo-Europeans whom we call Hellenes worked into southern Russia and eventually down into the Balkan peninsula; by this time places like Crete, the Nile valley, and the Tigris Euphrates valley were highly civilized. The Hellenes became civilized, too, in time; we know them as the Greeks. Meanwhile, peoples speaking a branch of Indo-European which we call Italic worked past the Alps and down into the Italian peninsula; they gave us Latin, and by descent, the Romance Languages. People we call Celts or Kelts, near-relatives of the Italic group if we may judge from the similarities of the languages, spread west through northern Europe, and even took over the offshore islands, England and Ireland. Another group, speaking what we call Proto-Germanic or Teutonic, followed them, overran them almost everywhere, and spread north into the Scandinavian peninsula. Those who migrated less, who spoke what we call Balto-Slavic, account for modern languages like Russian, Bulgarian, and Lithuanian, which has preserved the old Indo-European inflection system to a remarkable degree.

Thus the branches of the Indo-European language family account for most of the languages of Europe, some of the most important in Asia, and all of the languages likely to survive in Australia and in North and South America. Extensive charts can be found in most good dictionaries; for our purposes the concise chart on p. 402 will suffice. It should not be taken literally. The figure of speech of the family, by which we describe linguistic relationships, works well enough if we remind ourselves that it is a figure of speech, not an accurate statement. A parent language does not give birth to a daughter language, as a mother bears a child, at a certain time and place. Rather, divisions of a language drift apart, usually because the speakers have drifted apart, and since language is always changing, it changes differently in the two groups. For a time the two ways of speaking can be thought of as two dialects of the same language, but eventually they change so much that the speakers of one group cannot understand the speakers of the other, and we must recognize two languages, which of course will already have developed dialects.

24-5 **THE GROWTH OF ENGLISH**

When history dawned over northwestern Europe, the Celts were already established in England and Ireland. They were a relatively

SIMPLIFIED CHART OF THE INDO-EUROPEAN LANGUAGE FAMILY

The chart emphasizes western languages, especially those leading to English.

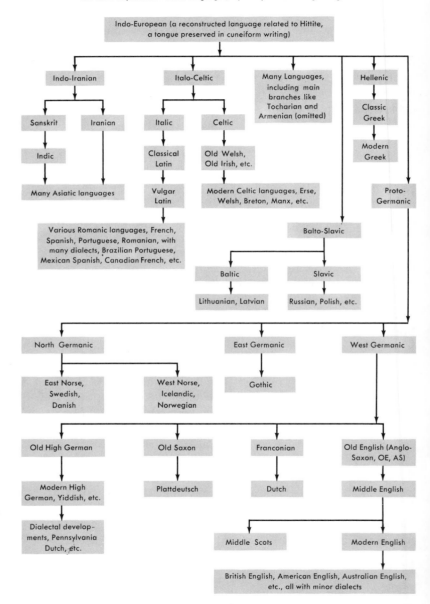

Indo-European (a reconstructed language related to Hittite, a tongue preserved in cuneiform writing)

Indo-Iranian

Sanskrit

Iranian

Indic

Many Asiatic languages

Italo-Celtic

Italic

Classical Latin

Vulgar Latin

Various Romanic languages, French, Spanish, Portuguese, Romanian, with many dialects, Brazilian Portuguese, Mexican Spanish, Canadian French, etc.

Celtic

Old Welsh, Old Irish, etc.

Modern Celtic languages, Erse, Welsh, Breton, Manx, etc.

Many Languages, including main branches like Tocharian and Armenian (omitted)

Hellenic

Classic Greek

Modern Greek

Proto-Germanic

Balto-Slavic

Baltic

Lithuanian, Latvian

Slavic

Russian, Polish, etc.

North Germanic

East Norse, Swedish, Danish

West Norse, Icelandic, Norwegian

East Germanic

Gothic

West Germanic

Old High German

Modern High German, Yiddish, etc.

Dialectal developments, Pennsylvania Dutch, etc.

Old Saxon

Plattdeutsch

Franconian

Dutch

Old English (Anglo-Saxon, OE, AS)

Middle English

Middle Scots

Modern English

British English, American English, Australian English, etc., all with minor dialects

unsophisticated group, mostly hunters and fishers. The Romans readily conquered those who lived outside the swamps and mountains, and brought them a measure of civilization, but the Romans left about 400 A.D., and Germanic peoples moved west to fill in the power gap. They brought their own Indo-European language with them, a language which was not much more influenced by Celtic than was English in America by the native American languages. These invaders came from two important tribal groups, the Angles, who came apparently *in toto,* and the Saxons, who left enough of their number behind to form Saxony on the Continent; there were also a few people known as Jutes, of whom we know little. They spoke Low-Germanic dialects, the dialects that existed along the North European coast; their language is often referred to collectively as Anglo-Saxon. We shall call it Old English to distinguish it from Middle English and Modern English.

These recently arrived Germanic peoples took several centuries to finish fighting with the Celts and to get over fighting each other, and to import much Mediterranean culture through France. They had been in some contact with the Romans on the Continent; one of their own crude roads they called a *weg,* as compared to our word *way,* which means some place one could go. One of the fine paved roads the Romans built they called by the Latin name, our word *street.* An inlet in the coast they called a *hafen,* our word *haven,* a place one was safe, but they had learned to call the marine installations the Romans built a *port* (Latin *portus*). In time they were converted to Christianity and began to borrow Greek, Latin, and French words associated with the church. They developed commercial and cultural connections with the Continent and borrowed more words, but not many. They endured a time of trial when they were overrun by some of their northern Germanic neighbors, the Norsemen, Danes and Norwegians, mostly; but these people eventually settled down, having brought with them other sorts of Germanic dialects which influenced the native speech, notably in the north and northeast. Then, as every schoolboy knows, the Normans conquered England in 1066.

The direct effects of this conquest on the language were not so great as are sometimes supposed, but the indirect effect was very large. The invaders were few in number, and most Englishmen went right on talking English, but French became the official language—the language of the court and culture, the language of big business; Latin remained the learned language. The Normans ruled, and words for government were Norman French, even *government* itself. The Normans directed commercial, educational, and ecclesiastical affairs, and words like *commerce, education,* and *ecclesiastics* stem from the French-Classical tradition, but common words like *learn* and *book* come from Old English, probably because native children were doing one with the other. Meat appeared on a wealthy Norman's table named with the Norman equivalent of our words *beef, veal, pork,* and *mutton,* but meat on the hoof was presumably tended by natives, who called the animals the Old English equivalent of *cow, calf, swine,* and *sheep*—*hog* and *pig* probably come from Norse and Dutch, but the principle is the same, for the common people were doing the work. Thus, learned or specialized words were borrowed, but the words that expressed the stuff of life continued to be native—*man, wife, child, house, bed, eat, live, die, love, fight.* Almost all the words language works with were native—*the, a, an, and, but, who, that, he, it, in, on, by.* Practically the only exceptions are *they, their,* and *them,* which seem to have come in with the Norsemen, and by 1066 can be thought of as native; they were not French. The result is that although borrowing from French, Latin, and Greek had begun before the Norman conquest and had somewhat increased after the Conquest, no great surge in borrowing took place until some two centuries after William won at Hastings.

Then the flood set in. By the fourteenth century, burgeoning England was developing close connections with the Continent, both commercial and cultural, and in that century more words were borrowed from French than in all the half-dozen centuries preceding. During the Age of Elizabeth another great wave of French and Latinate words swept in. By that time English had borrowed so many Gallicisms that it was running out of French to borrow; but when we could no longer borrow French words for armor, we borrowed Italian words for music, Latin words for botany and zoology, Greek words for physics and chemistry, and then French words again for food and fashions. We are still borrowing words from Latin and Greek and the Romance languages at a lively rate, especially in science and technology. The result is that a large percentage of the words in any English dictionary will be borrowed, mainly from Latin and Greek and the Romance languages; but the commonest words, the most useful words, are mainly native. They usually account for more than half of any piece of prose. To show how this goes, native words in the next sentence you read will be printed in italics. *The* result *would* differ *somewhat with the* subject *and the* author's style, *of* course; *if this* book *were about* philosophy, *the* borrowed *words would* probably *be more* numerous; *if it were about feeding pigs, they would be fewer; but the* results *could not be* changed *much, no* matter *what the* subject *nor how the* sentence *was written.*

The language changed in structure as well as in vocabulary. We have noted that Indo-European was a highly inflected language; the Indo-European forms and classes tended to combine in the Germanic languages, as they have in the Romanic, but Old English still retained some eight classes of nouns—depending on how many sub-classes you recognize—and about as many conjugations of two sorts of verbs. The adjective was still declined in two ways. But the language was already becoming notably distributive; apparently a speaker had to use the inflectional endings to be correct, but not much to be understood. After the Norman conquest English grammar started to change relatively rapidly; apparently languages change rapidly when they are fighting for their lives. For the next four hundred years or so, endings weakened and mostly disappeared, while distributive devices developed rapidly. For example, Old English had no form for the future at all; now we have many, made up by distributive means—*shall go, will go, am going to go, expect to go, am planning on going,* and the like. Such changes have continued ever since, and are presumably continuing still, but since about the time of Shakespeare these changes have been slower. Just at the time the grammar of the language was changing, the sounds, also, were changing relatively rapidly, and we have already seen that this was the great period of borrowing. Accordingly, we recognize three stages of the language which can be distinguished roughly as follows: Old English, from the beginnings (the earliest written work supposedly comes from about 675 A.D.) to about 1100; Middle English, about 1100 to about 1500; Modern English, about 1500 to the present. The names are abbreviated OE (Old English), ME (Middle English), and Mod.E. (Modern English). Modern English is often broken into Early and Late Modern English, dividing at about 1700.

We have noticed that the sounds also changed. As a matter of fact, most of the individual sounds did not change much, but the whole pattern of sounds changed enough so that Old English today sounds like gibberish to any but a student of the language, and even Middle English is not very intelligible. Many of the dialects can be understood only by a specialist. Most consonants remained unchanged; Old English had a consonant often spelled *h* which sounded something like *khkhkh*. It has disappeared, leaving behind it spellings like the gh in *thought, though,* and *enough.* Most of the so-called short vowels like those in *hill* and *get* have remained unchanged. Most of the so-called long vowels and diphthongs, however, have changed, and a phonetician would describe these changes by saying that they have moved forward and upward in the mouth. Vowels are made at different points in the mouth, depending in part on the position of the tongue; the sound heard as the first vowel in *mawkish* is low-back; the vowel heard in *meek* is high-front. This same vowel heard in *mawkish*, then, has moved toward *meek* but has not moved far enough to become the vowel in *meek.* For example, Old English had a word often spelled *rad,* which was pronounced about as a modern speaker would expect to say *rawd,* if there were such a word; it is our word *rode.* Similarly, the Old English word for *judgment,* pronounced like our word *dome* has come to be our word *doom.* In a word spelled *hat* and pronounced like our word *hot* the vowel moved forward so that the word became our *hate.* A word pronounced like our word *hay* and spelled *he* became our modern word *he.* Sounds that were already high and to the front became diphthongs; a sound like that in the word *moose* broke into a diphthong so that the word is now *mouse.* Similarly, a sound like that in our word *leek* became the diphthong in *like.* Roughly speaking, the vowels in Old and Middle English are about what those correspondingly spelled vowels would be in German or Spanish; the stressed or long vowels have moved forward and upward in what is called the Great English Vowel Shift.

Naturally, this description of sound changes in English is simplified; details and exceptions have been omitted. One other change must be noted, however; the stress in many words has shifted, and sounds have been lost or changed with shifts in stress. For example, every reader of the *Canterbury Tales* will recall that Chaucer rhymes words for *flower* and *liquor.* He could do this since the word for *flower* was then pronounced so that it would rhyme approximately with our word poor; the French word for *liquor,* spelled something like *licour,* ended with the same sound, and like many words from Old French, had an accent on the last syllable. But the pattern of English is to put the accent on the first syllable; the accent in Old French *licour* has moved forward in English *liquor,* which no longer rhymes with *flower* although it did 600 years ago. Especially in American English the tendency is to reduce all vowels in unaccented syllables to a neutral vowel like that heard in *of* or the second syllable of *sudden.*

24-6 SEMANTIC CHANGE

Having seen how our vocabulary came into being, we are prepared to see what it has become. How many words do we have? Nobody knows, because we cannot agree on what a word is; and even if we could, we are gaining new ones and losing old ones, and nobody has ever collected them all in one place. Nobody could count them fast enough to get an answer, and it would be wrong as soon as we could write it down—*sputnik* became an English word almost overnight. But we can approximate. Large general dictionaries of English enter about a half-million words, and there must be some hundreds of thousands of obsolete, slang, and highly specialized words. Most words have several uses; many have dozens. We can probably assume that there are or have been more than two million named uses in English. Now the curious fact is that most of these words have come to us in one way or another from Indo-European. True we got *John* from Hebrew, *chemistry* from Arabic, *kimono,* from Japanese, *woodchuck* from Algonquin, and a scattering of others from non-Indo-European languages; but the great bulk of our words came to us directly from Indo-European through Old and Middle English, or they were borrowed from languages that got them directly or indirectly from Indo-European. All the languages from which we have borrowed much have been Indo-European—Latin, Greek, French, Italian, Spanish, the Scandinavian languages, Dutch, German, even Indic and Russian, from which we are now beginning to borrow more. Did Indo-European have a large vocabulary? No, rather remarkably not, for so important a language. It was, after all, the language of a relatively unsophisticated people who did not need many names for things because they did not have many things; furthermore, they made so much use of decliners and classifiers that a syllable or two that embodied the core meaning could be made to serve many purposes. A relatively few hundred of them have been identified, and we have no reason to suppose there were more than a very few thousand. How have a few hundred Indo-European bases been blown up into many hundreds of thousands of named uses in English? Obviously, if we say that these words "came from" Indo-European we cannot define "came from" simply.

We might look at some words to see what has happened. A word that has grown greatly in use in recent years is *backlog;* manufacturers have backlogs of orders, judges have backlogs of cases, jobbers have backlogs of goods. But a century ago, apparently, nobody used the word in this way; a backlog was a device for radiant heating. It was put at the back of a large fireplace, and the lighter wood, including the forestick, was put in front of it so that the flames would make the front surface of the backlog glow and radiate heat. The curious reader will find a description of such a fire in Whittier's *Snowbound.* But the great backlog might burn for days, and perhaps for this reason became a figurative indication of something in reserve.

Neither did the parts of this word mean what they mean in backlog. The old Norse word *lag* did not mean wood; it is related to our verb *to lie,* and it meant *the lying thing.* That is, the *lag* or *log* meant the fallen tree after it was lying on the ground, and then the trunk of a fallen tree in any position. Logs do not necessarily lie in the log jam. Nor has *back* always meant back. It comes from an Indo-European base *begh,* meaning to bend (the asterisk indicates that the base is reconstructed), and as such it became the name for the part of the body that bends. But the bending is on the side away from the face or front of the human body, and thus anything opposite the front could become the back—but not always, for the backbone of a quadruped is at the top, and correspondingly the back of a handsaw is at the top in sawing. Once *back* had developed the meaning of opposite to the front, it acquired all sorts of other uses; to *back up* is to go toward the rear, but to *back somebody up* is to support him, presumably from the rear. Any good modern dictionary is likely to have columns involving *back,* from *back and fill* to *backyard.*

What is happening here? Many things; a word like *back* is being lived with, and growing to fit human needs. It means to bend, and by a sort of figure of speech it is attached to the thing that bends. But the thing that bends is at the side of the human being opposite the front, so that by generalization anything to the rear can be *back*. Once the word acquires this general force of *opposite-front* or *to-the-rear* it can become specialized again in a great variety of words and phrases like *back stroke, backhanded, backorder;* and by more figures of speech a bumptious kind of person becomes a *backslapper* and an old fashioned person can be *backnumberish*. The sorts of mental processes involved in these developments are too numerous to examine here, but anyone who will study what has happened to words will see that they grow in ways in which the human mind works. Among these are our use of generalizing from a particular example and specializing or particularizing from the general; along with these relatively pedestrian growths in use are sudden leaps in meaning which involve figures of speech.

24-7 **INDO-EUROPEAN BASES AND MODERN COGNATES**

Since words have descended into many languages, including Modern English and languages from which English has borrowed, dozens of words may go back to an Indo-European base, and they may retain similarities that help a writer to know more words and to use them with keener sense of their worth. Consider the descendants of the Indo-European base **derew-,* which meant tree or oak. This word descended into Proto-Germanic along with many others, and became OE *treow,* our word *tree,* which used to mean *wood* as well as a standing tree. It also became the name for things made out of "tree" in the sense of *wood;* that is, OE *treg* became our word *tray,* and OE *troh* became our word *trough*. It also became OE *treowe,* our word *true;* apparently the Old English people thought that being faithful was standing like a tree, very much as we now say *true as steel*. The Old English people also developed a verb with the idea, OE *trimian,* to make firm as a tree, which gives us modern *trim*.

Meanwhile, the same Indo-European base **derew-* was descending into other languages, from which we borrowed. Old Norse developed the word which we borrowed as *trust,* very much as we developed *true*. Latin had a word from **derew-* which we write as *durus,* meaning hard; before the day of metals, wood was considered hard. Figuratively, this word gives us words like *obdurate* meaning stubborn; and

Scotch *dour,* meaning hard, unbending, severe; and, through French, *duress,* meaning hardship; even *durum* wheat, which is relatively hard. It is probably related, also, to Latin *durare,* meaning to last, which gives us dozens of words like *endure, endurance,* and *durable.* All these words are what we call *cognates* of the words that come to us through Old and Middle English; that is, they were "born together," (Latin *co-gnatus,* which means born together).

Indo-European bases are symbols to conjure with. Once a writer knows that words like *truth, trust, dour, obdurate,* and *trim* all go back to an ancient word for tree and are associated with the reliability, hardness, and enduring qualities of a tree, he can use these words with more grasp and he can more readily learn words like *induration, duramen,* and *durative* which may be strange to him. The following is a list of Indo-European bases and some of the cognates that have descended from them. For almost any of these bases an industrious student could find hundreds of modern English words— try the cognates of any of the words spelled *can,* for example. The root ideas are given in parentheses.

*ar- art, arm, armada, armor, article, articulate (to join)

*au- ear, auricle, auricular, auriculate, auscultation (to perceive)

*aues- east, easter, aurora, aurum (to shine)

*bhudh-/men- bottom, profound, foundation, fundament, funds (soil)

*deigh- dough, duff, figure, effigy, lady (to knead)

*deik- toe, digit, diction, token, teach (to point)

*dekm- hundred, decade, century, cent, reckon, read, riddle (ten)

*ed- eat, ate, edible, edibility, comestible, obese (to eat)

*edont- tooth, teeth, dentist, dentistry, orthodontist, edentate (tooth)

*gan(dh)- can (noun), canister, canasta, canal, channel (reed)

*gene-/*geno- can (v), know, gnome, agnostic, could, uncouth, quaint, acquaintance, cognition, ignorant, connoisseur (to know)

*glogh- gloss, glossary, glottal, epiglottis, gloze (thorn)

*kali-/*gel- cold, cool, chill, gelid, gelatin, glacier, glace (cold)

*kel- hall, hold, hull, hill, hole, hulk, conceal, color, Colorado (to cover)

*kuon- hound, canine, cynic, canary, cynosure, kennel (dog)

*laub-/*lewp- leaf, loft, lodge, lobby, lobbyist (peel off, bark roof)

*leip- life, live, leave, liparoid, lipolytic (to endure)

*leuq- light, luminous, lunar, Loki, de luxe, luxury, lucid (shine)

*mel- meal, mill, malm, mollusk, mollify, Molinari (to grind)

*oqw- eye, oculist, optical, ophthalmologist, ogle (to see)
*pater- father, Pope, paternal, expatriate, padre, patron (pa-pa)
*ped-/*pod- foot, pedal, pew, pedestrian, gastropod (to go)
*penqwe- finger, quintet, five, Quinquagesima, quintessence, pentagon (five)
*pou- fowl, pullet, pauper, foal, fowler, puerile (small)
*pu- foul, putrid, pus, putrefaction, filth, defile (to stink)
*qeu- head, capitol, chapter, hump (to bend)
*(s)que- hide, hat, hood, hut, hoard, cuticle (to cut)
*rewos- room, rural, rustic, roister, ream, reamer (wide)
*seqw- say, see, seer, saga, saw (to see)
*slab- (from *leb-) sleep, labor, lapse, laboratory, elapse, collapse, elaboration, collaboration, relapse (to glide)
*wegh- way, vehicle, vehement, via, impervious, invoice, wain, wagon, convex, voyage, deviation, obvious (to go)
*wer- ward, ware, revere, guard, warden, warranty, guarantee, ware, guardian, reward, Ed, Teddy, disregard, wardrobe (to keep safe)
*wer-/*werbh- word, verb, verbal, verbatim, verve, verbosity, rhetoric, rhetorical (to say)
*werk- work, organ, playwright, wrought, erg, organize (to do)

EXERCISE 24

A. Recall that certain common words are likely to be native words from Old English through Middle English; check 24-5 to find out which sorts of common words are most likely to be native. Some borrowed words have become common, *factor, faith,* and *circumstances,* for example. Of these *factor* has become popular only very recently; *faith* became popular early. Perhaps you can guess why. Now examine the following list of words and divide them into two lists, one which you would guess to be native words from Old English, and one which you would guess to be borrowed. Then check the accuracy of your guesses against a good dictionary. Try to account for the words about which you are incorrect. CAUTION: words that appear in Middle English may have come from Old English (Anglo-Saxon) or they may have been borrowed, especially from Latin, French, or Old Norse; be sure you count as native only those from Old English or Anglo-Saxon.

an, and, aggression, alembic, aria, as, ate, barbiturate, best, blaze, brain, brontosaurus, carve, church, churn, cook, common, council, cyclometer, demoralize, dog, earth, emphasize, enthymeme, expose, fat, father, filterability, flexion, for, game, give, glaciation, hand, habitual, hen, her, hypocrite, in, interest, iota, it, king, know, labyrinth, land, like, language, lay, legislature, lung, man, manage, mimicry, mow, not, nominative, odoriferous, paternal, piano, pick, prosody, pure, read, refutation, revenge, ring, scissors, scorpion, she, smoke, snake, spectroscope, the, that, to, transcendental, translate, turquoise, up, uxorial, who, why, yacht.

B. Consult the list of Indo-European bases in 24-7, and select any three. Then find a hundred cognates that have come from these three bases into Modern English—for the more common of these bases it is possible to find up to a thousand apiece, counting phrases and rare or slang words. For additional information the best book to consult is Eric Partridge, *Origins,* 2nd ed. (New York, 1959). *Webster's New World Dictionary of the American Language* will give further information on the Indo-European bases. The *New English Dictionary on Historical Principles (Oxford English Dictionary)* gives the history of each word. The *Century Dictionary and Cyclopedia* is a good place to look for phrases and specialized words. There are many slang dictionaries, both English and American.

C. Recall that words have changed their meanings, and look up 24-6 to see how they have changed. Then look up five meanings for each of the following words, and mark them G (for generalization), S (for specialization), or F (for figure of speech), depending on how the meaning seems to have developed:

1. arm	4. hand	7. nothing
2. chair	5. home	8. run
3. date	6. man	9. table

D. Select two or three of the dictionaries listed above and in 25-1, preferring those which you have already found useful for etymological study. Then look up the following words, and write a brief paragraph about each, summarizing the most interesting facts you have discovered about the history of the word. Be sure to use at least one book which provides Indo-European bases.

atlas	explode	pants
canary	futhark	piano
change	infantry	pool
corollary	melancholy	quick
defense	mercury	stable
dollar	neighbor	travel

25

Vocabulary,
Meaning, Word Choice

For Guide to Revision, see page 427

Every successful writer needs an adequate vocabulary; we write with words.

Almost everyone has at least four basic vocabularies. First, he uses a relatively small number of words which we may call the *speaking vocabulary*. It includes words which will come to the speaker's tongue without his thinking much about them. A dull person is likely to use only a few hundred words in this way; even a moderately articulate speaker uses only a few thousand. Every literate person has a second vocabulary, a *writing vocabulary,* which includes the words in the speaking vocabulary, plus other words that he can call up. A good writer may employ a vocabulary of ten thousand, twenty-five thousand, perhaps fifty thousand words. A poor writer, on the other hand, may suffer from a vocabulary little larger than his speaking vocabulary. Every literate person has also a *reading vocabulary,* made up of words which he would not speak in conversation or use when he writes but which he knows when he sees them written. For most people the reading vocabulary is much larger than either the speaking or writing vocabulary—fifty thousand, seventy-five thousand, a hundred thousand words, perhaps more. The fourth vocabulary, the largest of all, we may refer to as the *acquaintance vocabulary*. It includes the other three, but it includes, also, a considerable number of words which the owner has seen or heard before but does not know much about. He may remember enough about them so that he can usually guess their meaning in context; he has a nodding acquaintance with the words, not much more. Vocabularies of this sort, of course, can be very large, often much larger than the reading vocabulary.

From the description of these four vocabularies, the student has probably guessed at least one way to improve his oral and written expression. Since speaking and writing vocabularies are relatively small and reading and acquaintance vocabularies relatively large, he has only to move words from his reading and acquaintance vocabularies into his speaking and writing vocabularies.

25-1 WORD HOARDS AND DICTIONARIES

In any deliberate attempt to improve vocabulary, the most useful aid is usually a good dictionary. At this writing, three desk dictionaries are much the best in their class. They are *Webster's New World Dictionary of the American Language* published by the World Publishing Company, *The American College Dictionary,* published by Random House, and *Webster's New Collegiate Dictionary,* published by the G. & C. Merriam Company. No one serious about his writing should be content with an inferior book, even though it is cheap. Of course there is no substitute for the bigger dictionaries, and students should know all the important ones. Of the so-called "unabridged" dictionaries, the *Webster's New International,* published by the G. & C. Merriam Company, is the best one widely used in this country. Two British dictionaries of about the same size are excellent in various ways: the H. C. Wyld *Universal Dictionary* and the *Shorter Oxford.* In many ways the most interesting American dictionary is the *Century Dictionary and Cyclopedia,* which runs to ten volumes. It is old but still a mine of valuable material. The great dictionary of the language, of course, is the *New English Dictionary on Historical Principles,* usually called the *Oxford English Dictionary.* For Americans it should be supplemented with the *Dictionary of American English,* and the more recent *Dictionary of Americanisms.*

No student should be content with meager dictionaries. Why starve when we have the Lord's plenty? A writer will remember words longer and use them more accurately the more he knows about them. Furthermore, using a book like the *Oxford English Dictionary* or Eric Partridge's *Origins* can be downright exciting.

25-2 USING A DICTIONARY

Any user of a dictionary should learn how much information he has available. He should examine the table of contents and preface and learn where to find foreign words and phrases, new words, proper names, abbreviations, and other special materials. He should learn the pronunciation system and find the list of abbreviations used in the book. A good desk dictionary should be adequate for at least the following uses:

(1) *Spelling.* Dictionaries record preferred current spellings for words and indicate where words can be divided between syllables and whether compounds are usually written as single words or with hyphens.

(2) *Pronunciation.* Dictionaries reprint each word with special marks to indicate the location of accents and the sounds of individual letters. The marks, called diacritical marks, are explained in the introduction, and usually examples appear at the bottom of each page of the text.

(3) *Word origins.* Every dictionary adequate for student use describes, using abbreviations explained in its introduction, the origins of words. Knowledge of derivations can be extremely useful in learning and remembering words.

(4) *Grammatical information.* The dictionary indicates, with abbreviations, the grammatical uses for which a word is considered suitable.

(5) *Usage.* Dictionaries endeavor to distinguish words which have general use from those which have not by indicating that certain words or certain usages of the word have limited currency. For variations in usage see 26-3.

(6) *Definition.* Most important of all, a dictionary endeavors to define words. A good desk dictionary should define most meanings of all but rare and highly specialized words. Some of the problems of meaning are discussed in 25-4.

25-3   INCREASING A WRITING VOCABULARY

A student who is familiar with his dictionary is prepared to observe the following simple procedures which will help him to increase his vocabulary.

(1) *Learn words which you will use.* You may be able to baffle your friends if you know the meaning of *ento-ectad,* but words completely strange to you are hard to learn, and unless you use them you are likely to forget them. Learn words which you encounter and recognize but cannot define or use.

(2) *When you learn a word, learn enough about it to make it yours.* Notice its various usages. Try to find out details about the origin and history of the word, where it came from and what has happened to it in English and American speech. For this, the *Oxford English Dictionary* is excellent; the *Century* and the others mentioned in 25-1 are also good.

(3) *Learn words by groups.* If you will learn related words together, you can learn several words, sometimes a dozen, as easily as you can learn one, often more easily. Suppose you were to look up the word *pictograph.* You would find that it is related to the words *picture* and *graph,* both of which you probably know, though you may have to find out what the Greek root *graph* means here. Any good dictionary ought to have twenty or thirty more words related to *picture* in adjacent columns; make out a list and learn them all as a group. In learning words by groups, knowing foreign languages helps. Latin and Greek are especially useful. Even if you do not know these languages, you can learn a few Latin and Greek prefixes; a list of common ones will be found in Exercise 25C.

(4) *Once you have learned a word, use it.* Many a good student, presented with a word he does not know, will look it up and immediately forget it. Do something deliberate to keep your words. Find a way to use them in conversation or in your next theme. Make up a list of words, put the list in your purse or pocket, and glance over it at some odd time every day for a week.

25-4   THE MEANING OF MEANING

Successful use of any vocabulary requires understanding of how words convey meaning. Strictly speaking, no word has meaning as a physical object can have length. The bars of metal in the Bureau of Standards, for instance, which determine our inches and feet, keep the same length at a given temperature, no matter who measures them, so long as the measuring is accurately done, but no words are kept at a controlled temperature in the Bureau of Standards. Words exist only in people's minds, and all minds are different. No word has a "meaning" which it inevitably calls up in everyone.

Theoretically Humpty Dumpty is justified in telling Alice, "When *I* use a word, it means just what I choose it to mean—neither more nor less." No authority can keep him from using the word *glory,* as he does, to mean *there's a nice knock-down argument for you.* Practically, however, Humpty is not communicating much. Words have no mystical connection with a particular "meaning," but communication is possible because at any time in history by common agreement people associate certain words with certain thoughts. We can communicate because we agree, closely enough for practical purposes, to let certain words symbolize certain ideas.

People can agree about meaning because words relate to things in the real world and are, relatively speaking, common and enduring, but the use and choice of words is complex because words are related to things through human minds, which are not all the same. A word is a symbol a human being uses to reveal his idea about something.

Referent   Thought   Word

                                             daisy

A writer or speaker can use *daisy* as a symbol to express his thought about a thing, a particular flower growing in a meadow, a referent. Speakers of English, by general agreement, use this symbol when they think of this particular kind of flower. The symbol would not work if the writer were thinking of a four-footed animal that brays or of a carved representation of George Washington. Neither would it work if he were writing in French or German. Conversely, any users of the language, readers or listeners, could interpret this symbol similarly.

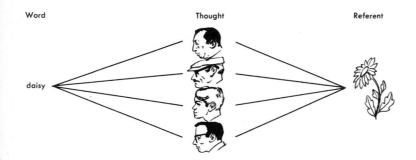

Word   Thought   Referent

daisy

417

Furthermore, a writer may have various thoughts about a referent he sees growing in a meadow, and he may choose a word quite different from *daisy*.

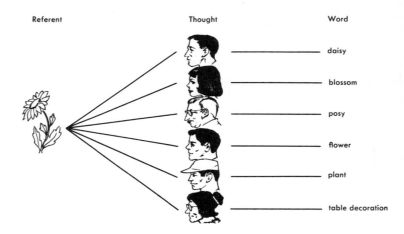

Referent	Thought	Word

daisy

blossom

posy

flower

plant

table decoration

Each of these words—and many others that might be thought of— has the same referent, but each conveys a slightly different thought about the referent. *Plant* indicates that the writer is distinguishing the referent less precisely than does *flower; posy* suggests something about the attitude of the writer; *blossom* and *table decoration* indicate special attitudes toward the referent. These differences illustrate some of the distinctions involved in word choice, distinctions between concrete and abstract words, between denotation and connotation, between different meanings in different contexts. They may even represent differences in the same person from day to day or minute to minute as his mood changes.

25-5 SYMBOLS AND WORD CHOICE

Modern philosophers, developing the theory of what they call symbolic transformation, suggest that the symbol was the tool with which man built civilization, the device with which he made himself human. Man, living in a complicated and seemingly confused world, was able to reduce his universe to something like order by using symbols. Symbols, which could attach to thoughts as well as to physical phenomena, enabled man to grasp relationships, to see wholes. Man is a symbol-making animal; by his ability to deal in symbols he became unlike other creatures, which seem not able to use symbols, but only to respond to signs.

The most significant result of man's discovery of symbols was language. We have already noticed that words are symbols, that a sequence of letters can stand for a thought about a flower and all sorts of things associated with a flower. But the process which created language continues to operate, and words, acting as symbols, readily develop new symbolic significances. Take, for example, a favorite remark among stock brokers, which runs as follows: "The bulls make money and the bears make money, but the pigs seldom do." Taken in the sense that we might call "literal," a bull meaning a male bovine and a bear a large ursine quadruped, the sentence makes no sense; neither of these makes money. But, of course, a bull is not here a bovine; *bull* is a symbol for an investor or a gambler who hopes to make money through a rise in the value of stocks he buys. Metaphorically, the word has developed new symbolic abilities which have become so crystallized that any good modern dictionary will list something of the sort as a meaning of the word. *Pig* is also a symbol, and in the sentence above we can guess readily what it means, but in this sense the word will not be found in dictionaries. That is, man's ability as a symbolmaker persists; man readily extends words to new symbolic uses and understands complex symbolic uses of words. Writers take advantage of man's continuing ability to make symbols.

Specifically, the symbolic power of words permits the writer to be both concrete and general, specific and abstract, at the same time. He can choose a specific detail which has the vividness of the concrete, but if he chooses sensitively he may also use a detail that has general symbolic overtones. In conversation we rely on symbolic associations even though the symbols have become trite. We use *whistle-stop* instead of describing abstractly a provincial town; we characterize a girl by saying that she wears bobby sox and blue jeans; we classify a restaurant by referring to its red-checked tablecloths. We speak of a person who would kick small dogs or would poison wells. Often, of course, such specific comments are accompanied by more general ones, but the well-selected specific detail is likely to give the desired impression more vividly and convincingly—perhaps even more accurately—than the general description. Katherine Brush, for example, in introducing a character mentions two specific details but makes no general statement about the person:

> Miss Levin was the checkroom girl. She had dark-at-the-roots blonde hair and slender hips, upon which, in moments of leisure she wore her hands, like buckles of ivory loosely attached.
>
> —*Night Club*

Somerset Maugham makes a general comment about a room he is describing, then illustrates with two specific details which become symbols:

> It was a room designed not to live in but for purposes of prestige, and it had a musty, melancholy air. A suite of stamped plush was arranged neatly round the walls, and from the middle of the ceiling, protected from the flies by yellow tissue paper, hung a gilt chandelier.
>
> —*Rain*

25-6 ABSTRACT AND CONCRETE

Drawing a picture of the referent of the word *daisy* is relatively easy, and the resulting picture may also portray the referent of the word *flower*. But a picture of the referent behind the "full" meaning of the word *flower* would be more difficult. It would have to include not only daisies but also irises and begonias and violets and the blooms on thistles, in fact everything in the writer's experience which made up the idea he was expressing by the word. Or consider drawing a picture of the referent behind the word *beauty*. The picture of the daisy might be a part, but dozens of other bits from the writer's experience would be necessary, and a picture would become virtually impossible.

Obviously, *flower* is more general than *daisy* and *beauty* is more general than *flower* (see 5-2). *Beauty* can also be said to be *abstract*, whereas *daisy* is *concrete*. Roughly, one can say that abstract words refer to generalities or to ideas, and that concrete words refer to things or objects. Or, in terms of the discussion above, concrete words stand for a thought of a referent which can be pictured or specified; abstract words go back to referents so complex or general that they cannot be visualized. These statements, however, require two qualifications. First, *abstract* and *concrete* are relative terms, like *general* and *specific.* Compare the following:

> There was *something* on the table.
> There was a *creature* on the table.
> There was a *tarantula* on the table.

Creature is more concrete than *something, tarantula* more concrete than *creature.* The ideas become more specific; the words become more concrete and increase in exactness and suggestiveness as they do so. Second, just as the general develops out of the specific, abstract expressions grow from more concrete ones. *Color* stands for a thought which would be hard to express if we had only more concrete terms like *red, yellow, blue, green.*

Consider the following sentence proposed by George Orwell to illustrate how some writers might translate a passage of the Bible:

> Objective consideration of contemporary phenomena compels the conclusion that success or failure in competitive activities exhibits no tendency to be commensurate with innate capacity, but that a considerable element of the unpredictable must invariably be taken into account.

The sentence exaggerates, but it suggests how abstractions piled upon abstractions can obscure ideas. Compare the passage from Ecclesiastes which Orwell has "translated":

> I returned, and saw under the sun, that the race is not to the swift, nor the battle to the strong, neither yet bread to the wise, nor yet riches to men of understanding, nor yet favour to men of skill; but time and chance happeneth to them all.

Instead of one general statement, the original uses five specific examples; instead of abstractions like *consideration, phenomena, conclusion, success,* and *failure,* the original uses more concrete words like *race, battle, bread,* and *riches.* Almost always, clear and accurate writing uses concrete words whenever possible.

25-7 DENOTATION AND CONNOTATION; SLANTING

Roughly speaking, a word's communication of a thought about a referent is the word's denotation, what is sometimes called its "dictionary meaning." *Daisy* and *flower* and *table decoration,* therefore, have different denotations; *flower* and *posy* can hardly be distinguished in denotation. Still, no botanist today would write that the "begonia bears monecius posies"; he would feel that the word *posy* is unsuited to scientific description. On the other hand, one might wish to suggest that certain wallpaper was old-fashioned by saying, "It was all cluttered up with pink posies." That is, each of these words can do something more than point to a particular thought. This power of a word to do more than designate, to make emotional and interpretive suggestions, is the word's *connotation*. Connotation is an essential part of the meaning of a word, to be distinguished from denotation only in analysis.

The connotation of a word always has an individual basis. To a garden lover, the word *flower* may suggest hours of pleasure in the sunshine, a sense of pervading joy, or even ecstasy. To someone else it may suggest Georgia O'Keefe's paintings, or if one has been ill from mimosa, it may even suggest nausea. But to a considerable degree, even though the basis of connotation is personal, most people share much of the connotative power of a word, for most of us have somewhat similar heritages and experiences. The word *home* connotes something different for each of us, but most people share feelings about the word, and would distinguish them from other feelings associated with *house*. Thus, to a degree, the emotional qualities of words can be used for communication, and the connotative power of words is so great that most good writers make conscious use of connotation.

In general, the connotations of words serve to emphasize certain characteristics of a referent or to reveal certain attitudes toward it. *Statesman* and *politician* may describe the same person, refer to the same referent.

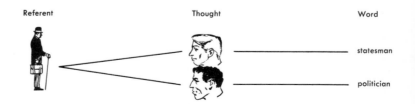

The thoughts expressed by the words differ, however; the words have become associated with emotional suggestions so that *statesman* emphasizes wisdom, dignity, vision, and integrity, and *politician* suggests intrigue, time-serving, and self-seeking. Through their connotations, the words present different views of the referent. Connotational meanings, therefore, are exploited especially in any writing or speaking which seeks to persuade, to move, or to stimulate emotion.

Concern for propaganda and analysis of propaganda have made our society particularly aware of the emotional qualities of words, especially as used in politics or advertising. Compare the following statements, which describe the same incident:

> Senator A ranted interminably this afternoon in a bigoted attack on the new budget.
>
> Senator A delivered a full and detailed address this afternoon in a spirited criticism of the new budget.

Through their connotations, the words in the first are clearly "slanted" or "loaded" against the senator; words in the second seek to move the reader to approve the speech. To suggest that "emotional" words should not be used is absurd, but the writer needs to be aware of their limitations and their weaknesses. From neither of the statements above does the reader know what Senator A did. The connotations of the words outweigh their denotations. Many similar words in English, especially words like *freedom, communist, authority, terrific,* or *sensational,* have developed such varied connotations that they can be used only with care and skill if the writer is to avoid distortion. Furthermore, misleading use of the emotional power of words is as false as any other kind of verbal lie because the connotations of a word are part of it. The writer who intentionally distorts the truth through his choice of "loaded" or "slanted" words should be challenged on his integrity rather than his skill with language.

25-8 FIGURATIVE LANGUAGE; METAPHOR

Irresponsible exploitation of connotations of words can distort truth, but skillful management of emotional meanings can make language more precise, more interesting, more intense. The importance of connotations can be seen especially in figurative language, in a device like the metaphor. Metaphor, or comparison in language, is more than embellishment; it is part of language itself. We use metaphors constantly in conversation (*He ran like a deer. He was a pig at the table*). Words develop through metaphors; we speak of the *hands* of the clock, the *foot* of the bed, the *head* of the household, the *legs* of a chair. Sails *belly*, and crowds *thunder* applause as the *shell shoots* across the *line*. We no longer think of the italicized words as figures of speech, but they developed as metaphors, and words are developing in this manner constantly, as we saw in Section 23. Metaphor, then, is a device by which connotations of words provide precise and vivid meanings. Consider the following relatively elaborate comparison from *Romeo and Juliet,* which uses one of the words considered above.

> This bud of love, by summer's ripening breath,
> May prove a beauteous flower when next we meet.

The metaphor is complex, but essentially it is using the word *flower* to express the referent usually expressed by *love*.

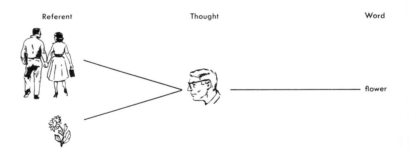

Referent   Thought   Word

flower

By using the word *flower* rather than the word *love,* Shakespeare emphasizes parts of both the connotational and denotational meanings of love. He makes us think of the "flowerlike" significance of love, its ability to grow, its beauty, its relation with time. The metaphor, in its context, allows the writer to exploit the emotional meanings of the words.

25-9   WORDS IN THEIR CONTEXTS

Words affect, and are affected by, the words with which they are used. The writer, then, needs to choose his words with care, selecting so that in both denotation and connotation they are appropriate in their contexts. Consider, for example, the following sentences:

My *love* is like a red, red rose.

The *love* of money is the root of all evil.

Greater *love* hath no man than this, that a man lay down his life for his friends.

Friendship is *Love* without his wings.

The score was forty-*love*.

God is *love*.

The word *love* appears in each sentence, but the meanings differ. The context, the company the word keeps, indicates its meaning.

The writer must choose his words with their contexts in mind. The lists of discriminative synonyms in dictionaries suggest how words fit different contexts (look up, for example, *joke, wit,* or *wise*). Even synonyms cannot be changed at random. For example, dictionaries list *exonerate* as a synonym for *clear*. Substituting *exonerate* would sharpen meaning in a sentence like *The attorney hoped to clear the ex-convict.* It would not serve in a sentence like *Mary cleared the dishes from the table.*

25-10 PRECISION AND VIGOR IN WORD CHOICE

As the discussions above indicate, choosing words with precise meaning and appropriate tone is not easy, but choice of the exact word often distinguishes good writing from mediocre. Almost any piece of good prose, such as the following, will illustrate:

> For Cooper was distressed by the new American world he found and bitterly resented many of its changes. He felt that America had retrogressed a century in these seven years, or perhaps he had stayed away too long, for he remembered Jefferson's saying that Americans might find themselves aliens if they spent more than five years out of the country. He had gone abroad in the days of the stagecoach, and the railroads were running on his return, while the scholarly John Quincy Adams had given place to Jackson and the piping times of ultra-republicanism. He was not prepared for the tawdry vulgarity that assailed him in the New York streets, or the flaring red of the bricks and green of the blinds, and this "rainbow capital" seemed to him a mean provincial town that could hardly compare with the second-rate cities of Europe. The scramble for money depressed him, and the general self-complacency, as if the "perfection of the people" had really been achieved, the mania for

change and speculation, the "gulpers" in the dining-rooms, the pigs that ran wild in the gutters and the rowdy press. For the yellow journals of the eighteen-thirties abounded in violent epithets, "offal," "garbage," "liar" and "bilious braggart," and Cooper himself was presently styled a "spotted caitiff" and a "leprous wretch," a "tainted hand," an assassin and a jackass. The most respectable editors, Bryant, for instance, assaulted one another on the streets. Cooper was disconcerted too by the coldness of the ordinary American manner, in contrast to the warmth and cordiality he had known in France, the lack of aesthetic sensibility, the timidity and wariness, so different from the freedom and frankness he had known of old. For when he referred to the bad pavements and the poor lighting of the town, his friends led him aside and begged him to be careful. It was unpatriotic to criticize American things. It was disloyal to suggest that the Bay of Naples could be mentioned in the same breath with the harbour of New York. It was shocking to compare the Alps with the Rockies. Yet, for all the bragging one heard in New York, there was little independence of mind, and England still did most of the thinking for the country.

—VAN WYCK BROOKS, *The World of Washington Irving*

Study of this passage reveals that certain words do a great deal. Some of the vividness of the picture James Fenimore Cooper found on his return grows from details, the pigs in the New York gutters, the author of *Thanatopsis* assaulting a fellow editor, but part of it grows from Brooks' choice of words. The country had "retrogressed a century" since the "days of the stagecoach." Modifiers make precise distinctions: "*piping* times," "*tawdry* vulgarity," "*flaring* red," or "*rowdy* press." Brooks uses words out of the day to picture the day, the "gulpers" in the dining rooms, and epithets for Cooper like "leprous wretch." One might notice the variety of words Brooks uses to indicate different degrees of disturbance in Cooper; sometimes he is "depressed," sometimes "disconcerted," and he "bitterly resented" the changes. One might notice, also, the impact of the word *led* in the passage, "his friends *led* him aside and begged him to be careful," and the nice distinction among *unpatriotic, disloyal,* and *shocking.*

25 W

VOCABULARY, MEANING, WORD CHOICE

Guide to Revision

Choose words as precisely as possible to fit their contexts.

Problems in word choice may vary from gross confusions of unfamiliar words to the necessity of drawing fine distinctions between synonyms. Mrs. Malaprop, a character in Sheridan's *The Rivals,* made herself famous and added the word *malapropism* to the language by misusing words she did not understand. When she complimented herself on a "nice derangement of epitaphs" and said that some one was "headstrong as an allegory on the banks of the Nile," she certainly did not mean to say *derangement, epitaphs,* or *allegory.* Slips in word choice may be as ludicrous as Mrs. Malaprop's, but less easily observed. They may result from ignoring connotations of a word, from failure to utilize concrete terms, or from failure to distinguish synonyms like *splash, slop,* and *spatter* which may be equally concrete but differ in meaning.

ORIGINAL

The capture of the ridge had seemed an *inhuman* feat.

[*Probably some kind of mental confusion with* humanly impossible *or* superhuman *accounts for the inaccuracy.*]

The inheritance brought them only *transitive* pleasure.

The Argentine government *interred* the cruiser.

Dr. Brinkley ran *a fowl* with other regulations concerning his practice.

REVISION

The capture of the ridge had seemed impossible.

[*It is difficult to guess precisely what the writer had in mind.*]

The inheritance brought them only *transitory* pleasure.

The Argentine government *interned* the cruiser.

Dr. Brinkley ran *afoul* of regulations concerning his practice.

427

Words similar in spelling or meaning are easily confused; distinctions between many common words must be learned (see Glossary and 29-7).

ORIGINAL	REVISION
The critic's statement *inferred* that he had plagiarized.	The critic's statement *implied* that he had plagiarized.
Every *affect* has a cause.	Every *effect* has a cause.
Most everybody was going to the party.	*Almost* everybody was going to the party.
There were *less* women than men in the class.	There were *fewer* women than men in the class.
Brigham found the *sight* for a new city.	Brigham found the *site* for a new city.
He did not understand the *illusions* to mythology.	He did not understand the *allusions* to mythology.
When he entered, her face turned a *livid* red.	When he entered, her face turned a *vivid* red.

25a "DIRECTION" IN WORDS   Dir

Words sometimes have meanings which will make sense in only one "direction." That is, if you mean that Irene likes jewels, you can say *Jewels have an attraction for Irene.* You cannot say *Irene has an attraction for jewels* without meaning something quite different, without using *have an attraction* with what might be called "false direction." Confusions of this sort are varied and usually develop from careless thinking and the kinds of basic errors considered in 13 and 15.

ORIGINAL	REVISION
The Elizabethan audience had a great *fascination* for wars and duels.	Wars and duels *fascinated* the Elizabethan audience.
I have a very *inadequate* feeling when I think of writing about this book.	I feel *inadequate* when I think of writing about this book.
Nor does an enemy of the prairie dog ever manage to approach the "town" *unawares*.	No enemy of the prairie dog can approach the "town" *undetected*.
Of course I am not *in reference* to the everyday loafer who comes and goes as he pleases.	Of course I am not *referring* to the common loafer who comes and goes as he pleases.

ORIGINAL (*Cont.*)

Once action is put forth the problems become disintegrated; therefore, let us *build up our weaknesses.*

Necessary financial reimbursements sent to the above address will receive my prompt attention.

REVISION (*Cont.*)

Prompt action will solve many problems; therefore let us *overcome our weaknesses.*

I shall promptly pay any bills sent to my address.

25b CONCRETE AND ABSTRACT WORDS   Spec

Some words are more concrete than others. They refer to real things, even to particular objects. A blow is more specific than an insult, a right hook to the ear more specific than a blow. "Chanel No. 5" is more specific than perfume. General and abstract words have their uses, but on the whole, vigorous writing is specific, concrete writing. Many a dull writer has only to substitute concrete words for his more abstract words to become interesting.

ABSTRACT

When we were in some fighting it was hard to know what was going on because so many things were happening that usually you did not know much about it until after it was over. You were excited, and though maybe you would know the things which were occurring, it was hard afterward to know just what had happened, especially around you.—Student theme.

MORE SPECIFIC

Who know the conflicts, hand to hand—the many conflicts in the dark, those shadowy-tangled, flashing moon-beamed woods, the writhing groups and squads, the cries, the din, the cracking guns and pistols, the distant cannon, the cheers and calls and threats and awful music of the oaths, the indescribable mix; the officers' orders, persuasions, encouragements; the devils fully roused in human hearts; the strong shout, *Charge, men, charge;* the flash of the naked sword, and rolling flame and smoke?—Walt Whitman's diary, slightly repunctuated.

ORIGINAL

I always used to like to go out camping when I was younger because Father was always doing funny things, and that always made us have a lot of fun. Father was always a funny man and he would do things you would not expect your father to be doing, and usually his things didn't work.

REVISION

Camping with Father was always fun, because he was sure to come lugging some contraption he had just invented, a chipmunk-repeller, which was supposed to keep chipmunks from devouring the soap—and did not—or an electrically driven decoy duck, which would get short-circuited halfway across the lake.

Abstract words are sometimes used as if they had no meaning at all, as blankets to cover meaning in the vicinity of the writer's idea. Such words go in and out of fashion, but the following are among those currently popular: *angle, aspect, claim* (verb), *contact* (verb), *point, factor, setup, situation, deal, phase, basic, regard, fundamental, force, rate* (verb), *worth-while, unique, put over, put across,* and *outstanding.* Blanket words are closely related to jargon and often appear in roundabout and wordy sentences (see 26).

ORIGINAL	REVISION
The question in this regard is directly related to the basic circumstances of the situation.	The question is basic.
The abnormal condition within Hamlet's mind is a governing factor which is the foremost force in molding his character traits.	The turmoil in Hamlet's mind altered his character. [*This may not be true, but it is apparently about what the student meant to say.*]
The coach stated that Jerry never rated very high with him because he never really came through in our particular setup.	The coach said that Jerry never adapted himself to our style of play.
He has familiarity with the medieval language picture and is an authority within the areas of that field.	He is an authority on medieval languages.

25c   COLORED, "SLANTED," OR PREJUDICIAL WORDS   Slant

In an oration once popular in high-school contests, Regulus addressing the Carthaginians referred to "the slimy ooze that stagnates in your veins," contrasting it unfavorably to the blood of the Romans. Obviously Regulus was not trying to be objective in his typing of Carthaginian blood. Similarly, when a mother says, "Now take your nice medicine," she is not necessarily describing her own impression of the medicine objectively. As they are here used *slimy, ooze, stagnates, nice* are colored, calculated to influence feelings, not to communicate truth. The connotations of words always influence their effect. Usually colored words are combined with ideas calculated to appeal to fears and prejudice. Notice the following:

> Rush me airmail without cost or obligation to me all the exciting facts about your amazing new "Pay-Check Protective System" that

pays me $400.00 a month for life with other valuable benefits. I understand that the remarkable dividends of this plan will give me money to help pay bills, keep me out of debt, and take care of my family's needs.

At times a writer may wish to play upon the emotions and the prejudices of others, but most writing is the better for being objective. Often, slanted words are so obvious in their intent that they fail to make even a convincing emotional appeal.

ORIGINAL

In high school there were some radicals who always stabbed any new worth-while project in the back just because they were rats at heart.

[*The writer probably does not know the meaning of the word* radical; *apparently, he is trying to discredit by calling names, but he is mainly discrediting himself.*]

My mother is a perfect angel with a saintly face and the most perfect disposition in the world.

[*Words like* angel *and* saintly *have some emotional force, but are vague enough to be unconvincing.*]

He had an unwholesome mouth that was disturbing to look at.

REVISION

There was one faction in our high school which tried to block any change that my group instituted.

[*The attitude of the writer has changed, and relatively objective words have replaced colored words.*]

Mother is seldom cross, never angry without good reason, and always helpful; years of smiling have left little wrinkles at the corners of her mouth.

[*Concrete terms clarify the passage and strengthen the appeal.*]

He had chalky teeth which looked as though they were decaying.

25d METAPHORICAL WRITING   Fig

Comparisons and figures of speech often make language brighter, more specific, and more precise. Many words have the meanings they do because they are old metaphors which are no longer recognized. *Outskirts* comes to us from the days when women wore more skirts than most women do now, and the "outskirts" were of course on the circumference. Much of the most vigorous, charming writing is metaphorical writing.

PROSAIC

Falstaff is so big and fat that he sweats a great deal when he walks too fast.

METAPHORICAL

Falstaff sweats to death
And lards the lean earth as he walks
                                    along.
—SHAKESPEARE, *Henry IV,* Pt. 1

PROSAIC (*Cont.*)

My roommate has a funny-looking face because his nose is short and kind of flattened.

The long mountains came down to the abrupt coast, and you could see them rather mixed up, running every which way. Some were angular, and some were rounded, and they all looked sad and depressing. Back from the shore where they were high the peaks were all snow-covered, and even nearer there were patches of snow and glaciers on them.

METAPHORICAL (*Cont.*)

My roommate's nose looks as though he always has it smudged up against a window pane.

These long mountains . . . lie, one after another, like corpses, with their toes up, and you pass by them, . . . and see their noses, tipped by cloud or snow, high in behind, with one corpse occasionally lying on another, and a skull or a thigh-bone chucked about, and hundreds of glaciers and snow-patches hanging to them, as though it was a winter battlefield.

—WORTHINGTON C. FORD,
Letters of Henry Adams

A metaphor can be a useful instrument. So can a stick of dynamite. Either can be dangerous. Avoid mixed metaphors, and avoid shifting metaphors so quickly that your reader is thinking about one figure of speech when you have gone on to another.

ORIGINAL

A creative person who has no political crystallization, not merely cuts the production end of his work, but loses a vital gut that is part of the social continuum.
[*Doubtless the man who published this to advertise an obscure magazine thought he was both profound and witty, but we only laugh at the poor artist, whacking off his production while slowly disemboweling himself, and all because he has not undergone crystallization.*]

Since then the snowball of knowledge has swept relentlessly on, stamping with each year another rivet of reliability and craftsmanship into the name of the House of Melarkey.— London trade advertisement.

REVISION

A creative artist who ignores contemporary politics limits himself as a creator and to a degree cuts himself off from society.
[*This is prosaic, perhaps, but understandable, and at the worst, not silly.*]

The House of Melarkey has advanced with the times, in experience, in craftsmanship, in reliability.

Some mixed figures, like those above, result from a misguided striving to write well. Much worse are the mixed metaphors caused by careless use of language.

ORIGINAL

He is always getting on band wagons, going off in all directions, and ending up clear out in left field.

We keep clipping the wool off the goose that lays the golden eggs, and instead of getting on the beam we pump her dry.

REVISION

He is impetuous.

Taking excessive profits inevitably destroys the source of those profits.

EXERCISE 25

A. On pages 434–436 are reproductions from *Webster's New World Dictionary of the American Language,* College Edition, the *American College Dictionary,* and *Webster's New Collegiate Dictionary.* Try to learn what you can about the contents of a good dictionary by comparing these pages in detail, beginning with *gab* and ending with *gable window.* Notice several sorts of information.

(1) *Word-list.* Does one dictionary include entry words not in another? Does one dictionary have phrases not in another?

(2) *Pronunciation.* Do the dictionaries agree in pronunciation? Are alternate pronunciations in the same order?

(3) *Etymologies.* Which book tells you the most about the origin and growth of a word? Which puts this technical information most clearly? Do the dictionaries include any Indo-European bases? (Indo-European, abbreviated IE., was the ancient ancestor of English). For this question you will need a few uncommon abbreviations, AS. (Anglo-Saxon), ME. (Middle English), Ar. (Arabic), L. (Latin), MD. (Middle Dutch), MHG. (Middle High German), OFr. (Old French), ON. (Old Norse), and abbreviations for modern languages like It. (Italian).

(4) *Meanings.* How do the meanings compare? Are the meanings in one more understandable than in another? More exact? Does one book treat certain sorts of words, such as obsolete words or technical words, better than another?

(5) *Uses.* All the dictionaries recognize several uses of the more common words. Does any omit important uses?

(6) *Encyclopedic material.* Dictionaries vary as to the amount of encyclopedic material they include. What seem to be the policies of these dictionaries? (One of them has two supplements at the end, one for biographical names, one a gazetteer.)

Now write an account of your findings, 300–500 words long, citing specific evidence.

gab (gab), *v.i.* [GABBED (gabd), GABBING], [ME. *gabben;* prob. < ON. *gabba*, to mock, reinforced by OFr. *gaber*, to boast, deride; the base occurs in AS. *gaffetung*, a scoffing, mocking & *gaf-spræc*, foolish speech; IE. base **ĝhabh- < *ĝhei*, etc., to yawn, have the mouth open], [Colloq.], to talk much or idly; chatter; gabble. *n.* [Colloq.], chatter; talkativeness.
   gift of (the) gab, [Colloq.], the ability to speak fluently; eloquence; glibness.
gab·ar·dine (gab'ẽr-dēn', gab'ẽr-dēn'), *n.* [var. of *gaberdine*], 1. a woolen, cotton, or rayon cloth twilled on one side and having a fine, diagonal weave, used for suits, coats, dresses, etc. 2. a gaberdine.
gab·ber (gab'ẽr), *n.* [Colloq.], a person who gabs.
gab·ble (gab''l), *v.i.* [GABBLED (-'ld), GABBLING], [< *gab* + *-le*, freq. suffix; ? suggested by MD. *gabbeln*, to chatter], 1. to talk rapidly and incoherently; jabber; chatter. 2. to utter rapid, meaningless sounds, as a goose. *v.t.* to utter rapidly and incoherently. *n.* rapid, incoherent talk or meaningless utterance.
gab·bler (gab'lẽr), *n.* a person who gabbles.
gab·bro (gab'rō), *n.* [It. < L. *glaber*, bare, smooth], any of a group of dark, heavy igneous rocks, composed chiefly of pyroxene and feldspar.
gab·by (gab'i), *adj.* [see GAB], [Colloq.], talkative; inclined to chatter.
ga·belle (gə-bel'), *n.* [Fr.; It. *gabella;* Ar. *gabālah*], a tax levied in certain countries; especially, a tax on salt, levied in France before the Revolution cf 1789.
gab·er·dine (gab'ẽr-dēn', gab'ẽr-dēn'), *n.* [earlier *gawbardyne;* OFr. *gauvardine, galvardine* < MHG. *walvart,* pilgrimage < *wallen*, to wander about + *vart* a trip < *varen*, to travel], 1. a loose coat or cloak made of coarse cloth, worn in the Middle Ages, especially by Jews. 2. gabardine.
gab·er·lun·zie (gab'ẽr-lun'zi; Scot. gȧb'ẽr-lün'yi), *n.* [Scot.; printing form of *gaberlunyie* (with printed *z* for *y* as in pers. name *Menzies*); earlier also *gaberloonie; prob. < Scot. Gaelic], a wandering beggar.
ga·bi·on (gā'bi-ən), *n.* [Fr.; It. *gabbione*, large cage < *gabbia*, cage, coop < L. *cavea*, cave, cage], 1. a cylinder of wicker filled with earth or stones, formerly used in building fortifications. 2. a similar cylinder of metal, used in building dams, foundations, etc.
ga·bi·on·ade (gā'bi-ən-ād'), *n.* [Fr. *gabionnade*], a defensive embankment or structure made of gabions.
ga·ble (gā'b'l), *n.* [ME.; OFr.; prob. < ON. *gafl*, gable; basic sense, "forked twig" seen in G. *gabel*, a fork], 1. *a)* the triangular wall enclosed by the sloping ends of a ridged roof. *b)* popularly, the whole section, including wall, roof, and space enclosed. 2. the end wall of a building, the upper part of which is a gable. 3. a triangular decorative feature in architecture, such as that over a door or window. *v.t.* [GABLED (-b'ld), GABLING], to put a gable or gables on. *v.i.* to be in the form of, or end in, a gable.

From Webster's New World Dictionary of the American Language, College Edition, Copyright, 1962, by The World Publishing Company.

GABLE

GABLE (sense 3)

gable roof, a ridged roof forming a gable at one end or both ends.
gable window, 1. a window in a gable (sense 2). 2. a window with a gable (sense 3) over it.
Ga·bon (gȧ'bōn'), *n.* a country in west central Africa, on the Gulf of Guinea: a former French colony, it is now a member of the French Community: area, 102,300 sq. mi.; pop., 420,000; capital, Libreville; also **Gabun**.
Ga·bo·riau, É·mile (ā'mēl' gȧ'bô'ryō'), 1835–1873; French writer of detective stories.

gab (găb), v., **gabbed, gabbing,** n. *Collop.* —v.i. **1.** to talk idly; chatter. —n. **2.** idle talk; chatter. **3.** glib speech: *the gift of gab.* [var. of *gob* mouth, t. Gaelic or Irish]

gab·ar·dine (găb/ərdēn/, găb/ərdēn/), n. **1.** firm, woven fabric of worsted, cotton, or spun rayon, with steep twill. **2.** a man's long, loose cloak or frock, worn in the Middle Ages. Also, **gab/er·dine/.** [t. Sp.: m. *gabardina,* ult. der. MHG *wallevart* pilgrimage]

gab·ble (găb/əl), v., **-bled, -bling,** n. —v.i. **1.** to talk rapidly and unintelligibly; jabber. **2.** (of geese, etc.) to cackle. —v.t. **3.** to utter rapidly and unintelligibly. —n. **4.** rapid, unintelligible talk. [freq. of GAB] —**gab/- bler,** n.

gab·bro (găb/rō), n., pl. **-bros.** *Petrog.* a granular igneous rock composed essentially of labradorite and augite. [t. It.]

gab·by (găb/ĭ), adj., **-bier, -biest.** loquacious.

ga·belle (gəbĕl/), n. **1.** a tax; an excise. **2.** (in France before 1790) a tax on salt. [t. F, t. Pr.: m. *gabela,* t. It.: m. *gābella* tax, t. Ar.: m. *(al-)qabāla* the impost]

Ga·bès (gä/bĕs), n. Gulf of, a gulf of the Mediterranean on the E coast of Tunisia.

ga·bi·on (gā/bĭ ən), n. **1.** a cylinder of wickerwork filled with eairth, used as a military defense. **2.** a cylinder filled w th stones and sunk in water, used in laying the foundations of a dam or jetty. [t. F, t. It.: m. *gabbione,* aug. of *gabbia,* g. L *cavea* cage]

ga·bi·on·ade (gā/bĭ ə nād/), n. **1.** a work formed of or with gabions. **2.** a row of gabions sunk in a stream to control the current. [t. F: m. *gabionnade.* See GABION]

ga·ble (gā/bəl), n., v., **-bled, -bling.** *Archit.* —n **1.** the end of a ridged roof cut off at its extremity in a vertical plane, together with the triangular expanse of wall from the level of the eaves to the apex of the roof. **2.** a similar end, as of a gambrel roof, not triangular. **3.** an architectural member resembling the triangular end of a roof. **4.** an end wall. —v.t. **5.** to build with a gable or gables; form as a gable (chiefly in **gabled,** pp.). [ME, prob. t. Scand.; cf. Icel. *gafl.* Cf. also OHG *gabala,* G *gabel* fork] —**ga/ble·like/,** adj.

Gables (def. 1)

gable end, (in a gabled building) the triangular wall space between the eaves level and the ridge, or the decorative wall carried up past the ends of a gable roof, and sloped, stepped, or scrolled to follow at a higher level its approximate shape.

gable roof, a ridged roof terminating at one or both ends in a gable.

gable window, 1. a window in or under a gable. **2.** a window having its upper part shaped like a gable.

Ga·bon (gȧbôɴ/), n. **1.** a republic in SW equatorial Africa: independent member of the French Community. formerly part of French Equatorial Africa. 403,000 pop. (est. 1959); 102,290 sq. mi. *Cap.:* Libreville. **2.** an estuary in this republic. Also, **Ga·bun** (gäboon/).

Ga·bo·riau (gȧbôryō/), n. Émile (ĕmēl/), 1833 or 1835–73, French novelist.

Ga·bri·el (gā/brĭ əl), n. one of the archangels, appearing usually as a divine messenger. Dan. 8:16, 9:21. Luke, 1: 19, 26. [t. Heb.: m. *Gabrī'ēl* the man of God]

Ga·bri·lo·witsch (gä/brĭ lüv/ĭch; *Russ.* gä/vrĭ lô/- vĭch), n. **Ossip** (ô/sĭp), 1878–1936, Russian pianist and conductor, in America.

ga·by (gā/bĭ), n., pl. **-bies.** *Colloq.* a fool. [orig. uncert.]

gad¹ (găd), v., **gadded, gadding,** n. —v.i. **1.** to move restlessly or idly about. —n. **2.** act of gadding. [? special use of GAD²] —**gad/der,** n.

gad² (găd), n., v., **gadded, gadding.** —n. **1.** a goad for driving cattle. **2.** a pointed mining tool for breaking up rock, coal, etc. —v.t. **3.** to break up with a mining gad. [ME, t. Scand.; cf. Icel. *gaddr* spike]

Gad (găd), n., interj. *Archaic.* a euphemistic form of *God* used as a mild oath. Also, **gad.**

gab (găb; *Scot.* gàb), *n.* *Scot.* The mouth.

gab (găb), *v. i. & n.* *Colloq.* Chatter; gabble.

gab'ar·dine' (găb'ẽr·dēn'; găb'ẽr·dēn), *n.* **1.** = GABERDINE. **2.** A woolen fabric closely resembling serge, but twilled on one side only; also, a similar fabric of cotton or rayon.

gab'bard (găb'ẽrd), **gab'bart** (-ẽrt), *n.* [F. *gabare*, *gabarot*.] *Obs. exc. Scot.* A lighter, barge, or similar vessel.

gab'ble (găb''l), *v. i. & t.;* GAB'BLED (-'ld); GAB'BLING (-lĭng). **1.** To jabber; chatter. **2.** To utter inarticulate sounds rapidly, as fowls. — **gab'ble,** *n.* — **gab'bler** (-lẽr), *n.*

gab'bro (găb'rō), *n.* [It., fr. L. *glaber* bare, smooth.] *Petrog.* Any of a family of granular, igneous rocks essentially of plagioclase with a ferromagnesian mineral and accessory iron ore, etc.

gab'broid (-roid), *adj.* *Petrog.* Resembling gabbro.

gab'by (găb'ĭ), *adj.* *Colloq.* Loquacious; talkative.

ga·belle' (gȧ·bĕl'), *n.* [F., through Pr. & It., fr. Ar. *qabālah*.] A tax; specif., an impost on salt, levied in France for several centuries prior to 1790, and in use down to the present day in China.

gab'er·dine' (găb'ẽr·dēn'; găb'ẽr·dēn), *n.* [Sp. *gabardina*.] **1.** A coarse loose frock or coat; — chiefly of medieval costume. **2.** The medieval Jewish gown or mantle. **3.** Var. of GABARDINE.

gab'er·lun'zie (găb'ẽr·lŭn'zĭ; *Scot.* gàb'ẽr·lün'yĭ, -lōōn'yĭ, -lōōn'ĭ), *n.* *Scot.* A wandering beggar.

ga'bi·on (gā'bĭ·ŭn; 58), *n.* [F., fr. It. *gabbione* a large cage, fr. *gabbia* cage, fr. L. *cavea*.] A hollow cylinder of wickerwork, iron, or the like. Gabions are filled with earth and used in building fieldworks, mining, etc.

ga'bi·on·ade' (gā'bĭ·ŭn·ād'), *n.* [F. *gavionnade*.] A work made with gabions.

ga'ble (gā'b'l), *n.* [OF., fr. ON. *gafl*.] *Arch.* **a** The vertical triangular portion of the end of a building, from the level of the cornice or eaves to the ridge of the roof. Also, a similar end when not triangular in shape, as of a gambrel roof. Hence: **b** The end wall of a building, as distinguished from the front or rear side. **c** A decorative member having the shape of a triangular gable, such as that above a Gothic arch in a doorway. — *v. t. & i.;* GA'BLED (-b'ld); GA'BLING (-blĭng). To furnish with gables; to terminate in a gable; as, a *gabled* roof.

Gable **a.**

gable roof. A roof which forms a gable at each end.

gable window. A window in a gable, or one with a gable.

Ga'bri·el (gā'brĭ·ĕl), *n.* [Heb. *Gab-hrĭ'ĕl*.] An angel of comfort to man (*Dan.* viii and ix), a herald declaring the coming of the Messiah. In Jewish and Christian tradition, he is one of the seven archangels. He is believed by Mohammedans to have dictated the Koran to their prophet.

ga'by (gā'bĭ; *dial. also* gô'bĭ), *n.* *Colloq.* A simpleton.

gad (găd), *n.* [ON. *gaddr* a sting, spike.] **1.** A goad; as, upon the *gad*, that is, suddenly, as if goaded. **2.** *Mining, etc.* A pointed iron or steel bar for loosening ore, etc.

gad (găd), *v. i.;* GAD'DED (-ĕd; -ĭd); GAD'DING. To wander about idly. — *n.* *Colloq.* A gadding, or rambling; — only in *on*, or *upon, the gad.*

Gad (găd), *n.* A softened form of *God*, used as a mild oath, as in **Gads'bod'i·kins** (gădz'bŏd'ĭ·kĭnz), **Gads'woons'** (-wōōnz'), **Gad'-zooks'** (găd'zōōks'), etc.

Gad (găd), *n.* *Bib.* See JACOB.

gad'a·bout' (găd'ȧ·bout'), *adj.* Gadding; roving. — *n.* *Colloq.* One who gads about.

gad'bee' (găd'bē'), *n.* A gadfly.

gad'der (găd'ẽr), *n.* One who roves about idly; a gadabout.

gad'fly' (găd'flī'), *n.; pl.* -FLIES (-flīz'). [1st *gad* + *fly*.] A fly that bites cattle; a horsefly.

gadg'et (găj'ĕt; -ĭt), *n.* A small contrivance, object, or device for doing something; also, a part of machinery.

Ga·dhel'ic (gȧ·dĕl'ĭk; -dē'lĭk; găd'ĕ·lĭk). Var. of GOIDELIC.

ga'did (gā'dĭd), *n* [See GADOID.] A fish of the cod family (Gadidae). — **ga'did,** *adj.*

ga'doid (-doid), *adj.* [NL. *gadus* cod + -*oid.*] Like or pertaining to the cod family (Gadidae), a large family of soft-finned, chiefly marine food fishes, including the cod and haddock, having a rather elongated body and a large mouth. — *n.* A fish of the cod family or of a group (Anacanthini) of teleost fishes that comprises the codfishes, hakes, and their allies.

gad'o·lin·ite (găd'ō·lĭn·īt), *n.* [After J. *Gadolin* (1760–1852), Finnish chemist.] A black or brown vitreous silicate of iron, beryllium, yttrium, cerium, erbium, etc. H., 6.5–7. Sp. gr., 4–4.5. It is a source of rare earths.

gad'o·lin'i·um (-lĭn'ĭ·ŭm; 58), *n.* [NL.] *Chem.* A metallic element, one of the rare-earth metals, found in combination in gadolinite and certain other minerals. Symbol, *Gd;* at. no., 64; at. wt., 156.9.

B. Your instructor will assign one of the following words to each member of the class:

above, *prep.*	lake, *n.*	sail, *v.*
appreciate, *v.*	legal, *adj.*	sick, *adj.*
apron, *n.*	make, *v.*	sun, *n.*
bedlam, *n.*	manufacture, *v.*	street, *n.*
bully, *n.*	noun, *n.*	tap, *n.*
cotton, *n.*	nobody, *p.*	tender, *adj.*
dead, *adj.*	over, *prep.*	tool, *n.*
find, *v.*	paper, *n.*	up, *adv.*
goose, *n.*	paternal, *adj.*	up, *prep.*
head, *n.*	quick, *adj.*	veal, *n.*
idle, *adj.*	read, *v.*	water, *n.*
judge, *v.*	red, *adj.*	wiggle, *v.*
kick, *v.*	road, *n.*	yank, *v.*

Look up your word in each of the following dictionaries: *A New English Dictionary on Historical Principles* (*Oxford English Dictionary*), *Dictionary of American English, Dictionary of Americanisms,* Wyld's *Universal Dictionary of the English Language, Century Dictionary and Cyclopedia, New International Dictionary of the English Language,* and *New Standard Dictionary of the English Language* (these last two are the so-called "unabridged" dictionaries published by the Merriam Company and by Funk and Wagnalls respectively). Use the questions in A above, and add to them the following:

Which dictionaries give examples of the use of the word? Which dictionaries give such systematic lists of examples that they constitute a history of the word in English or American speech?

Using your notes, prepare an oral report on your word, or write a 300–500 word paper, as your instructor directs.

C. The following are some of the more common prefixes from Latin and Greek used in modern English:

ab- (abs-)	cata-	hyper-
ad- (ac-, af-,	circum-	in- (il-, im-, ir-)
ag-, al-, an-,	com- (co-, col-,	inter-
ap-, ar-, as-,	con-, cor-)	intra-
at-)	contra-	intro-
ambi- (ambo-)	de-	mal-
ante-	di- (dis-)	multi-
anti- (ant-)	ex- (e-, ef-)	neo-
arch-	ex- (ec-)	non-
bi-	extra-	ob- (oc-, of-, op-)
para-	pseudo-	super-

per-	re-	supra-
peri-	retro-	syn- (sy- syl-, sym-)
post-	se-	trans-
pre-	semi-	tri-
pro-	sub- (suc-, suf-, sug-,	uni-
proto-	sum-, sup-, sur-,	vice-
	sus-)	

Be sure you know the use and meaning of each prefix, verifying in a good dictionary those about which you may be uncertain. Then choose five prefixes, and find at least ten words in which each of these occurs.

For more extensive lists of prefixes and suffixes, See Arthur Garfield Kennedy, *Current English* (Boston, 1935), pp. 337–345.

D. Look up each of the following words in a good desk dictionary and study the discriminative synonyms listed. For each word and each of its listed synonyms write a sentence putting the word in a suitable context.

1. anger	8. law	15. relevant
2. beg	9. lift	16. see
3. change	10. material	17. smell
4. copy	11. object	18. stick
5. crowd	12. power	19. think
6. debase	13. proud	20. weaken
7. guide	14. rebellion	

E. In the sentences below some words have been mistaken for other words, and some have been misunderstood. Make the necessary corrections.

1. Falstaff finally realized that he had been the brunt of a joke.

2. I am fighting because I want to make life better and happier for myself and my posteriority.

3. I decided that in regards to my future, my first duty was to go to college.

4. Their propaganda pictures showed our captured soldiers being treated with the upmost kindness.

5. His house looked like a mid-evil estate.

6. In *The Bishop Orders His Tomb,* Browning is satyrizing a Renaissance bishop.

7. In spite of my long slide down the glacier, my camera was in tact.

8. The marine biologist asked for a leave to investigate the debts of the sea, and his request was granite.

9. He announced his presence in a loud voice, and stood in the

middle of the room until I asked what he meant by his frontery.

10. I became so completely dissolved in our card game that I forgot all about the dog.

F. Correct the false direction of words in the following sentences:

1. He was afraid of how the discriminated groups might react.
2. Many results may be obtained which make their scientific value skeptical.
3. Shirley instilled an unreasonable fear of spiders as a small child.
4. You never know what your weaknesses are until you are applied to them.
5. When a point is trying to be made, a reader must watch the evidence.
6. The people who want more rigid rules for the girls in the dormitories are attributed to the older generation.
7. Jake yielded a very profitable income from these products crossing his bridge.
8. They were inculcated with the idea that they were well informed.
9. Fishing was once regarded as anything but a skillful art.
10. Enterprising publishers have now started bringing out a dearth of older detective stories.
11. Today, as never before, the church should have an unsurpassable bearing on modern civilization.
12. Massachusetts was one of the first states which was instigated by higher education for women.
13. From their difficult work teamsters derived the name "bull-skinners."
14. The first sight of a person coming up the hill is a ramshackle old barn.
15. Students are required to take some courses because it is known that the course will be profited by the students.

G. Each of the sentences below is followed by words which can be synonyms for the italicized words in the sentence. Indicate which could be substituted in the sentence and explain changes in meaning that would result.

1. Many members of the audience were *moved* to tears. (*incited, prompted, impelled, instigated, actuated*)
2. The general was not willing to pay the *price* of victory. (*value, charge, cost, expense, worth*)
3. Mary felt no *fear* as she faced the microphone. (*dismay, alarm, horror, anxiety, dread*)

4. The president did not have enough *power* to enforce the rules. (*potency, puissance, strength, energy, force*)

5. Her *pride* would not allow her to dress as the other girls in the house did. (*vanity, haughtiness, superciliousness, egotism, vainglory*)

6. *Examination* of the evidence showed that the jury had been wrong. (*inquiry, inquisition, scrutiny, investigation, proposition*)

7. The judge had no *sympathy* for law-breakers. (*pity, commiseration, condolence, tenderness, agreement*)

8. His devices were so *transparent* that nobody was deceived. (*translucent, lucid, diaphanous, limpid, luminous*)

9. The entire *company* joined in the song. (*group, throng, assemblage, flock, circle*)

10. Her dyed hair and *gaudy* clothes shocked the congregation. (*ostentatious, pretentious, tawdry, garish, flashy*)

H. The metaphors and similes in the following sentences vary in complexity and effectiveness. Study each one in terms of the referent-thought-word relationship discussed above (24-7). Then decide as specifically as you can which parts of the referent are emphasized or changed by using words metaphorically.

1. The moon was a ghostly galleon. . . .—Alfred Noyes

2. This man was hunting about the hotel lobby like a starved dog that has forgotten where he has buried a bone.—O. Henry

3. A wit's a feather, and a chief a rod;
   An honest man's the noblest work of God.—Alexander Pope

4. An honest God is the noblest work of man.—Samuel Butler

5. A pun is not bound by the laws which limit nice wit. It is a pistol let off at the ear; not a feather to tickle the intellect.—Charles Lamb

6.   Like our shadows,
   Our wishes lengthen as our sun declines.—Alexander Pope

7. I wonder why anybody wanted to wing an old woman in the leg.—Hilda Lawrence

8. More than a catbird hates a cat,
   Or a criminal hates a clue,
   Or the Axis hates the United States
   That's how much I love you.—Ogden Nash

9. So 'tis not her the bee devours,
   It is a pretty maze of flowers;
   It is the rose that bleeds when he
   Nibbles his nice phlebotomy.—John Cleveland

10. Let us go then, you and I,
When the evening is spread out against the sky
Like a patient etherized upon a table.—T. S. Eliot.

11. All of Stratford, in fact, suggests powdered history—add hot water and stir and you have a delicious, nourishing Shakespeare.
—Margaret Halsey

12. Our two souls, therefore, which are one,
Though I must go, endure not yet
A breach, but an expansion
Like gold to airy thinness beat.—John Donne

I. Revise the following passage by replacing the italicized words with other words which make us see, hear, taste, smell, or feel:

When I *entered* the *enclosure,* the *affair* was *going on.* I *found a place,* and was *feeling pretty good* if a *little uncomfortable* because of *the circumstances,* when I saw a *person* approaching me. She was a *female,* and *seemed to be in an agitated condition.* Her face looked *kind of funny,* and she *moved in a peculiar way.* She started *saying things* in an *odd kind of voice,* and I *realized* that she was in *an intoxicated condition.* Her *way of standing* was *unusual.* Then some *other persons approached,* including a *man,* who seemed to think he *was important around there.* He *spoke to me.* I also, was *in an agitated state* by now, so that I was *not sensitive to all that was transpiring,* but I heard *certain sounds from various people.* Somebody with a *repulsive face* was *admonishing* me. *One individual inquired* if I *was not aware* that I was an *improper person* to be *in these surroundings.* He *had a threatening attitude.* I *replied* that I *was unaware of the circumstances,* but that I would *accede to their wishes and retire.* As I *took my departure* I heard them *expatiating upon me.*

26

Usage and Economy
in Words

For Guide to Revision, see page 451

> They're cur'ous talkers i' this country, sir; the gentry's hard work to hunderstand 'em. I was brought up among the gentry, sir, an' got the turn o' their tongue when I was a bye. Why, what do you think the folks about here say for 'heven't you?' the gentry, you know, says 'heven't you'—well, the people about here says 'hanna yey.' It's what they call the 'dileck' as is spoke hereabout, sir. That's what I've heard Squire Donnithorne say many a time; 'it's the dileck,' says he.
> —George Eliot, Adam Bede

The diction of good writing has many qualities. Fundamental are the qualities of precise meaning considered above (see 25). Also important is "the dileck." Most important writing in English is in a dialect known as standard English, and the student needs to master it. Moreover, in any dialect, he needs to use language tersely, economically.

26-1 CORRECTNESS AND USAGE IN WORD CHOICE

The problem of correctness in language suggests the problem of correctness in clothes. Wearing the correct clothes, whether the wearer is promenading on Fifth Avenue or dashing for the South Pole, is less important than one's being clothed. But the choice of clothes is important; any lawyer knows that his clothes may sway justice, and dresses in one way for a judge, in another for a jury. Any doctor knows that his clothes are part of his bedside manner; many women are understandably concerned about when they should and should not carry gloves. Similarly, learning to write well is difficult and important; learning to write correctly is relatively easy and less important, but it has its uses and its peculiarities. In fact, among its peculiarities are that people become angry with one another about supposedly incorrect language, and many parents spend more time trying to make Johnny correct than they spend making him literate—which may be one reason Johnny grows up unable either to read or write with any competence. But if correctness in language can be exaggerated, no one denies that good usage is important or pretends that determining good usage is easy.

An older notion about correctness and usage prescribed that the language be kept pure. Usually, certain persons were set up, or set themselves up, to decide what was pure. They did not ask themselves very seriously what is meant by purity in language, but on the whole they assumed that whatever *was* was right, and that language should be logical. This now seems silly on the face of it, partly because we have learned more about language than was known formerly. Nobody suggests that Old English is purer than Modern English because it is older, or that we should all start speaking Indo-Hittite; and if it is illogical to imitate language that is a thousand years old why is it logical to imitate language that is a hundred years old, if oldness is a virtue? Who is to say which old forms should be preserved and which should not be? *He ain't* was approved usage two hundred years ago, although spelled without an apostrophe; after declining in favor, it is now returning to limited use. Our word *shall* was formally no auxiliary at all, to say nothing of its being preferred in some locutions to *will,* which also was not a sign of the future. In short, trying to determine modern usage by assuming that what was once correct is still correct will not work.

Perhaps to consider usage we should remind ourselves of some fundamental truths about language, truths which became apparent during our survey of language in Section 24. What is language? It is a medium, the principal medium, of human exchange. Who makes it? The users of the language make it. How do they make it? By using it, mainly by preserving it, but also by changing it gradually, apparently by adapting it to the changing needs of the users. Who determines usage? The users of the language. They determine what words mean because they agree roughly what the word can be used for; they determine grammar because they respect an unwritten agreement as to how words are put together; similarly, they determine usage, whether or not certain people say that one locution is right and another wrong. If enough users of a language use a certain locution in a certain way long enough and consistently enough, it will become "right" and other usages are in danger of becoming "wrong."

All of this means that *correct, right,* and *wrong* are often not very revealing words in discussions of usage, but it does not mean that there are no standards for usage. Obviously, people do not want language to change rapidly; apparently people understand that language is a means of communication, that it must have currency to communicate, and it can have currency only if it also has stability. People want to be able to do new things with language, but they also want most of the language today to be what the language was yesterday. They want to use language well, to learn to use it well, and accordingly they want good language to be known as good language, so that they can cultivate the good.

Usage is behind "correctness," but it does not offer a simple answer; we do not decide what to say by counting noses. We cannot say that an expression is correct because most people use it, or even because the "best" people use it. We can say that "correct" English is that English *which does what we want it to do*. In other words, a scientific understanding of language shows us that the question of "correctness" in the usual sense—in the sense of rules of conduct—is not an issue at all. We do not try to use good English *because* other people do or *because* someone has made a rule, any more than a carpenter cuts a board with a saw because other carpenters do or because someone has made a rule about saws. The carpenter uses the saw because it cuts better than a breadknife. All problems of language, then, involve usage, not because usage makes rules but because usage determines what a word or expression does, what effect it will have. The discussions in this book are attempts to describe the effects expressions will have and to point to some that will not work in serious writing. But an expression is not right or wrong according to which people use it. An expression is useful if it will do what the writer wants done; if not, it is inappropriate.

26-2 DIALECTS, IDIOM, AND USAGE

All languages, we believe, live and change by dialects, geographical and social; English, of course, is no exception. We have seen in Section 24 that dialects develop by geographical areas; they develop also by social groups. Usages often follow lines of social distinction, but they are also considered appropriate for certain purposes, in which case they may be referred to as *language levels*. Naturally, English has developed different pronunciations, different ways of putting words together, different meanings. A sidewalk is a pavement in England, and a footpath in Australia. If a Briton says "She lives *in* Oxford

Street," he means that the person referred to has Oxford Street as an address, but in the United States anybody who lives *in* the street has no address at all. What is a sack in the Middle West of America may be a poke in the South and something quite different in Army slang. "Where at do you'uns go of a Sunday" might be heard in some dialects of the Middle West, but it would sound strange in New York. There is nothing "wrong" or "right" about the customs of different areas, about the differences in dialect. Often the differences reflect genuine needs, and objection to them is absurd. In the eighteenth century one British writer commented condescendingly about a city in Georgia: "It stands upon the flat of a hill; the bank of a river (which they in barbarous English call a bluff)." The writer did not notice that *bluff* says in one word what had taken him nine. But the effectiveness of expressions used only in certain areas is limited. The student must realize that any expression common only in a particular dialect will have a special effect when used, and he must use it only when he wants that special effect. The dictionary labels some terms *dialectal* or *provincial* and sometimes names areas of use.

Since language lives and grows by custom, good speech rests upon the speech habits of the users of a language. These crystallized speech habits are called the *idiom of the language.* Most native speakers are entirely unconscious of the idioms which they have learned as naturally as they learned to breathe or to walk.

> I introduced him *to* my sister *at* Mary's party.
> I introduced him *at* my sister *to* Mary's party.

Any native speaker of English will know that the first of these two sentences is what we call "correct"—that is, it is idiomatic—but a foreigner who had learned English in school might find the second sentence as logical as the first. Most idioms have logic and good sense behind them. *To* and *at* differ, and in the first of the sentences above the two words are used in accordance with certain of their familiar uses. Many ideas, however, could be expressed logically in several ways, and the way sanctioned by idiom would seem to be nothing more than standardized custom. Some idioms are illogical; we say *The sun sets,* although logically we should say *The sun sits.* Logical or illogical, idiom is the language; there always has been and presumably always will be illogical idiomatic expression.

Since idioms grow from speech habits, they may change with time and place or may be characteristic only of the speech of limited groups of people. The appropriateness of some idioms, therefore, is hard to determine. Some have gained wide use in speech but are still suspected by conservative users of the language. *The teacher blamed the affair on Johnny,* for example, uses a common colloquial idiom, but the idiom might suggest to some readers that the writer was unaware of standard customs. Some would insist on *The teacher blamed Johnny for the affair.* An idiom like *I can't help but know . . .* is in wide colloquial use, but some speakers would object and prefer *I can't help knowing. . . .*

Variations and restrictions in usage develop in many ways. Workers coin terms which are easily understood among themselves but are not widely current. To printers, *pie* describes jumbled type, but to a sixteenth century divine *pie* referred to ecclesiastical rules, and to some drivers it means a truck owned by the Pacific Intermountain Express. Slang develops in groups: for instance, the rhyming slang of the underworld (*half-inch,* rhyming with *pinch,* means "steal"); the slang of jazz musicians (*gut bucket* for "bass viol"); the slang of college students (*bust* or *flunk* for "fail a course"). Some words also are barred from general use as impolite or obscene or irreligious, although society's attitude varies about specific words with changes in time and place. Most important, perhaps, some expressions, quite understandable and quite widely known, are popularly conceived to be used mainly by "ignorant" or "uneducated" or "vulgar" people. And many expressions are more or less characteristic of particular social groups in particular situations. Many such expressions may be useful or logical (*I can't hardly tell* is as clear as *I can hardly tell*), but the associations of usage attached to them make them dubious choices for serious writing. The locutions are limited and usually inappropriate for formal purposes. Dictionaries distinguish some variations by specifically naming an occupation or subject or by using terms like *professional, slang, obscene,* and the like.

26-3 USAGE VARIATIONS

Obviously, the ordinary person trying to decide whether to say "It is I" or "It is me" cannot examine all the complex variations of usage. Thus, some broad distinctions help, and we can notice three sorts of situations which give rise to three levels of language. Formal circumstances, important affairs, difficult subjects, and wide audiences require careful and reliable language. The Constitution of the United States has been weighed word by word for generations. Nobody would want it written in language which would rapidly change in meaning. A book on atomic power may be read anywhere in the world; it should be written in language which all speakers of English understand. An article in a good magazine will be read by all sorts of people; it should be written in language which has a common meaning for a bank president and for the freshman who talks college slang. An applicant for a position will wish to convince his prospective employer that he is a cultured, competent person; his letter of application should be written in the language of cultured people. Language of this sort is called *standard English*. Many situations do not require the precision of standard written English. Conversation, for example, has a limited audience and can be more informal, more idiomatic, more cognizant of special information and special attitudes of the speakers. It reflects our childhoods, our occupations, the various groups with whom we associate or have associated. It is used in various types of informal writing—informal articles, fiction, newspaper stories—and is sometimes called *informal English*. It is also characteristic of conversation and is sometimes designated *colloquial English*. *Colloquial* derives from the Latin word meaning *speech*. On a third level is the language, chiefly spoken, which is not socially acceptable for any serious use. It includes some regional dialects, some shop talk, some slang. It is often vivid and expressive, but it is limited in its use because it is conventionally associated with illiteracy and with the uneducated, and because it does not have general currency. It is referred to as *illiterate* or *vulgate English*.

These distinctions between three levels of language usage are, of course, only approximations. Obviously they overlap. Many slang expressions, for example, are classified by different persons as either vulgate or colloquial. The writer should not, however, neglect the existence of these levels in selecting his expressions. All kinds of expressions have their uses, but all are not useful in all situations. In other words, the appropriateness of an expression to the situation in which it is being used determines part of its effect. A word like *ain't* is avoided in standard English, not because it is "wrong" in some mysterious way and not because it is unclear. It is easily understandable and fills a need in the language, but it is traditionally connected with language on the vulgate level, and it cannot be used in standard English without seeming inappropriate. An expression or construction gains some of its "meaning" from its associations, and many expressions are appropriate at only one level of usage. Part of their meaning is involved in the suggestions they invoke. In this sense, then, an "error" of usage is not just an offense against polite society or a failure to do what "the best people" do; it is a failure to select words which do the jobs for which they are intended.

26-4 STANDARD ENGLISH

Anyone who hopes to do serious work in modern society should command the standard idiom of his native tongue, even though he must learn to do so. Language, like money, serves as a medium of exchange only if it has common currency, that is, only if it has a known and relatively stable value. If we cannot agree as to what a dollar is worth, we cannot trade much in goods, and if we cannot agree what a word is worth, we cannot trade much in ideas. Admittedly, no word has a fixed, absolute, and permanent value. Neither has the dollar, but it has been so stable and so widely accepted that business can be done with it. Similarly, some words have relatively reliable currency.

To write anything of importance, we must know what words, and what usages of these words, have sufficient currency to admit them to standard, acceptable English. The word *man* has meant an adult human male for more than a thousand years. It is standard English. Only recently has a *good guy* been an approved male; formerly, if a guy was not a piece of rope or wire it was a person who looked like a scarecrow. *Guy,* in the sense of *man,* is not acceptable standard English because its effectiveness in that sense is limited; it carries associations with nonstandard situations which are part of its meaning. In its newer, vaguer sense the word has not become part of the established body of standard English which can be relied on to maintain a relatively constant meaning.

Every student should be able to write and speak so that he will be understandable wherever his words may go, to New York or Dallas, to Cape Town or Liverpool. His writing should be understandable for longer than a few years. In this book, therefore, passages are revised whenever they are not clearly standard English, not because colloquial or vulgate writing is "wrong," but because students need to learn standard practices. They will continue to use informal speech in informal situations, but they need to be sure they know how to use more formal language when they need it.

26-5 ECONOMY IN WORDS

Even standard English works best when it is used efficiently. People in dreadful need of communication can usually make themselves understood in few words. "Help!" "Fire!" "Murder!" say more than "I am in need of assistance," "There is a conflagration," and "A person is being illegally dispatched." Of course complicated ideas and fine distinctions require elaborate treatment; they cannot be considered in few words, but the fewer the better, so long as the expression is adequate. Good writing results from a plenitude of ideas and an economy of words, not from a desert of ideas and a flood of vocabulary. Most writers, especially most beginning writers, should throw out words; but even well-constructed sentences can often be improved by removing nonessential or redundant words, substituting more direct sentence patterns for roundabout ones, and economizing on modifiers. The following will bear more than normal attention.

Cutting deadwood. Almost a sure way to improve composition is to resolutely cut out the words doing no work. Notice the italicized words in the following sentences:

> *It happened that* she was elected *to the position of* secretary *and this was* [of] the oldest club *that existed* in the city.
> Although he had always considered his sister *to be of the* awkward *type,* he found her *to be* a good dancer.

With the italicized words omitted, the sentences are clearer and sharper.

Direct expressions. Often shorter, more direct routes to meaning can be discovered. Notice, for example, the substitutions suggested in brackets for the italicized words in the following sentences.

> Mary's tears *had the effect of making* [made] Jim regret *the accusation which he had made hastily* [his hasty accusation].
> *By the time the end of the month rolled around* [By the end of the month] *it seemed to us a certainty* [we knew] that our first business venture would *be a success* [succeed].

A well-chosen verb or adjective may say as much as a wordy clause. *Economy in modifiers.* Every modifier added to a sentence decreases the impact of the others. Words like *very, really, surely, actually, merely, simply, great,* and *real* tend to accumulate in careless composition. Consider whether the modifiers italicized in the following sentence should be omitted.

> As I crept *hesitantly* out of the *dark,* dingy, *grimy* hotel and felt the *blazing,* withering sun on my back I was *very* sure I did not *really* want to spend a month in the city.

Often the effect of modifiers can be embodied in telling nouns or verbs. *Liar,* for most purposes, says everything in *a person given by nature or habit to disseminating untruths; canter* or *gallop* says more than *ride at a rapid pace.*

26-6 WORD ECONOMY AND ADEQUACY

Brief writing is not necessarily good writing; expression in a complicated world must usually be detailed, and details require words, many of them. Even publishers, who have to pay printing bills, often advise writers to "write it out," but granted that the writer uses words enough to express himself, the fewer words the better. Notice the following:

> Spring comes to the land with pale, green shoots and swelling buds; it brings to the sea a great increase in the number of simple, one-celled plants of microscopic size, the diatoms. Perhaps the currents bring down to the mackerel some awareness of the flourishing vegetation of the upper waters, of the rich pasturage for hordes of crustaceans that browse in the diatom meadows and in their turn fill the waters with clouds of their goblin-headed young. Soon fishes of many kinds will be moving through the spring sea, to feed on the teeming life of the surface and to bring forth their own young.
> —RACHEL L. CARSON, *Under the Sea Wind*

This is good writing, not because it is brief, but because it is economical. Miss Carson is saying something more than that the mackerel, after hibernating off the continental shelf, mysteriously wake up every spring; she is fitting the annual migration of the mackerel into the impelling cycle of the seasons; explanation requires detail, and details require words. The student might try going through this passage, endeavoring to remove one word without damaging the effect. In the last line, for instance, *teeming life* could be reduced to *life,* but the account would suffer. Note how much is implied in a passage like "hordes of crustaceans that browse in the diatom meadows." Word economy is not sparing words; it is putting them to work.

26 **Usage**

USAGE AND ECONOMY
IN WORDS

Guide to Revision

Use standard English; revise wordy constructions; eliminating dead-wood.

Most serious writing, formal or informal, requires standard usage.

ORIGINAL

Lots of people know they better keep an eye out for opportunities.

REVISION

Many people know they should look for opportunities.

Colloquial English which rests upon the usage in occupations and has never attained common currency is often called *cant*. It can be very useful, but should be used with caution in formal composition.

CONFUSING

Give the stiff the gandy.
[*If the context requires the use of a word like* gandy, *it should be put in quotation marks and explained.*]

In this groove winds the cable as the giraffe is let down into or drawn up out of the mine.

CLEAR

Tamp that railroad tie.
[Stiff *is a picturesque word for a railroad tie, but most people would not know what it means, and explanations can become awkward.*]

In this groove winds the cable, as the incline-car, the "giraffe," is let down into or drawn up out of the mine.
—DAN DE QUILLE, *The Big Bonanza*

451

Like other colloquial locutions, contractions are suited to intimate or nonchalant relationships. They have developed because they are convenient aids to speech, easy to pronounce, but they are not appropriate to formal writing.

ORIGINAL

We *don't* as yet have accurate relative heights for the tallest mountains, partly because mountaineers *haven't* agreed on a uniform method of measurement.

REVISION

We *do not* as yet have accurate relative heights for the tallest mountains, partly because mountaineers *have not* agreed on a uniform method of measurement.

NOTE: *don't* is sometimes confused with *doesn't* as a contraction.

don't = do not   doesn't = does not

One contraction is frequently misspelled.

it's = it is   its (possessive or genitive for *of it*)

26a   SLANG   Slang

Slang develops variously, notably because we like to play with words. We put old words to new uses or coin new expressions, largely for the sake of novelty or cleverness. The results vary. Occasionally a slang expression fills a genuine need, persists, and is accepted as part of the language. Often it is accepted by limited groups and remains current on the vulgate or colloquial level. Usually it has quick popularity and then disappears.

Using slang—especially if you make it up yourself—can be amusing, and the result vivid, but slang is characteristic of vulgate or colloquial language. For two reasons it is limited in its usefulness. First, it is usually known to so few people, in such a restricted group geographically or socially, and for so short a time that it can be used for only the most local and ephemeral purposes. Second, much slang is so general that it means almost nothing. The user of slang often does not know what he wishes to say, and the listener to slang does not know what, if anything, has been said.

SLANG

It's okay by all of us if the dean of women wants to throw the book at us,

STANDARD ENGLISH

None of us will object if the dean of women enforces the rules, but she

SLANG (*Cont.*)

but she better have the straight dope before she makes her move.

The bums on Capitol Hill better not steam-roller anything through about prayer-boning and sky-piloting, or try any shenanigans to keep other dopes from blowing off steam if they've got gripes.

STANDARD ENGLISH (*Cont.*)

should learn the facts before she acts.

Congress shall make no law respecting an establishment of religion, or prohibiting the free exercise thereof; or abridging the freedom of speech or of the press; . . . .—The Constitution, Bill of Rights, Article 1.

[*The framers of the Constitution studied composition more than two centuries ago, but they wrote standard English, and we still know essentially what they wanted to say.*]

Writers struggling for rare effects sometimes endeavor to coin words and are sometimes successful when they try, but inexperienced writers usually do better to use the half million words recorded in a good dictionary.

ORIGINAL

I would say that the second letter makes fun of the *overboardness* that the first writer went in his letter.

REVISION

I would say that the second letter makes fun of the *exaggerations* in the first letter.

26b   IDIOM   Id

Idiom is the result of custom in language. Usually it is logical, though not always, and to use the language a writer must learn idioms, whether they are logical or illogical. Native speakers have learned most idioms unconsciously, but writers with poor linguistic backgrounds have trouble. Furthermore, many idioms have become common colloquially but are not appropriate in standard English; certain of these are discussed in the Glossary (see 34).

ORIGINAL

He *hadn't ought to* go.

She told me *by* words of one syllable that the other girls had no affection *in* me.

REVISION

(1) He *should not* go.
(2) He *ought not* to go.

She told me *in* words of one syllable that the other girls had no affection *for* me.

Many expressions in English cannot stand popularity. Idioms, of course, and standard expressions appear over and over without losing their effectiveness, but slang or other attempts at cleverness or vividness emerge after overuse with as little vigor as any other stale joke. Metaphors which do not enter the language as new words often become trite. The writer who first referred to a wife as a *ball and chain* may have been amusing on the comic-strip level; the thousandth person who imitated him was not amusing on any level. Expressions which have been so tarnished by time that their charm, and often even their meaning, is gone are called trite or hackneyed expressions or clichés. Trite expressions are dangerous partly because they paralyze the mind. As ready-made channels for thought they invite the ideas of the writer, who can then cease thinking. An editorial writer commented in a discussion of academic freedom in a university:

> Any teacher who disagrees with his dean's academic views is not playing on the team and should turn in his suit.

The "team" metaphor was worn out long ago, but the writer fell into the set pattern so easily that he failed to analyze his own remarks. The convenience of the trite expression led him into an argument by false analogy (see 6c).

ORIGINAL	REVISION
When war first reared its ugly head, John Q. Public took it in his stride and played ball.	Faced with war, we did what had to be done.
In our day and age, in this great country of ours, progress has taken place by leaps and bounds.	America has progressed.
Back in the old home town and under the paternal roof, Jim found that, having struck it rich out in the great open spaces, the fatted calf was now prepared for the prodigal son.	Back home from the West, wealthy, Jim found that he had become suddenly popular.

Jargon is vague writing using blanket terms (see 25b), but it is notable in that the writer of jargon uses more words than he needs, apparently pleased with himself because the large, pompous words fill so many pages. He is not concerned with making the words say much. The writer of jargon says *the field of mathematics* rather than *mathematics, difficult in character or nature* rather than *difficult, in an intoxicated condition* rather than *drunk.* Favorite words of the jargon fancier include *case, factor, character, circumstances, conditions, situation, picture, line, persuasion, level, variety, degree, type, outstanding, worth-while.*

ORIGINAL

In the case of Jim, it was apparent that his condition was of a serious nature.

For reasons of safety, and in view of the circumstances which are unavoidably associated with the factors involved in a manufacturing enterprise, no young persons will be permitted within these premises if unaccompanied.

There were several instances where Hamlet could have put the quietus on the King, but he failed to come through because the situations were not applicable to the circumstances in his case.

REVISION

Jim was seriously ill.

For safety, no child under ten will be admitted without a parent or authorized guardian.
[*The words of the original say very little; they do not even proscribe two infants toddling in together. In the revision the words mean what they say.*]

On several occasions Hamlet could have taken revenge, but he wanted to kill Claudius in some act which would assure the King's going to hell.

A particular sort of jargonic writing has long been known as journalese because it reveals the flamboyant, careless superficiality which is characteristic of cheap journalism, though not of good newspaper writing. Avoid it by refusing to use words just to make an impression, by thinking clearly, and by endeavoring to say exactly what you think.

ORIGINAL

A new edition of State University hoopsters is slated to make its debut Saturday night to lift the curtain on the current hardwood season.
[*The trite substitutes for ordinary English do more to obscure than to brighten the passage.*]

REVISION

State University's basketball team will play its first game of the season Saturday night.
[*The revision may be flat sports writing, but the kind of journalese in the original does not give it life.*]

455

ORIGINAL (*Cont.*)

Four weary underground explorers dumbfounded their rain-stymied would-be rescuers last night by walking unheralded and unharmed out of the sub-Alpine "Hell's Hole" caverns where high water had trapped them for nine and one-half days.

REVISION (*Cont.*)

Four explorers, trapped in Alpine caverns by high water for nine and one-half days, reached safety unaided last night. Rain had prevented surface attempts at rescue.

26e WORDINESS   Wordy

Wordy writing is seldom wordy in only one way. Often a writer can revise a wordy passage best by thinking it through again from the beginning and trying to express the idea as simply and directly as possible. Good thinking, expressed in simple structures with carefully chosen words, will automatically remove wordiness.

WORDY

Although the story is in the supernatural class, Hawthorne manages to put over his point and show the effects on a person when he is confronted with the fact that everyone contains a certain amount of evil in their physical make-up.

CONCISE

Hawthorne uses the supernatural to suggest that there is some evil in everyone.
[*The original version was cluttered; with the verbiage cleared away, the writer can make the sentence direct and precise.*]

When someone is dead in a house it can always be seen that there is a change comes over you, there being so much to be done because of the death and the funeral and it is so sad. There is always quite a lot to do about the house, and then there is the adjustment factor because all of you have to get used to the situation of being without the dear one who was loved and is now gone forevermore.

The bustle in a house
The morning after death
Is solemnest of industries
Enacted upon earth,—

The sweeping up the heart
And putting love away
We shall not want to use again
Until eternity.
                    —EMILY DICKINSON

But if you get right down to the facts in the case, we cannot reorient this tract of real estate, nor can we determine what disposition is fated to be made in the future of this acreage fresh from God's hand, and last but not least we cannot render a decision as to whether or not this section of the earth's surface is to be employed for purposes other than those of the divine.

But in a larger sense, we cannot dedicate, we cannot consecrate, we cannot hallow this ground.
                    —ABRAHAM LINCOLN, "Gettysburg Address"

26f   REPETITION AND REDUNDANCY   Rep; Red

Repetition is often an effective device for emphasis, and it is often necessary. Repetition of a key word, for example, is preferable to the use of ostentatious synonyms. A paper on Shakespeare is bound to repeat words like *drama* or *play* or *Shakespeare,* and to avoid repeating the author's name with clichés like *the Bard* or *the Swan of Avon* is more obvious than the repetition. Careless repetition, however, particularly of easily noticed expressions, makes writing wordy and amateurish. Moreover, repetition of words is often a symptom of some fundamental weakness, of faulty sentence structure, of inadequate subordination, for example (see 15a).

ORIGINAL

Goldwyn added a little more spice by putting the beautiful girl in Walter's dreams. The girl made the play a little more interesting. He made the story move by adding comedy, and the people were a little more satisfied when they left the theatre. [*Repetition of* a little *in three successive sentences suggests language poverty.*]

REVISION

Goldwyn added spice and interest to the play by putting the beautiful girl in Walter's dreams. He made the story move by adding comedy, and the people were a little more satisfied when they left the theatre. [*The qualification in* a little *probably is not needed at all. Certainly its first two uses can be dropped.*]

Users of the library often use little care in handling books.

Users of the library often are careless in handling books.

He announced that if anyone wanted to argue that he should wait until the next meeting.

He announced that if anyone wanted to argue he should wait until the next meeting.

Excess words, especially those which double the meaning of neighboring words, are called redundant, and are usually the results of careless repetition or of inadequate knowledge of the full meanings of the words used. *Repeat again, continue on, return back,* and *diametrically opposite* are common examples of redundancy.

ORIGINAL

He was the first originator of the theory that we all now unanimously

REVISION

He originated the theory, now unanimously accepted, that under-

ORIGINAL (*Cont.*)

accept that understanding should be substituted in the place of punishment.

REVISION (*Cont.*)

standing should replace punishment. [*The following of the original are redundant:* first, originator, all, unanimously, substituted, in the place of.]

In this modern day and age of the present, one can never return back to the old methods of home industry of earlier times.

One cannot return to old methods of home industry.

That night the Badgers won their fourteenth straight victory without a defeat.

That night the Badgers won their fourteenth straight victory.

To these early, primeval inventors like Lenoir and Gurney we owe our modern, high-powered cars of today.

We owe the modern automobile to early inventors like Lenoir and Gurney.

26g   WORDINESS AND HUMOR   Humor

Like almost anything else, wordiness can be turned to humor. The American pioneer was amused by a word he devised, *segastuate,* by which he meant walk. In place of *someone had jimmied the kitchen window,* the following might conceivably be amusing: *It became apparent a party or parties unknown had gained entrance to the culinary regions by means of that instrument of ingress commonly known as a "jimmy."* Usually, however, the use of circumlocutions in the hope that overblown words will be funny leads only to boredom. A writer should use the device with the greatest caution.

WORDY

The tuneful canine when you hear him yodeling his native woodnotes wild in the dead of night, reminds one of the gentlemen of the press; to put it mildly they can sound like the last trumpet on the day of judgment.

CONCISE

Dogs are born journalists; their voices are like extras of dismay.
                        —CHRISTOPHER MORLEY

EXERCISE 26

A. Discuss the suitability of the italicized expressions in the following sentences for (a) campus conversation, (b) informal composition, and (c) formal composition.

1. My *girl-friend* knows so little about football she *thinks* "clipping" is charging six *bucks* for seats in the end zone.

2. A *stolid,* bald-headed gentleman was *staring* at me as though he thought he was *acquainted with* me, but was not *quite* certain.

3. *Here's* the *deal,* and you can *take it from me, it's a dilly.*

4. Whatever you want, she is *liable* to want something *of a different nature,* like *movieing* while you want to *shoot the breeze.*

5. *Irregardless* of my mother's warnings, I decided to *date* him.

6. I was so *enthused I figured I'd contact 'em first off.*

7. I *suggest* the *inclusion* of this *data* on the *agendas.*

8. She was *cute,* all right, but, *last but not least,* I *suspicioned* she *wasn't* the *swell dame* she was *cracked up to be.*

9. A *great number* of onlookers *blamed* the accident *on* Jim.

10. Maybe it's *okay lecturewise,* but *man,* I don't *dig* it.

B. The words listed below were once used in this country, but they were slang or colloquial and have now largely disappeared. Try to make a sentence with any you think you know. Then check your meanings against the meanings given in the *Dictionary of Americanisms.* The number after each word indicates the usage; for instance, *cutter, 2,* would refer to the second meaning of the word, "a device for checking a wagon going downhill."

1. out-Cherokee (under *Cherokee, v.*)
2. gorilla, 2
3. female tom
4. smoke, 3
5. muffy
6. rackabone (4 under *rack*)
7. monocrat
8. shell, 1
9. Hudson Dusters
10. bank whig, 2 (29)

Try to make up a list of similar words which you hear your companions use but which will probably not be understood in fifty years.

C. Substitute fresher, more expressive terms for the trite expressions in the sentences below. You may find that you must use more revealing words than those in the original, since trite expressions often become very nearly meaningless.

1. I slept like a log, and woke up at the crack of dawn, fresh as a daisy.

2. With her hair a sable cloud about her face, her peaches-and-cream complexion, her ruby lips, and her eyes like stars, she was as pretty as a picture.

3. Martha was a perfect baby, as happy as the day is long.

4. The wily southpaw zipped a fast one over the corner, and the old speed king had done it again. You can't hit 'em if you can't see 'em.

5. The last examination had put me out like a light, and accordingly, although I was down in the dumps—it was blue Monday for me— I determined to burn the midnight oil.

6. Crime never pays and true Americanism requires that we stamp it out, each and every time a crime wave raises its ugly head in this great and glorious land of ours.

7. And last but not least, in advertising you have to sell yourself; that is, to make it short and sweet, you have to hit the market smack on the nose.

8. We would willingly point with pride at the progress onward and upward in this land of the free; we have no inclination to drag a red herring across the trail to becloud the issue; but any lover of government of the people, by the people, for the people must view with alarm the state of the nation in this day and age, and unless we go back to the principles of the founding fathers, we are in grave danger of having our cherished liberties gone with the wind.

9. He took the unwelcome news like a man. He became sober as a judge, but I knew he was true as steel, all wool and a yard wide, and that he would snap out of it.

10. He was tall, dark, and handsome, with lean flanks and piercing eyes, always smelling faintly of good English tobacco and well-oiled leather, every inch a man's man.

D. Remove redundant words and phrases from the following:

1. It was the consensus of opinion that the statements were directly antithetical.

2. Her rendition was absolutely perfect.

3. While the nations work against one another, the presence of war is constantly at hand.

4. We hold diametrically opposite views on most questions.

5. My mother, she thought I ought to go to the cheaper college, but the differences in cost were infinitesimally small.

6. The way this story was written made it seem to make me feel that it could really have actually happened to me.

7. A girl should be able to make a living in her special particular line.

8. In spite of all the illegal crimes he had committed, the leader of the gang went entirely scot-free.

9. It is the one and only unique sacred white Burmese camel in the United States.

10. Formerly in the olden days the girls of the parish had to crawl through a small stone window to prove they had behaved themselves.

E. The passages below are wordy, many of them because they contain jargon. Rewrite them, making the sense clear in good English, if the passage suggests any sense. Some sentences may mean almost nothing, for blanket terms characteristically fill space with words, not with meaning. If a sentence has no discoverable meaning, write a sentence which says what you imagine the writer may have intended to say.

1. Though the evidence in the case seems to be that the crisis has passed and the Giants are over the hump of the slump that cost them great gobs of ground in the pennant chase, the Giant high command did not permit the chinks in the Giant armor turned up by the losing skid to go unnoticed. Quietly, behind the scenes, they are attempting to mend their fences, and you may be sure they will leave no stone unturned in their effort to batten down the hatches.

2. Another advantage of the cow is her ability to relax, and humans would be better off if they had this fundamental feature.

3. In this day and age the problem of drinking intoxicating beverages has had a much freer scope in recent years than was the case at an earlier period in time.

4. The person in search of worth-while science fiction material can find the basic circumstances at every facet of modern literature.

5. Some critics commented on his lecture to the highest degree.

6. Everybody should be capable of practicing in some line of work. Being able to support yourself is very important in this respect.

7. Although this may not be the over-all case, it does include the majority of advertisements, and the factors in the movement are to the extreme.

8. Reading—the anesthetic of a tired mind; the broadening of one's educational frame of reference; the opening of new and unfound fields of thought; a must in everyone's life.

9. The big day rolled around, but Hamlet, who had the inclination for abruptness of action, curbed his burning desires, and therefore slowness of action resulted.

10. I told her that if she wouldn't get on the beam and stop blowing up the insignificant factors in the case she had better get out of the picture.

Mechanics

At this moment the King, who had been for some time busily writing
in his note-book, called out "Silence!" and read out from his book
"Rule Forty-two. All Persons more than a mile high to leave the
court."

Everybody looked at Alice.

"I'm not a mile high," said Alice.

"You are," said the King.

"Nearly two miles high," added the Queen.

"Well, I sha'n't go, at any rate," said Alice: "besides, that's not a
regular rule: you invented it just now."

"*It's the oldest rule in the book,*" *said the King.*

—*Lewis Carroll,* Alice's Adventures in Wonderland

An oriental guest, to be polite, takes off his shoes, and after the
meal, belches. An American guest takes off his hat and refrains from
belching. The conventions differ.

Many of the mechanical aspects of composition are conventional, and
conventional only. Many of the "rules" represent codified good sense,
what Alice thought of as "regular rules." Others smack of the judicial
processes of the King of Hearts, but whether or not they are now "the
oldest rules in the book," they have been established by convention, and
conventions are necessary for clear communication. Ignoring conventions
may even be dangerous. Anyone in this country who consistently drives
on the left-hand side of the road will not stay long out of jail, a hospital,
or the morgue. Anyone who drives on the right-hand side in England is
in similar danger. A writer who fails to follow certain conventions, though
he may be physically safe, is in danger of being misunderstood.

Furthermore, although the mechanical conventions surrounding writing
are not the only conventions possible, sound reason stands behind each
of them, and *in toto* they offer the writer useful standardized devices.
Typed copy is double spaced because double-spaced copy is easier to read
than single-spaced copy and because it allows room for editing. Margins
are preferred because a crowded page looks messy. Manuscripts are written on one side of the paper because pages which must be turned over
lead to confusion and costly errors. Our conventions of capitalization are

not the only possible ones; German capitalizes all nouns and Spanish capitalizes no proper adjectives, but our system has its uses. With it, one can distinguish at once an *opal* from *Opal, Hamlet* from a *hamlet*. Our system of punctuation permits the writer to make his meaning immediately and sharply clear, and he can do so because conventions are standardized and recognized. There is a difference between "The man who customarily wears a beret. . . ." and "The man, who customarily wears a beret, . . ." although the difference is made clear by nothing but commas. The conventions of writing and the mechanics which embody these conventions help a writer because they put useful tools into his hands.

Almost all publishers and many publications have style sheets which cover matters of manuscript form, punctuation, capitalization, and even spelling; they include details of style which are too specialized to be covered by general rules. For instance, a builder's manual may have a style sheet including special punctuation for unusual measurements; bibliographies often have special style sheets which permit elaborate abbreviation of the information concerning the format of a book; a chemistry-journal style sheet will include abbreviations for compounds; newspapers record details of their style in stylebooks. For details of style not covered below, *A Manual of Style,* prepared by the staff of the University of Chicago Press (Chicago, 1949), has been standard practically since the first edition appeared in 1906. John Benbow, *Manuscript and Proof* (New York, 1943), is the manual for the American Oxford University Press. Useful for technical work is the *United States Government Printing Office Style Manual* (Washington, D.C., 1953); it is frequently revised.

The following chapters discuss punctuation and details of manuscript form and spelling.

27

Punctuation

For Guide to Revision, see page 469

Punctation marks clarify meaning and structure.

In *A Midsummer Night's Dream,* Shakespeare introduces a play produced by some well-meaning but ignorant people, with a prologue read as though it were punctuated as follows:

> If we offend, it is with our good will.
> That you should think, we come not to offend,
> But with good will. To show our simple skill,
> That is the true beginning of our end.
> Consider then we come but in despite.
> We do not come as minding to content you,
> Our true intent is. All for your delight
> We are not here. That you should here repent you
> The actors are at hand, and by their show
> You shall know all that you are like to know.

Some of this makes no sense, and some bad sense. Certainly the actors had not come to make the audience repent their attendance. Repunctuated, the passage is more appropriate.

> If we offend, it is with our good will.
> That, you should think. We come not to offend,
> But with good will to show our simple skill.
> That is the true beginning. Of our end,
> Consider then. We come. But in despite
> We do not come. As minding to content you,
> Our true intent is all for your delight.
> We are not here that you should here repent you.
> The actors are at hand, and by their show
> You shall know all that you are like to know.

Not every passage can be changed so much as can this by mispunctuation, but good punctuation can make meaning certain and reading more rapid.

27-1 STYLES IN PUNCTUATION

Until a century or so ago, punctuation in English was primarily rhetorical; that is, marks or "points" were stage directions for speaking, indicating where pauses of greater or lesser duration might occur in speech. In modern English, punctuation has become more standardized, working largely in a set of relatively consistent patterns to clarify meaning or help mark the grammatical structure of the sentence. The writer follows principles which make punctuation marks function almost as parts of common sentence patterns—for example, the comma used before *and* or *but* between independent clauses. Modern punctuation is not mainly a matter of marking the length of "pauses," although pauses and pitch changes clarify grammatical patterns in speech much as punctuation does in writing. Pauses and punctuation marks, therefore, often coincide, and often the student can get help with punctuation problems by considering how his expression would be pronounced. For example, the question of whether or not to put commas around a modifier can often be decided by considering how the sentence would be pronounced to convey the intended meaning. Consider:

> The two newspapers which had been competing for morning circulation were closed by the strike.

The writer thinking of the *which*-clause as restrictive would pronounce the sentence with no significant pause after *newspapers* and with rising inflection on *circulation;* he would use no commas. Thinking of the clause as non-restrictive, he would in speaking pause longer after *newspapers* and would pronounce *newspapers* with rising inflection on the first syllable; he would use commas before and after the clause to signal its non-restrictive meaning.

Even though practices in punctuation are less arbitrary today than they once were, when they depended greatly on the whim of the writer or even the convenience of the printer, fashions still vary—from writer to writer, country to country, and time to time. Some writers, for example, use a comma whenever there is the slightest chance that its inclusion might clarify; others punctuate more lightly, omitting marks whenever they can without obvious danger of being misunderstood. Some poets have sought particular effects by omitting punctuation or by using it in unusual ways. Some newspapers insist on a comma before the *and* in a series, some do not; book publishers generally use it. Books printed in England commonly have no period after *Mr;* books printed in America do. Writing being as flexible as it is, and human minds being as various and variable as they are, punctuation practice is not likely to be completely stable.

27-2 PUNCTUATION AND THE SENTENCE PATTERN

Nevertheless, punctuation of standard English expository prose is sufficiently standardized to make clear punctuation relatively easy. With some understanding of how punctuation works, some understanding of the meaning of punctuation marks, and understanding of a few statements that describe major uses of punctuation, the student can mark his writing with little trouble. To begin with, he needs to observe that punctuation is mainly confined to the four following general uses, most of them designed to help the reader focus attention on the main sentence pattern.

(1) Punctuation marks the ends of main sentence patterns—of sentences or of independent clauses in sentences. The period, question mark, and exclamation mark, with different meanings, indicate the ends of complete sentences. The semicolon, and sometimes the colon or dash or comma, indicate secondary breaks, breaks between independent clauses within the sentence.

(2) Punctuation tends to preserve the flow from subject to verb to complement by setting apart any elements which interrupt the thought of the pattern—non-restrictive modifiers, parenthetical expressions, and the like. Usually the comma is used for such purposes, although semicolons, dashes, and parentheses sometimes mark sharper separations.

(3) Punctuation separates co-ordinate elements not sufficiently separated by function words. Usually commas are sufficient for such separation, but sometimes a semicolon is used (see 27d).

(4) Punctuation has a number of conventional uses—to clarify statistical material, to mark bibliographical materials, to identify quotations, and so on. Most of these uses have been established by custom and are mechanical habits or traditions to be learned.

27-3 MARKS OF PUNCTUATION

The following marks are used in punctuation in English; their major uses are described in this chapter in connection with the discussions of particular punctuation problems.

. The *period* marks the ends of sentences not to be distinguished as questions or exclamations (see 27a). It has also a few conventional uses, mainly to mark abbreviations.

? The *question mark* (interrogation point) is used at the end of a direct question—not an indirect one (see 27a).

! The *exclamation mark* is used at the end of a complete or incomplete sentence to indicate strong emotion or feeling.

: The *colon* has mainly conventional uses, especially to introduce formal lists (see 27k); it sometimes separates independent clauses (see 27b).

; The *semicolon* mainly separates independent clauses (see 27b), although it sometimes separates items in series (see 27d).

, The *comma* is the most common punctuation mark in English, with a wide variety of uses.

— The *dash,* made with two hyphens on the typewriter, sometimes marks sharp breaks between clauses and sometimes sets off parenthetical material more sharply than a comma would.

" " *Quotation marks* enclose direct quotations, words reproduced as spoken or written.

( ) *Parentheses* have mainly conventional uses, but they also sometimes mark material to be sharply set apart within the sentence.

[ ] *Brackets* mainly have conventional uses to set off inserted materials. Since standard typewriters usually do not have brackets, brackets should be inserted by hand in typed material or made with the diagonal and underlining bars.

. . . The *ellipsis,* three periods, marks an omission, usually from quoted matter (see 27a).

27 P

PUNCTUATION

Guide to Revision

Use punctuation to reveal the sentence pattern and to clarify according to conventions.

Punctuation can be difficult; details of some conventional punctuation can be complex. But punctuation usually follows regular patterns and the following statements describe common punctuation patterns.

27a   END PUNCTUATION; PERIOD FAULT   P1; . ? !

Structurally the period is the most important device for punctuation, since it marks the end of any sentence not to be distinguished as a question or an exclamation. Use of a period to mark an expression not a complete sentence, sometimes called the *period fault,* usually reveals a basic error in sentence structure, the use of an inappropriate sentence fragment (see 12). Usually, also, the *run-together* or *fused* sentence grows from more serious trouble than mere lack of a period (see 27b).

The period is used after an indirect question, in which the question is not phrased verbatim but is part of a statement.

I asked her, "Will you go?" (*Direct question*)
I asked her if she would go. (*Indirect question*)

ORIGINAL

The question was whether Morgan would attack the center or make the long detour around Old Baldy and attack on the flank?
[*The indirect question should be followed by a period. If the question were put directly, it would be followed by a question mark.*]

QUOTATION WITH OMISSIONS

(1) The question was whether Morgan would attack the center or make the long detour around Old Baldy and attack on the flank.
(2) The question was this: would Morgan attack the center, or would he make the long detour around Old Baldy and attack on the flank?

Three consecutive periods (. . .) make a punctuation mark known as the ellipsis, inserted in the place of material omitted from a quotation. When the omission comes after a completed sentence or completes a sentence, the period needed to mark the end of the sentence is retained. In such instances, therefore, four consecutive periods appear.

ORIGINAL

Genius is the activity which repairs the decays of things, whether wholly or partly of a material and finite kind. Nature, through all her kingdoms, insures herself.

—RALPH WALDO EMERSON

REVISION

Genius is the activity which repairs the decays of things. . . . Nature . . . insures herself.

—RALPH WALDO EMERSON

The period is used, also, after most abbreviations: p.m., Mr., pp., Ave., St., U. S. A., ibid., A. D. Any good dictionary will include abbreviations in the word list or in a special section.

EXCEPTION: The period is not used after letters standing for recently created government bureaus: NLRB, CAP, ANZUS; after letters which represent scholarly or technical journals: PMLA, CA, MLR; after letters of radio stations: KLRB, WUISB, KATO; after MS (plural, MSS) for *manuscript;* certain unions and associations: WAA, AEF, CIO.

The question mark is placed after a direct question. It is not used after an indirect question.

ORIGINAL

By Sunday I could stand no more, and I said, "Aren't you ever going to leave."

Perhaps I was not very polite, but what could I do.

REVISION

By Sunday I could stand no more, and I said, "Aren't you ever going to leave?"

Perhaps I was not very polite, but what could I do?

The question mark is occasionally used after inserted interrogative material.

Anyone who loves his country—and who does not?—will answer a call to duty.

The question mark is used, sometimes in parentheses, to indicate that a fact is approximate or questionable, especially a date.

> *The Play of the Weather* (1533?) continues the convention. John Heywood, 1497(?)–1580(?), wrote the play.

Used as an attempted witticism or to mark sarcasm, the question mark is out of fashion and likely to appear amateurish.

> The next motion showed how wise (?) [*better omitted*] the committee really was.

A request or command which for politeness is phrased as a question may conclude with either a question mark or a period.

> Will you please sign and return the enclosed voucher? *or* . . . voucher.

The exclamation mark indicates emotion or feelings. It is seldom used except in reporting conversation, particularly after interjections like *Ouch! Murder!* Some beginning writers endeavor to make their composition more exciting by liberal use of exclamation marks. This device seldom works. Any prose which is so feeble that it must be propped up with punctuation had best be revised. Modern practice is to use the exclamation mark sparingly.

ORIGINAL

REVISION

"Help," she screamed. "My dress, in the cogs."
[*If the girl finds herself being dragged into power machinery, she may well be excited enough to warrant a few exclamation marks.*]

"Help!" she screamed. "My dress! In the cogs!"
[*The revision does not bolster weak prose; it makes clear at once the drama of the sentences.*]

And then! Just think! Out of the cocoon came a pale green luna moth! And still damp!!!
[*This is overblown. It may please children, but scarcely adults.*]

And then, out of the cocoon came a pale green luna moth, still damp.
[*The use of two or three exclamation marks together is best confined to comic books.*]

27b   INDEPENDENT CLAUSES; FUSED OR RUN-TOGETHER SENTENCE;
         COMMA FAULT OR SPLICE   P2; RT; CF; CS

Independent clauses, independent sentence patterns, are usually separated in one of three ways:

(1) They are marked with periods as separate sentences (see 27a).

(2) They are joined in a single sentence but separated by a semi-colon.

> We always like those who admire us; we do not always like those whom we admire.
> Man is certainly stark mad; he cannot make a worm, and yet he will be making gods by dozens.

(3) They are joined in a single sentence by a co-ordinating conjunction (*and, but, for, or, nor, yet, so*), with a comma preceding it (see 27c).

> Statesmen are not only liable to give an account of what they say or do in public, *but* there is a busy inquiry made into their very meals, beds, marriages, and every other sportive or serious action.

Notice that the semicolon is used even when the second clause is introduced by a connective like *hence, then, therefore, however, nevertheless, in fact,* or *moreover.*

> I do not have a taste for caviar; however, I should like to be able to afford to develop one.

Short, closely related clauses, especially when they appear in a series, are sometimes joined with only a comma.

> The rain falls constantly, the river continues to rise.
> The camera rolls back, the boom moves out, the water ripples gently, and the only one now to make a move outside the lighted circle is the man with the little fog can and the fan.

Occasionally, a colon separates independent clauses when the second clause specifies or exemplifies the idea of the first (see 27k).

A sentence in which independent clauses are joined without punctuation is sometimes called a *run-together* or *fused* sentence. Use of a comma between clauses when a semicolon or period is needed is sometimes called a *comma fault* or *comma splice.* The error usually involves more serious troubles than punctuation; it is a symptom that sentence patterns do not adequately relate ideas. Correction requires more than addition of a semicolon; it requires rewriting, often reducing one independent clause to a subordinate element.

ORIGINAL

The children tore the stuffed stockings from the mantel then they crept quickly back to bed.

[*The clauses can be made separate sentences, or separated with a semicolon (1); one clause can be subordinated (2); or one subject can be removed and the verb in the clause made part of a compound verb (3).*]

The hawk circled gracefully for a moment it seemed unaware of the scurrying chicks below.

The two boys cleared away the brush, then they pitched their tent and spread out their blankets.

[*The comma does not indicate a large enough break to signal the beginning of a new statement. The sentence can be revised by supplying a semicolon (1), by making one element dependent (2), or by constructing a single clause (3).*]

Talking is like playing on the harp, there is as much in laying the hand on the strings to stop their vibration as in twanging them to bring out their music.

He had been, he said, a most unconscionable time dying, however he hoped they would excuse it.

[*A conjunctive adverb* (however, moreover, therefore, then, hence) *is a modifier and does not obviate the need for a semicolon to separate the clauses.*]

REVISION

(1) The children tore the stuffed stockings from the mantel; then they crept quickly back to bed.

(2) After the children had torn the stuffed stockings from the mantel, they crept quickly back to bed.

(3) The children tore the stuffed stockings from the mantel and then crept quickly back to bed.

The hawk circled gracefully; for a moment it seemed unaware of the scurrying chicks below.

(1) The two boys cleared away the brush; then they pitched their tent and spread out their blankets.

(2) After they had cleared away the brush, the two boys pitched their tent and spread out their blankets.

(3) The two boys cleared away the brush, pitched their tent, and spread out their blankets.

Talking is like playing on the harp; there is as much in laying the hand on the strings to stop their vibrations as in twanging them to bring out their music.

(1) He had been, he said, a most unconscionable time dying; however, he hoped that they would excuse it.

(2) He had been, he said, a most unconscionable time dying; he hoped, however, that they would excuse it.

[*For position of the conjunctive adverb see 15b.*]

27c   INDEPENDENT CLAUSES WITH CO-ORDINATING CONJUNCTIONS   P3

Even when independent clauses have a co-ordinating conjunction (*and, but, for, or, nor, yet, so*) linking them, they are separated by a comma, which signals that a new clause is beginning rather than the presence of a compound complement or verb. Notice that in the following sentence the reader would momentarily misunderstand if the comma were omitted.

She fed all the peanuts to the elephant, and the monkey had to be satisfied with popcorn.

Without the comma the reader would miss the structure of the sentence until he came to the second verb, thinking momentarily that the monkey had shared the peanuts.

ORIGINAL

Jack had been brought up on golf and tennis held no interest for him.
[*Until he reaches* held, *the reader is not aware that a new clause begins with* tennis; *he assumes as he reads that Jack was brought up on both games.*]

REVISION

(1) Jack had been brought up on golf, and tennis held no interest for him.
[*Supply the comma.*]
(2) Since Jack had been brought up on golf, tennis held no interest for him.
[*Make one clause dependent.*]

The comma is not usual unless the conjunction introduces a clause; if it joins two verbs or complements the pattern is usually clear without punctuation (see 27n).

Jack spent his mornings playing golf and his afternoons playing tennis.

When long or complex clauses containing commas within them are joined, a semicolon is often needed along with a co-ordinating conjunction to mark the main division in the sentence.

ORIGINAL

Men have sworn at one another from earliest times, according to a Chinese classic on profanity, and to abstain from this natural exercise of the tongue is unhealthful but since elaborate swearing requires high intellectual ability, the ordinary swearer is cautioned to consider moderation.
[*Complicated clauses, containing commas within them, are joined here without punctuation.*]

REVISION

Men have sworn at one another from earliest times, according to a Chinese classic on profanity, and to abstain from this natural exercise of the tongue is unhealthful; but since elaborate swearing requires high intellectual ability, the ordinary swearer is cautioned to consider moderation.
[*A semicolon is needed to point out the major division of the sentence.*]

27d   PUNCTUATION IN A SERIES   **P4**

Commas separate words, phrases, dependent clauses, and sometimes very brief independent clauses (see 27b) when they are co-ordinated in a series of three or more.

She announced that she was staying in bed until noon, that she was not cooking lunch for anybody, and that she would decide later about dinner.

Some newspapers do not require a comma before *and* (*lettuce, endive and celery*), but most publishers and writers of standard English prefer the comma before *and* (*lettuce, endive, and celery*) on the ground that the omission of the comma is occasionally confusing.

Their menu includes the following: veal steak, roast beef, pork chops, ham and eggs.

She purchased the following: veal, beef, pork, ham, and eggs.

In the first sentence the reader may be uncertain whether or not the eggs are fried with the ham.

If all the items in a series are joined by connectives, no punctuation is needed (*lettuce and endive and celery*).

ORIGINAL

We distinguished highways, roads, trails, streets and alleys.
[*Acceptable in some informal writing; usually not preferred in standard English.*]

She planted stocks zinnias and delphiniums.

REVISION

We distinguished highways, roads, trails, streets, and alleys.

She planted stocks, zinnias, and delphiniums.

A combination like *bread and butter* within a series is treated as one element of the series.

ORIGINAL

We considered the following subjects: criticism, science, medical, and dental surgery, education, and educators, and law, and the courts.

REVISION

We considered the following subjects: criticism, science, medical and dental surgery, education and educators, and law and the courts.

Consecutive modifiers that tend to modify individually rather than to combine as a composite modifier form a series and are usually separated by commas. Compare:

The streetcar had badly constructed, old-fashioned seats.

The streetcar had grimy cane seats.

In the first, the adjectives seem to modify *seats* independently. As a rough test, insert the word *and* between them and see if the construction still produces a familiar pattern. If it does, as in *badly constructed and old-fashioned seats,* the modifiers are probably in series. In the second, however, *grimy* seems to modify all that follows it; the modifiers do not work independently in a series. *Grimy and cane seats* does not fill a familiar pattern for modifiers. As another rough test, reverse the order of the modifiers. Those in series can be logically reversed, *old-fashioned badly constructed seats;* those not in series cannot, *cane grimy seats.*

Numerals and common adjectives of size, color, and age seldom appear in series:

> Twenty-four scrawny blackbirds; two little girls; a spry old man; a pretty little girl

ORIGINAL

I canned dozens of gleaming many-colored jars of fruit.
[*The modifiers are in series;* and *could sensibly be put between them.*]

He bought a worn, old horse.
[Worn *and* old *do not modify separately.*]

The only available room was a dirty, vermin-infested, sleeping porch.
[Dirty *and* vermin-infested *modify in series, but* sleeping *is not part of the series.*]

REVISION

I canned dozens of gleaming, many-colored jars of fruit.
[*A comma should separate the items of the series.*]

He bought a worn old horse.

The only available room was a dirty, vermin-infested sleeping porch.
[*Only the two items in series are separated; each of them modifies* sleeping porch.]

The semicolon also substitutes for the comma to divide items in a series or list when the items are complicated and contain punctuation within them.

ORIGINAL

She told me that, in view of my prejudices, my poor health, and my interests, I would never be happy as a teacher, that I would find myself, at the end of a day, exhausted from policing dozens of squirming children,

REVISION

She told me that, in view of my prejudices, my poor health, and my interests, I never would be happy as a teacher; that I would find myself, at the end of the day, exhausted from policing dozens of squirming children;

ORIGINAL (*Cont.*)

and that I would find my evenings, during which I hoped to practice music, given over to school plays, the school band and orchestra, and playing command canasta with the superintendent's wife.

[*Since the sentence is long and involved, and broken only by commas, the reader has difficulty seeing at once the organization.*]

The Council included the following representatives: President John A. Rickert, administration, Professor George P. Barrows, faculty, Avery Warren, student council, and Janice Worley, W. A. A.

REVISION (*Cont.*)

and that I would find my evenings, during which I hoped to practice music, given over to school plays, the school band and orchestra, and playing command canasta with the superintendent's wife.

[*Semicolons separate the three dependent clauses, and mark the main divisions of the sentence.*]

The Council included the following representatives: President John A. Rickert, administration; Professor George P. Barrows, faculty; Avery Warren, student council; and Janice Worley, W. A. A.

27e PUNCTUATION OF NONRESTRICTIVE MODIFIERS   P5

When modifiers limit closely, especially when they supply the information that identifies or distinguishes subject or complement, they are called restrictive and are not set off by punctuation. Modifiers not essential to the subject-verb-complement combination, which supply incidental information (as this clause does), are called *nonrestrictive,* and must be set off by punctuation. Compare:

All the children who were in the front row received ice cream.
All the children, who were in the front row, received ice cream.

First of all, read the two sentences aloud. As we read the first, we raise the pitch of our voice on *row* and tend to pause after it. As we read the second, we raise pitch on the main syllable of *children,* drop it on *row,* and pause after both *children* and *row.* That is, we distinguish restrictive and nonrestrictive in speech by intonation. We can tell which are nonrestrictive by thinking how they sound and the punctuation helps us see how they should sound. The punctuation in writing reveals the meaning as the sound patterns do in speech. Both the sound and the punctuation show that the first sentence suggests that of all of the children assembled only certain lucky ones, those in the front row, were treated; *who were in the front row,* without commas, is read as restrictive. It restricts or limits children to the group it names, specifies certain children. The second sentence says that all the children received ice cream. The clause is nonrestrictive, as the commas indicate.

Sometimes, as in the sentences above, modifiers can be interpreted as either restrictive or nonrestrictive, but usually the modifiers make sense with only one kind of punctuation. A nonrestrictive modifier can be recognized because it can be dropped out of the sentence without distortion of the main meaning.

> The old house, badly out of repair, was hard to sell.

Omission of *badly out of repair* would not change the central idea of the sentence. But compare:

> An old house badly out of repair is not a good bargain.

Badly out of repair is required as part of the subject; it cannot be omitted without shifting the meaning. Punctuation on only one side of a nonrestrictive modifier is especially confusing because it separates essential parts of the main sentence pattern.

Following are some of the types of modifiers that are commonly nonrestrictive and therefore require commas:

(1) *Appositive modifiers*

> My brother, chairman of the board, opposed the stock issue.

Chairman of the board adds incidental information but is not essential to the subject-verb-object pattern. Sometimes, however, an appositive does restrict the subject and is not separated.

> My brother John is chairman of the board.

John specifies which brother, restricts *brother*.

(2) *Verbal modifiers*

> The catcher, having played twelve innings, was glad to be taken from the game.

(3) *Adjectives following the words they modify*

> The three books, dirty and charred, were all he saved from the fire.

ORIGINAL

I bought the material, that Mother had picked out.
[*The modifier identifies or defines the material; it is restrictive.*]

That evening which has always seemed the most terrifying of my life the dining room ceiling fell on us.
[*The modifier is not essential; it adds incidental information and is nonrestrictive.*]

My grandmother, who still had a powerful voice went to the door and shouted.
[*The subject,* grandmother, *is separated from the verb, and the modifier is not set off.*]

The meal badly cooked and awkwardly served was a failure.

We started running for the express station which was still several blocks ahead.
[*The punctuation is accurate only if the clause identifies one station of at least two.*]

She was the aunt, who had given me the turquoise earrings.

REVISION

I bought the material that Mother had picked out.
[*The restrictive use of the modifier is clear without punctuation.*]

That evening, which has always seemed the most terrifying of my life, the dining room ceiling fell on us.
[*The nonrestrictive modifier must be punctutated to set it apart from the main parts of the sentence.*]

My grandmother, who still had a powerful voice, went to the door and shouted.
[*Commas should appear both before and after the nonrestrictive modifier.*]

The meal, badly cooked and awkwardly served, was a failure.

We started running for the express station, which was still several blocks ahead.
[*In most contexts, the clause would be nonrestrictive.*]

She was the aunt who had given me the turquoise earrings.

Qualifying clauses, especially those beginning with *although,* are often non-restrictive even when they follow the main clause. When they are non-restrictive, they are usually set off by a comma; when they are restrictive, they are not punctuated.

ORIGINAL

Aunt Agnes dyed her hair, painted her eyelashes, and plucked her brows although she always wore shoe-length dresses.
[*The* although-*clause had best be set off with a comma.*]

I went, because I had to.
[*In most contexts the* because-*clause would be intended as restrictive.*]

REVISION

Aunt Agnes dyed her hair, painted her eyelashes, and plucked her brows, although she always wore shoe-length dresses.

I went because I had to.
[*The comma is unnecessary.*]

Notice, however, that even this *because*-modifier might be nonrestrictive in some contexts:

> "Did you go to the picnic?" "I went, because I had to."

The modifying clause supplies additional information, not that required to answer the question. Notice again that intonation supplies a practical clue; when the word before the modifier would be accented in speech and followed by a fairly clear pause, the sentence is likely to require a comma to indicate that the modifier is nonrestrictive. When no special accent falls on the word before the modifier and the main stress of the sentence is on the verb of the modifying clause, the modifier is probably restrictive.

27f   PUNCTUATING PARENTHETICAL MATERIAL   P6

Parenthetical expressions, which are usually nonrestrictive modifiers, should have punctuation before and after them to set them apart from the main movement of the sentence. General modifiers of the sentence like *of course, for example, that is, however, indeed,* and *in conclusion* need such punctuation unless they modify restrictively.

> He decided, however, not to throw the pie.
> The cape, as the illustration shows, reaches nearly to the ground.

When such modifiers are not set off with punctuation both before and after the modifier, the main pattern of the sentence may be obscured.

ORIGINAL

Dancing slippers of course are not very useful for a tramp through the woods.
[Of course *is parenthetical.*]

Politicians, generally speaking consider the desires of their constituents.
[*The expression must have punctuation both before and after.*]

The discussion is, indeed, silly.
[*The punctuation is not wrong, but it probably sets off the modifier more than necessary.*]

REVISION

Dancing slippers, of course, are not very useful for a tramp through the woods.
[*The parenthetical expression is set apart by commas.*]

Politicians, generally speaking, consider the desires of their constituents.

The discussion is indeed silly.
[*Probably the writer intends* indeed *to modify* silly *only, not to be parenthetical.*]

Parenthetical expressions which interrupt sharply or dramatically or which are not grammatically a part of the sentence are sometimes set off by dashes (see 27 l), or parentheses (see 27m).

27g   PUNCTUATION AFTER INTRODUCTORY MODIFIERS   P7

Introductory modifying clauses and other long or complicated modifiers are set off from the rest of the sentence by commas. The punctuation is especially necessary, even with a short modifier, if the reader might otherwise have difficulty identifying the point at which the modifier stops.

ORIGINAL

Before we had finished eating the salad and the fish were snatched away from us.
[*A comma would prevent momentary misunderstanding.*]

By daylight, we could find our way.
[*The comma does no harm, but the introductory modifier is short enough to make it unnecessary.*]

In the morning light filtered through the chinks in the ceiling.
[*Even though the modifier is short, the comma is needed to prevent misunderstanding.*]

Accordingly I resigned.
[*The introductory element is brief, but it is set off in meaning, and would be set off in reading.*]

Being without money and knowing no one in the town we slept on a park bench.

REVISION

Before we had finished eating, the salad and the fish were snatched away from us.
[*The comma marks the end of the modifier.*]

By daylight we could find our way.

In the morning, light filtered through the chinks in the ceiling.
[*The comma separates the two words which might otherwise be linked by their meanings.*]

Accordingly, I resigned.
[*The comma is preferable.*]

Being without money and knowing no one in the town, we slept on a park bench.

Often introductory modifiers are like restrictive and nonrestrictive modifiers in that the intonation intended provides a clue to punctuation. Consider:

Meanwhile the dog ate our dinner.

If we are thinking of the sentence as if there were a sharp rise in pitch on the first syllable of *meanwhile* and a pause after it, a comma after *meanwhile* would enforce our intention.

27h PUNCTUATION WITH GEOGRAPHICAL, TEMPORAL, AND METRICAL MATERIAL   **P8**

The comma has a number of conventional uses to separate parts of geographical, temporal, or metrical material, or other matter which may take a statistical form.

(1) Commas are used between all elements of a date. When a year is part of a date, it has commas both before and after it. Parts of a single element, such as the name of a month and the figure indicating the day, are not separated. With abbreviations both a period and comma are often required.

> They arrived by train at 10 A.M., Monday, January 17, 1956.
> Tuesday night, July 6, 1820, the debate began.

(2) Elements of addresses are similarly separated. When more than one element appears in an address, the last element is followed by a comma, unless the address is itself a separate unit, as in the address of a letter. Parts of elements, such as a street number and the name of the street following it, are not separated. Postal zone numbers are not separated from the cities in which they are located.

> He gave 1162 West Avenue, Cleveland 9, Ohio, as his address.

(3) Commas separate parts of measurements, divisions of a whole, and other statistical details. The last element of a series of divisions, like parts of a book, is usually separated from what follows, but the last part of a series constituting a measurement is usually not.

> He was six feet, eight inches tall.
> The sentence appears on page 11, line 28, of the new book.
> She must enter in Act III, scene 2, before the music begins.

ORIGINAL	REVISION
Mary was born January 4, 1952 in Chicago.	Mary was born January 4, 1952, in Chicago.
The play was first produced in December 1853 to a full house.	The play was first produced in December, 1853, to a full house.

ORIGINAL (*Cont.*)

He cleared the bar at six feet four inches.

Drive to 1062, Second Avenue.

REVISION (*Cont.*)

He cleared the bar at six feet, four inches.

Drive to 1062 Second Avenue.

27i   COMMA TO CLARIFY OR EMPHASIZE   P9

The comma is frequently useful to separate words which might be erroneously run together, to mark omission of a word used in a double capacity, or to emphasize structure when a connective is omitted.

ORIGINAL

Whatever is is right.
[*The two uses of* is *are confusing without separation.*]

The next day he told me what he meant what he had intended to say.

An hour of lecture presumes two hours of preparation, an hour of laboratory none.
[*Presumes* is *assumed between* laboratory *and* none.]

Admission ten cents.

REVISION

Whatever is, is right.
[*The words are separated for clarity, even though normally one would not separate subject and verb.*]

The next day he told me what he meant, what he had intended to say.

An hour of lecture presumes two hours of preparation, an hour of laboratory, none.
[*The comma makes the structure clear.*]

Admission, ten cents.

27j   PUNCTUATION WITH QUOTATIONS   P10

Direct quotations, words actually said or previously written, are enclosed in quotation marks.

"Get out," she said.
After his service in Korea, he agreed that "the paths of glory lead but to the grave."

This use is sometimes extended to include short expressions which quote speech from a special level of usage or from a particular person, or which call attention to a way of saying something.

We learned that the diners at the next table were "hepcats" waiting for the "squares" to leave.
A conservative oxford was at that time called an "opera pump."

The quotation marks are used because a quotation from some other speaking group is implied. Quotation marks are not generally used any longer as indiscriminate apologies for slang or colloquial English. In most instances, the slang should be used without apology if it is appropriate and omitted if it is not.

Quotation marks are sometimes used to indicate that a word is used as a word, but italics are more common (see 28f).

> The noun "boy" is the subject.

Quotation marks distinguish titles in two special circumstances: (1) when mechanical limitations, such as those in typesetting for a newspaper, make italics impractical; and (2) when a short work is to be distinguished from the larger work that contains it (see 28e, 31).

> Robert Frost's "Mending Wall" appears in *Poetry of America.*

Quotation marks appear before and after the quoted material. When a quotation runs for more than one paragraph, the mark of quotation begins every paragraph but closes only the last one. Long quotations are sometimes printed without quotation marks, in smaller type and indented; in typescript, the passage is indented and typed single-spaced.

Single quotation marks ('), the apostrophe on the typewriter, enclose a quotation within a quotation.

> The witness said, "I was just opening the door when I heard her scream, 'Drop that!' "

An indirect quotation is not placed within quotation marks, but a few words within an indirect quotation may be quoted directly.

> In his quiet way, he said that he was "excessively annoyed" with the gangsters next door.

ORIGINAL

I am sorry, she said, but those weeds you are lying in are poison ivy.
[*Material quoted directly should be set off by quotation marks.*]

Shaw pretended to believe that all man's civilization is founded on his cowardice, on his abject tameness, which he calls respectability.

REVISION

"I am sorry," she said, "but those weeds you are lying in are poison ivy."

Shaw pretended to believe that all man's civilization "is founded on his cowardice, on his abject tameness, which he calls respectability."

ORIGINAL (*Cont.*)

[*The latter part of the sentence is quoted directly.*

I told "her she ought to stop wasting her time."

[*The quotation is not direct; the direct quotation was something like "You'd better stop wasting your time."*]

She said I was in a hassel and that I had blown my top.

[*Hassel and* blown my top *are quotations from the character's manner of speech.*]

They were doing what they called trolleyizing the old tramway.

The old garden had been taken over by heather aster, the poverty weed.

[*Without quotation marks,* poverty weed *is taken as merely an alternative name.*]

REVISION (*Cont.*)

[*The quoted matter has been placed within quotation marks.*]

I told her she ought to stop wasting her time.

[*The quotation marks have been removed, since an indirect quotation is not enclosed.*]

She said I was in a "hassel" and that I had "blown my top."

[*The characteristic words have been enclosed within quotation marks.*]

They were doing what they called "trolleyizing" the old tramway.

The old garden had been taken over by heather aster, the "poverty weed."

[*Quotation marks might be used to show that the name is quoted from local speech.*]

When an expression like *he said* introduces a quotation, it is separated from the quotation by a comma.

The first little girl said, "Let's hide the body in that trunk."
I said, "I have always hated Pomeranians."

Sometimes a formal introduction to a quotation is followed by a colon (see 27k). But the comma is not used before an indirect quotation, that is, a quotation which is not verbatim.

I said that I had always hated Pomeranians.

ORIGINAL

"Tomorrow," Mother said "we are washing those curtains."

Then Juliet asked "Why is your name Romeo?"

Then Juliet asked, why his name was Romeo.

[*The quotation is indirect and should not be set off.*]

REVISION

"Tomorrow," Mother said, "we are washing those curtains."

Then Juliet asked, "Why is your name Romeo?"

Then Juliet asked why his name was Romeo.

[*The comma of the original separates verb from complement.*]

The position of the quotation mark in relation to other punctuation used with it is determined partly by logic and partly by arbitrary convention. Commas and periods are always placed inside quotation marks. All other punctuation marks are inside if they punctuate only the quoted words, outside if they punctuate an entire sentence containing a quotation.

> The rafters used a long handspike, which they called a "picaroon."
> He asked me to open the "boot"; I did not understand.
> "Are you ready?" I asked.
> Do you know who said that "life is but an empty dream"?

ORIGINAL

An upright contraption, known as a "moon box", was used to show an artificial moon on the stage.
[*The comma always goes inside the quotation.*]

"Are you afraid of the dark"? the child asked.
[*The question mark punctuates the quoted material and belongs inside the quotation marks.*]

REVISION

An upright contraption, known as a "moon box," was used to show an artificial moon on the stage.

"Are you afraid of the dark?" the child asked.

27k THE COLON   P11

The colon resembles in force the sign of equality in mathematics; that is, whatever comes before the sign is in at least one sense equal to what comes after it. It is most frequently used to precede a series which has already been introduced by a completed statement, often containing the word *following*.

> The common silk dress goods are the following: raw silk, taffeta, crepe de Chine, shantung, pongee, silk chiffon, silk organdy, satin, and silk velvet.
> I found that there were four kinds of girls in college: those that came to get married, those that came to get an education, those that came because their parents made them, and those that came because they did not know what else to do.

The colon is not needed, however, when the series immediately follows the verb as a group of complements.

ORIGINAL

The common silk dress goods are: raw silk, taffeta, crepe de Chine, shantung, pongee, silk chiffon, silk organdy, satin, and silk velvet.

[*The list is a complement and should not be separated from the verb it completes.*]

In high school I competed in the principal girls' sports, that is: in hockey, swimming, and basketball.

[*The colon properly introduces a formal series; here* hockey, swimming, and basketball *are in apposition with* sports.]

REVISION

The common silk dress goods are raw silk, taffeta, crepe de Chine, shantung, pongee, silk chiffon, silk organdy, satin, and silk velvet.

[*The colon which breaks the continuity of the subject-verb-complement pattern is omitted.*]

In high school I competed in the principal girls' sports, that is, in hockey, swimming, and basketball.

[*The meaning is at once clear with a comma, and accordingly the lighter punctuation is preferable.*]

The colon is occasionally used between independent clauses when the second part of the sentence has been introduced in the first.

> Two events occurred that spring to make Marie less happy in her new home: the mangy cat that had been her best friend was hit by a car, and the low spot near the garage which became a fine mud puddle after every shower was filled and leveled.

The colon is unusual in this use, however, unless the second part of the sentence clearly repeats or clarifies the first.

ORIGINAL

Almost everybody tries to come to Washington: everybody complains about the weather after he gets here.

REVISION

Almost everybody tries to come to Washington; everybody complains about the weather after he gets here.

The colon also has certain conventional uses, notably after the formal address of a letter (*Dear Miss Smith:, Dear Sir:*), in statements of time (*8:35*), and in citations from the Bible (*Genesis 5:1-3* or *Genesis V, 1-3*). For other conventional uses of the colon, see *A Manual of Style* (Chicago, 1949).

27 | DASH   P12; Dash

The dash (—), made with two hyphens on the typewriter, is used to mark sudden breaks in the flow of the sentence. It stops the reader abruptly, a little like a closet door bumped into in the dark. If, however, a walker in the dark discovers that his path is obstructed by a series of closet doors, he goes slowly, and even the closet doors lose their effect. Dashes are useful and versatile punctuation marks, but they should be used with care and restraint. Most commonly they have the following uses:

(1) A dash may emphasize a sharp break or change in thought, separating sentence elements or marking a break at the end.

> If he has any decency he will come and apologize—but has he any decency?
> He walked with quiet dignity up to the altar—and tripped on the first step.
> He knew the soldiers would march up in formation, aim their rifles, and then—

(2) A dash may set off parenthetical material (see 27f) when the writer desires a sharper separation than commas signify. Dashes are used to emphasize a dramatic or striking interruption; parentheses usually set off an insertion which is not grammatically part of the sentence (see 27m).

> The new queen of the·senior ball—and she was fully aware of her royalty—swept into the room.
> Some of them overlooked—if they ever knew—the dangers of driving with bad brakes.

The dash is especially useful if the modifier has internal punctuation.

> Often had he sighed, in Africa, for its drowsy verdant opulence—those willow-fringed streamlets and grazing cattle, the smell of hay, the flowery lanes.

(3) One English sentence pattern used occasionally lists a long series of subjects or modifiers followed by a dash and usually by a pronoun or other word summarizing the list.

> A brown, crusty turkey, fluffy mashed potatoes, jars of jam, pickles, ·and olives, and mince and pumpkin pies—all these and more appeared before Linda, as if she were in a dream.

(4) The dash is sometimes used between clauses when one clause introduces another, or it may introduce a list, less formally than a colon (see 27k).

Of the thoughts that flashed through my mind one persisted—if I screamed the children would wake up.

He bought samples of all the common silk dress goods—raw silk, taffeta, crepe de Chine, shantung, pongee, silk chiffon, silk organdy, satin, and silk velvet.

(5) The dash has various conventional uses, especially before a citation at the end of a quotation.

"Nothing endures, nothing is precise and certain (except the mind of a pedant)."
—H. G. WELLS, *A Modern Utopia*

It is used also in various kinds of informal tabular arrangements.

Humanities—fine arts, literature, language, philosophy.

Social sciences—history, political science, sociology, economics.

In current usage, other punctuation marks are avoided with a dash; for an exception see 27a.

ORIGINAL	REVISION
These discoveries,—evolution, relativity, and now atomic fission,—have given us a new conception of the world. [*The comma is not necessary with the dash.*]	These discoveries—evolution, relativity, and now atomic fission—have given us a new conception of the world.

Writers who are too indolent to decide what they wish to say, and thus how to punctuate, sometimes try to save themselves trouble by using dashes for everything, hoping that the reader will do the thinking that the writer should have done. The device seldom works. The prospective reader may well conclude that if the writer was too indifferent to decide what he wanted to say, the reader will be too indifferent to try to find out.

ORIGINAL	REVISION
Knowing only the most elementary principles of chemistry—I should never have attempted the experiment alone—However—I set up the equipment—and got out the necessary ma-	Knowing only the most elementary principles of chemistry, I should never have attempted the experiment alone. However, I set up the equipment and got out the necessary materials, not

ORIGINAL (*Cont.*)

terials—not knowing how explosive they were—especially in combination—
[*This is a jumble because the writer has not punctuated.*]

REVISION (*Cont.*)

knowing how explosive they were, especially in combination.
[*The dashes have been replaced by standard punctuation.*]

27m   PARENTHESES AND BRACKETS   P13

Parentheses enclose inserted material which does not fit into the grammatical structure of the sentence and which adds incidental information. In this book, for example, parentheses punctuate cross references or examples inserted into sentences. They can also enclose sentences or passages irrelevant to the main discussion.

> The statue bears this inscription: "To our bountiful lady, Margarita Fernandez." (Señora Fernandez was an Indian woman who married a Spaniard and at his death inherited his mining wealth.) It is an outstanding example of Spanish baroque.

Parentheses have various special uses such as enclosing numbers or letters in an enumeration.

> He cited reasons as follows: (1) no students had been allowed in the building in the past; (2) furniture was not well enough built to stand student use; and (3) students had adequate facilities without new quarters.

Punctuation goes inside the parentheses when it punctuates only the parenthetical material, outside when it punctuates the whole passage. Parentheses are used only in pairs. In most contexts they are best used sparingly.

ORIGINAL

He distinguished between the members of the family *Juniperus, Juniperus communis, Juniperus virginiana,* and the like, and the plants resembling juniper, such as retem, *Retama raetam.*
[*The words separated by commas seem at first to be words in a series.*]

To write you need a sharp pencil and a quick mind (the first of which can be easily acquired).

REVISION

He distinguished between the members of the family *Juniperus (Juniperus communis, Juniperus virginiana,* and the like) and the plants resembling juniper, such as retem (*Retama raetam*).
[*The parentheses clarify the sentence at once.*]

To write you need a sharp pencil and a quick mind, the first of which can be easily acquired.

ORIGINAL (*Cont.*)

[*Clauses within a sentence are usually sufficiently set off with commas.*]

REVISION (*Cont.*)

[*The comma is sufficient; for a sharper break, a dash would be preferable to parentheses.*]

Square brackets are used to enclose matter inserted into a direct quotation.

ORIGINAL

We hold these truths to be *self-evident* (the italics, of course, are mine), that all men are created equal. . . .
[*The parentheses imply that the inserted matter was part of the original and was there in parentheses.*]

REVISION

We hold these truths to be *self-evident* [the italics, of course, are mine], that all men are created equal. . . .
[*The inserted matter has been enclosed within square brackets.*]

Brackets are used for parenthetical material within matter within parentheses, to avoid the confusion of parentheses within parentheses.

27n   INAPPROPRIATE OR EXCESSIVE PUNCTUATION   P14; No P

Punctuation is intended to clarify; sprinkled indiscriminately through writing, especially when it separates closely related sentence elements, punctuation distracts or obscures. The mistaken notion that any pause in speech suggests a comma in writing is perhaps responsible for some useless punctuation. Punctuation that separates subject from verb or verb from complement is especially misleading. Commas setting off parenthetical or nonrestrictive material do not separate subject and verb so long as they appear both before and after the expression, but a comma on only one side of such an expression breaks the continuity of the sentence.

ORIGINAL

Hundreds and hundreds of tattered men, came tramping back from the war.
[*There is no good reason to separate the subject,* men, *from the verb,* came tramping back.]

Even Pearl, who had worn saddle

REVISION

Hundreds and hundreds of tattered men came tramping back from the war.

Even Pearl, who had worn saddle

ORIGINAL (*Cont.*)

shoes all her life bought a pair of high-heeled pumps.

[*The comma after* Pearl, *on only one side of the modifier, separates subject from verb.*]

REVISION (*Cont.*)

shoes all her life, bought a pair of high-heeled pumps.

[*When commas enclose the modifier, they set it apart and accentuate the subject-verb relationship.*]

Perhaps because final clauses sometimes modify nonrestrictively and are set off by a comma, students sometimes precede a clause used as a complement with a comma. Such a comma separates verb from complement.

ORIGINAL

Mary was afraid, that someone else would wear a pirate costume.

REVISION

Mary was afraid that someone else would wear a pirate costume.

The practice of using a comma before *and* between independent clauses should not be distorted into the notion that a comma always precedes *and*. Usually, a comma is not needed before *and* when it joins parts of a compound subject, verb, or complement.

ORIGINAL

My father, and John ran up the walk, and threw their arms around us.

He ran up the walk, and threw his arms around her neck.

REVISION

My father and John ran up the walk and threw their arms around us.

He ran up the walk and threw his arms around her neck.

The need for a semicolon between long, complex independent clauses does not require that a semicolon appear whenever an independent clause has any internal punctuation.

ORIGINAL

Of course, I looked in the drawer for the flashlight; but someone had taken it.

REVISION

Of course, I looked in the drawer for the flashlight, but someone had taken it.

EXERCISE 27

A. Supply appropriate punctuation in the following sentences. The meaning of some sentences may change with various sorts of punctuation.

1. One avocado did not ripen I don't know why the other one did
2. He was the worst dean I ever heard of with the alumni his putting the whole Sigma Nu house on probation is still a favorite story
3. He was playing left end you say so you say he was playing left end is that it
4. Two times two are four four times four are fifteen no four fours are sixteen or are they or is it is
5. I want you to wash the windows tomorrow you can go to the ball game if you want to
6. I said rats if they are eating the cake I don't want any of it
7. So you think you're pretty good do you feel like taking off your glasses and settling this outside.
8. Elmer Davis said when he resigned as a radio news commentator I am not leaving on account of political pressure or economic pressure only on account of blood pressure and my own at that
9. A certain truck carries the following signs this truck stops for a red light or a red head backs up 25 feet for a blonde and courtesy is our motto
10. Joseph Joubert is credited with the following some men find their sole activity in repose others their sole repose in activity
11. The following have registered thus far Alice Melarkey Los Angeles Muriel Jones St. Louis Florence O'Brien Seattle Florence Schmidt Syracuse and Helen Adney Atlanta
12. A number of changes account for the movement of beef raising into the southeast wornout cotton lands heavily cropped for years will not longer raise a high production crop successfully and meanwhile Texas ranchers finding they have insufficient pastures in this the driest year in a decade are glad to acquire additional grazing land in the eastern gulf states

B. The sentences below could be corrected by supplying adequate punctuation, but most of them would be improved by revision. Correct each by changing punctuation; then revise each by making one of the independent clauses dependent and compare the results.

1. It was cold and rainy outside, however, the house was warm and dry.
2. I was in the hospital during the time I was there I fell in love with the head nurse.
3. I finished washing all the dinner dishes then Mary said she thought we might mop and wax the kitchen floor.
4. I never learned the multiplication tables for this reason I have always been slow at mathematics.

5. The clerk opened the bank door at the time he did so the three robbers pushed their way into the bank.

6. The team lost the final game of the tournament, for this reason June cried herself to sleep that night.

7. The music stopped, all the girls ran for the chairs around the dance floor.

8. My sister was beautiful and talented however she did not win a trip to Atlantic City.

C. Punctuate the following sentences, paying particular attention to punctuation of nonrestrictive and parenthetical modifiers.

1. The tailored suit which I had brought home with me from Hadley's Bazaar a department store in New York City hung on me like a Hindu robe but everybody admired the outfit I had made a simple little dress I devised out of some coarse basket-weave that Aunt Lilly gave me.

2. The brook seeded with boulders and lined with brush looked exciting but hard to fish.

3. That summer I was employed as assistant to the playground director in Jordan Park the same park in which the previous summer I had refused to take part in the group games.

4. In our school Beeson County High School most of the students were interested in sports especially basketball and accordingly you did not ask whether a boy had anything in his head but only whether he was tall enough to hold his head six feet in the air.

5. Gladys who was the only daughter of a steel manufacturer used to make me angry and jealous showing off her new clothes.

6. She is the girl who won the 4-H scholarship.

7. The atoll a coral reef which barely broke the water was nothing to turn to for protection particularly in stormy weather.

8. We were told that the highway to Alaska which had just been opened the summer before was bumpy and provided little by way of accommodation gasoline meals or lodging.

9. After one hour saturate the curls with neutralizer for bleached, dyed, or overdry hair see instructions on the front of the folder.

10. The sorority which my mother favored was the only one that showed me any attention.

11. Then she started talking about a tepidarium whatever that is.

12. What we called the "coasting hill" a long grade that wound past the cemetery and down through the school yard unfortunately crossed Lake Street at the intersection by the feed and grain store a crossing which was much used by farmers on Saturday our only coasting day.

D. Supply the missing punctuation in the sentences below, and correct inappropriate punctuation; where two marks of punctuation are required, be sure you put them in the proper order. Some sentences are well punctuated as they stand.

1.   . . . the play's the thing
   Wherein I'll catch the *conscience* the italics are mine of the king.
2. Janice (a quiet girl who went out little) was very anxious to have dates.
3. I turned and ran toward the subway station,—or thought I did, for it was snowing so that I could not see,—then I bumped into someone.
4. If you will look up the citations I have given you Ephesians 2:6, 12, 20 you will see that Paul referred variously to his Lord.
5. Maximilian had three courses before him he could try to become a genuine ruler of the Mexicans for the Mexicans; he could take his scraps of a French army and flee; or he could go on living in indolent luxury, which would probably be ended by a firing squad.
6. Knowing what she did there was only one thing to do—give back the ring.
7. "The so-called Dixiecrats [dissident southern Democrats] hoped by this move to gain the balance of power."
8. Inside I saw: a cat, some kittens, and an old white-haired Negro.
9. Alice—the scrawniest little girl in our block—was growing up to be a beauty.
10. To distinguish the types of furniture, note the following: bamboo grows in sections and is hollow between the sections; rattan, a much stronger material, grows solid.
11. Is that what you mean by "whooping it up?"
12. They had something they called a "booby-hutch," which was defined as "a carriage body put upon sleigh runners."
13. "They the Pueblo Indians make a kind of bread called guayave which the white people call a 'hornet's nest.'
14. I decided to wear my new hat—but just as I was locking the door I noticed it was starting to rain.
15. If you want to be chigger-bitten, go: I am staying home.

E. Insert the correct punctuation in the following:

   When I was in Cuernavaca Mexico just before our entry into the second world war in May 1941 I heard a story of what became of one of Rivera's murals It seems that the proprietor of a fashionable restaurant ordered his walls decorated Since I do not wish to be libelous let us say that the restaurant was at 268 Morales Avenue which it was not The proprietor a small ingratiating excitable man considered various muralists interviewing them from the time he arose at 10 a m until he went to bed at 2 a m Finally he settled upon Rivera who was known to be fashionable with certain groups especially the foreigners The mural finished he awaited the approval of the dignified people in the town Members of the important old families who were eager to view the newest monument to local progress responded to his invitation They came in holiday mood and looked they left enraged They had seen their own faces painted upon the bodies of gangsters robbers cutthroats and quacks with small ceremony and no delay at all they rendered their artistic judgment If those pictures stayed up the most important people would stay out What to do The proprietor loved his murals for they had cost him much money he loved his business for it had brought him much money So he paced the floor which was new and only partly paid for and tore at his trim carefully waxed mustache At that he had an idea and with deft strokes painted bushy whiskers sprightly goatees and respectable muttonchops upon the faces of the abused citizens Should he not reason that whiskers that would render a mayor unrecognizable would also make him genial and as a result might he not be expected to eat the restaurant beefsteak But the device which the proprietor's mustache inspired was more ingenious than successful The outraged citizens were more outraged than ever not only had the proprietor insulted them by calling them bandits but he had further and doubly insulted them by implying that they grew bad beards As for Rivera he threatened to shoot the proprietor for desecrating art Torn between art and the artist between his patrons and their patronage the bedeviled proprietor saved at once his sanity and his business by having the whole room replastered.

28

The Manuscript

For Guide to Revision, see page 498

Follow standard practices or a special stylebook in preparing a manuscript.

Individual publications, newspapers, or college classes have special requirements for preparation of a paper, but any manuscript, whether submitted for publication, presented as a business report, or prepared to fill a class assignment, should be neat, standard in appearance, and conventional in capitalization, syllabification, and use of italics and numbers.

The following rules are standard and fit the requirements of almost any publisher or reader:

(1) Typewrite in black or write in black or blue-black ink on one side only of standard size (8½ x 11-inch) paper, unruled for typing, and ruled for handwriting with standard measure ruling, not the narrow ruling sometimes used for notebook paper.

(2) Double-space between lines of a typewritten manuscript. Most editors refuse to look at unsolicited copy which is not double- or triple-spaced. Keep tyepwriter type clean and use a well-inked ribbon.

(3) Make handwriting legible, distinguishing clearly between capital and small letters.

(4) Leave generous margins on all sides of the paper—at least an inch and a half at the top and the left and an inch at the right and the bottom.

(5) Indent about half an inch for each new paragraph—five spaces on the typewriter. In typing, leave one space after internal punctuation, two spaces after end punctuation.

Manuscripts submitted for publication usually carry a notation like the following in the upper right-hand corner of the first page:

> My Years in Jail
> John Doe
> 13 Skidrow Street
> About 92,000 words

Instructors specify requirements for papers submitted in class. Often brief papers are folded lengthwise and endorsed on what would be the front cover if the paper were a book. Longer papers are usually left flat, with information on the outside page. For class papers a notation like the following is usually required.

> Mary Edmonton
> English 101, Sec. 24
> Theme VI
> October 10, 1956
> Professor John Hancock

28 M

THE MANUSCRIPT

Guide to Revision
Check carefully the modern requirements for acceptable manuscript.

28a   CAPITALIZATION   M a; cap; lc

English has many conventions concerning the use of capital letters, often called "upper case" because they are found in the upper case of a font of hand-set type, as distinguished from small letters, referred to as "lower case." Styles and use of these conventions vary. Most American newspapers, for example, use what is called a "down" style; that is, they capitalize only the definitive part of a proper name unless the generic portion comes first (*Hudson river,* not *Hudson River; Northwestern university,* not *Northwestern University;* but *Uni-*

versity of Chicago). This system is intended to avoid excessive capitalization, since newspaper accounts are, of necessity, crammed with titles and names. It is used only by practicing journalists working for newspapers; the system is described in almost any basic journalism text. The style used for most literary, social, and commercial purposes, however, is an "up" style, and it is described in the following list of some of the most common uses of capitals in English.

(1) *Proper nouns* are capitalized. Clearly, to be useful, this statement requires definition of the word *proper noun*. The definition gives some trouble, not because the main distinctions involved in it are illogical, but because they are subtle enough to require clear thinking. For instance, Mrs. Hardy has a son, whom she names Thomas. Obviously, *Thomas Hardy* is a proper noun, the given name of one particular individual. Thomas Hardy writes some novels set in southwestern England near an imaginary town called Casterbridge. *Casterbridge,* also, is a proper noun. But suppose that a tourist wishes to visit the scenes of these novels, does he visit the Hardy Country or the Hardy country? Similarly, a river is named for Henrik Hudson. Is it the Hudson River or the Hudson river? Does it flow through the Hudson River Valley or the Hudson River valley? There is a women's college on the bank of this river; is the president the President of Vassar College, since there is only one such president at a time, or the president of Vassar College, since presidents are of common occurrence? Are the subjects taught in this institution American literature or American Literature, History of the Americas or history of the Americas?

The confusions arise in several ways, but partly because every object on earth exists as an individual. Every pebble on the beach is a separate pebble, but one of them becomes the basis of a proper noun only if it is given a name, Plymouth Rock, for instance. On this basis one can answer the questions in the previous paragraph. The area described in Hardy's novels is the Hardy country, because there is no definite, designated area which has been officially so named, as there is an area officially named Connecticut. For the same reasons, it is Hudson River, but Hudson River valley. The president of Vassar College is president, not President, unless she should sign herself, with her title, which then becomes Mary E. Smith, President of Vassar College. The subjects taught are American literature and history of the Americas, but if these subjects become titles of specific courses, then as titles they would be written American Literature and History of the Americas. The question is not whether the noun is the name of an individual object, being, sort, area, or anything else, but whether the noun is a name given to a particular unit, not shared by other units of its sort.

(2) *Words derived from names and closely associated with them* are usually capitalized. *American* derives from the name *America,* and although there are many Americans the word is capitalized.

(3) *Proper nouns which have become common nouns* are not capitalized.

In the early nineteenth century, sample forms for the British army were made out with the name *Thomas Atkins.* Eventually Tommy Atkins became the colloquial name for a British soldier; now *tommy* has become a common noun. Similarly, a Victrola was a trade name of an instrument manufactured by the Victor Company, but the instruments have become so common that any record player can be called a *victrola.* Salad dressing made of oil and vinegar is called French dressing, because French cooks developed and popularized it and Americans borrowed it from France, but if salads increase in popularity we may yet put french dressing on them. We use the Bible in church, but the incoming freshman student is expected to study the student handbook, often called the "freshman bible." Thus some words which are proper nouns become common nouns, at least in some usages. If the writer is uncertain whether a proper noun has become common, he should consult a good dictionary.

(4) *The first word of a sentence or a line of poetry* begins with a capital letter.

(5) *The pronoun I* is capitalized.

(6) *References to deity* usually begin with capital letters.

> To God the Father, God the Son,
> And God the Spirit, Three in One.

(7) *Initials and abbreviations* often require capitals (for details see 28b).

(8) *The first letters of principal words in titles* are capitalized (see 28e).

ORIGINAL

During my Second Year in High School, I took American Literature, European History, Mathematics, french, and Home Economics, and a new course entitled social problems. [*Words like* high school *and* literature *are not proper nouns, even though the writer is thinking of only one school and one literature.*]

We crossed over the Mount Vernon Road and down into the Coon River Bottoms. [*This capitalization is correct if* Mount Vernon Road *and* Coon River Bottoms *are given names.*]

I went to the Library and read a copy of the Library. [*The first* library *is not a proper noun; the second names a magazine and needs a capital and italics* (see 28e).]

In the Autumn the ducks move South out of Canada, and hunting is good in some parts of the west. [*Names of the seasons are not capitalized; the indication of a direction is not capitalized, but a direction as name of an area is.*]

God so loved the world that he gave his only begotten son. [*References to deity are usually capitalized.*]

REVISION

During my second year in high school, I took American literature, European history, mathematics, French, and home economics, and a new course entitled Social Problems. [Social Problems *is capitalized because it is a title given to a course, not a description of the material in the course.*]

We crossed over the Mount Vernon road and down into the Coon River bottoms. [*This capitalization assumes that the road is, let us say, Highway 56a but is called the Mount Vernon road because it goes to Mount Vernon, and the Coon River bottoms are the low land along the Coon River.*]

I went to the library and read a copy of *The Library.* [*The revised form makes clear the nature of each* library.]

In the autumn the ducks move south out of Canada, and hunting is good in some parts of the West.

God so loved the world that He gave His only begotten Son. [*Both the pronouns referring to sacred persons and the words naming them are capitalized.*]

28b ABBREVIATION   M b; Ab

In general, abbreviations are avoided in writing, except in footnotes, bibliographies, formal lists, compilations of statistics, tables, addresses, and the like. There are a few exceptions: common forms of address when used with proper names (*Mr., Mrs., Messrs., Dr., Jr., Sr., Ph.D.,*

LL.D., D.D., S.J.; but not *Rev., Sen., Gov., Prof.,* or *Pres.* in formal writing); *Before Christ* and *Anno Domini* when used with a date (B.C., A.D.); a few common standard abbreviations when used in informal, technical, or business writing (*cf., e.g., no., etc.*); some government agencies (*NLRB, OPA, ICC*). Except in footnotes, bibliographies, addresses, tables, and the like, the following are spelled out: names of states and countries (*California, United States*); details of publication (*volume, page, chapter*); addresses (*street, avenue, road*); months and days of the week (*December, Sunday*); business terms (*company, manufactured*); and other words not specifically excepted (*Christmas, mountain, fort, saint*). Contractions (*don't, aren't*) are inappropriate in formal writing (see 26). Characters or symbols used for *and* are not acceptable in standard writing.

ORIGINAL

The pol. sci. assign. for Mon. is something about the U.N. meeting in N.Y.

We ordered ice cream & cake for dessert.

During the Xmas vacation I got a job with a mfg. co.

Rev. McIntosh was in charge of the service.
[*The abbreviation is used only in newspaper writing and some informal writing.*]

Sen. Oldham announced a new govt. research grant to be administered by Prof. Jenkins.
[*First names should identify the persons when their names are first mentioned:* Senator John J. Oldham.]

Rome endured from 390 b.c., when it was sacked by the Celts, until 410 a.d., when it was sacked by the Germans.
[A.D. *and* B.C. *are always capitalized.*]

REVISION

The political science assignment for Monday concerns the United Nations meeting in New York.

We ordered ice cream and cake for dessert.

During the Christmas vacation I got a job with a manufacturing company.

(1) The Reverend Mr. McIntosh was in charge of the service.
(2) The Reverend Ira J. McIntosh was in charge of the service.
[*Formally, the titles* Reverend *and* Honorable *are preceded by* the *and accompanied by the first name or initials of the person or by the title* Mr.]

Senator Oldham announced a new government research grant to be administered by Professor Jenkins.

Rome endured from 390 B.C., when it was sacked by the Celts, until A.D. 410, when it was sacked by the Germans.
[*Note that* A.D. *precedes the date and* B.C. *follows it.*]

28c NUMBERS   M c; Num

Numbers which can be written in two words are written out in standard writing; thus, all numbers one hundred or below are written out.

Exceptions to this rule are:

(1) If several numbers are used in a passage and some of them are large, all of them are written in figures.

On a western highway, one passes through towns marked on the map with populations from zero up. For instance, traveling east on Highway 40, one leaves the San Francisco-Oakland metropolitan area, population 2,214,249; passes through Sacramento, 275,659; Verdi, 250; Mill City, 72; and Toy and Dad Lees, 0, since the Lees have moved.

(2) Figures are regularly used in certain standard contexts: for street and room or apartment numbers in addresses (*1238 Ralston Street, 14 West Twenty-third Street*); to designate portions of a book (*Chapter 10, page 371*); for dates (*January 10, 1838*), and for decimals and percentages when using words would become complicated (*3.1416, 57%*).

Figures are not used to begin a sentence, and numbers are not written both as figures and as words, except in legal documents.

For hyphenation in numbers see 29b.

ORIGINAL

1938 is remembered in our valley as the snowy year.
[*A figure should not begin a sentence.*]

The 4 of us moved into a little garden cottage at sixty-two Longfellow Avenue.
[*Write out numbers which can be expressed in two words, except in formulas like addresses.*]

There were 32 students in our zoology laboratory and only 27 microscopes, but after we got our first grades, 11 students dropped the course.

REVISION

In our valley, we remember 1938 as the snowy year.
[*The sentence is re-arranged to avoid the initial figure.*]

The four of us moved into a little garden cottage at 62 Longfellow Avenue.

There were thirty-two students in our zoology laboratory and only twenty-seven microscopes, but after we got our first grades, eleven students dropped the course.

28d DIVISION OF WORDS   M d; Div

A somewhat uneven right-hand margin is preferable to numerous divided words, or words incorrectly divided. In copy to be printed, hyphenation is uncommonly inconvenient, since the printer may not be sure whether the hyphen marks only the end of a line, or the end of a line which breaks a hyphenated word. When necessary, however, words may be divided between syllables. Syllabification is complicated. In general, it follows pronunciation, and consonants attach to the vowels following them (*pa-per, re-gard*); two consonants which represent two sounds go one with each syllable (*mis-ter, har-dy;* but *soph-o-more*); but prefixes and suffixes remain syllables by themselves (*ach-ing, ex-alt*), unless modern pronunciation has obscured a suffix (*chil-dren*). Double consonants are separated unless they are the ending of a word with a suffix (*rat-tle, swim-ming,* but *miss-ing*). Words of one syllable cannot be divided. Words should not be divided so that a single letter appears on either line. There are more rules and many exceptions; unless the writer is certain he should consult a good dictionary. When a word is divided, the hyphen appears at the end of the first line, not at the beginning of the second.

28e TITLES   M e; Tit

The title of a brief theme or other piece of writing should be centered on the first page, separated from the body of the composition by a blank line if handwritten, and by at least four spaces if typed. Principal words, usually all except articles and short connectives, are capitalized, but a title at the head of a manuscript is not underlined or enclosed in quotation marks. Titles of long manuscripts are placed on a separate title page.

When a title of a book, magazine, newspaper, play, poem, story, or moving picture appears within a manuscript, it should have capital letters to begin all words except prepositions and articles and should be underlined to indicate that it would be printed in italics (see 28f). Mechanical limitations sometimes necessitate variations; for example, newspapers tend not to use italics because they complicate typesetting. But modern practice more and more consistently prefers italics rather than other typographical devices to distinguish titles referred to in a text.

The *Times* reviewed *The Red Badge of Courage* enthusiastically.
Milton's *Lycidas* is a poem in the pastoral tradition.
The *Tribune* critic praised Judith Anderson's performance in *Macbeth.*

When a short work must be distinguished from the larger work
which contains it (see 31), quotation marks distinguish an article or
chapter from the periodical or book in which it appears, a short story
or poem from the volume in which it is printed.

> "How to Build Your Own Home" is a feature in the *Herald* every
> Saturday.
> *The New York Times* had a review of *Garland of Bays* called "The
> Robust Elizabethan Days."
> "Miniver Chevy" can be found in Robinson's *Collected Works.*

28f   ITALICS   M f; Ital

Italic type in printing, indicated in manuscript by single underlining of the words to be italicized, is increasing in popularity and respectability as a means of setting off certain words in the composition.
It is now regularly used for titles referred to in a manuscript (see
28e). It is used for all foreign words and phrases not yet Anglicized.
It is acceptable form for words used out of context and words to
which special attention is called. For most of these uses, quotation
marks were formerly used, and for some of them quotation marks may
still be used (see 27j).

Indiscriminate use of italics to emphasize certain words is to be
avoided, but italics can be used for emphasis and contrast.

> I said he was drunk? No! I said he was *not* drunk.

ORIGINAL

Soon, very soon, we shall start for
sunny California, hoping to have the
time of our lives.
[*Overuse of italics for emphasis destroys the emphasis.*]

After Professor Lovejoy's lecture, it
became "de rigueur" to have read
"The Road to Xanadu."
[*Italics are preferable.*]

REVISION

Soon, very soon, we shall start for
sunny California, hoping to have the
time of our lives.

After Professor Lovejoy's lecture,
it became *de rigueur* to have read *The
Road to Xanadu.*

ORIGINAL (*Cont.*)

Man is the subject of the sentence.
[*Italics should point to* Man, *used out of context.*]

Americans like to make new words out of old, to sleep in a motel and eat cheeseburgers.

REVISION (*Cont.*)

Man is the subject of the sentence.

Americans like to make new words out of old, to sleep in a *motel* and eat *cheeseburgers.*

EXERCISE 28

A. Correct the faulty capitalization in the following:

Texas, the largest State in the Union, has never been quite sure that it is part of the United States, and texas people have their own notions and are likely to live by them. Inhabitants of the lone star state are convinced that any texan can "lick his weight in wildcats" or ten times his weight in yankees, and texans have always had their own Ways of Thinking. Consider, for instance, old judge Bean, who called himself the Law west of the Pecos, meaning, of course, the Law west of the Pecos river. But when I speak of the independence of texans, I am thinking particularly of the individuality of the Buckaroos, or as they are sometimes called, "Cowpokes," up in the Panhandle Country. That, of course, is the area around the Town of Panhandle, but the whole Northwest part of the Sovereign State of Texas is sometimes called The Panhandle. And when I think of those Panhandle Buckaroos, I am reminded especially of the way they love their horses to the exclusion of everything else.

According to the story, one of these Buckaroos who lived in the northern part of Carson county, not far from the Town of Panhandle itself, heard about the moving picture *Gone With The Wind,* and decided he wanted to see it. He had heard it was about the civil war, and his Grandfather had fought in that War. Accordingly, he saddled his Palomino pony, rode into the town of White deer, and then down to Panhandle. At the Moving Picture Theater he found there was a Double Bill, and accordingly he sat through a showing of *Roaring riders.* He liked that because there were many good Quarter Horses in it. Then he saw the ravages of the union army, the burning of plantations, and Scarlet O'Hara baring her bosom to the camera. When he got back to the Ranch, somebody asked him how he liked Scarlet.

"all right, I guess," He said. He said nothing more for some time, and then he added, "jest been wonderin' how they got them horses out past them flames."

B. Correct the errors in abbreviations, contractions, and numbers in the passage below. Note which forms would be acceptable in colloquial writing but unsuitable in formal writing.

I've just purchased in a 2nd hand book store a copy of *Appleton's Guide* to the United States for eighteen ninety-two. It's full of entrancing old things, but since for the past 8 or 10 years our family has gone every summer to the Adirondack Mts., I was particularly interested in the description of those mts. The eds. point out that this sec. 30 yrs ago "was known even by name only to a few hunters, trappers, and lumbermen," but they're now able to give a detailed description of it. They correctly locate the area between L. Champlain and L. George on the E., and the St. Lawrence R. on the w. They also identify Mt. Marcy as the tallest mt. in the area, giving the measurement as five thousand three hundred thirty-four feet. They concede that this pk. is not so high as the Black Mts. of N.C., nor the White Mts. of N. Hampshire, but they point out that they're interspersed by more than 1000 lakes, the largest of which are more than 20 mls. long. These lakes're said to be infested with trout weighing 20 lb. or more. Hunting was also A-1; for instance, the hunter could take woodcock from Sept. 1st to April thirtieth, & the fine for shooting game out of season seems to have been only $25, which by our standards wasn't very high. The publication also gave instrs. that a "lady's outfit" should include "a short walking-dress, with Turkish drawers fastened tightly with a band at the ankle." Travel in the area was apparently done by boats, built a few ft. long, carried by the guides on their shoulders from lake to lake and from river to river.

C. Correct the faulty use or omission of italics in the following:

Among the curiosities of literature and thought is the career of Lord Monboddo, *baronet,* author af a book called Of the Origin and Progress of Language. He believed that human speech came from the speech of animals, and imported an *orangoutang* into Scotland, assuming that the animal represented *the infantine state of our species.* The *chimp,* as the animal was called, was presumably a representative of "Pongo pygmaeus" or Simia satyris. Lord Monboddo taught the animal to play the flute, after a fashion, but in Monboddo's words, he *never learned to speak.* The lord patiently tried to teach the animal to say "hungry" and "eat," but without success. The learned journals of the day, periodicals like the Quarterly Review and Blackwood's Edinburgh Magazine ridiculed poor Monboddo, publishing articles with titles like Misguided Jurist and *This Monkey Business.* Not until long after the publication of Darwin's Descent of Man did students of modern thought realize that Lord Monboddo had been ahead of his day. Among the milder satirists of the radical jurist was Thomas Love Peacock, who made genial fun of Monboddo and his orangoutang by inserting into his book Melancourt, a satirical novelette, a certain Sir Oran Haut-ton, whose name was of course a pun upon the French haut-ton, that is, high-toned.

29

Spelling

For Guide to Revision, see page 517

English writing records the spoken language; variations in spelling reflect language growth.

Language develops as speech. A written language follows a spoken language, as a record of speech. A system of writing, therefore, provides visual symbols to represent the varying sounds of speech, even to represent as far as possible changes in intonation or pauses or gestures. Such translation is not easy; representing all the possible shades of sound the voice can produce would require a system so cumbersome that it could not be widely used. Punctuation marks, for example, record some characteristics of a spoken sentence; marks to record all of them would be impossibly complex. A letter can represent a sound as distinguished from some other sounds, but an alphabet accurately representing every variation of sound would be impractically long. Furthermore, after a written language has developed, it acquires an identity of its own. Readers can use it without constant or direct reference to the spoken language, and it readily becomes more stable than the changing and developing spoken language.

29-1 WRITTEN ENGLISH AND SPELLING

Old English or Anglo-Saxon existed as a language long before it was reduced to writing, probably by priests, with an alphabet of Roman characters, supplemented by a few characters from old Germanic alphabets, such as the þ to represent the sound we now designate with *th*. Neither the spoken nor the written language remained changeless (see 24), but as the language developed, letters came to be more regularly associated with certain sounds and even some combinations of letters became fairly stable words. Still, no regularized system of spelling in English developed until sometime around 1650 to 1700. Even in Shakespeare's time a common word like *do* or *he* might be spelled in two or three ways on the same page. Printers sometimes added or omitted letters like *e* as a way of spacing lines.

In the seventeenth century people began to be concerned about stabilizing spelling, and the kinds of problems that still plague users of English became apparent. For example, native words and words borrowed early from other languages tended to retain spellings they had acquired in Middle English, even though pronunciation had changed. The final *e,* for example, often pronounced in Middle English, had become silent by the time of Shakespeare, but still appeared on many words. A spelling reformer like Richard Hodges observed in 1643 that the final *e* had lost its sound, but he also observed that in words like *mane* or *cane* or *pane* the silent letter was needed to indicate the sound of the vowel and distinguish the words from *man* or *can* or *pan*. It was apparent that *meet* and *meat* and *all* and *awl* and *rite* and *right* illustrated inconsistencies; once the differences in spelling had represented differences in pronunciation, but the differences in pronunciation had disappeared. Still the differences in spelling were useful to distinguish the words in writing.

English spelling became fairly well stabilized in the late seventeenth and early eighteenth century. It did not, of course, become entirely logical or consistent, in spite of many suggestions for reform. The frequent proposals in the seventeenth century that the double consonant in *saddle* or *fiddle* should become single was never adopted. On the other hand, the proposal by Thomas Mulcaster in the sixteenth century that the *re* ending become *er* in words like *letter* was confirmed by practice later, as was the proposal that *badde, bedde, lidde* and the like be standardized as *bad, bed, lid.* Alternate spellings *cry, crie, spy, spie, dy, die, ty, tie* both persisted through the seventeenth century; when spellings for the words became stable, they did not follow the consistent pattern that writers recommended; two kept the *y,* two *ie.*

Modern spelling has inherited these difficulties as well as others. It has added new complications; for instance, it has borrowed more and more words, often basing the spelling on the language from which the words were borrowed. The old spelling demon *phthisic* is spelled phonetically, but in a spelling based on the Greek; *schnapps* retains its German spelling. On the whole, however, English spelling is probably not so whimsical as it is sometimes considered, nor so difficult, at least for native speakers. Proposals for spelling reform continue to get support, and often they have an effect. Noah Webster, for example, managed to have a considerable influence on at least American spelling; *error, honor, terror* have become standard rather than the older British *errour, honour, terrour* largely through his efforts toward simplification. But most systems for a new spelling have had little influence; curing one inconsistency often causes another and any reform must meet the resistance of established habits plus large bodies of already printed materials. The student who has trouble with spelling is not likely to get help from simplified spelling. But after some serious and systematic effort, most students find that their problems are not so great as they might seem. Most spellings in English are at least partially phonetic, and anyone who knows the usual phonetic values attached to letters is likely to spell most words without trouble. Many other words follow general patterns which can be learned. Most adult spelling errors come from carelessness, for which the cure is obvious, or from trouble with a relatively small group of common but difficult words, which can be learned.

29-2 ANALYZING SPELLING PROBLEMS

Spelling ability is not necessarily an index to intelligence or education, but certainly the person who spells inaccurately works under a handicap. He is likely to be considered uneducated by anyone who catches him in errors, and he is likely to be limited in his writing, as he relies on simple but sometimes colorless words in order to be safe in his spelling. Some people are sufficiently eye-minded that they learn to spell unconsciously. By the time they have seen a word spelled correctly several times, they know it. Others have to work on spelling, not because they are slow or stupid but because their minds happen not to work in the way that records spelling automatically. But fortunately almost any intelligent person can learn to spell reasonably well if he will work at it. A "bad" speller is usually only a person who does not spell without learning, who has never been properly taught, or who has never tried hard enough to learn.

In spelling, as in almost everything else, there is no substitute for a good background. The more a student reads, and the better writing he reads, the better he is likely to spell. Similarly, a knowledge of other languages and of etymologies will help. Anyone who knows that *license* is related to Latin *licere* will not spell it *lisence;* deciding whether *innocence* and *inoculate* have one or two *n's* is not difficult for the person who knows that the first was formed from *in* and the Latin *nocere* and the second from *in* and the Latin *oculare*. But building background is a slow process, and even learning etymologies takes time. Furthermore, the sad fact is that a writer may be very learned and yet spell badly.

Most students who have reached college and still have spelling difficulties can progress best by analyzing their individual difficulties and working systematically on the basis of the analysis. The first step is to find out what words a writer misspells and, if possible, why he misspells them. Here a good teacher can help, but the student must do most of the work, and often he can do it best—after all, he knows himself as nobody else is likely to. He should first make a list of all words he looks up in the dictionary in order to verify their spelling and of all words he misspells, including all repetitions in either class. Misspelled words can be collected from corrected themes or from letters which the recipient has been asked to correct and return. There is always a way to get a list of one's misspellings; it should be based upon one's normal writing and should be extensive enough to be typical. For diagnostic purposes, the student should record his misspellings, not the correct spellings of the words, and he should record each misspelling of each word in order that the frequency as well as the nature of his misspellings will appear. Any diagnosis is likely to turn up problems like the following.

29-3 HABITUAL MISSPELLING

Following is a list of misspellings collected from two themes of a student who had spelling difficulties:

> recieve, to (*for* too), planatarium, too (*for* to), seperate, to (*for* too), recieve, to (*for* too), seperate, too (*for* to), Phillippine, too (*for* to).

Of course, good analysis requires a longer list, but even in so short a list the main difficulty is obvious. The student is misspelling the same few words over and over. All he has to do is to learn the difference between *to* and *too,* that *separate* is spelled *ar* instead of *er,* and that *receive* follows the rule of *e* before *i* after *c.* Anybody can learn that much in five minutes, and this "bad" speller could make a good start overnight by learning a few words.

Not every case of bad spelling is so simple as this or so easily helped. Most students with trouble not only misspell some words habitually but make errors for other reasons like those classified below.

29-4   CARELESSNESS

Consider the following list of misspellings from one theme:

> effect (*for* affect), Tes of D'Ubervilles, Tess of D'Uberviles, inan (*for* inane), Tamos, usally, Tess of Durbervilles, disipated, Tes of D'Urbyvilles, tradgedy, to (*for* too), principle (*for* principal), Tess of DUrbeville, berth (*for* birth), Tess of D'Urberville.

The girl who wrote the paper managed to spell one title six different ways—all of them wrong. That she did not know how to spell the title is not surprising, but she could have looked it up if she were not careless or lazy or both. She probably knows how to spell *inane, dissipated, Thames, tragedy,* and other words in the list, but she was too careless to bother to spell them correctly.

Hesitating during composition to spell every word correctly may impede writing, but there is no excuse for leaving misspellings uncorrected after the writing is done. An uncertain speller should scrutinize every word before he lets any written work out of his hands.

29-5   PHONETICS AND SPELLING

Consider the following list of misspellings:

> to (*for* too), goverment, ast (*for* asked), tradegy, airfiel, seperate, intrest, athalete, Scananavian, constriction company, preform (*for* perform), use to (*for* used to), could of (*for* could have), thing (*for* think), to (*for* too), affect (*for* effect), exackly, comdy, seperate, wend (*for* went)

There are some habitual misspellings—*to* (for *too*), *seperate*—but most of the remaining misspellings result from mispronunciations or from ignorance of phonetic values.

English spelling is not entirely phonetic. An ideal alphabet would have one letter for every sound and only one sound for each letter, but in English some letters may have many sounds, and some sounds can be represented in several ways. It is still true, however, that the phonetic value of the letters and the pronunciation of the words are, in general, the basis of spelling. No one who knows phonetic values and who pronounces carefully need be in much doubt about how to spell *perform* or *government*. In the list above, words like *asked, tragedy, airfield, interest, athlete, Scandinavian, construction, think, exactly, comedy,* and *went* are misspelled probably because the writer did not pronounce them correctly, and possibly also because he was not sure of the phonetic value of the letters. Anyone who makes errors of this sort should first be sure he knows the sounds associated with each letter. He should then be careful to know the words he uses and to pronounce them precisely. Temporarily, to fix troublesome words in mind, a speller may wish to pronounce the troublesome syllable with exaggerated stress: *prePAration, audiENCE, ATHletic, gov-ERNment.*

29-6 INDICATION OF VOWEL SOUNDS

Consider the following list:

> alright, geting, diner (*for* dinner), alright, doesnt, helpfull, combin, refering, occuring, excelence, noticeing, alright, permited, rideing, tradegy, laborously, Britanica, ninty, quanity, dominent, argueing, durring.

Some old friends like *all right* appear in this, and there is a sufficient variety of misspellings so that a much longer list would be required to be sure which represent a tendency and which result from careless-ness or are odd words habitually misspelled, but there is at least one noticeable tendency in this list. The writer does not accurately use consonants and vowels to indicate vowel sounds.

There are few reliable rules for the doubling of consonants and the use of additional vowels to indicate sounds, but there are tend-encies which are consistent enough to be useful. Medieval scribes often doubled a consonant if they wished to indicate that a previous vowel was short, especially if the consonant was not final, and added an extra vowel if they wished to indicate that a vowel was long. The scribes were not consistent in their practice, and we have not been entirely consistent in preserving medieval spellings, but modern practice is consistent enough to be useful. For instance, *dine* is distinguished from *din* by the extra final vowel. The writer of the list of words above seems not to understand this practice; otherwise he would not have confused *diner* and *d:nner,* which follow the rule, and he probably also would not have misspelled *getting, combine, helpful, referring, occurring, excellence, permitted, riding, Britannica, ninety, arguing,* and *during.* The rules covering these misspellings are somewhat complicated; the student who has difficulties of this sort should turn to 29g.

29-7 SPECIAL PROBLEMS IN SPELLING

The peculiarities of the language have given rise to special problems in English spelling. Consider the following list:

> lay (*for* laid), gread-grandfather, sensable, attendence, recieve, incidences, shipwreack, abbes (*for* abbess), recieve, sixty two, ponie's, dipthong, relient, primative, definate, dessert (*for* desert), playwrite, influance, perrequisites, presede, roll (*for* role), Britian, marketible, loose (*for* lose), recieve, lays (*for* lies), site (*for* cite), indistinguished.

There are several sorts of errors here, some of which, like the habitual misspelling of *receive,* have been mentioned above. Another type of error (*ponie's* and *sixty two*) results from ignorance of the plural forms in English (see 29c) and of the uses of the hyphen and apostrophe in spelling certain forms (see 29a, 29b). But the bulk of these errors come about through the confusion of words or parts of words which in some way resemble something else.

A few words the writer apparently does not understand. He wrote *gread-grandfather,* but he surely would not have written *gread mistake.* Similarly, he would not have referred to a collision on the highway as a *wreack,* nor would he have written *incidence* for a single happening. He is failing to understand the word or the parts of it, and his misspelling is a symptom of his poor grasp of vocabulary. Most of these words, however, present problems in spelling.

Some represent the confusion of homonyms, that is, of words having the same sound but different meanings, for example, *sight, site,* and *cite; to, too,* and *two; rite, write, right,* and *wright.* The cure for such errors is to look up all the homonyms in a good dictionary and learn enough about them to keep them separate, and then to find some way of associating the meaning with the spelling. Words which are not pronounced identically but are similarly spelled are confusing, especially if the difference in the spelling involves only a transposition or a doubling of a letter. Thus the following have always given trouble: *angle, angel; casual, causal; chose, choose; lose, loose; desert, dessert; canvas, canvass; accept, except; affect, effect.*

Spelling by analogy or etymology can be very helpful, but analogies may lead a writer astray, especially if they rest upon false assumptions. One of the most common misspellings is *definate* for *definite,* probably because of the large number of English words ending in *ate.* The misspellings like *pronounciation* and *renounciation* result from the analogy with the corresponding verbs. The spelling *primative* is probably influenced by the more common *primary.* The frequent misspellings *Britian* and *villian* are probably made by false analogy with many English words having *i* and *a* in this sequence, as in *Parisian, gentian, Martian.* Even very accomplished spellers will make occasional errors of this sort, but awareness of the problem helps to solve it, and thorough acquaintance with the word will cure individual difficulties.

The most numerous words that cause trouble through confusions are those that employ a syllable, often a prefix or a suffix, which can be spelled in several ways, or which differs but slightly from another syllable. Thus, *-ible* is confused with *-able,* and *-ents* with *-ence.* Is it *indistinguished* or *undistinguished, indistinguishable* or *undistinguishable?* Differences in meaning and use offer some help. The suffixes *-ents* and *-ants* are plurals, as in *residents* and *attendants; -ence* and *-ance* are evidences of an abstract noun, as in *residence* and *attendance.* Latin prefixes and suffixes tend to be used with Latin words, Anglo-Saxon affixes with Anglo-Saxon words. Thus we have *unable,* since both *un-* and *-able* come from Anglo-Saxon, against *indigestible,* since *in-, digest,* and *-ible* are Latin, but the rule is by no means consistent, as the confusion mentioned above in connection with words related to *distinguish* will illustrate. Frequently, *-able* follows words which are complete as they stand, whereas *-ible* follows syllables which have no meaning without the suffix (*acceptable, marketable,* but *terrible*), even though a silent *e* has been dropped from the word (*drivable*). Some tendencies can be observed, also, in the letters which suffixes follow, but many students find learning the words easier than learning the tendencies and the exceptions. For what the tendencies may be worth, here are the most common: *-able* usually follows hard *g* or *c* (*applicable*), *i* or *y* in the root word (*justifiable*); *-able* is common in words having a long *a* in a related word (*irritate,* and hence, *irritable*). The suffix *-ible* usually follows soft *c* or *g* (*tangible*), *miss* or *ns* (*sensible*); if the suffix can replace *-ion* in another word, without change of adjacent letters, *-ible* is usual (*perfection,* and hence, *perfectible*). The ending *-ar* is much less common than *-er* or *-or* (*grammar, calendar,* and a few others); *-er* is usual among words coming from Anglo-Saxon if the *-er* indicates a person's temporary or permanent occupation (*teacher, walker*); *-or* is the common ending, especially in words from Latin (*doctor, governor, motor*). Among the prefixes warranting unusual attention are the following:

per- (meaning *through* as in *perfect,* carried through to the end)

pre- (meaning *before* as in *prerequisite, predecessor*)

anti- (meaning *against* as in *antitoxin, anti-Russian*)

ante- (meaning *before* as in *antebellum, anterior*)

di- (meaning *twice* as in *dibase, digraph*)

de- (meaning *from* or *concerning, down* as in *depart, define*)

The endings *-cede, -ceed,* and *-sede* cause some confusion. The regular form in English is *-cede* (*concede, precede, recede*). The exceptions can be easily learned; one word ends *-sede* (*supersede*), and three end *-ceed* (*exceed, succeed, proceed,* but not *procedure*).

In modern English, especially in modern American English, all unaccented vowels tend to lose their quality and become a common vowel sound called *schwa,* the sound of the vowel in *the,* when *the* is not pronounced like *thee.* Thus, for many American speakers the vowel in the final syllable of *resident* and *attendant* has the same sound, which is the same sound they use for the next to the last vowel in *accommodate* and *government.* Since the same sound is here serving for *e, a, o,* and *er* (and it can serve, also, for *i, u, y,* and a number of others) phonetics will not help much directly. Indirectly,

phonetics can help, however. The word in which the vowel has become *schwa* can sometimes be associated with a related word in
which the vowel has retained the accent, and hence its quality. For
instance, although the *e* has lost its quality for many speakers in *resident* it has kept its quality in *residential*. A writer has only to sound
out *residential* to know that *residant* is incorrect. The pronunciation
of *inferential* indicates the spelling of *inference*. Less can be done
with the syllable written ʃʌn ʃən in phonetic script, which is variously
represented in *shun, percussion, complexion, cushion, direction, Hes-
sian, freshen.*

Obviously, spelling problems which rest upon any situation as complicated as that which gives us various uses for the same or similar
sounds are not likely to find resolution by simple means. Even here,
however, knowing one's weaknesses helps. The writer who knows that
he is likely to confuse *-ence* and *-ance* can give special attention to
words with these spellings, and eliminate the most troublesome, and
he can make use of some special devices, distinguishing the meaning
of homonyms, for instance, and associating words difficult to spell
with related words which the writer knows already, or can "sound
out."

29 Sp

SPELLING

Guide to Revision

Correct the misspelled word. Try to find out why you have made the
error, and learn the correct form so thoroughly that you do not repeat your mistake.

Most misspellings involve one of the causes discussed above: (1)
the writer is careless; (2) he habitually misspells certain words; or
(3) he has one or more of several different sorts of spelling difficulties, any of which can be cured or greatly reduced with a little attention.

For the first, the solution is obvious. For the second, there are also simple cures. Since relatively few words need be learned, they can be memorized. The writer can work from a list, eliminating words he knows. Furthermore, he can take advantage of some of our knowledge of how the mind learns. Anything repeated just before sleep is likely to be remembered in the morning. If the writer reminds himself just before going to sleep that *receive* is spelled *ei,* and does it on three successive nights, he is likely not to misspell it again. Anything repeated at intervals will be learned; a list of a few troublesome words can be repeated before every class, or every night while the writer is undressing. In a short time they will be learned for life, and the card with the list of words can be thrown away. A mnemonic device sometimes helps with particularly troublesome words. For instance, an old schoolboy device distinguishes *principal* and *principle* by suggesting that a high school *principal* might be a *pal* but a geometric *principle* could not. If the writer makes up his own device, it may work, no matter how silly it may sound. Often, learning many details about a word will make it easy to remember. The distinction between *affect* and *effect* is easier for the person who looks up the words in a good dictionary and understands all the differences between them.

Errors of the third sort are often more troublesome, but systematic work will decrease them. A first step is diagnosis of troubles (see 29-1 to 29-7). Some errors can be corrected by learning what are called "spelling rules," although strictly speaking these so-called rules are not rules at all, since spellings were not originally based on them. They are observations of spelling practice which has been more or less regular. All these rules have some exceptions, and for some rules the exceptions are so numerous that the rule is not worth learning. Rules in the sections below have enough application so that anyone who has difficulty spelling should simplify his problem by learning them.

29a THE APOSTROPHE   Sp a; Apos

The apostrophe is used to indicate an omission of one or more letters or figures.

> can't, isn't, o'clock, the gold rush of '49.

It is used also to indicate omissions in reports of dialectal speech.

"I rec'leck how y'r paw come courtin' like 'twar yestiday," she said.

Avoid overuse of the apostrophe in recording dialect; apostrophes clutter the page and confuse the reader. A writer is usually wise to indicate with an apostrophe only the most noticeable omissions in pronunciation.

Some contractions give especial difficulty because they are readily confused with possessive forms of pronouns which do not require apostrophes. Note the following pairs:

Contractions	Possessive pronouns
it's (it is)	its (The cat carried its kittens.)
they're (they are)	their (They ate their lunch.)
you're (you are)	your (Mind your manners.)
who's (who is)	whose (Whose little boy are you?)

ORIGINAL

You're supposed to pick it up by the back of it's neck.

[*The contraction* you're *requires an apostrophe; the possessive pronoun* its *does not.*]

REVISION

(1) You're supposed to pick it up by the back of its neck.

(2) You are supposed to pick it up by the back of its neck.

[*The contraction is suitable for informal writing only.*]

"I'm go'n' t' d'vide m' w'rk int' a duz'n per'ods," he said.

[*Even though the omissions actually occur in speech, so many apostrophes confuse more than they clarify.*]

"I'm goin' to divide my work into a dozen periods," he said.

[*There is no right number of apostrophes, and transcription of dialect is always difficult; but the best writers try to suggest, not to reproduce.*]

The apostrophe is now most frequently used as a sign of the possessive or genitive case. In a curious blunder, Renaissance grammarians supposed that a form like *the kingis book,* an alternate medieval form for *the kinges book,* should actually read *the king, his book.* They assumed that an *h* had been omitted; accordingly they used an apostrophe. They were wrong, but the practice has become standard modern usage.

To show possession in singular nouns and indefinite pronouns, provided possession is not shown by the preposition *of,* add an apostrophe and *s.*

Paul's temper, the cat's tail, anybody's opinion

For plural nouns which end in *s,* add only an apostrophe.

> the soldiers' rifles, the schoolgirls' idol

For plural and collective nouns which end with a letter other than *s,* add an apostrophe and *s.*

> the people's choice, all men's fate

Proper nouns ending in *s* follow the rule:

> Frances's earring, Carl Zeiss's best lens

but may have the extra *s* omitted if it would cause an awkward series of sounds.

> Xerxes' army, Moses' code, Keats' or Keats's poems

In compounds, the last part of the compound takes the possessive form.

> mother-in-law's visit, anyone else's rights

In words showing joint possession, only the last takes the sign of the possessive.

> Germany, France, and England's position; John and Robert's fight

A possessive form for each of two or more compound nouns indicates individual possession.

> Harry and Bert's bicycle (they own it together)
> Harry's and Bert's troubles (each has troubles of his own)

The apostrophe is often omitted in proper names which have become established.

> Columbia University Teachers College, Clayton County Old Folks Home

A few possessive forms, known as double possessives, use both the apostrophe and *of.*

> a friend of my father's, a cousin of Ann's

Nouns of specification in time, space, quantity, or value follow the rule for the apostrophe in the possessive.

> an hour's walk, a quarter's worth, Monday morning's *Journal,* five dollars' worth, at their wits' end.

An important exception should be noted. The possessive forms of personal and relative pronouns do not require the apostrophe. *His, hers, its, ours, yours, theirs,* and *whose* are used as possessives and do not have apostrophes.

ORIGINAL	REVISION
When June went to Ball State Teacher's College for a years work, she found that the warm wind's there made her hair curl. [*The apostrophe should be omitted from the proper name.*]	When June went to Ball State Teachers College for a year's work, she found that the warm winds there made her hair curl. [Year's, *a noun of specification, requires the apostrophe;* winds, *a plural, does not.*]
The Jones's dog chased the Macks's cat. [*The sense indicates that plural possessives are required.*]	The Joneses' dog chased the Macks' cat. [*The apostrophe after the regular plural forms the plural possessive.*]
A publishers joke suggests that the ideal book title would be *Lincolns Doctors Dog.*	A publisher's joke suggests that the ideal book title would be *Lincoln's Doctor's Dog.*
I became interested in my brother's-in-law troubles.	I became interested in my brother-in-law's troubles.

29b   COMPOUNDING; HYPHENATION   Sp b; Hy; -

When two words are used together to have a single meaning, they tend to combine in spelling, either as a single word or as a hyphenated word. The following examples illustrate how spelling differences signal differences in meaning:

The redcap wore a red cap.

The old stylebook was an old-style book.

The fairyland lady rented a room and became a fairy landlady.

He threw a big brown stone at the big brownstone.

Notice that in speech we distinguish the uses by stress; we stress the first syllable of *redcap,* but *cap* in *red cap;* we stress *stone* the first time it is used in the fourth example but stress the first syllable of *brownstone.* Often we can see a kind of logical need behind the development of compounds. Presumably the black board in the front of a school room was identified by its color so long that it naturally be-

came a blackboard to distinguish it from any black board that happened to be around. But often no logic of any sort is observable. One
can rationalize that *post office* has remained two words because there
is no other meaning from which it has to be distinguished; but what
of *courthouse*? There are, actually, no consistent principles for spelling compounds, but one or two tendencies in practice are general
enough to be useful.

(1) When two words function as an adjective or a verb with a
single meaning, they are regularly hyphenated.

> He was only six feet tall, but he made a seven-foot jump.
> One twentieth-century innovation was the pay-as-you-go tax plan.
> We hot-roll all the metal and double-rivet the joints.
> Macbeth was not caught red-handed, but he had a red hand.

Unless a compound adjective is formed from a word that has already become a single noun (*a backhanded compliment*), it is almost always hyphenated.

When the first of two modifiers modifies the second, however, the
modifiers are not hyphenated, especially if the first is an *-ly* adverb.

> The widely advertised camera took bad pictures.
> The wide-lens camera was easy to operate.

(2) With compound nouns, however, practices are much less consistent, and the dictionary is often necessary.

a. When the second word of a compound noun is stressed, the
compound is seldom written as a single word (*main stream, high
water, club steak, back road* but *headwaiter*).

b. Compound nouns are hyphenated only in special circumstances
—especially when the first word of the compound is a possessive
(*Dutchman's-breeches*), when the two words indicate parts
of a joint idea with neither modifying (*secretary-treasurer*),
and when a noun is joined to a word like *out* or *up* (*fade-
out, slip-on,* but compare *fallout, breakdown, markup,* and
countdown or *count-down*).

c. Compound nouns stressed on the first word follow no consistent
pattern, except that they tend to combine with continuing use,
especially if there is possibility of a confusion of meaning with
a non-combined pair of words (*highway, limehouse, mailman,*

mailboat, iceman, coalbin, gasman; but compare *garbage man, mail car, ice pick, coal oil, gas mask*).

Alternatives. If there are alternatives for the first element of a hyphenated compound, each of the alternatives may have a hyphen (*eight- and ten-paddle canoes, three- or four-ply roofing*).

Prefixes. Typically prefixes like *mis-, non-, dis-, anti-,* and *pre-* join words with no separation, but in a few circumstances hyphens are common. Hyphens usually separate a prefix ending with a vowel from a word beginning with the same vowel (*pre-eminent, semi-independent, re-elected,* but *co-ordinate* or *coordinate*). Hyphens sometimes separate other prefixes: (a) *ex* when it means former (*ex-president*), (b) a prefix with a proper noun (*anti-Nazi*), (c) a prefix which leads to a combination that might be confused with another word (*re-cover* to distinguish from *recover*).

Numbers. Compound numbers from twenty-one to ninety-nine are hyphenated. A fraction used as a modifier is hyphenated unless one element of it is already a hyphenated compound. Fractions used as nouns are usually not hyphenated.

Twenty-seven cattle, nine hundred and ninety-nine, a four-fifths majority, four fifths of the class, a three-sixteenths drill.

Hyphens are used to join the figures in inclusive dates (*1790-92, 1850-1900*) and to join inclusive figures when these appear in tabular form (*500-1000, 10,001-10,025*).

ORIGINAL	REVISION
The car sank hub deep in the newly-made road.	The car sank hub-deep in the newly made road.
[Newly, *which modifies* made, *should not be hyphenated.*]	[Hub-deep *is hyphenated; two words join to form a modifier.*]
Our slow baked bread has been slowly-baked.	Our slow-baked bread has been slowly baked.
Jim, back from the army, displayed his "ruptured duck" emblem.	Jim, back from the army, displayed his "ruptured-duck" emblem.
[*Combined as one modifier,* ruptured *and* duck *should be hyphenated.*]	
The alloy is rust, weather, and heat-resistant.	The alloy is rust-, weather-, and heat-resistant.
[*Alternatives preferably include the hyphen with each alternative.*]	

29c PLURALS

English vocabulary is made up mainly of (1) native words which have come from Anglo-Saxon, and (2) words borrowed from other languages. Roughly speaking, a piece of writing is likely to contain about equal quantities of each. The fact is of interest for spelling. Anglo-Saxon formed plurals in a variety of ways, but with few exceptions, all Anglo-Saxon nouns were reduced eventually to a single system, so that most native words form their plurals by adding -*s* or -*es*.

To form regular plurals, add *s* if the sign of the plural is not pronounced as a separate syllable (*boy, boys; regulation, regulations*); after a consonant, if the sign of the plural is pronounced as a separate syllable, add *es* (*grass, grasses; class, classes*); if the singular ends in *e*, add *s* (*house, houses; bridge, bridges*).

Some few nouns were not regularized in Middle English and retain archaic forms (*ox, oxen; deer, deer; brother, brothers* or *brethren; child, children*). For such words, consult a good dictionary; the *New English Dictionary on Historical Principles* includes interesting histories. Words ending in *o* formerly regularly added *es* (*tomato, tomatoes; Negro, Negroes; motto, mottoes*), but words recently borrowed usually have only the *s* ending in the plural (*radio, radios; banjo, banjos; solo, solos*). Thus words ending in *o* do not follow a reliable rule; exceptions must be learned. Proper nouns ending in *y* form the plural with the addition of *s*, and the *y* is not changed to *i* (*two Marys, all the family of Frys*). For common nouns ending in *y*, see 29f. In nouns having a final *f* or an *f* before a final silent *e*, the *f* is often changed to *v* before the sign of the plural (*wife, wives; loaf, loaves*); there are so many exceptions to this practice that it cannot be thought of as a rule (*sheriff, sheriffs; belief, beliefs*).

Words borrowed from other languages offer special problems. The English vocabulary is one of the most extensive ever built up, partly because English-speaking people have borrowed words very freely. Furthermore, English speakers tend to change words slowly, to keep a word relatively long in the form in which it has been borrowed. Eventually, of course, if the word becomes common, it becomes Anglicized, which means, among other things, that the plural is formed

by adding *-s* or *-es*. The transitional period does not greatly affect the
plurals of words from German, French, and Spanish, most of which
form plurals with *-s*. Words from Latin and Greek, however, are
somewhat complicated because they sometimes retain endings from
the complicated classical declensional systems. Latin words ending in
um usually form the plural by changing the *um* to *a* (*datum, data;
agendum, agenda*); *us* is changed to *i* (*focus, foci; cactus, cacti*); *a*
is changed to *ae* (*alumna, alumnae*). Foreign words eventually acquire
a plural form by analogy with English; that is, the plural ends in *-s*
or *-es*. Thus, for a time, there are two current forms; *focuses* is now
more common than *foci*. Sometimes foreign plurals are not recognized
for what they are, and they are treated as though they were singulars.
Thus one hears *This data is unreliable,* although *data* is plural and *is*
is singular; and one hears *The committee made up its agendas,* although *agenda* is already plural without the *s*. Eventually these
blunders may become standard speech (our accepted plural *children*
results from a similar blunder), but most of the foreign forms are
retained in writing.

Numbers, letters, and symbols become plural with the addition of
's (*two 2's; a row of x's*). Sometimes apostrophes are also used in
the plurals of words spoken of as objects (*if's* and *and's*), but the
current tendency is to form these plurals without the apostrophe
(*pros and cons, but me no buts*). These are the only plural forms
which use the apostrophe.

ORIGINAL

    High over our heads we saw dozen's
of vapor trail's from the plane's.
[*The apostrophe is used with possessives, but not with regular plurals.*]

    The louses were making life miser-
able for the deers.
[Deer *and* louse *have retained archaic plurals.*]

    Be sure to dot your is and cross
your ts.
[*Numbers, letters, symbols, figures,
and words out of context form the
plural with '*s.]

REVISION

    High over our heads we saw dozens
of vapor trails from the planes.

    The lice were making life miserable
for the deer.

    Be sure to dot your *i*'s and cross
your *t*'s.
[*Notice also that italics show that
the letters are used out of context.*]

ORIGINAL *(Cont.)*

The irate old man started throwing tomatos at all the radioes.

[*In general, words entering the language early, like* tomato, *form the plural with* es; *new words like* radio *add only* s.]

Mrs. Appleby brought all the little Applebies with her.

[*Proper names ending in* y *regularly do not change the* y *to* i *to form the plural.*]

REVISION *(Cont.)*

The irate old man started throwing tomatoes at all the radios.

Mrs. Appleby brought all the little Applebys with her.

29d SPELLING AND SOUND   Sp d

Errors in spelling frequently occur in words in which certain sounds are commonly unstressed or indistinct in everyday speech. The final *d* on participles, for example, sometimes gets lost and *prejudiced* comes out as *prejudice* or *used* as *use. Syllables* are slurred and *interest* is *intrest;* a word is mispronounced and *villain* is written *villian;* the common pronunciation of *could have* as a contraction, *could've,* produces the spelling *could of.*

ORIGINAL

We were suppose to get use to cold food.

Another performance would of been a failure.

REVISION

We were supposed to get used to cold food.

Another performance would have been a failure.

29e COMBINATIONS OF *I* AND *E*   Sp e

When *i* and *e* are combined to indicate the sound of *e,* the old rhyme reminds us

Put *i* before *e*
Except after *c.*

Thus we spell *relieve,* but *receive.* There are several exceptions, the most common of which can be kept in mind by remembering the following sentence: At his *leisure* the *sheik* will *inveigle* and *seize* the *weird* words *either* and *neither.* The standard spelling is *ei* when the symbol represents the sound of *a,* as in *weigh, neighbor.* In a few words having other sounds, *e* occasionally precedes *i,* as in *height, foreign, sovereign.*

29f COMBINATIONS OF Y WITH ENDINGS   Sp f

A final *y* regularly changes to *i* before an ending beginning with a vowel (*ally, allies; cry, cries; lucky, luckier*). There are many exceptions, mostly for obvious reasons. If *y* is preceded by a vowel, it usually is not changed (*monkey, monkeys; destroy, destroyer*). If the ending begins with *i*, the preceding *y* is not changed (*fly, flying, flies; fry, frying*). For proper names ending in *y*, see 29c.

29g DOUBLE CONSONANTS, DOUBLE VOWELS, FINAL SILENT E   Sp g

In general, (1) consonants are doubled only after short vowels; (2) silent *e, o, a, i,* or *y* marks a preceding long vowel. This statement grows out of medieval practice, which was very irregular, and it cannot be used in determining all spellings, but it has sufficient application to help the memory. The first part of the rule is complicated by the fact that some consonants are never doubled (*q, v, j, h, w, x*); others are seldom doubled except before an ending (*b, d, g, m, n, r, t*). Some consonants are usually doubled but not always (*f, l, s, c*—double *c* being spelled *ck*).Thus, we spell *cuff, hill, spell, hack, hiss,* BUT, *bed, dog, man, cur, get*. The second part of the rule is complicated by the various means of indicating a long vowel (*hoed, hose, speak, cede, read, day, maid*), and by the fact that these same indications of a long vowel sometimes stand for a short vowel (*head, dead*). As usual, there are many exceptions (*add, axe*).

A final consonant in an accented syllable having a short vowel is regularly doubled before an ending beginning with a vowel (*forgot, forgotten; omit, omitting; hug, hugged; slur, slurred*); in unaccented syllables the consonant is not doubled (*counsel, counseled; benefit, benefited*). Alternate forms are often admissible but are discouraged in American spelling; *travelled, traveller,* and a number of other doublings are common in British spelling. American practice avoids unnecessary doubling. If the vowel in the syllable is long, a following consonant is not doubled (*ride, riding; eat, eaten; steal, stealing; hate, hated*).

Final silent *e* is usually retained before an ending which begins with a consonant (*bore, boredom; love, lovely*); and dropped before an ending beginning with a vowel (*hate, hating; cure, curable*). There are exceptions, usually for good reasons. If the final *e* is preceded by a vowel, it is usually dropped regardless, to avoid an awkward sequence of letters (*true, truly; argue, argument*). It is often dropped if it might lead to mispronunciation when retained (*whole, wholly*). If the final *e* is used to indicate that a preceding *c* or *g* has the soft sound, that is, if it occurs before *a, o,* or *u,* it is retained (*notice, noticeable; courage, courageous*). There are also exceptions to the exceptions. *Judgment* is preferred in the United States to *judgement;* the *d* is sufficient indication that the *g* is soft.

EXERCISE 29

A. In the following paragraph, identify the specified forms to fill the numbered blanks:

(1) ———— have long been intrigued by their (2) ———— peculiar habits. A (3) ———— year allows him some (4) ———— leisure, when he is likely to wonder what a (5) ———— mind is like, and spend long (6) ———— reading (7) ———— description of the social organization of the (8) ———— and (9) ———— *Entymology,* available in (10) ———— translation. Maeterlinck, alone, provides a long (11) ———— reading, or for that matter, several (12) ———— reading, and raises curious questions. Why, for instance, with (13) ———— reputation for industry, does a bee spend time on a sunny afternoon in what is called "play," when this time is (14) ———— for the using? The beekeeper was likely to answer, "Why, indeed? (15) ———— strange (16) ———— and (17) ———— no accounting for (18) ———— doings." But (19) ———— work differently. The (20) ———— method requires the collection

(1) plural of *beekeeper,* (2) possessive plural of *bee,* (3) possessive singular of *beekeeper,* (4) form of *month* indicating extent, (5) possessive singular of *bee,* (6) plural of *evening,* (7) possessive singular of *Maeterlinck,* (8) plural form of *bee* in the possessive with *of,* (9) possessive singular of *Fabre,* (10) possessive singular of *Mattos,* (11) singular form of *evening* indicating extent, (12) plural form of *evening* indicating extent, (13) possessive singular of *it,* (14) appropriate possessive singular of *it,* (15) contraction of *they are,* (16)

and study of (21) _____; that is, in the case of the (22) _____, studying them when they are supposed to be at play. On any warm afternoon they can be observed before the hive in a sort of dance in the air, making figures like (23) _____ and (23) _____. The bee-keeper had assumed a few bees had become tired of industry, and danced around a little to feel better, but the (24) _____ (25) _____ showed that these (26) _____ were returning workers, laden with honey, who with a series of (27) _____ were informing their fellow work-ers where they got the honey. In short, the sup-posed "play" is the (28) _____ way of giving directions, what might be called *The* (29) _____ *Daily Market News.*

plural of *creature,* (17) contraction of *there is,* (18) possessive of *they,* (19) plural of *scientist,* (20) pos-sessive singular of *scientist,* (21) plu-ral of *datum,* (22) plural form of *bee* for the possessive with *of,* (23) plu-ral of *s* and *z,* (24) possessive plural of *scientist,* (25) plural of *record,* (26) plural of *bee,* (27) plural of *sig-nal* used with *of,* (28) possessive singular of *bee,* (29) possessive plural of *honey-bee,* form suitable for a title.

B. In the passage below italicized words include several compounds. Which should be (1) combined into a single word, (2) hyphenated, or (3) left as they are? For each, decide whether the current form can be determined by rule or must be sought in a dictionary.

After the second *World War,* a German *displaced person* whom we shall call Hans found himself in a *base hospital* and also in a *semi rigid plaster cast.* He was *thirty one* years old, *brim full* of energy, was *naturally curious,* and had a *North German* horror of waste. He contemplated his cast with a *sadly jaundiced eye.* It was a *hand made* cast, intended to restrict his *inter costal* muscles, and it was *nicely calculated* to hold the *spinal column* while at the same time there was space enough to allow *abdomino thoracic* movement. In fact, by con-tracting his stomach muscles, Hans could enjoy a *side glimpse* of his own navel. There was enough space, he decided, to allow him to insert a *hen's egg.* He ordered a raw egg for his *mid morning* lunch, and pro-ceeded to transform his cast into the equivalent of a *setting hen,* an *incubator cast,* if you will. That is, he tucked the egg under his cast, and it fitted nicely into his navel so long as he kept his *stomach muscles* contracted. But he was not a *mother hen* by nature. After *one day's* care, he relaxed and smashed the egg. He had the persistence of a *German born* scientist, however; he *back ordered* the egg, and was heard to remark, "I'll *mother hen* one of those things if I have to stay here until I've grown a *hen's nest* in my beard." Three weeks later he *hatched out* a little, downy, *baby chick*. He might, of course, have become a *duck incubator,* too, or started a *turkey flock,* even a whole barn yard, but he remembered that *turkey eggs* require a *five or six week* period, and he did not have room on his bed for a *duck pond.*

C. Dean Thomas Clark Pollock of New York University made an extensive summary of college misspelling, for which he used nearly 600 reports from college teachers, listing 31,375 misspellings, which included 4,482 different misspellings. Two salient facts emerge from this study: most words are misspelled very seldom, and most of the misspellings occur with relatively few words. More than a third of all the words were misspelled only once, but the 27 words misspelled more than 100 times each accounted for 5,097 misspellings; that is, less than 1 per cent of the words were involved in more than 16 per cent of the errors. Similarly, the 417 words misspelled more than 20 times accounted for more than half the misspellings. The moral of all this is that most young people who have trouble with spelling have their trouble with relatively few words, and learning to spell correctly may be easier than they think.

Following are the 308 word groups which account for twenty or more misspellings on Dean Pollock's list, printed in the order of the frequency with which the words were misspelled. They warrant careful study.

th*ei*r	sep*a*rate	success	simil*a*r
th*ey're*	sep*a*ration	succ*ee*d	pro*f*essor
th*ere*	beli*e*ve	succ*e*ssion	pro*f*ession
tw*o*	bel*ie*f	*its*	nece*ss*ary
to*o*	occa*s*ion	i*t's*	un*n*ece*ss*ary
t*o*	*lose*	privi*l*ege	beg*a*n
rec*ei*ve	*lo*sing	envir*o*nment	beg*i*n
rec*ei*ving	*write*	person*a*l	begin*n*er
e*x*ist	wri*t*ing	person*nel*	begin*n*ing
e*x*istence	wri*t*er	th*a*n	contro*l*
e*x*istent	de*scrip*tion	th*e*n	controll*ed*
occu*r*	de*s*cribe	princip*le*	controll*ing*
occu*r*red	ben*e*fit	princip*al*	arg*u*ment
occu*r*ring	ben*e*fi*t*ed	ch*oo*se	arg*ui*ng
occu*r*rence	ben*e*ficial	ch*o*se	proc*ee*d
de*f*inite	prec*ed*e	ch*oi*ce	proc*ed*ure
de*f*initely	refer*r*ing	*perf*orm	achi*e*ve
de*f*ine		*perf*orm*a*nce	achi*e*vement

controversy
controversial
all right
possess
possession
psychology
psychoanalysis
psychopathic
psychosomatic
analyze
analysis
equipped
equipment
affect
affective
rhythm
tries
tried
weather
whether
forty
fourth
criticism
criticize
apparent
sense
conscious
studying
varies
various
category
embarrass
excellent
excellence
grammar
grammatically
repetition
consistent
consistency
prevalent

intelligence
intelligent
realize
really
led
loneliness
lonely
prefer
preferred
surprise
explanation
fascinate
immediate
immediately
interpretation
interpret
thorough
useful
useless
using
noticeable
noticing
probably
imagine
imaginary
imagination
marriage
prejudice
disastrous
passed
past
acquire
busy
business
Negro
Negroes
among
height
interest
origin
original

conscience
conscientious
accommodate
comparative
decision
decided
experience
prominent
pursue
shining
practical
woman
acquaint
acquaintance
exaggerate
incident
incidentally
effect
government
governor
prepare
recommend
appear
appearance
convenience
convenient
mere
opinion
possible
ridicule
ridiculous
summary
summed
attended
attendant
attendance
coming
difference
different

hero
heroine
heroic
heroes
opportunity
paid
quiet
villain
accept
acceptance
acceptable
accepting
dominant
predominant
foreign
foreigners
independent
independence
particular
technique
transferred
discipline
disciple
humor
humorist
humorous
quantity
accident
accidentally
character
characteristic
characterized
hypocrisy
hypocrite
operate
planned
pleasant
athlete
athletic
challenge

fundamental	conceive	advice	guarantee
fundamentally	conceivable	advise	guaranteed
liveliest	consider	entertain	huge
livelihood	considerably	influential	indispensable
liveliness	continuous	influence	laid
lives	dependent	significance	length
philosophy	extremely	exercise	lengthening
speech	finally	involve	mathematics
sponsor	satire	leisure	remember
unusual	careless	leisurely	seize
usually	careful	sergeant	several
across	condemn	subtle	substantial
aggressive	maintenance	Britain	tendency
article	parallel	Britannica	whole
disappoint	permit	completely	accompanying
suppose	weird	dealt	accompanies
curiosity	efficient	divide	accompanied
curious	efficiency	excitable	accompaniment
desirability	friendliness	favorite	hear
desire	friend	interrupt	here
knowledge	fulfill	perceive	luxury
ninety	piece	persistent	moral
undoubtedly	temperament	reminisce	morale
optimism	carrying	suspense	morally
permanent	carried	amount	phase
relieve	carries	approximate	playwright
religion	carrier	curriculum	represent
together	happiness	disease	schedule
you're	response	especially	source
familiar	further	fallacy	capital
suppress	laboratory	financier	capitalism
where	oppose	financially	certain
whose	opponent	meant	certainly
author	propaganda	politician	chief
authority	propagate	political	counselor
authoritative	therefore	relative	counsel
basis	hindrance	scene	council
basically	approach	sophomore	divine
before	approaches		fictitious
	physical		primitive

regard
roommate
story
stories
strength
accustom
forward
pertain
safety
satisfy
satisfied
sentence
theory
theories
tremendous
vacuum
view
accomplish
arouse
arousing
despair
guidance

guiding
ignorance
ignorant
magnificent
magnificence
narrative
obstacle
shepherd
simply
simple
straight
synonymous
themselves
them
amateur
attack
attitude
boundary
clothes
expense
fantasy
fantasies

intellect
irrelevant
laborer
laboriously
labor
later
license
medieval
naturally
noble
peace
sacrifice
strict
symbol
actually
actuality
actual
adolescence
adolescent
against
appreciate
appreciation
experiment

field
hungry
hungrily
hunger
interfere
interference
likeness
likely
likelihood
magazine
maneuver
mechanics
medicine
medical
miniature
mischief
omit
persuade
those
thought
tragedy
yield

The Research
Paper

Nothing's so hard but search will find it out.

—*Robert Herrick*

Practice in research is not merely an academic exercise. Research is the basis of most serious intellectual activity in commerce, in engineering, in science, in government. The lawyer preparing a case works through previous cases, using indexes and summaries, and applies the information he collects to his particular problems. The sales manager proposing a new campaign to his directors investigates the past records of his own company, the policies of other companies, and general economic and psychological conditions, and finds information which will help him plan his own project and predict its results. The techniques vary, of course, with the materials, but the essential process behind much of the world's activity is research—acquiring knowledge about a subject and applying it to new circumstances from the point of view of a new thinker. The student working on an investigative paper, whether he is assembling a few facts for a short theme or preparing a thorough study of a limited subject, is learning a fundamental technique.

The investigative method is peculiarly the business of the sort of people who go to college, but it is also peculiarly important for life and success in college. Most of what a college teaches has been learned by investigation, and most of the skills a student learns—ability to handle language or figures or laboratory equipment—and most of the information he absorbs are designed to equip him to find out more, and to report what he finds. The student in college needs not only practice in finding out about the world, about its past, its present, and its future, but also an understanding of how to use evidence when he has it. The longer investigative paper described in the following pages is, of course, only a more extensive project in research than many papers the student has already written. But the longer paper has certain advantages as practice in student writing. Much bad writing is bad because the writer has nothing to say; for the investigative paper the writer has only to study his subject enough and he will inevitably have something to say.

Strictly speaking, a student in a basic writing course is not likely to do research. Research presumably adds to the sum of the world's knowledge, and a young writer is usually too inexperienced and a basic course is too brief to permit productive research; but even a beginner can use an investigative paper to learn orderly methods of working and of handling material. That is, he can learn the essential procedures, even though his results are not publishable. In addition the research paper offers opportunities for intensive practice of a number of generally useful skills.

Among the most useful are the techniques discussed in Chapter 30 for recording the essence of a piece of writing in a précis or in a summary. Methods of taking notes and keeping them in convenient order are useful generally, as well as in academic work. The research project also can help the student learn something of the many uses of the library. Libraries are treasure houses of information, and nobody suspects how much a good library contains until he has learned to use one well. The student who says, "There is nothing in the library on my subject," is usually not making a comment on the library; he is usually commenting on his own inability to use it. The research paper also provides the student with an opportunity to learn how to select material for a restricted subject, how to record facts accurately, how to order and relate material, and how to evaluate it for a specific purpose. It teaches him how to document work in a scholarly manner. In one sense this is a specialized and restricted technique, since most people do not spend most of their lives writing scholarly or scientific papers, but in another sense it is a generally useful ability since a student who has learned to document well has learned, along with the technical details required, to judge evidence and its relevance, and to distinguish among the known, the probable, and the doubtful. The research paper also helps the student apply principles of organization and development to units larger than the paragraph; and since the investigative paper rests upon the ordered results of research, it provides a clear laboratory example for the study and application of the principles of handling material. Furthermore, a paper intended to report the results of attempted research encourages restrained, clear, objective expression. Any student who has prepared a library project will have become aware that almost everything about his subject is to a degree uncertain, but that much worth saying can be found within this uncertainty. He is likely to discover that he needs new ways of indicating just how certain or uncertain he may be. Faced with the necessity of explaining truth which is varied and to a degree uncertain, he is likely to write more precisely than he has ever written before.

30

The Précis and Summary;
Taking Notes; Plagiarism

Systematic summaries and notes promote careful reading and provide accurate materials for writing.

Education requires reading, understanding, remembering, and using written materials, and the student needs all the help he can get in these processes. Available techniques include the précis, useful both as an exercise to insure close reading and as a way of recording material for future reference. A briefer summary may be even more useful for keeping records of the ideas in source material, but, in any case, note-taking should be systematic and orderly if the student is to avoid inaccuracy or plagiarism.

30-1 THE PRÉCIS AND SUMMARY

The word *précis* is French, related to our word *precise* and to a Latin word which meant "cut off in front." A good précis embodies the idea of both words; it is "cut off" in the sense that it is intended to give the essence in brief compass of a longer piece of writing, and it should be as precise as a relatively brief restatement can be. Its origin suggests its character. The précis arose from reports sent back by diplomatic representatives abroad, and if the student will put himself in the position of a representative of the State Department in a foreign country he should recognize the qualities of a good précis. Consider, for instance, the position of a diplomatic attaché in a South American capital who fears a revolution accompanied by an attack from a neighboring country. The State Department will want his opinion of the situation, but it will also need evidence divorced from opinion, because any decision must take into account both of the countries, factions within the countries, international organizations, and a host of other governments, along with a variety of interests, including our own. Decisions will be made in Washington, and those who decide will need accurate and proportioned understanding of the situation in Latin America. Right decisions require reliable information, but time may not permit lengthy reports—revolutions may not wait. Accordingly, the attaché prepares précis of all important documents, and as he writes he must be as objective and penetrating as possible, endeavoring to reflect his originals accurately, without distortion or bias, and losing nothing vital, as a small mirror can reflect a large room without distortion or omission. In words, the accuracy of the mirror is not possible, but for a précis, precision is still the ideal.

The précis has uses outside the diplomatic corps. It may provide excellent classroom exercise which requires the student to read carefully enough to transfer the essential thought of a piece of writing into his own words, an exercise which requires both close reading and precise writing. The précis can also provide a record of a document which the student wants to preserve in some detail, for review for a class or for use in a research paper. A précis of Section 24-3 of this book on *The ancestry of English* might read as follows:

> Knowledge of the origins of English, acquired only recently, has revolutionized current thinking about language. Although scholars two centuries ago worked with language, describing the language of their own times, they knew too little of languages other than their own to develop general principles. The Greeks, for example, had good grammars of Greek but only limited knowledge of other languages. The Biblical tradition—tracing language from Adam to the Tower of Babel to modern tongues—dominated other thinking, even that of Noah Webster.
>
> Earlier scholars did have some knowledge of languages around them. They had observed the origins of French, Italian, Spanish, and Portuguese in Latin and the borrowings of Latin words from Greek. Scholars did not, however, make full use of this knowledge. Particularly they did not speculate about what had happened before historic times, before Latin; at least they did not before the nineteenth century. During the nineteenth century, however, new observations led to new questions which led to new knowledge about language. The key observation was that the ancient Indic language, Sanskrit, resembled Latin and Greek in a number of ways, even though there was no reason to think that the languages had influenced one another in earlier times. This observation was extended to the observation that similarities extended through several lan-

guages; a set of comparisons by the American philologist William Dwight Whitney includes: *three*, English; *tri*, Lithuanian; *tri*, Celtic; *tres*, Latin; *treis*, Greek; *thri*, Persian; and *tri* Sanskrit. Evidence like this led to modern theories of the growth and descent of languages. The method used to develop notions of language growth is essentially to reconstruct earlier languages on the basis of conjectures about what must have existed earlier to account for what exists now. For example, to account for the modern *oeil*, French; *ojo*, Spanish; and *occhio*, Italian, scholars could have predicted the existence of a word like the Latin *oculis*, eye, even if they had not known it. By the same methods, figuring out what must have existed to account for the development of modern words, scholars reconstructed a hypothetical ancient language called Indo-European, presumably spoken some thousands of years before Christ in central Europe. Even though recent discoveries of similarities between ancient Hittite and the conjectured Indo-European language have led to new theories, Indo-European remains important as a reconstruction of an early ancestor of English.

This précis reduces the original to a little less than half its length, omitting much of the illustrative material such as most of Whitney's table of cognates. Sometimes a longer, more detailed précis is required. Sometimes, however, especially in taking notes, a briefer summary is useful. The section might have been reduced to:

> Earlier scholars, even in the Greek or Hebraic traditions, did not know enough about languages other than their own to develop broad theories about the origin and growth of languages. In the nineteenth century, observations of similarities between Latin and Greek and Sanskrit led to observations of remarkable similarities in various words in a number of quite widely separated languages. Working back from existing languages, scholars reconstructed what once must have been a common ancestor of a whole group of modern languages, calling it Indo-European. This hypothetical language is generally agreed today to approximate the now lost language that was the early ancestor of the language family to which English belongs.

The summary contains much less detail, but it would serve to remind a reader of the main notions contained in the passage.

Whether the writer is producing a full précis or a brief summary, a few general principles should be observed:

(1) The précis or summary should reflect the ideas of the original accurately and honestly. It should not distort the point of view or attitude of the original.

(2) The précis should be put into the words of the writer; it should not be a series of excerpts from the original. Since the purpose of the précis is to stimulate the student to digest a piece of writing and then reproduce the ideas in a briefer form, lengthy quotations almost never are appropriate; one difficulty is that the phrasing of the original is likely to be out of proportion in the shorter version.

(3) If any short expressions are taken verbatim from the original, they should be scrupulously labeled with quotation marks.

(4) The précis, especially, should develop a unity and form of its own, as a brief essay or paragraph on the same subject as the original.

30-2 TAKING AND PRESERVING NOTES

For the preparation of a paper, the student sometimes needs to make a précis or summary of a book or article to which he can refer later. More often, however, he is investigating a specific topic and he needs to take brief notes on material which contributes to his particular interests. Often the success of his project depends on his working out a system for orderly handling of notes. The wrong way to take notes is to write them down consecutively in a notebook. They soon become a jumble. They occur in whatever order they occurred in the book from which the information was taken—usually not the order which the investigator will require. They are unidentified. They cannot be classified, particularly if the investigator writes on both sides of a sheet of note paper. As a result, the investigator knows only that he "has that somewhere" and has to spend half his time hunting for notes he cannot find. Most research workers find that cards or uniform slips provide the most practical means of taking and preserving notes; they permit the most flexible system, and in the end are the most economical. The procedure takes a little time to learn, and using it makes the recording of material a little slower, but in the end it more than pays for itself. The investigator should begin by providing himself with cards or slips; usually three-by-five bibliography cards prove to be too small. Four-by-six cards will serve many purposes, but some writers prefer half-sheets of paper; if slips are used, the paper should be heavy enough to be handled easily, and slips should be cut uniformly so that they can be filed. The following are fundamental rules for using the system:

(1) *Copy notes directly onto the cards.* Copying notes into a notebook and then transcribing them to cards wastes time and encourages error.

(2) *Write only one piece of information on a card.* If a card contains only a single piece of information, it can be classified by subject with cards containing similar information, no matter from what source it comes. Thus the investigator has all his material on one aspect of his subject filed together.

(3) *Identify the source of the information on the card.* The investigator needs to know from what work his information comes so that he can identify it as he proceeds. Probably the majority of research workers use the following system: they record the author's name and an abbreviated form of the title. A reference to page 166 of the first volume of Christopher Ward's *The War of the Revolution* might be identified on the note card as Ward, *Revolution,* I, 166.

(4) *Be sure to indicate clearly on the note cards any passages taken verbatim from the source.* Apparent plagiarism results if the investigator fails to mark a direct quotation on his note card, forgets that the passage was written by somebody else, and writes it into his paper as his own work. Whenever even a two- or three-word phrase is taken directly from a source, it should be enclosed in quotation marks on the note card.

(5) *Indicate with key words the nature or use of the material taken.* When the card is complete, it should be filed according to subject matter. For this purpose, the investigator should adopt a number of words under which material can be filed; usually these words are headings of his outline.

The following card contains material on the importance of clothing and supplies in the Revolutionary War. Clothing and supplies, of course, are subjects of all the cards and need not be entered on any of them. One important subtopic of the subject, however, is the importance of uniforms. Thus *uniforms* becomes the first key word to identify the note. *American* subdivides the cards concerning uniforms, and *from France* further identifies this note.

Note restricted to one subject; other notes
from the book appear on separate cards.

Key words classify note
by subject matter and
indicate how it can be
filed.

Uniforms—American—from France

   *Large shipment of clothing, shoes
from France, October, 1778. Blue and
brown coats faced with red. "This was
the first time that anything like
uniform dress for the whole army
had been possible."*

Quotation marks en-
close material taken
in the author's words.

Ward, Revolution, II, 594.

Source identified by last name
of author and short title.

30-3   RECORDING MATERIAL IN NOTES

Much of the labor of collecting material is routine; there are sound
and unsound methods of working, and the investigator has only to use
sound methods. But the selection of material is not routine. It requires understanding, alertness, and self-training. Consider the following passage from Mark Twain's *Roughing It.*

> He [Hyde] said it was pretty well known that for some years he
> had been farming (or ranching, as the more customary term is) in
> Washoe District, and making a successful thing of it, and further-
> more it was known that his ranch was situated just in the edge of
> the valley, and that Tom Morgan owned a ranch immediately above
> it on the mountainside. And now the trouble was, that one of those
> hated and dreaded landslides had come and slid Morgan's ranch,
> fences, cabins, cattle, barns, and everything down on top of *his*
> ranch and exactly covered up every single vestige of his property,
> to a depth of about thirty-eight feet. Morgan was in possession and
> refused to vacate the premises—said he was occupying his own
> cabin and not interfering with anybody else's—and said the cabin
> was standing on the same dirt and same ranch it had always stood
> on, and he would like to see anybody make him vacate.
>
> "And when I reminded him," said Hyde, weeping, "that it was
> on top of my ranch and that he was trespassing, he had the infernal

meanness to ask me why I didn't stay on my ranch and hold possession when I see him a-comin'! Why didn't I *stay* on it, the blather-
ing lunatic—by George, when I heard that racket and looked up
that hill it was just like the whole world was a-rippin' and a-tearin'
down that mountainside—splinters and cord-wood, thunder and
lightning, hail and snow, odds and ends of haystacks, and awful
clouds of dust! Trees going end over end in the air, rocks as big as a
house jumping 'bout a thousand feet high and busting into ten million pieces, cattle turned inside out and a-coming head on with their
tails hanging out between their teeth!—and in the midst of all that
wrack and destruction sot that cussed Morgan on his gatepost
a-wondering why I didn't *stay and hold possession!* Laws bless me,
I just took one glimpse, General, and lit out'n the country in three
jumps exactly."

Let us assume that the investigator wishes to make use of this passage in a paper intended to reveal the peculiar qualities of Mark
Twain's humor. He can, of course, copy out the whole passage as it
appears here; that would take time. He might produce a précis or a
summary, but this might not serve his purposes. He might, for example, wish to preserve more of the original's phrasing for possible
quotations in his paper than a good précis would contain. He might
make a note like the following:

T. makes a rancher called Hyde give very funny account of how
another ranch landed on top of his. Good picture of way landslide
came down mountain, using exaggeration and wild details.

A note like this is almost worthless. It is too general to be of use;
Twain's humor has disappeared from it. Compare:

T. makes rancher named Hyde tell how in a landslide "Morgan's
ranch, fences, cabins, cattle, barns, and everything" slid down and
"exactly covered up every single vestige of his property, to a depth of
about thirty-eight feet." Morgan refused to vacate, saying cabin "was
standing on the same dirt and the same ranch it had always stood
on," and asked Hyde why he had left when he "see him a-comin'."
What Hyde had seen was "just like the whole world was a-rippin'
and a-tearin' down that mountainside," bringing with it "odds and
ends of haystacks . . . trees going end over end in the air, rocks
as big as a house jumping 'bout a thousand feet high and busting
into ten million pieces, cattle turned inside out and a-coming head
on with their tails hanging out between their teeth!" In the face of
this, Hyde "lit out'n the country in three jumps exactly."

The quotation has been reduced to less than half, but the most picturesque details have been preserved. Furthermore, the material can

be used without fear of plagiarism because material which has been quoted exactly has been kept within quotation marks.

Selection of the material to be recorded on note cards, then, depends first of all on the purpose of the investigator. He can select sensibly because he knows what he is looking for. A few basic rules, however, may help him to take notes adequately and efficiently.

(1) *Adopt a system and follow it scrupulously.* The investigator must doggedly resist the temptation to "just jot this one down in my notebook," or to "just remember this one until I get a chance to write it down."

(2) *Avoid taking unnecessary notes.* Hours spent collecting material not pertinent to the paper may be educational, but they do not get the job done. Some material important for a general understanding of the subject will soon become so familiar that the investigator will not need it in his notes. The sensible research worker reads generally upon a subject before starting to take notes, and skims through a book before collecting material from it.

(3) *If in doubt, take the note.* Taking just the right material, just enough material and no more, is hardly possible. The investigator will save time by taking too much rather than too little. Copying a few extra words takes a few minutes, but trying to get a book after it has been returned to the library and someone else has borrowed it may take hours.

(4) *Take concrete, specific, exact material.* Occasionally generalities are useful, but, on the whole, the more specific the notes, the more useful they will prove to be. Facts, figures, dates, statistics, verbatim quotations, or factual digests are useful. Most beginners are wont to collect too much general material, not enough concrete, objective material.

(5) *Distinguish sharply between material which you quote and material you digest; if you quote, quote exactly.* Knowing when to take material verbatim and when to summarize is difficult. In general, however, the investigator may find that he wants word-for-word accounts of the following: material that has been very well phrased; material which is extremely important for the discussion; and controversial material, especially if the writer expects to examine the statement and comment upon it adversely. Scrupulously enclose any quoted material within quotation marks.

(6) *Be accurate and neat.* Type or write legibly; take especial pains with titles, figures, the spelling of names, or with any material in which blunders cannot be caught by context.

(7) *Double-check every note card.* A wrong page number or an omitted title can cost hours of time and frustration in locating a quotation. And if the final paper contains misquotations, misspellings, or mispunctuation in copied material, the reader cannot be expected to have much confidence in any of the conclusions of the paper.

30-4 PLAGIARISM AND INTELLECTUAL MATURITY

At least one matter which has entered into the previous discussions in various ways calls for more detailed treatment: plagiarism. It is the academic and literary equivalent of burglary, taking another person's property and treating it as though it were one's own. It is not restricted to reporting research, but at least in student writing it is most likely to appear there, particularly insofar as it is concerned with intellectual maturity. Some plagiarism involves unadulterated dishonesty; the student, being overworked, lazy, or incompetent, copies printed material or another student's work and submits it as his own, knowing quite well what he is doing, but hoping he will not be caught. He is a petty criminal, and he deserves the contempt that society reserves for petty criminals as well as the treatment that the law endeavors to provide for them. But this book does not purport to be a treatment of morals or ethics, and most student plagiarism, particularly in papers resting upon library investigation, stems not so much from dishonesty as from intellectual immaturity. Since intellectual maturity is surely one of the goals of higher education, it warrants careful attention.

That many students grow up intellectual copycats is not to be wondered at; they have been taught no better. With young children this is inevitable; small children have to be told, and they may learn most readily by repeating what they are told. They have to assume that everything they are told is true, and they early learn that, relatively speaking, it is likely to be. But of course a time comes when they ought to outgrow this childishness. Sometimes they are not much encouraged to do so; they go on through the secondary schools praised if they can produce a "correct" answer, even though the answer is something they have parroted out of a book or a lecture without knowing what it means and without being expected to know. They continue to take matter out of textbooks and to record it in lecture notes, and again, they may be encouraged to regurgitate this jumble uncritically in examinations. Many examinations are calculated to encourage original thinking, but under the pressure of an examination, routine correctness may be preferred to judgment, and even an intelligent student may go on for years without discovering that higher education is training of the mind, not stuffing the mind with relatively reliable statements which can be reproduced on stated occasions. Thus the student may be slow to recognize that at last he is being treated as an adult and that he is expected to act like an adult and assume the responsibilities of an adult.

Thus intellectual honesty and intellectual maturity go together. Most students want to be intellectually honest, but they may not know how; they may not have trained their minds to distinguish that which they believe they know from that which they are accepting because they are assuming that a writer knows and the subject is strange or difficult. Or they may not have become much aware that they should not steal another man's phrasing and treat it as their own. They may never have learned to paraphrase intelligently and carefully; they may not even have learned to be careful to distinguish their own material from other people's material, and thus they become unwitting criminals, but criminals all the same.

Perhaps an example may be instructive; the following is from Alexis Carrel, *Man the Unknown.*

> The life of all great mystics consists of the same steps. We must accept their experiences as described by them. Only those who themselves have led the life of prayer are capable of understanding its peculiarities. The search for God is, indeed, an entirely personal undertaking. By the exercise of the normal activities of his consciousness, man may endeavor to reach an invisible reality both immanent in and transcending the material world. Thus, he throws himself into the most audacious adventure that one can dare. He may be looked upon as a hero, or a lunatic. But nobody should ask whether mystical experience is true or false, whether it is auto-suggestion, hallucination, or a journey of the soul beyond the dimensions of our world and its union with a higher reality. One must be content with having an operational concept of such an experience. Mysticism is splendidly generous. It brings to man the fulfillment of his highest desires. Inner strength, spiritual light, divine love, ineffable peace. Religious intuition is as real as esthetic in-

spiration. Through the contemplation of super-human beauty, mystics and poets may reach the ultimate truth.

The following is one student's paraphrase of the passage:

> All the great mystics go through the same steps, and we have to accept their experiences. For people who have lived a life of prayer the search for God is personal, and they get outside the world around us. Mysticism is the greatest adventure that one can dare, and although a mystic may be called a hero or a lunatic, he is concerned with a higher reality. Mystics are splendidly generous people, and religious intuition is as real as esthetic inspiration.

This is a weak paraphrase, mainly because it does such scant justice to Carrel, but secondarily because it could scarcely be used without some plagiarism. The student has not understood the passage, but he has recognized that it contains intelligent comment. Accordingly, he has gone through it, picking up familiar words and stringing them together so that they make a sort of sense, although certainly not the sense that Carrel intended. When he changed "mysticism is splendidly generous" to "mystics are splendidly generous people" he was misunderstanding the use of "generous" and hence the whole sentence. He ignored whole passages, probably because they made no sense to him, but he incorporated verbatim the sentence "Religious intuition is as real as esthetic inspiration," probably in a sort of desperation, and because the comparison appealed to him; but by using it as the closing idea he distorts the meaning of the whole. Furthermore, when he comes to write his paper he would probably be attracted by these words and write them into his paper without indication that they constitute a direct quotation.

Now notice another purported paraphrase:

> Only those who have themselves led the life of prayer, that is, the mystics, are capable of understanding its peculiarities, because the search for God must inevitably be a personal undertaking. A man who endeavors to reach an invisible reality both immanent in and transcending the material world throws himself into the most audacious adventure that one can dare. Nor should anyone ask whether mystical experience results from auto-suggestion, hallucination, or a journey of the soul beyond worldly dimensions in its unions with higher reality. Mysticism, being splendidly generous, brings its fulfillment in inner strength, spiritual light, divine love, and ineffable peace, and mystics may share with poets the ultimate truth.

In one sense this is much better; the student has gained some grasp of what Carrel is saying, and if he has stolen unabashedly, he has at least had the taste to steal Carrel's best passages and not to corrupt them much. But, obviously, if he treats this paraphrase as his own notes and makes any use of it, plagiarism of a good many sorts is inevitable.

An adequate paraphrase of a paragraph like this may well be beyond the student's ability, but any student should be able to take better notes than these paraphrases represent if he will consider the following injunctions:

(1) Endeavor to understand a passage as a whole before attempting to paraphrase any of it.

(2) State in your own words anything you summarize, and note carefully that your wording is not colored by the original.

(3) When you can provide no adequate summary of your own, or when the wording of the original is so good that you wish to preserve it, scrupulously surround it with quotation marks.

The following paraphrase may not be adequate, but it could be used without plagiarism:

> The activities of mystics, although they may strike more worldly people as strange, or even as insane, have their justification in that mystics, like poets, "may reach the ultimate truth." We must assume that mystics are describing their experiences to us honestly, and that only those who have experienced a mystical life can understand it. The mystic "throws himself into the most audacious adventure that one can dare"; mysticism is "splendidly generous," and the mystic's end is to "reach an invisible reality both immanent in and transcending the material world," and thus to cultivate "inner strength, spiritual light, divine love, and ineffable peace."

EXERCISE 30

A. Read carefully the following selection, including the footnotes:

> The silk craze swept the country in the late 1820's. Silk was a useful and valuable product. Silk came from cocoons of the silkworm. Silkworms lived on the mulberry leaf. The mulberry grew abundantly in the South and West. "Wherever the mulberry finds a congenial climate and soil, there, also, the silkworm will flourish. Such a climate and soil, and such a country is ours, throughout its whole extent from its East-

ern to its Western shores." [1] Therefore farmers could always be sure of one big cash crop. "How long will it be before the old fields of the [p. 186 ends] middle and southern states will be converted into mulberry orchards, and the United States into an exporter instead of an importer of silk.—We answer, not twenty years!" [2] Every agricultural periodical printed dozens of articles annually on the culture and profits of silk. By 1839 there were at least five periodicals in the country devoted mainly or exclusively to silk growing,[3] besides numerous manuals on the subject. From these publications the newspapers regularly copied long extracts on silk and often added enthusiastic editorials and letters.[4] When the Ohio legislature appointed a committee to find a staple crop to enhance the state's wealth, the committee felt it could make no better recommendation than silk and sugar beets.[5] Apparently the great silk boom existed on paper rather than in reality, and the Midwest never became a serious competitor with the Orient.

—R. CARLYLE BULEY, *The Old Northwest Pioneer Period, 1815–1840* (Bloomington, Ind., 1951), I, 186-87.

[1] *The American Silk Grower's Guide* (Boston, 1839), 25.

[2] *Cleveland Herald,* March 26, 1833, quoting the Baltimore *American Farmer.*

[3] *Ohio Farmer and American Horticulturist,* July 15, 1839. These were the *Journal of the American Silk Society and Rural Economist,* Baltimore; *The Southern Silk Grower,* Baltimore; the *American Silk Grower,* Philadelphia; the *Silk Culturist,* Hartford, Connecticut; and one at Keene, New Hampshire.

In 1826 silk was taken up seriously by Congress. The Secretary of the Treasury was ordered to prepare a manual on the growth and manufacture of silk, and in 1828 six thousand copies were printed. (U. S. *House Executive Documents,* 20 Congress, I session, No. 158.) In 1830 a national school was proposed by Congress with M. D'Homergue, of France, as instructor in sericulture. The House of Representatives Committee on Agriculture issued a report on silk culture in 1830 (U. S. *House Reports,* 21 Congress, I session, No. 289), which included D'Homergue's directions. Reviewed by James Hall in *Illinois Monthly Magazine,* I (1830–31), 145-58.

[4] For instance, the *Hamilton (Ohio) Advertiser,* May 4, 1827, ran a two-and-one-half-column editorial on silk culture.

[5] *Cincinnati Daily Gazette,* February 20, 1837.

Notice that this passage, including the footnote reference, can be variously useful for students with various interests; make note cards for the passage as recommended below. Be sure to record the sort of concrete, specific material which will be useful in lively, objective composition. Be sure to get all titles and references exact. Be careful to use your quotation marks and your quotation marks within quotation marks so that you will later be in no doubt as to just what was quoted verbatim and from whom. Try your hand also at providing key words with which to file the cards.

1. A card for a paper to be entitled "Early Agricultural Journalism in Maryland."
2. A card for a paper to be entitled "Federal Attempts to Aid the Farmer in the 1820's."
3. A card for a paper to be entitled "The Early History of Keene, New Hampshire."
4. A card for a paper to be entitled "D'Homergue in the New World."
5. A card for a paper to be entitled "Hartford as an Early Center of Culture."

If you were writing an article called "The Great Silk Craze," how many cards would you probably make for this single entry? What might be the key words for the different cards? Make one of the cards.

B. Study carefully the following paragraph from Edward Sapir's *Language:*

Strictly speaking, we know in advance that it is impossible to set up a limited number of types that would do full justice to the peculiarities of the thousands of languages and dialects spoken on the surface of the earth. Like all human institutions, speech is too variable and too elusive to be quite safely ticketed. Even if we operate with a minutely subdivided scale of types we may be quite certain that many of our languages will need trimming before they fit. To get them into the scheme at all it will be necessary to overestimate the significance of this or that feature or to ignore, for the time being, certain contradictions in their mechanism. Does the difficulty of classification prove the uselessness of the task? I do not think so. It would be too easy to relieve ourselves of the burden of constructive thinking and to take the standpoint that each language has its unique history, therefore its unique structure. Such a standpoint expresses only a half truth. Just as similar social, economic, and religious institutions have grown up in different parts of the world from distinct historical antecedents, so also languages, traveling along different roads, have tended to converge toward similar forms. Moreover, the historical study of language has proven to us beyond all doubt that a language changes not only gradually but consistently, that it moves unconsciously from one type towards another, and that analogous trends are observable in remote quarters of the globe. From this it follows that broadly similar morphologies must have been reached by unrelated languages, independently and frequently. In assuming the existence of comparable types, therefore, we are not gain-saying the individuality of all historical processes; we are merely affirming that back of the face of history are powerful drifts that move language, like other social products, to balanced patterns, in other words, to types. As linguists we shall be content to realize that there are these types and that certain processes in the life of language tend to modify them. Why similar types should be formed, just what is the nature of the forces that make and dissolve them—these questions are more easily asked than answered. Perhaps the psychologists of the future will be able to give us the ultimate reasons for the formation of linguistic types.

Criticize the following attempts to paraphrase this passage:

1. Trying to put the thousands of languages and dialects spoken on the surface of the earth into a limited number of types makes it necessary to ignore certain contradictions in their mechanisms, and hence classification becomes a useless task. In assuming the existence of comparable types, therefore, we are gainsaying the individuality of all historical process. Perhaps the psychologists of the future will be able ultimately to put the languages of the world into types.

2. Although Sapir recognizes that speech, like all human institutions, is too elusive to be ticketed, he believes that endeavoring to type sorts of speech develops constructive thinking. He points out that historical study of language has proven that a language changes not only gradually but consistently, and that accordingly, we must assume that similarities in language in different parts of the globe represent powerful drifts that move language, like other products, to balanced patterns, in other words, to types.

Now try to write a more adequate paraphrase of not more than a hundred words.

31

Collecting Material

Careful, orderly, systematic investigation saves time and promotes accuracy in any research.

A research paper is a creative project. It is a record of the writer's thinking and organizing and relating of ideas, and it requires imagination and judgment; it is not merely a mechanical reproduction of mechanically collected data. Nevertheless, the job is complex enough that certain systematic procedures are necessary to save the writer from confusion and inaccuracy. Some of them are routine methods that have been tested enough to prove their efficiency; others are conventions of procedure and recording which must be followed in order to give the final paper ready clarity.

31-1 CHOOSING A SUBJECT

A subject for research should have at least these four qualifications: the subject must be within the range of the student's capabilities; it must be conducive to objective treatment; it must be sufficiently restricted to permit detailed work, and it must be chosen with a view to the limitations of the library and other sources of information. The first of these limitations will exclude many technical subjects, since the specialized knowledge required even to read the available publications may require years of preparation. The study of an American Indian language would require a knowledge of phonetic and phonemic structural analysis; discussing the nature of matter would require a knowledge of both higher mathematics and atomic physics. Many aspects of most subjects, however, can be studied by any literate person.

A research paper should be objective, and objectivity inevitably requires rigid restriction of the subject. Objectivity, of course, is always relative; it represents an ideal, not an achievable reality, but the writer can endeavor to be objective, and some subjects are more amenable to objective treatment than are others. *Why I Believe the Republican is the Best Party* is not a likely subject for research. The writer is not prepared to be objective; he has already made up his mind. Neither is he likely to provide much objective evidence; psychologists may some day have objective evidence on how political opinions are formed, but the writer is probably not prepared to study the subject in an objective way. Furthermore, even subjects amenable to objective study cannot be studied objectively unless they are sufficiently restricted to permit objective treatment in the space available. Unless he restricts his subject the writer may never get beyond his introduction or a few generalities whose validity he has never tested. This, of course, is the same problem discussed earlier (see 1-2), but in choosing a subject for research it becomes acute because beginning students seldom suspect how much material is available on almost any subject. Below are subjects obviously too broad, with suggestions for restricting them:

Physics	Some Dangers in Disposing of Atomic Waste in Desert Areas
Nursing	The Care of the Wounded at Gettysburg
Architecture	The Early Impact of LeCorbusier on American Architecture
Shakespeare	The Background and Meaning of "Hoist With His Own Petard."

The last qualification will not be important for most subjects, provided the student has a good library at his disposal. The holdings in well established libraries are so great that the beginning student, although he may at first have difficulty locating the most useful material, is likely soon to find himself buried in material and wondering how he can reduce his subject further. Libraries in small or new colleges, however, may be inadequate, and may force the student to abandon an otherwise promising subject, and some libraries, especially in institutions with a technical or professional bias, may be so restricted that the general collection of books is inadequate. Some subjects carry their own restrictions; material of military importance may be restricted for reasons of security, and rare manuscripts or old newspaper files may not be available for general use. On the other hand, the student may wish to take advantage of special materials locally available. He might, for example, write the history of his home town, using materials collected in the state historical society, or he might write the biography of a figure prominent in his community, using local newspaper files.

31-2 LOCATING MATERIAL

For most investigations, the student will find the major part of his sources in libraries. Although librarians labor to have their materials in good order and readily available, libraries are inevitably complicated because the world's knowledge is complicated; thus the problem of finding material usually resolves itself into the problem of using the research tools in a library. Printed material is classified according to the manner of its publication. For purposes of arrangement, printed material is divided into books, periodicals, and pamphlets and bulletins. The investigator should satisfy himself as to which of these media will contain the material he wants, and he should use the appropriate tools to locate all the material of each sort which may be pertinent to his study.

Most important material is eventually published in book form and is most readily available in that form. The best tool for locating books is usually the card catalogue in the library, which for most libraries lists all available books (but *not* the articles in periodicals nor the pamphlets). Books in the library will be entered alphabetically by the last name of the author if the author is known, by the first letter (except *a, an,* or *the*) of the title, and by the subject of the book. For instance, Eric Partridge's *The World of Words* will be catalogued under *Partridge, Eric,* as author; under *World of Words, The,* as title; and under *Language and languages, English language—History, Americanisms,* and other divisions of learning as subject. If there is more than one author, a book will be entered once for each author; sometimes a book will be entered for an editor; usually a book will be entered for more than one subject, since most books discuss more than one. The subject cards in a library catalogue are very helpful, but they can never be exhaustive, and the investigator must expect to use a card catalogue as a useful means of getting started, not as the final list of his appropriate books. The research worker should always look up several synonyms of his subject. For instance, if he is working on *words,* he should also try *language, speech, vocabulary, diction, etymology, usage* and the like.

31-3   CLASSIFICATION OF BOOKS; CATALOGUES AND BIBLIOGRAPHIES

So that they can be easily located, books in libraries must be arranged according to some system. Many American libraries use the Dewey Decimal System or a variation upon it. Large libraries often use the Library of Congress numbering system or a system adapted to their peculiar needs. The numbering and the classifications vary, but the theories of the systems are similar.

By the Dewey Decimal System, for example, all books are divided into ten groups (except fiction and biography, which are classified under *F* and *B* respectively), the first group being general books and the nine others, books in nine general areas of knowledge which supposedly include all subjects. Each of these groups is in turn divided into ten, and this subdivision again into ten. Thus the top row of the number for Partridge's book would be 410. The number means that this book falls within the broad subject of language, 400 in the Dewey system; 1 as the second digit indicates the English language, and 0 as the third digit indicates that the book is general. The second row of the call number identifies the individual book, with a capital letter for the author's name, numbers to identify the book within the latter group, and the initial of the first important word of the title (*P259w*). A third line of the call number may add the date of first publication. Thus the call number of Partridge's book would be:

410
P259w
1944

This call number is put on the spine of the book itself and recorded on the book's catalogue cards; every book in the library can be identified and located by a call number.

Library cards provide a variety of information about the book and its author. A typical author card looks like the following:

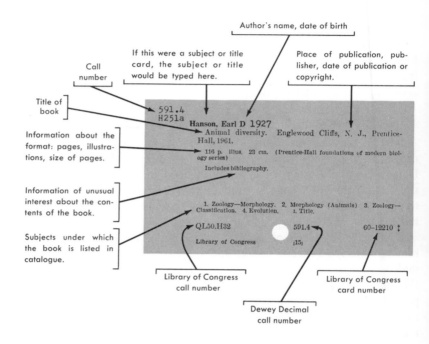

Author's name, date of birth

Call number

If this were a subject or title card, the subject or title would be typed here.

Place of publication, publisher, date of publication or copyright.

Title of book

Information about the format: pages, illustrations, size of pages.

Information of unusual interest about the contents of the book.

Subjects under which the book is listed in catalogue.

591.4
H251a
Hanson, Earl D 1927
Animal diversity. Englewood Cliffs, N. J., Prentice-Hall, 1961.
116 p. illus. 23 cm. (Prentice-Hall foundations of modern biology series)
Includes bibliography.

1. Zoology—Morphology. 2. Morphology (Animals) 3. Zoology—Classification. 4. Evolution. I. Title.

QL50.H32   591.4   60–12210 ‡
Library of Congress   [15]

Library of Congress call number

Dewey Decimal call number

Library of Congress card number

31-4 PRINTED CATALOGUES AND BIBLIOGRAPHIES

If books are not available in the local library, they may be obtained from other libraries, borrowed by interlibrary loan, or if they are important and in print, purchased. For these purposes, printed catalogues of the great libraries and printed bibliographies are indispensable. Three are the most useful for general work. The catalogue of the Library of Congress is available in some libraries on cards and has also been printed with supplements which bring the whole up to more than two hundred volumes. The catalogue of the British Museum has also been issued in supplements, though not yet brought down to date; it is excellent for older books, for British and Continental books, and for rare books. The *Cumulative Book Index* lists current books in English; in annual and cumulative five-year volumes it is known as the *U. S. Catalog of Books in Print*. Other bibliographies can be found through *Bibliographic Index: A Cumulative Bibliography of Bibliographies, 1938–* (New York, 1939–). Some libraries have a union card catalogue made up of cards for books in many libraries. Bibliographies for many subjects may be located conveniently through Constance M. Winchell, *Guide to Reference Books,* 7th ed. Chicago, 1951; supplements, 1954, 1956, 1960; 8th ed. in preparation.

The student should also be alert for bibliographies and bibliographic footnotes in books. These are often the best sources because they are prepared by experts in particular subjects. A good beginning bibliography can usually be found in an authoritative encyclopedia.

31-5 PERIODICAL AND NEWSPAPER INDEXES

With rare exceptions, magazine articles are not included in the card catalogues of libraries or in the general bibliographies. They must be located through special indexes. Magazine articles are often extremely important, more important than the writer who knows only popular magazines is likely to expect. There are scholarly, technical, scientific, and professional journals in all subjects of any consequence. They print highly technical material, some of which is never reprinted in book form, and they report the latest findings before this material can possibly be incorporated in books. Thus, extremely important information is available first in periodicals, and some very important material is available only in periodicals.

Good periodical indexes are "cumulated"; that is, they are constantly re-edited and republished in accordance with a system which keeps them up to date. For instance, the *Reader's Guide to Periodical Literature,* which indexes relatively popular magazines, appears every month. In February of any year, the library will receive a small number which indexes the January issues of magazines, and in March a number which indexes the February issues. In April, however, a larger number will arrive, in which all the issues of January, February, and March have been re-edited into one list. Thereafter one-month numbers will continue, but in August there will be an issue for six months. The following January there will be a number which cumulates the entire preceding year. Similarly, there will be two-year, three-year, and five-year cumulations, by which time the book has become so large that the cumulation begins all over again. In this way, the index can be kept constantly up to date, but the user does not have to thumb through the numbers for each month. The investigator should be sure, however, that he uses all the copies of the index to cover the time in which he is interested. He should be sure, also, that the periodicals he needs are indexed in the periodical index he is using; there will be a list somewhere, usually in the front of any volume. Most periodical indexes use a highly skeletonized style; the user should consult the list of abbreviations. Not all indexes are cumulated so frequently as is the *Reader's Guide,* but the principle is the same.

The following are the most useful indexes to periodical material published in English:

Poole's Index to Periodical Literature, 1802–1907. A pioneer work indexing leading English and American periodicals, this set is still valuable for its date; for more recent times it has been replaced by the next two items.

Reader's Guide to Periodical Literature, 1900——. The most useful general index in English, although it includes fewer serious or specialized periodicals than the *International Index.*

International Index to Periodicals, 1907——. Unusually useful for investigative papers of the sort under consideration, since it includes extremely important American and foreign periodicals in the sciences and humanities. It does not index highly specialized or technical journals.

Indexes to special subjects. Almost every field of study, and every subdivision of a large field of study has a specialized periodical index. Many of these are published in an issue of a periodical; for example, the most widely used current bibliography of the study of language and literature is that published in an annual number of the *Publications of the Modern Language Association,* and bibliographies of periods are likely to appear in journals of more restricted interest. Specialized indexes, not all of which are cumulated, include the following:

Agricultural Index, 1916——. Includes pamphlets.

Annual Bibliography of the Modern Humanities Research Association, 1924——. Discontinued during the Second World War, but presumably reorganized for publication.

Art Index, 1929——.

Book Review Digest, 1905——. Indexes reviews, with excerpts; not cumulated.

Dramatic Index, 1909——.

Education Index, 1929——. Includes both professional and academic journals.

Engineering Index, 1906——. Indexes, also, many subjects related to engineering.

Essay and General Literature Index, 1900____. Invaluable for locating essays by subject, fiction by theme, and the like.

Industrial Arts Index, 1913____. Indexes a large number of trade, technical, and industrial periodicals, many of them obscure. Includes pamphlets.

Official Index of the Times (London), 1906____. Cumulation has varied; now quarterly; for earlier references, see *Palmer's Index to the Times Newspaper,* 1868____.

New York Times Index, 1913____. Cumulation available, but not in all libraries.

Public Affairs Information Service, 1915____.

Work in Progress in the Modern Humanities, 1938–42; presumably to be revived.

(For additional indexes, see Winchell, *Guide,* 31–4, above.)

31-6 BULLETINS AND PAMPHLETS

Bulletins and pamphlets vary, both in the manner of their publication and in their value; accordingly, libraries handle them in different ways, and they are often difficult to locate. Some bulletins come out more or less regularly and in series. For example, the Bureau of American Ethnology publishes what are called *Bulletins.* They may run to hundreds of pages of important original research not elsewhere available. On the other hand, a pamphlet issued to describe the beauties of a lake resort may be almost worthless. Accordingly, such questions arise as when is a pamphlet a pamphlet and when is it a book or a periodical? Which so-called pamphlets are worth cataloguing, which are worth keeping but not worth spending much money cataloguing, and which should be thrown away? No simple statement can be made about pamphlets, but something can be said. Some pamphlets are treated as though they are books, and are catalogued in the regular way and appear in the card catalogue. Practice varies, especially with the purposes of the library. In a university library having an active anthropology department, the Bureau of American Ethnology *Reports* and *Bulletins* are likely to be catalogued. In a public library they are likely not to be. If they are not catalogued as individual volumes, they are likely to be catalogued as a series with authors and titles on a central card under the name of the series. As indicated above, some pamphlets are listed in periodical indexes, even though they are not periodicals. Government bulletins—and they include quantities of extremely important material—appear in the

United States Document Catalogue. Many libraries collect documents
by subject, especially on local topics.

31-7 REFERENCE BOOKS

Some books are so useful for ready reference that most libraries
keep them on special reference shelves or at a reference desk. The
most important works in all fields, including reference works, can be
located through Winchell, *Guide to Reference Books,* cited in 31-4.
Some reference works are so useful that everyone should know them
without reference to Winchell.

Dictionaries. For the most important dictionaries of English, see 25-1.
Encyclopedias and specialized dictionaries. Encyclopedias and specialized
 dictionaries are good to start with but not to finish with. They should
 be used mainly to acquire a reliable introduction, for brief bibliographies, and to verify routine details. They should not be used as
 crutches to avoid serious investigation.

Useful general encyclopedias include the following:

Encyclopaedia Britannica, 14th ed., 1929, 24 vols. This work is in continuous revision, so that important articles may be quite recent;
 some articles are signed. Scholarly articles in the eleventh edition are
 still valuable, as are some in the thirteenth. For many purposes this
 is the best general encyclopedia in English.
Encyclopedia Americana, rev. ed., 1945, 30 vols. In many ways similar
 to the *Britannica;* less detailed on most subjects, but often more detailed for American material.
New International Encyclopedia, 2nd ed. 1914–16, rev. 1922–30, 25
 vols. Older and briefer than the two previous items and with fewer
 signed articles, but useful.

Encyclopedias are available in most important European languages, some
of them excellent. In addition, some encyclopedias, although limited by
area or a sectarian approach, are yet sufficiently inclusive so that they
serve for general reference work. They include the following:

Catholic Encyclopedia, 1907–22, 17 vols.
Encyclopedia of the Social Sciences, 1908–12, 12 vols. and index.
 1949–50, 13 vols.
Hasting's *Encyclopedia of Religion and Ethics,* 1908–27, 12 vols. and
 index.
New Schaff-Herzog Encyclopedia of Religious Knowledge, 1949–50,
 13 vols.

Encyclopedias and handbooks of more specialized subjects can save time
and trouble:

Bartlett's *Familiar Quotations,* 12th ed., 1948.
Grove's *Dictionary of Music and Musicians,* 5th ed., 1954, 9 vols.
Handbook of Chemistry and Physics, 1914——.
Harper's Dictionary of Classical Literature, 1897.
Mencken's A New Dictionary of Quotations, 1942.
Oxford Companion to American Literature, 3rd ed., 1956.
Oxford Companion to English Literature, 3rd ed., 1946.
Oxford History of Music, 2nd ed., 1931–38, 6 vols.
Mythology of All Races, 1916–32, 13 vols.

Collections of biographical accounts in English include the following:

Dictionary of National Biography (called *DNB*), 1882–1949, 22 vols.
Treats important British figures no longer living.
Dictionary of American Biography (called *DAB*), 1928–1936, 20 vols.
and index. Supplements, 1944, 1958. *American* refers to the United
States.

Briefer accounts are included in the following:

Who's Who, 1849——. Biographical accounts of British subjects and
some others of great prominence.
Who's Who in America, 1899——. For living citizens of the United
States. For names not in the general volume, see *Who's Who in New
England,* 1915——; *in the East,* 1943——; *in the Midwest,* 1949——;
in the West, 1949——.
Who Was Who, 1897——. Useful for those not included in *DAB;* supple-
ments roughly by decades.

Similar works are available in the native language for most large countries.
More specialized dictionaries of biography include the following:

American Men of Science, 9th ed. 1956.
Century Dictionary and Cyclopedia, 1911, 12 vols.
Current Biography, 1940——.
Directory of American Scholars, 2d ed., 1951.
Twentieth Century Authors, 1942——.
Webster's Biographical Dictionary, 1943.

Almanacs and Yearbooks. Some publications bring within ready compass
statistics and miscellaneous information about a variety of subjects of
general, and especially of current interest. Most of them are revised
annually, with statistics brought down to date for the previous year or
the most recent compilation. They include the following:

Facts on File, 1940——. A weekly digest under headings like *Sport,
World Affairs.*
Statesman's Yearbook, 1864——. Standard; strong international bent,
with emphasis on political and commercial subjects.

Statistical Abstract of the United States, 1878——. The most extensive body of general statistical information readily available in English.
World Almanac and Book of Facts, 1868——. Perhaps the best of a number of almanacs published by newspapers; another good one is that published by the *Chicago Daily News*. These are cheap; every student should have one on his desk.

A number of encyclopedias publish annual supplements, surveys for the year; they include the following: *Encyclopedia Americana, Encyclopaedia Britannica, New International Encyclopedia.*

31-8   THE TRIAL BIBLIOGRAPHY

The first step in any investigation is the preparation of a trial or preliminary bibliography. This bibliography has several uses. Through it the investigator discovers what has already been learned about his subject, and accordingly, what is left for him to do. It provides him with a general view of his subject and its relationships, with the titles of the most important works on his subject, and with an orderly way of working. Since he now has a list of all the best known works, he can start with the more general and the more important.

To make a trial bibliography, the investigator should make intelligent use of available bibliographical and reference tools. First, he should look up the subject in some general works, in encyclopedias, for instance. Next, he should consult the card catalogue, using first the subject entries. If there are general works on the subject, they should be consulted in a preliminary way for bibliography. Anyone who has written on the subject should be looked up in the card catalogue as an author; for if a man writes a book on a subject, he may include information on the same subject in another book, although too little to warrant a subject card in the catalogue. Meanwhile, the investigator should be considering other sorts of publications. Is the subject of such nature that there would be magazine articles on it? If so, what index would cover magazines that might include articles on the subject? Would there be pamphlets or documents on the subject?

For instance, let us assume that a writer has realized that the system of roads in the United States is one of the great achievements of man and has decided to learn more about road building. He looks up *roads, transportation,* and *road building* in several encyclopedias. He discovers that modern methods of building roads have developed in the last two centuries, and he then looks up social histories, like Traill's *Social England,* and books on transportation. In some of these he finds extensive bibliographies and bibliographical footnotes, and he makes cards for these (see 31-9). In one of them he notes that when Josiah Wedgwood's dishes became popular all over Europe, Wedgwood built private roads, because the public roads were so bad that he had to pack his dishes on muleback, and when packs slipped off mules, that was the end of the dishes. The writer is interested and tries to find out all he can about Wedgwood and his ware. He looks him up in the *DNB* and finds biographies of him and bibliographical suggestions for further investigation. He discovers that there is an elaborate series of British local histories, called the *Victoria County Histories,* and he surmises that the county history for Wedgwood's shire will tell him something about the roads of the area and probably refer to more detailed studies which will include Wedgwood's roads. By now the writer is well on his way to locating the material for an investigative paper on the manner in which ornamental vases contributed to the revolution in road building. From now on he has only to use reference works intelligently and faithfully.

There are two things the investigator should not do. He should not begin by asking the librarian, "Is there anything in the library on building roads?" There are hundreds, thousands of works in any good library on building roads, but the librarian does not have time to prepare a list of them. That is the investigator's job, not the librarian's. Similarly, the investigator should not try to get his work done for him by writing an authority for information; he should not write the county engineer, "Please tell me all you know about building roads." Most of what an investigator wants to know is in published form; his job is to find it.

31-9 BIBLIOGRAPHY CARDS

As fast as the investigator locates titles which may be pertinent to his subject, he should prepare his bibliography. Most competent investigators use a system something like the following:

They provide themselves with small cards or slips of paper of uniform size; three-by-five-inch cards are customary. They use one card and only one for each book, article, or pamphlet. On it they write the name of the author first, exactly as it appears on the title page except that the last name is put first. They record the bibliographical information in accordance with a style like that described below. They often add the library call number for the book, for their own con-

venience, and any brief comment they may wish for their later use.
A bibliography card for a book looks like this:

Full name of author,
last name first

Title underlined to
indicate italics

Place and date of pub-
lication, to identify the
edition used.

Indication of volumes
when there are more
than one.

WARD, Christopher

The War of the Revolution

New York: Macmillan, 1952. 2 vols.

973.33
W21
1952

*(Detailed descriptions of
battles. Full accounts of
personnel involved.
Bibliography.)*

Call number

Comment for later reference

Some bibliographies include other information. Most bibliographies
omit the publishers for books out of print or books published more
than fifty-six years ago and hence out of copyright.

A bibliography card for a magazine article looks like this:

WOLLE, Francis

Title of article in
quotation marks

"What the GI's Did to Homer"

Title of magazine
underlined

College English, XIII (1952), 438–444

in Roman numerals
Volume specified

*(The experience of a professor of Eng-
lish with convalescent GI's who
discovered that Homer knew about
war.)*

Year of magazine
in which article
appears

Pages occupied
by article

The month of issue and the number of the magazine are sometimes added.

A bibliography prepared on cards of this sort can be expanded indefinitely without becoming confused. The cards can be kept in a file drawer for ready reference; they are usually filed alphabetically by the author's last name (alphabetically by the first important word of the title if the work is anonymous).

31-10 BIBLIOGRAPHICAL FORM

A bibliography of the principal works consulted, including all those cited in the paper, is customarily appended to a long documented composition. The entries should follow a standard form, and the form should be used in entering information on cards of the preliminary bibliography. Styles for bibliographies vary in details according to the field of investigation and the publication for which the paper is written. All publications of any consequence have a style sheet, which formalizes practice; if a writer knows he is writing for a specific publication, he should acquire the style sheet of that publication and follow it. Described here is one of the standard styles. Others vary in details, some using periods rather than commas between items or omitting the parentheses around publication data, but the student should become familiar with the common practice of taking a style and following it scrupulously, even though on another occasion he may be asked to follow a different style. The recommendations below, which follow the style sheet adopted by the Modern Language Association, are widely used for literary and humanistic studies.

Some bibliographical entries, especially those in elaborate series, become complicated, but the basic entry is as follows: last name of author, comma; remainder of author's name and collaborators, period; title of book, underlined (for print, in italics), period; place of publication, comma; date of publication, period. The following is a typical bibliographical entry:

> Hockett, Charles F. *A Course in Modern Linguistics*. New York, 1958.

If the publisher is included, the style becomes as follows:

> Hockett, Charles F. *A Course in Modern Linguistics*. New York: Macmillan, 1958.

If the work runs to more than one volume, the number of volumes and the inclusive dates should be given as in the following:

> Baker, Ernest A. *The History of the English Novel.* 10 vols. London, 1924–39.

The following entry provides a form for a work having more than one author and for a work having a subtitle:

> Bernbaum, Ernest, Samuel C. Chew, Thomas M. Raysor, Clarence D. Thorpe, and René Wellek. *The English Romantic Poets: A Review of Research.* New York, 1950.

If the edition is not the first, this fact may be noted as follows:

> Baugh, Albert C. *A History of the English Language,* 2nd ed. New York, 1957.

Works for which the author is not given on the titlepage may be listed under *Anon.* for anonymous, but are usually entered by title; if the author is known but his name does not appear on the titlepage, it may be inserted within square brackets, and with a question mark if the identification is uncertain, as follows:

> [Wesley, John?]. *The Complete English Dictionary.* Bristol, Eng., 1764.

The same rule usually applies if an anonymous work has an editor, but an edition, particularly one cited for the editor's notes, may be alphabetized under either the title or the editor, as follows:

> *Beowulf* and *The Fight at Finnsburg.* Ed. Fr. Klaeber. New York, 1928.
> Klaeber, Fr., ed. *Beowulf* and *The Fight at Finnsburg.* New York, 1928.

A similar style serves for translations, as follows:

> *Translations from the Chinese.* Trans. Arthur Waley. New York, 1919.

If the date of publication cannot be determined, it may be replaced with n.d., for *no date.* If it is not on the titlepage, most styles permit using the copyright date as the date of publication. If the date is not given but is known, it may be inserted within square brackets, and if it is uncertain it may be followed with a question mark. Some publications in series are sufficiently complicated bibliographically that no brief statement will provide for all contingencies, but much can be inferred from the following entry:

> Young, Karl. *The Origin and Development of the Story of Troilus and Criseyde,* Chaucer Society, 2nd Ser., No. 40. London, 1908 [for 1904].

For other examples, see *The MLA Style Sheet,* compiled by William Riley Parker (New York, 1951), pp. 14–17.

For articles and selections, this standard bibliographical form is adapted to account for the name of the article, which is enclosed within quotation marks, and the name of the book or periodical, in italics, as follows:

> Wolle, Francis. "What the G.I.'s Did to Homer," *College English,* XII (1952), 438–444.
> Lewis, C. S. "Hamlet: The Prince or the Poem?" *Hamlet: Enter Critic,* ed. Claire Sacks and Edgar Whan. New York, 1960. pp. 170–187.

It will be noted that the article and the periodical are treated as a continuous description, with commas instead of periods, and that the page numbers in the periodical or the book must be included. If the volume number is given, the abbreviation for pages is not used. For a periodical the number or other identification may be included, and must be included unless the whole volume of the periodical is paged consecutively, as follows:

> Marriott, Alice. "Beowulf in South Dakota," *The New Yorker,* XXVII, iv (1952), 42–45.
> Updike, John. "Recital," *The New Yorker* (June 10, 1961), 29.

If pages are interrupted, they may appear as follows: 6–18, 81, 90.

31-11 FOOTNOTE FORM

Footnotes do not become a problem until the student starts to write, but for simplicity they may be reviewed here, since footnote form closely follows bibliographical form. In general, the two differ in four ways: (1) the name of the author is not reversed, since no alphabetizing is involved; (2) the page or pages referred to must be included; (3) the footnote carries a superscript number, and (4) the style presumes that the footnote is a sort of a statement, and hence the punctuation is changed so that terminal periods do not appear within the footnote citation—periods will, of course, appear after abbreviations and between sentences in a discussional footnote. The basic bibliographical note given above would appear in a first footnote as follows:

> [1] Charles F. Hockett, *A Course in Modern Linguistics* (New York, 1958), pp. 46–53.

> [1] Charles F. Hockett, *A Course in Modern Linguistics* (New York: Macmillan, 1958), p. 219.

If the author's complete name has been given in the text, it may be omitted from the footnote, as follows:

> [1] *A Course in Modern Linguistics* (New York, 1958), p. 89.

If the work runs to more than one volume, the volume must be identified, but the abbreviation for page or pages is not used:

> [2] Ernest A. Baker, *The History of the English Novel* (London, 1939), X, 63.

Other details, such as editors and translators, are inserted as in the bibliographical form, but separated from each other and from the remainder of the citation by commas. Similarly, the footnote form for articles in periodicals and for briefer pieces within a collection reflects the bibliographical form, as follows:

> [27] Francis Wolle, "What the G.I.'s Did to Homer," *College English,* XII (1952), 441.

> [13] C. S. Lewis, "Hamlet: The Prince or the Poem?" *Hamlet: Enter Critic,* ed. Claire Sacks and Edgar Whan (New York, 1960), p. 183.

> [35] Alice Marriott, "Beowulf in South Dakota," *The New Yorker,* XXVII, iv (1952), 44.

If he knows the source of a reprinted article or monograph, the writer may well include this in his footnote, as follows:

> [13] C. S. Lewis, "Hamlet: The Prince or the Poem?" *Hamlet: Enter Critic,* ed. Claire Sacks and Edgar Whan (New York, 1960), p. 183; repr. from *Proceedings of the British Academy,* XXXVII (London, 1942), 1–18.

If the writer is relying on material not available to him, but cited in a secondary work which is available, he may cite as follows:

> 28 Thomas Campbell, *Essays on English Poetry* (London, 1848), p. 39; cited in Albert C. Baugh, *A History of the English Language,* 2nd ed. (New York, 1957), p. 224.

For simplicity in dealing with periodicals which do not follow the familiar pattern of volume numbers and consecutive pagination, or which have relatively complicated subdivisions with pagination within the subdivisions, an acceptable form is as follows:

> 47 "The Problem of Atomic Energy" (editorial), *The New York Times,* March 4, 1951, Sec. 4, p. 8.

Common dictionaries and encyclopedias arranged alphabetically may be cited without the conventional bibliographical details as follows:

> 39 *Encyclopaedia Britannica,* 14th ed., under "Jonson, Ben."

> 40 Sidney Lee, *DNB,* under "Marlowe, Christopher."

All these forms serve for the first citation from a given work; thereafter the citation is abbreviated for convenience. Currently, the best practice is to use the author's last name, a shortened title, or both, mentioning this abbreviation in the first footnote from the work. For example, if an article concerns the works of one figure, the title may be reduced to *Works* and footnotes handled as follows:

> 17 *The Complete Works of Chaucer,* ed. Fred N. Robinson, rev. ed. (Cambridge, Mass., 1957), p. xii, hereafter cited as *Works.*

> 21 *Works,* p. 547.

Similarly, a work may be cited by the abbreviated title, or if only one work is cited from an author, by the author's name. The first work cited above might well be abbreviated Hockett or *Linguistics.*

> 1 Charles F. Hockett, *A Course in Modern Linguistics* (New York, 1958), pp. 46–53; hereafter cited as Hockett.

> 5 Hockett, p. 275.

Earlier practice encouraged reference to a work already cited by one of the following abbreviations: ibid., loc. cit., and op. cit., usually not now printed in italics. Modern practice is to discourage use of these abbreviations, since they can be confusing and save little or no space; if they are used they should be employed as follows:

> [14] Albert C. Baugh, *A History of the English Language,* 2nd ed. (New York, 1957), p. 38.

> [15] Ibid., p. 65.

> [22] Baugh, op. cit., p. 91.

> [24] Baugh, loc. cit.

The abbreviations must be used with the following restrictions. *Ibid.* is the abbreviation for *ibidem,* meaning "in the same place," and hence can be used only to refer to a single citation in the immediately preceding footnote. *Op. cit.* is the abbreviation of *opere citato,* meaning "in the work cited," and hence can be used for a work recently cited, but for a different page in that work. *Loc. cit.* is the abbreviation for *loco citato,* "in the place or passage cited," and hence does not include a page number and can be used only if the citation refers to the same page or passage identified in the previous citation.

Highly specialized writings, notably scholarly, scientific, and technical studies, usually employ letter abbreviations for standard journals and reference tools; *Publications of the Modern Language Association* becomes *PMLA; Webster's New World Dictionary of the American Language* becomes *WNWD,* and the *Library of Congress Catalogue* becomes *LC.* These abbreviations are permissible only if they are indicated in a footnote as above, if they are included in a list of abbreviations in the book or periodical, or if the work is intended for a very restricted body of readers, all of whom can be expected to know the abbreviations. Usually they are appropriate in student writing only if they are individually identified in the first footnote citation to the work.

For reference, the prescriptions for footnotes in the Modern Language Association *Style Sheet* are reprinted below, minus the footnotes:

For Books

    a. Author's or authors' names in normal order, not as though they were being alphabetized, followed by a comma. By always giving names in the fullest form known to you, or at least the most usual form, you may save your reader many minutes of searching in a library catalogue, e.g., for "H. M. Jones."

b. *Title of the chapter or part* of the book cited, enclosed in quotation marks (not underlined), followed by a comma inside the final quotes. This detail is rarely necessary except in references to articles in collections, Festschriften, etc.

c. *Title of the work,* underlined, followed by a comma unless the next detail is enclosed in parentheses. Some abbreviation of the title is permissible in cases of books with unusually long titles; but the first few words should always be cited intact, and any later omissions *within* the portion cited should be indicated by three periods (. . .). Always take the title from the title page, not from the cover or running title. If there is a subtitle, underline it as well and, if necessary, supply appropriate punctuation (usually a colon). If there are typographical peculiarities in the title (e.g., an italicized name of a play), you may normalize them, using quotation marks or roman for something there italicized.

d. *Editor's or translator's name* in normal order, preceded by "ed." or "trans." (without parentheses), followed by a comma unless the next detail is enclosed in parentheses. If the editor's or translator's work rather than the text is under discussion, give his name *first* in your reference (followed by a comma, followed by "ed." or "trans." without punctuation) and the author's name *after* the title, with a comma and "by."

e. *Edition used,* whenever the edition is not the first, in Arabic numerals (e.g., "4th ed."), followed by a comma unless the next detail is enclosed in parentheses. Unless you are concerned with your author's changes of opinion, or with differences in text, you will of course have used the latest *revised* edition or will inform your reader of your inability to do so.

f. *The series* (if unnamed on the title page), not underlined and not in quotation marks, followed by a comma, followed by the number of this work in the series (e.g., "VII" or "Vol. VII" or "No. 7"), followed by a comma unless the next detail is enclosed in parentheses. If, however, your reference is to part of a collection or section of works named on the title page, the more general title is also underlined and may be introduced by "in."

g. *The number of volumes* with this particular title, if more than one (e.g., "3 vols.") and if the information is pertinent. It is usually not pertinent when your reference is to a specific passage rather than to the book as a whole.

h. *Place(s) and date(s) of publication,* within parentheses, the place followed by a comma; but if the publisher's or bookseller's name is also supplied, it follows the place of publication, preceded by a *colon,* and followed by a comma. Except in articles with a bibliographical slant or purpose, or except when acknowledgment for permission to quote must be made, it is usually pointless to add the name of the publisher, for this information rarely aids in identification of the book. Some scholars, however, regularly include the information for all works still in the copyright period (i.e., published within the last 56 years), assuming a legitimate interest by the reader. In listing places avoid ambiguity (e.g., Cambridge—Mass. or Eng.) or vagueness.

i. Volume number, if one of two or more, in capital Roman numerals, preceded and followed by a comma, unless it is necessary to give the date of a single volume (in parentheses, followed by a comma). Use the volume number alone (without "Vol.") if the page number follows, e.g., "III, 248–251."

j. Page numbers in Arabic numerals (unless the original has small Roman numerals), preceded by a comma, followed by a period unless an additional reference is required, e.g., "p. 47, n. 3." The numerals are preceded by "p." or "pp." only for works of a single volume.

Articles in Periodicals

a. Author's name in normal order, followed by a comma. Here it is not so important as in the case of books to give the name in the fullest possible form, but if only initials are given, give them all (and, in typing, leave a space between them).

b. Title in full, enclosed in quotation marks (not underlined), followed by a comma inside the second quotation marks.

c. Name of the periodical, abbreviated in accord with good usage, underlined, followed by a comma.

d. Volume number (without "Vol." preceding) in capital Roman numerals, followed by a comma unless the next detail is enclosed in parentheses. Volume numbers of newspapers and weekly or monthly magazines may be omitted and the complete date given instead—with commas, not parentheses.

e. Issue number or name (e.g., "Autumn") if the pagination of the issue is separate and if, then, the month of publication is not also given.

f. The year (preceded by the month, if needed; see *e*), enclosed in parentheses, followed by a comma. The year should always be given unless it has been noted in your text, for it tells the reader at once how recent the study is and serves also as a useful check on the volume number in the act of location. If the volume covers more than one year, give only the year of the number involved.

g. Page number(s) in Arabic numerals, without "p." or "pp." preceding, followed by a period unless an additional reference to a footnote is needed.

EXERCISE 31

A. Using the style recommended and information in the examples above, correct the following as bibliographical entries:

1. A Course in Linguistics by Charles F. Hackett, published by the Mac Milan Company, Inc., in New York early in 1958

2. Fong, Doreen Yes Hung; The Joy of Chinese Cooking, New York, Greenberg, publisher. It has no date, but it was new in 1951.

3. Otto Jespersen, *Language,* its nature, development, and origin, (New York, the MacMillan company, 1922, pp. 85.

4. G. N. Clark, "Social and Economic Aspects of Science in the Age of Newton. Economic History 3. 1937. pp. 362–79.

5. Davidson, Martin: *The Stars and the Mind,* a study of the impact of astronomical development on human thought, 210 pages long. (London: 1947)

6. August Goll, *Criminal types in Shakespeare, Journal of Criminal Law and Criminology* 29, (1938) 492–516.

7. Ruth Leila Anderson, *Elizabethan Psychology and Shakespeare's Plays,* University of Iowa Humanistic Studies (1927) III, number 4.

8. Greenlaw, Edwin. The New Science and English Literature in the seventeenth century. 331–54. Johns Hopkins Alumni Mag. XIII, 1925

B. Assume that you have footnote references to the works in 31A in sequence as follows:

Fong, p. 86; Davidson, p. 21; Jespersen, pp. 89–91; Greenlaw, pp. 121–23; Jespersen, p. 181; Clark, p. 371; Anderson, p. 16; Jespersen, pp. 186–190.
Prepare the appropriate footnotes.

C. Below are twenty titles of reference works and twenty questions which have answers in the books. For each question indicate which reference book would be likely to supply the answer.

1. *World Almanac*
2. *Statesman's Yearbook*
3. *Encyclopaedia Britannica*
4. *Dictionary of National Biography*
5. *Dictionary of American Biography*
6. *Catholic Encyclopedia*

7. *Statistical Abstracts*
8. *Facts on File*
9. *Hastings Encyclopaedia of Religion and Ethics*
10. *Harper's Dictionary of Classical Literature*
11. *Dictionary of Americanisms*
12. *New English Dictionary on Historical Principles*
13. Winchell, *Guide to Reference Books*
14. *American Men of Science*
15. *Bibliographic Index*
16. Bartlett's *Familiar Quotations*
17. *Who's Who in America*
18. *New York Times Index*
19. *Mythology of All Races*
20. *Grove's Dictionary of Music and Musicians*

1. When was the sonata first popular as a type of musical composition?
2. What is the educational background of the present Secretary of State of the United States?
3. What is the history of the word *mugwump*?
4. Who is currently head of the government of Venezuela?
5. Where is the original of the Magna Carta?
6. When did the term *sans-culotte* develop with a political meaning?
7. What is the title of a standard bibliography of English history?
8. When did a wrestling team from Notre Dame last compete at the University of Michigan?
9. What beliefs are associated with the god Krishna?
10. Who discovered electric welding?
11. What is the story told of the Virgin of Guadalupe?
12. Is it true that Watt became interested in steam engines while watching his mother's kettle?
13. Who wrote, "Ring out wild bells to the wild sky"?
14. What were the twelve labors of Hercules?
15. Who were the Nobel Prize winners of 1961?
16. Is there a prepared bibliography on diamond cutting?
17. How does it happen that Buddhism has become common in China but has lost popularity in India?
18. What college or university did the head of your department of physics attend as an undergraduate?

19. What was the sixteenth-century meaning of the word *fond*?
20. What Greek plays deal with stories of the family of Atreus?

D. By using conventional reference aids, answer the following questions and specify where you found each answer.

1. What is the most recent history of India in your library?
2. When the conflict between Juan Domingo Perón and the Roman Catholic Church led to fighting in the streets of Buenos Aires, which of the armed forces supported Perón?
3. Is there a concordance of Omar Khayyám? If so, when was it published?
4. Locate and name two recent magazine articles on trout fishing.
5. When was the word *gig* current to refer to a rowing boat used for racing?
6. How many students attended the University of Wisconsin last year?
7. According to classical mythology, who was the great-great-grandfather of Jason?
8. What is the source of the quotation: "Great wits are sure to madness near allied"?
9. What was the height of the winning pole vault in the most recent Western Conference outdoor track meet?
10. What is the height of the tallest mountain peak in Europe?
11. In what city did the word *hoodlum* originate?
12. In Jewish religion, what is the length of the knife to be used in Shehitah, or the ritual slaughtering of animals?
13. What was the maiden name of the wife of one of the senators of your state?
14. Who are the authors of a bibliography of the writings of Washington Irving published in 1936?
15. Of what type is the government of Liberia?
16. What is the most recent article published on extracting salt from sea water?
17. Where was Winston Churchill born?
18. What was Tennyson's first published book?
19. Where did the word *blizzard* come from?
20. Of what New York periodicals was Noah Webster once editor?

32

Writing A
Research Report

Evidence should be organized for clarity, and the report should be
written with grace and objective restraint to reveal the significance
of the material.

Any serious investigation usually results in a report; in fact,
the purpose of the investigation may be to provide a report. The report involves special problems. It is likely to result in a relatively long
composition; reports of research may run into many volumes, although
of course most of them do not, but they involve the principles of organizing longer papers discussed in 9, and the student may do well
to review that material before he writes a report of any extensive investigation. The report should be written in paragraphs (see 1–3),
and, for whatever reason, teachers know that students who have
learned to write paragraphs may forget this useful ability when they
are absorbed in endeavoring to organize and control a considerable
body of material which they have collected but have not thought
through very fully. These are, of course, routine techniques of composition, but some writing skills are more than usually characteristic
of a skillful writer of research reports.

32-1 STYLE IN THE INVESTIGATIVE PAPER

The handling of materials in any research report should be objective and relatively impartial, and the style should reflect this objectivity. If the writer has opinions to express, he should label his opinions clearly. In general, research reports are made in the third person.
Best practice now allows the use of the first person to avoid excessive
use of the passive voice where circumstances require some discussion
of the author and what he did—for instance, in describing how equip-

ment was set up, or why an investigation was conducted in a certain way—but a research report should be couched in generally objective terms.

The need for writing skill becomes acute in almost any research report, and developing the essential technique gives the young writer excellent training. The reader of any difficult or controversial report wants always to know whether the author is sure that he is right, whether his evidence is sound. But writers cannot always be sure; they do not always have adequate evidence. Thus the writer should make clear what he knows certainly and why; he should also make clear what he is saying because the evidence is extremely good, although inconclusive; and he should identify any observations which are guesses, which he has made just because they are his best guesses, subject to revision. Keeping the reader constantly aware of the writer's own estimate of the conclusiveness of his statements is not easy, and it can become cumbersome, although it need not be. Writing need not be pedestrian because it is exact and careful, and part of the secret of a good objective style grows from learning to keep the reader informed, unobtrusively, of the writer's own estimate of his material. The devices for doing this are legion, too numerous to be detailed here, but the beginning writer will do well to study competent pieces of serious writing, in magazines like *Harper's* and *The Atlantic,* for instance, and in scholarly and scientific journals.

Another problem bothers almost every beginning research worker: what should he do when the authorities disagree? They do disagree. Most important problems cannot be settled certainly and finally, and even for minor questions the evidence is often contradictory. If the writer finds no reason for preferring one of his disagreeing sources, he can present the evidence on all sides and cite all authorities in his footnotes. If he thinks one argument is better than the others, he can present it and then cite opposing evidence in a footnote. Even if he is sure that one side is right, he should cite any opposing opinions in footnotes.

Of course these are aspects of the same problem, and they may appropriately be considered together. Notice the following, an excerpt from a popular discussion of American English.

> That this meaning of the word *lumber* was brought to America
> is evident from its survival in some local dialects as well as from a

good deal of early legislation. The *Boston Records* for 1663 show
that the inhabitants were cautioned to "take care that noe wood,
logges, timber, stonnes, or any *other* lumber be layed upon the flatte
to the annoyance of any vesseles," and a similar law was passed in
1701 against encumbering any street, lane, or alley. Certainly in a
pioneer community with building going on constantly, cut timber
would inevitably be piled in the streets from time to time, and the
circumstance that this was so often the offending impediment seems
to have led to a specific association of *lumber* with cut or milled
wood, in contrast to uncut logs or possibly standing trees, as is suggested by the report of Sir Edmond Andros, written in 1678: "The
Comodityes of the Country to ye westward are wheat . . . pipe
staves, timber, lumber & horses."

—ALBERT H. MARCKWARDT, *American English*

Since the book is intended for popular reading, Marckwardt does
not provide footnotes, but the passage indicates that documentation
is essentially a quality written into the prose itself, a characteristic of
style to which the footnotes are only an important appendage. Exact
documentation is not possible, because without footnotes Marckwardt's sentences would become too cluttered with details if he were
to provide all bibliographical information, but the essential documentation is there. The writer quotes his sources exactly, and he gives
enough evidence of source so that we are convinced he is founding
his observations upon carefully selected fact, and we are even provided with rough citations. Marckwardt mentions these sources
urbanely, making no great to-do about them; but any examination of
his terminology will reveal that he is constantly assessing his evidence
and making us quietly aware of when he feels confident and when
he is making a plausible guess. He starts by saying that the survival
of the meaning in America "is evident," and he indicates that he has
two sorts of evidence, survival in dialects and direct legislation. He
then cites two specific instances in which building materials cluttering
up streets or the waterfront were called *lumber;* here he makes flat
assertions, but he is very careful what he asserts. He says the "inhabitants were cautioned," and he apparently assumes we will presume that the caution was needed. He points out that the caution
might well be needed in a pioneer community. So much for his background; he is now ready for his main conclusion, the reason for his
paragraph—how did a word which meant something like *rubbish*
come to mean "cut or milled logs"? He believes he has the answer,

but the answer is only inferred; he has no direct, reliable evidence for it, and accordingly he makes his proposal, but cautiously: "The circumstance . . . seems to have led to a specific association. . ." He has some collateral evidence, but this also is not conclusive, and accordingly he uses the phrase "as is suggested." That is, though Marckwardt does not in this passage have the advantage of being able to use footnotes, he has written the essence of his documentation and his estimate of the worth of his evidence into the text itself; this is sound practice, even when the writer is writing for an audience that welcomes footnotes.

The next passage is from a documented history of the English language, with the footnote numbers changed to avoid confusion:

According to the same chronicler [1] William the Conqueror made an effort himself at the age of forty-three to learn English, that he might understand and render justice in the disputes between his subjects, but his energies were too completely absorbed by his many other activities to enable him to make much progress. There is nothing improbable in the statement. Certainly the assertion of a fourteenth century writer [2] that the Conqueror considered how he might destroy the 'Saxon' tongue in order that English and French might speak the same language seems little less than silly in view of the king's efforts to promote the belief that he was the authentic successor of the Old English kings and in the light of his use of English alongside of Latin, to the exclusion of French, in his charters. His youngest son, Henry I, may have known some English, though we must give up the pretty story of his interpreting the English words in a charter to the monks of Colchester.[3] If later kings for a time seem to have been ignorant of the language,[4] their lack of acquaintance with it is not to be attributed to any fixed purpose. In the period with which we are at the moment concerned—the period up to 1200—the attitude of the king and the upper classes toward the English language may be characterized as one of simple indifference. They did not cultivate English—which is not the same as saying that they had no acquaintance with it—because their activities in England did not necessitate it and their constant concern with continental affairs made French for them much more useful.

—ALBERT C. BAUGH, *A History of the English Language*

[1] Ordericus Vitalis, ed. Prevost, II, 215.

[2] Robert Holkot, on the authority of John Selden, *Eadmeri Monachi Cantuariensis Historiae Novorum siue sui Saeculi Libri VI* (London, 1623), p. 189.

[3] The story was considered authentic by so critical a student as J. Horace Round ("Henry I. as an English Scholar," *Academy,* Sept. 13, 1884, p. 168), but the charter has since been proved by J. Armitage Robinson to be a forgery. Cf. C. W. David, "The Claim of King Henry I to Be Called Learned," *Anniversary Essays in Medieval History by Students of Charles Homer Haskins* (Boston, 1929), pp. 45–56.

[4] We do not know whether William Rufus and Stephen knew English. Henry II understood it although he apparently did not speak it (see below, p. 144). Richard I was thoroughly French; his whole stay in England amounted to only a few months. He probably knew no English. Concerning John's knowledge of English we have no evidence. As Freeman remarks (*Norman Conquest,* II. 128), the royal family at this time is frequently the least English in England and is not to be used as a norm for judging the diffusion of the two languages.

We may note some similarities and some differences between Marckwardt's and Baugh's paragraphs. Most notable, perhaps, is that they read very much alike. Marckwardt has no footnotes, and Baugh's treatment can be read without them. Both paragraphs read smoothly; like Marckwardt, Baugh can keep his reader constantly aware of where his evidence comes from and how much he, as a scholar, trusts it. He is constantly evaluating this evidence; he is aware that chroniclers have varied in statements about William the Conqueror and his attitude toward English. He notices the testimony of one chronicler that William at forty-three tried to learn English and he observes that "there is nothing improbable in the statement," but recognizing that chroniclers are not always reliable, he makes no commitment himself. He records but declines to accept the opinion of another writer, partly because the person lived long after William, partly because William's own actions seem to belie the statement. He rejects out of hand a legend concerning William's son; the chronicle reporting it has been proved a forgery. As for the knowledge of English possessed by other twelfth-century figures, he offers his own guess as "simple indifference." He does not labor his uncertainty; he does not say, "Of course this is just an opinion, and every man is entitled to his own opinion, but I have read a good many chronicles and scholarly studies, and I have tried hard to produce a fair answer, and for what it is worth, this is my best estimate." He implies all this, however, when he says "the attitude . . . may be characterized. . ." That is, scholarly writing that carries footnotes is much like scholarly writing which has no footnotes; it should be clear, orderly, well balanced, factual, judicial, urbane, and the reader should be able to follow it with or without the footnotes.

On the other hand, footnotes provide the scholarly writer distinct advantages; we might observe how Baugh exploits them. He can, of course, be more precise; he can cite works exactly, giving the edition, the volume and page; he can quote long titles intact, can cite more than one source for a fact, and all this without interrupting the flow of his prose. He can save space and the hurried reader's time by banishing some details to the footnotes. For example, he rejects the story of Henry I besting the monks of Colchester in a few words because he can provide the details in the footnote. He has examined the evidence and has found it so convincing that he need not equivocate; if the reader is not content to trust Baugh as a scholar, he probably will be convinced when he reads the footnote; if not, he has the references, and can pursue the question. Baugh does not need to defend his position in the text; but Marckwardt presumably would not have felt he could be so cavalier. What about those people who had read the story of Henry I in some old history book and had believed it all their lives? Doubtless, without footnotes, the writer would have felt he had to interrupt his account to explain why he doubted this story; the footnote permits the writer to make his decision and get on with pertinent parts of the discussion.

Somewhat different is the last footnote, because it allows Baugh to introduce material which, without footnotes, he would probably have felt provided enough of a digression so that he would have had to omit it. Some writers use footnotes even more extensively for this purpose than does Baugh; Van Wyck Brooks, for example, in a charming series of books on early America, has loaded his footnotes with bits of information not directly on his subject, but allied to it, and so engaging that many readers find the footnotes the juiciest parts of the books. This sort of thing can be carried too far; a scholarly writer should not use footnotes for any sort of gossip that comes into his head, but notes do permit a research worker to pass on bits which he has turned up that are not quite germane to his central purpose.

32-2 DOCUMENTATION

What should be documented? The ability to use footnotes deftly, to determine what requires documentation and what is so clear or obvious that no support is necessary, is one of the marks of a judicial mind and of a good research worker. In general, a research writer may think of his composition as a building set upon pilings; he needs a piling, that is, a footnote reference, under every key point in the structure. These points must be supported so that they are absolutely solid; the points in between need no support, but are held up by internal structure. Statements on which the writer's argument rests must be supported from beneath; the others should not be cluttered with footnotes. In general, footnotes can be profitably used for the following:

(1) *The source of a significant quotation.* In carefully documented writing, all direct quotations used as evidence should be identified with a footnote. Material quoted for embellishment need not be identified in a footnote. For instance, suppose a writer begins a discussion as follows:

> "In the beginning was the word"; whether or not we now accept this statement literally, words have been at the beginning of many ideas, and hence they have been at the beginnings of what grew out of the ideas.

The quotation from the New Testament does not require a footnote. Most readers would recognize it, and in any event it is only a stylistic device. If, however, the passage were used as evidence of the Greek veneration of language, it should carry a footnote.

(2) *The source of information not sufficiently familiar so that most readers would know it or be able to find it readily.* There need be no footnote for the date of Shakespeare's death or the name of the twenty-fifth president of the United States. Anyone who does not take the writer's word for such details can find them in dozens of reference works. But all major assertions in a serious discussion should be supported by footnotes.

(3) *Controversial matter and opposing views.* Any serious investigation is likely to lead the writer into fields where there are differ-

ences of opinion. Whether he takes sides or not, the writer should be sure that both sides are represented in footnote references.

(4) *Details or statistics that would interrupt the paper.* Statistics, figures, tables, or other supplementary data are sometimes placed in footnotes, where they are available for reference but do not interrupt the movement of the paper. With discretion, details too good to miss but not quite on the subject may be added in footnotes. Additional evidence intended for the unusually skeptical critic may be placed in footnotes.

32-3 CONVENTIONS OF THE RESEARCH PAPER

Footnotes are usually numbered consecutively through a brief paper or through a chapter of a long work. They are not now usually indicated by asterisks, daggers, and other printer's marks, because this system does not admit sufficient flexibility. Neither are footnotes now often numbered by pages; the numbers in the copy do not correspond with the numbers on the printed page, and mistakes are easy. Customarily a superior figure (made on the typewriter by turning the platen half a line) is placed in the copy directly after the word, passage, sentence, or paragraph to which the footnote refers. A similar number appears immediately before the footnote. The footnote begins, like any paragraph, with an indention, and like any sentence, with a capital letter. Footnotes are placed in one of three positions: (1) especially in papers not intended for publication they may be placed at the bottom of each page with a rule above the first note on the page; this system is convenient enough for the reader, somewhat irksome to the typist, who must estimate the space he needs at the bottom of each page; (2) they may be placed at the end of a brief paper, at the end of a chapter or a book; this arrangement is convenient for the writer and the typist, but may be maddening to a reader or an editor, who has to read with four stacks of manuscript in front of him; (3) they may be placed immediately after the line containing the citation, and ruled above and below; this method takes a bit more space, but is growing in popularity, especially for material intended for print, because it is the most convenient for the typist and a reader or editor.

Graphs, tables, and other illustrations or tabulated inserts are imperative for many technical papers, and much complicated material is best shown in visual or tabular form. The writer should always consider whether a table or an illustration will not make his meaning clearer. Inserts of this sort should usually be labeled for ready reference in the text. Use *plate* to refer to a full page (Plate IX), *figure* for an illustration in the text (Figure 8), and *table* for a tabular or graphic arrangement (Table 3).

Some abbreviations and standardized signals can be employed to save space in footnotes, and formerly Latin words and their abbreviations were used for this purpose, but the practice of using English is growing. Even if the Latin is used, modern practice permits dispensing with italics. A list of these symbols can be quite long (see *MLA Style Sheet,* pp. 20–22), but a student writing an investigative paper is not likely to need any but the most common. For most purposes, those in the following list will suffice:

p., pp.—page, pages.
l., ll.—line, lines.
v., vv.—verse, verses.
vol., vols.—volume, volumes.
no., nos.—number, numbers.
cf.—compare.
n.—note, footnote.
supra—above; preferred to ante; the English is now often preferred.
infra—below; preferred to post; the English is now often preferred.
c.—copyright; used when the date of a copyright is known but the date of publication is not.
c., ca.—circa, about; used in approximate dates (ca. 1888).
ff., et seq.—and following; not used in the best practice to complete a citation to pages; inclusive page reference (pp. 86–93) is preferable.
passim—at intervals through the work or pages cited.
sic—thus; may be used after an obvious error in a quotation to indicate that the error was in the original; best used sparingly; when inserted in a quotation, should be enclosed in brackets.
n.d.—no date.
ed.—editor, edited, edition.
tr.—translated by, translation.
rev.—revised.

32-4   SAMPLES OF RESEARCH OR INVESTIGATIVE REPORTS

Below are portions of two investigative papers of the sort that are commonly required in composition courses, written by students but somewhat revised for style. In form, they represent two variations on the form recommended in Chapter 31; in content they provide two applications of what have come to be known as "controlled research" pamphlets. These pamphlets, a development within recent years, present some distinct advantages: they avoid overburdening the library and discommoding students who cannot obtain books for which there is sudden demand; and they permit more careful study of the techniques of handling evidence, since the whole class is working on a common body of limited material. Many courses in composition now rely exclusively on one of these pamphlets to provide materials for one or more research projects; other courses use these pamphlets, but encourage the student to extend his subject by some work in the library. Still other courses, based on the theory that no student ever learns enough about how to use a library, require the student to dig out all the material himself, with no help from a specially collected body of material. Doubtless each sort of course has its virtues.

Of the selections which follow, that entitled "Young Man on a Horse" was written entirely from one research pamphlet; that entitled "A Yet Unexorcised Ghost" started with a research pamphlet and a paperback copy of the play, but the students were then required to continue their investigation in the library. For style as to the inclusion of publishers in the footnotes, and in the placing of the footnotes, the student should follow the form prescribed by the instructor. For the types of investigative paper the first should offer suggestions for papers written from research pamphlets; the second suggests procedures for papers involving library reference, whether or not the paper starts from a pamphlet of controlled research materials.

YOUNG MAN ON A HORSE

by

Agnes Arnold

It was the third day at Gettysburg, mid-afternoon. Major General George E. Pickett's rebel-yelling Confederates had stormed Cemetery Ridge, and were boiling over a stone wall and a rail fence which had provided some protection to Brigadier General Alexander S. Webb's troops, holding the Union center. If they succeeded, if the charging men in gray could stay there, if they could establish a front around the clump of trees to which they had marched across open fields, the Union forces would be split, the Army of the Potomac cracked and faced with disruption or extinction. Nothing adequate for defense would stand between General Robert E. Lee and his undefeated Army of Northern Virginia and the populous Northern cities, Philadelphia, New York, Boston. If Pickett's men had stayed on Cemetery Ridge, Lee could quite probably have dictated, from either New York or Philadelphia, the terms on which the United States of America was to become two countries rather than one.

A half hour later, the decimated remnants of Pickett's men who "had moved across that field of death as a battalion marches forward in line of battle upon drill," [1] were fleeing, those who could run or crawl. Perhaps the

---

[1] George E. Pickett, *Soldier of the South: General Pickett's War Letters to His Wife,* ed. Arthur Crew Inman (Boston: Little Brown, 1928), p. 70, hereafter referred to as Pickett; repr. *The Third Day at Gettysburg: Pickett's Charge,* ed. Alan M. Hollingsworth and James M. Cox (New York: Appleton-Century-Crofts, 1959), p. 97, hereafter referred to as *Third Day.* This paper is written entirely from documents reprinted in the latter work; when pagination can be inferred in the original publication, exact pages will be given; otherwise they will be given only for *Third Day.*

COMMENT

Miss Arnold uses an extensive introduction. Usually, such a long introduction would be quite inappropriate in a paper of moderate length, but her approach may be justified because it provides a dramatic opening to a semi-popular presentation and at the same time allows the author to introduce material which is to prove useful in the body of her paper.

The first part of the first footnote will serve as a typical example of a reference to a book which includes the publisher; since the author expects to use material from this book again, a short form is provided, and since this is the only piece of writing to be cited from Pickett, the name of the author provides the easiest form for brief reference. If the author were citing two books by Pickett, an appropriate shortened form would be "Pickett, *Letters*". The second half of the footnote introduces the collection of documents assigned, to which the student is restricted. The footnote can be taken as a model for reference to a book having no author; a shortened title of the book serves for subsequent citations. Many collections similar to *Third Day* have page numbers in the text to indicate the end of each page in the original; they thus permit exact references to the

most dramatic account of what turned the tide is that of Frank Aretas Haskell, a young Wisconsin civilian turned lieutenant, writing to his brother, H. M. Haskell.[2] Lieutenant Haskell was returning from an attempt to deliver a message when he stopped to view what he called the "tremendous" conflict, and observed that there was "no wavering in all our line." His account continues,

> Wondering how long the Rebel ranks, deep though they were, could stand our sheltered volleys, I had come near my destination, when—great heaven! were my senses mad? The larger portion of Webb's brigade—my God, it was true—there by the group of trees and the angles of the wall, was breaking from the cover of their works, and without orders or reason, with no hand lifted to check them, was falling back, a fear-stricken flock of confusion! The fate of Gettysburg hung upon a spider's single thread.[3]

Haskell goes on to tell how "a great magnificent passion" overcame him as he saw how "the damned red flags of the rebellion began to thicken and flaunt along the wall," and he dashed to stem "the tide of rabbits," commanding them to face about and fight, and beating with his sword on their "unpatriotic backs." Soon General Webb came sweating up on foot and "did all that one could to repair the breach," but his men were "falling fast." The Confederate flags "were accumulating at the wall every moment" now, and Webb had only three small regiments with which to oppose them. "Oh, where is Gibbon? where is Hancock? [4]—some general—anybody with the

---

[2] *The Battle of Gettysburg* (Wisconsin History Commission, November 1908), pp. 122–30; *Third Day,* 66–70.

[3] *Third Day,* p. 68.

[4] Major General Winfield S. Hancock was in command of the Second Army Corps, of which Brigadier General John Gibbon was second in command, and in direct command of the second division; Webb commanded the second brigade within this division. Generals Hancock and Gibbon were thus Webb's immediate superiors, as well as Haskell's. *Third Day,* 152–53.

original by using only the reprint, but this device is not employed in *Third Day.* If the author were writing for publication she would be expected to consult the original, but the student here is working within the restrictions of a class exercise.

Miss Arnold was instructed to accumulate footnotes at the bottom of each page.

In footnote 2 the author can refer to the original and the reprint since the reference is to the whole passage. The author is not yet ready to state her main idea, but she is centering attention on the central figure.

For footnote 3 the author is able to cite only *Third Day* exactly, since the ends of pages are not marked in the reprint. The instructor may indicate that, to save time, references may be restricted to either the original or the reprint, although strict scholarly practice would require providing both.

This footnote raises a more important question: how much of the original should the writer quote? She has elected to quote verbatim the description of the flight from the wall, partly because it is a dramatic scene dramatically recorded, but also because some of the later discussion is to hinge on this scene. She could, of course, have gone on quoting, but the whole passage would run to several hundred words, and

power and the will to support that wasting, melting line?"

Haskell had no troops under him, but he was aide to General Gibbon,[5] and thus had a sort of derived authority, so long as nobody asked questions. He set about trying to find help. The most copious body of reinforcements would have been the First Army Corps, which had not as yet been engaged, commanded by Major General Abner Doubleday,[6] but Haskell concluded that Doubleday was "too far and too slow," and he recalled, also, "on another occasion I had begged him to send his idle regiment to support another line battling with thrice its numbers, and this 'Old Sumpter Hero' had declined." [7] What about Hall?—Colonel Norman J. Hall, of the Seventh Michigan Infantry, commanding the third brigade, was stationed immediately to Webb's left.[8] His men had been under heavy attack, but "the fire was constantly diminishing now in his front." [9] Haskell located Hall, sword in hand, who agreed to "move my brigade at once," and soon five regiments were marching to the rescue of Webb's three. But this was not enough—how about Harrow? Brigadier General William Harrow was in command of the whole second division, and in addition—although Haskell did not know this at the time—he was now in command of the entire Second Army Corps,[10] since both Hancock and Gibbon had been severely wounded. Harrow could not be found, presumably because he had gone back to headquarters to relieve Hancock and Gibbon, but Haskell did

much of it is not germane to the writer's eventual purpose. Accordingly, she gives her own running account, but she inserts within it words, phrases, whole sentences from the original which preserve the flavor of Haskell's account, although she has reduced the original by about ninety per cent. One might notice that the author is writing sentences and is identifying all sources within the text of the article, but making no great to-do of her documentation. The citation is started unostentatiously in the sentence beginning "Haskell was . . ." by inserting the words "what he called the 'tremendous' conflict." No citation is necessary here because we get to it in the next sentence, and the two passages are related by "His account continues." After the quoted passage no further citation is necessary, because "Haskell goes on to tell" lets us know that the remaining details come from the next page or two.

Footnote 4 is informational; we need to know who these officers are. The author has worked out their relationships by studying the data supplied in the appendix.

Footnote 5 provides an example of a reference to a complicated title. Titles of this sort are not common, but they are relatively more common in scholarly and scientific

---

[5] *The War of the Rebellion: A Compilation of the Official Records of the Union and Confederate Armies,* series 1, vol. XXVII, part 1 (Washington, D.C., 1889), p. 30, hereafter referred to as *Official Records,* ser. 1, XXVII, pt. 1.; *Third Day,* p. 62.

[6] *Third Day,* p. 151.

[7] *Third Day,* p. 69.

[8] *Third Day,* pp. 42–43, 47, 153.

[9] *Third Day,* p. 69.

[10] *Third Day,* pp. 43–44, 152.

not stand on ceremony. He managed to get men from the Nineteenth Maine, the Fifteenth Massachusetts, the First Minnesota, and the Thirty-second New York Militia to follow him, and "all that I could find I took over to the right at the *double quick*." Arrived he saw that the Union troops had been pushed well up the ridge, that in their confused milling they were suffering terribly from the Confederate troops firing from the wall from which Webb's regiments had fled. Haskell endeavored to organize a charge on the wall, but with some difficulties, as his description reveals: [11]

> My "Forward to the wall" is answered by the Rebel counter-command, "Steady men!" and the wave swings back. . . These men of Pennsylvania, on the soil of their own homesteads, the first and only to flee the wall, must be the first to storm it. "Major—*lead* your men over the crest, they will follow." "By the tactics I understand my place is in the rear of the men." "Your pardon, sir; I see *your* place is in the rear of the men. I thought you were fit to lead." [12]

Under Haskell's urging, a color-sergeant dashed toward the wall and was shot down, but others followed him, gained the wall, breached it, and soon Pickett's charge was thrown back. The battle was won, and although nobody knew it yet, the issue of the war was determined.

---

[11] *Third Day,* p. 70.

[12] I have not been able to identify this major. The regiments referred to were the 69th and 71st Pennsylvania, but the skeletonized outline of the Union command provided in *Third Day,* pp. 151–155, includes no majors for these units. Captain William Davis, reporting for the 69th Pennsylvania, reported that "our major" was wounded. *Official Records,* ser. 1, XXVII, pt. 1, p. 432. The major, of course, had a point; troops were being constantly disrupted by the loss of their officers, who were obviously prime targets. For example, Pickett retired with only one field officer unhurt; he lists seven colonels and nine lieutenant colonels killed or seriously wounded. Pickett, p. 71; *Third Day,* 97.

writing than in most prose, and they are sometimes complicated enough so that they do not fit into a standard style. When in doubt the writer should give enough of the bibliographical details so that the specific volume can be certainly identified.

If the author were here trying to make a parade of her knowledge she could seed this passage with footnotes, but she wisely restricts them to the quotations which involve a change of page reference. If she were using abbreviations in footnotes she could use *ibid.* here. The instructor had designated a style not using abbreviations like *ibid.,* and *op. cit.*

One might notice that the author continues to keep the story dramatic by quoting bits from Haskell's account, but moves the story rapidly by relying mainly on her own summary. This procedure is the more appropriate because the essay depends in part on what Haskell did, how much of a hero he was; and since the writer's case is to hinge in part on the validity of Haskell's account as against Webb's official report, details are necessary but are best in Haskell's words. She could, of course, have reproduced Haskell's entire letter, but long undigested accounts are not usually so useful as more succinct versions with brief quoted passages.

Such was the high tide of the Confederacy as Haskell professed to have seen it, but his part in saving the day at Gettysburg for the Union forces found no reflection in the report of General Webb, whose troops he had relieved. On the surface, Webb's report appears to be brief, factual, and reliable. His command suffered in the bombardment, he reports, and then sustained the brunt of Pickett's charge. He continues,

> The Sixty-ninth Pennsylvania Volunteers and most of the Seventy-first Pennsylvania Volunteers, even after the enemy were in their rear, held their position. . . but the enemy would probably have succeeded in piercing our lines had not Colonel Hall advanced with several of his regiments to my support. . . The conduct of this brigade was most satisfactory. Officers and men did their whole duty. . . I saw none retire from the fence.[13]

Webb makes no mention of Haskell.

One cannot help wondering why. Was Haskell so in love with his own Homeric account of the battle that he grossly distorted it? His being able to hear the commanders on both sides of the fighting above the thundering of thousands of men firing at each other rather suggests that he may have imagined some of what he reported. Was he handsomely making himself a hero for the family back home? Did he have an exalted notion of himself? Or did Webb deliberately suppress any mention of Haskell? He did mention Hall, but Hall was a general, and obviously protocol required mentioning superior officers; was Haskell's performance sufficiently routine for a lieutenant so that it did not warrant individual notice? Or did Webb have some reason for belittling Haskell's assistance? After all, if we are to accept Haskell's account, he saved Webb's forces from defeat and probably from destruction; he may well have saved the day for the Union forces, and he quite probably saved Webb himself from death or capture. Webb may have had

The author faced the problem here, also, of what material to put into the footnotes and what to keep in the text. The observation that Haskell was to learn only later why he could not find Harrow might have been relegated to a footnote, as could that about Hancock and Gibbon having been wounded. But on the whole the text should be readable without the footnotes, and apparently the author felt that her audience would want to know this much about Haskell's dilemma and the reasons for it.

Again, in footnote 11, the author has elected to quote a considerable passage, partly because it will prove germane to the central idea of the paper. One might notice the way she introduces this passage, keeping attention on what Haskell is doing and identifying the quotation with the phrase "as his description reveals."

Footnote 13 presents a somewhat different problem. As will appear below, the author has become convinced that Webb was a liar, even though he may have been a sort of white liar, trying to protect the reputation of his troops, and his manner of doing this may have made him look rather less trustworthy than, in fact, he was.

Now the author is ready to state her main idea. It is announced by the topic sentence, "One cannot help wondering

---

[13] *Official Records*, ser. 1, XXVII, pt. 1, pp. 428–29; *Third Day*, p. 46.

both psychological and professional reasons for preferring to ignore Haskell's services.

Closer examination of the available documents may cast some light on these questions. First we might notice that at least two details in Webb's report are suspect. He says, as we have seen, that "officers and men did their whole duty," and "I saw no one retire from the fence." The first of these statements cannot be true; Captain Davis, reporting for the Sixty-ninth Pennsylvanians, was doubtless making the best of the situation when he wrote, "our troops, with few exceptions, met them bravely," [14] and Colonel Smith, reporting for the Seventy-first, mentioned that a captain and a private, "are under sentence of court martial," an admission which surely suggests they had done something less than their duty. Webb's other observation is even more suspect; when he says, "I saw no one retire," he must be deliberately using language to deceive. Possibly he did not see them; Haskell says the general arrived after "the larger portion of Webb's brigade" had fled. In the smoke of battle he may not have seen them, or he may have been appropriately bringing up the Seventy-second Pennsylvania, which had been held in reserve; he may have told the truth when he said he did not *see* them, but he certainly knew they had retired. If he did not know it, he must have been one of few men in both armies who remained in ignorance; Union commanders on both sides of him reported the retirement as one of the routine details of the battle, and Confederates, both in Pickett's charge and out of it, recorded the Union retirement.[15] Webb must have col-

---

[14] *Official Records*, ser. 1, XXVII, pt. 1, p. 431.

[15] Particularly convincing is the highly circumstantial account in a personal letter from a Confederate officer. He records that "Armisted's men rushed across the wall and pursued the enemy . . . we pushed up to the wall, and could almost see the Yankee gunners leaving their places and running in our lines for safety." Charles T. Loehr, "The Old First Virginia at Gettysburg," *Southern Historical Society Papers*, XXXII (1904), 35–37; *Third Day*, p. 94. One might notice, also, Hall's

why," which directs the reader's attention to the main problem of the paper, although not too belligerently. The author makes her point and lets us know where the article is going without saying "I shall now endeavor to prove to you. . ."

After a paragraph that presents us with the alternatives, a paragraph which becomes, in effect, a topic sentence for the whole paper, the writer makes clear how the article is to be organized.

Here the author faces one of those problems that may baffle young writers—what should one do when the evidence is contradictory? Of course, what the young writer does not know is that there is almost always some contradictory evidence, even on such matters as when a person like Shakespeare was born. For many of these questions the evidence has been sifted, and readers are given results of the sifting of evidence; whereas the writer is now faced with the problem of doing the sifting. Did Webb's men run, or did they not? In this case the decision is easy: Webb's superior said they retired, even after receiving Webb's report; his fellow officers said the men retired; the attacking Confederates said the same thing, and so did people who wrote letters and had no notion that they were giving evidence. They were just telling their

ored his account to protect the reputation of his men, and quite possibly of himself.

If so, one may raise the question, also, as to whether Webb did not gloss over some of Haskell's exploit for similar reasons. We know that Webb was not in all details a reliable reporter; was Haskell? Here we might consider at least two sorts of evidence: what corroborative evidence does Haskell's report receive from the reports of other observers, and how reliable does Haskell seem to be, particularly when he is dealing with his own achievements? As for the first, a modern reader of the contemporary reports gains the impression that a large part of the Union army was recounting Haskell's exploits, and if so, the information must have come to Webb's attention, for the general's report is dated more than a week after the battle,[16] whether or not he noticed Haskell in the fighting. . . .

sketch of the battle lines at this point, which show Webb's troops drawn well back from both the stone wall and the rail fence. *Official Records,* ser. 1, XXVII, pt. 1, pp. 473–441; *Third Day,* p. 49. Hancock's official report recorded that "the most of that part of Webb's brigade posted here abandoned their position"; presumably he had received Webb's report when he made his. *Third Day,* p. 78.

[16] *Official Records,* ser. 1, XXVII, pt. 1, p. 428; *Third Day,* p. 45.

friends what happened. Only Webb seems to have tried to suggest that his men did not retire, and he does this in such a way that one suspects he is twisting words to tell the literal truth while telling what amounts to a lie. Accordingly, the writer says confidently that Webb's men did retire, and addresses herself to the crucial problem of whether it is possible that Webb did not know this.

The author has now established her first point, that Webb was not above distorting evidence if he had good reason to do so. But that he distorted evidence to protect his men does not establish that he distorted evidence to belittle Haskell. Here we need more direct testimony, and the author recognizes that we have evidence of two sorts: (1) Webb is not an entirely reliable witness, but is Haskell any better? and (2) do the reports of other witnesses confirm Haskell's account of himself in any entirely convincing way? Since the second is more objective, she starts with that, reviewing the testimony, or lack of it, in the reports of officer after officer who either mentions Haskell or would have been in a position to see what he did.

A Yet Unexorcised Ghost

by

James Assuras

Centuries have elapsed, if we are to take the plot of *Hamlet* for fact, since the troubled shade that purported to be the spiritual remains of the elder Hamlet was satisfied with Claudius's death and laid to rest. But not so, Shakespeare's ghost in *Hamlet;* he still stalks the halls of criticism and puzzles the mind of at least an occasional playgoer. Now and then a critic cries out against this "most unnatural murder" in killing off the essential nature of a poor ghost no longer able to defend himself. Even we who merely view the play may be reminded that although the play seems to end in a way partially calculated to please the Ghost, was it truly his will to have the court heaped with corpses, including those of his son and her mother? Had the Ghost, a supernatural being, plotted this blood-bath? If so, was he a servant of justice, albeit rough justice? Was he a devil inducing people to commit murder and die without time to repent? Was he a soul on his way to heaven or hell who could slip back to earth occasionally to tidy up his unfinished earthly affairs? In short, who or what was this ghost, provided he was anything more than a convenience for the plot, a convenience that Shakespeare did not bother to think much about?

The critics apparently do not agree, and so far as I have been able to discover, they have produced five different sorts of answers, some of which subdivide into alternate answers. He may have been, as he purported to be, King Hamlet's soul,

Doom'd for a certain term to walk the night,
And for the day confined to fast in fires,
Till the foul crimes done in my days of nature

COMMENT

Appropriately, Mr. Assuras has compressed his introduction and his statement of his problem into his first paragraph. He lets us know that the Ghost in *Hamlet* presents one of those perennial uncertainties, and indicates the lines along which he expects to investigate it. He does not anticipate his conclusions, if he is to reach any, quite probably because he cannot make brief, certain inferences. Had he had such conclusions, he might have preferred to announce them at once; for example, he might have begun, "The Ghost in Hamlet has long presented a vexed question, but new evidence has come to light which allows us to assert with some confidence that the Ghost was a benevolent Episcopalian ghost sent in answer to a prayer by the Archbishop of Canterbury." Of course, the evidence permits no such conclusion, but theoretically, the material of a paper like this can be arranged either inductively or deductively.

Citations to most works must refer to a specific page in a given edition, and often one edition and only one will be standard, and by common agreement all references will be to that edition. There is no such edition of Shakespeare, of the Bible, or of a number of other common works, but if the

Are burnt and purged away. (*Hamlet*, I, v, 9–13) [1]

---

[1] I employ here, and throughout, the spelling and line numbering in *The Complete Works of Shakespeare*, ed. Hardin Craig (Chicago, 1951), hereafter referred to as *Works*.

Even so, was he a Roman Catholic soul in Purgatory, or a Church of England soul? [2]

---

[2] The distinction is extensively drawn in Lily B. Campbell, *Shakespeare's Tragic Heroes* (New York, 1952), p. 121, hereafter referred to as Campbell.

Granted that he is the soul of a deceased king, is he on a personal mission of revenge, of kingly justice, or is he the emissary of some higher power who has sent him to intervene in affairs of state? [3] The Ghost may be a devil,[4]

---

[3] The latter interpretation has been presented in I. J. Semper, "The Ghost in Hamlet," *The Catholic World,* CLXII (1946), 313.

---

[4] Robert H. West, "King Hamlet's Ambiguous Ghost," *Publications of the Modern Language Association,* LXX (1955), 1107–17.

---

as Hamlet himself recognizes:

> The spirit I have seen
> May be the devil: and the devil hath power
> To assume a pleasing shape; (II, ii, 627–29)

He may also be a figment of Hamlet's diseased mind, the result of melancholia,[5] and this ex-

---

[5] This is, of course, having too much "black bile," something more than melancholy in the modern sense; see *The Oxford English Dictionary* (1933), under *melancholy;* Alban H. Doran, "Medicine," *Shakespeare's England* (Oxford, 1916), I, 422; Virgil K. Whitaker, *Shakespeare's Use of Learning: An Inquiry into the Growth of His Mind and Art* (San Marino, Calif., 1953), p. 264, hereafter referred to as Whitaker; Walter Clyde Curry,

work is divided into chapters and verses, into acts and lines, or into some other recognizable divisions, page references are not necessary.

The student was instructed not to include publishers in his bibliography and footnotes; footnote 2 may be taken as a standard reference to a book having a known author if the publisher is not to be included. For style if the publisher is included, see Miss Arnold's paper above. Mr. Assuras was instructed, also, to rule footnotes into the text.

Footnotes 3 and 4 may be taken as samples of footnotes based upon articles, footnote 3 a reference to one page, footnote 4 a reference to more than one page.

No footnote is required for the second quotation from Shakespeare; the edition has been identified in footnote 1, and we have here the act, scene, and lines.

Footnote 5 is complicated, giving a number of references. A note of this sort can be useful to both writer and reader; for the writer, the footnote serves to provide bibliographical details for works to which he expects later to refer a number of times, and for the reader it provides a group of references should he care to embark upon his own study of an interesting sideline. One might notice that in addition to examples of references to a book and to

Chaucer and the Medieval Sciences, rev. ed. (New York, 1960), pp. 7–20, 147–48, hereafter referred to as Curry; W. W. Greg, "Hamlet's Hallucination," *Modern Language Review,* XII (1917), 393–421; for a briefer reference see W. W. Greg, "A Critical Mousetrap," *A Book of Homage to Shakespeare,* ed. Israel Gollancz (London, 1916), p. 80; repr. *Hamlet: Enter Critic,* ed. Claire Sacks and Edgar Whan (New York, 1960), the latter will hereafter be referred to as *Enter Critic.*

planation has the advantage that it accounts for Gertrude's not seeing the Ghost, but what of Horatio, Marcellus, and his stout companions? Were they also melancholics? A fourth solution has been advanced in a brilliant essay by G. Wilson Knight,[6] that the Ghost is "the Em-

---

[6] "The Embassy of Death: An Essay on Hamlet," *The Wheel of Fire* (London, 1930), pp. 35–50; repr. *Enter Critic,* pp. 157–69. See also Robert Ornstein, "The Mystery of Hamlet: Notes Toward an Archetypal Solution," *College English,* XXI (1959), repr. *Enter Critic,* pp. 196–99. A somewhat similar interpretation is implied in G. R. Elliott, *Scourge and Minister: A Study of "Hamlet"* (Durham, N. C., 1951), pp. 30–32.

---

bassy of Death," a sort of symbolic character who sets the death motif which Knight believes dominates the play. Recently Maynard Mack has suggested that the Ghost represents reality.[7]

---

[7] "The World of Hamlet," *Yale Review,* XLI (1952).

We might review these theories in order.

Assuming that the Ghost is a genuine spirit, we have first to ask if the shade is a benevolent or malevolent creature, and here the problem is greatly simplified if we can assume that the Ghost is a Catholic spirit, since that Church has laid down four clear criteria for identifying a benevolent ghost. . . .[8]

---

[8] Campbell, pp. 123–26.

---

a magazine article, there are citations for an article in a book and for a standard reference work, *The Oxford English Dictionary.* Since this is a standard work, bibliographical details are not necessary; and since it is arranged alphabetically, page references are not necessary; the writer need only say "under *melancholy.*" He does identify the year, however, since there was an earlier edition of this work known as the *New English Dictionary.* Had the author been referring to a work like the *Encyclopaedia Britannica,* which has been edited many times, he would have needed to identify the edition.

For footnotes 6 and 7 the name of the author is mentioned in the text, since Knight and Mack are critics with some reputation, and the reader may well want to know who is espousing these theories; but since their names are included in the text, they are not required in the citation. Mr. Assuras is here following sound practice; the text should be readable without the footnotes.

With his problem surveyed, the author turns to his first subdivision, and in footnote 8 he is able to take advantage of the fact that for most of the works he expects to cite he has already provided the bibliographical information.

BIBLIOGRAPHY

Campbell, Lily Bess. *Shakespeare's Tragic Heroes: Slaves of Passion.* New York, 1952.

Craig, Hardin, ed. *The Complete Works of Shakespeare.* Chicago, 1951.

Curry, Walter Clyde. *Chaucer and the Mediaeval Sciences.* Rev. ed., New York, 1960.

Doran, Alban H. "Medicine," *Shakespeare's England.* Oxford, 1916. I, 413–433.

Elliott, G. R. *Scourge and Minister: A Study of* Hamlet. Durham, N. C., 1951.

Greg, W. W. "A Critical Mousetrap," *A Book of Homage to Shakespeare.* Ed. Israel Gollancz, London, 1916. pp. 179–80.

———. "Hamlet's Hallucination," *Modern Language Review,* XII (1917), 393–421.

Hamlet: Enter Critic. Ed. Claire Sacks and Edgar Whan. New York, 1960.

Knight, G. Wilson. "The Embassy of Death," *The Wheel of Fire.* London, 1930.

Mack, Maynard. "The World of Hamlet." *Yale Review,* XLI (1952), 502–23.

Ornstein, Robert. "The Mystery of Hamlet: Notes toward an Archetypal Solution," *College English,* XXI (October, 1959), 30–35–36.

The Oxford English Dictionary. Oxford, 1933.

Semper, I. J. "The Ghost in Hamlet," *The Catholic World,* CLXII (1946), 510–17.

Shakespeare, William. See Craig, Hardin.

West, Robert H. "King Hamlet's Ambiguous Ghost." *Publications of the Modern Language Association,* LXX (1955), 1107–17.

Whitaker, Virgil K. *Shakespeare's Use of Learning: An Inquiry into the Growth of His Mind and Art.* San Marino, Calif., 1953.

The bibliography as here reprinted is restricted to the works cited thus far in the paper. The complete bibliography, of course, includes the remainder of the works cited, but does not include other books which the author consulted but which he did not cite directly. Occasionally, a writer may wish to include in his bibliography a work to which he is greatly indebted, although in such a general way that he has no occasion to use a footnote reference to it. Usually, however, such a work will appear in some footnote giving general references, or it can well be omitted from the bibliography.

The edition of Shakespeare is here entered under the editor because the writer expects to cite Craig's notes. If the work were entered under *Shakespeare,* a cross reference from *Craig* would be appropriate. As to the place of publication, several American cities appear on the titlepage of this Shakespeare, but they are only the various offices of the publisher. In such entries, usually only the first city is used. When a book is published in two countries, both cities may be used, as in the following: William D. Bayles. *Caesars in Goose Step.* New York and London, 1940.

Extending the number of cities in which a book is issued can become complicated and does not usually help in identifying the volume.

Since there are entries for two works by Greg, the second may be introduced with a long dash.

For consistency, since he entered Shakespeare under *Craig*, perhaps the author should have listed *Enter Hamlet* under *Sacks* and *Whan*, or at least provided cross references under the names of the editors. His inconsistency is perhaps defensible since he is not citing the editors and he uses the abbreviated title in footnotes.

For standard works like the *Oxford* most of the bibliographical details may be omitted, but since there are two printings of this work with some revisions, enough details are included to identify the impression.

If Shakespeare's works had not been entered under *Craig* they could have appeared as follows: Shakespeare, William. *The Complete Works of William Shakespeare*. Ed. Hardin Craig. New York, 1951.

Appendix:
Ready Aids To Revision

Easy writing's curst hard reading.
                                    —*Richard Brinsley Sheridan*
Plays are not written; they are rewritten.
                                    —*Attributed to George M. Cohan*
If you want to be read more than once, do not hesitate to blot often.
                                    —*Horace*

According to Ben Jonson, the players praised Shakespeare because ". . . in his writing he never blotted out a line." Jonson, who knew his Horace, answered "Would he had blotted a thousand" and criticized the players because they chose "to commend their friend by wherein he most faulted." But Jonson probably took the players too seriously, because there is evidence that Shakespeare revised often before he submitted his plays, during rehearsal, and even while they were in production.

Frequently the difference between a mature writer and a novice is that the writer takes his revisions seriously. The novice, once he has worked through a beginning and middle to an end, is likely to be so relieved or astonished by his accomplishment that he loses enthusiasm for further work. Or he may rationalize indolence with the myth that sanctity protects prose fresh from the pen. He may look on his composition as a fragile bit of creation, ready to crumble if touched, but prose endures mauling and is the better for it. What the beginner may call a theme, or article or novel, the accomplished writer probably calls a first draft. He knows that however good the first draft may be, however much he may have thought about it and agonized over it, he can improve it by rewriting as often as necessary.

For revision, at its most useful, is more than correcting small blunders; it is reconceiving, rethinking. This is one reason, no doubt, that classical critics recommended putting any composition aside for nine years before giving it to the public. The writer needs some time to get away from his initial enthusiasm, some time to mature. Unfortunately, the student writer cannot wait nine years before revising each first draft; an instructor is likely to assign a theme and expect to receive it a few days later. Nor is the need for speed confined to the classroom; a defense lawyer might willingly save his client from the electric chair for nine years while he polishes his brief, but no presiding judge would be likely to grant so long a recess. However, revision is possible and profitable in shorter time.

The final sections of this book are appended as aids to the student who needs to revise fairly quickly and soon after he has begun his course. Even under the pressure of assignments, the student should prepare a first draft as long as possible before the paper is due, letting the ideas cool and settle a day or two before they are reworked. But sometimes even a day or two for rethinking is not possible. Furthermore, revising involves all aspects of composition—the organization and development of the ideas as well as the vigor of the diction and the directness of the sentence structure. This appendix is intended to help the student meet these practical problems. It suggests that by orderly and careful revision, both before and after the instructor reads a paper, the student can do a great deal to improve his writing, even at the beginning of the course.

Section 33 contains three sorts of materials. The first, intended to help the student do his own revising, consists mainly of questions. If the student will ask them seriously and try to answer them objectively and in detail, he may see his composition, or part of it, in a new light. The second portion is intended to help the student profit from the suggestions he receives, to interpret the code system used by the instructor so as to understand as fully as possible the teacher's recommendations. The section closes with a check chart. If the student will keep it up, filling the blanks every time a theme is returned, he may discover trends in his writing that will help to direct his review.

Section 34 is a glossary of terms often used carelessly or illiterately. The student may use the glossary as a ready reference for locutions of which he is uncertain, or the instructor may use it as a convenient device for calling the student's attention to common errors in usage.

33

Revising and

Correcting the Theme

Every piece of writing requires revision: a college composition needs at least two revisions, one before it is submitted and a second after the instructor returns it.

A student learning composition is like a man thrown into mid-ocean to practice swimming. He has to write while learning to write. While he practices organization he must remember to spell and punctuate according to the conventions, and while he checks pronoun reference he must watch the development and coherence of his paragraphs. Nobody has found a simple solution to this dilemma, but careful and repeated revision helps.

33-1 CHECK CHART FOR REVISION

For a college theme, the student might well ask himself the following questions, checking against his paper each time as objectively as he can.

1. Did the subject prove too big or too little or unsuitable?
2. Have you brought the material sharply into focus about a main idea?
3. Have you made each paragraph a developed unit?
4. Have you developed your subject adequately and logically?
5. Are style and tone appropriate and consistent?
6. Are sentences clear and direct? Could any profitably be revised from a passive or expletive pattern?
7. Have you chosen words that mean what you want to say?
8. Have you corrected mechanics? Be sure of the spelling of each word, using a dictionary when necessary.

The following suggests how a revision of a portion of a first draft might look:

The ~~stock market~~ crash, *however,* ~~of 1929~~ was only the begin*n*ing ~~of the great de-pression~~; in the summer of 1932 the depression reach its lowest point, both economically and psychologically. The first signifi*c*ant event ~~to start the ball rolling for the epoch~~ of the great depression was the stock market crash in October, 1929. ~~The clerks in wall Street brokers' offices worked late into the night posting records of an unprecedented volume of sales.~~ Apples began to ~~be sold~~ *sell apples* on the street. ~~by~~ unemployed citizens. In New York, as well as in other cities, bread lines appeared, displaying the extreme poverty suffered by some people.

As early as January, 1932, ~~there was a~~ demonstrat*ed* ~~ion~~ at the national capital. ~~conducted by~~ 10,000 unemployed men. When destitute families lacked sufficient funds even to buy a few pounds of coal, *a relief bureau had to provide* ~~they gave them~~ fuel. People began crowding into banks, fearing failures and hoping to rescue any savings they had.

The opening sentence is moved to improve continuity in the paragraph.

Spelling errors are corrected.

Unnecessary words are deleted.

A comma is supplied.

A sentence not relevant to the main idea of the paragraph is dropped.

Word order is changed to make the sentence active.

The sentence is shifted to regular actor-action order and moved to the end, where it provides a transition to the next paragraph.

The sentence is revised to correct vague pronoun reference.

When the draft has been thoroughly revised, it should be carefully and neatly copied, and then the final version should be checked for typographical errors or blunders introduced in the process of copying.

33-2 CORRECTING THE THEME

Even though the student has carefully revised his theme, the instructor is likely to add corrections and suggestions. Inside the front cover of this book is a chart of key numbers and abbreviations which may be used in correcting themes. An alphabetical list of the abbreviations will be found inside the back cover. A reference chart to the rhetorical sections of the book also appears on the inside front cover. To profit from his instructor's corrections, the student should correct his paper according to the following procedures:

1. If your instructor uses abbreviations to mark corrections, refer to the alphabetical list inside the back cover and find the number of the section to which each abbreviation refers.
2. If your instructor uses numbers as symbols, or after you have found numbers corresponding to his abbreviations, turn to the section of the book headed by each number indicated on the paper. To locate the sections, refer to the numbers at the tops of the pages.
3. Study the section of the book to which the instructor has referred you, comparing examples in the *Guide to Revision* sections of the book with your own paper until you are sure you understand his recommendation.
4. Then rewrite each passage as it should be written.

The student should note that profitable correction often requires more than rewriting misspelled words or changing punctuation. The writer derives the greatest benefit from carefully reworking sentences and paragraphs. A mark like *Coh* or *3* in the margin of the paper, for instance, indicates to the student that the portion of his theme so marked lacks coherence; it tells him to strengthen continuity between ideas, to devote special study to Section 3 in the text, and to rewrite the passage so that it holds together. If the mark *Sub* or *15* appears in the margin of the paper, the student needs to devote special study to Section 15, where he will find a discussion of methods for improving sentence structure through the proper employment of subordination; it is possible that to achieve this improvement he will need to combine two or three sentences by reducing a clause to a phrase or a

single word. The following selection from a student theme has been
marked with the abbreviations listed inside the back cover.

```
                   The public is fooled every day by a
 Ref c   variety of people ranging from the glib
         medicine man to people working for high        Hy
         geared political machines.  The inteligence    Sp
 Agr     of these people vary widely.  The people
         they fool are often more inteligent than       Sp
 CF      they, however, their skills are so great
         that they overcome even the inteligent         Sp
 Sp      man.  Inteligence is not acquired, but
 Sp      knowlege can be acquired, (due to) man's       Dev
         ability to learn. Salesmen often state         Coh
         as fact information about their products.
 Sub     Often these are untrue.
```

The opening for the theme is not promising, and frequent errors in
structure and mechanics have been marked. To correct them, the
student should check each abbreviation in the list inside the back
cover. He will discover, for example, that *Ref c* indicates faulty word
reference and is discussed under 19c in the text. He can find 19
quickly by using the numbers at the tops of the pages. *Hy,* the student
will find, indicates faulty hyphenation and is discussed under 29b,
and *Agr* refers to faulty agreement of subject and verb and is discussed under 21. The third sentence from the end is marked *Dev,*
which refers to relevance of the development and is discussed under 5,
but it contains an expression, *due to,* circled and not otherwise
marked. Whenever no abbreviation or number is used with a marked
passage, the student should look up the marked expression in the
glossary (34) or index, where he will find an explanation or a reference.

A theme may also be marked directly with the numbers which appear above portions of the book and at the tops of pages and are summarized in the chart inside the front cover. The following selection from the theme begun above has been marked with numbers.

> Many methods are used to influence
> people. These methods include as one of   15a
> the most popular the use of propaganda.
> Pamphlets, newspapers, magazines, books,
> posters, billboards, radio, movies and   27d
> television are all mediums for the
> spread of propaganda. For example, know-
> 15c   ing the kinds of things audiences want to
> see also
> 17c   hear, many facts are distorted by radio
> commentators. There are many kinds of in-   17a
> 5, see   formation which are distorted for propa-
> especially
> 5-2   ganda purposes.

The student can look up 15a and find a suggestion that the sentences be combined, with one subordinated to the other. The reference to 27d points out an omission of a comma in a series, and 15c marks a dangling modifier. The instructor has also suggested that the writer see 17c, which refers to overuse of passive sentences. The reference to 5 calls attention to a weakness that is apparent throughout the theme, overuse of general rather than specific development.

The instructor has used another kind of symbol here also, the hyphenated number 5-2. Hyphenated numbers head discussions of writing methods and procedures rather than specific instructions for improvement. Sometimes, however, an instructor may think that the writer could profit from study of these sections and will refer to them. A reference chart appears on the front endpapers.

33-3 RECORD OF THEMES AND RECOMMENDATIONS FOR REVISION

Mechanical proficiency alone will not make a writer competent, but mechanical proficiency is necessary. It can be acquired—if the writer will learn to understand his errors, will learn how to avoid them, and will concentrate on correcting habitual mistakes. The chart on the following page is intended to help the student analyze his weaknesses, to give him a guide for special study, and to help him know what to look for in theme revision. Use the blanks at the bottom of the chart for other subjects marked frequently in your papers.

THEME NUMBER	1	2	3	4	5	6	7	8	9	10	11	12	13	14	15
GRADE															
Organization, 8															
Paragraphing, 2-3															
Development, 5															
Fragment, 12															
Run-together, 27b															
Postponed subject, 17a															
Passive sentence, 17c															
Predication, 13															
Parallelism, 14															
Subordination, 15															
Dangling modifier, 15c															
Reference, 19															
Pronoun form, 18															
Verbs, 20															
Agreement, 21															
Words, 24-26															
Adjective, adverb, 22															
Punctuation, 27															
Manuscript form, 28															
Spelling, 29															
Possessive, 29a															
Hyphenation, 29b															

34

Glossary of Usage

For Guide to Revision, see page 610

Prefer literate English suitable in its context.

Anyone who wishes to browse among eighteenth-century writings on language may amuse himself by observing an ordained divine vilifying a bishop's diction as "barbarous," by noticing that one learned grammarian derides another learned grammarian's locutions as "vile," and by remarking that the American lexicographer, Noah Webster, found the observations of the British lexicographer, Samuel Johnson, "extremely erroneous." Such vigorous denunciation and counter-denunciation among cultured students of language is no longer in fashion, but the discriminating use of English is no less important for that. In fact, however the grammarians of the eighteenth century belabored one another, the evidence seems to be that eighteenth-century people were relatively tolerant of linguistic variety. Standards there were. People being what they are and language being what it is, there probably always have been and always will be standards, but practical standards of English usage are perhaps more rigorous now than formerly. Although serious students of language are not now much inclined to shout that X is right but that Y is horrible and Z is stupid, the practical penalties, social and financial, attached to questionable usage are probably greater today than they have ever been before among English-speaking peoples.

All this is complicated by the fact that we no longer presume that there is one impeccably pure and eternally best way to say anything. Using language well, even using language in a manner that is labelled "correct" as opposed to "incorrect" is not simple. It follows no rigid rule; good usage grows, if it grows well, from wide knowledge and deep understanding of one's native tongue. Thus a glossary of usage, like the following one, is almost an impertinence. Nobody can prescribe language for everybody; notably, nobody can, in a few pages, lay down rules and inclusive pronouncements. Therefore, this glossary is intended mainly as a convenient list for ready reference. It is not exhaustive, and it is not intended as a set of prescriptions.

Earlier sections of this book have insisted that English is a rich and subtle means of thinking and communicating, and that shortcuts to its mastery are not to be expected. Similarly, good usage presents complex problems, but one simple and useful distinction can be made: that between what is often called *standard* and *non-standard* English, between *literate* and *vulgate* speech. Roughly speaking, these two sorts of English are used by two sorts of people; literate English is used by cultured people who know how to use the language in an acceptable way and take the pains to do so. Vulgate is the language of those who do not know how to speak and write acceptably, are not able to do so, or will not bother. We should notice one further distinction; even the users of literate English do not always use the same English. A judge will speak in one way dictating an opinion, in another way dictating an official letter, and in different ways still when he talks with an old friend or his teenage son. Generally speaking, his English —which must, of course, all be called literate English—is more or less formal, depending upon the occasion.

The following glossary, then, is intended roughly to distinguish literate English, and within this body of literate usage to suggest varying degrees of formality and informality.

34 **Gloss**

GLOSSARY

OF USAGE

Guide to Revision
The following list describes customary usage for certain troublesome expressions.

Accept, Except. To accept means "to receive"; *to except* means "to exclude."

He decided *to accept* the bribe.
They agreed *to except* the controversial paragraphs of the motion.

Except is also a function word to indicate an exception.

They all quit *except* Johnny.

Actually. Frequently used as a meaningless word.
Ad. Informal shortening of *advertisement,* not appropriate in formal English.
A.D. Abbreviation of *Anno Domini,* in the year of Our Lord, used for dates after the birth of Christ when dates A.D. and B.C. could be confused. Being Latin, it preferably precedes the date (A.D. 43).
Adapt, Adept, Adopt. To adapt is "to adjust," "to make suitable."

The children *adapted* their habits to their new home.

Adept means "skilled, proficient."

She is *adept* at typing.

To adopt is "to accept" or "to take as one's own."

The resolution was *adopted.*
He *adopted* the mannerisms of his teacher.

Adviser, Advisor. Both spellings are in current use; the *-er* spelling is perhaps more usual.

Affect, Effect. *Affect* is a verb meaning "influence." *Effect* is usually a noun meaning "result," but it may be used as a verb meaning "cause" or "bring about."

The weather *does not affect* her disposition.
The weather has no *effect* on her disposition.
The envoys tried *to effect* a compromise.

Agenda. The word is from Latin, where it means "things to be done," and is thus plural. Following the pattern of English a new plural *agendas* is developing, but is still not standard.

Aggravate. Used in formal English to mean "intensify" or "make worse." Used informally in the sense of "annoy" or "provoke."

INFORMAL: The children *aggravated* her.
FORMAL: The children *annoyed* her.
FORMAL: The new ointment only *aggravated* the disease.

Alibi. Formally used only in the legal sense, an indication that a defendant was elsewhere at the time of a crime; colloquially, "an excuse."

All (of). Constructions with *all of* followed by a noun can often be made more concise by omission of the unnecessary *of*. Usually *of* is retained between *all* and a pronoun.

He could not bribe *all of them* with *all* the money in the world.

All right, Alright. Alright is a common misspelling for *all right,* accepted in modern dictionaries only with reservations.

Already, All ready. *Already* is a single modifier meaning "before some specified time." In *all ready, all* modifies separately.

The team was *already* on the field.
They were *all ready* for the kick-off.

Alumnus, Alumnae. An *alumnus* is a male graduate; *alumni* is the plural of *alumnus,* and is usually used for groups including both males and females. An *alumna* is a female graduate; *alumnae* is the plural form of *alumna.* The contraction, *alum,* is not acceptable in standard English.

Among, Between. The formal distinction that *between* is used of two and *among* of more than two has not been rigidly observed, at least informally, for *between.*

The men divided the reward *between* Bob and me.
The book records differences *among* (or *between*) synonyms.

Amount, Number. *Amount* indicates a sum or total mass or bulk. *Number* refers to a group of which individual parts can be counted; it is a collective noun, singular when designating a unit, plural when designating individuals.

A *number* of friends were in the lobby.
The *number* of his crimes is astounding.
A large *amount* of wheat had been stored.

And which, And who. Standard only when the following clause is co-ordinate with a previous clause introduced by *which* or *who*.

FAULTY: That was the first car I owned, *and which* I expected to cut down for a "hot rod."
STANDARD: The car, which was the first I ever owned *and which* I expected to cut down for a "hot rod," was . . .

Angle. Currently popular in a number of colloquial expressions, rapidly becoming trite.

SLANG OR COLLOQUIAL: He knew all the *angles*. What's the *angle* on this?

Anxious. Formerly restricted in meaning to "apprehensive," "worried"; still sometimes suspect formally in newer sense of "eager."

FORMAL: He was *eager* (not *anxious*) to enter the game.

Anybody, Any body; Anyone, Any one. Combine the words to make the noun form; separate if the first portion is a modifier.

Anybody may come.
Any body in the burning ruins . . . .
Anyone could do that.
Any one infraction of the rule . . . .

Anywheres. Substandard; omit the *s*.
Apt. See *Liable*.
Area. Overused, usually redundantly, to refer to a subject or discipline.

He was a student *in* (not *in the area of*) agriculture.

Around. Informal when used for *about*.

There were *about* (not *around*) a thousand people present.

As. Useful as a conjunction indicating contemporary times but overused for *since, because, for,* or *that,* usually imprecisely.

She was happy, *because* (not *as*) she had found the book.
I do not know *that* (not *as*) I believe you.
As I rounded the corner, the car stopped.

For confusion of *as* and *like,* see 23c.

Aspect. Overused; see 26d.

As to. Awkward as a substitute for a more precise preposition such as *about* or *of.*

> He spoke to me *about* (not *as to*) the nomination.

At. Redundant and to be avoided in questions with *where.*

> Where was he? (not *Where was he at?* or *Where at was he?*)

Athletics. Plural in form, but often considered singular in number.

Auto. No longer much used as a colloquial shortening of *automobile; car* is a more common short form.

Awful, Awfully. Overworked as a vague intensive: *awfully good, awfully bad.* Since the words are overworked, their effectiveness is blunted. In formal English awful means "awe-inspiring."

Bad. When used as subject complement, sometimes confused with the adverb *badly* (see 22a).

> She felt *bad* (not *badly*) all day.

B.C. Abbreviation of *before Christ,* used to mark dates that could be confused with dates in the Christian era. It appears after the date (52 B.C.)

Be. Sometimes preferred to *is* in clauses of condition in formal writing (*if this be true*).

Because. Standard to introduce a modifier, not a noun clause (see 13c).

> The reason I ride the elevator is *that* (rather than *because*) I am lazy.
> I ride the elevator *because* I am lazy.

Being as, Beings as. Nonstandard usage for *since* or *because.*

> *Because* (not *being as*) I live here, I know what I am doing.

Beside, Besides. Beside is used as a preposition, meaning "by the side of." *Besides* may be an adverb or preposition, meaning "in addition to" or "except."

> He had to sit *beside* the teacher.
> It was too late to go to the dance, and *besides* I was tired.

Between. See *Among.*

Blond, Blonde. A tendency remains in writing to preserve the feminine *e* ending of the French word. As a noun *blond* refers to men, *blonde* to women.

Broke. Used to mean "out of money," *broke* is slang, not standard English; "financially embarrassed" as a substitute is trite and affected.

Bunch. Colloquial and overused to mean "group."

> A *group* (not a *bunch*) of students . . . .
> A large *amount* (not a *bunch*) of material . . . .

Burst, Bust. Standard principal parts are *burst, burst, burst. Bust* or *busted* in the sense of "burst" is nonstandard.

But, Hardly, Only, Scarcely. Negative words not used in standard English with another negative (see also *Double negative*).

> He *had* (not *didn't have*) but one alternative.
> He *knew* (not *didn't know*) only one answer.
> I *hardly* (not *don't hardly*) think so.

But that, But what. Used for *that, but that* is redundant and *but what* is nonstandard.

> He did not doubt *that* (not *but what* or *but that*) she would finally agree.

Can, May. In formal English, *may* refers to permission (*Mother, may I go swimming*) and *can* to ability (*I* can *swim across the pool*). Informally, *can* is commonly used for both meanings, and even formally *can* sometimes refers to permission to distinguish from *may* referring to possibility:

> I *can* (I have permission to) go swimming.
> I *may* (possibly I shall) go swimming.

Can't help but, Can't hardly. A double negative (see *But, Hardly,* etc.) used only colloquially.

> I *cannot help thinking* (not *cannot help but think*) she is honest.

Case. Overworked in expresions like "in this case" or "in the case of" (see 26d).

Censor, Censure, Censer. To censor means "to examine," especially to examine printed matter for possible objections. *To censure* means "to reprimand" or "to condemn." A *censer* is a receptacle for incense, especially in religious ceremonies.

> Half the story *was censored.*
> The students condemned their treasurer in a vote of *censure.*
> Choir boys carried the *censers.*

Certain. Redundant in expressions like "this certain person" or "in that certain instance."

Circumstances. Currently misused and overused in jargonic writing; use a more exact expression.

> He was *in great difficulty* (not *in very difficult circumstances*).

Cite, Sight, Site. To *cite* means to "refer to." *Sight* means "view" or "spectacle." A *site* means a "location."

> He *cited* an old legal document.
> The mountains below were a beautiful *sight*.
> We visited the *site* of the new building.

Claim. Overused; see 26d.

Combine. Non-standard as a noun meaning "combination."

> Several business houses *combined* (not *formed a combine*) to supply the needs of the new college.

Complected. A non-standard substitute for *complexioned*.

> She was *light-complexioned* (not *light-complected*).

Conscience, Conscious. Conscience is a noun referring to a sense of rightness. *Conscious* is an adjective meaning "awake" or "aware" or "active mentally."

> Let your *conscience* be your guide.
> I was not *conscious* of his fear.

Contact. Currently overused and loosely used, especially overworked as a verb synonym for *talk with, telephone, ask about, advise, inform, query, write to, call upon.*

Continue on. Redundant as a verb with a separable suffix; omit *on*.

Could of. Sometimes, because of its sound, mistakenly written for *could have*.

> He *could have* (not *could of*) looked up the word in the dictionary.

Council, Counsel, Consul. Council means "advisory board" or "group." *Counsel* means "advice" or, especially in law, "the man who gives advice." A *consul* is a "government official."

> He was elected to the administrative *council*.
> The dean *counseled* him to leave school.
> He was American *consul* in Brazil.

Couple. Colloquial in the sense of "two" or "about two."

> I gave him *two* (rather than *a couple*) dollars.

Cute. Overworked colloquially as a vague way of expressing approval.

> She was an *attractive* (or *charming* or *pleasant* or *lovely,* rather than *cute*) girl.

Data. Originally the plural form of Latin *datum,* often considered singular in colloquial usage, but still plural in standard English. *Strata* and *phenomena* are plurals of the same sort.

> *These* (not *this*) data *confirm* (not *confirms*) the theory.

Date. A useful colloquialism, rapidly becoming standard, meaning "appointment" or "to make an appointment," or "the person with whom an appointment is made," especially if the appointment is social and with a person of the opposite sex.

Deal. Currently overworked as a vague slang term for any transaction or arrangement or situation. A more specific term is preferable. *Great deal* is only loosely used as an equivalent of *many.*

Definite, Definitely. Currently overworked as vague intensifiers in expressions like "a definitely fine party."

Different from, Different than. *From* is idiomatic when a preposition is required; *than* introduces a clause.

Do. An extremely useful verb sometimes carelessly used in idioms in which it cannot function (see 13a).

> Everyone has an ambition he wants to *fulfill* (rather than *do*).

Disregardless. Substandard; use *regardless.*

Don't. Contraction of *do not* not acceptable after *it, he, she,* or a singular noun.

> It *does not* (or *doesn't* in conversation, not *don't*) seem wise.

Double negative. Although a double negative is conceived in some languages as a device for enforcing the negative sense, two negatives are not used in the same negative statement in modern standard English.

> We *did* (not *didn't do*) nothing wrong.
> We did not see *anybody* (not *nobody*) on the pier.

Two negatives are used in the same statement in English to give varying emphasis to a positive idea.

> It was not impossible to see their meaning.
> I was not totally unimpressed by the speech.

Doubt. *Doubt that* implies a negative; *doubt whether* (informally *doubt if*) assumes that there is room for doubt.

I *doubt that* he will come (presumably he will not).
I *doubt whether* he will come (probably he will not, but he may).

Due to. Like *owing to* or *on account of, due to* is originally an adjective modifier (The delay was *due to* the icy roads). Its use adverbially is not generally accepted as standard English, athough it has long been common in introductory adverbial phrases (*Due to* unavoidable circumstances, the delivery has been delayed). *Because of* is the preferable adverbial idiom.

Because of (not *due to*) the icy roads, the bus was late.

Each other, One another. Many careful writers distinguish, using *each other* to refer to only two and *one another* to refer to more than two.
Effect. See *Affect.*
Either, Neither. Usually singular in number (see 21a) and used to designate one of two, not one of more than two (see also *Each other*).

Any (not *either*) of the three books has the information.

Enthuse. Colloquial but overworked for *be enthusiastic* or *make enthusiastic.*
Equally as. A wordy confusion of *as good as* and *equally.*

My cake was *as good as* Sue's.
The cakes were *equally* (not *equally as*) good.

Etc. Abbreviation for *et cetera* meaning "and so forth," or "and the like," appropriate only when statistics or lists justify abbreviations. *And etc.* is redundant, *et* means "and."
Exactly. Currently popular as a meaningless word. The person who asks "exactly what is poetry?" probably does not want to be told "exactly," even if he could be.
Except. See *Accept.*
Expect. Non-standard in the sense of "suppose" or "suspect."

I *suppose* (not *expect*) that his paper is finished.

Extra. Non-standard in the sense of "unusually."

The coffee was *unusually* (not *extra*) good.

Fact, The fact that. Often overused as a roundabout way of saying *that.*

He was aware *that* (not *of the fact that*) everybody disliked his plan.

Factor. Often jargonic; see 26d.
Famed. Used for *famous* or *well known, famed* usually suggests journalese or amateur writing.

Farther, Further. A distinction, not universally made, prefers *farther* as the comparative form of *far* in expressions involving space and *further* to mean "in addition." Modern dictionaries recognize the interchangeable use of the two words.

Feature. Used to mean "emphasize" or "give prominence to," *feature* is becoming standard usage, but the word has been so overworked in this sense by journalists and press agents that it bears watching. In expressions like "Can you feature that?" the word is slang.

Fellow. Colloquial in the sense of "man," "friend," "person," "individual."

Fewer, Less. Fewer is used in distinctions involving numbers of individuals, *less* in relation to value, degree, or quantity.

The course will not be offered for *fewer* than ten students.
The receipts were *less* than the expenditures.

Field. Overworked and often redundant when used to refer to a realm of knowledge or subject.

He was an expert *in* (not *in the field of*) chemistry.

Figure. Colloquial for *think, expect, suppose, conclude, believe.*

I did not *expect* (not *figure*) the course to be difficult.

Fine. Colloquial as an adverb.

She sang *well* (not *fine* or *just fine*).

Fix. In standard English a verb meaning "make fast" and, more recently, "repair." The word is colloquial as a noun meaning "predicament" and as a verb meaning "intend" or "prepare" (I was *fixing* to go).

Folks. Colloquial for *people* or *relatives.*

Formally, Formerly. Formally means "in a formal manner"; *formerly* means "previously."

We had to dress *formally* for the party.
She was *formerly* a singer.

Funny. Overused, and imprecise in the sense of "strange," "odd," "unusual," "perplexed." A more exact word is preferable.

Get, Got. Useful verbs and the basis of many standard idioms, but also used in many colloquial and slang expressions (The song *gets* me. The pain *got* him in the back. Better *get* wise). Used to mean "must" or "ought to," *got* is colloquial and usually redundant.

We *must* (or *have to,* not *got to*) finish by evening.

Good. An adjective, not to be confused with *well,* the corresponding adverb (see 22a).

Good and. Non-standard as an intensive.

> He was *very* (not *good and*) angry.

Gotten. Alternative form for *got* as past participle for the verb *get.*

Guess. Many dictionaries now accept *guess* in the sense of "believe," "suppose," "think," but some writers restrict it to colloquial usage.

Had of. Nonstandard for *had* (see also *Could of*).

> I wish he *had* (not *had of*) told me.

Had ought, Didn't ought, Hadn't ought. Nonstandard redundant forms for *ought* or *should.*

> He *ought not* (or *should not,* not *hadn't ought to*) say that.

Hang. Principal parts of the verb are *hang, hung, hung,* but to refer to death by hanging, they are *hang, hanged, hanged* in formal English.

> We *hung* the new picture.
> The murderer *was hanged.*

Hardly. See *But, Hardly,* etc.

He or She. The combination is not usual as an equivalent for *one. He,* alone, is usually preferred.

Healthful, Healthy. A distinction gradually breaking down restricts *healthful* to mean "conducive to health" and *healthy* to mean "possessing health."

Heap, Heaps. Colloquial in the sense of "a great deal."

Heighth. Common misspelling for *height.*

Hisself. Vulgate for *himself;* not acceptable.

Honorable. Used as a title of respect, mainly for people of prestige in political office. It is usually preceded by *the* and used only with a full name (*The Honorable John H. Jones* or *the Honorable Mr. Jones* not *Honorable Jones* or *the Hon. Jones*).

Human. Originally an adjective, *human* is now often used as a noun meaning "human being." Some modern dictionaries accept the noun use as standard, although others label it colloquial.

Idea. A handy word which careless writers readily overuse. A more exact word is often preferable.

> *My purpose* (not *my idea*) is to become a nurse.
> *The theme* (not *the idea*) of the book is that crime never pays.

If, Whether. If implies uncertainty; *whether* implies an alternative.

> *If* he will trust me, I shall tell him.
> I shall tell him, *whether* or not he believes me.

If is not used with *regardless.*

Even though (not *regardless if*) he is a doctor . . . .

Imply, Infer. *To imply* is "to suggest a meaning"; *to infer* is "to draw a conclusion from evidence."

The attorney *implied* that the witness was lying.
The jury *inferred* that the attorney was trying to discredit the witness.

In, Into. *In* implies rest or motion within a restricted area; *into* is preferable to indicate motion from the outside to the inside.

She lives *in* town.
We drove *into* town.

In back of. Redundant; prefer *behind.*
In regards to. Nonstandard; use *in regard to.*
Individual. Loosely used, and often overused, as a synonym for *person;* best used as a noun to emphasize that persons are separate and unique.

Students are not merely names in a card file; they are *individuals.*

Infer. See *Imply.*
Inferior than. Nonstandard; use *inferior to.*
Ingenious, Ingenuous. *Ingenious* means "having or giving evidence of resourceful intelligence." It can be used of either persons (an *ingenious* strategist) or things (an *ingenious* device). *Ingenuous* means "naïvely frank." Except for things closely associated with people (an *ingenuous* proposal), it is used only of persons.
Inside of. Redundant as a compound preposition; omit *of.*
Invite. Restricted in standard usage to use as a verb, not acceptable as a substitute for *invitation.*

I asked Joe for *an invitation* (not *an invite*) to the dance.

Irregardless. Nonstandard; use *regardless.*
It. Usually to be avoided in impersonal constructions, especially in locutions like "*It* says in the book . . . ," in which *it* seems to have an antecedent but does not (see 19a).
Its, It's. *Its* is the possessive form of *it.* It's is the contraction of *it is.*
Kind, Sort. Singular words, which formally can be modified only by singular demonstrative adjectives, *this* or *that.* Plural forms, *those kinds* or *these sorts,* are used, and colloquially *kind* and *sort* are commonly treated as if they were plural (*these kind*).
Kind of. Colloquial as the equivalent of *somewhat, rather.*
Kind of a. Colloquial.

Lay. For confusion of forms of *lay* and *lie,* see 20a.

Lead, Led. Lead is the present tense of the verb. Because of the similarity in pronunciation, the past tense, *led,* is often misspelled as *lead,* the name of the mineral.

> He *led* (not *lead*) the horse to water.

Less. See *Fewer.*

Let, Leave. Both are common in a few idioms (*leave,* or *let it* alone), but in other idioms, especially when the verb carries a sense of permission, *let* is standard.

> *Let* (not *leave*) them stay.
> *Let us* (or *let's* not *leave us*) go soon.

Liable, Apt, Likely. Interchangeable informally, but often distinguished in careful writing.

> She is not *likely* (rather than *liable* or *apt*) to tell her teacher.

Strictly, *liable* means "responsible for" or "subject to."

> He is *liable* for the damage he caused.

Apt means "has an aptitude for."

> Marie is an *apt* pupil.

Lie. For confusion of forms of *lie* and *lay,* see 20a.

Like. For debatable use as a conjunction, see 23c.

Line. Jargonic or slang or redundant in certain current uses.

> *He sells books* (not *Selling books is his line*).
> I want to buy something *similar to* (not *along the lines of*) the dress in the window.
> He *was deceiving her* (not *handing her a line*).

Literally. An antonym, not a synonym of *figuratively.* The student who wrote, "I was literally dead when I got in," did not say what he probably meant.

Loan. Now generally accepted as a synonym of *lend;* many careful writers, however, use *loan* only as a noun and prefer *lend* as a verb.

Locate. Provincial as a synonym for *remember* or *take up residence.*

Lot(s) of. Colloquial as a synonym for *many.*

Love. Currently misused as a synonym for *like.* Use an exact word.

Mad. Colloquial in the sense of "angry." Use *angry* or a more exact word like *vexed, furious, annoyed.*

Math. Clipped form of *mathematics,* not appropriate in formal writing.

Might of. Use *might have,* (see *Could of*).

Mighty. As a synonym for *very* not acceptable in standard English, although common in certain areas as a colloquialism.

> She was a *very* (not *mighty*) pretty girl.

Moral, Morale. Moral is a modifier, concerning the preference of right over wrong; *morale* is a noun suggesting good spirits and a healthy attitude.

> George Washington was a *moral* man.
> The victory improved the soldiers' *morale.*

More than one. Logically plural, sanctioned by custom as singular except when the meaning clearly requires a plural verb.

> *More than one* man is eager to marry her.
> If there are *more than one* apiece, they should be divided as equally as possible.

Most. Colloquial as a synonym for *almost.*

> I am home *almost* (not *most*) every evening.

Movie. Gaining in popularity as a synonym for *motion picture* but not generally accepted for formal discourse.

Muchly. Nonstandard; use *much.*

Must. Currently overworked as a noun.

Myself. For use as a substitute for *I* or *me,* see 18e.

Nature. Jargonic in certain current wordy expressions (see 26d).

> The job was *difficult* (not *of a difficult nature*).

Neither. Used of two; see *Either.*

Neither . . . nor. Used as correlatives.

> She could *neither* set up her experiment *nor* (not *or*) conduct it.

Nice. Colloquial as a synonym for *affable, agreeable, amiable, congenial, considerate,* and so on through the alphabet. Prefer a more exact word. Carefully used, *nice* means "precise," "exact," "discriminating."

Nice and. Colloquial as an intensive.

> The coffee was *pleasantly* (not *nice and*) hot.

None. None as a subject takes a singular or plural verb depending upon its meaning.

Not . . . as. Some writers on usage have objected to this construction. They prefer

He is *not so* (rather than *not as*) dull as his younger brother.

Either construction is now generally considered acceptable.
Nowheres. Substandard; omit the *s*.
Number. Use with caution.

Many (*dozens* or *hundreds* or *thousands,* but not *a great number*) of students will participate.

Of. Confused with *have.* See *Could of, Might of.*
On. Sometimes redundant with dates.

I shall see you Tuesday (rather than *on Tuesday*).

On the part of. Often a clumsy equivalent of *by;* see *Part.*
One. Used in English in impersonal constructions, although it sometimes seems stiffly formal. It may be replaced by *he,* and *one's* by *his,* for a second reference.
Only. For the position of *only,* see 15b.
Orama, Orium. Faddish suffixes overused in various advertising coinages: *seafoodorama, lubratorium* (for a filling station).
Out of. Prefer *out* (*out* the door; not *out of* the door).
Outside of. Redundant as a compound preposition (*outside* the barn, not *outside of* the barn). *Outside of* is colloquial in the sense of "except."

He failed all his examinations *except* that in chemistry (not *outside of* chemistry).

Outstanding. Overworked; see 26d.
Over with. Colloquial in the sense of "done," "finished with," "ended," "completed."
Over-all. Useful as a synonym for *general,* but currently overused; accurately used in a phrase like *the over-all length.*
Part, On the part of. Often used in wordy writing.

WORDY: There was some objection, *on the part of* the administration, to the moral tone of the skits.
REVISED: The administration objected to the moral tone of the skits.

Party. Not usually acceptable in composition as a synonym for *person;* used in legal papers (party of the first part) and by telephone operators (Here is your party).
Past, passed. Past is the modifier or complement; *passed* the verb form.

His troubles were *past.* She *had passed* all the tests.

Per cent. Acceptable forms either *per cent* or *percent.*

Phase. Often jargonic; see 26d.

Phenomena. Plural; the singular is *phenomenon* (see 29c).

Phone. Informal; in formal composition use *telephone.*

Phone up. Substandards; use *telephone, call on the telephone,* or for more familiar uses, *call up.*

Picture. Currently overused in the vague sense of "I gave them the whole picture." More specific writing provides the cure: "I told them why I needed five dollars."

Piece. Colloquial in the sense "a short distance."

Plan on. Colloquial in some uses (*plan to go,* not *plan on going; plan to see,* not *plan on seeing*).

Plenty. Not acceptable as an intensive (*excellent,* not *plenty good*).

Point. Overworked as a blanket word.

He had many admirable *characteristics* (not *points*).

Poorly. Colloquial in the sense "in poor health."

Prejudice. A noun, not to be confused with *prejudiced,* a modifier.

He was *prejudiced* (not *prejudice*) against John.

Presence. The noun form corresponding to *to be present* (The chairman requests your *presence* on the platform); to be distinguished from *presents,* plural of *present.*

Principal, Principle. The two words should be distinguished. *Principal* can be a modifier meaning "first in importance" (I answered his *principal* objections), or a noun naming somebody or something first in importance (a high school *principal,* the *principals* in the fight). *Principle* is always a noun (The law of the conservation of matter formulates a fundamental *principle* in physics; Machiavelli has been accused of having no *principles*).

Prof. Slang when used as a common noun (I like the course, but not the *prof*). Acceptable in journalistic and informal writing as an abbreviation with a full name (*Prof.* George B. Sanders, but *Professor* Sanders). Best formal style requires that *professor* be written out in all titles.

Proved, Proven. Proved is the only form having historical foundation, but *proven* is also commonly accepted. The verb *to prove* is often used carelessly of statements which are not proved; often *to suggest, to imply,* or *to indicate* would be more accurate.

Providing. In older usage, not admitted as a synonym of *provided,* a conjunction meaning "on the condition."

Put across. Blanket term for *explain, prove, demonstrate, expound, argue, make clear, establish,* and the like.

Quite. Generally accepted, although often unnecessary, in the sense of "entirely" (*quite* dead, frozen *quite* to the bottom); colloquial in the sense "somewhat," "rather" (*quite* cold, *quite* a big job).

Raise. For confusion of forms of *rise* and *raise,* see 20a. *Raise* is now generally accepted as a synonym of *rear* in the sense "bring to maturity," but many writers prefer *rear* when referring to human beings.

Rate. Currently overused and misused; slang in some usages (He does not *rate* with us).

Re. In the sense "about," used for formal purposes only in legal documents and skeletonized commercial writing.

Real. Colloquial as an intensive (It was a *real* nice clam bake). Use *really, very,* or a word expressive enough so that it needs no intensive.

Really. A useful word frequently overused and misused so that it clutters sentences.

INEFFECTUAL: He had been *really* traveling.
REVISED: He was gasping for breath because he had been running.
REDUNDANT: It was *really* true.
REVISED: It was true.

Reason is because. See *Because* and 13c.

Reason why. Usually redundant (The reason why I like to swim. . . .); omit *why.* In many sentences *reason,* also, can be omitted and the structure strengthened (see 13c).

Reckon. Dialectal and inexact as a synonym for *believe, suppose, assume.*

Regard, regards. Often overused; see 26d. *Regards* is nonstandard in constructions like *in regards to.*

Respectfully, Respectively. Respectfully means "in a respectful manner" (*respectfully* submitted); *respectively* means "in the specified order," "severally" (The balloons were identified as 4b, 5a, and 2g, *respectively*).

Reverend. Used in standard English with the first name or initials of the person described or with the title *Mr.* (see 28b), in formal usage preceded by *the.*

The Reverend William Dimity; the Reverend W. L. Dimity; the Reverend Mr. Dimity.

Right. Informal as an intensive in expressions like "right away"; prefer *immediately, at once, promptly,* etc. A localism in the sense of "very."

It was a *very* (not *right*) good fight.

Rise. For confusion of forms of *rise* and *raise,* see 20a.

Said. Pseudo-legal affectation as a modifier; if necessary, use *this, that, these,* and the like.

Having rejected *the motion* (not *said motion*), the committee adjourned.

Same. As a pronoun used with *in, same* is sometimes useful in legal documents, but sounds affected in most writing.

Having made his bed he must lie *in it* (not *in same*).

Scarcely. Not to be used with another negative (see *Double negative*).

There *was scarcely* (not *was not scarcely*) any butter.

Seem. A useful word, often misused or overused, especially as a qualification in constructions like "it would *seem* that."

The evidence *suggests* (not *would seem to suggest*) that Shakespeare was once a schoolmaster.

Seldom ever. Redundant; omit *ever.*

Set. For confusion of forms of *sit* and *set,* see 20a.

Set-up. Slang in the sense of "an easy victory," and currently overused in jargonic writing to mean anything related to organization, condition, or circumstances (I liked the new *set-up*).

Shall. Commonly indistinguishable from *will;* for the distinction sometimes maintained, see 20b.

Shape. Colloquial in the sense of "condition," "manner."

She was *well trained* (not *in good shape*) for the tournament.

Should. For distinctions between *should* and *would,* see 20b.

Should of. Mistaken form of *should have;* see *Could of.*

Show. Colloquial as a synonym for *chance, opportunity;* colloquial also as a synonym for *moving picture, play.*

Show up. Not acceptable in standard English in either the sense "arrive" (Jim did not *show up*) or the sense *"expose"* (He is no gentleman, and Mary *showed him up*).

Sic. For uses of *sic* see 32-3.

Sign up, Sign up for, Sign up with. Not acceptable in formal English.

Sit. For confusion of forms of *sit* and *set,* see 20a.

Situated. Often used redundantly.

The house was *in* (not *situated in*) the tenement district.

Situation. Wordy and jargonic in expressions like "the team had a fourth-down situation."

Size. Not generally accepted as a modifier (*this size of dress,* not *this size dress*).

So. Avoid the excessive use of *so* to join independent clauses (see 15).

So as. Not to be confused with *so that* (see 23b).

Some. Not acceptable in standard English to indicate vague approval.

It was *an exciting* (not *some*) game.

Somebody's else. The sign of the possessive appears on the last word (see 29a). Use *somebody else's.*

Sometime, Some time. One word in the sense "occasion," "some other time"; two words in the sense "a period of time."

> Come up to see me *sometime.*
> The repairs will require *some time.*

Somewhat of. Somewhat is most commonly an adverb (*They were somewhat slow*); *somewhat of* is not a standard idiom.

Somewheres. Substandard. Omit the *s.*

Sort. See *Kind.*

Sort of, Sort of a. Both are clumsy and colloquial as modifiers.

> I was *rather* (not *sort of*) tired.
> He was *an amateur* (not *a sort of a*) plumber.

Speak, Speech. The difference between the vowel sequence in the verb *speak* and the noun *speech* is fruitful of spelling errors.

State. Currently misused as a loose equivalent of *say, remark, observe, declare.* Carefully used, *to state* is "to declare in a formal statement."

> The board *stated* that the coach's contract would not be renewed.
> The coach *said* (not *stated*) that practice would be postponed until four-thirty.

Stationary, stationery. Stationary is a modifier meaning "not movable" or "not moving"; *stationery* is a noun meaning "writing materials." They can be distinguished by remembering that l*etters* are written with station*e*ry.

Such. Overused as a vague intensive (see 16b). It was *a very* (not *such a*) warm day.

Suit, Suite. Suit, the commoner word, can be either a verb (*suit* yourself) or a noun (a tailor-made *suit*). *Suite,* only a noun, has several specialized uses. (The ambassador and his *suite* occupied a *suite* of rooms.)

Suspicion. A noun, not appropriately used to supplant the excellent verb *suspect.*

Sure. Colloquial as an intensive.

> He was *certainly angry* (not *sure sore*).

Swell. Not acceptable in standard English as a modifier; use *good, excellent,* or, preferably, some more exact modifier.

Take and. Not standard in most uses.

> He *whacked* (not *took and whacked*) down the hornet's nest.

Take sick. Not generally accepted in standard English; prefer *became ill* or a more exact expression.

Terrible, Terribly. Overused and misused; colloquial as general intensives (She is a *terribly* sweet girl) and as blanket words signifying anything unpleasant (I had been vaccinated and felt *terrible*).

Terrific. Recently misused and overused; not a general synonym for anything *large, impressive, dramatic, significant, dexterous,* or *important;* a word so abused that it can now scarcely be used in its standard meaning, "causing terror."

That. Omission of *that* from the introduction of a clause can be confusing or unidiomatic (see 16a).

That there. Substandard; omit *there.*

Their, There, They're. Commonly confused in spelling. *There,* which can be remembered by its similarity to *where,* means "in that place" (Lie *there,* Nipper). *Their* is the possessive of *they* (see 18-2). *They're,* the contraction of *they are,* is not acceptable in formal composition.

These. *These* should be avoided as a substitute for *the* (see 23g).

These kind, These sort. See *Kind.*

They're. See *Their.*

This. *This* should be avoided as a substitute for *the* (see 23g); for reference of *this,* see 19a.

This here. Substandard; omit *here.*

Tho. A variant spelling of *though,* not preferred for formal composition.

Those. Avoid *those* as an intensive with no reference.

He looked back fondly on *his* (not *those*) old college days.

Thusly. Affected or nonstandard for *thus.*

To, Too, Two. Distinguish the function word *to* (*to* the game, learn *to* read) from the adverb *too* (*too* sick, *too* hot), and the numeral *two* (*two* seats on the aisle).

To be. For the faulty use of forms of *to be* in an equation see 13b.

Tooken. A confusion for "took and" or for "taken," which is usually redundant and nonstandard.

Toward, Towards. Alternative forms; *toward* is more common in the United States.

Trait. Redundant in *character trait;* use *trait* or *characteristic.*

Try and. *Try to* is preferred in standard English.

Type. In formal English, *type* is a noun or verb, although colloquially it is often an adjective (*a ranch-type house*).

This type of research (not *this type research*) yields results.

Unique. For the use of *unique,* see 22b.

Up. Useful in verb-adverb combinations (see 20-2); can frequently be separated from the verb, but often the sense is clearer and the construction smoother if *up* is kept close to the verb.

AWKWARD: He made his mind up.
REVISED: He made up his mind.

Used to. The *d* is elided in speech but not omitted in writing.

We *used to* (not *use to*) go to the beach every summer.

Used to could. Vulgate for *used to be able.*

Very. The most useful intensive, but since it is usually only an intensive, with relatively little meaning, it is as likely to weaken writing as to strengthen it. Most good writers use *very* sparingly. The older practice was to forbid the use of *very* before a past participle without an intervening *much* (*very much pleased,* not *very pleased*). The distinction is still maintained in much formal writing.

Wait on. Except in the sense of "serve," use *wait for.*

We have been waiting *for* (not *on*) you.

Want for. In most constructions, omit the *for.*

I *want* (not *want for*) you to meet her.

Ways. Colloquial for *way* in the sense "a distance."

It was a long *way* (not *ways*) to the road.

We. The editorial *we, we* used for *I* or to stand for a newspaper, is generally confirmed to journalistic writing; *we* is common as an impersonal subject meaning "people in general," or "the writer and the reader."

Weather. Frequently confused in spelling with *whether* (I asked him *whether* or not we could depend upon fair *weather*).

Well. An adjective in the sense "in good health," "cured" (The patient is now recovered, and is quite *well*); an adverb corresponding to the adjective *good,* but not to be confused with it (see 22a).

She played her part *well* (not *good*).
The blueprints look *good* (not *well*).

What. Should not be confused with *that* (see 23b).

When. Avoid the *when*-clause in a definition (see 13c).

Where. Colloquial when substituted for *that.*

I noticed in the paper *that* Senator Jones is a candidate for re-election (*not* I see by the paper *where* Senator Jones is up for re-election).

Where at. In most constructions, omit the *at.*

Where is he? (not *Where at is he?* or *Where is he at?*).

Whether. See *If.*

Which. For *which* after *and,* see *And which;* for the use of *which* to refer to human beings, see 23.

While. Often carelessly used as a synonym for *although* or *and* (see 23b).

Who, Whom. Pressure of sentence pattern encourages the replacing of *whom* by *who* (see 18). For distinction between *who* and *which,* see 18-1.

Who's, Whose. Who's is the contraction of *who is; whose* is the possessive form of *who* (see 18-1). In all but the most formal contexts, *whose* may replace the awkward *of which.*

The dog, *whose nose* (not *the nose of which*) was full of porcupine quills. . . .

Will. Sometimes distinguished from *shall;* for the distinction, see 20b.

Wire. Informal for either *telegram* or *telegraph.*

–Wise. Currently in vogue and overused as an informal suffix for almost everything: *The meal was good tastewise.* Often the uses sound as absurd as this example.

Without. Colloquial as a substitute for *unless.*

I will not stay *unless* (not *without*) you raise my wages.

Wood, Woods. In the United States either is acceptable as a synonym of *forest.*

Worst kind, Worst way. Not acceptable in the sense "very much."

Worth-while. Overused blanket word; see 25b.

Would have. Often awkward.

If they *had* (not *would have*) done that. . . .

Would of. Mistaken form of *would have* (see *Could of*).

You. To be used with caution in impersonal constructions (see 21d).

You-all. Colloquial Southern form as the plural of *you;* not acceptable for formal composition.

Index